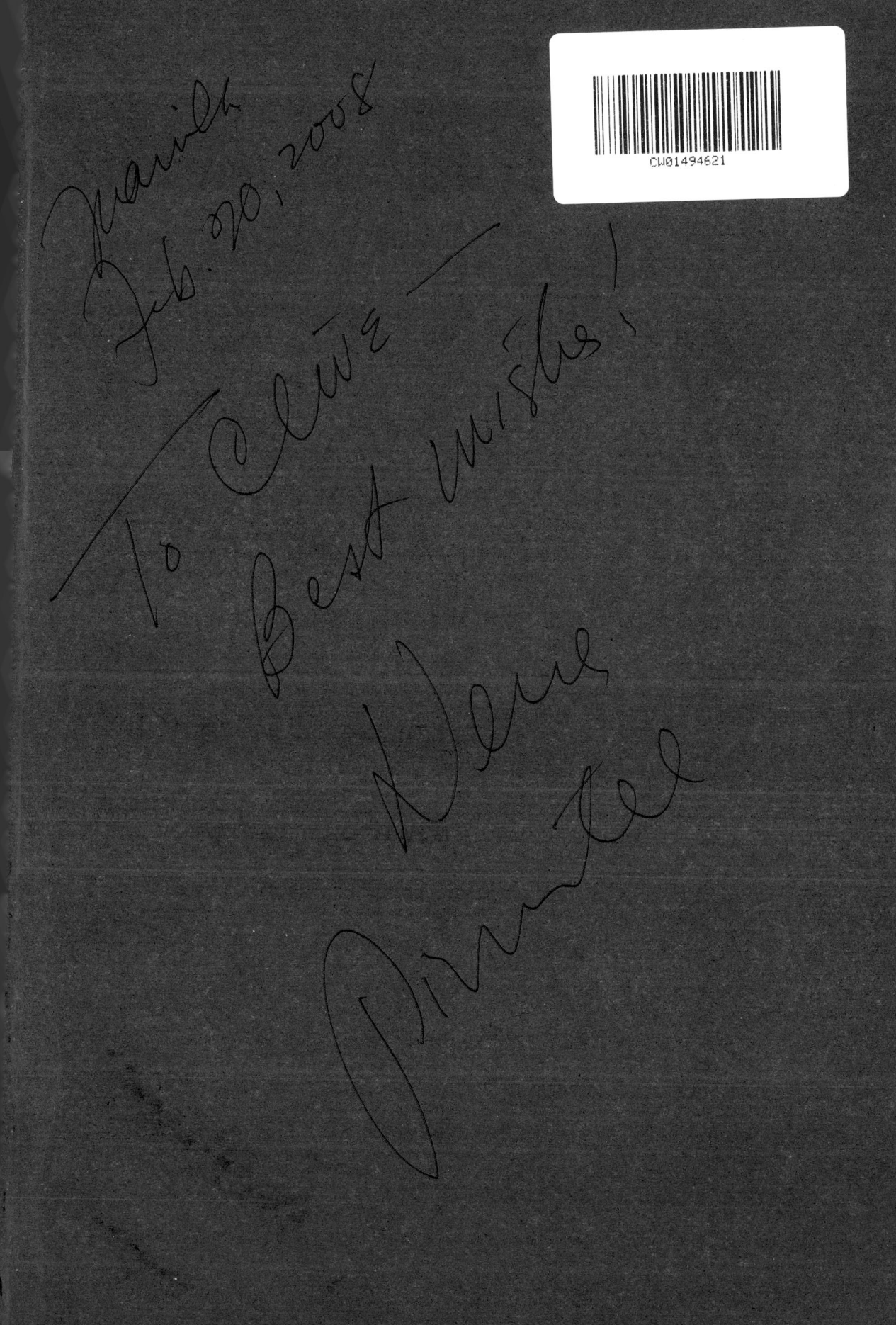

Manila
Feb. 020, 2008

To Clive —

Best wishes!

Dennis

Martial Law
in the Philippines:
My Story

By Aquilino Q. Pimentel, Jr.

For information address inquiries to Lorraine Pimentel Borghijs at this email address: *Lorraine.Pimentel@cgu.edu* or to Cacho Publishing House, Union corner Pines, 1501 Mandaluyong. Tel: 631.8361 Fax: 631.5244

First Edition

Cover Design by Joanna Cortez

Printing History
10   9   8   7   6   5   4   3

ISBN: 971-19-0222-2 (De Luxe hardcover edition)
          971-19-0223-0 (softcover)

— *Contents* —

OTHER BOOKS BY THE AUTHOR

CACHO PUBLISHING HOUSE

The Local Government Code of 1991:
The Key to National Development

OTHER PUBLISHERS

The Barangay and the Local Government Code

The Cooperative Code of the Philippines:
Theory, Law and Practice
(Atty. Mordino R. Chua, co-author)

Handbook on Cooperatives

— *Foreword* —

Many people have written and will continue to write about the infamous martial law years from 1972 to 1986, when the freedoms of every Filipino except for the powers that be were curtailed, and those who dared defy the rules of the dictator were arrested, detained, and in many instances, summarily executed. But not many can tell the story of martial law with the passion of Nene Pimentel, who was one of its more prominent and battle scarred opponents.

Perhaps this book should have been entitled *Living to Tell the Tale,* with apologies to Gabriel Garcia Marquez who has written an autobiography with the same title. For Nene chronicles a life that was put more and more at risk as his opposition to martial law deepened, from the early days as a young delegate to the 1971 Constitutional Convention, on to his stint as mayor of Cagayan de Oro City, and as an elected member of the Batasang Pambansa from which he was ousted by the martial law Comelec for alleged electoral fraud.

In between, he was arrested and detained four times and once placed under house arrest. With each arrest and detention, his star rose so that by 1986, when Marcos fled and the government was ours, Nene, the feisty and much admired mayor from Mindanao, was a household name synonymous with the national cry for freedom, justice and democracy.

Nene was one of my more reliable advisers in the run up to the snap elections. I relied on his experience and considered his principled political judgment whenever I had to make a big decision. He was a good soldier who bit the bullet if it meant the unification of the Opposition. When I announced my choice of Doy Laurel as my running mate during the snap elections in 1986, Nene accepted it manfully, even if I had told him earlier that he was my choice to run as Vice President.

Nene tells it all in his personal account of those days which were both exciting and terrifying. It took courage and daring and much faith to stand up to the dictator, and Nene had large reserves of these. I will always be grateful to Nene for being there for our country — and for me — when the going was rough. In particular, I appreciate his willingness as my first Secretary of Local Government, to absorb the political blows from our massive purge of entrenched local officials identified with the Marcos regime with our appointment of officers in charge when we took over the government after the dictator fled in 1986.

Thank you, Nene, for telling us your story. While it evokes nostalgia in those of us who marched with you during the martial law years, it should inspire present and future generations of leaders to take the road less traveled and march to the different drum of principled politics.

CORAZON C. AQUINO

— *About the Author and the Book* —

Of the thousands who were arrested and detained in military stockades for opposing Marcos' martial law rule, Nene Pimentel stands out as the outstanding out-and-out recidivist in championing democracy when it had few friends.

Nene's book recalls in the most vivid terms the horrors of that period, 1972-1986, when Filipino inhumanity towards Filipino broke all records before and since. Nene writes movingly about it, not only because he witnessed it but also because he endured it as few of its victims did.

A champion of freedom to the bone, Nene was among the first to question the constitutionality of Proclamation No. 1081 imposing martial law despite the clear futility not to mention the terrible risk it entailed. He was promptly picked up and detained in Camp Crame.

In the first elections for the Interim Batasan Pambansa, Ninoy Aquino, Nene Pimentel and other Opposition leaders did the unthinkable; Ninoy from his prison cell. They ran against the martial law regime and won the election so that with only 30% of the votes tallied, Marcos ordered the Comelec to declare all his KBL candidates the winners. The great guns of the Opposition, the venerable Lorenzo Tañada, Soc Rodrigo, Pimentel and others[1] promptly staged a protest march, which ended up, of course, in jail; this time in Camp Bicutan.

Nene returned to his roots in Cagayan de Oro, where he had studied under the Jesuits. He ran for mayor against the Marcos candidate and won. But the Commission on Elections made it difficult for him to take his seat. And when he was finally able to do so, it did not take long before Marcos ordered him arrested and detained again — this time far from his beloved Cagayan de Oro, in a military camp in Cebu City.

If experience is the best teacher, Nene seemed impervious even to life's simplest instruction. Nene ran again in the second election for the Batasan Pambansa. Marcos dispatched the big leaders of the region to finish him off in the polls. Nene won again. And was again arrested for the fourth time. Happily, his beloved people of Cagayan de Oro "coming from all walks of life" bailed him out.

By then, his trials and tribulations were etched on a face that had acquired a permanently doleful expression — "the face of martial law," some people called it, the poster boy of defiance to dictatorship.

Nene did not enjoy winning and losing anyway. Nor did he like getting arrested and detained, even if it seemed like that. Indeed, as far as Nene was concerned, life was not trying to teach him the obvious, which was to quit; a lesson he couldn't learn. On the contrary, it was Marcos who just couldn't learn — in election after election that the dictator stole from Nene and the Filipino people — to uphold the Constitution and the laws. Nene wasn't being bullheaded. He was just being persistent, like a tireless teacher of mentally challenged students of democracy like Ferdinand Marcos.

Nene's book comes out way overdue and certainly none too soon. It is a reminder of what we once lost, and of the cruelty and cupidity of those who took it away. It is a reminder very much needed at this time when democracy is again under threat, coming from one who didn't just see it all but was very much a part of the history he retells.

Nene's story continues into the period after the restoration of democracy, when he continued his unfinished fight against martial law's most recalcitrant legacies. There was the high and unpardonable debt for the obsolete Bataan Nuclear Power Plant, that monument of Marcos folly that was built on an earthquake fault at the price of two new ones, which Nene had opposed and now wanted repudiated.

There was the nationwide political network that Marcos had established throughout the country to maintain the dictatorship, which traditional politicians in her camp wanted Cory Aquino to adopt as her own. In the teeth of their warnings, Nene successfully implemented a sweeping purge of all local executives. As a result, the repeated coup attempts against Cory Aquino in Manila failed to get any support outside the capital, neither from civilians nor the military in the provinces a total vindication of Nene's intransigence.

Nene's profound nationalism manifested itself when his stand against the extension of the US Bases and thereafter against the Visiting Forces Agreement made him the only senator who voted twice against a foreign military presence in the country.

There are as many ways to defend democracy as the myriad ways to undermine and destroy it that we continue to witness especially these days. Although Nene's book reminds us of when democracy faced its most obvious threat from military rule, it has important things to teach us about the more insidious threats that democracy faces today. And not the least of these lessons is that the courage and integrity of even a few remain freedom's best defense.

Get hold of it, read it, keep it always in view. Before a collective experience can become a shaping influence on a people, someone must first make sense of it for them. Nene Pimentel has done that preeminently well in this book.

JOKER P. ARROYO

---

[1] *Author's note: Joker Arroyo was a leader of that march and was jailed along with Tañada, etc.*

—— *Author's Note* ——

Writing a book, a writer once said, is like giving birth to a child.

As a member of the male specie, I suppose that giving life to a book would be the closest experience men can vicariously have of parturition, an act exclusively reserved for the female genus.

While babies are born usually after nine months in the womb, this book took more than two years of actual writing.

In the process, I lost weight. I neglected to exercise regularly. I developed creaking joints, symptoms of carpal tunnel syndrome and pain in my eyes. I missed several social and political engagements. For a straight year, I even failed to visit my hometown Cagayan de Oro City in Mindanao and that led many of my contemporaries there to wonder if I was still alive.

But there were video clips to view and martial law tomes, bundles of clippings, yellowing source documents and bits of scattered personal notes that had to be read, collated and used as bases of the facts, opinions and conclusions that are now in the book. There were also many friends whose views on the struggle against martial law had to be verified. Acknowledgment of their invaluable contribution is done where possible in the pertinent passages of the book.

That said, I cannot but plead guilty to my unpardonable failure to accommodate so many requests for interviews by television, radio and print journalists and political science students and numerous invitations to weddings, political gatherings and other social activities.

I must also apologize for the overuse of the words "I", "me" and "myself" in the book. Even as this is a first person account of the events that I witnessed directly when martial rule ravaged the land or which I learned from primary sources, I tried to minimize frequent references to myself. But as the reader can see, I did not quite succeed.

Finally, the book focuses on the events unfolding in the country from September 21, 1972 when President Marcos declared martial law until he left the country in 1986. The book, however, also discusses the circumstances that led Marcos to plant the seeds of authoritarian rule in the Constitutional Convention that began its work in 1971 and the acts by which he strengthened his one-man rule even after he had supposedly lifted martial rule in 1981. The book, therefore, encompasses a period of some 15 years. I tried my best to recall the statements and the acts of the key players of martial rule in that parlous period of our history. Some of them are still alive as the book goes to print. What they did after martial rule is not within the purview of the book. Other tomes will tackle those matters at some future time.

— *Acknowledgment* —

This book could not have been written without the support of many friends who were personally involved in the struggle against martial law. They recalled many incidents that would not have been possible for me to remember by myself. Aside from those who are cited in the book as major sources of information, special thanks are due to:

(a) Boy Abragan, Cris Lanorias, Rey Teves, Cesar Ledesma, Omeng Maglangit, Ben Ranque and my nephew, Roel Regalado from Mindanao. They recalled many names of colleagues in the struggle and dates of incidents mentioned in the book;

(b) Nits Amihan, Endong Dilag and my friend, Pete Josol from the Visayas. They gave information on events only they possessed, and

(c) Mayor Jojo Binay, former Constitutional Convention Delegates Oca Santos and Celso Gangan from Luzon. They evoked vivid images of the confrontations we had with the authoritarian ruler.

I also appreciate the gentle editorial help of Coylee Gamboa. Without her guidance, there would be numerous repetitive passages that as a politician I am prone to and more grammatical oversights in the book than is the case. I must have given her nightmares because I rewrote passages in the book that had already been reviewed by her.

The interviews that my daughter, Maria Petrina, did with Cory Aquino and Cardinal Sin provide substantial insights on their roles in the fight against the Marcos dictatorship. These are cited in the last Chapters of the book.

Clarissa Lascano Aquino did mind-boggling research that minimized errors of names, places and dates. Clarisse also helped Rey Ronda do the work of indexing the book under the supervision of my daughter, Inde. To them all, I must say 'Thank you."

Of the numerous volumes about martial law in the country, I found most helpful: Ed Olaguer's *Light A Fire II;* Manuel Martinez's, *The Grand Collision;* Conrad de Quiros's *Dead Aim: How Marcos Ambushed Philippine Democracy;* Jovy Salonga's *A Journal of Struggle and Hope;* Alfonso P. Policarpio Jr.'s, *Ninoy, the Willing Martyr;* editors Tina Montiel's & Susan Evangelista's *Down from the Hill;* Raymond Bonner's, *Waltzing with a Dictator;* Sterling Seagrave's, *The Marcos Dynasty;* Primitivo Mijares's, *The Conjugal Dictatorship of Ferdinand and Imelda Marcos;* and Neni Sta. Romana-Cruz's, *Tales from EDSA.* A long bibliography is appended to the book.

Errors of fact or interpretations of events in the book are solely mine.

Among the errors of fact that were found after the release of the first edition of the book are the following:

On page 135, 6th paragraph, 2nd line — Ricky Razon should read Ricky Delgado and

On page 339, photo caption — Barangay Captain Orly Cabaring should read Barangay Captain Romeo Edadis, and the unidentified lady is actually Dr. Estela Garcia.

I apologize to the gentlemen and the lady concerned.

— *Dedication* —

To my beloved wife, Bing, without whose undying love and unstinted support neither this book nor the struggle for freedom that it speaks of would have been possible;

To my children, Gwen, Maripet, Koko, Jac, Terelou, and Inde, who despite my risking their lives and futures during the martial law regime, gave me and their mother unquestioning devotion;

To my grandchildren, Dominique, Trina, AC, AL, Komart and Preet and their generation in the hope that our sad experiences in the martial law years need not be their lot ever.

And posthumously:

To my father, Aquio and my mother, Peting, whose simple lives of honest toil helped charter the course of my own; and Nanay Mameng, who willingly acted as a surrogate parent for our children in those times of acute need; and

To my parents-in-law, *Daddy* (*Dr*. Justo de la Llana), and *Mama* (Remedios del Carmen), who eased the burdens of my struggle against martial law in innumerable ways.

Part I

The Clash Begins

1972: *STUDENTS STAGE violent demonstration against Marcos government*

Chapter 1:

The Setting

I f there was any one person who touched my life profoundly in 1972, it was President Ferdinand E. Marcos. Not that he was a special friend or hero of mine. He was neither.

In fact, my respect for him began to ebb after the 1969 presidential election when he became the only president of the country ever to have been re-elected to another four-year term. The reason for my disenchantment was the widely held belief that Marcos won re-election through dubious methods that included massive overspending, the use of goons and outright fraud. Then, in September 1972, roughly a year before the end of his constitutionally mandated non-extendible second term, Marcos committed the ultimate sin. He declared martial rule and that criminal act vaporized whatever esteem I still had of him.

Small-Town Dabbler

Naturally, Marcos did not have me in mind when he proclaimed martial law. As a small-town dabbler in politics, I was surely outside his political radar screen, which focused — and rightly so — on nationally known politicians like Senators Benigno S. Aquino, Jr., Jose W. Diokno and Lorenzo Tañada, who were capable of challenging his political preeminence.

Still, I had this problem with martial rule. And it was basic. The problem was that the very concept of Marcos's martial rule clashed violently with my deeply held belief — honed at the Jesuit-run Xavier University Colleges of Liberal Arts and Law in Cagayan de Oro City — that it is democracy, not one-man rule, which enhances the value of human life and assures the equal protection of the rights of the people. That was the reason why from Day One, I resolved to oppose the authoritarian rule of Marcos.

My educational background and my familial religious upbringing, however, circumscribed my options in resisting the Marcos regime. Indeed, even as I hated the dictatorship, I detested even more the thought of using the gun to depose the regime. As a believer of Mahatma Gandhi's *Satyagraha* (firmness in the right principle of active nonviolence), I was totally convinced that nonviolent means were the only acceptable way I could oppose martial rule and I resolved to do so no matter what.

'Think of Your Children'

A lawyer friend with whom I discussed my resolve to oppose the martial rule, argued that if appeals to my personal security were not sufficient to deter me from doing so, I should think of my children. "Who will support them if Marcos should punish you for your obstinacy?" he asked.

"In that case," I said, "God will have to provide for them. I believe that supporting one's family subsists only if one is not prevented by an insuperable cause." I told him, "Since martial rule will deter us from living normal lives, that circumstance is justification enough for our inability to comply with our normal obligations." But, even before the words completely left my mouth, I knew that I sounded too idealistic, if not actually irrational.

Nonetheless, because we had no domestic precedents to go by, I took martial rule to mean that Marcos could do whatever he wanted with our lives because he had supplanted the Rule of Law with the Rule of the Gun. Thus, from the moment Marcos declared martial rule, I believed that my family and I would have to live from day to day. I believed we no longer had the luxury of planning long-term for our family. I told my wife, Lourdes "Bing" de la Llana, that, from then on, we would not borrow money unless absolutely necessary as I did not want any indebtedness of ours to become a "pressure point" that Marcos could use against me.

Super Typhoon

At home, Aquilino, my father — who knew how mule-headed I can sometimes be — weighed in with his view that martial law was like a super typhoon that sweeps down anything standing in its path. In his view, I should learn from how the bamboo outlasts typhoons. "The bamboo," he said, "bends low, sways with the gale-force wind and survives." However, I could not agree with the view of my old man, even if he had my best interests at heart.

A human being, I told myself, was not a bamboo. He was a million times more important than a bamboo. And, therefore, if a person followed his conscience and did what was good, he'd get over the trials that come his way, including the "super typhoon" called martial law.

Even the "acknowledged political leader" of Misamis Oriental at the time, Sen. Emmanuel Pelaez, echoed my father's advice when I sought his opinion on martial law at his law office near the Luneta in Manila. He told me that the best position we could take was for us "to be neither too

MY FATHER, Aquilino Pimentel

near nor too far from the dictatorship." That view, in my opinion, meant straddling the fence, which was unacceptable to me.

Hence, despite the dire forebodings of my father and friends, including my fellow Constitutional Convention delegate, the Jesuit priest, Pacifico Ortiz, a man steeped in the ways of the Spirit and wise in the ways of the world, I resolved to do what my conscience told me to do: resist the dictatorship, but in the ways of peace whenever and wherever the opportunity would arise. I did just that all the way until the peaceful People Power I revolution deposed Marcos in 1986. Happily, by the grace of God and with the support of my family and friends, I survived martial law and lived to tell this story.

Starting Law Practice

When martial rule was declared, four of our six children — Gwendolyn, Maria Petrina, Aquilino Martin and Aquilino Justinian — were in grade school. The two youngest, Teresa Lourdes and Lorraine Marie, were not yet of school age.

My wife Bing and I did not know what was in store for us, as a family, and much less, for the nation. At that time, our family was in Manila where, as a delegate to the Constitutional Convention, I was actively participating full-time in the process of amending the country's 1935 Constitution. Before I was elected as a delegate to the Constitutional Convention, I had a fairly active law practice based in Cagayan de Oro where a daily trial load of a case or two was routine.

Immediately after passing the Bar in 1959, I began my practice of law. I did general criminal and civil law practice. Between the two, I was really more attracted to the practice of criminal law. I enjoyed handling the defense of criminal suspects, especially those who could not afford "expensive counsel." The way I was attracted to fight for the cause of the downtrodden was almost instinctive, probably like that of a red ant drawn to sugar.

First Case

I remember the first case that I handled was for a boy who was probably not more than 14 years of age when he was accused of stealing empty sacks from a hauling truck. I got him acquitted and was paid with a dozen eggs.

There was also the case of the woman who had been jailed for *estafa* or swindling. She had bought a portable radio by installment from a well-to-do businessman in Cagayan de Oro and could not make the installment payments. From that civil obligation, a criminal case was concocted that brought her behind bars. It was a fairly routine criminal case, but for the fact that she was nursing an infant child in jail because she could not pay bail for her provisional liberty.

Judge Agustin Antillon appointed me her counsel *de officio*. I had her acquitted on the argument that her failure to fulfill a civil obligation could not ripen into a criminal liability.

I received nothing for my effort, not even a "thank you" from my client. All I remember were the tears that filled her eyes when she heard the verdict of not guilty. That small court victory earned for me the eternal enmity of the business-man and his family, who could not comprehend my handling a case against their interests as they were my father's friends.

Dean of Law

As the years went by, my law practice earned enough for the needs of my family in Cagayan de Oro. I also taught law at Xavier University, from which I had graduated with a Bachelor of Arts degree in 1956 and with a Bachelor of Laws degree in 1959. Two years out of law school, I was appointed the dean of the College of Law by the university president, Fr. James McMahon, SJ.

Circa 1962: XAVIER UNIVERSITY COLLEGE of Law Faculty with me as Dean. (Left to right): Gabriel La Viña, Francisco Fuentes, Judge Benjamin Gorospe, me, Judge Bernardo Teves, Pablo Magtajas, my father, Aquilino Pimentel and Francisco Velez. First batch of the law students under my deanship in two rows at the back.

Five years later, I resigned as dean to devote my time to the practice of law more fully and to delve into local politics on the side. I must say that Fr. McMahon's assurance — that, in the event that my sorties into the political arena failed, I could always go back to the College of Law as a member of its faculty — emboldened me to try my hand in the local electoral politics of Misamis Oriental and Cagayan de Oro. Fr. McMahon true to his word took me back to the college when the city and the provincial electorates turned down my first two attempts at local politics for vice mayor and board member respectively. It was "their loss," I told Bing, "not mine."

Chapter 2

My Family

Life as a practicing lawyer was fun. I liked it immensely. I found it intellectually stimulating to stand on my feet in a courtroom, trying to unravel an opposing party's claim while parrying the thrusts of opposing counsel who, in turn, would try to demolish our side's theory of the case. I also liked the practice of law in Cagayan de Oro and the nearby provinces in that I could bring my kids to watch the trials I was handling (without the hassle of too much traffic as we traveled to and from home). I wanted the kids to witness for themselves what it meant to be a trial lawyer. I also made it a point for them to come with me when I made occasional visits to the shanties of my squatter clients to give them a view of life in the raw.

I think the kind of life that Bing and I lived rubbed off on our six children. Two, Gwen and Koko, are lawyers like me. Aside from a law degree from the University of the Philippines, Gwen also has a Master's in Public Administration from the same school. She is a lawyer in the Office of the Solicitor General, a position she got when Francisco Chavez, one of the most active law practitioners in the country, was its head. Prior to getting his law degree also from UP, Koko finished a Bachelor of Science in Mathematics at the Ateneo de Manila. He is a law practitioner in Manila.

The rest have pursued other disciplines. Maripet, an Economics graduate of Ateneo de Manila University, also holds a master's degree in Mass Communications and a California Teachers Credentials, both from California State University, Northridge. She is currently a public school teacher in Los Angeles, California. Jac finished his Bachelor of Science in Biology at Ateneo de Manila and then went on to take up Medicine at the University of the East. He did further studies in Orthopedic Surgery at the University of Cincinnati and is now an orthopedic surgeon practicing in Cagayan de Oro. Terelou, an AB-Psychology and Law graduate of Xavier University in Cagayan de Oro, is the general manager of the Filipino Songwriters and Composers Association of the Philippines in Manila as of the time this book is written. Inde, the youngest, graduated from the Ateneo de Manila University with a Bachelor of Arts degree in Interdisciplinary Studies and has two master's degrees, one in Communication, Culture and Technology from Georgetown University in Washington, DC, and, the other in Comparative Politics from the Claremont Graduate School in California.

Inculcating Responsibility

I believe that Bing and I have instilled in our children a certain degree of responsibility for them to aspire to become productive citizens, and to respect and be concerned for people regardless of their station in life. One of the things that we tried to inculcate in them was for them to think things through and to argue rationally, rather than cry about problems confronting them. To get them used to the idea that other people may have different ways of looking at things, Bing and I would sometimes present a problem and discuss it with them as if they were lawyers. We would then have them take sides and produce their own "witnesses" as it were to prove their case. In that respect, I think that we had some success in training them to think on their feet. Even our second-to-the-youngest, Teresa, more excitable than her siblings, often managed to put her emotions under control.

As parents, we are proud that Koko topped the Bar Examinations in 1990 and Jac topped the Orthopedic Examinations in 1998. We are equally proud of the scholastic and professional achievements of our daughters who sometimes exhibit my bullheadedness in the things they believe in but, happily, are balanced by the charity of their mother.

Five of our children are now blissfully married: Gwen to Luis Gana, a lawyer; Maripet to Baljit Brar, a businessman in Sacramento; Koko to Jewel Lobaton, a medical student at the Far Eastern University's College of Medicine; Jac to Malyn Fernandez, a doctor of medicine who did further studies in Dermatology at the Thomas Jefferson University in Philadelphia; and Inde to Alain Borghijs, a PhD in Economics from the University of Antwerp in Belgium.

We also take pride that our children, at relatively tender ages, began to show concern for others. I remember driving with my kids in a sudden downpour on the way back to Cagayan de Oro from Iligan City where I had a case as counsel for a poor family whose shanty we visited after the court hearing. My son, Jac, probably just five years old at the time, told me that he pitied my client's family. "Why?" I asked. "They would be totally drenched by the heavy rains by now," he replied.

On another occasion, I brought Inde and her playmate, a neighbor's daughter of her age, to visit a squatter area in Metro Manila. As we entered the place of the squatters, the strong stench of poverty assailed our nostrils and hovels made of cartoon boxes greeted our eyes. Inde's friend blurted out that the place was *pangit*, ugly, which Inde, barely four years old at the time, did not allow to pass. She told her friend not to say that "because the residents might be offended."

I attribute their concern for the plight of the less fortunate to the fact that I exposed them to the real-life situations of my poor clients. Now and then, Bing and I also tried to impress upon them that there were just too many hungry children on earth that they should thank the Lord we still had enough to eat on our family table. Once, I showed them a clipping from *Life* magazine that showed an emaciated, skin-and-bones child, a victim of famine in an African country. I asked them to write what they thought of the picture. Bing would judge the best essay for which there was a prize (a few pesos). I remember that it was Jac, now a doctor of medicine, who won the contest, with his lines, "I pity the boy. I want to help him."

1972: MY FAMILY, Jac, Maripet, me, Terelou, Bing, Inde, Gwen and Koko

Downside of Law Practice

The practice of law, however, had its downside. I found the tendency of some clients to dictate to their lawyers to build their cases on falsehoods particularly abhorrent. It was difficult to turn down paying clients who wanted me to handle their cases by any means to ensure victory. But turn them down I did because the motto of my alma mater, *Veritas Liberavit Vos* or the Truth Shall Set You Free, which greeted my eyes when I first entered the gates of Xavier University as a high-school freshman in 1948, remained indelibly chiseled in my mind. Thus, even in the practice of law, I could not dissociate myself from the thought that truth was always the best, if not the only, basis for bringing cases to court or for establishing lasting relationships out of court. Tactfully, I had to tell many a prospective paying client to try other lawyers whenever I sensed that they wanted me to engage in underhanded methods in the handling of their cases.

There was another thing that I could not abide in the practice of law. That was the arrogance of some judges who treated lawyers appearing before them as if they had no dignity at all. Those judges would shout at lawyers or show utter disrespect to them, apparently in the mistaken notion that by doing so, they asserted the superiority of the Bench over the Bar. I remember telling one such judge during a hearing that, if he wanted me to respect him, he should also respect me because respect was a two-way street. Luckily, he did not cite me for contempt. Had he done so, I would have challenged him all the way up to the Supreme Court because I believed that my comment was fully justified by the circumstances.

Protecting Lawyers

To provide an avenue for lawyers in Cagayan de Oro to defend ourselves from oppressive judges, we organized the Cagayan de Oro Association of Practicing Attorneys (Coapa). To make sure that the judges knew that Coapa meant business, we not only stood up against autocratic judges in the courtroom, but we also brought our complaints to the Secretary of the Department of Justice directly or in written petitions. Once, when Justice Secretary Vicente Abad Santos visited Cagayan de Oro, we, in behalf of the members of Coapa, asked him to summon Court of First Instance Judge Benjamin Gorospe to appear at our meeting with him. Judge Ben was a distant relative of my father. I explained to Abad Santos that some of our members had certain complaints against the judge and that it was best that Gorospe be summoned so he could hear our complaint personally and not think we were bad-mouthing him behind his back. Incidentally, the complaint had to do with courtroom behavior of the judge and not with corruption or some such serious breach of the law.

Abad Santos acceded to our request and asked Gorospe to attend the meeting. When the judge arrived, we related to Abad Santos the Coapa members' complaints about the judge's courtroom behavior. Gorospe, apparently, did not want to engage us in a prolonged discussion, so he promised the secretary that he would change the way he acted in his court. And he did.

The Coapa effectively sent a message to the judges that we were not their peons and that we expected to be treated with civility and respect when we appeared before them to litigate the cases of our clients, just as they could expect the same civility and respect from us as officers of the court.

Constitutional Principles

In the practice of civil and criminal law, I found the provisions of the Constitution most rewarding in many of my attempts to vindicate the fundamental rights of my clients. Time and again, I used constitutional principles, particularly due process, even in common criminal cases or ordinary civil cases. While I did not earn as much money in legal fees by practicing law in Cagayan de Oro as I would much later in Manila (for some six years after the 1995 elections when I was cheated out of a seat in the Senate through *dagdag-bawas*), law practice in general gave me great personal fulfillment.

My law practice in Cagayan de Oro, supplemented by Bing's teaching at Xavier's grade school, provided us with sufficient income to meet the simple joys of life — like going to church or the movies together, swimming in the sea or picnicking in a secluded mountainside near our home. We also earned enough to matriculate our kids at the grade schools of Xavier University and Lourdes College, a girls' school run by the Religious of the Virgin Mary (RVM) sisters.

To our delight, the Social Security System rated us "creditworthy" in 1963, within three years of our married life. That meant we could borrow from the SSS to fund the construction of our family home. The loan enabled us to construct a simple house that still stands today as our home in the city. Incidentally, we paid every centavo of the principal and the interest of that loan in 1972, the year of the declaration of martial rule. I asked Bing to pay off the loan then because I did not want to give Marcos or his minions the pleasure of using that loan to pressure me to do his bidding.

The Rule of Law

Looking back, I found that my having read law and my having practiced it rather extensively deepened my belief that the Rule of Law anchored on the Constitution was the best way to protect the rights and liberties of our people. And I tried to use my knowledge of the law to fight against the martial law dictatorship of Marcos, indeed without much material success but with great personal satisfaction.

Part 2

Revising the Constitution

VOTE—

AQUILINO PIMENTEL JR.

for DELEGATE to the CONSTITUTIONAL CONVENTION

ON NOVEMBER 10, 1970

Dear

You must have heard that I am a candidate for delegate to the Constitutional Convention. As such, I wish I could see you personally and talk with you about the ideas I humbly believe should be inserted into our Constitution. And then beg for your support.

However, time is running out on us as the election will be held on November 10, 1970 or barely two months from now.

Hence, I do not know if I could still get in touch with you personally. And so, out of necessity, I have to resort to this letter to do what I would gladly do in person, time permitting.

MY PLATFORM

Basically, I stand on the platform of Christian Democratic Socialism.

To be more specific, these are SOME of the ideas I would want to work for on the Convention Floor, if given the opportunity:

(1) the adoption of the PRINCIPLE OF MAN'S STEWARDSHIP OF PRIVATE PROPERTY. Under this principle, we would try to eliminate the theory of absolute ownership of private property — to emphasize the Christian concept of property.

Thus, we would still recognize MAN'S RIGHT TO OWN property. But his RIGHT TO USE that property would be regulated so that he could use his property only for beneficial purposes. Following this theory, the government may compel the rich to invest their money in projects that can give work to people.

Also, businessmen may be compelled to share their profits with their employees.

(2) the adoption of the PRINCIPLE OF COOPERATION as a vehicle to solve our economic problems.

Briefly, this means that the Government would encourage and support Cooperatives, like Credit Unions, Consumer's Cooperatives and the like.

(3) the power to appoint Judges and Fiscals should be lodged with the Supreme Court to prevent political interference in the administration of justice.

(4) the grant of more powers to local governments and the elimination of useless, wasteful and irrelevant local governmental entities.

(5) the limitation of the Presidential term to only one without reelection.

(6) the limitation of the right to reelection of other elective officials to only one reelection to prevent the formation of political dynasties.

(7) the adoption of a unicameral lawmaking body and abolishing the 100-day limit to the yearly regular session of our Congress to make Congress work throughout the year.

(8) to revamp the General Auditing Office and grant it more powers.

MGA KAIGSONAN, ITUBOY TA SI

MLBN. AQUILINO "Nene" PIMENTEL

Pagka
DELEGADO

TUNGOD KAY SIYA ADUNAY

KATAKUS

1. VALEDICTORIAN, Ateneo de Cagayan High School - 1952
2. VALEDICTORIAN, Bachelor of Arts, Ateneo de Cagayan - 1956
3. GOLD MEDALIST, College of Law, Xavier University - 1959

KASINATIAN

1. PANGULO, Cagayan de Oro Association of Practising Attorneys - 1964 - 1970
2. DEKANO, College of Law, Xavier University - 1962 - 1967
3. MAGTUTUDLO, College of Law, Xavier University - 1960 - 1967
4. PANGULO, Ateneo Alumni Association - 1963
5. PULI - PANGULO, Jaycees of Cagayan de Oro - 1962
6. ABOGADO, Mindanao Press and Radio Association
7. MAGSUSULAT, Mindanao Star

KALIGDONG

1. REGIONAL CHAIRLEADER, Christian Family Movement - 1968 - 1969
2. PULI - PANGULO, Cursillo Movement sa Misamis Oriental - 1969 - 1970
3. MIEMBRO, Knights of Columbus

KASINGKASING

1. ABOGADO, Credit Union Movement
2. COORDINATOR, Mga Manlalaban nga Kristianos alang sa mga dinaug - daug nga kabus
3. FOUNDER, Legal Aid Bureau, Cagayan de Oro Association of Practising Attorneys

---

1970: HAND-OUTS IN MY CAMPAIGN for delegate to the Constitutional Convention

Chapter 3:

The Campaign

In 1970, two years before the proclamation of martial law, Marcos called for a Constitutional Convention to amend the 1935 Constitution, which had governed the nation for the last 35 years. The premise was that we needed a new constitution that would capture the soul and the aspirations of the Filipino. The argument was that the 1935 Constitution was "a colonial document" because it had provisions allowing the presence of the US military bases in the country and requiring the approval of the US President to make it effective even after the Filipino people ratified it.

I wanted to help craft that Constitution. So I ran for the position of delegate — one of four — to represent the city of Cagayan de Oro and the province of Misamis Oriental at the Constitutional Convention. From the start of the campaign, I decided that I was not going to hock my soul to any politician or businessperson in the campaign. Bing and I sold a parcel of land, which I had received as "attorney's fees" some years back, and that money served as my campaign kitty in my quest for a seat in the Convention.

My supporters produced and distributed campaign leaflets that proclaimed me as a person who had four "Ks" going for me. In the Visayan language, these were: *katakus* or competence; *kasinatian or* experience; *kaligdong* or integrity; and *kasingkasing* or a heart for the people. Aside from the self-serving propaganda materials that my campaign staff dished out by the thousands, I also had an eight-point program that I expounded on without let up throughout the campaign period.

Eight-Point Platform

My eight-point platform proposed the: (1) adoption of the principle of stewardship of property; (2) propagation of cooperatives; (3) transfer of the power to appoint judges from the President to the Supreme Court; (4) conversion of the General Auditing Office into a Commission; (5) limitation of the term of the president to only one without re-election; (6) limitation of the right of re-election of other elective officials to one term; (7) reduction of the voting age to 18; and (8) extension of free medical services to the people.

The eight principles are now embodied either in their entirety or in essence in the Constitution that governs the country today or are found in existing laws. In the campaign, surprisingly, it was the principle of stewardship of property that stirred the most controversy — principally among wealthy individuals and the business community. I found the resistance to the proposal rather surprising because I had intended it merely to underscore the principle that property created certain obligations on the owner to use it not only for his or her benefit but for the benefit of others also. Critics tagged the stewardship principle as communist-inspired. Thus, it was inevitable that, during the campaign, my opponents labeled me as a communist, which was absolutely untrue. I got more flak for this proposal later when I formally introduced it in the Convention.

Campaign Difficulties

I found the campaign for election as a delegate to the Convention extremely difficult. Although the election was supposed to be nonpartisan, the big politicians in my province and city — who were all Marcos men — publicly made known their choices to the people and their short list excluded me. While they did not raise the hands of their candidates, which was the usual way politicians endorsed their electoral bets, they nonetheless announced their preferences in public forums.

The political kingpin of my province, Senator Pelaez, for example, did his utmost to prevent me from winning. This he did by announcing openly through the radio that he was supporting five candidates to the Constitutional Convention, even though Misamis Oriental and Cagayan de Oro were entitled to only four delegates. His bets were: Felino Neri, a former acting secretary of foreign affairs, Fausto Dugenio, a former congressman; Eudoxio Along, his longtime lawyer-secretary; Rolando Piit, a lawyer and scion of a well-to-do family in Cagayan de Oro; and Pablo Reyes, a popular practicing lawyer and civic leader in the province and city. The five were all top-caliber candidates and eminently qualified to represent the province and the city in the Convention. But why did Pelaez endorse five when the province and the city were entitled to only four delegates? He supported five so that, if the people did not like any of his first four choices — Neri, Dugenio, Piit and Along — they could eliminate one of them and vote for Reyes as their alternative candidate, instead of me.

Marcos's and Pelaez's heavyweight political henchmen in the province and in the city, namely, Rep. Pedro Roa and Gov. Concordio Diel, generally followed Pelaez's lead and intervened in the Constitutional Convention elections. Roa batted for three of Pelaez's candidates, namely, Dugenio, Neri and Piit. The only Pelaez candidate that Roa did not endorse was Along. I was grateful for that omission because, theoretically, the people could write me down as their fourth choice.

Governor Diel, however, endorsed the four principal candidates of Pelaez. To help condition the minds of the electorate not to waste their vote on me, Diel publicly predicted that I would land No. 6 among the candidates. His line reflected the sentiment of the Aglipayans, a sizeable religious group in the province, led by Bishop Camilo Diel, a brother of Governor Diel. The Aglipayans had mounted an "anybody but Pimentel" campaign. Even the employees of the Presidential Assistant for Community Development, a national government office, singled out Piit as the only candidate they would support to block my getting the top position of the four delegate-seats for the province and the city.

Black Propaganda

Black propaganda was also directed against me, principally to dissuade Aglipayan voters from voting for me. It pictured me as a *Catholic* candidate who would discriminate against the Aglipayans and the non-Catholics — all because I was advocating the adoption of the principle of stewardship of property. That was, of course, utter falsehood. But that was the way it was in the politics of Misamis Oriental and Cagayan de Oro: outright lies, half-truths and vote buying were *de rigueur* even then.

However, compared with other places, politically speaking, our province and city were still better situated. At least in Misamis Oriental and Cagayan de Oro, political controversies were settled not by the bullet but by the ballot. In the province and city, the political lords were not warlords. Nobody at that time was killed or physically harassed or harmed for partisan political reasons. And people of different political persuasions could campaign publicly for their candidates without being run out of town or having their meetings broken up by armed goons.

Winning Support

In the end, all the efforts of my political opponents to block my election or to thwart my topping the list of delegates failed. Despite a lack of funds, being denied support by the recognized political leaders of the province and city, and the absence of a solid organization that hampered my campaign, the people of Misamis Oriental and Cagayan de Oro stunned Pelaez and his political leaders by voting overwhelmingly for me as their No. 1 delegate to the Convention on Election Day, November 10.

By early evening of that day, when the election returns started to come in by radio, I told Bing that we were going to make it. We went with our children to the Xavier University chapel to give our thanks to the Lord and then we repaired to a movie house to relax as we awaited the final results.

The final election returns, indeed, showed that I had won first in Cagayan de Oro and in 20 municipalities of the province. I was second in Gingoog City and in one town, and third in two other municipalities. Overall, I had a lead of some 14,000 votes over Piit, the next-ranking delegate.

In that campaign, I learned that — although difficult — it was possible to land an elected position without necessarily compromising one's fundamental beliefs. I also learned that some people were capable of supporting candidates like me with "no strings attached."

Friends like Edgardo Neri Marfori and his wife, Lilia Acero, for instance, literally launched my candidacy by lending me their one and only van which enabled me to campaign throughout the province, accompanied only by another friend, Edwin Padla, who doubled as my driver and personal assistant. There was also lawyer Frederico Gapuz, who volunteered his incomparable talent for organizing a political campaign. He scheduled where I should go, at what particular time and what topics I should discuss before the people.

There were many more who helped — like the Jesuits, the parish and secular priests, seminarians, nuns, pastors of different denominations except the Aglipayans, fellow lawyers and kindred souls — but who are remembered here more in spirit than in word. Their acts of kindness, I recall as vividly today as if written on stone, even as those took place more than 24 years ago — acts that I can never repay.

End of Pelaez Politics

When I finally got to the Convention, in my naivete, I found it utterly incredible that some delegates from other parts of the country had spent millions just to land seats in the Constitutional Convention. It was a rude awakening on my part into the world of *realpolitik*.

My election as a delegate to the Constitutional Convention in 1970 was my entry point to the public offices that I subsequently held. I was elected mayor of Cagayan de Oro City in 1980 and a member of the Batasang Pambansa, the unicameral legislative body, in 1984, during the martial law years. I was appointed Minister of Local Government by President Corazon Aquino in 1986. Thereafter, I was thrice elected as a Senator of the Republic, in 1987, in 1998 and in 2004.

It may also be said that my successful ventures in politics spelled the end of the political supremacy of Pelaez in our province. In the local elections of 1980, for instance, the old Pelaez reliables gave way to new politicians in both Misamis Oriental and Cagayan de Oro. Although Pelaez never really wanted me to succeed in politics, let me say that I found him a fairly decent man swimming among less decent men in the turbulent seas of the country's politics.

Relocating to Manila

Even before the work to amend the 1935 Constitution started in mid-1971, Bing and I had to relocate our family to Manila. We did not want to leave our children behind in Cagayan de Oro as they were all still of tender age.

With a Master's in Guidance, Bing applied for guidance counseling positions in private schools to help support the family. Fortunately, she was accepted at St. Mary's College in Quezon City and later at the Ateneo de Manila University, where she was named head of its Placement Office in 1975. Later, in 1980, she resigned from the Placement Office when we went back to Cagayan de Oro to try my luck as a mayoral candidate in the first local elections that President Marcos called since the proclamation of martial rule. But that was eight years later, reckoned from the start of the sessions of the Constitutional Convention.

To save on house rent, my father-in-law, Dr. Justo de la Llana, and my mother-in-law, Remedios del Carmen, so kindly agreed to swap houses with us. Dr. de la Llana, a graduate of the Indiana University School of Medicine in the US, had been a Health Department doctor and had overseen much of the work of public hospitals in Mindanao. My parents-in-law and their youngest daughter, Tess, who was then a college student, lived in our house in Cagayan de Oro, while we stayed in their home in Project 8, Quezon City, for the duration of the work of the Convention. Their generosity in sheltering our large family in their residence — as many other Filipino clans do for their extended families — speaks volumes of how we as a people take to heart the principle espoused by both the Church and State that the family is the foundation of society. I also believe that it is from the family that the core values of caring for one another, loving one's neighbor and dealing honestly with others flow into the body politic.

Comelec Proclaims Winners

A few days after Election Day, the Commission on Elections proclaimed most of us who had won as duly elected delegates to the Convention. That meant that we were fully qualified to assume the functions of our office on June 1, 1971, the day set for the Convention to begin its work.

There was a seven-month period before the date fixed by law for our assumption of office so that we could prepare for the Convention. That was exactly what we as delegates-elect decided to do: prepare for the Convention by holding pre-convention meetings in Manila.

I left Cagayan de Oro for Manila soon after my proclamation by the local Comelec. Some friends thought that I left for Manila to participate in the pre-convention meetings. While that was also true, there was another reason for my early departure.

On November 5, five days before elections, I suddenly became ill with high fever. To prevent our political opponents from capitalizing on it, Fred Gapuz and Bing kept me from public view by booking me at the Vista Hermosa, a hotel owned by my friends, Ed and Lili Marfori. The location of the hotel on top of a hill some distance away from the heart of Cagayan de Oro sort of helped keep my ailment "confidential" for the rest of the election period. I stayed at the hotel until Election Day, recuperating from an attack of what turned out to be Bell's palsy, which caused my right cheek to sag slightly.

When the elections were over, Bing and I decided to go to Manila to get further medical treatment for me. Doctor Juan Alcazaren patiently nurtured me to recovery. By the time the Convention opened, there was hardly a trace of Bell's palsy on my face. The doctor was so kind; he did not charge me a centavo. He said that all he wanted of me was to do my job in the Convention for the good of the country.

Chapter 4

Pre-Convention Meetings

Our pre-convention meetings began as a get-together, get-to-know-one-another kind of gathering. It was good that we had those meetings because these provided a good avenue for the exposure of the kind of delegates every province, city or district had sent to the Convention. Some immediately identified themselves as the garrulous breed that waffled at the spur of the moment on whatever topic and drowned their audience with a torrent of words. Others were a little more circumspect and spoke only when they thought they had something important to say. Still others acted as if they were born to silence and were created by the Almighty just to nod sagely or frown majestically at the goings-on of other delegates.

While I found the mix of the wordy, the silent and the wise among the delegates interesting, I was prepared to work with them *as is*. They were, as far as I was concerned, the people's choices in a democratic election that was perceived as one of the more honest elections ever held in the country up to that time. Hence, my liking or not liking the way my co-delegates were packaged either by their handlers or by God was immaterial.

Preparing for the Opening

In January 1971, the pre-convention caucuses buckled down to more serious work, which was to prepare for the Convention's opening session on June 1. To get some order in the pre-convention meetings, we chose a "permanent secretary" in the person of Delegate Napoleon Rama. Rama was nationally known as a courageous writer of the popular weekly, the *Philippines Free Press*, long before he was elected as a delegate. For many of us delegates-elect, his principal attraction was that his *Free Press* articles were fearlessly critical of Marcos.

Rama was not the only aspirant to that position. Sonia Aldeguer, a daughter of House Speaker Pro-Tempore Jose Aldeguer contested his bid. She lost by a few votes. Rama's election as the permanent secretary of the pre-convention meetings telegraphed the sentiment of many delegates that they did not want anyone associated with Marcos to occupy positions of power in the Convention. Sonia's father, Jose, was a known supporter of Marcos in Iloilo.

On January 23, we met at the Philippine Columbian to discuss the proposed draft rules to govern the Convention sessions in June. The draft rules were supposed to have been crafted by a committee of delegates the week before. As things turned out, there were no draft rules. What was furnished us was a proposed agenda for the opening day of the Convention.

I closely monitored the proposed agenda. I liked the idea of having Comelec Chair Jaime Ferrer do the opening remarks. Ferrer's handling of the Constitutional Convention elections had impressed me deeply. After his opening remarks, the Convention chairman would be elected and the Convention committees formed.

I was glad no one suggested inviting Marcos to grace the opening session of the Convention. Talk was rife that Marcos would to be invited to it. But, during that particular meeting, nobody mentioned it. The invitation to Marcos to attend the opening session of the Convention and give the main speech was a later development.

Different Views

At the January 23 pre-convention meeting, I saw how the views of the Metro Manila-based delegates were so different from the views of us delegates who represented areas outside the metropolis. The difference surfaced when the venue of the Convention sessions was tabled. Three proposals were made.

Delegate Pacifico Ortiz suggested that our sessions be held at the Manila Hotel for P260,000 a month. Whoever chose Ortiz to suggest Manila Hotel as the venue of the Convention was a public relations genius. Ortiz, a Jesuit priest, was a respected figure not only in religious and academic circles as a former president of Ateneo de Manila, but also in the rarefied air of high national political offices as the chaplain-advisor of Manuel Luis Quezon, the first President of the Commonwealth of the Philippines. Moreover, in a country where 85% of the people were Catholics, few would dare question the motives of a priest like Fr. Ortiz. I was, however, startled that we should even consider the Manila Hotel as a possible site when the country was reeling from economic difficulties.

The second proposal made by Delegate Jose Concepcion, Jr., was for the Convention to be held at the Quezon City Hall, where we could rent floors sufficient for our needs for P40,000 a month. That, I thought, was a little more justifiable.

Delegate Heherson Alvarez suggested a third alternative. He proposed that the Convention hold its sessions at the University of the Philippines "for nothing." In my naivete, I considered the Alvarez proposal the best. At the time, however, it hardly created a ripple. I did not quite realize then that our colleagues — even those who proclaimed themselves as public servants — actually wanted to work in comfortable, if not luxurious, circumstances. We failed to settle the venue of the Convention sessions in that meeting.

It was not until February 8 that the venue was finally decided by the 286 delegates present of the maximum of 320 delegates who were elected in the districts defined by law. Ortiz presented the proposal anew to hold our sessions at the Manila Hotel with the come-on that the hotel management had reduced the monthly rent by P100,000 from the P260,000 previously offered to us. I argued against it, saying:

The rental of P160,000 a month for the Manila Hotel represents about 16% of our annual budget of P12 million. We probably will be hard put to explain our decision to the people, most of whom are living below the poverty line.

My objection was booed down. The overwhelming majority chose the Manila Hotel as the Convention site. Only 50 of us opted for UP.

After the vote, Delegate Antonio Raquiza of Ilocos Norte told me that he saw difficult times ahead of our work in the Convention in view of the lack of sensitivity of many delegates to the "poverty and misery of our people" that I had adverted to. While I was pleasantly surprised by Raquiza's remark, I reminded myself to be cautious in my dealings with him because he was a publicly known Marcos leader.

The choice of the Manila Hotel as the Convention site, in my view, defined the general character of the delegates as being unprepared to sacrifice for the people. Inferentially, it also foretold the kind of Charter that would eventually come out of the Convention.

Considering the taste for *la dolce vita*, showed by the majority of the delegates who chose the Manila Hotel as the convention site, I feared as early as then that we could never craft a progressive Constitution that would address the basic problems of the nation. We had not even begun to discuss basic proposals for inclusion in the proposed Charter. Still, with 50 of us voting for a less expensive venue for the Convention, I thought we had a good number that could

1971: *I DENOUNCE THE PROPOSAL that the Manila Hotel be the site of the Convention. Delegate Eriberto Misa of Surigao del Sur tries to stop me. Among those listening are (left to right): Andres Flores, Jorge Kintanar, Nap Rama, Antonio de Pio and Francisco Albano. I was booed for my efforts.*

make things difficult for the majority to ram through anti-people proposals when the Convention actually began its work.

Marcos Reaching Out

After settling the venue, what was uppermost in the minds of the delegates was the cocktail party in Malacañang to which Marcos had invited the delegates. Many of us wanted to go to the cocktails for a variety of reasons — some to hobnob with the Marcoses, and others, like me, a *provinciano*, just to see what Malacañang looked like. I had never been there before. That was, I thought, as good a time as any to have a close look at the palace and see Marcos again (he had visited me at my home in Cagayan de Oro when he ran for the presidency for the first time in 1965) and Imelda at close range.

At the Maharlika Hall of Malacañang, Marcos assured us of his support to make the Convention a success. Although I avoided a handshake with Marcos by staying away from him, I was not so lucky in evading Mrs. Marcos. She was a busy hostess that night, flitting like a butterfly from one table to another, posing for pictures and greeting the delegates, especially those of us who came from the Visayas and Mindanao in *Visayan*, our local language. The lady, I thought then, was going for the presidency when Marcos's term ends in 1973.

The Malacañang party did not last long. By 7:30 that evening, we went back to the Manila Hotel to join the Philippine Constitution Association, which unilaterally decided to enlist us as members to help "protect and defend the Constitution" merely because we had been elected delegates to the Convention. In less than two years, I would regret my enlistment as a member of Philconsa because the association did nothing to protest the proclamation of martial rule by Marcos. Instead, the association, whose numbers were boosted by the wholesale membership of delegates, echoed the Marcos line that martial law was the only way to create a "new society" or, as Marcos had put it in a more sanguine manner, to "make the nation great again!"

Convention Presidency Aspirants

In between the pre-convention meetings and the formal opening of the Convention, a number of known aspirants for the Convention presidency began to emerge. The front-runners were former President Carlos P. Garcia of Bohol, former President Diosdado Macapagal of Pampanga, Raul Manglapus and Teofisto Guingona, Jr., both of Rizal. On the side, the names of former Supreme Court Justice Jesus Barrera and Salvador Araneta, both also of Rizal, were floated as possible candidates for the Convention presidency.

Since the start of the pre-convention meetings, I supported Manglapus. I was, thus, often present in his strategy caucuses. Our basic game plan was to prevent a Marcos choice from getting the Convention presidency. The only way we could do that was to unify the Manglapus group with the Guingona faction. Only then, I said, would we have a chance to gain the support of a sizeable number of uncommitted delegates and prevent a Marcos *tuta* or lapdog from being elected to the Convention presidency. While the Convention presidency was not a position of vast political power, placed in the hands of a Marcos partisan, it could be used, at least symbolically, as a prop of the Marcos regime. Moreover, it would then be easier for pro-Marcos proposals to be written into the new Constitution.

Negotiating with Guingona

I played an active role in the Manglapus negotiations with Guingona. My position was that Guingona should withdraw in favor of Manglapus. One critical meeting between the Manglapus and Guingona panels was held at the Manila residence of Delegate Luis Lorenzo of Bukidnon, a Guingona partisan.

We had a seven-man panel for Manglapus, composed of Delegates Dean Feliciano Jover Ledesma of Manila; Ricardo Nepomuceno, Jr., of Marinduque; Ceferino Padua of Rizal; Wilfredo Cainglet of Zamboanga del Sur; Jose Leviste, Jr., of Batangas; Antonio de Guzman of La Union; and myself. In the Guingona group were: Jose Mari Velez of Rizal; Sonia Aldeguer of Iloilo; Augusto Sanchez of Rizal; Antonio Araneta, Jr., of Manila; Augusto Saguin of Zamboanga del Norte; Luis Lorenzo of Bukidnon; Bren Guiao of Pampanga; and Jose Bengzon, Jr., of Pangasinan.

Our panel's collective argument was that Guingona would only split the "Progressives" — meaning us, delegates, who proclaimed ourselves as beyond the control of Marcos — and scuttle the chances of our candidate to win the Convention presidency. Dean Ledesma opened the discussion by arguing that Guingona should give way to Manglapus, who had "more stature" than he. Ledesma meant that, Manglapus, a former senator, had better political credentials than Guingona who had not been elected to public office other than as delegate. Velez and Sanchez, however, got heated up and said that, if stature were the gauge for the Convention presidency, then we should all vote either for Garcia or Macapagal who were former presidents of the land.

When my turn to speak came, I reminded our colleagues that, in our negotiations, we were looking for the more *independent* candidate, one whom Marcos or other vested interests could not manipulate. And there were only two choices: Manglapus or Guingona. All references to others were simply immaterial. I explained that, between the two, Manglapus had demonstrated the more independent stance in political as well as economic issues.

Saguin and Sanchez, however, countered that Manglapus had a tainted record in public office as he had been ousted as a senator for "overspending." There was no arguing the point because it was a fact. Manglapus listed all that had been spent for and by him, thereby bloating his campaign expenditures beyond the limits set by law.

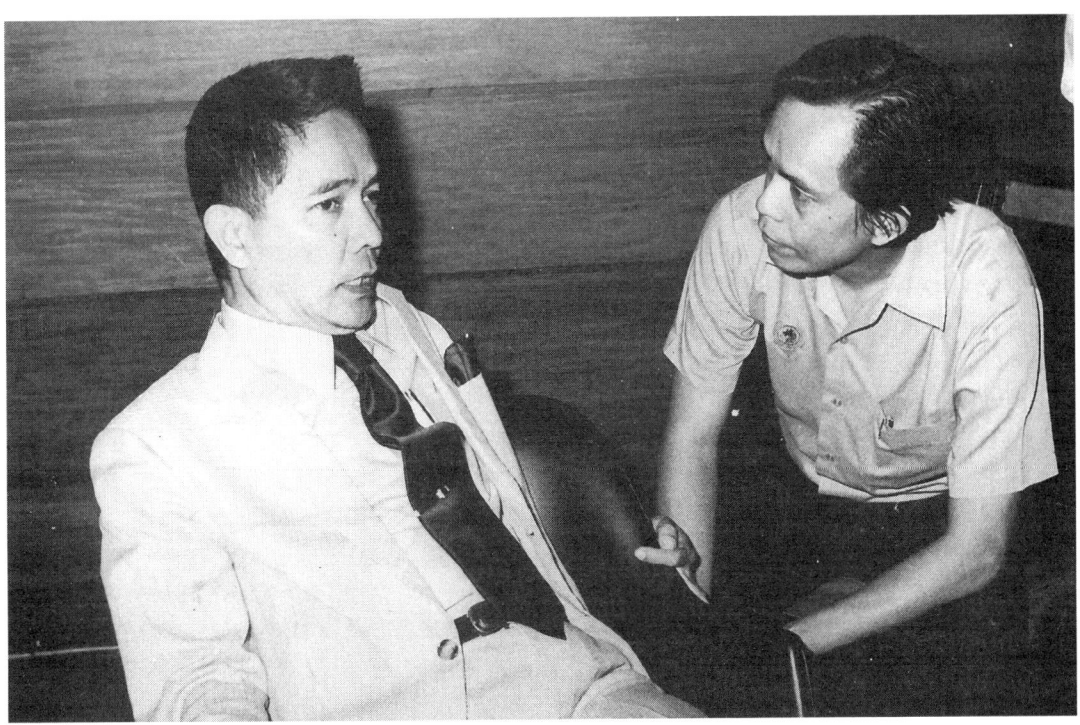

1971: *I SUPPORTED RAUL MANGLAPUS'S bid for the Convention presidency.*

The discussions went on interminably since neither panel would give way. Near midnight, Jose Leviste, Jr., suggested that perhaps the best thing was for Manglapus and Guingona to settle the issue between them in private. The proposal was the only one that both factions agreed on without argument. Fatigue, as we all found out, had a way of compelling even the most hard-line negotiators among us to go the way of reason. We then retired for the night.

Manglapus and Guingona met at 8 o'clock the following morning in Tony de Guzman's office. Hours later, we heard the good news. Guingona had agreed to withdraw in favor of Manglapus and would settle for the position of President Pro-Tempore of the Convention. Our joy was, however, short-lived. There was a hitch. Delegate Sotero Laurel said that he was also aspiring for the position of President Pro-Tempore and would not give way to anyone.

With Sotero Laurel's refusal to back off, the Manglapus and Guingona factions agreed to leave it to the first balloting on the floor of the Convention to decide who between the two of them would continue contending for the Convention presidency and who would withdraw and back up the other. We committed to support the one who received at least 10 more votes than the other as our common candidate for the Convention presidency.

With the pact between Manglapus and Guingona in place, I turned my attention to another contest. Felino Neri and Domocao Alonto, both from Mindanao, wanted to launch their candidacies for President Pro-Tempore.

I supported Neri's bid. As a former secretary of foreign affairs, he had, in my view, the credentials and good name to give honor to the position. Neri asked me to be part of his negotiating panel, which included Delegate Fanny Cortez Garcia of Surigao del Norte and Neri himself. Alonto's group also had three members: Sergio Tocao of Cotabato, Ramon Tirol of Davao del Norte and Alonto himself.

Like the negotiations between Guingona and Manglapus on the Progressives' candidate for the Convention presidency, the Neri-Alonto discussions went nowhere. We finally agreed to refer the matter to Senator Pelaez, the recognized leader of the Minsupala (Mindanao-Sulu-Palawan) political aggrupment. In the event, even Pelaez failed to resolve the issue. Neri and Alonto both ran and lost when the election of the President Pro-Tempore was held.

Macapagal's Resolution

During one of our pre-convention meetings, Macapagal filed a resolution to disqualify past and present Presidents of the Republic, their spouses and their relatives from running for offices under the proposed Constitution. The resolution was one of a number of proposals that the Manila media red-flagged as the Ban-Marcos resolutions.

The Macapagal resolution was criticized by the media as a ploy to attract the non-Marcos delegates to his candidacy for the presidency of the Convention. Although that was probably Macapagal's immediate goal, intrinsically, the proposal to ban Marcos and his relatives from running for public offices under the forthcoming Constitution had merit. It was believed that, if Marcos and his immediately family were banned from running for public positions under the proposed Constitution, Marcos would most likely adopt a hands-off policy instead of interfering in the affairs of the Convention. The delegates could then do their work freely. Marcos supporters in the Convention, however, vigorously objected to the move to ban their leader. They argued that it was wrong to include a provision in the proposed Constitution that sought to disqualify a particular individual or group of individuals from public office.

The several proposals that sought to prohibit Marcos and Imelda from running for public office under the new Constitution were eventually consolidated into a single Ban-Marcos Resolution. The Ban-Marcos Resolution became one of the two most contentious issues to hit the Convention. The other was the so-called Quintero exposé, which is discussed in greater detail in Chapter 6.

Controversy on Inviting Marcos

There was one other issue that had to be threshed out in our pre-convention meetings. That was the question of whether or not Marcos should be invited to attend and speak at our opening session. The issue was so controversial that it riled many delegates. Some delegates wanted Marcos invited out of courtesy to him as the President. Others wanted him invited out of loyalty to him as their leader. But there were a good number of us who did not want to have him present at the opening session.

Put to a vote, the motion to invite Marcos not only to attend the opening session of the Convention but also to deliver the main speech was approved by the majority. In his book, *The Grand Collision*, which was about the political battles between Marcos and Benigno S. Aquino, Jr., Delegate Manuel F. Martinez of Romblon recorded:

> The motion to invite won by a narrow margin, 117 to 101. About a hundred (delegates) were absent or abstained. It was the first of the slam-bang skirmishes on Marcos that was to plague the whole of the Convention.

1971: I ARGUE AGAINST PLAN to invite Marcos to the opening session of the Constitutional Convention. (Front row): Alfredo Abueg; (next row) Pablo Trillana and Jose Nolledo; (third row) Arturo Pingoy, Rodolfo Ortiz and Margarito Teves

Martinez was right. Indeed, the delegates were either for or against Marcos — not only as a person but also for the things he espoused. I voted against inviting Marcos, not because he did not deserve to be invited but because I wanted to help stave off the rising perception that the Convention was so early on already showing signs that it was nothing but a convenient tool to perpetuate Marcos in office. Because of the vote to invite Marcos to speak at the opening of the Convention, the original plan to have Comelec Chair Jaime Ferrer do the honors was simply forgotten. It was a pity because I thought that Ferrer had done a fairly good job in ensuring trustworthy elections for the Convention the year before. Because he was such a credible government official, I believed that he could have given us a message to inspire us to go beyond our own interests and focus on the nation's interest when we began our work to amend the Constitution.

Chapter 5

Inside the Convention

1971: *AT THE CONSTITUTIONAL CONVENTION with Convention President Diosdado Macapagal. (Left to right): Ric Sagmit, Dandy Tupaz, Ding Tolentino, me, Romy Capulong, President Macapagal and Tony Tupaz*

On the morning of June 1, 1971, the Convention opened its sessions at the Manila Hotel with Senate President Gil Puyat and House Speaker Cornelio T. Villareal as the joint presiding officers. Marcos was the guest of honor and principal speaker. He delivered a surprisingly brief speech, mainly — and hypocritically, I thought — about the need to craft a constitution that was Filipino in character to protect the interests of the people. He also pledged to create a "moral climate" whereby he could "support" the Convention to achieve "national unity."

Much of what Marcos said was lost on me because I was irritated that he had been invited to address the Convention. Some of our fellow delegates actually walked out of the convention hall as Marcos was about to speak.

Among them were: Jesus Barrera, Juan R. Liwag, Heherson Alvarez, Bonifacio Gillego, Romeo Capulong, Ernesto Rondon, Augusto Kalaw, Raul Roco, Geronimo Cabal, Enrique Voltaire Garcia, Jose Mari Velez, Antonio Araneta and Alejandro Lichauco.

I was tempted to join them, but eventually, I decided it was not the proper thing to do. Marcos, after all, was the President of the Republic. Although I did not like him, I thought the walkout was boorish even if, at that time, media pundits hailed it as an act of courage.

It was, thus, with great effort that I stayed put on my seat to listen — with little success — to what Marcos had to say. I convinced myself it was right to hear Marcos out now that he was the guest not only of the delegates who voted to invite him but also of the entire Convention. My discomfort at the opening rites was not caused solely by Marcos's presence. Part of it was due to my old ill-fitting black pair of pants that was redone by my tailor in Cagayan de Oro.

Outside the halls of the Convention, two competing groups of students demonstrated. The radicals called for revolution instead of a convention, while the moderates cried for reforms. Presaging by more than a year the demise of the Convention, 37 mock coffins with lit candles were lined up by the radicals in front of the Manila Hotel. The demonstrations inconvenienced both the delegates and the guests. Many had to take the side entrances to the Manila Hotel to avoid nasty confrontations with the demonstrators.

Electing Convention President

After the opening ceremonies, we adjourned for the day. The next morning, with Juan Liwag of Nueva Ecija presiding, we elected the Convention President in an executive session, that is, a closed-door session with the public excluded, as provided in the rules. The rules also called for runoff elections if no candidate got the majority. Runoff elections meant a second or a third balloting would be held with the elimination of the tail ender in every balloting until the majority went for the winning candidate. The rules likewise forbade speeches by those nominating their candidates for the various elective positions, as well as speeches by the nominees themselves.

The ban on speeches was ostensibly predicated on the need to save time. Actually, the reason for the ban was that the Marcos bloc feared that Carlos P. Garcia, their candidate, would be put to a disadvantage if the nominees were allowed to speak. Garcia was not a particularly good platform speaker except in the Visayan language and he would have suffered in comparison with Manglapus, who could mesmerize any audience with an impromptu or prepared speech in English, Spanish, Tagalog, Cebuano, Iloco, Hiligaynon and a dozen or so dialects. Garcia would have paled even against Macapagal, who invariably drew applause from political crowds with his kilometric sentences — the kind that built up to a crescendo like a staircase to the heavens before cascading back to earth — in English, Spanish, Tagalog or in his native

Kapampangan. Having heard Macapagal perorate, I knew that, had the nominees been allowed to speak, Macapagal would have left not only himself but also his audience breathless.

Four Candidates

The four delegates who finally contended for the Convention presidency were Garcia, Guingona, Macapagal and Manglapus. A fifth contender, Salvador Araneta, surfaced, but only his close associates thought he might win.

Garcia was generally perceived as the Marcos candidate. His followers thought that he could garner the highest number of votes at the first ballot, but not the majority required by the rules. Ingeniously, they assigned a number of Garcia diehards to vote for the weakest candidate (in their view, Guingona) at the first balloting so that they could eliminate the stronger ones (Macapagal and Manglapus, in descending order) from contending in the runoffs. Marcos was, arguably, at the lowest ebb of his popularity then, so that it was also convenient for some of the delegates to dissemble their commitment to him by posing as supporters of Macapagal, Manglapus or Guingona.

Manglapus Edged Out

The ploy worked. In the first balloting, Garcia received 95 votes; Macapagal, 69; Guingona, 66; and Manglapus, 65. The result meant that Manglapus would have to bow out of the race.

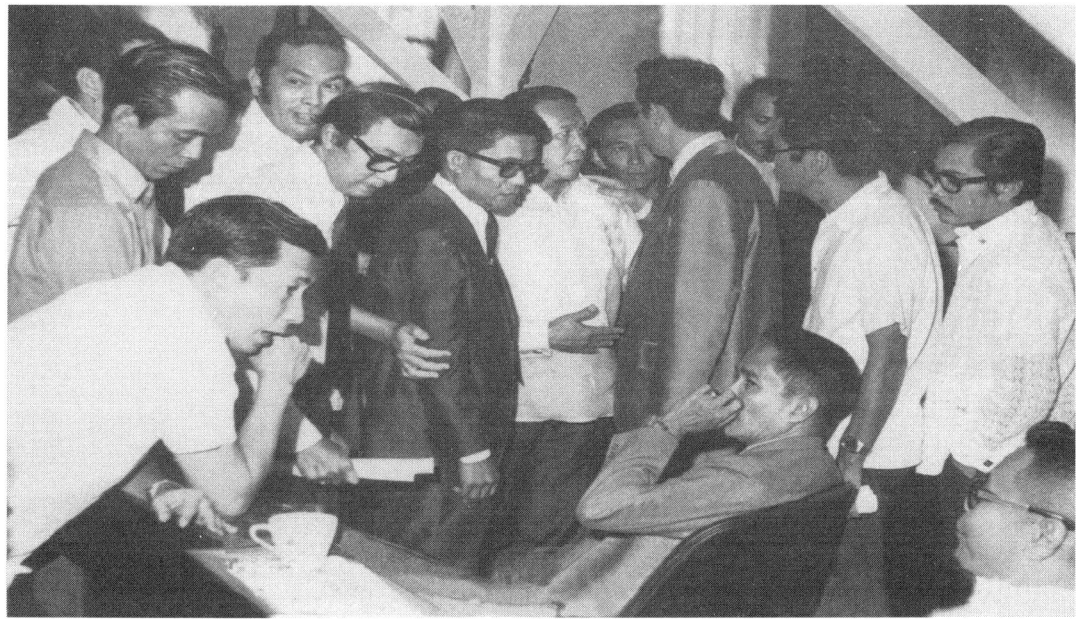

1971: RAUL MANGLAPUS, (in coat, seated), our candidate for president of the Convention, mulls his next move after he was edged out of contention by Tito Guingona (in coat) who stands to his right. I stand (2nd row from left) dejected by our unexpected loss to Tito. To my left are Dante Sarraga (smiling because he was for Tito), Totoy Nepomuceno, Ernie Rondon, Wilfredo Cainglet, Tony Bacaltos, Augusto Kalaw, Eddie Alanis and (rightmost) Boni Gillego.

But, between Manglapus and Guingona, things were not that clear. As mentioned earlier, when negotiating the terms of their unification, they had agreed that one would withdraw in favor of whoever led by 10 votes.

What complicated the issue was that during the counting of the votes, Guingona's followers offered Manglapus a new deal — whoever trailed the other even by only one vote would withdraw. When Guingona's followers made the offer, Manglapus was leading Guingona by eight votes. It appeared to be a good bargain, so Manglapus agreed. Unfortunately, the final tally showed Guingona leading Manglapus by one vote. Thus, a tempest in a teapot developed over the issue of whether or not Manglapus should go into the second balloting.

Many of Manglapus's followers urged him to go into the second balloting. I disagreed. I said that it was important for Manglapus to keep his commitment to Guingona. Happily, Manglapus agreed and asked me to convey his decision to bow out of the race to Pacifico Ortiz, who headed the Election Committee of the Convention. Ortiz told me that Manglapus should put his decision in writing. I got him to write it down and showed it to Ortiz. Ortiz was about to announce Manglapus's withdrawal when Guingona's followers objected to the wording of the withdrawal. They said Manglapus had merely withdrawn from the race, but had not expressly stated that he was withdrawing in favor of Guingona. I went back to Manglapus and asked him to add the words "in favor of Delegate Guingona of Rizal." Ever the gentleman, Manglapus wrote the phrase requested without making any fuss. I brought the amended letter to Ortiz. However, Ortiz doubted that the added words had actually been written by Manglapus because the ink used was not of the same color as that used in the original letter of withdrawal. I told Ortiz that those were indeed the words of Manglapus and that I vouched for the authenticity of the added words. It was only after I signed as a witness to the document did Ortiz announce that Manglapus had withdrawn from the race and was backing Guingona.

Guingona Loses

Guingona then went into the second balloting as the candidate of the Progressives. Although he showed a terrific performance by besting Macapagal, Guingona actually received only 93 votes to Garcia's 127 and Macapagal's 86. In the third balloting, with Macapagal eliminated, Garcia took the Convention presidency with 185 votes to Guingona's 118.

The tactics employed by Marcos partisans led by Delegate Antonio Tupaz of Agusan del Norte were ever so subtle that we, the supporters of Manglapus and Guingona, did not quite know what hit us. The Marcos "boys" showed us, the so-called Progressives, that we were all wet behind the ears in the art of hard politics.

It was only after the election for the Convention presidency that we, in the Manglapus camp, started to suspect that Antonio de Guzman of La Union was a Marcos mole in our ranks. In addition, we also thought that Arturo Barbero of Abra was another Marcos agent posing as a Manglapus follower. We, however, did not take what they did as a personal affront. We took it as a lesson learned that, in the political arena, some people act according to the adage that "all is fair in love, war and politics."

After Garcia was elected President of the Convention, in quick order, Sotero Laurel of Batangas was chosen President Pro-Tempore; Ramon Diaz of Camarines Sur, chair of the Steering Council, and Enrique J. Corpus of Zambales, chair of the Sponsorship Committee.

Garcia's *Sursum Corda*

After the elections of the other officers, Garcia delivered his inaugural speech as Convention President. It was simple and brief. He stressed that the immediate need of the Convention was for delegates to understand that "unity in diversity" was indispensable in our work. It was a message borne out of wisdom that, in a country like ours with diverse languages and cultural backgrounds, the constitution we were about to craft must respect those differences if we were to unite our people.

Garcia ended his talk with a strange sounding phrase that I did not hear clearly. It was only after I asked Delegate Jose Feria that I learned he had said, *"Sursum corda."* This was a Latin exhortation said during Catholic Masses, meaning "lift up your hearts," after which the congregation was expected to say "amen." No "amens" were uttered in response to Garcia's speech. There was only polite applause.

Garcia immediately took over the job of presiding at the session after his inaugural speech. It was, in my mind, a bad omen of things that Garcia did not hear a motion from the floor to adjourn the session until three in the afternoon of the following Monday. He announced, much to our amusement at the time, that he did not "wish to take up any other matter" and that if nobody would object, he would adjourn the session until next Monday at 3 p.m.

Laurel Presides

The Monday that Garcia spoke of came, but when the session opened at the scheduled hour, it was not Garcia but President Pro-Tempore Sotero Laurel who called the session to order. Laurel explained that Garcia was "a little indisposed" — that was why he had to preside over the proceedings.

We proceeded to discuss more rules to govern the Convention during the session until early evening when we adjourned. I then went to Manglapus's office to discuss some proposals with him. He was not there but I saw Delegate Jose Concepcion, Jr. rushing into the office. He was also looking for Manglapus, but because the latter was not around, he sprinted out of the room towards the session hall. I followed him there and found many delegates milling around and wearing long faces. They all seemed to be talking at the same time. Then I learned that Garcia had died of a heart attack minutes earlier.

I rushed back to Manglapus's office to leave the sad news with his secretaries to relay to him. Manglapus, however, was there and already knew of Garcia's demise. I suggested to him that the resolution we had prepared that afternoon asking Garcia to define his stand on the Ban-Marcos Resolution be withdrawn for the sake of propriety, considering the circumstances. But it turned out that the resolution had been released to the media. So we assigned Vicente Calejesan, a Manglapus student volunteer, to call the editors of the newspapers and the managers of the TV and radio stations to "kill" the story.

As the night deepened, Ricardo Nepomuceno, Jr., Jose Leviste, Jr., Bonifacio Gillego, Samuel Occeña, Jose Concepcion, Jr., and Margarito Teves gathered at Manglapus's office to discuss the repercussions of Garcia's death and the other developments of the day. Inevitably, the discussion turned to the possibility of Manglapus's vying again for the presidency of the Convention. I cautioned against making the intent public as Garcia had yet to be interred. It would not be in good taste, I said. Our colleagues agreed and we broke up our impromptu caucus on that note.

Manglapus Redux

The Convention had a week-long recess in deference to the demise of Convention President Carlos P. Garcia. After Garcia's interment, the election for the vacant position was held on June 29. This time there were only three candidates: Macapagal, Manglapus and former Supreme Court Justice Jesus Barrcra. Guingona had graciously announced his support for Manglapus.

Barrera, although a well-respected jurist, was considered merely a spoiler of Manglapus's bid for the presidency. He was egged on to run for the presidency by the radicals who reviled Manglapus as a "clerico-fascist."

We, who supported Manglapus, believed that this time our candidate would trounce the other contenders, especially since Guingona had thrown his support behind him. Macapagal, however, was no pushover. He won the support of many Garcia followers, led by Tony Tupaz and Gilberto Duavit.

Macapagal Wins

In the event, the delegates chose Macapagal to succeed Garcia. He won with 160 votes. Manglapus was second with 120 and Barrera, a distant third with 18 votes. There was no runoff election this time, because, with 160 votes, Macapagal had garnered more than the required majority. There were less than 320 delegates present at the Convention because some had not yet been proclaimed.

The superstitious viewed Macapagal's election to succeed Garcia as a manifestation of destiny. Macapagal had succeeded Garcia as President of the Republic in the elections of 1961.

With the election of Macapagal and other officers of the Convention, we settled down to work on a new Constitution for the Republic. On the side, we also filled the other elective positions in the Convention.

One of those positions was that of Floor Leader. Pablo Reyes of Misamis Oriental and I both aspired to be Floor Leader. In order not to strain our relationship, I suggested that our fellow delegate from our province and city, Rolando Piit, decide who should be our candidate for Floor Leader. Piit suggested we toss a coin to settle the issue. Reyes and I agreed. Reyes won and I stepped aside so that we could all support Reyes as our candidate. Reyes lost to Delegate Edmundo Cea of Camarines Sur.

Convention Blocs

As we began our work in the Constitutional Convention, the delegates started to group themselves into three major blocks: the radicals, the moderates and the conservatives or "reactionaries," as the radicals were wont to call them.

The radicals espoused the view that imperialism, colonialism and feudalism were the basic causes of the nation's ills. In their eyes, the US was the quintessential imperialist that sucked the blood of the nation first through colonialism and subsequently through neocolonialism. The US took over from Spain as our colonial masters in 1898. Upon the restoration of our political independence in 1946, in their view, the US took on the role of neo-colonizers by which it became the principal propper of the feudal character of Philippine society. In other words, by combining their interests with the local elite who controlled the wealth of the nation, the US continued to exercise undue influence over the economic, social and political life of the nation. The radicals peppered their rhetoric with the word "revolution" as the only way to save the people from utter poverty and further exploitation by the elite.

The moderates, on the other hand, were those who advocated change in the country incrementally. For instance, to provide land for the landless, the moderates proposed land reform — not confiscated but paid for with just compensation — and, to soften the harsh features of capitalism, they advocated, among other things, state support for cooperatives, profit-sharing and a family living wage, and the creation of a citizen's army in lieu of the standard Armed Forces.

The conservatives were those who were resistant to change or who merely advocated cosmetic changes in the legal structures of the country. For example, they proposed shorter terms of office of elective officials and using English as the language of the Constitution.

As a novice to the ways of Manila-based political sophisticates, I was attracted by the sloganeering of the radicals: "down with imperialism" or *"ibagsak ang imperialismo"*; "down with colonialism" or *"ibagsak ang kolonialismo"*; and "down with feudalism" or *"ibagsak ang pyudalismo."* Their anti-imperialist stance gave life to the demand to dismantle the US military bases in the country, which I supported. And their anticolonial position sought to free the country's economy from the perceived clutches of the colonial or neocolonial forces represented by the US and its allies. That I also found to my liking.

To do away with feudalism, the radicals urged the confiscation of big landed estates and their distribution to the landless. They also advocated that other means of production be transferred to the working class to end a few privileged families' stranglehold on the economy. I backed the land reform concept of the moderates, not the radicals. I also disagreed with their idea that the means of production should be completely transferred to the hands of the proletariat or the working class. It was my position even then that capitalism could have a human face. I was, for instance, a firm believer in cooperatives, profit sharing and family living wages to help the people escape the mire of poverty.

Manglapus's Influence

Lacking a more thorough grounding on how nations develop economically without sacrificing their democratic political moorings, I did tend to gravitate towards the radical bloc, which political observers believed were dominated by the so-called Left. I could not, however, cast my lot totally with the Left. Much of the reason was my admiration of the views of Manglapus, the dynamic guru of the Christian Democrats.

I guess genetics also tilted the balance in favor of the moderates. I was the son of Petra Quilinging, a public school teacher from Batac, Ilocos Norte, whose innate religiosity (she was always praying) could not but rub off on me. Besides, my father Aquilino, a lawyer, believed in reformation, not revolution, as the way to change the ills of society. Moreover, one of the greatest influences during my college days at Xavier University was Fr. William F. Masterson, SJ. Masterson always underscored the need for us not only to love our country but also to respect life. Thus, the farthest I traveled along the ideological path in the Convention was from center to left of center.

MY MOM and me

Manglapus's influence on me was reflected in the resolutions that I filed during the Convention. Among these were: Resolution No. 202, which called for the adoption of a principle to change the concept of property ownership from absolute to mere stewardship; No. 720 to repeal the death penalty; No. 3051 to enfranchise the 18 year olds and make them eligible for election or appointment to local government offices; and No. 1162 to exempt conscientious objectors from compulsory military service.

I also filed Resolution No. 1374 to secure for all employees in govern-

1971: *I FILED A RESOLUTION to lower the voting age to 18 and to provide family-living wage to workers. Listening from left, Arsenio Yulo, Sotero Laurel and Emilio de la Cruz. To my right, Jose Feria.*

ment service or private enterprise not only a minimum but a just living wage, and to guarantee a family living wage for employees with families. And I authored No. 691 to make it a policy of the State to encourage and support the organization and development of cooperatives.

Although there was nothing peculiarly Christian-Democratic about it, I also filed Resolution No. 3945 to compel the publication of the country's foreign loans and their terms and conditions which were approved by the Committee on Investments. In my opinion, it was vital that the people be informed of the loans secured by the government from abroad.

I authored other resolutions that had no Christian Democratic ideological content, but were important for their intended impact on the nation.

For example, I filed Resolution No. 200, which proposed that an article on local governments be included in the new Constitution. It was the forerunner of the Local Government Code that I authored and sponsored in 1987 during my first term as senator. And, foreshadowing the ban on presidential re-election embodied in the 1987 Constitution, I also authored Resolution No. 692 to limit the President to only one term. In the same resolution, I proposed that other elective officials be limited to only one re-election.

To spur owners to make their lands productive, I filed Resolution No. 1978 to empower the State to tax undeveloped or idle lands more heavily than developed or cultivated ones. A similar provision is now found in the Local Government Code. I got them calendared and approved at committee level. Those were proposals that I believed deeply in and which I had espoused when I campaigned as a candidate for the Convention.

I authored or co-authored with my friends in the Convention many other resolutions, but the ones cited more or less mirrored the basic ideas that I believed should be embodied in the proposed Constitution.

I found out early on in the work of the Convention that a delegate like me — who had no close allies to rely on to push for the things I wanted done — literally had to adopt rough tactics to accomplish his or her ends. I arrived at that conclusion after Resolution No. 320, which I filed on June 10 along with 21 other delegates as co-authors, languished in the bowels of the secretariat for more than two weeks before it was calendared for action on the Convention floor.

The Aquino Exposé

The resolution was in response to Sen. Benigno Aquino's exposé in a privilege speech he delivered at the Senate. Aquino bewailed the transfer of some P26 million from the Public Treasury to the House of Representatives, allegedly to fund the candidacies of certain delegates supported by leaders of the Nacionalista Party. We sought to obtain from the Treasurer of the Philippines certified true copies of the treasury warrants covering payments of the P26 million to the House.

Although I had no connection with Aquino then, I thought the Convention had a vital interest in his exposé, because the reputation of the delegates, unless cleared, would be tarnished by it. After several days of waiting futilely for the Secretariat to calendar the resolution, I decided to make a fuss about the "studied failure" of the Convention leadership to submit my resolution for debate on the floor.

I moved that a special order be issued to calendar the resolution. Put to a vote, the "nays" sounded louder than the "ayes," so I asked for a show of hands. A majority of the delegates approved my motion to calendar the resolution. But the resolution was not automatically taken up on the floor. I had to make myself obnoxious to Macapagal and his Floor Leaders Edmundo Cea and Estanislao Fernandez to get the resolution discussed on the floor.

Cea and Fernandez twice attempted to talk me out of pushing for the resolution. Their argument boiled down to pragmatics. They said we were "treading on dangerous grounds as the Convention was in the process of asking for more funds from Congress." I told them bluntly that they could defeat the resolution on the floor, but I would insist on sponsoring it.

Cea and Fernandez then maneuvered to insert other matters in the calendar for priority discussion. On July 1, when it became obvious that their strategy was to prevent discussion of my resolution at all costs, I asked for recognition by Macapagal who was presiding.

Macapagal recognized me — to his regret, I suppose — because I immediately rebuked him and the Floor Leaders "for trying to suppress dissent on the floor." That, I said, ran counter to his public promise when he was elected President of the Convention that he would "listen to contrary views."

In the end, the resolution was voted down. I expected the outcome, considering the conservative nature of the delegates. While I lost the vote on that one, I did not, however, consider my efforts a total failure. It helped educate me on the refinements needed to succeed in democratic debate in a collegial body, which I put to good use in the Senate soon after People Power I ousted Marcos from the presidency in 1986.

Stewardship Concept of Property

In the Convention, what really got the ire of powerful interests in the country was my introduction of a formal resolution for the adoption of the stewardship concept of property. The proposal — and I — became the targets of free-fire from the conservative sectors of our society.

The Philippine Association, which counted among its members the biggest foreign and local conglomerates, took the lead in attacking the proposal. The association feared that, once adopted, it would put to risk business investments in the country. In the association's view, the proposal would give the government a *carte blanche* to confiscate or nationalize businesses.

The association's opposition acquired a face in the person of Andres Soriano, Jr., one of the country's most successful businessmen and the head of

1971: ADVOCATING THE ADOPTION of the Stewardship Concept of Property. At my back, Mercedes Cojuangco Teodoro; at my right Domacao Alonto (in dark coat) and Sergio Tocao. At my left, Augusto Cesar Espiritu and in front, Elfren Sarte.

the San Miguel Corporation. He also owned substantial interests in the *Philippines Herald*, which generally echoed his denunciation of the stewardship principle.

Inside the Convention, influential delegates like Carlos Ledesma, a former president of the National Federation of Sugarland Planters, Miguel Cuaderno, a former Central Bank Governor, and Leonardo Siguion Reyna, a lawyer of the major oil companies, articulated the opposition of the association.

To my surprise, even the biggest organized peasant movement in the country, the Federation of Free Farmers, led by Jeremias Montemayor, a recognized authority on agrarian problems and a Vatican consultant on those issues, opposed the adoption of the concept of stewardship of property, the *Manila Evening News* said in its editorial on May 9, 1972. Also opposed were the Manila Jaycees, who simplistically assailed the concept as "misleading and a shorthand expression of abstract ideas" that should be avoided. There were also those who, lacking civilized breeding, hurled vile personal vituperations against me. An unsigned venomous letter, purportedly sent by people who called themselves "Bacoleños," belittled the proposal and called me names.

Of those who opposed the concept, I was most disappointed by the criticisms of the respected legal giant, Sen. Ambrosio Padilla. I did not know the extent of Padilla's conservatism until he delivered a privilege speech in the Senate, calling the proposal "communistic."

While I never had a chance to discuss the issue with Soriano, I had a debate on the issue with Senator Padilla in a meeting organized by the Institute of Social Work of the University of the Philippines. The senator was his usual articulate self when he espoused the view that the principle could lead to abuse by the government. He even called it unchristian.

I replied that the proposal was not meant to stand alone as the guiding principle of ownership of property. I said the principle, if adopted, would still have to be fleshed out by legal enactments to ensure that it would not be abused by those in power. Moreover, I said, the principle was a most Christian one because Christianity taught that all things are owned by God and man is only a steward. Therefore, man should use property in his hands not only for his benefit but for society's as well.

Alfredo Salanga, Jr., in an article titled "Con-Con: Left Turn?" in the *Asia-Philippines Leader* on January 21, 1972, discussed the proposal at some length. Quoting sources from the Philippine Association, Salanga said the stewardship proposal had "shocked the business community with its 'ultranationalistic and socialistic drift.'"

My reply, which also found space in the same article, pointed out that the proposal was nationalistic, but not necessarily ultranationalistic. I said:

> [It is one way that Filipinos can be] made supreme in our own land. Unless the nationalist principle is given a push in the new Constitution, parity agreements, alien military bases and free enterprise would make us a neo-

colony of foreign interests forever. The principle may be a socialistic principle, but it is the only way we can narrow the gap between the "haves" and the "have nots."

The stewardship proposal also had well-known defenders. Fr. Francisco Araneta, SJ, former head of Xavier University, openly supported it in behalf of the Association for Social Action. Some journalists, like Rodulfo Tupas of the *Sunday Times Magazine* and Gerry Gil, a columnist of the *Philippines Herald*, also refuted the charge that the proposal was a communist principle.

The national interest generated by my proposal on stewardship was music to my ears. As a *provinciano*, I suddenly found myself thrust into the maelstrom of a national debate over a proposal that I thought was really not that controversial. In fact, I felt flattered that the June 12 issue of the *Manila Times*, the No. 1 daily in the country, published in full a statement that I made entitled, "A Check on Appetite: Stewardship of Property."

In that statement, I refuted the allegations leveled against the proposal. For instance, I took a swipe at proposals to substitute the stewardship concept with what I thought was a more effete suggestion called the "social responsibility of the wealthy," as advocated by the Philippine Business for Social Progress. I said the social responsibility theory would not do because, as the proponents suggested, it "would leave to the conscience of the property owners to devise how they would share their bounty with the less fortunate." If that happened, I argued, "We would wind up exactly where we are now — meaning nowhere, insofar as alleviating the state of the property-less is concerned."

I said that the better idea was the stewardship concept of property as embodied in the report of the Constitutional Convention Committee on Declaration of Principles. I pointed out the error of the argument that "the concept robs the individual of all his rights to property." I said, "The concept explicitly recognizes the right of man, every man, not just some men, to own property."

Neither was it correct, I asserted, for those who opposed the concept to say that it concentrated all of man's rights in the State. I argued:

> On the contrary, the concept merely grants additional powers to the State to restructure ownership as its traditional powers of eminent domain, taxation and police power have been found wanting. The insinuation that the concept would create "an all-powerful State" is not right. The State cannot, without laws authorizing it, touch property even under the principle of stewardship. And such laws would have to conform to the requirements of due process....

I ended with a pitch:

The switch from the absolutist concept of property to mere stewardship would place in our society "a controlling power on the will and the appetite of men," especially those who were more favored by circumstance so that property may be more justly and equitably distributed.

Eventually, the partisan political agenda of the Marcoses to keep themselves in power through the Convention sidetracked the major economic or social proposals, which sought to change the socio-economic milieu of the country. Before the fight for supremacy in the Convention degenerated into a pro-and anti-Marcos strife, the delegate blocs — the radicals, the progressives and the moderates — representing various economic and social persuasions were actively recruiting adherents.

National Language

Meanwhile, a big fight was brewing among delegates on the issue of the national language. Most of the delegates from Luzon favored Tagalog as *the* national language, or at least the basis of the national language. In general, the delegates from the Visayas and Mindanao wanted English as the national language.

Inflamed rhetoric reverberated in the halls of the Convention about the need to show our love of country by writing the Constitution in our native tongue. The other side argued that one's love of country need not be measured by his or her mastery of the native tongue. Rizal, it was pointed out, wrote most of his memorable writings in Spanish, not in Tagalog, the language of his boyhood and of his family.

I thought that it was important that we developed our own language and use it in all our official communications, even in our court trials. In my experience as a trial lawyer, I found it unnatural that people litigating their rights in criminal or civil proceedings usually needed interpreters to translate their testimonies to English. There was something terribly wrong with the situation when people going to court could not even litigate their grievances in our native tongue. I found an ally in Ricardo Sagmit, Jr., who supported my stand that it was crucial that the Constitution be written in the national language so that it could be more easily understood by the people. As a fellow practicing lawyer, Sagmit also found it untenable that people should be compelled to use a foreign tongue to vindicate their rights.

I voted to adopt Tagalog as the basis for our national language and to write the Constitution in our own native tongue. Furthermore, I proposed that the Constitution should be rendered in the major languages, which should have the same force and effect as the English or the Tagalog version of the Constitution.

For a while, I was ostracized by many of my delegate friends from the Visayas and Mindanao. But I stuck to my decision because I believed that people would understand one another better, learn the basic things in life faster and perhaps facilitate the development of the nation if we had a common national language by which we could easily communicate with one another.

Three Blocs Vie for Power

The emergence of the three major competing groups in the Convention was a victory of sorts for Jaime Ferrer, the Comelec chair in the Convention elections of 1970. Ferrer saw to it that the elections were clean and honest. He went around the country warning all political parties and candidates not to inject partisanship in the Convention elections. He also insisted that the candidates woo the voters in the same forum under the sponsorship of the Comelec or any civic or nonpartisan, nongovernment organization. As a result of Ferrer's Comelec strict-neutrality approach, a good number of the delegates were elected not on the basis of the partisan support of the Nacionalista Party or the Liberal Party, the two major political parties at the time, but on the basis of the qualifications and platforms of the candidates.

Thus, early in the Convention, it was not the two political parties that vied for power. In fact, the political parties were sort of sidetracked in that three blocs contended for power: the radicals, the progressives and the moderates.

Faulty Oath?

In the midst of discussions on matters of national interest, like a discordant note of a wayward trumpet in an opera, somebody sued the Convention in the Supreme Court. The dispute was over the allegedly faulty oath of office that we took as delegates. The oath that I took on June 1, 1971, which was standard for all of us, simply stated:

> I, Aquilino Pimentel Jr., of Cagayan de Oro Misamis Oriental, having been duly elected Delegate of the Lone District, Misamis Oriental, to the Constitutional Convention, do solemnly swear that I will well and faithfully discharge to the best of my ability the duties appertaining thereto; that I will uphold the independence and integrity of the Convention; that I will bear true faith and allegiance to the people of the Philippines whose welfare, security and happiness I will hold uppermost in the Constitution I will help to amend; and that I impose these obligations upon myself voluntarily, without mental reservation or purpose of evasion.
> So help me God.

President Macapagal administered the oath of office to us on June 1, 1971, during the opening session of the Convention. The complaint alleged that the oath was unconstitutional because it did not contain the standard phrase required of the oaths of office of all public servants, "to uphold and defend the Constitution of the Republic." The Supreme Court, however, made short shrift of the complaint and dismissed it as being without merit.

Before long, the three blocs' contest for supremacy based on fundamental principles and basic beliefs dissipated in the face of the challenge from a more powerful group that inexorably gained the upper hand in the Convention. This was the group that worked for the insertion of provisions in the proposed Constitution that would perpetuate the Marcoses' hold on government.

The members of the group aggressively raided the ranks of the conservatives and the moderates. They had the advantage of having Marcos in their corner. They had perks to offer to, privileges to confer on and political power to share with whoever was willing to support Marcos's continued stay in Malacañang. They were also not beyond employing bribery and blackmail, as Eduardo Quintero of Leyte denounced in a brief privilege speech on the floor of the Convention on May 19, 1972. The speech that began in the hushed tones of an old man rocked the Convention to its foundations, rattled Marcos to the bones and woke the nation from its lethargy.

Chapter 6:

The Quintero Exposé

1972: IN HIS PRIVILEGE SPEECH, Delegate Eduardo Quintero displays some peso bills (in his left hand) sent to him to make him support the adoption of the parliamentary form of government and desist from supporting the Ban-Marcos resolution. Listening intently to his left are Delegates Jesus Matas and Bren Guiao. Eyeing Quintero with suspicion further right is Delegate Casimiro Madarang.

Eduardo Quintero caught many of us by surprise when he said in a privilege speech that money had been given to certain delegates by some people "acting as agents" of an unnamed principal. Only Macapagal, Vicente Sinco and a handful of Macapagal's close allies, mostly trusted Liberal Party colleagues, knew beforehand that Quintero would say something earth-shaking on that day.

In fact, with Macapagal presiding, the May 19 session began rather inauspiciously. After the roll call, Ramon Tirol took his turn to sponsor the resolution for the adoption of a parliamentary government. Tirol took about 10 minutes to discuss his point that the parliamentary form was more accountable than the presidential form and, therefore, more conducive to nation building.

Quintero followed Tirol as the next speaker in favor of the adoption of a parliamentary government. He had a prepared speech but read only a brief portion, after which he asked that the undelivered parts be inserted in the journal of the Convention. Those of us who were following the proceedings thought that Quintero wasted his opportunity to expound on the merits of the parliamentary government, but we knew it was a normal practice for delegates to ask that their statements be considered read and "inserted in the journal" of the Convention. We liked that rule because it saved us a lot of time reading our speeches or listening to those of our colleagues, especially if the purpose was simply to ensure that posterity would remember us as having said something during our stint as delegates.

'A Matter of Collective Privilege'

After Quintero's sponsorship speech was entered in the journal, Floor Leader Gregorio Puruganan moved to suspend the session for five minutes, during which he went into a brief huddle with Macapagal. When the session was resumed, Puruganan moved for the suspension of the debates on the parliamentary form of government. The motion was approved without any objection. Puruganan then moved that Quintero be allowed to speak on "a matter of collective privilege."

Since Quintero was recognized to speak on a matter of personal and collective privilege, I assumed he would discuss issues that involved the name, honor and the integrity of the Convention delegates. Incidentally, before that day, many of us barely knew there was a delegate by the name of Quintero. And the few who really knew him saw Quintero as a mild-mannered former diplomat, an elderly statesman who could give sage advice to his juniors in the Convention. The only telltale sign something big was about to happen did not come from Quintero. It came from Macapagal. He ran his right hand swiftly over the bridge of his nose thrice, a mannerism that Ricardo Sagmit, Jr., a delegate from Macapagal's home province, Pampanga, said betrayed his innermost tensions.

Since the Convention had been in session for almost a year, collective privilege speeches were common interventions and did not attract much attention. Many delegates, in fact, were not in the session hall, but in the coffee shop of the hotel, relaxing. Even those of us who were in the session hall did not initially pay close attention to his speech. Quintero's age — he was turning 72 in a few days — and his deliberative manner of speaking did not attract attention to what he was saying.

But, when he revealed that some delegates had dinner at Malacañang on January 6, all ears turned to him. Many delegates stopped talking among themselves and those who were standing slowly slid into their seats to listen to him more closely. The other delegates in the coffee shop started to filter into the session hall. With bated breath, everybody waited for Quintero to name the delegates who had attended the Malacañang dinner. But he did not. He explained that he mentioned the dinner to make clear that, contrary to rumors fanned by media reports, the delegates at the dinner received only tokens from Marcos, like a cigarette lighter, a black wallet containing P2 and a brown lady's wallet with P1 in it.

Had Quintero ended his speech on that note, his exposé would not have created the impact that it did. However, he went on to deplore "the attempt of certain quarters to influence the delegates with the use of lobby money that placed the dignity and the integrity of the Convention under the cloud of doubt." With that assertion, the visual and aural faculties of all the delegates were glued on him.

Quintero then proceeded to reveal bits of evidence of someone's intervening in the work of the Convention. In measured tones, Quintero said that, "since March 19, 1971 and on several occasions, thereafter," he had received, through "some delegates who acted as 'agents,' various amounts totaling P11,150."

Sepulchral silence received Quintero's public admission that money had been passed on to him by "agents," some of whom were delegates. Questions on the identities of the delegate-agents and their principal raced through our minds, overtaking the pace of his delivery. Quintero kept us in suspense. He did not name the delegate-agents. Neither did he name the principal for whom they had acted. He merely said he was turning over the money given him to the Convention secretariat as physical evidence of his revelation.

The omissions were a letdown for us, in the anti-Marcos bloc, because we eagerly expected more direct disclosures from him. The pro-Marcos bloc just as avidly hoped that he would simply end his privilege speech.

We in the anti-Marcos bloc were also dissatisfied that Quintero did not submit to the Secretariat the envelopes that contained the money given to him. As a lawyer, I knew the envelopes were important documents to complete the evidence.

We also lamented that Quintero did not categorically assert that the money given him and the other delegates was a part of Marcos's attempt to manipulate the work of the Convention. At the time, the rumor mills were churning out endless gossip that the pro-Marcos bloc in the Convention would insert provisions in the new Constitution to ensure Marcos's stay in power longer than the two successive presidential terms of four years each allowed by the 1935 Constitution. Marcos was first elected as president in 1965 and was re-elected in 1969. His two-successive-term limit, as prescribed by the 1935 Constitution under which the Convention was working, would be reached by 1973. Nonetheless, we were pleased that he provided the basis for a more detailed probe into the alleged manipulation.

On the other side of the political divide in the Convention, the Marcos bloc was furious that Quintero dared to put into its records the so-called *payola* (word used by the Manila press) that was only bruited about earlier in rumors.

The reactions of the opposition political leaders to the Quintero expose as publicized by the Manila media were predictable. Sen. Jose Diokno said that his speech "confirmed the existence of a plot to bribe the delegates." Other politicians like

Vice President Fernando Lopez and Senate Minority Leader Gerardo Roxas expressed similar views. As far as the public was concerned, the Quintero speech strengthened the prevailing belief that Marcos would look for a way to enable him to stay in power longer than what the 1935 Constitution allowed.

Form of Government

To many of us, the adoption of a parliamentary government became the chief indicator of whether or not Marcos controlled the Convention. If a parliamentary government were adopted, the country would see more of Marcos as its Prime Minister. In fact, pro-Marcos operators in the Convention argued that the 1935 Constitution's prohibition against Marcos's running for a third term would not apply to him under the new Constitution as the ban applied to the presidential, not parliamentary, form of government. Under the parliamentary form of government, Marcos would be running for head of government as Prime Minister, not as head of government and of State in the presidential type.

Quintero's speech gave a tremendous boost to our stand against Marcos's running again for president or prime minister or another public office under the proposed Constitution. Nonetheless, I found myself in an awkward position. I was still making up my mind whether or not I would support the adoption of the parliamentary form of government. In fact, I had not filed any proposal to adopt one form over the other. What I filed was a proposal to limit the president to one term. But, as the debates progressed, I was inclined to support the parliamentary form. I was not, however, prepared to accept the proposal of the parliamentarians in the Convention that the President should only have ceremonial powers.

I argued that the President, even under a parliamentary form of government, should be vested with certain powers. I cited, as examples, the powers to promulgate laws, to ask for a reconsideration of the acts of parliament, to appoint the top officers of the Armed Forces, and to be the commander-in-chief of the Armed Forces. I pointed out that those powers were lodged with the Presidents of Italy, France, West Germany and India, leading examples of parliamentary governments.

The Marcos partisans did not really care whether the parliamentary form of government hewed closely to the European or any other model or not. The only consideration weighing heavily in their minds was that, whatever form of government the Convention adopted, it should not oust Marcos and Imelda from power in 1973. As mentioned earlier, 1973 was the deadline for Marcos's non-extendible second term, as fixed by the 1935 Constitution.

Quintero's privilege speech on May 19 only hinted that a powerful hand was manipulating the Convention. The direct imputation that the Marcoses were behind the bribery of the delegates came days later. Initially, Marcos's reaction was a studied "hands-off policy" denial that he had anything to do with it. His spokesman, Press Secretary Francisco Tatad, said:

1972: *THE COMMITTEE ON PRIVILEGES maps out our plan to investigate the Quintero expose. Chairman Eduardo Sison (center) is flanked by committee members (left to right), Manuel Concordia, Augusto Legaspi, Decoroso Rosales, Jose Feliciano, Raymundo Baguilat, Romualdo Mendiola, me and Jose Madrilejos, Jr.*

Malacañang does not know anything about these envelopes and anybody interested should ask those who gave them. Malacañang denies any connection with anyone who allegedly gave the envelopes to the delegates.

Privileges Committee Probes Exposé

Quintero's privilege speech was referred to the Convention Committee on Privileges for investigation. The committee, headed by Chairman Antonio Sison, had nine other members, namely: Raymundo Baguilat, Manuel Concordia, Jose Feliciano, Augusto Legaspi, Jose Madrilejos, Jr., Romualdo Mendiola, Decoroso Rosales, Ceferino Padua and me.

Just as a number of things in my life happened without any deliberate planning on my part, I became a member of the committee, probably the last, because no one else wanted to be in it. The committee was entitled to 15 members, but the most it could get were 10 delegates, including the chairman.

Other delegates shunned it because it had the unattractive duty of investigating any wrongdoing or unethical conduct of delegates. As delegates, we knew that decisions on the ethical behavior of our fellow delegates would create a no-win situation for the committee members. If the members exonerated delegates under investigation, the public would in all likelihood damn them. And if the panel punished the offending delegates, the latter and their allies in the Convention would damn the committee members, too. Furthermore, the committee was not a high-profile one that worked in the glare of media klieg lights. As a rule, its investigations were done *in camera* or in executive session, with only the members of the committee in attendance, and its decisions were to be normally couched in the most diplomatic language possible, something that would hardly make the headlines.

For instance, prior to the Quintero exposé, the committee investigated media reports in March 1972 that some delegates were using their offices for gambling and womanizing. The *Herald*, on March 4, front-paged an article titled, "Delegates Forsake Work to Gamble." In its March 5 issue, *Taliba*, a Tagalog afternoon daily, headlined: *"Delegado Nagdadala nang Babae"*, "Delegate Womanizes." The *Bulletin*, the *Manila Times* and other newspapers carried similar stories. Because Manila was well covered by radio and television, the news reports that the Convention delegates were wasting the people's money in gambling and womanizing reached the entire archipelago.

Because of their salacious hints, the news reports acquired a life of their own and became more demanding of public explanation. Macapagal was thus impelled to direct the Privileges Committee to investigate the allegation that some 15 unnamed delegates were converting their Manila Hotel offices into a gambling casino.

Pursuant to the Macapagal directive, Sison, as chairman of the committee, called an emergency meeting on March 6 to consider what we should do. The committee approved my suggestion that we should invite Vicente Foz of the *Manila Times*, Jose Carreon of the *Herald*, Ben Lara of the *Bulletin* and Mel Parale of *Taliba*, to shed light on their reports that "gambling and womanizing" were prevalent in the premises of the Convention.

Reluctant Witnesses

The newsmen came in response to our summons, but were not of much help. They claimed they had no direct knowledge of the gambling and womanizing of the delegates. They said their sources were delegates whom they refused to identify because they had to protect their sources. It was frustrating to hear the newsmen repeating their "mantra" that they would not reveal the sources even if their articles put all the delegates in a bad light. In defending their stance, the newsmen to a man said that their duty was simply to report what they saw or heard about the goings-on in the Convention. It was not their duty to prove what they wrote about.

Nonetheless, one newsman, Carreon of the *Herald*, testified that an informant told him that some 10 to 15 delegates frequented Room 208 and that their gambling activities took place three or four times a week, usually between 9 to 11 o'clock in the morning. In criminal law, Carreon's testimony by itself would be considered hearsay information and would not suffice to "convict" an accused. But, taken with other testimonies like that of Delegate Timoteo Ruben of Misamis Occidental, who was a priest, and that of Foz of the *Manila Times* and the other witnesses, I believed we had more than enough basis to at least admonish certain delegates or even reprimand them. After all, we were not investigating a criminal case. We were holding a probe on the ethical conduct of certain delegates.

Ruben also told the committee that, on certain evenings, from his room (210), which adjoined Room 208, he could hear mahjong tiles colliding. Foz testified that he had seen card games being played in some rooms assigned to delegates on the second and third floors of the hotel. Like his other media colleagues, however, Foz declined to name the delegates concerned.

Parale testified that he did not have any personal knowledge of gambling in the Convention premises, but had heard of it from delegates who were "unimpeachable sources." Sison elicited from Parale the admission that the latter had been invited several times to join some delegates in card games in their offices. Parale, however, also declined to name the delegates.

I believed that we could have asked the newsmen to be a little more specific were it not for the committee members' collective fear of incurring the wrath of the media. Thus, the committee members simply glossed over the need to get the crucial information from the newsmen.

After we heard the testimonies of Ruben and the newsmen, we did an ocular inspection of Room 208. Although we found no gambling paraphernalia there, we saw some boxes with the name of Arturo Pacificador. When the committee reconvened, I moved that Pacificador be invited to our next meeting. Madrilejos objected, arguing implausibly that "what the members (of the committee) saw during the ocular inspection was not at issue." He was clearly wrong on that point. Precisely, an ocular inspection meant subjecting a place involved in a controversy to visual scrutiny, after which the inspectors would report what they had seen to the body that had ordered the inspection. Feliciano, however, intervened and suggested that, instead of formally inviting Pacificador, he should just be asked if he would voluntarily testify regarding the boxes bearing his name in Room 208. Sensing that the Feliciano suggestion would carry the day, I refrained from pushing my motion.

Shortly before Quintero did his exposé, the committee dismissed the gambling and womanizing charges against the unnamed delegates. I thought that we should have delved deeper into the matter and imposed sanctions on the offending delegates. But no delegate who was suspected of having gambled or of having brought women for sexual purposes into the premises of the Convention was summoned to the hearing. Even Pacificador was not summoned.

In my dissent to the findings of the committee dismissing the gambling and womanizing incidents, I said:

> The report suffered from inconclusiveness because we did not exhaust all avenues to seek out the truth. Because we had not done so, I said, the impression was inescapable that the committee was halfhearted in discharging its functions; wishy-washy in the execution of its mission; and slipshod in arriving at its conclusion.

But I was a minority of one and my opinion did not change the stand of the committee. With the Quintero exposé referred to our committee, I did not think that we could live up to the expectations of the people, considering our poor track record in the investigation of the gambling and womanizing delegates.

Quintero Speech Stresses Convention

After the formal referral of Quintero's speech to the Committee on Privileges, Macapagal ordered the resumption of the session so the debates on the parliamentary form of government could continue.

Samuel Occeña of Davao, however, moved that Quintero be compelled to reveal the names of the delegates who had attended the Malacañang party on January 6. Macapagal ruled that, since the Quintero exposé had been referred to the Committee on Privileges, the matter would be taken up by it. Macapagal then ordered the debates on the parliamentary form of government to proceed as if Quintero had not said anything that imperiled the Convention.

Macapagal's decision to continue the plenary session was a well-calculated move. It was meant to send a message to the people that, regardless of what Quintero said, the Convention under his leadership intended to craft a new Constitution for the nation. In fact, the following day, Macapagal told a press conference that, assuming that 40 delegates actually prostituted the Convention, the remaining 277 delegates would make up for misdeeds of the 40. It was a good sound bite, but as events later showed, Quintero's speech had already doomed the Convention in the minds of the people.

Anyway, at the plenary session, Sammy Occeña did not agree with Macapagal's decision to continue the parliamentary debates as if Quintero had not exploded a political bombshell. He, therefore, presented another motion, this time to defer the debates on the form of government "until after the Quintero exposé was acted upon" by the committee. Macapagal, however, would have none of it. Suspending the session for a few minutes, he succeeded, after talking with Occeña, in making him withdraw his motion.

With the Occeña motion out of the way, 11 other delegates, Geronimo Cabal, Oscar Leviste, Clemente Abundo, Rebeck Espiritu, Liningding Pangandaman, Pedro Exmundo, Jesus Reyes, Wilfredo Cainglet, Gregorio Tingson, Francisco Astilla and Godofredo Ramos, took turns in sponsoring the parliamentary government resolution. As the minutes recorded it, the Convention adjourned at 8:01 on the evening of May 19, as if Quintero's revelations were all a part of a normal day.

Quintero's First Appearance

Things in the Convention, however, were far from normal on that day. While the delegates went on to debate the merits and demerits of a parliamentary government, the Committee on Privileges met in Room 402 of the Manila Hotel. Breaking the Convention rule that forbade committees from meeting while the plenary session was in progress, Chairman Sison convened the Privileges Committee at 3:45 p.m., but nobody questioned it because of the critical issues raised in Quintero's speech.

Sison told us he wanted to provide Quintero with a speedy avenue to amplify on the revelations he had made an hour earlier. Immediately after Macapagal referred his privilege speech to our committee, Sison asked Quintero to meet with us.

While waiting for him to arrive, Sison asked for suggestions on how we should proceed with the investigation. I suggested that it be done in public, not in executive session, so the people would know what we were doing. I also urged that the investigation be conducted continuously so the people would not suspect the committee of being a party to any attempt to whitewash the Quintero revelations or delay the completion of the investigation. My twin proposals were accepted without objection. So were Padua's and Madrilejos's suggestions that

1972: QUINTERO (rightmost, sideview) meets Privileges Committee for the first time. There were kibitzers but the committee members were all present.

Quintero's speech be reproduced and that he be made the first witness of the committee.

Before long, Quintero appeared. Without delay, Sison asked the committee members to direct questions at him. Feliciano, Concordia, Padua and Madrilejos asked several questions. They wanted to know if Quintero knew why money was passed on to him. They also wanted him to name the 39 other delegates who were at the Malacañang party on January 6 when they were given the presents that Quintero mentioned in his speech.

I found Quintero less than forthcoming. He fended off the questions by insisting that the committee should first consider the matter of his exposé carefully before delving into its details, like asking him the names of the recipients of money from Malacañang. He wanted to be given time to think about the repercussions of his testimony. To Madrilejos's insistence that he name names, Quintero testily replied that he did not want to be "bamboozled" into a cross-examination at the time. He then asked that the investigation be postponed as he was leaving for Leyte to visit a brother who was very seriously ill.

Although Quintero looked like a walking bag of bones, he managed to stay for about an hour with the committee. I found his appearance all too brief and inconsequential. Before he left, I moved the committee members be made to state categorically whether or not they were present at the Malacañang party referred to by Quintero. The motion placed all committee members on the spot.

My purpose was to prod all members to state for the record if any of us were present at the party because, in my opinion, anyone who was present should automatically be inhibited from participating in the investigation. I also wanted to send a message to the Convention that we intended to search for the truth of the exposé, no matter who got hurt. The motion was approved and, one by one, the members of the committee, had to respond.

Nine of us — Sison, Padua, Feliciano, Concordia, Legaspi, Madrilejos, Mendiola, Rosales and I — categorically stated we were not in Malacañang on January 6. Baguilat said he "was in Malacañang sometime, but was not sure of the date" and asked that he be given time to verify his records. Padua asked Quintero if he had seen Baguilat at the Malacañang party on January 6. Quintero said he could not remember. Had Quintero replied in the affirmative, either Padua or I would have moved to disqualify Baguilat from the committee. In a subsequent meeting of the committee, Baguilat made it of record that he had not been present at that Malacañang party.

Quintero's appearance before us on the afternoon of May 19 was the first of his personal appearances before the Committee on Privileges to substantiate the statements he had made in his privilege speech. As he left, Quintero assured us that he would "cooperate with the committee" and would return in two or three days. In fact, it took him 10 days to do so.

Overconfident Timetable

Later that day, Chairman Sison confidently told the media that he thought "the investigation would end in about two weeks." He added, "The committee can come up with a report in three days from the termination of the hearings." Subsequent events showed this was not to be the case. For one thing, Quintero's frail state of health prevented his appearing before us on many days set for the investigation. For another, the publicity that hounded Quintero after his exposé and those suspected to have been involved in the scandal complicated the already complex issues of his May 19 privilege speech.

For instance, on Sunday, May 21, Domingo Veloso of Leyte issued a press statement in which he admitted giving Quintero "sums of money on different occasions." Veloso explained that he had given the money "without any consideration whatever, except our friendship." Veloso's explanation was a little too credulous, but it presaged the Marcos line that Quintero's woes arose out of his financial difficulties from which he had asked friends to bail him out.

Veloso's gambit drew an unexpected response from Quintero in Tacloban City on May 22. In a classic in the art of befuddling an issue, Quintero said Veloso had indeed given him money but Veloso's publicized reasons for doing so were different from what the latter had actually told him. Quintero did not elaborate on those reasons other than to say that he would first confer with Veloso to avoid any misunderstanding.

Then, like a master magician pulling rabbits out of his hat, Quintero, without any preliminaries, dragged the name of Jaime Opinion of Eastern Samar into the *payola* scandal. He identified Opinion as one of the agents who had passed on "lobby money" to him. He said he hoped Opinion would be as "honest and frank" as Veloso. That bothered me because, if Quintero thought Veloso was "honest," was he saying that the latter had given him money "because they were friends" as Veloso had claimed? In any case, Opinion furiously denied his accusation and threatened to file libel charges against him.

To further complicate our committee work, on May 22, the first session day after the Quintero exposé, Sotero Laurel delivered a privilege speech demanding that the Committee on Privileges submit a report on the exposé forthwith. If it needed time, "the committee should be given three hours to do so," he said. Sison replied that the committee had not even begun its investigation, hence it could not comply with Laurel's demand.

On other session days, similar demands were made on the committee to submit its report soonest. Time and again, Sison had to explain that Quintero was still in Leyte or that he was ill and unable to testify. The impatience the delegates expressed on the floor or elsewhere for the early submission of our report pressured all of us in the committee to conduct and conclude the investigation soonest.

Crafting the Rules

In the last days of May, while Quintero was still in Leyte, we crafted the rules to govern the investigation. Up to the Saturday of that week, we worked continuously to refine the procedure of the investigation. We argued lengthily as to whether or not the committee rules should be submitted to and approved by the Convention. We finally agreed that we should approve the rules and only furnish the delegates with a copy.

1972: *DELEGATE CEFERINO PADUA reaches out to me to help fight off moves to expel him from the Committee on Privileges. Between him and me are Jose Feliciano and Convention Secretary Jose Abueva. May be seen in picture (from left) are Jesus Barrera, Antonio Velasco and Sam Occeña.*

Other contentious issues emerged during our discussions on the rules, but one stood out over the rest. It was the question of whether or not we should accept Quintero's statements given after his speech as an integral part of his exposé. Quintero had intimated that he had a diary containing some of the information that he referred to in his speech. I argued that the entire contents of the diary of Quintero" should be considered as a valid basis for the investigation to proceed. Put to a vote, the proposal won 5-4, with Chairman Sison abstaining. Padua cast the vote that spelled victory for our side.

Padua's pronounced anti-Marcos attitude and vote, which broke the tie on whether or not Quintero's diary and other statements should be a valid basis for the investigation to proceed, brought him the ire of Marcos's delegates. Soon after the committee vote, Arturo Pacificador questioned Padua's membership in the committee on the Convention floor. Ostensibly, the move to oust Padua was due to the fact that he was a member of five committees, one more than the number the Convention rules allowed per delegate. Because his continued membership in the committee was challenged, Padua, a decent man, inhibited himself from participating in the investigation. The inhibition was not enough to quench the Marcos partisans' thirst for blood. On June 15, they forced a decision on Padua's membership in the committee and, by a vote of 118-92, ousted Padua from it, a clear signal of the fate that awaited the committee decision on the Quintero exposé.

Although I saw Padua as an invaluable ally in our search for the truth in the Quintero investigation, his ouster actually made the committee more credible as a probe body because now the members were evenly divided into the pro-Marcos bloc, composed of Baguilat, Legaspi, Madrilejos and Mendiola, and the anti-Marcos group, namely, Concordia, Feliciano, Rosales and me. Sison as chair was the "X" factor, who could cast his swing vote either way in case of a tie.

Regardless of our perceived biases, we worked hard to adopt reasonable rules to govern the conduct of the Quintero investigation. Among other things, upon my motion, we agreed to bar our fellow delegates from appearing as counsel before the committee or from speaking for or against the issues raised by Quintero during our committee hearings. The rule did not sit well with a number of our co-delegates. Most delegates, however, just bristled at the thought that they could not air their views at the investigation but did nothing about it. Still, during one committee meeting, my father's cousin from Surigao, Vicente Pimentel, who was known for his hot temper, voiced his disagreement with the ruling. He said so and started to perorate about the right of delegates to participate in the hearings of committees. Chairman Sison ruled him out of order, but he persisted in talking. Sison then ordered Sergeant-at-Arms Humberto Garganera to escort him out of the hall. But when Garganera approached him, he lunged at Garganera and would have pounced on him were it not for the intervention of other delegates.

Enforcing the Rules

Sison's firm insistence on enforcing the rules restored order. From then on, only the members of the committee and the delegates named by Quintero or their non-delegate counsel were allowed to freely participate in the committee investigation. Sison let it be known to the non-committee member delegates who wanted to intervene that they could not just barge into the committee hearings without getting embarrassed unless they had the chair's permission.

Even without other delegates' complicating the proceedings of the committee, we had enough controversial issues to keep the Quintero investigation lively. In one committee hearing, I moved to invite Mrs. Marcos to be a witness after Quintero named her as a source of the money. I said it was important for us to hear her side, otherwise she would not have the chance to air her story and the records of the committee would be incomplete. Madrilejos and Legaspi objected to it on the technicality that to summon Imelda would in effect assume we had already established the truth of Quintero's allegations.

My motion was lost as only Feliciano, Concordia and I supported it. Aside from Madrilejos and Legaspi, Rosales, Baguilat and Mendiola voted against it. Although the words of the motion were explicit enough, the intent was not that manifest. I also wanted to find out that early, if in a crunch, our anti-Marcos ally, Rosales, would stand by us or not. When he voted against my motion, I thought we had lost him to the Marcos bloc. In fairness, however, in the end, he voted against efforts to terminate the Quintero investigation inconclusively and, more importantly, against the ratification of the proposed Constitution in an act of rare courage, which he displayed for all to see, along with a handful of our colleagues.

Meanwhile, Quintero's brother died in Tacloban City so he could not return to Manila and appear before the committee on May 23 as previously agreed. To see for ourselves how Quintero was doing, we — Chairman Sison, Feliciano and I — flew to Tacloban on May 25. Thanks to Chino Roces, the publisher of the *Manila Times*, who lent us the plane *Newsboy*, we got to Tacloban in no time at all. We met with Quintero at his house. We wanted to get his commitment to formally substantiate his charges before the committee on the following Monday. Quintero demurred, saying he could not attend any hearing on Monday but could do so on Tuesday. Fearing that delays in his appearance might provide the occasion for him to change his story, I suggested that, if he could not personally testify before the committee, perhaps he should just submit a deposition, a sworn statement taken in question-and-answer form before a notary public.

Quintero, however, said that taking his deposition in Tacloban could complicate things and delay the submission of his testimony. For one thing, he added, he "could not afford to pay the services of lawyers who would take the deposition." For another, he said we should just wait for him to return to Manila on Monday, which was only a couple of days away. The most that we could get from him was his assurance that he would identify the delegates who gave him money. We saw no need to press the point of his returning to Manila before the end of the period of mourning for his brother. It was obvious also that Quintero was ill, so we decided to fly back to Manila and wait for him there.

By 5 o'clock that afternoon, we were back at the convention where Sison reported what had transpired between Quintero and us in Leyte. Sison told the Convention that, on May 29 and 30, the committee would start its formal investigation of Quintero's exposé.

Manglapus Committee Approves Marcos Ban

With the Quintero issue hogging the headlines, the 19-18 vote of the Manglapus's Committee on Suffrage and Electoral Reforms to ban Marcos from running for any public office under the proposed Constitution hardly made it to the front pages of the national dailies. With three abstentions and one member who did not vote, the approval was too close a call for our comfort.

While it was only a committee vote, it sent a strong message that there were still some delegates who stood up for the rights of the people and who had not supinely capitulated to Marcos.

The Manglapus committee Ban-Marcos report did not escape Marcos's attention. Marcos condemned it as being motivated by the "personal ambitions of his political enemies rather than what was good for the country."

It was noteworthy that, among those who supported the Ban-Marcos proposal at the Committee on Suffrage and Electoral Reforms level, Manglapus, Padua, Jose D. Calderon, Feria, Concepcion and Velez stood by their libertarian principles throughout the martial law era. The others either shifted loyalties or muted their resistance to the Marcos regime after martial law was proclaimed.

On the other hand, those who voted against the ban at the committee level, namely, Victor Ortega, Honofre Restor, Elizabeth Chiongbian-Johnston, Antonio Ceniza, Agaton Yaranon, Jr., Lourdes Trono, Federico Ablan, Benjamin Reyes, Romeo Gonzaga, Eduardo Sison, Liningding Pangandaman, Roseller Lim, Damian Aldaba, Emilio Macias II, Pedro Exmundo, Julio Ozamiz, Amado Garcia and Ramon Encarnacion, came out boldly in support of martial law upon its declaration in September 1972. They supported Marcos all the way until the latter was toppled from office in 1986 in the wake of the first People Power revolution in the country.

Attempt to Remove Me

Emboldened by their success in ousting Padua from the Privileges Committee, groups identified with Marcos wanted me removed from the committee as well. The *Manila Evening News* of May 26 headlined, "Pro-FM (Ferdinand Marcos) men move to disqualify prober," meaning me. The item stated that "the insidious scheme" was intended to result in a "whitewash of the case." It was "reportedly hatched by pro-Marcos elements to secure the expulsion of Delegate Aquilino Pimentel, Jr., of Misamis Oriental before the Committee on Privileges resumes its investigation of the Quintero exposé on Monday. *Taliba* carried a banner story to the same effect.

Surmising about the reasons for the moves to expel me, the *Evening News* said:

> It was Pimentel who filed a move to purge the Committee on Privileges of known sympathizers of President Marcos. It was also Pimentel who recently wrote a dissenting opinion against what he called a "whitewash" of a report which investigated the womanizing and gambling activities of certain delegates....

When the newspaper got my side, I said that the move to expel me could have been instigated by those who feared I would try "to ferret out the whole truth regardless of whose heads [would] roll." It was a good thing the intention remained a mere threat.

Quintero's Affidavit

On Monday, May 29, Quintero arrived on board the *RPS Romblon*. He dreaded flying, so Convention President Macapagal got a naval cutter to pick him up from Tacloban and ferry him back to Manila. Macapagal, Sison and I met him at the pier where he reiterated his promise to be present at the committee hearing the following day. He looked pale, thin and wobbly, but he gamely agreed to make a brief appearance at the Convention.

When Quintero entered the session hall, the debate on the report of the Committee on National Integration, chaired by Lamberto Mordeno of Agusan del Sur, was suspended to allow him to address the plenary session. He made a short statement, thanking Macapagal and the Philippine Navy for the use of the cutter to ferry him to Manila. He apologized to the Convention for upsetting the delegates with his exposé. His apology, instead of putting to rest the issues cited in his privilege speech, actually raised a lot of eyebrows as to what he actually meant. Did he mean he had made a mistake in making the exposé? Was he backtracking on his charges? Before we realized it, he wound up his speech with the assurance that he would "tell the truth" before the committee after he shall have undergone medical treatment. We understood the remark to mean that he would present himself before us the following day.

After that short visit to the Convention, Quintero was brought to the San Juan de Dios Hospital in Pasay City. But Quintero did not get the rest that his physical condition demanded. Some members of the committee — Feliciano, Baguilat, Legaspi and I — followed him to the hospital with Convention Secretary Jose Abueva. The committee directed us to get a copy of his affidavit amplifying on the statements he made in his privilege speech. Quintero gave a copy of his affidavit to Abueva without sharing its contents with the committee members and several news people at his bedside. The affidavit was meant to be read officially before the committee at its session the following morning.

To our surprise, on Tuesday, May 30, the Manila media carried reports that Quintero had identified the persons who had given him money. Twelve of the money-givers were delegates. The *Bulletin's* Ben Lara wrote, "Ailing constitutional convention Delegate Eduardo Quintero revealed yesterday the names of the persons who had allegedly given him money in a suspected lobby now rocking the Charter meet."

Apparently, without waiting for the committee to formally convene and hear Quintero, enterprising journalists got a copy of his affidavit and disclosed its contents. The affidavit was more specific than his privilege speech. In it, Quintero directly named Imelda Marcos, House Speaker Nicanor Yñiguez and Mrs. Paz Mate, wife of Congressman Artemio Mate of Leyte, as being among the persons who had caused the delivery of money to him in connection with his work in the Convention.

Most of those he named were delegates from the provinces of Leyte and Samar, Mrs. Marcos's political bailiwicks. He identified them as Gabriel Yñiguez, Domingo Veloso, Jaime Opinion, Ramon Salazar, Damian Aldaba, Antero Bongbong, Flor Sagadal and Federico de la Plana. Later, Quintero added the name of Francisco Astilla of Leyte as one of the delegates who had also received a monetary dole out.

In his affidavit, Quintero likewise named Constantino Navarro, Jr. of Surigao del Norte, Venancio Yaneza of Masbate, Augusto Syjuco, Jr., of Rizal and Casimiro Madarang of Cebu as participants of the *payola* network in the Convention.

Committee Visits Quintero in Hospital

At the committee hearing at 10 a.m. on that day, Chairman Sison informed us that, according to Macapagal, "upon the advice of his doctor," Quintero could not attend the investigation because he was too ill to do so. After much debate, we decided that the committee as a whole would visit Quintero at San Juan de Dios Hospital.

Actually, only a delegation composed of Feliciano, Mendiola and Convention Secretary Abueva went to the hospital to talk with Quintero shortly before 11 o'clock. By 11.30, they were back. They told the committee that they found Quintero too ill to attend the investigation. Instead, Quintero reiterated his request for Abueva to deliver a copy of his new affidavit to Sison.

But, as indicated earlier, the Manila media had already reported the contents of the new Quintero affidavit in their morning editions. Quoting the affidavit, the major dailies and the tabloids asserted that Marcos used bribery as a means of getting some delegates to support the proposal to shift to the parliamentary government, under which he would not be banned from running again to head the government as Prime Minister. Quintero was also quoted as saying that, on one other occasion, Marcos himself asked him to support the adoption of a parliamentary government and that he was a direct witness to several efforts of pro-Marcos operators in Malacañang to get some delegates to switch their support to Marcos.

At our committee meeting, I moved to have the Quintero affidavit accepted by the committee and read publicly. Feliciano seconded the motion, but Madrilejos, Rosales and Sison objected. Much of the discussion centered on arcane constitutional issues about the right of the parties mentioned to cross-examine Quintero — as if by reading the affidavit, the persons named in it would lose their right to question Quintero, which was not the case at all.

Rosales, however, moved that the whole committee go to the hospital immediately and ask Quintero to affirm his affidavit, after which it would be read publicly. The Rosales motion was approved 5-4. Concordia, Padua, Feliciano, Rosales and I voted for it, while Legaspi, Madrilejos, Mendiola and Baguilat opposed it.

At 12:30, the committee convened in Quintero's hospital room. Sison read the three-page affidavit to Quintero and asked whether it was his. Under oath, Quintero affirmed it was his affidavit and the signature was his.

When we resumed the committee hearings at the Convention, Sison asked Abueva to read the Quintero affidavit into the committee records. This was supposed to be a simple procedure. It was not. Delegates Roseller Lim of Zamboanga del Sur and Victor de la Serna of Bohol prevented its immediate reading. Lim and de la Serna said that their clients, Bongbong and Yñiguez, who were named in the Quintero affidavit, would be subjected to trial by publicity if it were read as ordered by Sison.

Vicente Pimentel joined Lim and de la Serna in railing against the reading of the Quintero affidavit. Their arguments also questioned Padua's membership in the committee. Lim read into the records Pacificador's letter objecting to Padua's membership on the ground that Padua was a member of more committees than the Convention Rules allowed.

In the midst of the provocative and irascible arguments raised by Lim and Vicente Pimentel, Chairman Sison calmly told them that, at the hospital, Quintero had identified the affidavit that was being read and that its reading had already been agreed upon by the members of the committee. Sison, ears reddening, told them that their remarks were out of order. As for Padua's membership, Sison said the Steering Committee to which the Pacificador letter had been referred had not yet ruled on the issue.

It took three hours of impassioned discussion before Lim, Vicente Pimentel and de la Serna withdrew their objections to it. By six o'clock of the day, the affidavit was finally read in *toto* into the records of the committee.

Quintero Names Marcoses

After Quintero amplified his speech with an affidavit and other statements in which he explicitly named Marcos and Mrs. Marcos as being behind the moves to control the Convention for their personal agenda, Marcos exploded with vehement denials. He berated Quintero for his supposed ingratitude, especially to Mrs. Marcos. He said that she had merely tried to help tide him over his financial difficulties.

Aside from naming Mrs. Marcos as the source of the money that flowed into the pockets of some delegates, Quintero also said that Marcos himself had asked him to withdraw his support for the Ban-Marcos resolution. While he did not tell Marcos that he would do as he requested, he told him that he would consider it.

Understandably, Marcos went ballistic over Quintero's revelations. "Vicious lies," the *Bulletin* quoted Marcos on the Quintero affidavit that linked his wife, among other people, into the mess. The man, in Marcos's words, "was simply being used by my political opponents." The delegates identified by Quintero also vehemently denied delivering money to him for the purpose of influencing his vote on any matter being taken up in the Convention. One of those mentioned by Quintero,

Leyte Congressman Artemio Mate, repeated what he had said to the media days before that, if indeed he had given Quintero money, it was for the purpose of bailing him out of his financial predicament.

Chapter 7

Marcos Retaliates

At this point, Marcos no longer limited his furious reactions to the Quintero speech to verbal rebuttals. He had the National Bureau of Investigation raid the house of Quintero in Sta. Ana, Manila, on May 31.

The *Manila Times* of June 1 bannered the story: "Quintero's home raided; Bagful of money 'found' by NBI." The quotes on the word 'found' were worth a hundred paragraphs and aptly described the national pulse that people just did not believe the money (P379,320 in cash) was Quintero's. It was commonly held that the money had been "planted" by the NBI agents. That it was part of Malacañang's countermoves against Quintero became more plausible as the circumstances of the raid emerged. For instance, it was Leyte Rep. Artemio Mate, an ally of the President, who executed the affidavit used by the NBI to secure a search warrant that Judge Elias Asuncion of the Manila Court of First Instance issued. It was no coincidence either, Senator Aquino said in a statement to the media, that Asuncion, a native of Ilocos Norte, had gotten his Manila assignment through the intercession of Marcos when Marcos was still a senator.

Senator Aquino called the raid a brazen attempt to silence Quintero. He pointed out that the NBI had been used to harass anti-Marcos people in the past and was being used now to harass Quintero.

People laughed at the administration's patently crude attempt to portray Quintero as a massive bribe taker or grafter. In the coffee shops, talk spread that the money the NBI agents "found" in an unlocked drawer in the anteroom of Quintero's bedroom was actually P500,000, but only P379,320 was turned over to the authorities. Gossip had it that P120,680 had gotten lost between Quintero's house and wherever the money was initially brought.

The raid was only the beginning of Quintero's woes. The NBI used their "discovery" of the P379,320 to file anti-graft charges against him before Jose Flaminiano, the city fiscal or prosecutor of Pasay City. Marcos ally, Congressman Mate of Leyte, surfaced as the complainant against Quintero for his alleged accumulation of "unexplained wealth." As mentioned earlier, Quintero had named Mate's wife as one of those who had given him money.

The Supreme Court, however, came to Quintero's rescue. On June 6, during its Baguio City summer sessions, the Supreme Court issued a restraining order that barred Judge Asuncion and Fiscal Flaminiano from acting on the bribery charges filed against Quintero and prevented the NBI from using "in any proceeding" the P379,320 and other things seized from Quintero's house on May 31. From his hospital bed, Quintero told the Manila press that the issuance of the Supreme Court's injunction was a "happy moment" for him.

The Quintero exposé even at this point had already fatally wounded the Convention. The exposé, however, also had a beneficial effect on the Convention. It provided a tremendous boost for the approval of the Ban-Marcos resolutions that sought to disqualify Marcos, Imelda and their next of kin from running as candidates for any public office under the new Constitution. The resolutions were subsequently consolidated into one Ban-Marcos proposal.

Ban-Marcos Resolutions

The Ban Marcos resolutions were actually the more direct challenge hurled by the anti-Marcos bloc in the Convention against the Marcoses. Napoleon Rama of Cebu was generally credited as the main author of the Ban Marcos resolution, with Juan Liwag of Nueva Ecija as a coauthor. In fact, Jose Mari Velez of Rizal had authored a similar resolution some days earlier and Macapagal had also filed a resolution to ban Marcos from running again for the presidency in the early days of the Convention.

Rama's resolution, however, attracted the most media attention because, aside from the fact that Rama was a media man himself, he got more than 160 delegates to initially affix their signatures on it. He said he gathered that much support for the resolution by personally contacting the delegates. "Marcos", he claimed, "was alarmed when he learned that the resolution gained the support of half of the full membership of the Convention." It was then, Rama said, that Marcos ordered his henchmen to "counterattack." He said Marcos wanted the signatories to withdraw or to vote against it at "the appropriate moment." Quintero's claim that Marcos had asked him to withdraw his support for the Ban-Marcos resolution buttressed Rama's conclusion. The Cebu delegate, however, also made another charge that certain delegates were given cars as inducements to withdraw their support for the resolution. In this accusation, Rama failed to identify a single delegate who had allegedly received a vehicle from Marcos for that purpose.

Rama's resolution got a shove from Macapagal's own version of the Ban. The Macapagal version, however, surfaced in the wake of his campaign for the Presidency of the Convention against Garcia, Guingona and Manglapus. Thus, Macapagal's motives were suspect from the day of its filing. While Rama personally welcomed the Macapagal version, he said that Macapagal vacillated when he pressed him to calendar it for plenary debate. Macapagal, he said, put up one reason or another why it was not yet timely to submit it to the floor. It was unfortunate, Rama said, that Macapagal was not as forthcoming as he was in espousing the Ban-Marcos proposal because, in his opinion, it was the "litmus test" to determine whether the delegates were free representatives of the people or paid agents of Marcos.

On July 7, two and a half months before martial law was declared, the parliamentary form of government was finally tabled for voting. It won by a vote of 158 over 120, with three abstentions. Thirty-four delegates were absent and Macapagal, as the *Manila Chronicle* of July 8 put it, "did not vote."

Switching Sides

In an article titled "How They Voted," Vicente Foz of the *Manila Times*, disclosed that "71 delegates switched votes to parliamentary as against 11 who changed their support to the presidential system." The immediate effect of the vote was for the Convention to use the draft on the parliamentary government as the working basis for debate, instead of the draft on the presidential form.

In the item "Reversals on the Ban," which the *Manila Times* published on August 30, I argued that the motives of the delegates who changed their minds on the issue of the form of government may not normally be impugned, but under the circumstances, those motives were open to question. The article was in response to the argument of Ramon Gonzales of Iloilo, who said in an earlier news item that "changing minds for the better" was no crime. I pointed out that, under the circumstances, where there was widespread belief that an "invisible hand" was manipulating the delegates and where Quintero asserted that monetary dole outs were regularly distributed to the delegates to defeat the ban, the burden was on the shifters to show the righteousness of their cause.

As expected, the delegates named by Quintero in his exposé, voted for the adoption of the parliamentary form of government. The parliamentary government proposal did not have a provision to ban Marcos, which was probably the main reason that caused them to vote for it. In fairness, though, our judgment on the motives of the other delegates did not apply to the likes of Heherson Alvarez, Augusto Cesar Espiritu and his brother Rebeck, Vicente Sinco, Adolfo Azcuna and Ramon Gonzales. They probably supported the adoption of the parliamentary government in the belief that, with or without Marcos, it had built-in safeguards against abuses by people in power.

I was among those who voted for a presidential government. While I had serious second thoughts about the propriety of readopting the presidential government that gave rise to a Marcos dictatorship, I made the formal switch to the presidential form when it became apparent that Marcos was manipulating the Convention to get support for the parliamentary government proposal. I saw that a parliamentary government for the country would extend Marcos's hold on power because — as his supporters argued

— what the 1935 Constitution prohibited was a third term of Marcos as president, but not a new term for Marcos as prime minister.

After the vote was tallied, I found myself in the company of the losing delegates who were previously inclined to support the adoption of the parliamentary government but who eventually voted for the presidential form. Among them were Raul Manglapus, Sotero Laurel, Ernie Rondon, Manuel Martinez, Augusto Sanchez, Elfren Sarte, Jose Mari Velez, Eubolo Verzola, Richard Gordon, Romeo Capulong, Bonifacio Gillego, Salvador Araneta, Jose Aruego, Sedfrey Ordoñez, Pacifico Ortiz, Melchor Padua, Jr., Anacleto Badoy, Jr., Fernando Bautista, Gaudioso Buen, Jose Concepcion, Jr., Timoteo Ruben and Oscar Santos.

There was an attempt to muddle up the issue raised by the Ban-Marcos proposals and this took the form of the Ban-the-Delegates resolution filed primarily by Domingo Guevara. He wanted the Ban-the-Delegates resolution tackled ahead of the Ban-Marcos proposals. Along with many other delegates, I voted for the proposal to ban ourselves from running for any office under the proposed Constitution. While I knew that Guevara was being used by Marcos partisans to deflect public attention from the necessity of banning Marcos, I still thought we should give the people no reason to doubt our sincerity in purging ourselves of personal motives when we voted on critical resolutions in the Convention. But, we lost in that effort also.

The adoption of the parliamentary form of government was widely seen as a "Victory for Marcos," as the *Chronicle* said in its issue of July 9. Under the byline of Jose U. Macaspac, the article stated that "the adoption of the parliamentary form will afford him a chance to prolong his stay in power."

Along with Capulong and Rondon, I issued a statement deploring the decision of the Convention to use the parliamentary form of government as basis for our debates. In our statement, we said the proposed Constitution that was now emerging had a "Marcos label."

Vote on the Ban

By the first week of September, it became clear that the Marcos forces were in control of the Convention. On September 6, they wanted a vote on the consolidated proposal to ban Marcos as they were confident that they had the votes to defeat it.

The consolidated version had two main paragraphs. The first paragraph stated that, "No person, who has at any time, served as President of the Philippines under this or the previous Constitution shall be eligible to occupy the same office or that of prime minister." The second paragraph provided that "the spouse of such a person shall be ineligible to occupy either office during the unexpired portion of his term in the immediately succeeding regular term."

As worded, the first prohibition would cover Marcos and Macapagal, as Marcos was the incumbent president and Macapagal was a former president. The modifying phrase "of the Philippines" was clearly a surplusage as the Convention could not possibly cover any other President except of the country. The practice of officialdom to refer to our laws as applying to "the Philippines" was a carry-over from our Commonwealth past. As a colony of the US, our lawmakers and the bureaucracy were careful to craft the language of their enactments and communications as dealing only with the people of the country and not with the people of the US.

The second paragraph assumed that the person subject of the prohibition would necessarily be a "he." The drafters of the Ban probably never imagined that women could ever be President, or they were believers in the archaic notion that the noun "man" includes "woman" and the pronoun "he" includes a "she."

The run-up to the showdown on the Ban-Marcos issue was nerve-racking to many of us. Talk of delegates' shifting their support for the ban to the side against it was rampant. We did not know whom to trust anymore. Then there were threats to oust Macapagal from the Convention presidency if he took to the floor to argue for the ban. We, however, got Macapagal to be the main speaker for the affirmative side. We wanted him to do the chore because, as president of the Convention, his words carried some weight in and outside the Convention, and also because we wanted him to assume a more pronounced anti-Marcos role.

Macapagal Sums Up

Macapagal did not fail us. On September 6, his summing up of the reasons in favor of the Ban as an amendment to the parliamentary government resolution was both eminently reasonable and emotionally eloquent. In essence, Macapagal said the ban must be incorporated in the proposed Constitution to ensure its ratification by the people. The ban, he said, was also necessary because it was "not good for the country to allow the chief executive and his lady to stay too long in power." The ban, he added, must include the spouse of the president, because to allow her to succeed her husband would set the stage for the abuse of power to ensure her victory. Addressing the President directly by name, Macapagal asked Marcos to display "humility" and "wisdom" by not seeking reelection for the good of the nation.

Appealing to the emotions of his audience, Macapagal said that, since Marcos and he had rendered service as presidents of the country, he had no "unfriendly intent towards him and the First Lady." Macapagal said that he was motivated by "a well-meaning wish that you, with whom I share the honor of belonging to the institution of the presidency, may win the approbation of posterity to which I myself aspire." He warned us, his fellow delegates, that our votes on the ban issue would seal the "fate of our

Convention." The ban, he said, was the only resolution that he had filed and that he was taking the floor because of its vital importance to keep the faith of the people in the Convention. True to form, Macapagal ended his speech with this kilometric sentence without pausing for breath:

> As the future of our nation is compressed in your vote, as it were, I pray that in this historic moment of grandeur or mediocrity, you be equal to the challenge; that as the roll is called, you vote not as an individual whom history will just pass by but rather that you be counted in the roster of those who shall become a part of the greatness of our race for voting with courage and wisdom to uphold the unalloyed and vibrant principle of democracy which is embodied in the proposed prohibition.

While Macapagal was no John F. Kennedy or Winston Churchill, we who supported the ban and the audience that packed the session hall enjoyed his oratory and applauded him vigorously. Despite his forceful speech in support of the ban, however, we lost by a vote of 155 to 131. There was a 24-vote margin as the *Manila Times* reported on September 7. In disgust, Rama, Capulong, Rondon and I issued a statement that:

> In voting down the anti-dynasty proposal, the Convention has proclaimed itself as a kennel serving the interest of one man against the interest of the nation.

We picked up the "kennel" description of the Convention from cartoons in the *Philippines Free Press* magazine that occasionally depicted the delegates as *mga tuta,* lap dogs, of Marcos.

Despite our loss, I was gratified by a survey conducted by Delegate Jose Concepcion Jr., which was published in the *Manila Times* of September 11. It showed that in Mindanao, delegates from: Bukidnon, Luis Lorenzo; Cotabato, Anacleto Badoy; South Cotabato, Tomas Falgui; Sulu, Benjamin Abubakar; Davao del Norte, Gaudioso Buen, Jesus Matas and Camilo Sabio; Davao del Sur, Leon Garcia, Jr., Dominador Carillo, Samuel Occeña, and Ismael Veloso; Zamboanga del Norte, Ernesto Amatong, Adolfo Azcuna, and Augusto Saguin; Zamboanga del Sur, Maria Clara Lobregat and Vincenzo Sagun; Lanao del Norte, Francisco Abalos and Luis Quibranza; and Misamis Occidental, Timoteo Ruben and Julio Ozamiz, voted for the Ban. I was especially happy that our two colleagues from Misamis Oriental and Cagayan de Oro, Rolando Piit and Pablo Reyes, supported the Ban. Had Felino Neri been alive at the time, I was certain that he would have voted with us.

I found it personally elating that my friends — Felix Alfelor, Jr., of Camarines Sur; Celso Gañgan, Isabela; Jose Leviste, Jr., Batangas; Manuel Martinez, Romblon; Elfren Sarte, Albay; Augusto Sanchez and Ceferino Padua, Rizal; Ricardo Sagmit, Jr., Pampanga; Oscar Santos, Quezon; Melchor Padua, Jr., Ilocos Sur; and Romeo Capulong and Ernesto Rondon, Nueva

Ecija — voted for the Ban, along with other anti-Marcos colleagues.

Surprise Votes

Surprise votes cast in favor of the ban included those of Richard Gordon of Zambales; Edgardo Angara, Quezon; Victor de la Serna, Bohol; Licurgo Tirador, Iloilo; Lilia de Lima, Camarines Sur; Margarito Teves, Negros Oriental; Gregorio Tingson, Negros Occidental; Raul Estrella, Masbate; Pablo Trillana, Bulacan; and Emil Ong, Northern Samar. I use the word "surprise" because I thought they would vote against the Ban. Angara, for instance, was at the time the principal partner of the ACCRA law office, which had the then Secretary of National Defense Juan Ponce Enrile as an unnamed partner. That Angara voted for the Ban was to me simply amazing.

Fifteen days after the vote on the Ban, Marcos proclaimed martial rule and squashed all attempts by the radicals and the moderates combined to control the Convention and seek a reconsideration of the vote for a parliamentary government. Under martial rule, the Convention became putty in his hands.

Privileges Committee Dismisses Probe

Our committee, for instance, was unable to complete our Quintero investigation freely. With the country reeling under martial rule, the proceedings of the committee froze like a block of ice in dead winter in the Alaskan seas. Some of our colleagues were picked up and detained by the military and the rest of us did not quite know what was going to happen next.

The majority of the members of the committee no longer felt it "wise" or "safe" to pursue the investigation. Moreover, it was also true that Quintero was unable — all these months — to complete his testimony before the committee. Thus, even if some evidence showed that Marcos money had flowed into the pockets of certain delegates, Chairman Sison, by a committee vote of 5-4, terminated and dismissed the investigation on November 27, 1972, primarily on the technicality of Quintero's failure to submit to cross-examination by the committee members and by the delegates he had named.

Legally, Sison's report terminating and dismissing the investigation was understandable. By Sison's count, Quintero attended only four out of 24 hearings of the committee from May 19 to November 27. My notes, however, record that Quintero met with us seven times. Aside from the dates mentioned by Sison, we met with him as a committee at the Manila Hotel on May 19; in Tacloban City as a subcommittee of three on May 25; and at the San Juan de Dios hospital on May 30, again as a subcommittee. These meetings had to do with the investigation of the Quintero privilege speech, but were not mentioned in the Sison report. It was true, however, that because of ill health, Quintero failed to attend many of the scheduled committee hearings.

But it was the penultimate paragraph of the Privileges Committee Report that threw its otherwise valid premises askew. The paragraph read:

> The Committee feels that the Delegates whom Quintero singled out in his exposé as well as the other persons whom he named, including the First Lady (Mrs. Marcos), were mere victims of circumstances beyond their control. It behooves upon (sic) the Committee, as an act of justice to reverse that unfounded judgment against them by recommending, as it hereby recommends, complete exoneration of all those persons who Delegate Quintero named from any and all charges he made.

I had developed a high regard for Chairman Sison when we began working together in the Committee on Privileges. The rosy esteem, however, dwindled to a misty memory when martial law was proclaimed. After the imposition of martial law, like many of our colleagues, I noticed a shift in his approach to the Quintero investigation, which was also evident in the way, the delegates as a whole did our work. The purple paragraph, which lawyers called "the dispositive part" of the report revealed what was in Sison's heart.

There was absolutely no basis for dismissing the Quintero exposé on the ground that Mrs. Marcos and the delegates named by Quintero were "mere victims of circumstances beyond their control." How the handing out of money to him from Mrs. Marcos through the delegates could be justified as having been committed under "circumstances beyond their control," I will never understand. Neither was there any fact or circumstance to justify the report's findings of "unfounded judgment against them" or any basis for recommending the complete exoneration of the persons named by Quintero.

I think that Sison and the members of the committee — Baguilat, Madrilejos, Mendiola and Legaspi — went overboard in their rationalization to clear Mrs. Marcos and the delegates named by Quintero. The simple explanation for their spineless decision to dismiss the Quintero charges was that martial law had been in place since September 21. I could expect that Baguilat, Madrilejos, Mendiola and Legaspi to come up with that irrational conclusion, but not Sison. That he led or joined them to pen the obsequious report could only be attributed to the power of martial law to twist the positions of otherwise rational people into grotesque rationalizations.

However, four committee members — Concordia, Feliciano, Rosales and I— did not agree with the report. While we did not elaborate on our dissent, the report that Sison filed with the Convention on November 27 tellingly carried only his signature and those of the four other members of the committee, not ours.

The dismissal of the Quintero exposé caused an explosion of unbridled joy among the delegates whom he had implicated. The delegates concerned delivered paeans to their "vindication," which at the time - and in recollection, even today - sounded so hypocritical to me. In more prosaic terms, the hairs on my arms stood shakily on end when I heard the self-serving delegates speak of their "just" exoneration from the Quintero charges.

From then on, the Convention inevitably slid into opprobrium in the minds of the people who saw it as a useless exercise that cost the country millions of pesos only to prove itself a willing tool to perpetuate Marcos in power.

Subtle Pressure, Too

Although the committee dismissed the Quintero charges, in my opinion, Marcos indeed tried to influence the outcome of the Convention by passing money to some delegates. In fact, I was also the object of attempts to get me to join the Marcos bloc not by pressuring or bribing me directly but in a more subtle way. The overture came when the release of our per diems as delegates — we were paid P100 per session attended — was delayed. The delay created some financial pressure on me because I depended mainly on the per diems to enable me to do my job as a delegate.

An item in the *Bulletin's* April 2 column of Apolonio Batalla captured my predicament:

> One of the disappointed delegates to the Constitutional Convention is Aquilino Pimentel from Cagayan de Oro. He gave up a lucrative law practice in order to be a delegate. Then the Convention was rocked by some scandals and finally the P100-a-day allowance for delegates was suspended. Since he could no longer afford to live in Manila he went back home.

Since I did not know Batalla personally and had no public relations man to publicize what I did or did not do in the Convention, I had no idea where he got the information that I went back home as if I abandoned my work as delegate. Batalla's kind words notwithstanding, his conclusion was incorrect. The truth is that I went home only for the duration of a few days' break in our work as delegates. Furthermore, when I ran for delegate to the Convention, I had braced myself for the worst. Although the suspension of the payment of our allowances, added to the strains of my work, I considered it as just one of the hazards of the job.

A delegate friend of mine who was one of the pillars of the pro-Marcos group in the Convention offered to bail me out. He said that he had P30,000, which I could get from him "without strings attached." Under the circumstances, the amount was a princely sum to me. Nonetheless, I declined his offer, remembering Homer's lesson of the Trojans' bearing gifts. I told him I did not need any assistance from Marcos because my family and I were "prepared to eat rice and salted fish if need be," rice and salted fish being the standard fare of the poor. My answer packed more wallop in Visayan, *"Andam kami mokaon sa kan-on ug guinamos kung kinahanglan"* as it graphically described the lengths to which a person would go to prove a point. My friend saw the futility of enticing me to his cause and subsequently dropped the offer. To this day, we remain friends.

In sum, the exposé stung Marcos more bitterly because it was Quintero, rather than other delegates, who had done it. Quintero represented the province of Leyte, where Imelda was born and where she and her relatives had begun building their political dynasty with Marcos's rise to power. Quintero's revelations, in addition to the affidavit that he executed later on, were the first direct assertions that Marcos actually interfered with the work of the Convention by devious means. Quintero's exposé had also one unintended effect. It removed the ideological distinctions among the factions contending for power in the Convention. Now there were only two: the anti-Marcos and the pro-Marcos forces.

As the Convention wound up its work, it became evident that Marcos had carefully planned the placement of his people in leadership roles in strategic committees. Two eminent examples were Venancio Yaneza, who headed the Committee on Transitory Provisions, and Domingo Veloso, chair of the Committee on Legislative Powers. Both Yaneza and Veloso were unabashed Marcos partisans.

Quintero revealed in his statements that he had been asked to vote for Yaneza as chair of the Committee on Transitory Provisions as envelopes filled with money changed hands in a meeting of delegates that he attended. The Transitory Provisions Committee was crucial because it was the Committee where the role of the incumbent President (Marcos) would be defined under the proposed Constitution during the transition period from the presidential to the parliamentary government. Domingo Veloso was elected chair of the Committee on Legislative Powers, where the form of government, whether presidential or parliamentary, would first be settled. Indeed, the Committee reports of Yaneza and Veloso made no mention of the Ban-Marcos proposals.

Big Business Supports Martial Rule

Outside the halls of the Convention, the people were ambivalent about martial rule. While there was no free polling of the public view, it was clear that some of the more politically inclined sectors of society were threatened by martial rule. Others wanted to give Marcos a chance to bring about the New Society that he promised to create through the proclamation of martial rule. But big business, especially the American Chamber of Commerce, roared loudest its approval of the declaration. It was an unmistakable sign that the US government favored Marcos's move. There were at least two reasons for its approval: one was America's desire to keep the US military bases in the country and the other was its wish to protect its huge investments here.

More directly, the American Chamber of Commerce was worried by a Supreme Court decision dated August 19, 1972, about a month before the proclamation of martial rule. The Supreme Court was asked by William Quasha, an American citizen, to rule on the issue of whether or not his rights over a parcel of land that he had purchased here in 1954 would lapse in 1974 when the 1946 Parity Rights Amendment to the 1935 Constitution expired. The Parity Rights Amendment allowed US citizens and their corporations to exploit, use and develop all agricultural, timber and mineral lands of the public domain, waters, minerals, oils, all forces and sources of potential energy, and other natural resources of the country, and to operate public utilities.

In Quasha, the Supreme Court ruled that

> under the 'Parity Amendment' to our Constitution, citizens of the United States and corporations and business enterprises owned of controlled by them can not acquire and own, save in cases of hereditary succession, private agricultural lands in the Philippines, and that all other rights acquired by them under said Amendment will expire on 3 July 1974.

With that Supreme Court ruling, under the existing Constitution, there was no legal remedy by which the Americans could get an extension of their rights under the Parity Agreement. While they had allies in the Convention, there was no sign that the Parity Agreement would be extended by an amendment to the Constitution. Additionally, the unanimity of the Supreme Court ruling in the *Quasha* case deterred any move to get it reconsidered.

Thus, when Marcos declared martial rule, the American Chamber of Commerce immediately lauded the event to the high heavens. And the Chamber subsequently got what it wanted. The rights of the Americans under the Parity Agreement were extended. Marcos also issued Presidential Decree No. 92, which liberalized, among other things, the requirements for immigration and foreign investors, as well as Central Bank requirements on capital repatriation and profit remittances.

Voting on the Constitution

In the halls of the Convention, with the Quintero exposé dismissed under questionable circumstances and the Ban-Marcos resolution defeated decisively by the votes of the "compromised" delegates, Marcos ordered his hit men — or in the words of Delegate Augusto Caesar Espiritu, "the Marcos politburo"— in the Convention to prepare the 1973 draft Constitution for its ritual approval by the delegates and, thereafter, for its pro-forma submission to the people for ratification. The Marcos politburo was headed by Gilberto Duavit, while the members, Espritu said, were Arturo Pacificador, Emilio de la Cruz II, Antonio Tupaz, Antonio de Guzman, Vicente de Guzman, Jose Bengzon and Venancio Yaneza.

Put to a vote on November 27, the proposed Constitution was overwhelmingly approved. There was only a sprinkling of "nay" votes and one "refusal to vote." The "ayes" or the "yes" votes had been carefully nurtured by Marcos. As Quintero had pointed out, Marcos was not beyond bribery to get his way in the Convention. Not only that. Marcos also exerted blatant pressure on us delegates by causing the arrest and detention of some of our colleagues upon the proclamation of martial rule. On the date of the voting on the draft Constitution, some delegates were still detained at Camp Crame and Fort Bonifacio. Likewise, Marcos promised that the delegates voting for the proposed Constitution would automatically become members of the new parliament that he would convene after its ratification. Many of the delegates who voted "Yes" were lured into doing so by the promise that Marcos eventually did not comply with. In the case of Ricardo Sagmit, Jr., of Pampanga, he told me that he shed tears when he voted "Yes". He explained that Macapagal convinced him to vote "Yes" on the argument that "it was better to fight the dictatorship from within rather than from outside the government." It must also be said, however, that some voted "Yes" to weather the storm of martial rule, hoping to come out of it in one piece. That said, I still cannot understand to this very day why a sick delegate had to come out of a hospital in a wheel chair with a brace on his neck only to vote "Yes" to the proposed Constitution, which he knew we delegates had not freely adopted. He was a pathetic sight.

No Votes

The "nay" votes were basically acts of sincere conviction that the proposed Constitution would devastate the democratic structures of government, and that a Marcos dynasty would ensue and cause the enslavement of the people. Indeed, many delegates believed that Marcos was preparing Imelda and their children, Bongbong, Imee and Irene, to take over the reins of government after him. At the very least, the more perceptive saw Marcos was grooming Imelda as his heir apparent in the event that he could not stay on as president in the immediate future.

On the day of the voting (after the third and final reading of the proposed Constitution), 14 heroic delegates voted "No." They were Dakila Castro of Bulacan; Juan T. David, Manila; Ramon Diaz, Camarines Sur; Marcelo Fernan, Cebu; Andres Flores, Cebu; Leon M. Garcia, Jr., Davao; Sedfrey Ordoñez, Nueva Ecija; Pacifico Ortiz, Rizal; Rolando Piit, Misamis Oriental; Decoroso Rosales, Samar; Jose Santillan, Cavite; Margarito Teves, Negros Oriental; Jose Suarez, Pampanga; and Pedro Yap, Cebu. They were "heroic" because they not only voted "No" to what I saw was a flawed Constitution, but they also cast their negative votes in public and in person, meaning that they stood up to be counted on that crucial day when the draft Constitution was submitted to the delegates for final approval. The strength of their character was very much in evidence that day because they could have absented themselves and explained their absence later with all kinds of reasons. Or they could have voted in writing. But they came to the Convention and said "No" to the proposed Constitution. There were others who valiantly voted against the proposed Constitution even as they were behind bars in the military prison camps, having been arrested upon the declaration of martial rule. Among them were delegates Napoleon Rama of Cebu; and Jose Mari Velez, Teofisto Guingona, Jr. and Alejandro Lichauco, all of Rizal.

Refusal to Vote

The "refusal to vote" was mine. Pursuant to the parliamentary procedure known as a "roll call vote," I stood up when my name was called and went to the nearest microphone to record and explain my vote. Abraham Sarmiento, a vice president of the Convention, as presiding officer, repeatedly asked what my vote was. I said with all the calm I could muster that, for the record, I found the draft to be "a bastardized travesty of Constitution. Hence I refuse to vote."

Sarmiento ordered that my vote be recorded as an "abstention." It was probably the basis of an Associated Press report, which said the new constitution "was approved by a vote of 271-14, with one abstention." The news report identified me as the "abstainer." Sarmiento made the order probably to soften the defiant tone of my vote and lessen the risk of my being arrested. Either that or, he believed that conventional parliamentary practice allowed only three kinds of votes: "aye," "nay" or an "abstention." My refusal to vote did not fall under any of the three. Nonetheless, in retort to Sarmiento's order, I immediately asked that my vote be recorded not as an abstention but as "a refusal to vote." The reason, I said, was that under the strictures of martial law, we, the delegates were not really free to vote as the representatives of the people in the Convention.

The lopsided vote in favor of the proposed Constitution was attributable mainly to the fear factor that was brought to bear upon the delegates. Augusto Caesar Espiritu wrote in his book, *How Democracy Was Lost,* that he and many of his allies in what he called as the "Independent-Progressive group" in the Convention voted in favor of the Constitution because they feared they would be arrested if they did not.

Espiritu said some of his friends, like Romeo Capulong and Raul Roco, who were on the list of people to be arrested upon the proclamation of martial law, had been removed from the list. It was of common knowledge in the Convention that their names had been expunged from the "wanted list" of delegates upon the intercession of our fellow delegate, Edgardo Angara of Quezon. Angara had unqualified access to National Defense Secretary Juan Ponce Enrile, the main executor of martial law, who was then his partner in the ACCRA law firm.

Espiritu said that when he asked Capulong and Roco whether or not they were made to pledge to vote for the approval of the draft Constitution in consideration of the removal of their names from the arrest list, Roco gave a negative reply but added that it "was assumed" that they would do so. And they did.

Theologians Consulted

For Espiritu and a number of their colleagues in the Independent-Progressive bloc, approving the proposed Constitution did not come easy. Some wrestled with their consciences and actually consulted "moral theologians." After the consultations, Espiritu said those delegates were convinced that there was nothing morally wrong if they voted for the proposed Constitution because the irresistible pressure of martial law prevented them from taking any other course of action.

The times were so abnormal that ordinary standards did not suffice to guide most of our colleagues in casting their votes. In my case, I arrived at my decision by simplifying the issue. I did not find the need to consult any moral authority but my conscience. I asked myself was I free to vote under the circumstances? My answer was "No." Would it be good for the country if I voted to approve the Constitution? Again, my answer was "No." And was there anything I could do about it, considering that the country was under martial law regime? My answer was "Yes." There was something I could do. And that was to refuse to give my assent to the things that the regime wanted to extort from me as a delegate to the Convention. Hence, when my name was called, I put it very plainly on record that I was casting a "refusal to vote" for the new Constitution.

Incidentally, those who voted for the approval of the Constitution were assured of seats in the proposed the Interim National Assembly, the unicameral legislative body created by the Convention, which Marcos said he would convene upon approval of the new basic law. That was an additional, if not *the*, come-on for the practical-minded among the delegates to join the Marcos bandwagon in the Convention. Marcos, however, did not convene the INA. He had now crowned himself the absolute authoritarian ruler of the country and there was nothing that the duped delegates could do about it.

Plaza Miranda Bombing

Actually, the stifling of the people's freedom had already begun even before Marcos placed the country under martial rule in 1972. He suspended the privilege of the writ of habeas corpus, the constitutional guarantee against arbitrary arrest and indefinite detention, on August 21, 1971, after the bombing of the opposition Liberal Party meeting at Plaza Miranda in Quiapo, Manila. Two fragmentation grenades were lobbed on the stage of the Liberal Party rally at Plaza Miranda that evening, killing some spectators and seriously injuring many of the opposition party's stalwarts, including its 1969 presidential standard bearer, Sen. Sergio Osmeña, party president Sen. Gerry Roxas, and LP senatorial candidates Jovito Salonga, Eva Estrada Kalaw, Edgar Ilarde, John Osmeña and Ramon Mitra, Jr. Also wounded was Ramon Bagatsing, who was running for election as mayor of Manila.

Recalling the incident, I could not help but think that, but for the grace of God, I could have been one of those directly imperiled or injured in the bombing incident. Senator Roxas had personally invited me to attend that rally in my capacity as the Liberal Party chair of Misamis Oriental. Since

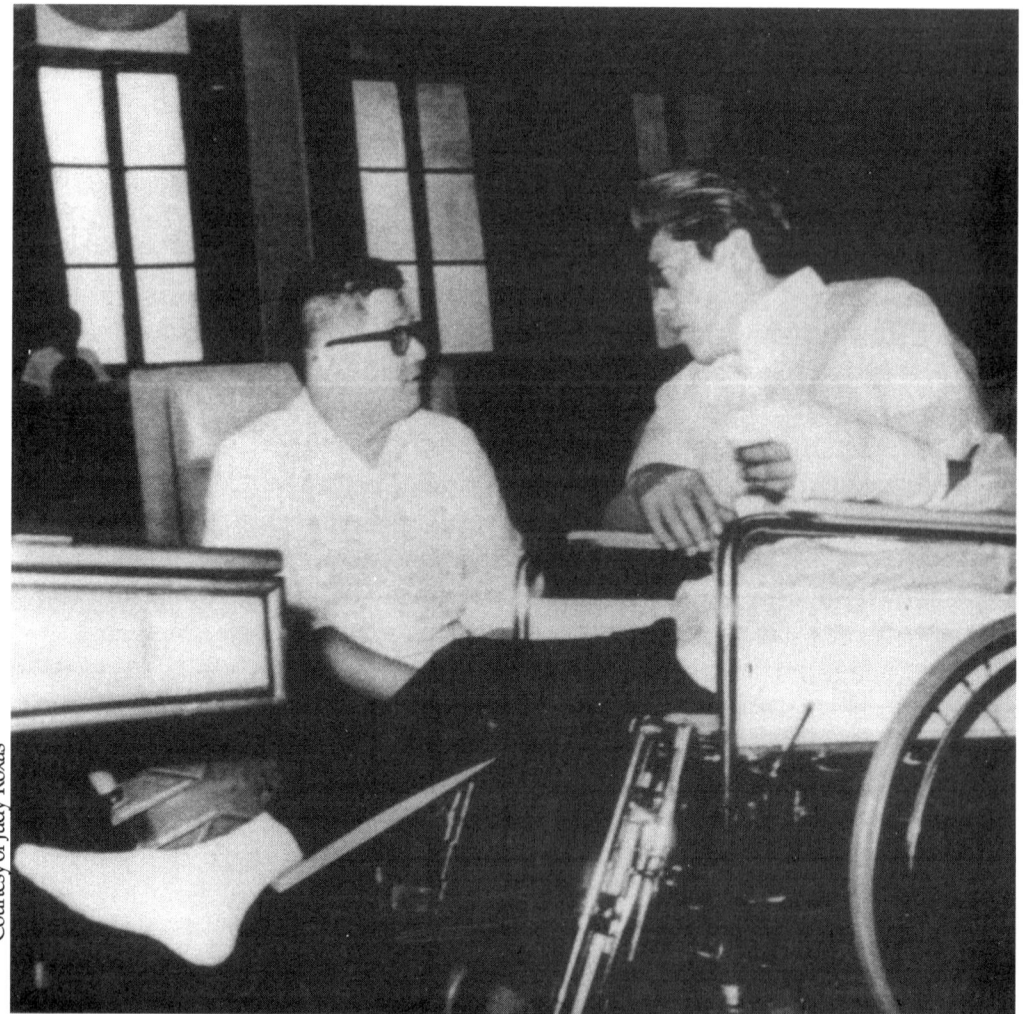

Courtesy of Judy Roxas

1972: *NINOY TALKS WITH GERRY ROXAS days after the Plaza Miranda bombing. Gerry was one of those seriously wounded in the incident.*

political parties prided themselves in the support of their ward leaders from all over the nation, I would have, in all likelihood, been asked to sit on the stage. Had I been there on the stage at Plaza Miranda that fateful evening, I could have been among those injured. The immediate reason why I was not there was, I believe, simply providential. My friend, Honesto Salcedo, who was to accompany me to Plaza Miranda, arrived late at the place where we had agreed to meet. We were in a taxi on our way to Plaza Miranda when we heard of the bombing over the radio.

After the bombing of the Liberal Party rally at Plaza Miranda and without waiting for the result of any investigation on who was responsible, Marcos immediately blamed the communists. He then suspended the constitutional privilege of the writ of habeas corpus.

Since there were yet no credible findings on the identity of the Plaza Miranda bombers, people speculated as to who did it. Some believed sardonically that Marcos himself had ordered the bombing. Senator Roxas expressed the anger and the frustration of the people when he said that he was "holding President Marcos personally responsible for the brutal and senseless carnage that occurred at Plaza Miranda."

Even the police appeared clueless as to the perpetrators of the crime. They linked certain notorious gangsters in Metro Manila, particularly the so-called Big Four, to the bombing and had them arrested and placed in detention at the Philippine Constabulary headquarters in Camp Crame, Quezon City. The Big Four, a criminal syndicate, was reportedly composed of Luis Asistio, Kit Pascual, Totoy Antonio and Benigno Urquico. I met one of them at the camp a year later and he told me the Big Four had nothing to do with the crime. He said that if Marcos really believed that they were involved in the offense, they would have already been tried, sentenced and executed for the Miranda bombing.

Anyway, at the time, leftist student activist groups competed with the moderates in organizing marches and demonstrations that called the Marcos government to task for arresting fall guys. They charged that Marcos wantonly violated the people's civil liberties guaranteed in the Constitution while he blatantly enriched himself and his family through corrupt practices. Along with Tito Guingona, Ernie Rondon, Romy Capulong, Jose Mari Velez, Voltaire Garcia, Jerry Barrican and other delegates, I sometimes spoke at those rallies. I also had time to accept speaking engagements outside Metro-Manila where I discussed not only the issues against Marcos but also my pet proposals in the Convention like the stewardship of property. For example, I spoke on those issues before the Rotary Club of General Santos City. I went to that affair upon invitation of my compadre and friend, Mario Nery, and his wife, Inday Salcedo.

Four months later, in January of 1972, Marcos lifted the suspension of the privilege of the writ of habeas corpus. We joined activists of all stripes to rejoice over its lifting. Little did we or the people know or even suspect that Marcos lifted it to deflect public attention from his next move to consolidate power in his hands by placing the country under martial rule.

On a personal note, we, the delegates from Misamis Oriental and Cagayan de Oro, were saddened that, on January 2, our colleague, Felino Neri, died. His death left Rolando Piit, Pablo Reyes and me to represent the people of the province and city in the Convention.

Part 3

Martial Law Imposed

Courtesy of Judy Roxas

1972: *KEPT OUT OF THE SENATE by martial law proclamation (left to right): Senators Doy Laurel, Eva Estrada Kalaw, Monching Mitra, Gerry Roxas and Jovy Salonga.*

Chapter 8:

Bombings & Arrests

I heard of the declaration of martial law at dawn on September 23, 1972, through my friend and fellow delegate, Ernie Rondon. Ernie had a daily radio program during which he frequently lambasted Marcos for real or, I suspect, even imagined wrongdoing. Unlike his true persona, in the announcer's booth, Ernie was a fire-breathing dragon who instinctively inveighed against official wrongdoing, no matter who did it. But, on September 23, when he went to the radio station to do his program, he found the station closed, with several soldiers guarding it. He managed to phone me that martial law had been proclaimed and that we had better go into hiding.

Convention Site Bombing

Subsequent events showed that Marcos had signed the declaration of martial law on September 21 but shortly before that date, there was a series of bombings in Metro Manila. To us delegates, the biggest scare were the September 18 blasts that hit the Quezon City Hall, where the Convention had transferred from the Manila Hotel.

The first bomb exploded in the washroom of a trial court on the sixth floor at about 3:50 p.m. Minutes later, another bomb went off in the rest room of the session hall of the Convention on the 14th Floor. Jesus Matas of Davao del Sur had just finished his sponsorship of his amendment to the proposed form of government when the bomb exploded. Delegates, their staff members and the spectators in the gallery scampered for safety. I sat transfixed at my desk, but seeing that everybody was heading for the exit, I followed the fleeing throng.

Quickly but in an orderly fashion, we descended 14 stories to the ground floor. The following day, the newspapers reported that 25 people had been wounded in the blasts.

Delegate Roger Panotes of Camarines Norte told the media that the Convention should declare a recess and reassess the situation. I disagreed. I felt that, despite the atmosphere of terror, we should continue to do our duty to craft a new charter. To quit now "would be a supreme abnegation of duty," the *Manila Times* edition of September 19 quoted me as saying. Macapagal decided the issue by announcing that the session would be suspended for the afternoon, but would be resumed the following day.

The question of the moment, however, that begged an immediate answer was: Who did it? Jose Nolledo of Palawan told the media that, right after the explosions, he saw two men sporting crew cuts, rushing out of the City Hall. The implication was that the bombings were the handiwork of the Marcos military. Soldiers at the time were required to have their hair cropped close to the scalp.

Delegate Manuel Concordia was more specific. He said that he saw four soldiers board a Philippine Constabulary truck, which sped away right after the bombs went off. Delegate Augusto Caesar Espiritu surmised that Marcos's group had caused the explosions "to sow fear among the population and to find an excuse for imposing martial law or suspending the writ of habeas corpus."

With the spate of bombings, people believed that the stage was being set for the declaration of martial rule. On the 21st of September, 32 of us delegates, along with priests, nuns and members of the national media, placed a full-page ad in the *Manila Times*. In it, we said:

> Whoever is behind the bombings, there is no need for President Marcos to exercise emergency power, or to suspend the writ of habeas corpus or declare martial law and make himself a dictator to stop them.

Oplan Sagittarius

Earlier, Ninoy Aquino delivered a privilege speech in the Senate denouncing Marcos's plan to place the country under martial rule. Ninoy based his statement on a copy of *Oplan Sagittarius*, which a source had given him. Marcos denied that he planned to impose martial law and said that *Oplan Sagittarius* was merely a contingency study undertaken by his think-tank. Subsequent events proved Ninoy right. Marcos imposed martial rule.

It took months before we in the Opposition learned that the declaration of martial law had been plotted by Marcos with the active collaboration of 12 men who enjoyed his confidence. His 12 co-plotters were Defense Minister Juan Ponce Enrile, Generals Fabian Ver, Fidel Ramos, Romeo Espino, Rafael Zagala, Ignacio Paz, Jose Rancudo, Tomas Diaz and Alfredo Montoya, Rear Adm. Hilario Ruiz, Col. Romeo Gatan and businessman Eduardo Cojuangco.

The persons in the cabal were later called the "Rolex 12." Marcos gave each of them expensive Rolex watches as tokens of his gratitude for their wholehearted support in hatching the plot. Without exception, the 12 benefited from the authoritarian regime of Marcos.

Reality of Martial Rule

Marcos justified the immediate proclamation of martial law on the ground of an alleged ambush supposedly directed at Defense Minister Enrile on September 20. Enrile was not in the car. Only his driver was in it but was not hurt in the incident. The circumstances of the ambush strained belief in its veracity.

Years later, after he had severed relations with Marcos, Enrile admitted that the ambush had been faked. It was a ruse that he agreed to because Marcos needed the incident to justify the immediate imposition of martial rule on September 21.

The problem for me and the other anti-Marcos delegates at the time was not whether or not the ambush was for real. The immediate problem was the reality of martial rule that was confronting us. In our minds, or at least in mine, the urgent concern was that we should make ourselves scarce in the next several days so as to elude the military authorities who might have been ordered to arrest us.

We needed time to think things through and figure out what we could realistically do under the circumstances. My difficulty was that I did not know where to hide. The names of friends came to mind, but considering the circumstances, I did not even want to ask them to hide me in their houses for fear of endangering their own security. The next best thing I could think of was to go to Ernie Rondon's home in Project 6, Quezon City, which was not far from my in-laws' place in Project 8.

Ernie was already at home when I got there. We discussed what we should do. He suggested we go into hiding together which was fine with me. He then called a friend of his to tell him that he and a colleague, would be going over for a visit.

In less than an hour, we were at the house of his friend. After explaining the real purpose of our visit, his friend, without any hesitation, agreed to shelter us. We stayed in his friend's house for two uneventful days, Saturday and Sunday. With no sign that any police or military officers were looking for us, we got bored and decided to surface on Monday and attend the activities of the Convention at the Quezon City Hall.

When we arrived at the convention hall, nobody appeared to have noticed that we had not been visible for the last two days, probably because those were nonworking days. Only close friends like Cefe Padua, Meling Padua and Noli Santos cared enough to caution us against provoking Marcos because some of our colleagues like Bren Guiao, Natalio Bacalso, Tito Guingona, Jose Marie Velez, Joe Concepcion, Jose Nolledo, Nap Rama and Alejandro Lichauco had already been picked up and detained by the military. They also told us that Romy Capulong and Sonny Alvarez were being hunted by the military.

Counsel for Ernie

After the morning session, Ernie invited me for lunch at his house. He apparently thought he was not in any danger anymore of being arrested by the military. But, as we started to eat, plainclothes military men swooped into his home without warning and arrested him. They asked him who I was. He told them that I was a friend from the province who had come to visit him. Not surprisingly, the soldiers took his word for it and paid no attention to me. Then they whisked him away in an unmarked vehicle towards Camp Crame.

With Danny, his brother driving, Thelma, Ernie's wife, and I followed the military vehicle in their family car. We wanted to assure ourselves that he was brought to the camp and not elsewhere to be "salvaged," a military term that meant being extra-legally executed. We left Camp Crame after learning he had been brought to the gym where political detainees were being held. Later, Thelma asked me to file a petition for *habeas corpus* with the Supreme Court to ask for Ernie's release as his detention was arbitrary and without valid basis.

I did as Ernie requested. The petition was set for oral argument a few days later at the Supreme Court. Some years back, I had done some limited practice before the Supreme Court and had orally argued before it. I remember doing the oral argument in a case to invalidate the detention of lawyer Angel Quimpo of Cagayan de Oro. Quimpo was sued for libel by Senator Pelaez, who was also from our province, Misamis Oriental.

But, that was before martial law when we were quite free to say anything relevant to any case that we argued before the Supreme Court. With martial law being enforced, the circumstances were vastly different. In Ernie's petition, for instance, we were directly impugning the legal authority of the Marcos martial law government to arrest people without judicial warrants and detain them indefinitely without criminal charges being filed against them formally. No less important was the issue of whether or not Ernie, a civilian, could be tried by a military tribunal for subversion under a decree that Marcos had issued.

My main difficulty in Ernie's petition was that the legal precedents I could use seemed inapplicable under martial rule. Conventional judicial wisdom of the time, for instance, held that before people could be arrested legally, they had the right to confront the witnesses against them in a preliminary investigation conducted by a prosecutor or by a judge. Only thereafter could criminal cases be filed against the persons concerned and warrants for their arrest be legally issued by the proper courts. But Ernie was arrested without any preliminary investigation and, as far as I could gather, no case had yet been filed against him. Moreover, since he had been arrested ostensibly for subversion, would a military tribunal have the power to try him even as civilian courts were still functioning?

As I prepared to argue his case, I had no idea what to expect from the Supreme Court. I found comfort in some US Supreme Court decisions like *Duncan vs. Kahanamoku*, which ruled that "military trials of a civilian charged with crimes, especially when not made subject to judicial review, are so obviously contrary to our political traditions..." and *US vs. Quarles*, which ruled that "the assertion of military authority over civilians cannot rest on the President's power as commander-in-chief, or on any theory of martial law."

There was also what lawyers call the leading case of *Ex Parte Milligan*, that was decided in 1896 by the US Supreme Court. Milligan was detained by a martial law order of President Abraham Lincoln during the American Civil War, despite the fact that the courts were functioning in the area where the former was detained. Lincoln justified his actuations on the ground, that as commander-in-chief of the Armed Forces during a time of war, he had the power to detain people at will. In *Milligan*, the US Supreme Court disagreed with Lincoln and found his detention in violation of the guarantees of the US Constitution. The US Supreme Court, in the case, said the Constitution of the United States was "a law for rulers and people, equally in war and in peace, and covers with the shield of its protection all classes of men, at all times and under all circumstances." The hitch, however, was that *Milligan* was decided after, not before, the US Civil War was over.

How the fundamental guarantees of the Constitution would operate under martial law conditions, I could not foretell. My worst fears were that the Supreme Court would not invalidate Marcos's martial law edicts, especially after the justices had unanimously upheld the validity of his suspension of the privilege of the writ of habeas corpus in late 1971.

When I got to the main gate of the Supreme Court on the day of the oral arguments, I immediately saw that things did not look good for us, the lawyers of the petitioners. First, we were subjected to body searches and glares by the civilian security guards manning the gate — rude treatment that we had never experienced before in our dealings with the Supreme Court. That made us feel like criminals, not officers of the court, the status that we lawyers enjoyed prior to the declaration of martial law. Then we were told that we could not bring or use tape recorders or private stenographers to take notes of the oral arguments. To me, those were ominous signs that the Supreme Court was dealing overcautiously, if not timorously, with the legal challenges against martial rule that we had brought for its adjudication.

In the argument room of the Supreme Court, I saw lawyers Joker Arroyo, Sedfrey Ordoñez and Francis Garchitorena. They filed briefs for their clients who had likewise been picked up and detained by the military as a consequence of the declaration of martial law. Joker was the lawyer for Joaquin "Chino" Roces of the *Manila Times*, Teodoro "Teddy" Locsin of the *Philippines Free Press*, Max Soliven, one of the best-read columnists of the *Manila Times*, and other big guns of the media; Sed Ordoñez was counsel for Sen. Ninoy Aquino, and Francis, for Sen. Jose Diokno.

Strong Language

When it was my time to argue, I went straight to the point and minced no words, saying it was the duty of the Supreme Court to free Ernie, my client, for the reason that there was absolutely no cause in law or in fact for his arbitrary arrest and continued detention. It was the Supreme Court's duty to rule in favor of protecting the political rights of my client by invalidating his arrest and detention, I said, "unless the Court would rather abdicate its power to safeguard the rights of the people against abuses of the executive."

After the oral arguments, Joker, who later became my counsel in many cases when my libertarian stance clashed with the edicts of martial rule, commented that he thought I had used rather strong language and that I risked being cited for contempt of court. Fortunately, the justices were preoccupied with the weighty implications of the issues raised in the cases at bar and were not sidetracked by my rough remarks.

The hearing took more time than usual because Ernie's petition was but one of the many heard on that day and the justices appeared interested in making the more fundamental issues raised in the petitions surface. Anyway, after the oral arguments, I saw Ernie before he was taken to the military bus for the trip back to the camp; but instead of my consoling him, it was he who consoled me. He knew I was downcast because the decision of the Supreme Court did not appear to be forthcoming, so he tried to cheer me up by saying I had argued his case well. But the thought that everything I had learned in law school and the legal precedents decided by the Supreme Court no longer seemed to matter weighed heavily on me. Without the Rule of Law being observed, I thought to myself, I might as well be a dock hand or a taxi driver eking out a living by the sweat of my back and who did not need to stand up for some vague constitutional precepts or legal norms.

At this time, there was no legislative recourse, either. Marcos had already padlocked Congress upon the declaration of martial rule.

Chapter 9:

Opposing Ratification

On December 1, Marcos ordered that a plebiscite be held on December 15 for the ratification of the proposed Constitution. He assured the people that there would be free and open discussion on the proposed fundamental charter, the official copy of which he received from Convention President Macapagal on November 29.

I was emboldened by Marcos's announcement that people were free to campaign for or against its ratification, although I knew by instinct that the word of Marcos could hardly be given credence. Nonetheless, I did not want to pass up the chance to condemn the abuses of martial rule in public. Thus, I spoke in a number of meetings organized by concerned citizens in Metro Manila. In fits of braggadocio, I usually wound up my talk by asking the "spies of Marcos in this crowd to kindly record what I said of him and report it to him directly so he does not get my message wrong." Sometimes, I would get interviewed on camera by the government television, Channel 4. But, more often than not, the TV crew would only get a blurred shot of me for a few seconds and then pan the camera to the anchor, who would then give his interpretation of what I had said.

Aside from campaigning in Manila against the proposed Constitution, I decided to bring the issues to Cagayan de Oro. As I was leaving for home, I learned from Delegates Tito Guingona and Joe Calderon that the delegates had individually been given P11,400 as "campaign funds" for the ratification of the proposed Constitution. I found out that some 40 of us had been excluded from the bonanza. The exclusion, my notes record, "made me happy because I could tell the people I did not make illicit money out of the Convention."

Speaking Out in Cagayan de Oro

I had accepted several invitations from private groups in Cagayan de Oro to discuss the proposed Constitution. But, when I arrived in the city, I found that most of the meetings had been canceled. In the space of a week, for example, meetings at Lourdes College, the Liceo de Cagayan, the East Rotary Club and the Catholic Seminary were all canceled. So were the convocations in a college in the municipality of Balingasag and in the town plaza of Manticao.

The only significant meeting in Cagayan de Oro that I addressed on the ratification of the proposed Constitution was held at the provincial capitol. It

1972: *IN CAGAYAN DE ORO, denied bigger forums, I conduct small teach-ins to explain why the draft Constitution should be rejected by the people.*

was not canceled primarily because the main organizer was Concordio Diel, the pro-Marcos provincial governor. Aside from the governor, other top officials of the province, the provincial board members, the judges, the prosecutors, a few mayors and, of course, the ubiquitous military officials and intelligence officers were there. The meeting was obviously intended as a forum to impress the people that the government was fulfilling its role to disseminate information on the pros and cons of the proposed Constitution.

They invited me to speak at the meeting only because I was one of the four delegates to the Convention — in fact, the No. 1 delegate — representing Misamis Oriental and Cagayan de Oro. The other delegates were Felino Neri, who died before the Convention could finish its work, Rolando Piit, who voted against the proposed Constitution, and Pablo Reyes, who voted for it.

Since Piit no longer spoke out after martial rule was imposed, it would have looked bad if the organizers only invited as speakers those who advocated the approval of the proposed Constitution. They, therefore, sent me an invitation. They did not think I would accept it. In fact, I kept them guessing whether or not I would attend the meeting. In the event, I showed up while the meeting was going on. All the speakers before me, I was told, extolled Marcos as the savior of the nation and the proposed Constitution as the vehicle by which Marcos would institutionalize the New Society.

Since I was already there, Diel had no choice but to give me a chance to talk. I spoke passionately against the ratification of the proposed Constitution. I told the audience that its ratification would mean the beginning of the end of our democratic rights and the institutionalization of a Marcos dynasty.

As was usual with government-sponsored gatherings, the audience was composed mostly of government people. Such a crowd would normally be antagonistic to anyone speaking against the prevailing government line. Nonetheless, I saw that some people in the audience, mostly those seated at the middle to the back rows, could not resist applauding certain points I raised, but this they did in a most unusual manner. They didn't show their hands to clap; they kept their hands between their thighs while clapping, which muted the sound of their applause. I understood that to mean that they empathized with my stand, but they could not manifest it because the place was swarming with military agents and the threat of arrest was ever present under the conditions of martial rule.

After the rally, I was told that the provincial commander of the Constabulary, Col. Guillermo Oppus, was so incensed by what I had said that he wanted to arrest me immediately after my talk. Oppus probably could not imagine anyone talking in such disrespectful terms towards Marcos, his commander-in-chief, the way I did in his presence. Governor Diel reportedly convinced him not to arrest me, lest it prove that Marcos's promise of free discussion of the proposed Constitution could not be relied upon. I escaped arrest that time by the skin of my teeth. I would not be as lucky the next time around.

'Show of Hands' Referendum

The period for the free debates on the proposed Constitution did not last its course. It was cut short by an order of Marcos. He worried, and rightly so, that the abuses and the anomalies of his regime were being exposed through the open discussion of the merits and demerits of the draft Constitution. Even the cautious leader of the Liberal Party, Sen. Gerry Roxas, was speaking out openly against ratification. As early as December 9, 1972, in a printed statement disseminated by mail and courier, Roxas said:

> Under the proposed Constitution...the powers of government are overly concentrated in the Prime Minister, thus negating the established democratic principle of checks and balances.

Marcos followed up his order stopping the debates with another order — to submit the draft Constitution forthwith to the people for ratification. This was all right with us. The problem was that Marcos ordered that the ratification be done by a show of hands in the Barangay or Citizens' Assemblies, not by secret ballot in a formal plebiscite, as ordained by the 1935 Constitution. Marcos resorted to the show of hands to pressure people to ratify the draft Constitution. He let it be known that his martial law apparatus was monitoring how people responded. The implication was that, if they did not vote as he wanted them to, they could get into trouble with the martial law enforcers.

As an avid student of history, Marcos knew that the referendum was the favored method used by authoritarian rulers like Napoleon Bonaparte and Adolf Hitler to consolidate power in their hands. The French simply nodded when Napoleon crowned himself emperor of France in 1804, while the Germans applauded when Hitler made himself the *Fuhrer* of the German *Reich* in 1934. Marcos followed the way his idols, Napoleon and Hitler, did it in their respective countries: concentrate power in his hands by the use of referenda. In all, Marcos ordered the holding of two referenda in 1973 and one each in 1975, 1976 and 1977. In the 80s, he became a little more formalistic in that he ordered the holding of separate "plebiscites" in 1980, 1981 and 1984, all of which were intended to strengthen his hold on the levers of government. In a space of 12 years, Marcos ordered the Constitution that he caused the Constitutional Convention to adopt in 1973 to be amended eight times, a record in the history of the country's constitutional amendments.

Overwhelming 'Approval'

On January 17, 1973 Marcos announced that the proposed Constitution had been "approved" overwhelmingly, that is, by more than 95% of the vote through a show of hands in the barangays. The 95% approval was certainly spurious and there were no authentic records to support that conclusion. The report that was supposed to have been submitted to Marcos by a certain Francisco Cruz of Pasig, the president of the so-called National Federation of Barangays, was nowhere to be found.

The Supreme Court said so in the case of *Josue Javellana vs. Executive Secretary et al.* and five other cases that were decided on March 31, 1973. In those cases that dealt with the validity of the ratification of the proposed Constitution, the Supreme Court found that Cruz was not even a member of any barrio or barangay council. Hence, he could not have been the president of a national federation of barangays. To top it all, the Supreme Court said that, despite its order for the government to produce Cruz's report, no such report was submitted to it.

My lawyer friend, Fred Gapuz, who stood up for a free discussion of the proposed Constitution, told me this story shortly after barangay consultations were held in various places in Misamis Oriental and Cagayan de Oro. Gapuz said:

> The people attending the consultations were asked to raise their hands if they wanted rice and sardines. Many did. The agents of Marcos then reported that there was overwhelming approval of the draft constitution. On the basis of those unverifiable reports, Marcos then issued Presidential Proclamation No. 1102 that the proposed Constitution had been ratified on January 17, 1973.

The "show of hands" method of ratifying the proposed Constitution did not sit well with Comelec Chairman Jaime Ferrer. Since Ferrer was hardly one to hide his displeasure at official misconduct, and this was one of the worst he had seen, he submitted his letter of resignation on December 19, 1972. Marcos took time to assess Ferrer's discontent in an attempt to keep him under the control of his administration. But, after the so-called ratification of the Constitution, Marcos replaced Ferrer as Comelec chair with Leonardo Perez on May 28, 1973. Having now anchored his martial law powers in the newly "ratified" Constitution, Marcos no longer saw the necessity of observing the substantial requirements of the Constitution that lawyers love to quibble about. To Marcos, it was sufficient that the people were made to believe that the formalities of the Constitution — like getting their approval of the proposed fundamental law, even by a show of hands — were being followed.

The Custodial Committee

As we were winding our work in the Convention, Macapagal organized a Custodial Committee to compile, preserve and publish the records of the Convention. The Convention records were a treasure trove of documents that could be used to interpret the provisions of the Constitution and Marcos saw the need to have full and exclusive access to those records. Thus, he supplanted Macapagal's Convention Custodial Committee with a Malacañang Custodial Committee by issuing Executive Order No. 406. He had his man in the Convention, Delegate Gilberto Duavit, to chair it. He also had another reliable Marcos man in the Convention, Delegate Pacificador, as a member of the Committee.

Soon after the Duavit-led Malacañang Committee was created, the records of the Convention were brought to the National Shipyard and Steel Corporation (Nassco) building. At that time, many of us delegates did not know what Marcos was up to, but we heard that the Nassco building was where Pacificador held office. We naively thought that the records were brought there merely for safekeeping by him. What happened after the records were transferred shocked us. Pacificador's office got burned and Convention records were reportedly gutted by fire. We never knew how many precious Constitutional Convention documents were lost. But we in the Opposition could make an educated guess why the records were burned.

The records were the original or source documents to prove or disprove facile claims of Marcos drumbeaters that the Convention had intended to grant Marcos ample powers to do at least two things that were now being disputed: to use the referendum instead of a formal plebiscite for the ratification of the new Constitution as required by the 1935 Constitution, and to name his own successor. Earlier, Pacificador had publicly claimed that Marcos had those powers and he cited alleged discussions in the Convention to prove his point. Macapagal refuted Pacificador's assertions in a written 10-page statement, a copy of which he shared with me. In retrospect, Macapagal's penchant to write down his thoughts on government was most beneficial since the martial law government gagged the media back then. In sum, Macapagal said that the records cited by Pacificador had been fabricated.

Macapagal pointed out that, had the Convention records not been burned, the so-called debates of Pacificador with Antonio de Guzman, Rodolfo Ortiz and Midpantao Adil — which favored Marcos's stand on the referendum and his alleged right to name his successor — would easily be exposed as a hoax. Macapagal concluded that, in his best judgment, "the proceedings cited by Pacificador (had been) falsified."

Back then, I suspected that, aside from simply setting the records straight, Macapagal was trying to prod Marcos to convene the Interim National Assembly. As the Convention President, the INA was Macapagal's brainchild and getting it convened became an obsession with him. If the INA did not get convened, Macapagal felt he would lose face with the delegates, many of whom had signed the new Constitution upon his prodding. It was, thus, natural for him to urge Marcos to convene the INA. He also probably thought that its convening would hasten the normalization of the country's political situation. Whatever might have been his true motives, I agreed with Macapagal's views that Pacificador's arguments in support of Marcos's moves to have the draft Constitution approved by referendum instead of by plebiscite and to name his successor were based on falsified entries in the records of the Convention. Marcos's henchmen had resorted to falsification to provide a fraudulent constitutional basis for certain acts of Marcos after the declaration of martial rule.

Delegate Manuel Concordia, a loyal supporter of Macapagal, confirmed in one of the meetings of our Opposition group, that some of the minutes of the Convention had been "invented." Concordia knew what he was talking about. He was a member of both the Custodial Committee that Macapagal had created and later of the Malacañang committee formed by Marcos, which eventually took custody of the records.

Concordia disclosed that he was paid P20,000 for six weeks' work as a member of the Marcos committee, which took hold of the Convention records. He said he was asked to agree to the insertion of some fabricated deliberations by some delegates on certain pro-Marcos provisions of the new Constitution after the declaration of martial rule. He said that he refused to do so. Consequently, he was eased out of the committee and no longer informed of its activities.

In any event, Marcos had his wishes realized. The proposed Constitution was ratified through a referendum rather than by a plebiscite. He now had more than enough bases in the new Constitution to back his exercise of authoritarian powers.

Moros Rebel

While the mainstream opposition in Manila challenged the proclamation of martial rule and the other edicts of Marcos with legal arguments before the

Supreme Court, the Moros of Mindanao fought martial rule with lethal bullets in the provinces of Lanao, Cotabato, Maguindanao, Basilan and Sulu. The proclamation of martial rule triggered what developed into the most wide spread Moro rebellion in the country.

Previous Moro rebellions were mostly tribal affairs. The Tausugs of Sulu, the Maguindanaos of the Cotabato provinces and the Maranaos of the Lanao provinces took turns in fighting the Spanish colonizers from the murky years of Magellan's "discovery" of the country in 1521 up to the time the US bought "the Philippine Islands" from Spain for $20 million under the Treaty of Paris in 1898. The change of our colonizers from the staid Spaniards to the more aggressive and better-armed Americans did not intimidate the Moros. Legend has it that Gen. John Pershing, who eventually became the only US army six-star general, had the .45 caliber pistol invented so that his officers and men in Sulu could stop the Moro juramentado, the precursor of the Iraqi suicide bombers. The Moro juramentado was said to be unstoppable by the Krag rifle that was the standard firearm issued to US soldiers at that time. True or not, the fact is that the Moros continued their armed resistance against the American colonizers from the turn of the 20th century up until the Japanese war. When Japanese troops occupied the country, the Moros turned against them, too, but now in cooperation with other Filipino — and American — guerilla groups.

In 1945, the Japanese War ended. The following year, on July 4, 1946, US President Franklin Delano Roosevelt restored our independence pursuant to the provisions of the Tydings-McDuffie Law. But even as we had regained our independence from the US, Moro arms continued to challenge the government of the Republic even up to the more recent times. In fact, within a month after the declaration of martial law, Moro rebels under the banner of the Moro National Liberation Front overran the government installations in Marawi City on October 20. Early the following year, particularly on February 7, MNLF fighters also took the town proper of Jolo, the capital town of Sulu, and the fighting soon spread to the provinces of Maguindanao and Cotabato. Government troops retook Jolo only after razing it to the ground.

Marcos had to reinforce the government troops in Mindanao by sending an estimated two-thirds of the fighting men of the Marines and the Army to restore a semblance of order in the Moro areas in the island. The Moro rebels, however, kept the government troops at bay. Nur Misuari who had assumed the leadership of the MNLF estimated years later that the Marcos government spent no less than US$3 billion just to fight the Moro rebels to a standstill. The approximation of the dollar costs of the MNLF rebellion was probably overstated but not the estimates that more than 40,000 were killed in the rebellion and half a million refugees fled from the areas of conflict to the safer parts of Mindanao and the Visayas and even to the Federal State of Sabah in Malaysia.

The MNLF rebellion kept the Marcos forces occupied in the provinces of Lanao, Cotabato, Maguindanao, Basilan, Sulu and Tawi-Tawi for the remaining months of 1973. At this time, the rest of the country in general appeared to think that martial rule was a good thing as, at the very least, it imposed some order in Luzon, the Visayas and in the Christian dominated areas of Mindanao.

While we in the political opposition did not approve of the bloodletting that accompanied the MNLF rebellion, some of us, like Jimmy Ferrer, did not believe that we should limit our opposition to Marcos only through the electoral process. He told me soon after he was relieved as Chair of the Comelec by Marcos that it should be fairly easy to blow up some passenger planes by the use of C4 plastic bombs. I listened as patiently as I could to Ferrer who discoursed on the evils and the corruption of the Marcos regime and on certain violent means that could end it sooner than later. But, I told him that I was not prepared to go the route of violence in my opposition to Marcos although I said there could be others – without identifying them – who would probably be persuaded to do so.

In any event, by and large, we in the legitimate opposition were more inclined to blame Marcos rather than the Moro rebels for the escalation of violence in the Moro dominated provinces. We saw martial rule as the trigger that eventually blew up the fuse of the Moro tensions that had been building up through the years.

Chapter 10:

My First Arrest

I was in Cagayan de Oro when Marcos announced that the people had ratified the new Constitution by an overwhelming vote through the referendum that he had ordered. A few days after the Marcos announcement, I went to the Lumbia airport of Cagayan de Oro to fly back to Manila on January 28 to wind up my affairs with the Convention.

While waiting for my flight, I heard my name paged over the public address system. I was asked to go to the ticket counter. I did as requested, thinking there might have been something wrong with my booking. But, at the ticket counter, a middle-aged man in civilian clothes met me. I identified him in my notes as Jose A. Santos, a Counter Intelligence Service officer. He was accompanied by another CIS agent by the name of Franco Espartero.

Santos told me casually that Espartero and he had come to arrest me. I had no choice but to go with them. Santos said they would take me to Manila on the morning flight. In the meantime, reinforced by heavily armed soldiers, they were taking me to Camp Alagar, the Constabulary Camp in the city, where I would be detained for the night.

I asked if it would be possible for us to pass by my house so I could tell my wife and kids about my arrest and to pick up a few articles of clothing and toiletries. They agreed. When we got to my place, I immediately went to our room where Bing was having a siesta. She was surprised to see me as she thought I had already taken the flight to Manila. I told her, as calmly as I could, that soldiers had arrested me at the airport and that they were at the *sala* of our house. I added that she should not cry. I had to ask this particular favor of her because if I saw her cry it would have weakened my resolve to continue opposing martial rule.

Bing accommodated my request and took my arrest in stride. Even the children, whom she had psychologically prepared, continued playing as if nothing unusual was happening in our home. Perhaps, they had taken to heart Bing's repeated admonition that, if one day Marcos ordered my arrest, they should not panic or be ashamed because I was not a criminal. I was only standing up for the rights of our people.

Soon friends like lawyers Fred Gapuz, Berchmans Abejuela and Ricardo Tapia, my close associates in the Coapa, came to our house on time to witness the soldiers ransack my library in search of "subversive" books that would incriminate me. The soldiers confiscated, among other volumes, *The Red Book of Mao,* a book on Che Guevara and another on the Huk rebellion. Through the years, I had collected those books among many volumes that dealt with political science, history and biographies of people who affected the lives of others.

When Bing noticed that they were zeroing in on books with revolutionary themes, she pulled a book out of a shelf and asked them to seize it also. The book was titled *Today's Revolution: Democracy,* which they refused to take. Their refusal was understandable because the book was authored by Marcos who had intended it as a justification for the imposition of martial law.

During a break in their search for subversive materials in our house, Bing offered the soldiers *puto* and coffee. The soldiers were probably too embarrassed to partake of the *merienda* that they told me we had better leave now for Camp Alagar. We got to the camp in no time at all. The arresting team had me confined at the office of Capt. Jun Medina.

I had difficulty sleeping there. I noted in my improvised diary that I missed Bing and our children and that "my heart was wrenched with pain when they took me away." I remembered what the poet Kahlil Gibran had written: "love knows not its own depth until the hour of separation." How true it was, but I tried to present a brave front in the presence of the arresting officers. I did not want them to know that I had an Achilles heel in my being forcibly separated from my family.

Cagayan de Oro being a relatively small place, the news that I was arrested spread like wild fire in a dry, kindling prairie. I saw our neighbor, Tia Nena Vamenta, cry as I was being taken away. Later, I was told that an old friend, Bontong Novales, also cried in utter frustration that he could not do anything for me under the circumstances.

At Camp Alagar, where I was detained for the night, friends like Philip and Jacob Montesa, Erasmo Damasing, the Adaza brothers Cecilo and Guerrero, Enriquito Beja and Digno Roa came to visit me, in addition to Fred Gapuz and Ric Tapia who had accompanied me to the camp. Many of those who visited me handed me a few pesos as *pabaon* or emergency money. The generosity of my friends boosted my spirits even as I saw no end in sight to my travails at that time.

There was, at least, one adverse comment on the circumstances of my arrest. It came from lawyer Francisco X. Velez, who told mutual friends that I deserved to be arrested because I was "playing hero" or *"pa-hero-hero"* in the Visayan language. But there were many others who assured me of their support through Bing, not only verbally but also in writing. One poignant note was written by a Jesuit priest, Hudson Mitchell, which I reproduce here because, to my regret, I was never able to thank him for it before he died in a plane crash on February 5, 1975. He wrote:

Feb. 2, 1973

Dear Bing,

When I returned Tuesday, I learned about Nene's being taken to Manila. I can appreciate how concerned you must feel about it. This note is just to say that I share your concern and promise to remember you and Nene during these anxious days.

Nene is a brave and honest person. You have every reason to be proud of him. If every citizen were as honest and brave, it would be a new society indeed. It is especially distressing that after being guaranteed freedom to speak openly on the proposed Constitution without fear of reprisal, that his frankness and courage should now be used to his disadvantage. Nevertheless I am convinced that his honesty will be recognized at last. Too many know him to permit any real harm to come to him.

Sincerely,
Hudson Mitchell, SJ

On the morning of January 29, the arresting team brought me to the Lumbia airport for the flight to Manila. Bing and the kids were all there to see me off. Our youngest, Inde, was asleep in Bing's arms. In general, our elder children, Gwen, Maripet, Koko, Jac and Terelou carried themselves well although Maripet shed tears now and then while Jac showed his emotions by bussing me on the cheek every so often.

Abadilla's Office, Camp Crame

Before long, I was flown to Manila on board a Philippine Air Lines flight and we arrived at the domestic terminal without any hitch. The arresting team brought me straight to Camp Crame, the national headquarters of the Philippine Constabulary. There, I was placed in the custody of the unit headed by the dreaded Capt. Rolando Abadilla, who had acquired a reputation of violently dealing with those who opposed martial rule.

By sheer luck, I was not brought to Abadilla personally. An officer led me to a crowded room where he found a vacant desk with a typewriter. He sat behind the desk and asked me to sit on a chair in front of it. He typed his questions and my answers. An agent named Ortega interrupted with his own questions, which I tried to answer as best I could. From the questions, I sensed they were trying hard to link me with underground "subversives" with whom I had no dealings whatsoever. One of the persons they wanted me associated with was a certain "Boy," whom I vaguely remembered as someone who had married into the family living next door to my in-laws' place in Quezon City. Boy had disappeared after martial rule was declared and neither his family nor I knew what happened to him.

While I knew that the real reason for my arrest was my public and vocal opposition to martial rule, it was only when the questioning got deeper that I sensed what the immediate cause was.

The investigating officer asked me about a lunch that I had attended some weeks before at the house in Quezon City of my fellow delegate, Jose Calderon. I did remember that lunch. Calderon had invited Delegate Manuel Molina and me to his house. The questions of the officer suggested that we were plotting a revolution on that occasion. I denied that, saying we merely discussed how we could legally obtain the release of Boy, the son of Calderon, who had been picked up by the military. I knew that Boy was arrested not because he was involved in any subversive activity but because he was Calderon's son. As a wealthy businessman who was openly critical of martial rule, Calderon was especially vulnerable to pressure.

Days before the lunch, I accompanied Boy as his lawyer to answer the summons of Gen. Prospero Olivas, whose office was in Camp Crame. It was the most useless act as a lawyer that I have ever done in my entire life. Minutes after we were allowed into the general's office, I was asked to go out and leave Boy behind. I was tempted to argue that my client had every right to be assisted by his counsel, but decided to keep my peace, remembering we were under the constraints of martial rule. In the event, Molina and I failed to secure Boy Calderon's release. I did not know it then, but I was to join the Calderons — father and son — at their detention place in a matter of weeks.

I told the officer who was questioning me that, after talking about what we lawyers could do to free Boy Calderon, we discussed the legal ramifications of the ratification of the new Constitution. We also talked about what we could do to continue our peaceful opposition to it. We certainly were not plotting any violent upheaval against the government.

The officer also insinuated there was a connection between me — or perhaps us who did not support the Marcos initiatives in the Convention — and the would-be-assassin of Imelda Marcos. Days before my arrest, somebody hacked Imelda with a bolo as she handed out certificates of commendation during a program. Only the timely intervention of her security people and Tourism Minister Jose Aspiras, who wrestled the would-be-killer to the floor of the stage, that prevented her receiving fatal injuries.

The investigator was obviously eager to connect us to the would-be-assassin to butter up to his superiors. I was not of much help. There simply was no conspiracy between me and my colleagues who had opposed Marcos in the Convention on the one hand and Imelda's would-be-assassin on the other. In fact, all I knew about the incident was what I had seen on TV. I remember casually mentioning it to Bing then that I hoped the military would not attribute the assassination attempt to us. Also I thought then that it was asinine for Imelda's security people to have shot him dead when he had already been completely subdued. With the overkill, they would never know what had motivated him to attack her or if he had acted alone or in conspiracy with others.

When the interrogation was over, I asked for a copy of my statement. I was not given any. No reason was offered for the refusal. Under the circumstances, my notes recorded that I "resigned myself to God."

Actually, I easily fielded the "fishing expedition" questions of the interrogating officer. There was nothing in my answers that could legally incriminate me, or anyone, at the Calderon lunch. I learned later that martial law authorities knew who were present at the lunch because they had Calderon's house placed under surveillance. Intelligence agents posing as gardeners of a nearby house monitored who went to the Calderon home on that occasion. Indeed, I recalled seeing some crew-cut, sunburned and shabbily clothed individuals leisurely pulling out or pretending to cut grass beside the sewage canal of the house across Calderon's.

The amateurish interrogation done, the officer told me to stay in the office and await further orders. Initially I did as I was told, but the security was so lax that I walked out of the office to go to the camp chapel to pray. I came back to the office after some 30 minutes without anyone having missed me. I suppose the reason for my military guards' laxity was that even the soldiers who arrested me apparently believed in my innocence. I did not realize it then but what I did was foolhardy. Had my absence been discovered, the authorities could have ordered that I be placed in isolation or, worse, shot on sight. In any case, my arrest was probably merely intended to intimidate me and deter others who might be tempted to follow our example of defying martial law, even verbally. The most effective weapon of martial rule, in my view, was not the actual but the threatened arrest of people without court warrants and the thought that those arrested could be imprisoned indefinitely.

While awaiting my transfer to a detention cell, I slept on empty tabletops after office hours in Abadilla's office. That was the nature of my "accommodations" for a couple of days until Calderon sent over a chaise lounge to serve as my bed at night.

Loneliness & Doubt

The daytime bustle in the office of Abadilla kept me preoccupied with my problems with the government. I had to think of what to say to investigators that would not implicate others or incriminate myself, and that would not be outright lies. The hardest time for me, as I suppose it was for other detainees, was when the darkness that follows dusk began to set in and there was only quiet in the office where I was being held. Then I would begin to think of my wife and my children and recall the simple joys of just driving around with them, singing children's songs and doing word puzzles on the commercial advertisements that we saw along the way. I would lull myself into sleep by repeating in my mind that I missed and loved them very much and entrusting myself to God's care.

During those lonely hours, doubts would assail my mind as to whether or not what I was doing was right. To cope with the situation, as in other times of stress, I resorted to prayer. Not formalized prayer, but short and spontaneous ones, particularly of surrender to the Lord. Pangs of sorrow that I had caused so much trouble to Bing and our children who, at the time, were still growing up often weighed heavily on my mind in those hours of solitude. Prayer helped me from breaking down.

The feeling of loneliness that sunk into my mind while I was detained in the office of Abadilla was not caused by the absence of people. Abadilla's office was full of people, some of whom were also detainees like me, but they were all complete strangers to me. We were under orders not to converse with one another. We were undergoing "tactical interrogation". Thus, our jailors did not want us to compare notes or talk with one another.

On one morning as I was passing water into a makeshift urinal in a shed abutting the office of Abadilla, I noticed a strapping young lad who had the looks of a peasant waddle, rather than walk, towards the space beside me. Then when he was by my side, he emitted an agonized whimper as if he was in great pain. I asked him in a whisper, "What happened to you?" He answered in a low voice that he had been tortured the night before by his jailors. "They inserted the sharp edge of a paper fastener into my penis," he said. Since there was nothing much that I could do for him, I left the toilet and said a private prayer for the poor fellow.

In my case, the interrogation/booking process took three days, including medical examination and fingerprinting. The examination was rather superficial. The doctor only did a bronchial stethoscope and blood pressure examination on me ("130/90," the doctor said), after which he pronounced me as fit as a fiddle. The fingerprinting went smoothly.

Enrile's Signature

Then I was brought to the Judge Advocate General Service where the only "unusual" thing in the whole process had to do with a Lieutenant Nicholas who informed me — without my asking — that their office could not "review" my case because the warrant for my arrest had been signed by Defense Minister Enrile himself. The lieutenant probably intended to intimidate me with the seriousness of the charges that brought me to Crame. He apparently equated the gravity of the charges with the signature of Enrile on the arrest warrant. Enrile's signature on the warrant for my arrest was actually no big deal.

Under pressure of martial law, the Constitutional Convention leadership overturned the rule that only judges could issue warrants of arrest, search and seizure. As a result, under the Marcos Constitution, the Minister of National Defense was also empowered to issue those warrants. The Convention adopted the change after an intense debate that was decided by a phone call to Malacañang.

Macapagal was presiding at a plenary session debate on a resolution to vest the Minister of National Defense with the power to issue warrants of arrest in the same manner that judges were authorized to do so. Delegate Jose

Suarez warned against it. He said that to allow other officials to share that judicial power could "signal the death of civil liberties in the country (and) be an instrument of harassment." Suarez's argument carried the hour and his motion to reject the proposal was approved by a vote of 96-87.

Macapagal then had the session suspended. He stepped down from the rostrum and walked towards the seat of Delegate Duavit, Marcos's head-man in the Convention, who was seated two rows in front of me. I heard Macapagal ask Duavit what he thought Marcos's reaction would be to the Suarez amendment, which denied the power to issue warrants of arrest to the Minister of National Defense. Duavit excused himself from Macapagal's presence and went to the nearest phone a few feet away from our seats and placed a call to someone, presumably, Marcos in Malacañang. I did not hear the telephone conversation between Duavit and the person he called, but almost everybody who saw him make the call assumed he had phoned Marcos himself.

After the call, Duavit talked with Macapagal — beyond our hearing. Subsequently, the Suarez amendment was reconsidered. The power to issue warrants of arrest was no longer limited to judges. Other officials authorized by "law" could now also do so. The law envisioned in this regard was not a law as the term was normally understood — an enactment of the legislature. "Law" under martial law conditions now meant a decree or any other issuance of Marcos that he intended to have legal force and effect.

In the event, the power to issue warrants in the form of an Arrest, Search and Seizure Order (ASSO) was vested by a Marcos decree on the Minister of National Defense. The ASSO became the legal cover for the indiscriminate arrest and indefinite detention of people who were considered enemies of the martial law government. As Marcos had intended it, the grant of power to issue warrants of arrest to the Minister of National Defense intimidated not only the Convention leadership but also a good number of delegates who subsequently approved wholesale numerous pro-Marcos provisions in the proposed Constitution.

I was among the first 800 individuals who were arrested by the military under an ASSO #797, dated January 26, 1973 in which I was classified as a "subversive." Being arrested through an ASSO meant that the military or police were authorized to pick me up and detain me immediately without any preliminary investigation by a Department of Justice prosecutor or fiscal or even by a judge — a right previously enjoyed by people before martial rule. Since the ASSO classified me as a "subversive," even if I was a civilian, under Marcos's decrees, I was now a fit subject of military tribunal proceedings.

Before my arrest by ASSO, speculation was rife among us delegates as to why Macapagal, a former President of the Republic, appeared to have capitulated to the authoritarian rule of Marcos. I, for one, thought he should have put up a more spirited resistance to the Marcos regime. We were certainly disappointed that he did not.

Ric Sagmit was one of those who expressed grief that Macapagal was not pre-pared to oppose Marcos's declaration of martial law more openly. Sagmit said he visited Macapagal at his office at the Quezon City Hall on the first working day after the declaration of martial rule.

He recounted the incident:

> I told the President that this is your moment of history. The country needs a leader to oppose this power grab of Marcos. Take the lead, Mr. President, and I will follow you.
>
> President Macapagal replied that I was still young and that there is a time for people to step back so that they could fight on another day. He said that there is no use bucking an irresistible force (martial law). It is better to work things out so that we will be a part of the power structure of the government, he added.
>
> In my opinion, he missed an opportunity for greatness.

Incidentally, Sagmit recounted that the moment Macapagal sensed that he was going to discuss the imposition of martial rule, the latter pulled out a transistor radio from a pocket of his suit and tuned it to a radio station that played some music. "I could hardly hear him or my own voice," he said, but Macapagal explained that "it is necessary to drown out bugging devices that martial law agents could have placed in the office."

In any event, some delegates assumed unkindly that, like plain citizens, Macapagal dreaded the possibility that Marcos would order his arrest and detention. I am not too sure that he was moved by fear. What was more plau-sible at the time, I think, was the theory that Macapagal was motivated by more practical considerations than the fear of being arrested. He wanted a kind of power-sharing with Marcos so that he would be the President of the Republic even with minimal powers under the new Constitution while Marcos could be the Prime Minister with real powers of government. If that were so, he was in for a rude awakening. Marcos had no intention of sharing power with anyone. He wanted power consolidated in his hands under the new Con-stitution, as events subsequently showed.

The Gym

After my initial detention in Abadilla's office, I was ordered confined in the Camp Crame gym. There I met delegates Jose Calderon and Manuel Molina who had been arrested earlier than I. Molina corroborated what I had told the investigating officer that we were at lunch at Calderon's home on January 19 principally to map out our legal defense of Boy, Calderon's son. Molina added that we also decried the submission of the draft Constitution "as approved by the Con-vention" to Marcos personally by Macapagal in his capacity as the president of the Constitutional Convention.

We could not imagine how Macapagal could maintain a straight face and tell Marcos that he was submitting to him the draft Constitution as if it were the product of a free convention when it was certainly not. It was common knowledge that after Marcos placed the country under martial rule, a select group of delegates and non-delegates had taken over the drafting of the new Constitution to ensure that it contained provisions that facilitated Marcos's continued exercise of power.

In the Gym, I also met some friends and made new ones like Amadeo Seno, the famed law practitioner from Cebu; Ernesto Granada, a widely read columnist of the *Manila Chronicle*, who wrote scathing articles against Marcos; Roberto Ordoñez, a newsman of another national daily; Luis Taruc, the erstwhile supremo of the Huks, a guerilla organization that fought against the Japanese and, subsequently as communists, against the government; and Homobono Adaza, a clamorous lawyer from Camiguin. They were, like me, detained under that all-inclusive criminal charge of having engaged in "subversive activities."

There I also met the longest-serving detainees in the country, Angel Baking and his bosom friend, Samuel Rodriguez. They had just finished serving long prison terms for rebellion when Marcos suspended the writ of habeas corpus in August 1971. In the wake of the suspension, they were both re-arrested and detained without any explanation from the authorities as to why they were being deprived of their liberty again. Their sad plight continued when martial law was proclaimed. The military used the proclamation as the justification for their continued detention. The military authorities apparently considered them a threat to the State and that was it.

Baking was the most learned man I had the privilege of meeting. He could talk philosophy as if he were born to it, or science, especially social science, as if he had mastered it in some Ivy League school in the US, which he did not but which he learned, according to him, "in the best school any person can go to — the school of experience." On one occasion, he told me, tongue in cheek, that the gym was "perhaps the only prison in the country where the inmates all claimed to be innocent." He beamed the sarcastic observation towards some detainees, who, prior to their detention, had "loudly protested US domination or the militarization of the country, but who now dissembled their stand to save their skin." It was a pity, he said, that instead of considering their detention as subversives as "a badge of honor," they were now ashamed of it.

Rodriguez was Sancho Pancha incarnate to Baking's role as Don Quixote in their quest for a just society. My impression was that he followed Baking wherever he thought they should go — including going to the hills to fight a revolution, which they did in the 1950s and for which they were convicted for rebellion and had served more than 20 years in prison. But Sancho Pancha or not, in my opinion, Rodriguez was also one of the most compassionate and down-to-earth human beings I had ever met. Like a mother hen caring for her chicks, Rodriguez always made it a point to inquire what happened to any detainee who missed any meal or why a detainee seemed to have lost his appetite. He also dispensed street-smart advice to us.

On one occasion, he advised against a plan of some of our fellow detainees to file a complaint against a lieutenant who had shouted at a detainee for failing to answer a roll call. He sagely counseled that complaints against more serious grievances would lose steam if we dissipated our efforts on such a trivial matter.

In another incident, we were upset about the guards' order that disallowed the delivery of local newspapers to us. The availability of local newspapers was one of the little amenities that made life for us in the gym a little bearable. We thought that the guards were preventing us from getting outside information and were being unduly harsh. We wanted to complain to the camp commander.

Rodriguez said that censoring the news was farthest from the minds of the guards. They could not have even thought of it. In fact, he said, the order was not directed towards the detainees, but to the gardeners who received the newspapers from the delivery boys and brought the papers to us. The guards saw the gardeners as the conduits through whom many things such as soap, cooking oil, toilet paper or, worse, drugs were passed on to the detainees. Hence, Rodriguez suggested that, instead of charging the guards with violating our "right to information," perhaps the better thing to do was to assure the guards that no other items would be passed through the gardeners to us aside from the newspapers. Or, if the guards wanted, we could ask them to assign somebody to get the newspapers for us. For a fee, Rodriguez added with a wink. We followed his counsel and we got our newspapers.

Crude Facilities

There were three washrooms in the gym, which housed 170 detainees at the time that I was there. There was always a long line of people waiting to use the toilets every morning. To beat the queues, I would do my thing in the early dawn, between two and three o'clock. Truth to tell, the schedule created no extra hardship for me because I had very little sleep in the overcrowded gym. People talked endlessly into the wee hours of the morning. Even as I tried mightily tried to lull myself into dreamland, I could still hear them. There was also the problem of cigarette smoke, which my nostrils abhorred and which seemed to perpetually hang in the air inside the gym. That caused me sleepless hours. Worse, water was scarce. There was never enough for the needs of the detainees. Water pressure was very low in the daytime, so that some detainees would wait for the break of dawn to collect the precious liquid. When they did, the racket caused by pails banging against one another or against the cement floor made sleep for me so much more elusive.

The scarcity of water was such that there was a time when I went without bathing for two straight days. I felt that I smelled awful — what with the heat of summer sun beating down on the gym and the accumulated stench of ill-washed detainees within its walls.

On March 19, after patiently waiting for my turn, I finally got a vacant shower stall. There I removed my clothes and my black-dialed Rolex watch and put them on the top frame of a divider that provided a degree of privacy to whoever was taking shower. After the shower, I put on my clothes and left to go back to my bunk. I paused for small talk with a group of old friends and a new bunch of detainees that included some policemen from Quezon City. The policemen were arrested on charges of having drowned some criminal suspects in a well. After a while, I realized that I had forgotten my wristwatch at the showers. I rushed back only to find that my prized possession was gone. I was truly saddened by the loss of the watch because it took me several months of practicing law before I could buy it.

I went back to the group and told them that I had lost my watch at the showers some minutes ago. The policemen asked me to describe the watch and I did so without any thought of recovering it. Our conversation group broke up as I proceeded to my bunk. A few minutes later, the cops came with my watch and gave it back to me without asking for any payment. Naturally, I thanked them profusely for it.

Cynics would probably say the policemen themselves did it. But since they were with the group I was conversing with, I was inclined to believe the cops merely intuitively knew who did it and got my watch returned. I recount the story not only because of its intrinsic merit as a human interest item but also because it validated the proposition that I had always believed in: the police should be local, not national, as Marcos had mandated under martial rule. The local police recruits would personally know who the peace-loving people and who the hoodlums were in their localities. It would thus be easier for them to enforce the law in their home ground than for police officers who came from other places.

Precious Moments with Inde

Despite its inconveniences, I began to adjust to the reality of being a detainee in the custody of the Constabulary in the gym. It was not all gloom for us detainees. We also had fun.

Now and then, we were allowed to play ping-pong or badminton for exercise. But my greatest source of joy then was when Bing, my children, my mother-in-law, sisters-in-law Ate Laling, Ate Mel and Meg, and other relatives and friends visited me and brought me stories of what was happening outside the gym. To the credit of Bing and my in-laws, they never brought any bit of unsettling news. They were always positive in their outlook and never once betrayed any sign that they saw my situation as hopeless.

I was particularly anxious to know how Bing and the children were faring and it brought me great relief to hear it directly from her that she was coping with the problem of my detention with grace. The children, she would tell me, were all doing well in school and they were all fairly healthy. And more importantly, that they were behaving as normal children did.

Due to financial difficulties, Bing could only bring our youngest daughter, Inde, then aged two, to visit me with more frequency than our older children. Early on in my confinement, the general rule was that we could meet our guests at the chicken-wire fence that separated the detention yard from the visiting area: we, the detainees, on the inner side of the fence and they, the visitors, on the other. We could only touch fingers with our visitors through the chicken-wire mesh. Because Inde was then only two years old, the guards kindly allowed her to be put on a revolving disk (like the "Lazy Susan" that Chinese restaurants have on their tables) where visitors placed the things they wanted to send to their loved ones on the other side of the fence.

Thus, I managed to have the immense pleasure of taking my youngest daughter into my arms, caressing and kissing her as I usually did at home before my detention. Since I could not take her for a walk, we would spend a few

1973: BING BROUGHT INDE to see me and I knew that all would turn out well in the end.

precious minutes together holding hands. I would coax her to tell me if she had any new playmates or ask anything that I thought she could respond to in her tender age. The problem was that those moments of happiness with Inde were completely dependent on the mood of the guards. When they said, "enough," that was it. I had to put my daughter back on the rotating disk and send her to Bing at the other side of the fence.

One of the most painful memories of my incarceration in Crame took place on March 20, almost two months to the day of my arrest. I was playing with Inde when the guards announced that all visitors had to leave.

Inde did not understand why she and Bing had to go home without me. So she pulled my little finger and asked me to go home with them. She said it in the vernacular,"*Sama ka na, 'Tay. Uwi na tayo.* Come with us, Pop. Let us go home." In my notes, I wrote, "I had to whisper to her that I cannot go home yet because the soldiers might get angry. Her face betrayed bewilderment. Apparently, she did not understand the reason I gave. So I told her that I still had some work to do in the camp. She nodded her little head in seeming understanding. I had to exert all effort to keep the tears in check. "Those were scenes," my notes for the day concluded, "that I'd bring to my grave."

Nonetheless, I thanked the Good Lord — and the guards — even for those fleeting moments of blissful tenderness that Inde and I had together. Nobody, not the intelligence agents, not the guards, not the whole world would have guessed that, for me, those all-too-short interludes of pure love between me and my daughter recharged my belief that things would, in the end, turn out right.

For the moment, however, I had to contend with the vicissitudes of daily life in detention. Even as the visits of Bing, my children, family and friends brought immense happiness without measure to me, their having to leave when the visiting hours ended also brought a tremendous sense of emptiness into my life.

At that time, the end of my detention at Camp Crame was uncertain and martial rule was to unravel many years yet into the future. When she could not visit, Bing and I communicated through letters that were sometimes allowed by the camp authorities. I wrote Bing now and then to inquire how the kids were behaving and to the kids, too, to tell them to study their lessons well. I told the boys to play basketball or other sports and the girls to learn how to play the piano, and I urged all of them to behave, obey and take care of their mother. I also suggested to Bing to sell whatever we had, "my books, typewriter, tape recorders, etc., to meet" her needs and those of the kids.

Despite my absence, Bing took good care of the children. How she managed to do it, I could hardly imagine. But she did bring them up responsibly and well. Whenever she had to go to Manila to visit me, the kids were taught to take care of themselves and they learned fast to budget the little money she left behind for their food and other needs. It also lifted my spirits immensely when Bing's letters mentioned the support that she was getting from friends like Mordino and Dadi Cua, the Jesuit priests in general — and in particular, Fr. John Gordon, Fr. Jack Ryan of the New York Jesuit Province, Fr. Francisco Araneta — and several anonymous supporters whose generosity kept our family's body and soul together during those difficult times.

Teardrops

I found the gym to be a rather humane place of confinement, probably because most, if not all, of the detainees were political, not criminal inmates. And we could also play some indoor sports like badminton, which gave us some exercise. My favorite playing partner was Matoy Seno who always let out a loud guffaw whenever I smashed a shuttlecock with a shout: "Take that, you, Marcos, you!" One of my greatest satisfactions was when we played doubles where Matoy and I beat Bono Adaza's team by three points, a feat that was duly noted in the entry of my notes for February 17, which happened to be my wife, Bing's, birthday.

Matoy Seno, Bono Adaza and I tended to gravitate towards one another probably because we spoke the same language, Cebuano, and shared the same passion for law practice. Also, at core, we were all sentimental individuals who were not above pretending that we were tough and beyond tears. But the truth was that we shed tears whenever any event or circumstance touched our "soft spots" (Matoy's words).

On March 13, for instance, Matoy told me that he cried when his visitors from Cebu that morning relayed his children's assurance that "they would not cause their mother any trouble." That bit of news, so terse and so blasé, caused the tough old legal warrior of Cebu to cry. I also saw Bono Adaza become teary-eyed when he talked of his children being deprived of his company. And no matter what some people may think of him, I can vouch for his devotion to his kids. He was one active law practitioner in Cagayan de Oro, for instance, who enjoyed driving his children to school and picking them up after school despite his busy court schedule.

I also know that Bono was a loving husband to his wife, Margot. I remember watching his face light up with joy when Margot managed to visit him at the gym on February 25. He was so obviously happy that the lines which had perpetually furrowed his forehead momentarily disappeared. He seemed to have forgotten, for the time being, that he was in detention in a military camp. The bliss that enveloped his whole person, however, evaporated like morning dew before the rising sun when the visiting time was over and Margot had to leave. In my notes of the day, I said:

> [Bono] appeared upset. I had to convince him to take supper with me in an effort to let him know that he still had friends to help ease the burden of loneliness even in the camp.

In my case, privately, I shed tears whenever I read letters that Bing or the children were sick and I was not there to care for them. Probably, it was the fact that I was so utterly helpless to do anything about the predicaments of my loved ones that pushed copious tears out of my eyes so involuntarily.

Shedding tears was not a phenomenon that was common only to us lawyers, Matoy, Bono and me. Even the grizzled rebel Baking showed deep emotions at times. I witnessed it once when he told me that he felt bad about his and Rodriguez's "over incarceration" because the Supreme Court did not act on their petition for habeas corpus, which challenged the legality of their detention. In my notes of February 9, I wrote that he "was on the verge of tears and his voice cracked" when he made this observation. While the cause of Baking's distress appeared to be a legal matter, I thought there was a tinge of self-pity in it. In any case, as Matoy Seno, the wizened courtroom strategist, philosophized:

> No matter how tough a man is, he has a soft spot somewhere in his body. The moment that spot is touched, he cannot help but cry, and crying is therapeutic. I cried this morning and felt a lot better afterwards.

'Amnesty'

From mid-February up to mid-March, we were subjected to psywar tactics by military officers led by a Colonel Dimaya, who told us that there was only one way by which we, detainees could get out from our confinement and that was by our applying for amnesty. Amnesty is a legal device where the State would, in effect, forget that a person amnestied had committed a crime. But before anyone could be granted an amnesty, he or she would have to apply for it, own up to having committed an offense and renounce membership in subversive organizations. Without amnesty, Dimaya threatened, we would rot in detention forever. My immediate reaction, was that I found applying for amnesty abhorrent. First, I committed no crime. And second, I did not belong to any subversive organization from which I could validly renounce my membership.

The military officers, however, were so insistent that by the deadline for amnesty application, most detainees especially the young activists applied for amnesty. In my notes, I recorded that only three detainees did not apply for amnesty: Angel Baking, Sammy Rodriguez and I.

Days before the deadline for the application for amnesty, on March 11, Bono Adaza told me that he would apply for amnesty, and if anybody asked, he would explain why he did it. Tears rolled down his cheeks when our conversation turned to his children, whom he obviously missed. I can only guess that his amnesty application had to do more with his desire to be reunited as fast as possible with his family than for any other reason.

Soon after the deadline for the amnesty application passed, I was transferred from the gym to the cell of hardened criminals. I believed that the transfer was the offshoot of my refusal to file for amnesty.

Brigada IC

Since I was a political, not a criminal, detainee, I saw the order transferring me to the cell of hardened criminals as a ploy to make me more pliant in the hands of the jailors. I was not happy with the transfer. Despite the obvious discriminatory treatment against me, I followed without complaint the order sending me to *Brigada* IC, which was located in another building inside the camp. Since my arrest, I had resolved not to complain unless things really got unbearable. As things turned out, I was in for pleasant surprises at the *brigada.*

The cell to which I was assigned could accommodate a maximum of maybe 25 inmates. When I was confined there, the cell had easily more than 40 convicts of various heinous crimes like murder, robbery, rape, drug trafficking and a suspect of the Plaza Miranda bombing, Flavio Binauro. As in the other cells of criminal convicts, *Brigada* IC had a *capo* or boss man, or in the local prison lingo, *ang mayor*, the mayor. In our brigade, the *capo* was Bening Urquico, one of the "Big Four" reportedly running criminal syndicates in Metro Manila. Urquico was arrested and detained, I was told, upon the declaration of martial law with the other three.

In my cell, I did not know who gave the order, but I was given a cot to sleep on. And every morning, for the duration of my stay there, a hot cup of coffee materialized on the floor beside my cot when I woke up. When my blanket needed washing, there was always somebody who did it. What I remember most of all was that my fellow cellmates — hardened criminals all — were, without exception, kind to me. Quite likely, they heard that I was a political detainee, a lawyer and a Constitutional Convention delegate who had stood up against the Marcos regime openly and without equivocation. Whatever it was that moved them to extend the hand of kindness to me, they personified the innate goodness of people that comedian Will Rogers said existed in every person, no matter how bad he or she was perceived to be by others. To paraphrase Rogers, I found out that, indeed, killers did not always kill nor liars always lie even among hardened criminals.

Incidentally, the breakfast fare for us, detainees, was okay by my standard: *pan de sal*, two pieces of sardines, jelly and coffee. The other meals were enough to fill up the stomach, but did not have much else to commend them. That early in the life of martial rule, there was already talk that the meal allowances for the detainees were subjected to under-the-table cuts by several layers of authority. And, among the self-appointed pundits in the ranks of the detainees like the newsman Bobby Ordoñez and Ernie Rondon, it was an article of faith that corruption would undo martial rule sooner or later.

Aware that I was a practicing lawyer by profession, my cellmates often asked me what I thought of the criminal cases that caused their detention in Camp Crame. I would tell them, as patiently as I could, the legal ramifications of their cases. I gave them some threads of hope to cling to so that, when times became normal, they could challenge the validity of their incarceration. If that was the *quid pro quo* for their treating me with so much unbelievable kindness, I can only thank the Good Lord for giving me a chance to live for a time with "the dregs of society." The opportunity has shown me that jails do not necessarily blot out the inherent goodness of people. Anyway, I felt as if I were the incarnation of Tom Hagen, the consigliore in *The Godfather*, Mario Puzo's classic story of the Mafia.

In the days that I was in the cell with hardened criminals, I was not allowed out to sun myself or to exercise in the open air. The only recreation tolerated by the guards was gambling or television viewing. I hate to believe that, as a people, we are inveterate gamblers. But, in detention, I saw evidence of the propensity of our people to gamble their time away, just as I saw the same vices in the world outside prior to my detention. It is, in fact, a matter of common knowledge that young boys in the streets of Metro Manila go for what the Tagalogs call *cara y cruz*, in the same manner that young boys in the Visayas or Mindanao play *hari o corona*, gambling games which roughly translate as heads or tails. Their fathers, whether in Luzon, the Visayas or

Mindanao, go for *sabong* or cockfighting, Black Jack or other card games. And their mothers go for mahjong, bingo or other games of chance.

The culture of gambling in our detention cell was not much different from that went on in the homes of many people. The inmates in my cell bet on card games of all sorts. When the cards were confiscated by irascible guards, the more imaginative inmates bet on the coin or the stick on which a fly would first alight. They also placed bets on which team would win a basketball game on TV. Usually, the inmates of our cell placed bets against the inmates of the cell across ours, especially in championship games.

In our detention *brigada*, the prison TV was placed in the narrow corridor that separated our cell from the other cell that was also occupied by convicts. It was set at an angle so that the inmates of the two cells could view the games. I had my own TV set — not really my own but — lent to me by lawyer Wencelito Andanar and his wife, Titos Marfori, daughter of my dear friends Ed and Lili Marfori. I had tried to dissuade them from lending it to me because I was not much of a TV watcher. On their insistence, I relented and that made TV watching a little more convenient for my cellmates.

In my life out of detention, I considered watching TV a waste of time. But after I saw a TV sports-news clip of Sonny Jaworski, one of the greatest basketball players of the country, trip on the hard court, tumble over his head twice, only to rise and continue playing as if nothing happened, I gradually became a fan of televised basketball games.

In our detention cell, since there was not much else to do, I would join my cellmates in watching the televised games, especially between Crispa and Mariwasa, two of the big teams of pro basketball in the country. One incident that sprang from a bet between the inmates of our cell and those of the other cell on the outcome of a basketball game between Crispa and Mariwasa is forever etched in my mind.

The inmates of our cell bet on Crispa, while the inmates of the other cell chose the other team. My cellmates raised P1,000, a princely sum in those days, to bet against them, I must say, without any contribution from me. I begged off because I had and still have an innate aversion to gambling.

It was a ding-dong ball game, with the lead changing sides many times, and very thrilling for me. In the end, Crispa won by two points. Naturally, there was a lot of shouting, clapping and plain charivari celebrating our team's victory in our cell. Before long, we noticed with surprise that the inmates of the other cell were also jumping in jubilation.

The mystery cleared up when the leaders of the other cell claimed they had also bet on Crispa. Somebody was lying, but for sure my cellmates weren't. In seconds, my cellmates were pulling bladed weapons of all sizes and shapes hidden under their mattresses. I saw real kitchen knives, army jungle bolos, and improvised bladed weapons made out of sharpened spoons and forks.

I suppose that the inmates of the other cell were also retrieving all sorts of bladed weapons from their secret hiding places. A bloody melee would have ensued but for the timely arrival of the guards who raided both cells and confiscated the weapons. I said a short prayer of thanks to the Lord that a bloodbath had been prevented. I could have lost my life on an absolutely inconsequential matter in which I only had a very peripheral participation and that was to cheer every time our team scored.

Hospital Ward

Soon after that incident, I received an order transferring me to the camp hospital. I was glad the order came when it did. I was actually getting sick in the cell, primarily for lack of sleep. I could also feel the right side of my face getting numb again since I was not fully cured of Bell's palsy that I had more than two years before. Additionally, our daily meal rations had deteriorated in quality and quantity. For breakfast in the *brigada*, we now had four pieces of *pan de sal* and a cup of coffee. No more sardines. The order to transfer me to the camp hospital was, thus, heaven sent. Privately, I guessed that Jose Calderon's human hand was in it.

I did not know Calderon personally before the work of the Convention began. I only read of him as the chair of the Namarco, the National Marketing Corporation, which dealt mainly with stabilizing the price of rice, corn and other basic commodities. In the Convention, Calderon, the senior delegate of the province of Nueva Vizcaya, got a seat beside mine — not by choice but by lottery — which the Convention secretariat prescribed as the seating arrangements of the delegates. Since he was a Liberal Party official, I saw him as a kindred spirit because I was the Liberal Party chair of Misamis Oriental prior to the election of the delegates to the Convention. As delegates, we also had something in common: we both opposed the martial rule of Marcos. Now, we found ourselves as fellow detainees, courtesy of Marcos.

Arrested ahead of me, Calderon unfortunately or maybe even fortuitously, suffered from several ailments including heart palpitations and high blood pressure that at times manifested themselves in painful nonstop hiccups. It was thus easy for his personal doctors to convince the Camp Crame doctors to allow him to be confined as a patient at the camp hospital.

Calderon was a basically kindhearted person. Since he probably felt responsible for my being in detention, he worked it out so that I was transferred to the hospital. Since at the time I looked as if I had just survived a famine, the camp doctors certified that I should also be confined at the camp hospital.

Although I was never one to ask for favored treatment from my jailors, it would be the height of hypocrisy to say that I did not like the idea of being transferred from my cell at the *brigada* to the Camp Crame hospital. To my discomfiture, however, for the first few days at the hospital, I was even more closely guarded than when I was at the cell of hardened criminals. A guard would follow me to the bathroom, insist that I keep the door half-open and knock persistently when he thought that I was taking too long to do my morning rituals. He was, of course, being unduly strict with me. Knowing, however, that there was no legal remedy against the difficulties that I was facing, I decided to take things as they came without complaining.

After a while, the strict security measures for me ended without my knowing why. Overall, I found the hospital ward a far better place in terms of comfort and facilities than the gym or the *brigada*. We also had better food — courtesy mainly of Calderon, whose son, Boy, was also detained there. Moreover, the doctors, in general, were kindly persons who were genuinely concerned over how we were doing physically.

In my case, the doctors would now and then give me a physical. Their common verdict was that I needed vitamins and—"rest," which they believed would cure my occasional dizzy spells. Although given professionally, I found their prescription ironic. How could they expect me to "rest" in detention while I had a family of six children to take care of outside? I also needed an optometrist or an eye specialist to remedy the imbalance in the sight of my left and right eyes. Anyway, as far as space was concerned, the ward was all right as there were but nine beds, which left an area of roughly two feet between beds.

Aside from the injustice of my confinement, there was no substantial cause for me to complain regarding the hospital ward, where I was now detained. In fact, we had funny moments there, too. On April 7, for instance, I was dozing off in bed at 12:30 midnight when the night duty guard, a Constable Cristobal, used a phone in our ward. In a voice that could awaken even the dead, he spoke in Ilocano to somebody at the other end of the phone asking when his (Cristobal's) mother was leaving. The disturbance, however, lasted for less than five minutes. Boy Calderon and I had a good time the following morning mimicking the intonation of the guard.

Rough Treatment

Our confinement in the ward would have been pleasantly passable were it not for one incident when a military doctor — not one of our doctors — treated a wounded prisoner rather roughly in our presence. The man was brought on stretcher a little after 8 a.m. on April 3. He was barely alive, I thought. We learned that he had been shot three days earlier in an encounter between his group, supposedly a unit of the New Peoples Army, and a combined Constabulary-National Bureau of Investigation team in the province of Bataan.

A fetid smell heralded his arrival at our ward. It turned out that his arm had been shattered in the shoot-out and was rotting. His condition needed the immediate attention of doctors. Unfortunately, while there were other doctors in the camp hospital, the military bureaucracy demanded that his condition be first examined by a particular doctor, a major (whose name I failed to note) who was not yet around. There was nothing much anybody could do for the wounded man who was obviously in excruciating pain, judging from the groans that emanated from his throat now and then. In the meantime, the foul odor of rotting flesh was becoming more intense by the minute, which made breathing difficult for all of us.

Finally, after an hour and a half, the doctor came. His aides took off the soiled bandages. The air in the ward became more pungent with the nauseating odor. I could not help but empathize with the wounded man when the doctor insensitively lifted his broken arm as if there was nothing wrong with it, causing him to emit an agonizing cry. In time, the dressing was completed and the doctor ordered the nurse to give him Demerol, a painkiller.

While I did not experience any "manhandling" even remotely similar to that suffered by the wounded man during my detention at the gym or in Brigada IC, along with other political prisoners, I underwent rough treatment. For instance, in the gym, our jailors would time and again subject us to debasing treatment just to show their complete mastery over us, their prisoners. For instance, they would call the roll of detainees at dawn and we had to jump out of our bunks just to prove we had not escaped. Once, a brownout threw our detention area into pitch darkness. The guards surrounded the place with drawn arms, beamed the headlights of several military vehicles on us and ordered us to squat or sit on the floor. The guards were probably applying the Pavlovian principle so that, like dogs, we could be trained to obey whatever they wanted us to do.

Even as I knew that the martial law authorities had that power to keep me in detention for as long as they wanted. I also knew I had the power to say "No" to any attempt to make me compromise my opposition to the martial law regime. Hence, I consoled myself with the thought that Marcos could, indeed, jail my body all he wanted, but I would not allow him to imprison my spirit. The line of a poem "walls do not a prison make" kept ringing in my ears as I prepared myself for a prolonged detention at the pleasure of my jailors.

My Release

Their pleasure of keeping me confined in Camp Crame ended abruptly three months after my arrest. Without any official explanation, I was told I could get out of the camp. All I had to do was sign a commitment that I would report to my jailers at the camp once a week. The officer who processed my release papers said I must have a Metro Manila address so my release could be implemented immediately. The problem was that I no longer had any home address in Metro Manila as Bing and our kids had returned to Cagayan de Oro. And I did not want to use my in-laws' place as my contact address because they were too advanced in age to be bothered by the military, should my jailors come looking for me.

Since I was told that I must have a Manila address, I decided to use the address of my brother-in-law, Judge Himerio B. Garcia, husband of Bing's elder sister, Ate Laling. Inwardly, I was also hoping his position as a circuit criminal court judge would, at least, subliminally convince my jailors that I was not the subversive I was pictured to be. In hindsight, I think I should not have done that as it placed Judge Garcia at some risk. Guilt by association, after all, was a rule that martial law authorities thought sacrosanct. In any case, I used Judge Garcia's address as my contact address in Metro Manila. To his and his wife's credit, they were so kind that I never heard a word of reproach from them.

After I gave Judge Garcia's address, I was released without any further fuss. Even then I was already planning to go home to Cagayan de Oro simply because that was where my family was. There was however, a big problem.

My release papers, signed by the Chief of Constabulary, General Fidel V. Ramos, placed me under "the supervision of the CG (Commanding General), ISAFP (Intelligence Services Armed Forces of the Philippines), or his authorized representatives to whom (I) shall report upon release and as often as directed thereafter." The ISAFP required me to report weekly to Camp Crame. This reporting requirement posed a huge difficulty because, if I had to go home to Cagayan de Oro, there was no way I could come back to report to the Camp every week. I simply could not afford the airfare. And I could not take the boat just to be with the family in Cagayan de Oro and return by boat also to report to Crame — the travel time made that arrangement unfeasible.

A REUNION OF DETAINEES after our release. Seated (left to right), Manuel Almario, Jose Nolledo, Nap Rama and me. Standing: Ernie Rondon and Joe Concepcion. Background at left is Ernie Granada.

1940: *MY MOTHER, the school teacher (front row), with her Grades I and II students at the Julao-Julao Primary School in Cagayan, Misamis Oriental. I am 3rd from her left in the front row.*

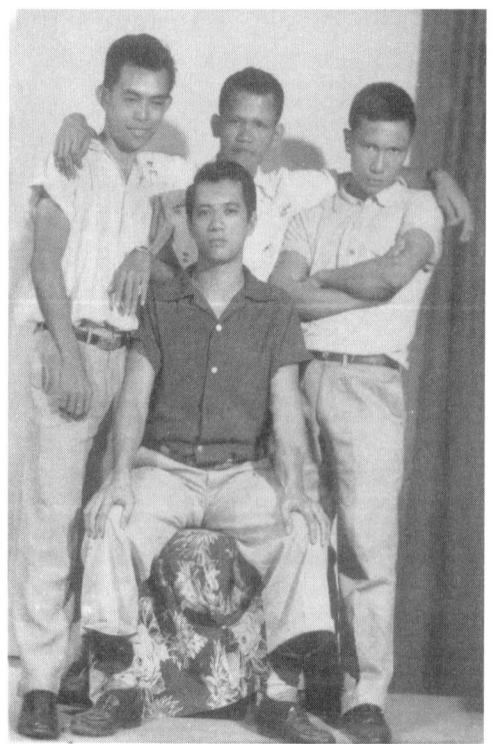

CIRCA 1954: *WITH MY "GANG": standing from left to right, me, Bodo Nagac and Dan Bautista. Seated, Boni Ramirez.*

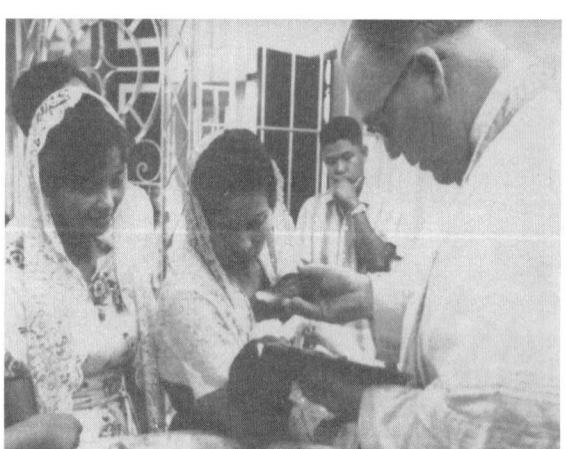

1961: *FR. WILLIAM F. MASTERSON, SJ, baptizes my eldest daughter Gwen. Holding Gwen is her godmother, Inday Nery. Baby Vamenta stands next to Inday. At the back is Faeling Floirendo.*

MY FATHER (standing beside me), married a second time after my mother died. Nanay Mameng, the grandmother our kids knew, sits (left to right) with Gwen, Maripet and Koko in the arms of Bing.

1972: *I BOOST KOKO'S morale at a math contest in his school, Claret.*

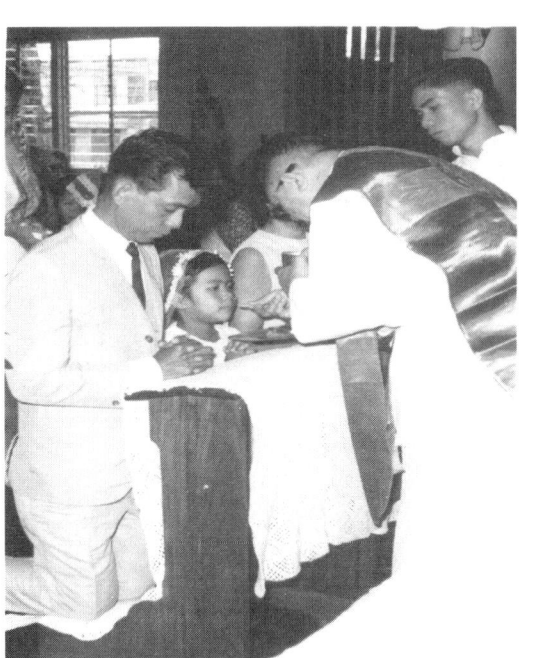

1969: *MARIPET RECEIVES her first communion from Fr. Cicero Cebrero, SJ.*

B

1975: *INDE, our youngest daughter at fighting five.*

1973: *JAC TRIES piloting Manong Pepe Calderon's chopper.*

1974: *TERESA AND I ready to swim.*

1978: *BING'S FAMILY with in-laws, (seated, left to right) Meg, Mama, Dad and Boy. Standing (left to right) me, Bing, Tess and Butch Emata, Mely and Gani Tadeo, Laling and Judge Himerio Garcia, Pat and Jun Idhaw. Inset, Perla, wife of Boy. Days after this picture was taken, Dad passed away.*

C

1964: KNIGHTS OF COLUMBUS general assembly in Cagayan de Oro. I stand 4th from the right (back row). My father and Ed Marfori are third and fifth from left (front row) respectively.

1965: CHRISTMAS MERRYMAKING before martial law. Koko (1st baby on the left) carried by his nanny; Gwen (1st little girl from left), Bing behind her; and Maripet (3rd from right), sleeping in my arms.

D

Part 4

Marcos Digs In

Chapter 11:

Reshaping My Law Practice

Happily, Delegate Jose Calderon came to my rescue. Upon his release a couple of weeks after mine, he took me into his mining business as his lawyer. This gave me sufficient reason to reside in Metro Manila and enabled me to report to Camp Crame weekly. The requirement was still inconvenient, but it no longer entailed enormous financial costs.

I had a fairly commodious office at the Fil-Am Resources Building, the main office of Calderon's companies, near Escolta, Manila. My new job also gave me leeway to interact with my friends from the Constitutional Convention days, like Ernie Rondon, Tito Guingona and Oca Santos whose office was only a few buildings away from mine. We were, what one might call, inveterate anti-martial law activists, and every now and then, we would sit down after office hours in a coffee shop and discuss what the prospects were of ending martial law. To express our continuing dissent — which nobody noticed — Ernie Rondon and I pasted "Freedom!" stickers on the bumpers of our cars.

In July, I wrote Defense Minister Enrile, through the Judge Advocate General at Camp Aguinaldo in Quezon City, asking that I be issued final clearance papers. I informed him I had complied with the "requirement of periodic reporting to the authorities." I asked for my "final clearance papers" because — although I did not tell Enrile — Calderon intimated to me that he wanted me to go with him on a business trip to Singapore and the US. I did not receive any reply from Enrile nor from the Judge Advocate General. But when Calderon and I eventually left for Singapore and then for the US, I was not prevented from leaving.

The reporting requirement was finally scrapped on September 24, 1974 by the Central Reporting Office for Temporarily Released Detainees in Camp Aguinaldo, Quezon City. A certification signed on that date by Lt. Col. Melquiades Alimagno attested that:

> Aquilino Pimentel Jr., TRD [Temporar(il)y Released Detainee] No. 80111 had already complied [with] the conditions imposed upon him.

The statement was good as far as it went, but the next phrase was completely untrue. The phrase averred that I had "reformed and subscribed to the tenets of the New Society." Consequently, the order said that I was now "given the privilege not to report to this office" anymore.

Apparently, in the mind of our military custodians, being "reformed" meant that I now "subscribed to the tenets of the New Society." That was a complete misstatement. It was a good thing that I was not there when the certification was released. Moreover, the certification carried only the signature of Lieutenant Colonel Alimagno and I was not required to affix my conformity to it. Otherwise, in all likelihood, I would have balked at it. At the very least, I would have asked that it be reworded. And my reservations would have complicated the process of my "full release" from the restraints imposed on my freedom of movement by the military.

The term "full release" under martial law conditions was really just a play on words. Nobody was fully released from the might of the military under martial rule. But it was still good for me to have the certification because, one, it freed me from the obligation of periodic reporting to the Central Reporting Office at Camp Crame and, two, it facilitated my travel to places within the country and even to destinations abroad.

Startling Fact

The Alimagno certification also stated a rather startling fact. The certification said that I was the No. 80,111[th] detainee who was temporarily released. If true, then there were more than 80,111 people who were rounded up as detainees under martial law. Our estimates at the time placed the number of martial law detainees at no more than 20,000. Apparently, we were far off the mark.

From my own experience with the "Central Reporting Office for Temporary [sic] Released Detainees [Cenrepo]," I can say that their recordkeeping was woefully inaccurate. For instance, a month after my reporting requirement was terminated, Maj. Genaro D. Rosales, chief, Cenrepo, Camp Aguinaldo, in a mimeographed letter dated November 13, 1975, ordered me "to report at [that] office on November 22, 1975 at exactly 9:00 o'clock in the morning." The order couched in pidgin English said the officer wanted "to know what activities you have embraced and conformed wholeheartedly had been released the beneficial programs of the NEW SOCIETY [sic]." While I could not fathom exactly what the preceding phrase meant, the order clearly threatened that if I failed "to comply as required, [my] release papers will be nullified and voided," and, more ominously, "this Office will be constrained to order [my] rearrest."

I received the order two days after I was supposed to report to Cenrepo. I would have panicked were it not for the fact that my own records showed that I had complied with the reporting requirement and that I had been relieved of having to report to Cenrepo by Lieutenant Colonel Alimagno, a higher-ranking officer than Major Rosales. Also, in May 1974, more than a year before the Rosales order, Col. Emilio P. Melendres of the Constabulary Headquarters at Camp Crame certified that I had "no criminal or derogatory records in this Headquarters as of this date." I do not recall how the problem played out eventually, but to my great relief I did not hear from Cenrepo ever again.

Corporate Lawyer

In a matter of weeks, I was settling down into my life as a corporate lawyer for Calderon's companies. But, truth to tell, I found it boring even as I was earning enough to support the growing needs of my family of six children. I did not find poring over the fine lines of corporate contracts and negotiating with would-be investors of much interest to me.

Upon the suggestion of Calderon, or Manong Pepe as I started to call him, I accompanied him to Los Angeles, California, via Singapore, to assist in his negotiations with a big mining and oil exploration company, Atlantic Richfield. Atlantic Richfield wanted to do exploration work in his gold and copper mining concessions. After the negotiations, which took only a week, we flew to New York to visit his daughter, Lilia Calderon Clemente. Lilia was making waves in the New York Stock Exchange where, at the time she was in charge of the investments portfolio of the Ford Foundation, among other things.

Perks of the Job

The opportunity to go to the US was one of the more pleasant aspects of my job as a lawyer of Manong Pepe's companies. In New York, I went to visit the great museums of the city. At night, I was able to watch some of the popular plays on Broadway. I remember the feeling of excitement when Lilia accompanied me to watch the play, "Let My People Come!" In my naivete, I thought it had a biblical theme!

While in New York, I received a call from my brother-in-law, Dr. Vicente (Boy) de la Llana and his wife, Perla, inviting me to visit them and their children in the Bahamas. Since he was doing quite well there as a government doctor, he bought me a round-trip ticket from New York to the Bahamas and provided me with some pocket money also. The only hitch was that I did not

1974: MY BROTHER-IN-LAW, Dr. Boy de la Llana, his wife, Perla and two of their children, Abigail and Alex in the Bahamas.

have a visa to the Bahamas. Boy assured me that it was all right. He'd meet me at the airport and get me out without any hassle.

I flew from New York to Florida and from Florida to the Grand Bahamas. But when I got to the Bahamas airport, Boy was not yet there. Since there were not too many passengers, I was soon at the booth of an immigration officer who naturally asked me where my visa was. I explained that my brother-in-law, Dr. Vicente de la Llana, was fetching me. Happily, in a moment, Boy materialized behind the immigration officer who readily gave me a few days of visa-free stay in the Bahamas.

I had a good time in the Bahamas with Boy, Perla and their two children, Abby and Alex. It was the first time I tasted conch shell meat raw with only vinegar and salt, a la *kinilaw*, a dish of raw fish, which is a favorite of Visayans back home. At a beach resort, I saw a mini-mountain of conch shells, a mute testimony of Bahamian appetite for the shellfish. I also met a couple of Filipino doctors, Romeo Fernandez and his wife Emma, and Joel Pedroche and his wife Rose. They were well-respected professionals there.

Boy and Perla gave me a tour of the West End of the Grand Bahamas and showed me the Xanadu Hotel, owned by the eccentric US billionaire Howard Hughes. Boy said that Hughes occupied the top three floors, including the penthouse of the hotel.

The work with Manong Pepe was not too heavy a stuff. It afforded me some light, enjoyable moments, but I still was not comfortable in it. I shared the unease that I felt about my work with newly found friends like Raul Gonzalez, who would become one of my lawyers in the legal battles I fought against the Marcos regime. I told Raul that I did not think my potential as a lawyer was being utilized to the full.

Teaching Law

As God's grace would have it, Dean Feliciano Jover Ledesma of the San Beda College of Law plucked me out of my predicament and asked me to teach Criminal Law and Evidence at night. Dean Ledesma, a fellow delegate to the Convention, knew that I was the dean of the College of Law of Xavier University in Cagayan de Oro and that I had some experience teaching law.

Since I loved teaching, I jumped at his offer. Teaching law kept me happily occupied especially because Dean Neptali Gonzales of the Far Eastern University's Law School also asked me to teach Criminal Procedure and Evidence at night. I had fun with my students analyzing the ramifications of criminal law, the law on evidence and procedure, and denouncing Marcos on the side. My hours were now more or less spent fruitfully.

Soon, I earned enough money to buy a small house in a lower middle class subdivision inappropriately named Fairlane (after a Ford model car that no longer exists) in Marikina where, incidentally, my family and I still live. Later, we were able to buy a compact car for my use, followed by the purchase of a second car, a van, which Bing drove for the family.

Probably my presence in Fairlane was beginning to be felt by the Marikina politicians because Osmundo de Guzman, the mayor of the town, whom I had not met, sent a pre-filled "Oath of Office" in which he was appointing me as a "Purok Leader in the Barangay Council of Fairlane Subdivision." I did not accept the proffered appointment because I had no intention whatsoever of working with the Marcos government. At the time, neither de Guzman nor I knew that, 11 years later, I would cause his removal from office and name his replacement after Marcos was toppled from the presidency in my capacity as the Minister of Local Governments under the presidency of Cory Aquino.

Lawyer for the Poor

In the meantime, although I was enjoying teaching law and doing some corporate legal work, my new preoccupations did not quench my thirst to put my legal knowledge to help the poor. That was why, when I was asked to act as the lawyer for the National Secretariat for Social Action (Nassa) of the Justice and Peace Commission of the Catholic Bishops Conference, I accepted with alacrity. It was there as a lawyer for Nassa that I saw an opportunity to make my legal profession, even under conditions of martial rule, relevant to the cause of social justice under the guidance of Bishop Julio Labayen and Msgr. Ralph Salazar. These two men of the cloth helped sharpen my concern for the poor in the country. Edith Torres, who acted as my secretary, Wilerico Manao and Doy Medes were some of my Nassa co-workers who showed me what love for the poor really meant.

As a lawyer for Nassa, I handled cases for farmers who were being eased out of their farm holdings in Central Luzon by big corporations without just compensation and for the homeless along the "riles" or railroad tracks in Manila who were being evicted out of their shanties without due process. I also acted as counsel for fisher folk who were challenging the intrusion of big time fishing companies into their fishing areas in Laguna and elsewhere in the country. I lawyered, too, for the members of a cooperative in Southern Leyte who were fighting against exploitative acts of their coop leaders. Their problem was complicated by the intervention of powerful local politicians associated with the Yñiguez clan in favor of the erring coop leaders. I was to meet the patriarch of the Yñiguez clan, Nicanor, a decade later at the Batasang Pambansa. My legal views were also solicited by a progressive labor organization in Zamboanga on how best labor and management could harmonize their efforts to attain industrial peace.

Now and then, small successes crowned my efforts at seeking justice for the marginalized sector, even under the hostile environment of martial law, like getting compensation for the farmers of Central Luzon or stalling the inhuman demolition of squatter shanties without due process. But, more often than not, my knowledge of the law did not suffice to bail out many of the poor whom Nassa sought to serve.

Since I was not one to lose hope, I did not spend time moping over the cases that we could not win. For me, what was important was that, at the time when some oppressed individuals needed me, I was, by the grace of God, there to extend a helping hand to them, no matter how feeble. I did so without demanding legal fees. Whatever they could afford was fine with me, even as I made them understand that it would be more in consonance with their own dignity if they offered something — no matter how meager — to their lawyer. Dole-outs even in services to the poor, I believed then as I do now, serve even more to degrade than to help them.

The legal experiences that I had in the service of the poor proved beneficial later in my work as mayor of Cagayan de Oro and then as a legislator. As mayor, I made use of the methods I learned in Nassa in dealing with "squatters" humanely. As a legislator, I used the insights that I had gathered from Nassa when I sponsored or supported pro-poor legislations such as Republic Act No. 7160, which, among other things, set aside 15 kilometers from the shoreline into the open sea as a reservation for "small-time" fisher folk; Republic Act No. 6938, which provided the way for the poor and the marginalized to get organized into cooperatives to help themselves get out of the poverty rut, and Republic Act No. 7279, the Urban Development Housing Act.

Nassa also gave me the opportunity to write occasional articles critical of the Marcos regime for the *Nassa News*, a monthly in-house paper. One such article, "Prices, Taxes, Wages and Martial Law" was front-page material in the *News*. In the article, I pointed out that, while Marcos's avowed purpose of imposing martial law was to save the Republic and reform it, six years since then, he failed to achieve the objectives. On the contrary, citing Central Bank statistics, I said that, under martial law, the prices of basic commodities were rising; the peso lost its real value and the real wages of workers declined; and the tax burdens of the people grew increasingly heavier.

I purposely began the article with those statements as a premise for its closing paragraph:

> In the years prior to martial law, governments had been ousted through the ballot on the issues of spiraling prices, rising taxes, loss of the value of the peso and the diminution of the real wages of workers. But now under martial law conditions, it was problematic how the people could pass judgment on the government on those issues without honest-to-goodness elections being held.

I added that, ultimately, "the people will have to grapple with the problem — and provide the solution to it. After all, they are sovereign — a key concept in republicanism," which Marcos threw overboard when he imposed martial law in September of 1972.

Chapter 12:

Consolidating His Rule

The year 1973 was a busy one for Marcos as he began to institutionalize and consolidate his one-man rule. On January 26, for instance, he had the "results" of the ratification of the new Constitution by the Barangay Citizens Assemblies announced in Malacañang.

Francisco Cruz, a person purporting to be the president of the *Katipunan ng mga Barangay* (League of Barangays), read the "results" as follows: Yes, 14,976,561; No, 743,869 and Abstentions, 802,991. How he had arrived at those figures was never explained. Neither was it shown that he was a duly elected leader of any one of the more than 41,000 barangays in the nation, let alone, how he became the president of the Katipunan. Those things did not in the least bother Marcos. He cheekily proclaimed that, as Cruz had announced, 95% of the voters approved the new Constitution by referendum.

The INA Dissolved

At the Malacañang meeting, Marcos announced a ticklish decision: the dissolution of the Interim National Assembly (INA), created in the Transitory Provisions of the new Constitution, and its replacement by the Interim Batasang Pambansa. Many delegates who voted for the approval of the new Constitution had done so in the hope that they would become members of the INA. They were naturally aghast at this development. The fears that lurked in their minds when they approved the new Constitution that Marcos would put one over them had come to pass. Nonetheless, they realized that they could not do anything about it. Like Faust, who made a pact with the devil and rued his error, they regretted, after the fact, the covenant they had entered into with a master manipulator who outfoxed them all, even with their much-vaunted collective practical wisdom, legal genius and business acumen. Unlike Faust's malevolent partner, theirs was not some twin-horned prince of darkness in hell. He was of flesh and blood, and was the actual occupant of Malacañang, the seat of power in the country, Ferdinand E. Marcos, the President and Prime Minister of the Republic.

The dissolution of the INA was the first concrete manifestation that Marcos did not want to share his newly acquired powers with any entity, much less the INA, which theoretically had the power to enact laws. The delegates concerned could have raised howls over it. However, they realized that Marcos now possessed all the aces in his hands. He had accumulated all the powers of government that he needed to browbeat them into meek submission. Thereafter, Marcos stood the Rule of Law, the linchpin of democratic government, on its head. His word was now law. And that was the sad story of how he begun to build up his autocratic rule, which ironically also eventually caused the unraveling of his grandiose dreams for the country.

Marcos Rewards Disciples

It must be said, however, that Marcos did not forget to reward his most faithful disciples in the Convention. Delegate Dandy Tupaz, who was in Malacañang on the occasion, revealed that Marcos invited 20 delegates to the meeting where he named Jaime Opinion, Casimiro Madarang, Venancio Yanesa and Lindy Pangandaman (who later became ambassador to Saudi Arabia) to the Commission on Elections, a vital cog in the drive for the legitimacy of his administration; Gerardo Espina, to the Export Processing Zone; Arturo Pacificador, to the National Steel Corporation; Midpantao Adil and Mangontawar Guro, to the trial courts; Rey Fajardo to a military support organization called Tanglaw; Godofredo Ramos, to the Court of Appeals; and Emilio de la Cruz II, to Malacañang Palace, with the rank of undersecretary.

Dandy Tupaz added:

> Marcos spotted Espina after the latter eloquently spoke on issues related to the problems of the INA delegates who had supported Marcos in the Convention. Marcos was impressed by Espina's presentation and that was why he appointed him to head the Export Processing Zone.
>
> Amante and Esparrago did not seek any appointment to the Marcos government. They were interested only in securing timber license permits.

Among the delegates who witnessed the appointments were: Edelmiro Amante, Mateo Esparrago, Jr., Constantino Navarro, Jr., ReynaldoVillar, Cesar Sevilla, Homobono Sawit, Salvador Britanico, Gregorio Puruganan, Natalio Castillo, Jr., and Antonio Tupaz.

The appointments were certainly rewards for services faithfully rendered. I did not find it surprising that Marcos acted the way he did. I remembered what Marcos told me in my house in Cagayan de Oro when he visited me when he was seeking the nomination of his party for the presidency. He said that his critics could fault him "with all the crimes in the book, except ingratitude." He meant to assure me that, if I supported him, he would be grateful. However, I supported Raul Manglapus for the presidency against Marcos. It was, thus, providential that I never got close to him personally or politically, otherwise the course of my life could have turned out differently.

In any case, the appointments were his way of saying "Thank you" to the delegates and "Stay with me, there will be more." The appointments momentarily assuaged the hurt feelings of the members of the now-defunct INA. It somehow reassured them that they had a direct lifeline to Marcos through their newly appointed colleagues for their political and personal concerns.

Series of Referenda

Despite the unprecedented concentration of powers in his hands as the head of State and of the government, Marcos still found the new Constitution inadequate for his needs. Like a suitor unsure of the love of his beloved, he ordered a series of referenda to amend the Constitution, the first of which was held in July 1973, only six months after its so-called ratification in January.

The July referendum asked a two-pronged question: "Do you approve of President Marcos prolonging his term beyond 1973, and completing the reforms he commenced under martial law?"

Even if the question really contained two clauses, the voters were required to answer only with either a "Yes" or a "No" without qualifications. It would not have been possible for the voters to write "No" to the first clause if they were against Marcos's prolonging his term but "Yes" to the second clause if they favored his completing the reforms he had initiated under martial law or vice versa.

In the event, the Comelec proclaimed that 90.67% of the voters voted "Yes" in favor of the question. The affirmative vote rendered the two-term presidential limit in the 1935 Constitution inapplicable to Marcos in connection with his intent to lead the nation under the new Constitution. It also removed any legal or constitutional obstacle to Marcos's pursuing the reforms he envisioned for the "New Society" as he pleased.

The results of the referendum, however, were flawed not only because of the suspiciously high percentage of the "Yes" votes, but also because the constitutionally prescribed method of amending the Constitution through a plebiscite was not followed. Moreover, under martial law, people were under duress to vote in favor of what Marcos wanted, otherwise they could be harassed by the martial law authorities or by their personal enemies who might have had close connections with the regime. That said, Marcos gained the legal cover he needed to justify his staying on as president even when his term under the 1935 Constitution ended in mid-1973, and to do whatever he thought was needed to achieve the aims of his New Society.

Voting at the referendum was compulsory. Unsure of how an ex-detainee like me should act under the circumstances, I decided to play it safe and voted in the precinct nearest the rented house where my family and I lived in Project 6, Quezon City. But I did not fill up the ballot as we were supposed to do. I just wrote the unsolicited advice (now paraphrased for politeness' sake) that Marcos should go to the place where Satan reigned supreme and where I unkindly thought he belonged.

Aside from that one incident of weakness, I did not ever again vote in any of the other referenda that Marcos called to amend the Constitution. Despite the warnings of martial law authorities that those who did not vote would be imprisoned, there were many voters who defied the threats. Others, in fact, openly called for a boycott of the referenda. I did not join the boycott movement. On one referendum day in 1975, I took Calderon's chopper and flew to inspect a mining prospect up north. I had the chopper fly to the top of the Cordilleras and made an impromptu visit to the fabulous rice terraces of the Igorots. It was the first time I saw the breathtaking engineering feat that the Igorots did some 2,000 years ago and that without benefit of formal schooling. By the time I flew back to Manila, the referendum was over. Nobody took the trouble of charging me criminally for not voting.

Even though all the powers were now in his hands, courtesy of the new Constitution, particularly the Transitory Provisions, Marcos continued to tinker with it and to plug all the loopholes whereby his exercise of those powers could be legally questioned. He ordered three other referenda to strengthen his martial law powers in 1975, 1976 and 1977 to further expand his authoritarian rule. Although he went through the formalities of asking the people to freely express their views in the various referenda, they were necessarily constrained by the simple fact that martial law was still in effect. The threat of being arrested without a warrant and of being detained indefinitely continued to hang over their heads.

In February 1975, the referendum asked if the people approved of:

(1) The means through which President Marcos exercised his powers through decrees, orders and instructions;
(2) His continuing to exercise those powers; and
(3) His replacing elected local authorities when their terms expired on December 31 or the holding of local elections.

At the end of the voting day, the Comelec proclaimed that the people responded with an overwhelming 87% "Yes" vote to Questions No. 1 and No. 2, and a less enthusiastic 69% of the vote to Question No. 3.

The 87% support for Questions No. 1 and No. 2 gave Marcos the presumed basis to continue ruling the country by martial law fiats, while the 69% of the vote in favor of Question No. 3 gave him the option to remove local officials and replace them with individuals of his choice (which he did by the end of the year) or to call for elections (which he did five years later).

We in the Opposition persistently questioned the validity of resorting to a referendum to amend the Constitution from the first time it was used in 1973. The Supreme Court, however, laid the issue to rest on February 1, 1975, when it unanimously dismissed a petition challenging Marcos's authority to use the referendum for that purpose.

Even as he knew that he was winning in the play for power by using referenda to amend the Constitution, he also saw the need to pay lip service to the perceived public demand to clean up his government of corruption. In October 1973, the year following the declaration of martial law, Marcos directed the *Tanodbayan* or Ombudsman, which was created in the new Constitution, to start purging the government of corrupt officials. But, like his September 26 decree placing the rice and corn farmlands in the country under a land reform program and his October 21 edict ordering the emancipation of tenants, his main objective was to make the people believe that he had noble aims for his martial law proclamation. Incidentally, in the same year, Marcos also began the process of contracting for the building of a nuclear power plant to get the country out of reliance on fossil fuel as a major energy source. He had studies made that showed that the country should have one nuclear power plant of 600 MW, which could be built for $245 million. The studies seemed well-intentioned but for the fact that, by 1974, he was talking of two nuclear power 600 MW plants instead of one and at the cost of $500 million per power plant.

Media Clampdown

Subsequent events showed how deceptive his rhetoric was on the need to shift from fossil fuel to nuclear power as a source of energy. Foreign news-papers, particularly, the *Washington Post*, the *Asian Wall Street Journal* and the *New York Times* revealed that a relative of Marcos by affinity, Herminio Disini, got paid a huge commission for the nuclear power plant deal. As a result, the opposition to the Marcos government's nuclear power plant deal with Westinghouse started to escalate among the people. Senator Tañada led the fight against the project. Several years later at the Batasang Pambansa, I called for the scrapping of the Bataan Nuclear Plant.

Before the issue reached the Batasan, the people in general were kept ignorant about the nuclear plant deal for the reason that, since day one of martial law, Marcos made a thorough job of controlling the media in the coun-try. Social critic Renato Constantino, in his article, "The State of the Philippine Press," wrote:

> Media closed down by martial law totaled eight major English papers, four vernacular and Spanish language newspapers, 14 English language dailies, 60 community newspapers, 66 TV channels, 20 radio stations, 292 provincial radio stations. [The] TV and radio facilities of the ABS-CBN, the Philippines' largest network owned by Marcos's rivals, the Lopezes, were immediately seized and confiscated by the military.

Of the weekly magazines that were shut down by the martial law regime, easily the most popular was the *Philippines Free Press*. A no-nonsense magazine that spared nobody — high or low — from its withering criticisms, it was published by Teodoro Locsin. Leon O. Ty, Napoleon Rama and Teddyboy Locsin, Jr. were the stellar writers of the weekly. It was a measure of Marcos's displeasure at the tirades of the *Free Press* that Locsin, the father, and Rama were picked up and detained by the military upon the declaration of martial law.

Among the 14 English language dailies that were shut down at the onset of martial law, two were my favorites: the *Manila Times*, published by Joaquin

"Chino" Roces, and the *Manila Chronicle,* published by the Lopezes and edited by Armando Doronila.

Roces and one of his columnists, Max Soliven, were jailed. The son of Eugenio Lopez, Geny, who ran the family's media empire, was also arrested, along with columnist Ernesto Granada of the *Manila Chronicle,* one of Marcos's most bitter critics. Armando Doronila, the editor-in-chief, was not detained. He was simply thrown out of work after martial law agents padlocked the *Chronicle.*

To eke out a living, Doronila worked with the UP Center of Strategic Studies. He had wanted to get out of the country but did not have an exit permit. It took him three years to get his exit permit. With it, he left for Australia where he resumed writing for the *Melbourne Age,* "the largest Australian daily" (Doronilla's words).

Like Doronila, three friends of mine from Cagayan de Oro who were making their names as respected media practitioners in Manila found themselves locked out of their jobs upon the declaration of martial rule: Cip Apolinario of the *Manila Times,* Nestor Torre and Joe Gabor of the *Manila Chronicle.* Joe's name was, at the time, already a byword in news photography in the country.

Other people in radio and television were also arrested and detained for various lengths of time. On the average, they were released after two months.

While the closure and harassment of the media outlets began on the day martial law was declared, it continued throughout the martial law period in various degrees of intensity.

In 1973, Marcos also launched a program called *Balikbayan,* literally Homecoming, which was the brainchild of Tourism Minister Jose Aspiras, mainly to earn the goodwill of the expatriate Filipinos. The program received the support of our *paisanos* abroad, particularly those residing in the US. Aside from the promised fare discounts, the *balikbayans* were assured of welcome as returning heroes in their hometowns.

Chapter 13:

Resistance Jells

The Marcos propaganda machine went into full gear glorifying the achievements of martial rule in its second year. But, resistance to it also started to jell.

Marcos was himself immensely responsible for the rising tide of opposition to martial rule not only because the people began to see the excesses of his administration but also because he was getting careless in his public pronouncements. There was one slip, for instance, that Marcos made in Malacañang on June 22, 1973, when he addressed a group of reserve officers. According to the *Daily Express* of the following day, Marcos said:

> There is no real emergency in the country today. The situation in Mindanao had been reduced to occasional sporadic clashes between government troopers and armed men who are out to terrorize the countryside.

We in the Opposition retorted, "If there was no real emergency in the country at that time, why retain martial law?" We also charged that the martial law regime was engaged in "the manufacture of popular consent and fictitious majorities." We reiterated the same issues years later as martial law sunk its roots more deeply into the body politic. In a 16-page manifesto, prepared principally by Sen. Jovito Salonga and Jesuit Provincial Horacio de la Costa, we questioned Marcos's methods of securing the people's support for the regime. Along with Senators Gerry Roxas, Soc Rodrigo and Eva Estrada Kalaw, Congressman Rogaciano Mercado, Tito Guingona, Sedfrey Ordoñez, Charito Planas, Alejandro Lichauco, Abraham Sarmiento and others, I signed the manifesto.

Marcos was in no mood to reply to our rhetorical questions that were also totally ignored by the controlled media. In Mindanao, however, contrary to the rosy picture of the country that Marcos tried to paint, the Moro National Liberation Front (MNLF) was actually waging a war of attrition against the government. That was something that neither he nor the media could ignore for long.

The US-Based MFP

In the meantime, the resistance to Marcos spread outside the country especially to the US. In the US where most expatriate Filipinos had relocated themselves, our former colleague, Delegate Raul Manglapus, organized an anti-Marcos movement that was eventually named, the Movement for a Free Philippines. Two former delegates, Boni Gillego and Sonny Alvarez, and Willy Crucillo, who had migrated to the US before martial law was imposed, assisted him.

Organizing the MFP did not come easy. Alvarez said it took two years of hard work before the US-based anti-Marcos Filipinos got formally organized into the MFP, with Manglapus as its leader. Among the problems they encountered was the fact that many Filipinos residing in the US were of Ilocano roots — like Marcos. The Ilocanos were more or less inclined to support Marcos without reservation, unlike the other Filipino ethnic groups there.

To keep their struggle relevant to the domestic resistance to the Marcos regime, the MFP leadership reached out to the Manila-based Opposition. One day, I received a mimeographed letter addressed to me and to the in-country Opposition leaders whose names were blacked out for security reasons. The letter was signed by Manglapus and Alvarez. The gist of the message was that, at its convention in Chicago in October 1974, the MFP took the stand that the 1935 Constitution was still valid and could be used as the basic law when the Marcos regime collapsed. Their core assumptions were that the Marcos government would collapse and, when it did, the 1972 Constitution "expurgated of its undemocratic provisions" could be submitted for "genuine ratification by the people" and used as a basis for the tentative governance of the country.

At that time, I viewed the MFP position — to put it mildly — as plain daydreaming. There were then no visible signs in Manila in late 1974 that the Marcos martial law regime faced an impending collapse in the near or distant future. We were, in fact, prepared to see the struggle against martial rule continue from the regime of Ferdinand Marcos to at least Imelda's as his successor. Since the MFP was 10,000 miles away from the country, I thought that its leaders could dream big and talk even bigger because they were beyond the reach of Marcos's dreaded police. And, even if it was not verbalized, I also sensed that there was a feeling of insecurity among our leaders in the legitimate Opposition in Manila. The reason for the unease was the fact that we were so badly disorganized that the birth of the MFP threatened to overshadow our in-country leaders' efforts to dismantle the martial law regime peacefully.

We were also apprehensive that if we established formal links with the MFP, there was the real danger that, if they advocated outright violence against the martial law regime, that would give Marcos the excuse to crackdown on us, the local Opposition, more forcefully. While they were out of the country and beyond his reach, we were in the country for easy picking by the martial law authorities. I also saw from our discussions that there was a palpable disinclination to consider the MFP as equal partners in the struggle against Marcos. At best, the MFP was seen as a useful group to disseminate internationally our position as *the* peaceful Opposition to the Marcos regime. Nonetheless, in our discussions, we acknowledged the important contributions of the MFP to restore democracy to the country. At the very least, we thought of them as propagandists in the mold of Marcelo H. del Pilar who, in exile, spoke for and wrote about the rights of our people during the Spanish colonial era.

Incidentally, Manong Pepe Calderon's and my visit to his daughter Lilia in New York enabled me to meet with Sonny Alvarez. We met in one of the plazas of New York. I did not immediately recognize him among the people walking through the park until I saw him beckoning to me. He acted as if he was being tailed by Marcos agents. He had a soft felt hat on and wore a thick jacket that looked like it had seen better days. Certainly, his attire was a far cry from the sartorially elegant clothes he usually wore when he attended the Convention sessions before martial law was declared. I could see that New York was not a hospitable haven for him and his wife, Cecille Guidote.

Sonny and I talked about the situation at home but only in generalities. I told him about the meetings of the Opposition in Manila and told him of the threats of our being arrested any time the Marcos dictatorship wanted to round us up. I told him also about the apparent lack of interest on the part of the people to resist the martial law regime contrary to Ninoy Aquino's prediction that people would rise up against it.

I asked him how he got out of the country but he was not so forthright about it, except to say that he escaped from the Marcos police so narrowly that he brought only enough clothes in a small bag, which he toted all the way to the US.

It was only after the fall of Marcos that Alvarez told me that he also escaped through the "back door," that is, through the Sulu Sea, but not as the other escapees did. He said:

> I hid in the houses of friends for six months after martial law was declared. Businessman Ricky Delgado went out of his way to help me escape. After successfully eluding the Marcos military on land, I hitched a ride in a small vessel in Manila that was bound for Hong Kong through Kota Kinabalu in Sabah. The captain of the ship agreed to smuggle me out of the country after I assured him that I was a social democrat, not a communist.

From Hong Kong, Sonny went to Paris where "at that time," he said, "no visa was yet required of Filipinos." In Paris, he lay low for a while, waiting for a chance to go to the US by any means because his girlfriend, Cecille Guidote, whom he later married, was already there. His main problem was that he had no travel documents for his visa application for the US. Fortunately, a friend lent him his passport. By switching his photograph for that of his friend, Sonny now had a passport that looked genuine enough. Unfortunately when he presented the passport to the US consul in Paris to ask for a visa to the US, the latter, who had been assigned to Manila, got suspicious. The consul wanted to know why he did not apply for a visa in Manila. Before things got out of hand, Sonny told the consul that he should indeed apply for a visa in Manila. He hurriedly got back his fake passport from the incredulous consul.

Continuing his story, Sonny said:

> I finally got my visa for the US through another US consulate in a country in Europe. After I entered the US, I continued using the name of my friend for some years, until the United Nations Commission on Refugees granted me a refugee status. Then I began working with the Movement for a Free Philippines.

I also met former Delegate Romy Capulong in that trip to New York. He was one of the more perceptive delegates to the Convention who spoke and joined demonstrations against Marcos before martial law was imposed. Ernie Rondon, Romy Capulong and I had developed into fast friends during the Convention and we used to issue common statements on critical issues of the day.

In our conversation, I sensed that he was now taking a more violent line against the Marcos regime. He no longer believed that peaceful change was possible. Marcos, he said, could be brought down only by force. Since I knew that I had to go home to Manila while he was staying in the US, I tried to be very cautious about the way I talked of the Marcos regime. I told him that the Opposition group in Manila was meeting often to let people, if not Marcos himself, know that not everyone agreed with his authoritarian rule and that our leaders could provide a peaceful viable alternative to him.

High Drama Escape

During our meeting in New York, Romy did not tell me how he eluded the Marcos police in Manila to get an asylum in the US. Like Alvarez, it was only years later that he revealed the details of how he had slipped through the dragnet of the Marcos police, not once but three times. It was high drama. In his words:

> On the day martial law was announced, at around 5:30 a.m. of the Saturday morning, September 23, 1971, Ernie Rondon telephoned me in the duplex house I was then renting in UP Village. He said that the radio station where he was supposed to do his usual broadcast was guarded by uniformed and heavily armed military men. He said that martial law must have already been declared. I then had myself driven by my cousin, Ely Sta. Maria, to the house of my friend, lawyer Jose Ricafrente, which is also in the UP Village. There I lay low for a while. Upon arrival at Ricafrente's house, I sent Ely back to fetch my wife Nene and our two kids, Alexander and Eduardo, then 11 and 8 years old, respectively. We eluded the military raiding team by barely an hour. That was my first successful evasion of the clutches of the military.

> We hid for about two months. Then, we linked up with Raul Roco
> and other Constitutional Convention colleagues who also opted to go
> into hiding rather than get arrested. News spread that there was a
> shoot-to-kill order against those who were in hiding. Roco and I then
> asked for "sanctuary" in Edong Angara's house in White Plains. He allowed
> us to stay in the basement of his house.

The Angara mentioned by Romy Capulong was none other than Edgardo
Angara, a colleague of ours in the Constitutional Convention. At the time, he
was probably the closest delegate to Defense Minister Enrile. Romy continued:

> [While we were staying in Angara's house,] Roco and I mapped out our
> plan to escape through Zamboanga and then to Kota Kinabalu with the
> help of Maria Clara Lobregat, also a colleague in the Convention. Then,
> one evening Angara, who [had] just [come] from a party attended by
> Enrile, told us that we could opt to surface and resume our work in the
> Convention without being arrested.

With Angara's assurance that they would not be arrested, Romy Capulong
and Roco emerged from hiding and went back to work as delegates to the
Convention. Angara was as good as his word and no attempt was made to
arrest them while the Convention sessions lasted. After the Convention adjourned, Romy Capulong practiced law again. He said:

> I reestablished my law practice...first with Juan Liwag and later with
> young associates whom I recruited from UP. I had a fairly comfortable
> law practice with eight associates, occupying almost the entire fifth floor
> of San Luis Terraces Building on Kalaw St., Ermita.
>   On October 26, 1979, at about 12:30 p.m. Abadilla and his team raided
> my law office. I was having lunch with Liwag at the nearby Manila Hilton
> Hotel when the raid took place. (I learned later that the raiders wanted to
> arrest me before 12 noon, but were delayed because they first went to the
> wrong building, the San Luis Building, that was located on same street.)
>   Upon the advice of Liwag, we went to his law office [in] Gotiangco
> Building and figured out what to do....We called up Jovy Salonga and
> Pepe Diokno. Ka Pepe advised me against confronting the raiding team
> (which was my initial reaction) and to go into hiding instead. I followed
> his advice.
>   From my law office, the raiding team proceeded to my house [on
> Matimtiman St.] in Sikatuna Village, looked for me there and searched my
> house. They also confiscated my car and never returned it.

Romy told me he did not know why his law office was raided, but his having been associated with the insiders of the Aquino campaign must have been one of the reasons. This was the second time that he had successfully eluded the Marcos police. In the meantime, his political friends worked behind the scenes to get him off the martial law arrest-list. Romy said:

> Liwag and Gov. Eduardo Joson, both of whom had already joined Marcos and the KBL, volunteered to intercede for me with Marcos to lift the arrest order. I told my two elders from Nueva Ecija that I already decided to leave the country with my family to do some hard thinking and serious reassessment of my politics and my career. I [had] a relatively good law practice, but I was not happy. The judiciary had become very corrupt and rotten. The lifestyle of my two teenage[d] sons was giving me nightmares.

Romy gave Convention President Diosdado Macapagal credit for actually making it possible for him to leave the country.

> [Macapagal] assigned to me an ex-Coast Guard officer who knew how Manila-Hong Kong cargo liners operated. The officer arranged my trip to Hong Kong from Manila through one of the cargo vessels without going through immigration procedures and with minimum disclosure of my identity. From Hong Kong, I boarded a Korean Airlines flight to Los Angeles. In Los Angeles, Raul Daza met me at the airport, brought me to his house and contacted the other US-Filipino expats, including Manglapus, Alvarez, Psinakis and Gillego.

That was his third and final flight to freedom. As an active patent-law practitioner, Romy had an updated visa to the US. So did his wife and two sons, who had left earlier aboard a regular flight to New York. While they found life a little difficult early in their stay in the US, in a matter of months, they were all given work permits and, more importantly, Capulong was allowed to practice law in New York and other states.

'Back Door' to Freedom

Whatever route any would-be escapee took, he or she needed an exit permit to leave the country, a visa to enter the country of destination, credible reasons for the trip and enough dollars to cover the expenses. More often than not, the exit permits and the visas had to be forged and reasons for going out the country invented. To succeed, the would-be escapee also needed to have the proper contacts at the stopovers and at the final destination.

Exiting through the Sulu Sea "back door" was an extremely hazardous endeavor. Aside from the pirates who would kill hapless voyagers and rape women who crossed their paths in the Sulu Sea, there was always the possibility that a government patrol craft could intercept the *banca* or the boat being used in the escape and apprehend any would-be-escapee.

Despite the inherent dangers of going through the Sulu Sea, many of our friends took the risk. Boni Gillego, Charito Planas, Gaston Z. Ortigas, Pacita LaO Manglapus, wife of Raul, and their three teenage sons, Raul Jr., Bobby and Francis, Gerry Jumat and his wife Boots Ayson, shook off the dust of the martial law regime through that route.

I shared vicariously the joy of their successful escapes. I saw their flights to freedom as a series of breathtaking kicks to the solar plexus of the Marcos regime. Gillego, Planas and Ortigas told me of the harrowing experiences they went through in their getaways. They shared with me their hair-raising chance encounters with people who knew them but who did not appear to have recognized them, or their near brushes with military agents. Gillego and Ortigas had to disguise themselves, the latter donning a wig, and had to use assumed identities. Charito wore a nun's habit. Mrs. Manglapus was "Portia Molina" in her escape, while Gerry and Boots Jumat used their ethnic connections with the Tausugs of Sulu and Sabah to elude the Marcos police.

Citing the sagas of our friends' run to freedom in the few pages of this book barely acknowledges the anxieties, the difficulties and the dangers that they underwent.

Among the most exciting stories of my friends who fled the clutches of martial law were the serial escapes of the Manglapus family. As mentioned earlier, when martial law was proclaimed, Raul, the father of the family, was on a stopover in Tokyo on the way to the US where he had speaking engagements. His family and friends persuaded him not to return to Manila.

Joey Ortiz, a Philippine consulate official, assisted Manglapus upon his arrival in Washington, DC. Ortiz risked his job — he eventually lost it — to help the man regularize his status as a political refugee in the US.

Ortiz recounted that he tried to register Manglapus in a hotel under an assumed name. The check-in clerk, a Filipino, who saw Manglapus standing behind him, asked Manglapus in Tagalog, *"Hindi ba kayo si Senator Manglapus? Are you not Senator Manglapus?"* From then on, Ortiz said, the fugitive from Marcos's martial law regime had to use his real name.

Back in Manila, Mrs. Manglapus and their three sons and one daughter tried every "legal" avenue to join him in the US — to no avail. In desperation, Mrs. Manglapus and her sons then decided to use the "back door" to get out of the Marcos gulag. Tina, their daughter, was left behind because she had gotten married to Ben Maynigo and was on the family way.

It was a journey full of fearful imponderables. From the time they boarded a commercial flight from Manila to Zamboanga City on March 23, 1974, the danger of being recognized dogged them. Mrs. Manglapus had a name and face that were known by many people and the probability of her being spotted by martial law agents was great. She was, after all, the wife of Raul, the implacable and popular foe of the regime who continued his resistance even in the US. Moreover, they lived in Dasmariñas Village, a posh subdivision in

Makati, where they had for a neighbor, Juan Ponce Enrile, the Defense Minister.

The Manglapuses, however, had a support group that was as dedicated as they were to the cause of freedom. First and foremost were Gerry Jumat and Boots Ayson, who later became his wife. Also in the group were: the parents of Jumat; Oblate Bishop Antonino Nepomuceno of South Cotabato; Luis Jose and Maria Feria, loyal friends of Raul Manglapus; and others who have remained anonymous to this very day.

Gerry and Boots Jumat recounted how Mrs. Manglapus and her sons began their escape. In Gerry's words:

> Boots accompanied Mrs. Manglapus, who was now using Portia Molina as an alias, and her sons on the flight from Manila to Zamboanga City, where they stayed overnight. The following day, Boots flew back to Manila. Then, Mrs. Manglapus, her sons and I chartered a small plane to fly to Sibutu as "tourists."
>
> In Sibutu, we were jolted by the story that Enrile, the Minister of National Defense, was on the island the day before. We interpreted his visit to mean that the military unit in the island was active and must have been primed by the minister to be on the lookout for all kinds of antigovernment activities. But the nuns, who hosted us in their convent overnight, kept our presence a well-guarded secret until it was time to leave the following morning for Sitangkai.

Gerry's parents, who did barter trade between Sulu and Sabah, hired a *kumpit*, a motorized boat, to bring the would-be escapees to Sitangkai.

Meanwhile, back in Manila, with the assistance of Chino Roces, Boots hatched a disinformation campaign about the disappearance of the Manglapuses. The two fanned the rumor that Mrs. Manglapus and her sons slipped out of the country with the assistance of the Central Intelligence Agency (CIA) through the Clark Air Force Base, a US military facility, in Central Luzon. The CIA angle was purposely used, according to Boots, to remove the suspicion that Mrs. Manglapus and her sons left through the Sulu Sea, with her assistance and that of the Jumats.

In Sitangkai, where they stayed overnight, Gerry recalled:

> The following morning we hired a bigger *kumpit* to take us to Tawau in Sabah, Malaysia. The trip to Tawau was uneventful. But when we arrived at Tawau, Pacing (Mrs. Manglapus) and her sons were not allowed to disembark because they did not have the proper papers. The immigration requirement, however, did not apply to us, residents of Sulu and Tawi-Tawi.
>
> Because I was from Sulu, I was allowed to get off the *kumpit*. I contacted the parish priest of the local Catholic Church, Fr. John Lee, (now Archbishop

of Kota Kinabalu). I told him of the problem of the wife and sons of Raul Manglapus, a prominent political leader in the Philippines, who was in exile in the US. Through the intercession of Fr. Lee, Pacing and her sons were allowed to disembark and go to the priest's convent where, for the first time in several days, they were able to freshen up and have a hot meal.

With Fr. Lee's permission, I used his phone to call Raul in Washington and told him that his wife and sons were in Sabah. Raul was happy over the development.

From Sabah, Gerry said the Manglapuses flew to Kuala Lumpur, a journey facilitated by Mr. Ong, a Malaysian legislator who was a friend of Senator Manglapus. Once they were in Kuala Lumpur, the Manglapuses got to the US without too much trouble.

After the Manglapuses left Sabah for Kuala Lumpur, Jumat went back to his job as a vice president of the Notre Dame University in Cotabato. On the side, he also worked as a consultant of Adm. Romulo Espaldon, whom Marcos had appointed regional director of Region IX, which included the provinces of Sulu and Tawi-Tawi.

For the next three years, Boots Jumat said, the cover story that Mrs. Manglapus and her sons had fled through Clark Air Force Base worked. She and Gerry resumed their normal activities as if they had nothing to do with the escape of the Manglapuses. Then, one day, things changed. Boots recounted:

> I received an invitation from the Frederich Ebert Foundation of West Germany to participate in a cooperative conference in Java, Indonesia. Since I was also a consultant to the Civil Service Commission for Region IX, I thought that it would be best if I could have my regular passport changed to a government one. With a government passport, I felt I could move around more freely.

That turned out to be a mistake. At the time, getting or changing passports and applying to leave the country were tedious processes. In the case of Boots, her application to change her passport from a regular to a government one got the attention of the National Intelligence Services Agency, whose reputation at the time was beginning to rival that of Hitler's dreaded *Schutzstaffel*, the SS.

The NISA agents summoned her and, without specifying what she was supposed to have done that merited their attention, suggested that she had done something to embarrass the government and that she might as well confess whatever it was. Then they confiscated her passport and aborted her trip to Indonesia. Coincident with Boot's problem with the NISA, rumors were circulating in Manila to the effect that Mrs. Manglapus and her sons did not leave through Clark but through the South with the help of "a Christian UP student" and "a Muslim." The descriptions of Mrs. Manglapus's confederates fitted Boots and Gerry, respectively.

Fearful that the fiction they had peddled about Mrs. Manglapus's and her son's escape to freedom was about to be exposed, Maring Feria used a safe phone to ask Manglapus's advice on what Jumat and Boots should do. Gerry recalled, "The reply of Manglapus was that we should pack up and leave through the southern 'back door' and take with us, his daughter Tina and her family."

That was how the second phase of the Manglapus family escape came to pass. In the words of Gerry Jumat:

> We planned our "great escape" [for] two months. Then, on October 26, 1975, we implemented it. Tina, her husband Ben and her daughter Tanya flew to Zamboanga City "to visit friends." The following day Boots and our two kids, Wally (one year old) and Lara (two years old), left for Tawi-Tawi via Cotabato, Jolo and Siasi, on board a commercial boat. They rendezvoused in Sitangkai.

There was a hitch that Gerry did not anticipate. He could not accompany them on the day of their getaway. His employer, Admiral Espaldon, had instructed him to accompany him to a meeting with Region IX's governors, city and municipal mayors. It was too late to call off the plan, so Tina, her husband Ben Maynigo and their daughter Tanya, and Boots Jumat and her two infant children, Lara and Wally, went to Sitangkai, accompanied by some members of the Jumat clan.

It was only after three days, when the meeting was over, that Gerry caught up with his family and the Maynigos in Sitangkai. From there, accompanied by his father and several relatives, they took a faster and bigger *kumpit* to Tawau. They also took with them two teenage Spaniards, Luis and Carmen, who were their student wards in Zamboanga City.

When I told Gerry that it seemed foolhardy for them to have taken the two foreign students along in their escape, he disagreed. In fact, he said, the presence of the two Spanish students lent credence to "our cover story that we were touring our guests who wanted to see the sights in the Sulu Sea."

Gerry mentioned a detail of their escape that, to my knowledge, was hitherto unspoken. He said two armed groups secured them from pirates and other predatory elements all the way from Sitangkai to the outer edge of the Philippine waters, that is, up to where international waters began. That was ordinary enough. But his next revelation was startling.

> Our convoy boats were manned by armed men working for the government Constabulary and MNLF ranks, who were my cousins and close relatives.

Gerry's comment that both government troopers and MNLF rebels provided security for them showed that, in the Sulu Sea, the divide between the government and the rebels was not that deep. It could be bridged now and then by blood ties and, I heard, other interests like monetary payments.

Nonetheless, when their escorts left them, Gerry said they were harassed by fully armed pirates in a speedy pump boat. The pirates operating in the area were reputedly under the protection of some military officers and they specialized in harassing barter traders. He said, "Luckily, they knew us and we knew them. Thus, we were spared from harm."

That evening, when they reached the shallow waters of Tawau, they had another scary encounter, this time with a Malaysian Navy Patrol boat. Gerry recalled:

> [The boat] fired a warning shot at us, apparently because our boat had no light at all. Our gas lamp had run out of kerosene. The Navy boat then focused its search light on our *kumpit*. We were all afraid. We stopped the boat and a couple of the Malaysian officers boarded our *kumpit* and investigated us. When I spoke to them in Tausug, they warmed up to us. In friendly tones, they asked for our identification papers and passports. My brother and mother and my uncle showed their residency and barter traders permits. (My father had gone back to Sitangkai with our convoy). They asked why we had our suitcases and other people (the Spanish youths) with us. Without waiting for our answer, they concluded we were escaping from Marcos regime. Surprisingly, they now acted even more friendly with us. They said they knew my parents and our other relatives residing in Tawau. They then advised us to anchor our *kumpit* beside their patrol boat for protection and told us not to proceed to the mainland since it was already midnight.
>
> The following morning we continued our trip to Tawau. When we got to Tawau, we were not allowed to get out of the wharf until further verification and clearance. But Carmen and Luis, our Spanish students, were allowed to get out of the wharf since they had passports. They contacted the parish priest, Fr. John Lee, about our arrival. Then, they called Raul Manglapus in US to let him know that we were in Tawau. Fr. John Lee, who welcomed Mrs. Manglapus and sons some three years back, came to see us, after which the Spanish students continued their trip to Europe through Malaysia.

Without the generous assistance of Fr. Lee, Gerry said that their sufferings would have been unbearable. He continued:

> When we were finally allowed to disembark, Fr. Lee received us in his residence. We stayed with the priest for one month before the Red Crescent finally placed us in a hotel for another six months.

Overall, our stay in Tawau was pleasant. The head of the Special Branch of the Sabah police was related to my mother. He treated us very well. He assigned a plainclothes officer to provide security for us in our hotel. He also took us out for lunch or dinner occasionally.

1980: SAFE IN THE US, left to right, Boots, Lara, Gerry and Wally

Eventually, they were allowed entry to the US after Jimmy Carter was elected President. Gerry said:

> [I remember] the kindness shown to us by the First Secretary of the US embassy, Frank Bennet, who treated us with compassion. He even accompanied us in boarding the plane for Hong Kong. From there, we got to Seattle as our port of entry. We were finally free of Marcos's martial rule.

The successful flights of the Manglapuses, the Jumats and many other fugitives from the martial law government, demonstrated that the control that Marcos's authoritarian regime had over the lives of our people in Luzon, the Visayas and most of Mindanao did not extend to the Moros who had been plying the route to Sabah since the dawn of history to do brisk barter trade with the Sabahans. The Moros did not allow the restrictions of Marcos's authoritarian regime under martial to interfere with their pursuit of profit. Gerry Jumat's testament also affirmed that the Malaysian government was, at that point, not at all sympathetic to the Marcos government.

In the US, the Jumats gave unstinting support to the MFP that eventually became the biggest anti-martial law organization for Filipinos in North America.

Church Guidance

Here at home, the people in general kept silent in the face of the oppressive acts of the martial law government. Many looked up to the Church for guidance. Ten months after the declaration of martial law, in July 1973, the Catholic Bishops Conference of the Philippines issued a pastoral letter that defined their position vis-à-vis martial rule. Though short of our expectations for an outright condemnation of Marcos's experiment, the pastoral letter nonetheless raised the spirits of those of us who did not accept the facile premises for which martial law was imposed. Signed by the president of the CBCP at the time, Teopisto V.

Alberto, DD, Archbishop of Caceres, Baguio City, the pastoral letter quoted with approval an earlier document, "The Ministerial Priesthood," that the Synod of Bishops had issued for the guidance of "priests and the entire Church." That document declared:

> Together with the entire Church, priests are obliged to the utmost of their ability, to select a definite pattern of action, when it is a question of the defense of fundamental human rights, the promotion of the full development of persons and the pursuit of the cause of peace and justice; the means must indeed always be consonant with the Gospel. These principles are all valid not only in the individual sphere, but also in the social field.

The Catholic bishops' reference to the need to defend human rights and to promote the full development of persons and the pursuit of peace and justice, even under conditions of martial law, gave us in the Opposition some consolation, if not hope, that we were doing the right thing. The bishops concluded with a caution that the goals of Marcos in the creation of a "New Society" must be achieved with justice, truth and Christian charity:

> We speak of justice. For in the current striving to bring about a "new society," there is ever the danger that basic human rights will be pushed aside and ignored, due processes of law conveniently bypassed in the name of reform.
>
> We also speak of truth. For if our people are to participate with freedom and dignity in the making of decisions that touch their very lives and persons; if they are to develop as a people in the integral manner we have been talking about here; then their right to the truth must be respected at all times.
>
> And lastly, and above all, we speak of charity. For it is Christ's love that we have been concerned with here all along: a love based on justice and on truth; a love that impels us to commit ourselves to the great task of development and evangelization. Under conditions prevailing in the country today, this means for all of us, both as individuals and as community, unstinting service to the common good of all our people, be they Christian or Muslim, native or foreign-born, rich or poor. It is in this service that we will incarnate that selfsame charity in our lives and give witness to its transforming power.

While the pastoral letter did not directly condemn martial rule, it urged "the people of God" to adhere to the basic teachings of the Church on truth, justice, peace and love in the pursuit of the principles for change in the lives of our people. The pastoral letter did not satisfy all my longings for guidance by the Church on the matter of the morality of martial law, but it was, in my mind, better than no guidance at all.

Whether or not the martial law authorities construed the pastoral letter as a direct challenge to them, the following year, specifically on August 24, 1974, the military raided the Sacred Heart Novitiate in Novaliches. They arrested the Jesuit Provincial Benigno Mayo, SJ, Fr. Jose Blanco, SJ, and 20 student members of Kasapi. Their travails are recounted in the 2005 book, *Down from the Hill, Ateneo de Manila in the First Ten Years Under Martial Law, 1972-1982*, edited by Cristina Jayme Montiel and Susan Evangelista.

On September 1, 1974, Cardinal Sin hit the Marcos administration in his homily during a Mass concelebrated with 75 other priests at the Manila Cathedral before 5,000 people. Quoting the *Philippine Clipper*, special issue of September 1974, Montiel and Evangelista said that it was "the first time a major leader of the hierarchical Church took a clear stand against Marcos."

The "clear stand" that Sin took against Marcos did not lead to an outright defiance of the martial law regime by the Church. It, however, led to sporadic acts of truculent behavior — as we shall see — by members of the clergy and the religious against perceived acts of oppression by the martial law regime.

In an attempt to ease the tension between the martial law government and the clergy, Marcos, accompanied by Defense Minister Enrile and Press Minister Tatad, met with Bishops Mariano Gaviola and Hernando Antiporda of the CBCP, Fr. Benigno Mayo, SJ, and Fr. Simplicio Sumpayco, SJ, on October 29, 1974. As a result of the meeting, the following day, 13 of the 21 arrested in the Sacred Heart Noviate were released.

Chapter 14:

Diversionary Tactics

A believer in the carrot-and-stick approach, Marcos also tried to divert the people's attention from the harsh realities of martial rule by staging various kinds of public entertainment.

The *Extravaganzas*

For instance, under the sponsorship of Imelda, the first Miss Universe Pageant was held in Manila in July of 1974. With Marcos's approval, the pageant became a semiofficial affair of the government. All government agencies were impressed into supporting it.

Since there was no official statement as to how much the pageant would cost, speculation was rife that Imelda had set aside P40 million — of commingled government and private funds — for the pageant.

Then, in October of 1975, as if the country had all the money in the world for him to splurge as he wished, Marcos underwrote $4 million of the cost needed to stage *The Thrilla in Manila* heavyweight boxing championship fight between Mohammad Ali and Joe Frazier. The exorbitant spectacle was another example of how the arrogance of power scuttled whatever pretence Marcos had of love for the people. Unfortunately, again, the denunciations of the Opposition did not quite bother either Marcos or, for that matter, the public. The people loved the show. They seemed to agree with his line that the expense was worth the publicity because tens of thousands viewed the fight from their television screens and saw how "martial law was good for the country."

And, in 1982, the year before the assassination of Ninoy Aquino, with Marcos's approval, Imelda caused the building of the Film Palace to accommodate the Manila International Film Festival at the cost of $25 million.

The extravaganzas were nothing short of scandalous considering the palpable poverty of the people. We in the Opposition called the Marcoses as the reincarnation of Nero who, legend had it, played his fiddle while Rome burned. The Nero analogy was not that farfetched because, in the rush to complete the Film Palace, many workers were buried alive in fast-drying concrete when a floor collapsed on them. Instead of having the hapless victims rescued, the authorities ordered the construction to proceed without delay so that the deadline for the completion of the Film Palace could be met.

Our condemnations did not stop the pageant, the Thrilla or the film festival. The people did not seem to mind. The nation talked about the spectacles for several weeks.

Imelda's Role

For almost two and half years since the imposition of martial rule, Marcos played coy about the role of Imelda in his scheme of things. But, in 1975, he issued a decree vesting Imelda with succession rights to his position as the authoritarian ruler of the country. He named her as the chair of a commission that would govern the country in the event of his death or permanent incapacity. Then, in November, he appointed her governor of Metro Manila.

The appointment was in response to a supposedly widespread clamor of barangay officials in Manila. The endorsement of the barangay officials enabled Marcos to create a semblance of grassroots backing for her appointment. Marcos also got the business people — not that they were unwilling for business reasons — to endorse her as the best qualified person for the job. As Metro Manila governor, Imelda now had jurisdiction over the four cities of Manila, Quezon, Pasay and Caloocan and 13 towns of Makati, Mandaluyong, Malabon, San Juan, Navotas, Pateros, Taguig, Parañaque, Las Piñas, Muntinlupa, Pasig, Marikina and Valenzuela.

Earlier, Marcos had sent her on numerous missions as his emissary. In that capacity and in quick succession, she visited Nepal, Egypt, Algeria, Saudi Arabia, Bolivia, Cuba and Libya. Her trip to Libya had to do with the then on-going peace negotiations between the Moro National Liberation Front and the government. Some details of her involvement in the peace effort are discussed in the next few pages of the book.

The visits of Imelda as a super diplomat to those countries were unmistakable signs that Marcos was grooming her as his successor. In the same breath, Marcos wanted the US to know that he was now looking beyond the traditional Philippines-US ties to the world outside for new economic and even military deals.

Imelda Courts China

But it was as Marcos's personal representative to China that Imelda made her most important diplomatic coup. In September 1974, he sent Imelda to China to get Mao Zedong and Prime Minister Chou En-lai to consider the Philippines as an ally rather than as a Cold War enemy.

In that mission, Imelda was immensely successful. She charmed Mao, even if at that time, the latter was "seriously ill," according to his physician, Dr. Li Zhisui, who mentioned Imelda's visit in his book, *The Private Life of Chairman Mao*. With the apparent approval of Mao, Imelda set the stage for

Marcos's state visit to China in 1975 to formalize the establishment of diplomatic ties between the two countries.

Here at home, we in the Opposition hoped that Imelda's China visit would, at least, disturb the Americans into reconsidering the erroneous support they had extended to Marcos's declaration of martial law. Upon the declaration of martial law, the American Chamber of Commerce in Manila almost simultaneously lauded the move. We believed that the chamber would not have done so if US President Nixon had not given his imprimatur to the imposition of martial rule. But, more directly, we also knew that the American Chamber of Commerce was worried about the Philippine Supreme Court decision of August 19, 1972. Less than a month before the proclamation of martial rule, the Supreme Court ruled that US citizens and corporations would lose their so-called Parity Rights by 1974.

Our concerns over Imelda's China visit soon gave way to dismay over another Supreme Court decision in December 1974, which upheld the Marcos proclamation of martial rule. Although we sort of expected the adverse ruling, just the same we were hoping against hope that Ninoy Aquino's questioning of the validity of his being tried by a military tribunal as a consequence of the declaration of martial law would provide some hope for our continuing reservations on the validity of the martial law proclamation. In the event, the Supreme Court accepted Marcos's reasons for the proclamation and dashed all hopes that we could again raise constitutional issues against it.

State Visit to China

On June 7, 1975, with Imelda by his side, Marcos made a historic state visit to China to formally establish diplomatic ties with its communist government. It was the first ever visit to China by a Philippine president. The visit was well publicized by the domestic press. At the time, the public perception here at home was that the US did not want the country to establish diplomatic relations with China. The US had announced its full commitment to support Chiang Kai-Shek, the leader of the Kuomintang government, even after Mao's forces drove him away from the mainland to Taiwan. But for pragmatic reasons, Marcos saw the need to shift the country's ties from Taiwan. While Taiwan was a source of support for the economic development of the country, China was, in the minds of Marcos's military analysts, a potential, if not an actual though covert, source of support for the New People's Army rebels, who by now styled themselves as "Maoist" communists.

The establishment of the country's diplomatic relations with Mao's China bound us to a one-China policy. By recognizing Mao Zedong's government, Marcos had to officially sever our diplomatic ties with Taiwan. In fact, the country's ties with the latter were not cut off completely. They were merely downgraded from full diplomatic relationships to one on economic and cultural matters.

In Manila as in many parts of the country, the downgrading of Taiwan's diplomatic relationship with the country did not come easy. Chapters of the Kuomintang Party that had sprouted in the Philippines from the time Chiang rose to power in China lobbied against the downgrading of the country's relationship with Taiwan. Well-placed Filipino-Chinese business magnates told national and local officials in no uncertain terms that they could get more economic support from Taiwan than from Mainland China.

In my home city, Cagayan de Oro, the Filipino-Chinese Federation split into two: one, pro-mainland China, and the other, pro-Taiwan. The pro-mainland Filipino-Chinese in the city were predominantly the younger generation and the pro-Taiwan faction was composed mostly of the older Filipino-Chinese. The split in the membership of the Filipino-Chinese Federation in Cagayan de Oro also happened in many parts of the country.

There was, however, no turning back on the country's diplomatic recognition of China. China eased the difficulties by posing no objection to the maintenance of our economic and cultural relations with Taiwan. Eventually, Taiwan and its Kuomintang chapters in the country gave up their resistance to the establishment of Philippine-China diplomatic relations. Inevitably, the flag of the People's Republic of China replaced the flag of the Republic of China at the Chinese Embassy in Manila.

Soon, however, a downside of the new relationship began to manifest itself. As the reality began to sink into the minds of the Filipino-Chinese community that the world, including the Philippines, recognized only one China, the Chinese-Filipinos saw wider trade opportunities in Mainland China than in Taiwan. That led to the huge Filipino-Chinese investments in the mainland that remain to this day.

By formally recognizing China, Marcos telegraphed the message to the US that the country's options for economic and military aid had widened. If China's assistance in those areas should prove unavailing, there was also the Soviet Union to which he had sent Imelda earlier to mend fences, principally with the Russian bear. A year after the establishment of foreign relations with China, Marcos formally inaugurated diplomatic ties with the Soviet Union.

It was his way of piling up pressure on the US to give his regime more aid. He used the proposed extension of the US leases of the military bases in the country as a major bargaining chip. It was also true, however, that he pragmatically hoped that by befriending China, he could convince the latter not to extend assistance — moral, financial or war materiel — to the New People's Army that, ironically, his proclamation of martial rule had energized. It was a common knowledge that the proclamation of martial rule was the single most important factor which drew more recruits to the NPA than any other circumstance. Whereas before the proclamation, it was widely accepted that the NPA only had at most a few hundred fighters in the 1970s, by the time Marcos was ousted in 1986, NPA armed partisans had grown to roughly 15,000.

In the course of his 1975 State Visit to China, both Chairman Mao and Prime Minister Chou En-lai assured Marcos that China did not "export revolution." Happy in the thought that they had converted China into becoming a firm ally, Marcos and Imelda came home to a triumphal welcome. The media predictably extolled Imelda, principally for her "diplomatic triumph" and rightly so because it was her personal diplomacy that apparently beguiled Mao and softened the hostile attitude of his government which had long considered Marcos as a *tuta* of the US in Southeast Asia .

Mijares's Defection

Before Marcos's partisans could fully savor the success of his and Imelda's diplomatic mission to China, an announcement made by the US-based Movement for a Free Philippines dampened their euphoria over the event. The MFP in a widely publicized statement, proclaimed that Primitivo Mijares, Marcos's erstwhile chief media censor, would testify against Marcos before the US congressional subcommittee on International Relations on June 17, 1975.

His impending testimony before the subcommittee sent Marcos and his top executive assistant, Guillermo de Vega, a former close associate of Mijares, into a tizzy. In a crude attempt to dissuade the latter from testifying, De Vega called him up by phone from Manila and offered him $50,000 to back off. Mijares had an American lawyer listen in on their phone conversation during which he said the offer was too small but he would think about it if it was raised to $100,000. De Vega fell for Mijares's gambit and said he would be sending the amount through the Filipino consul in San Francisco, Trinidad Alconsel. Alconsel subsequently phoned Mijares to say he had opened a joint account with Mijares and had deposited the money in the account in a bank in San Francisco.

Although Mijares was generally considered a "tainted source," his defection from Marcos and his subsequent testimony against Marcos before the US congressional subcommittee were pleasant to hear for two reasons. One, defections from Marcos were rare and far between. Fear inhibited Marcos's associates from dissociating themselves from his administration. And, two, because the local media was controlled, any news against the Marcos regime was good.

I had not met Mijares personally before his defection. He and I only met in San Francisco after he testified before the subcommittee. We got together at an eatery inside a US military facility on Yerba Buena, an islet beneath the San Francisco Bay Bridge.

It was cloak-and-dagger stuff. Coded calls were exchanged between Mijares and some friends, particularly Steve Psinakis and Charlie Avila, who acted as go-betweens. The venue was identified and the time was fixed with a minimum of words. I arrived at the appointed time and, on the dot, he also materialized at the meeting place with a soft hat covering his head and a part of his forehead. After we shook hands, he pointed to an American who was following him at a distance. "He's an FBI agent," he told me with a tinge of pride in his voice, "assigned as my security."

Without my asking, he said:

> I can no longer stomach the corruption that characterized the martial law government. I am now convinced that Marcos proclaimed martial rule to perpetuate himself and his family in power. I am also bothered by the massive human rights violations in the country.

Most of the time, I merely listened to him. When I was able to, I injected the thought that he was doing the country a great service by exposing in the US the anomalies and abuses of the Marcos administration. Because the media was controlled at home, people had very little access to news of the massive corruption and widespread wrongdoing of the Marcos government. I said that, through his exposé, people back home would surely get a glimpse of how Marcos and his cohorts had abused their powers and had bled the country dry.

As we parted, Mijares told me that he was finishing a book that would detail his accusations against Marcos and Imelda. The book, *The Conjugal Dictatorship of Ferdinand & Imelda Marcos,* was published in 1976 after he gave his testimony before the International Relations subcommittee of the US Congress.

Mijares's book was banned in the country, but a number of copies managed to wind up in the hands of the anti-Marcos crowd. I got a copy of the book duly autographed by the author. I found it hastily-written. Several passages duplicated the same criticisms against Marcos and Imelda. The book could have benefited from good editing and Mijares, having been a newspaperman himself, would have seen the need for it. Considering the circumstances, however, he probably did not think that having the book edited first was worth the delay. With the enormous martial law powers now in the hands of Marcos, nobody could really blame Mijares if he thought that Marcos would prevent its publication by any means. Whatever its defects, the book contained so much valuable information from a direct witness of the workings of the martial law government, its abuses, the corruption and shenanigans of Marcos, the grandiose schemes of Imelda, and the peccadilloes of some of the brightest stars of the martial law government, some of whom are alive as these lines are written. Marcos survived the Mijares exposé but it certainly shook him up

Nixon Resigns, Marcos Woos Ford

In 1974, the Watergate scandal caused US President Richard Nixon to resign. We the Manila Opposition hoped that the resignation would diminish US support for Marcos. In our view, Nixon was an unabashed supporter of Marcos's martial rule. When the news of Nixon's resignation came to the attention of Marcos and Imelda, she reportedly quipped that it was a pity that Nixon had to resign because he "was a friend." Now a new US president, Gerald Ford, had taken over and Marcos did not know what to expect from him.

Unwilling to leave things to chance, Marcos made every effort to invite the new US President to make a state visit to Manila. Craftily, he wanted to be as close personally to Ford as he had been to Nixon. After intense lobbying by the Philippine Embassy in Washington, DC, and the broad hints that Imelda gave to US congressional leaders about the urgency of reaffirming and strengthening US-Philippine relations, Ford made an official visit to Manila in December 1975.

In Manila, Ford assured Marcos that he considered the relationship of the US and the country as written on stone. In turn, Marcos told Ford that the establishment of diplomatic ties between China and the Philippines did not diminish the ties that historically bound the US and the Philippines. Ford's visit to Manila was a big plus for Marcos's martial law government. Marcos and Imelda drummed it up for nothing less. And the people lapped it up.

My own gut feel then was that the people saw that even Uncle Sam was shoring up Marcos's regime and was willing to give him a chance to accomplish what he had promised to do when he declared martial law. He promised to create a New Society where the little man would have an equal chance as the oligarch to get a space under the sun. With Ford's support for the Marcos regime so clearly manifested in his state visit to the country, we in the Opposition realized that we were in for a long struggle.

Courting the Moros

In Mindanao, the Moro rebels continued to battle it out with the government. Aware that the rebellion of the Moros of Mindanao could dissipate the foundations of his "New Society," Marcos made several moves to ease the Moro-secessionist struggle. In quick succession, he decreed the enactment of a Muslim Family Law Code. He ordered the grant of amnesty to the MNLF and MILF combatants who had taken up arms against the government. He created the Amanah Bank to grant loans without interest to Moro borrowers.

The Moro rebels, however, viewed those moves as superficial peace offerings. In general, they continued to confront the government violently until 1976 when Marcos secured a peace agreement — more of a truce, really — with the MNLF under the prodding of Colonel Khadaffi, the Libyan leader.

Earlier, to assure that the other sectors of society would not feel left out of the magnanimity of his martial rule and to gain their sympathy, Marcos ordered in September 1974, the release of more than a thousand martial law detainees, including Sen. Jose W. Diokno, one of those whom he had ordered arrested immediately on the day martial law was proclaimed.

Hostage-Taking in DC

Before 1974 came to a close, two incidents embarrassed the government no end.

The first incident occurred on November 18 in Washington, DC. It had to do with the hostage-taking at gunpoint of the Philippine Ambassador, Eduardo Romualdez, at the Philippine Embassy by Napoleon Lechoco, a Filipino-American. Lechoco vented his ire on Romualdez for the government's alleged harassment of his family. He believed that officials in Manila were preventing his son from going to the US in retaliation for his anti-martial rule stance.

Eventually, Lechoco surrendered to the DC police after he was assured that his son was already on board a plane bound to the US. Lechoco was subsequently tried, convicted and sentenced to several months in jail. After serving 15 months, he got a retrial and was acquitted on the ground that evidence favorable to him had been suppressed, allegedly upon the urging of the State Department, then headed by Secretary of State Henry Kissinger. Kissinger was said to have considered Marcos too invaluable an ally to offend and had thus sacrificed truth and justice in the Lechoco case to advance what he perceived to be in the national interest of the US.

The hostage-taking of the country's ambassador by Lechoco agitated the Filipino community in the US against the Marcos government even more. The Marcos-controlled media in Manila, however, generally ignored the incident.

In any case, we were elated by the Lechoco caper because of its immense propaganda value against the Marcos regime. The US government saw that there was a growing disaffection of the people against the Marcos regime, not only in the Philippines but even on US soil.

Hunger Strike

Then, while the police authorities in Washington DC, had their hands full with Lechoco's holding Ambassador Eduardo Romualdez hostage, also on November 18, (Philippine time), two detainees in Fort Bonifacio staged a hunger strike that caused a tremor in the presidential palace even if the controlled press hardly gave it a line.

The hunger strike shook Malacañang because it got wide publicity in the US media and positive reactions from members of both Houses of the US Congress. The reason the hunger-strike got noticed by US legislators was that the hunger-strikers were Sergio Osmeña III, son of Sergio, Jr., the LP presidential candidate against Marcos in 1969, and Geny Lopez, son of Eugenio, the business magnate who had severed his connections with Marcos shortly before the declaration of martial law.

The two had been detained since 1972 on the suspicion that they had plotted to assassinate Marcos. Although he had detained them for more than two years, Marcos was not eager to get them to trial He had another agenda. Coffee shop talk had it that he wanted to use their detention as a leverage to prevent the Osmeñas from financing any destabilization attempt against him and enable him to get his hands on the economic empire of the Lopezes.

For a while, the scheme appeared to work. The Osmeñas in Cebu kept their distance from opposition politics. At some point, Lito Osmeña, nephew of Sergio, Jr., even allied himself with the Marcos regime as a candidate for a regional office and John Osmeña, brother of Lito, went into voluntary exile in the US. The Lopezes, on the other hand, capitulated to the pressure of Marcos. They handed over their holdings in Meralco, the giant electric company servicing Metro Manila, the ABS CBN radio and television network, *The Manila Chronicle* and other businesses to the Romualdezes, Marcos's in-laws, and other cronies just so Geny would be released.

Marcos, however, reneged on the agreement to release Serge and Geny, according to Eugenio Lopez, the father. Thus, the hunger strike.

The hunger strike was "Geny's idea," Osmeña said. From the way, he described it to me, it sounded like a well-orchestrated operation, much like the D-Day landing at Normandy on June 6, 1944, which ended World War II in Europe.

If the Normandy landing involved not only the Americans but also the British, Canadians and other allied troops in its planning and execution, so did the hunger strike involve not only the Lopez family and the big leaders of the opposition in Manila but also the anti-martial law Filipinos in the US and sundry members of the US Senate and House of Representative.

In their planning, the hunger strikers targeted four fronts: legal, medical, political and religious.

Before Lopez and Osmeña began their hunger strike, their two lawyers, Senators Tañada and Diokno worked the legal front by lobbying again with Defense Minister Enrile for the release of their clients. On the medical front, they had Gabby, a son of Geny, research the effects of a hunger strike on the body. Gabby told them that the breakdown of body functions sets in after three weeks of total fasting, and that a person could go on a hunger strike for 60 days but he or she could lose consciousness in 50.

Gabby suggested that they could take "glucose tablet to feed their brains with glycogen and slow down the deterioration of their immune system." He added a historical fact to persuade them to do so. He said Mahatma Gandhi took salt and bicarbonate of soda during his famous fasts which eventually led Great Britain to grant India independence. If Gandhi succeeded in getting freedom for India by his fasts, Osmeña and Lopez believed that they could also get Marcos to grant them their freedom by their hunger strike.

On the political front, two in-laws of the Lopez family took charge of publicizing the strike. Chita, Geny's wife, gave updates in Manila on the condition of the two hunger strikers mainly to local "subversive organizations" (Serge Osmeña's words). In the US, Steve Psinakis, Lopez's brother-in-law, turned it into a media event.

The hunger strike was hardly mentioned in Manila by the controlled press. It, however, attracted media attention in the US not only as a result of the efforts of Psinakis but also because Raul Manglapus, leader of the US-based Movement for a Free Philippines, lobbied US senators and congressmen in Washington, DC, to send cables to Marcos demanding the release of Osmeña and Lopez.

Twenty-six US senators, some real big names like Alan Cranston, Hubert Humphrey, Edward Kennedy, George McGovern, Walter Mondale, Birch Bayh, James Fulbright and Adlai Ewing Stevenson, responded positively and cabled Marcos asking that Osmeña and Lopez be released. From the US House of Representatives, 30 members, including Stephen Joshua Solarz, Tom Harkin, Leo Joseph Ryan, Edward Irving Koch, Robert F. Drinan, Leon Edward Paneta, Peter Wallace Rodino, Morris King Udall, Bella Savitzky Absug, Paul Tsongas and Andrew Jackson Young, Jr., demanded that Marcos free the hunger strikers.

On the religious front no less than Jaime Cardinal Sin openly demanded that Osmeña and Lopez be released. The Cardinal, in fact, tried to visit them at Fort Bonifacio, but he was not allowed to do so.

Ten days into the hunger strike, however, Osmeña and Lopez called it off after Marcos promised that they would soon be released, along with other political detainees. Marcos did release "other" political detainees but, untrue to his word, he did not free the two. Osmeña said years later that their hunger strike had not been in vain. He explained:

> For one thing, the hunger strike embarrassed Imelda no end. She was in the US for a visit at the time it started. Moreover, it also resulted in the release of some 1,022 detainees on December 5, 1974.

There were claims that Senator Diokno was released as a result of Osmeña's and Lopez's hunger strike. Diokno, however, was released earlier, that was on September 11, 1974. In any case, unlike Aquino, whom he continued to detain, Marcos felt that Diokno was no threat to his rule. He considered him more of a legal theoretician than an anti-martial rule tactician. And he was right. While Diokno provided the most cogent philosophical and legal reasons for opposing martial rule, he never advocated or organized any group to topple martial rule by the use of force.

In any case, other notable detainees were released as a result of the hunger strike. They included Jake Almeda Lopez, a senior executive of the Lopez business conglomerates; Charito Planas, an aggressive lady lawyer, and Renato Tañada, son of Senator Tañada, the acknowledged leader of the legitimate Opposition to the Marcos martial law regime.

The authorities made a big show of the release of the detainees in a public ceremony that was presided over by, the Chief of the Constabulary, General Fidel V. Ramos.

Purging Local Officials

At that time, no elections had been held since the proclamation of martial law. The four year-terms of local government officials elected in 1971 would expire at the end of 1975. Some local officials then asked for the holding of local elections. Immediately, Local Government Minister Jose Roño doused cold water on the suggestion. To justify his position, he made the barefaced assertion, reported by the *Daily Express* of October 18, 1975, that there would be no local elections "because the people (did) not want them held." With a sophistry unrivaled in the annals of the country, Roño justified his conclusion by referring to a referendum held earlier in the year. He said:

> By a vote of 15,321,799, the people opted for the presidential appointment of local officials whose terms expire in December (of 1975) while only 3,278,085 voted for (the holding of) elections."

In truth, in that referendum as well as in others that were held under martial law conditions, the people were not free to express their views.

Actually, Roño was simply setting up the stage for Marcos to replace the local government officials as he pleased, which he started to do in the year that followed. It was a personalized selective process whereby Marcos ousted the local executives whose loyalty to him he doubted and retained those whose loyalty was unquestionable.

Among the first casualties of the Marcos purge of local officials were City Mayor Reuben Canoy of Cagayan de Oro, who was replaced by Concordio Diel; Mayor Pedro Espina of Surigao City, by Constantino Navarro, Jr.; Governor Carlos Fortich of Bukidnon, by Angelo Lopez; Governor Antonio Luspo of Camiguin, by Dioscoro Quiblat; Governor Brigido Valencia of Pampanga, by Juanita Nepomuceno; and Governor Patricio Dumlao of Nueva Vizcaya, by Osias Cadiente.

Marcos tried to pin a more objective reason for the purge of the cited local government officials: corruption, inefficiency or simple undesirability. A closer look at the names of those that Marcos ordered removed in the first phase of his purge of local officials showed that the mayors and the governors concerned had one thing in common: they were more or less "independent-minded." It was also true that some people who were personally close to Marcos maneuvered to have them replaced.

As Marcos was gaining some public relations points with his drive against so-called erring officials, in late September 1975, we in the Opposition were agog over reports that Minister Enrile was going abroad on an indefinite leave of absence. We thought that Enrile had a falling out with Marcos. It proved to be wishful thinking on our part. According to subsequent media reports, Enrile left his office for a while to avoid creating the impression that he was personally protecting his son, Jackie, who was involved in the killing of another youth. Subsequently, Jackie was cleared of the charges and Enrile was back in office in mid-October.

In late October 1975, however, a genuine shocker rocked Malacañang. Guillermo de Vega, a top aide of Marcos, was shot dead in his office in Malacañang. De Vega was the Marcos official who telephoned Primitivo Mijares to request him to desist from his plan to testify before the US Congress on the anomalies of the Marcos government. The superstitious among the people surmised that De Vega's killing presaged the collapse of the Marcos government.

The year, nonetheless, ended with a big economic propaganda bang for the Marcos government. Kawasaki put up the Philippine Sinter Corporation, a multi-billion dollar investment in Misamis Oriental. Although Kawasaki put in a lot of money into the project, we in the Opposition were not altogether pleased by it. We were not happy about the prospects of many towns in Misamis Oriental being polluted by the operation of the sintering plant. The Japanese, we learned, did not want the plant to be put up in Japan precisely because sintering iron ores to produce processed materials for steel manufacturing was a heavy pollutant. In any event, our concerns resonated only with nongovernment activists who saw the plant's potential for ruining the health of the residents living nearby.

For my family, 1975 was — but for martial law — not a bad year. I was working as a lawyer in Manong Pepe Calderon's companies, teaching law in San Beda and assisting farmers, fisher folk and the urban poor on the side. Bing was also employed with St. Mary's College. The children were all in school, doing well. And, thank God, we were all in good health. There were moments when we enjoyed ourselves as family. For instance, Koko, my third child, then 11 years old, who was not very demonstrative, found time to send me a note with the greeting, "To the greatest man alive because he is my hero" on my birthday in December of the year. Gwen, Maripet, Jac, Teresa and Inde were just as profuse in their birthday greetings to me, which made me forget my abhorrence of martial law for the day at least.

Part 5

The Interim Batasang Pambansa

1978: *NINOY GREETS ME in a reception room in Fort Bonifacio after he asked me to be one of his Laban candidates for the Interim Batasang Pambansa in Metro-Manila.*

Chapter 15:

Martial Law Contradictions

The next year, 1976, was hardly congenial to the struggle for freedom. Marcos pursued peace initiatives to pacify the Moro rebels but at the same time, he saw the need to eradicate whatever remained of the free press to promote his authoritarian rule. And while he denied it, torture of detainees became fairly endemic to his regime.

Tripoli Peace Effort

Marcos knew that his authoritarian rule could not last long if he had to face a war on two fronts: the MNLF in many parts of Mindanao and the NPA in some provinces of the country. Between the two groups that were now fighting the martial rule government, he saw the MNLF as the more malleable rebel force than the dogmatically ideological NPA communists. Thus, he sought to establish peace or, at least, a truce with the MNLF. As was mentioned in Chapter 14, he sent Imelda to Libya to mend fences with Col. Maumar Khadaffi, the Libyan leader, who was believed to be the main funding source of the MNLF and to Saudi Arabia and Pakistan to touch base with the leaders of those nations that were known havens of Moro rebels.

In Libya, Imelda turned out to be an effective diplomat. She got Khadaffi to oversee the government negotiations with the MNLF in Libya and on December 23, 1976, Khadaffi had Misuari sign the so-called Tripoli Agreement that was intended as a roadmap to peace in Mindanao. Deputy Minister of National Defense Carmelo Barbero signed it in behalf of the government.

Marcos, however, never intended to implement the Tripoli Agreement. Instead of creating only one Autonomous Region for Mindanao as embodied in the Agreement, he organized two: one for the Moros of mainland Mindanao and another for the offshore Moros of Basilan, Sulu and Tawi-Tawi. It was a classic case of the "divide and rule" tactic that past masters of the art of colonization from Julius Caesar to the more recent British colonizers of many lands in Southeast Asia had employed.

To provide a legal cover for his moves, Marcos insisted that the Agreement be ratified in a plebiscite among the people of the provinces and cities proposed to be included in the Autonomous Regions. The provinces and cities that voted in favor of the plebiscite would be included in the autonomous regions. The results were predictable. The non-Moro provinces and cities opted for exclusion from the Autonomous Regions and only the predominantly Moro provinces voted to be included. Misuari and the hard-line MNLF commanders did not like what happened because they had wanted to project that they were fighting not just for Moro peoples of Mindanao but for the Christians and the Lumads as well. The problem with that posture was that most Christians and Lumads did not want to be placed under a Moro-dominated government. I remember one facetious argument which nonetheless carried weight among the non-Moros: if the Christians and the Lumads voted for inclusion of their areas in the Autonomous Regions they would then be prohibited from eating "lechon" (roasted pork).

Although Misuari and some MNLF leaders saw through the Marcos ploy, other MNLF commanders decided to play along with him, their decision made easier by the perks and privileges in the form of logging concessions, sardine importation quotas, and other largesse that Marcos heaped on them. But even as certain MNLF commanders and their troops dallied with Marcos, the NPA engaged government troops in several skirmishes in non-Moro provinces not only in Mindanao but also in the Visayas and Luzon. Some NPA leaders and sympathizers would see me at later dates in attempts to recruit me to their side in the struggle for the restoration of freedom in the country.

Church-based Media Harassed

With more absolute powers now in his hands, Marcos decided to tough it out with media outlets — no matter how small — that began to show signs of independence. Like an oncologist who uses radiation to root out cancer cells still embedded in the body of a patient, Marcos now wanted even insignificant news outlets excised from the ranks of the legitimate media. He ordered the military to harass and padlock the more vociferous ones like *The Communicator, The Signs of the Times* and the *Political Detainees Updates* in Manila and much later, *Ang Bandillo (The Announcer)*, in Bukidnon. These were Church-based media organizations that dared to publish items irksome to the Marcos regime, particularly the military.

The Communicator was a weekly newsletter that the Jesuits published with Fr. James B. Reuter as editor. The newsweekly "chronicled the behavior of the government, printing facts not available in the Marcos-controlled media." On December 5, 1976, Col. James Barbers of the Western Police District and Lt. Col. Rolando Abadilla of the Metrocom served the orders issued by Defense Minister Enrile to close down the publications office of *The Communicator*. Barbers and Abadilla were assisted by Lt. Col. Laurel Valdez, Jr., Lt. Panfilo Lacson and Lt. Dennis Nazaire of the Metrocom and by officers of the WPD, Lt. Col. Narciso Cabrera and Maj. Vicente Vinarao, the *Daily Express* reported on December 6, 1976. Incidentally, Abadilla was implicated in the murder of a shoemaker in an article that appeared in *The*

1976: JIM REUTER, SJ, editor of The Communicator, turned the tables on his accusers.

Communicator. His personal motives in carrying out the closure order were rather obvious.

Days later the military formally charged Fr. Reuter with subversion, inciting to rebellion, and dozens of other charges arising from the publication of *The Communicator.* The trial lasted for 12 days during which the Marcos-controlled press played up the charges — obviously in a bid to cow other publications into toeing the government line.

As events subsequently showed, the government, made a monumental blunder in bringing Reuter to trial. The international press picked up Reuter's trial and gave it more attention than the government wanted. The international attention alarmed Marcos and his publicists. Criticisms against his regime coming from sources within the Catholic Church and published by the international media placed him in a bad light, especially in the eyes of the US. And, more than anything else, Marcos wanted international approbation and US support to continue for the martial law government.

It did not come as a surprise then that, in the case of Reuter that the Marcos government flip-flopped. Instead of pursuing the case against him to its predetermined conclusion, Marcos ordered the termination of the case and granted amnesty to him and his co-accused.

In a sense, Reuter gave the Marcos regime no choice. He had earlier turned the tables on his accusers through his counter-affidavit, a document that allowed a person under investigation, to explain his or her side. With clear logic and concise statements of facts, Reuter's counter-affidavit demolished the charges leveled against him and the other individuals who worked with *The Communicator.* Reuter, for instance, explained that one of the articles objected to by the military entitled, "Please burn this!" was not at all subversive. The title of the story was the ending of a note from a girl who described the travails of her boyfriend who had been in prison since the beginning of martial law. The girl, he said, was simply questioning why her boyfriend was still in detention.

Fr. Reuter then raised the issue in his counter-affidavit:

(Was) it an obligation, for everyone living in the Philippines under the present regime, to be silent about anything that is done by the government or by the military? If any person voice(d) a protest of this kind, (was) this subversion? Was any protest against the government, or against this regime or against the military, subversion?

It was a devastating argument that the military could not refute without coming out badly in the exchange. That is why, in the end, the regime ordered the termination of the investigation of the respondents. In a sense, the amnesty was granted not to give a respite to Reuter and his co-accused but to provide the government with graceful exit from the mess they had created.

Before the happy ending to his travails, Fr. Reuter, true to his calling as a leader, assumed full responsibility for every issue and for every article published in *The Communicator* and exculpated his co-respondents, Sr. Elizabeth Farley, RSCJ; Nelia R. Paculan; Lina D. Lomibao; Blesila Angels; Sr. Mary Aurelie Cortes, SPC; Rosario Castro Aquino; Jaime Jamero; Isagani Diaz; Sarah Manapol; Joan Espay; Lucina Sarmiento; and Fr. Paul Sheehan, SJ.

Bing and I were surprised that Sheehan, who officiated at our wedding and was my religion teacher in the Ateneo de Cagayan High School in Cagayan de Oro, was implicated by the military for the alleged subversive items published by *The Communicator*. Like Reuter, Sheehan was no subversive even in the context of martial law. At the personal level, I felt so useless that I could not do anything to help him out of his problem.

Subsequently, however, we were gladdened by the report that the charges filed against him and his co-accused eventually fell apart not only because those were based on very tenuous grounds but also because trying Reuter, Sheehan and company proved a rather difficult task even for the martial law government. Reuter, particularly, was not only an accomplished media practitioner in the country, he also had numerous contacts abroad. And his contacts abroad made sure that every move that he made to defend himself and staff of *The Communicator* was given adequate publicity.

The Signs of the Times, a mimeographed publication of the Association of Major Religious Superiors of the Philippine (AMRS), was likewise closed upon orders of Defense Minister Enrile. According to the *Daily Express*, Enrile's order was issued pursuant to a recommendation of Maj. Gen. Fidel Ramos, chief of the Constabulary. According to the newspaper, Ramos found:

[The articles of the two publications were] evidently scurrilous libel against the government of the Philippines and the duly constituted authorities thereof, and...tend(ed) to suggest or incite rebellious conspiracies or riots and (led) or tend(ed) to stir up the people against the lawful authorities or disturb the peace of the community.

As was done to *The Communicator*, the closure of *The Signs of the Times*, was also carried out under the supervision of Col. Barbers of the WPD and Lt. Col. Abadilla of the Metrocom.

In a statement published by the *Times Journal* of December 8, 1976, Enrile justified the closure of *The Signs of the Times*. He said:

> [The publication was closed for] knowingly print[ing] subversive propaganda and systematically perpetrat[ing] libel...by deliberately printing materials notoriously known to be false, or in reckless disregard as to whether they were true or not.

The Provincial of the Jesuits at that time, Fr. Joaquin Bernas, was quoted in the same newspaper that the closure of the periodicals was "a clear violation of the freedom of the press and expression in the most blatant manner." Violation of press freedom or not, the periodicals stayed closed. But if people thought that the closures of the *Communicator* and the Signs ended the friction between the restive churchmen and women and the martial law government, they were wrong.

Ten months later, on October 5, 1977, 15 members of various religious orders — eight men and seven women — who were current or past members of the executive board of the AMRS were summoned to attend a preliminary hearing of the charges against them at Camp Crame in Quezon City. The men were Fr. Toti Olaguer, SJ; Fr. Benigno Mayo, SJ; Fr. Lope Castillo, MSC; Fr. Florante Camacho, SVD; Fr. James Noonan, MM; Bro. Rolando Dizon, FSC; Fr. Benjamin Ortazon, CM; and Fr. Carlos Oeteghem, CICM. The women were Sr. Christine Tan, RGS; Sr. Emelina Villegas, ICM; Sr. Carmel Carpio, MM; Sr. Angela Ansaldo, RA; Sr. Irene Dabalus, OSB; Sr. Avelina Alcaneses, FMN; and Sr. Natividad Asuncion, DC. They were made to explain their role in the publication of the Signs *of the Times.*

Within the same period, the military closed down two Church-affiliated radio stations: DXBB, run by the diocese of Malaybalay, Bukidnon; and DXCD, owned by the Maryknoll fathers in Davao. The personnel of the two radio stations were summoned by military authorities to answer charges of sedition and subversion, but as predicted by Fr. Reuter, nothing came out of the investigations of *The Signs of the Times* and of the radio stations. Bishops Joseph Regan of the Tagum Diocese and Francisco Claver of the Malaybalay Diocese denounced the closures of their radio stations as nothing but pure government harassment.

Bishop Francisco Claver, SJ, of Malaybalay, Bukidnon, best captured the essence of the struggle against censorship when, in June 1978, he urged in a pastoral letter for the Bukidnon diocese that Christians must "proclaim the truth from the housetops."

The Bishop said:

> [The proclamation of the truth] was decreed to be a crime from the very beginning of martial law. It had to be. For the political structure that rose up

ready-made from its imposition was founded on untruth and it has been
propped up from then on with further untruths. It was not, thus, surprising
that the slightest criticisms written or broadcast over radio rattled the martial
law regime not because of their wide circulation or reach but because the regime
was scared of hearing the truth.

In Kibawe, Bukidnon, following the closure of DXBB, Fr. Godofredo
Alingal, SJ, the parish priest, introduced an innovation to news propagation
to his parishioners. He constructed a huge blackboard in front of the church
where items deemed relevant to the times were written for all to read. His
parishioners loved the idea and called it the "Blackboard News Service."
Some powerful people, however, apparently, hated the idea. Years later,
after receiving many death threats, Alingal was shot dead inside his convent,
a martyr to the cause of truth and freedom.

PDU in Hit-List

Also in the hit-list of the military was a mimeographed publication,
the *Political Detainees Updates*, of the Task Force Detainees of the Philippines.
Task Force Detainees was supervised by a gutsy nun, Sister Marianni
Dimaranan, SFIC, under the auspices of the AMRS. *PDU* had its offices at
the compound of the Religious of the Virgin Mary sisters in Quezon City.
As its title suggested, the paper documented the arrest, detention and torture
of detainees. It also branched out into the reporting of the salvaging, massacre
of civilians, involuntary disappearances and other human rights violations.
It was no wonder that the military was not too happy with the publication
even if it only had a modest circulation. They had Sr. Marianni "invited" to
report to Camp Crame and kept her in detention there for three months.
Before and after that detention, she, her office and the convent of the St.
Joseph's Sisters of which she was a member were placed under constant
surveillance.

Sister Marianni, however, refused to be cowed. She continued her work
with *PDU* and later assumed the chair of Task Force Detainees that published
the *PDU* continuously despite the constraints of martial rule. Off and on,
the harassments against the Task Force Detainees came. On September 8,
1982, a group of fully armed men in plainclothes, led by a certain Lt. de la
Cruz forcibly entered the Task Force Detainees' Iloilo office. The raiding
team carted away the filing cabinets, including the documents and files,
office equipment, relief goods and cash amounting to P1,200.

Some of the Task Force Detainees workers were killed or simply
disappeared during the martial law years. A Task Force Detainee worker,
24-year-old Rizaldy Maglantay of Ibajay, Aklan, was "salvaged" or
extrajudicially executed by military men on August 3, 1985. He died of
multiple stab wounds. Another employee, Albert Enriquez, a fifth-year civil

engineering student in Lucena City, was abducted by plainclothes military men on August 29, 1985. He was not seen again.

The *PDU* was so committed to the truth that it named the tortured and the torturer whenever it had documents to prove its allegation. It pointed to the Military Intelligence and Security Group (MISG) of the Metrocom at Camp Crame as the main perpetrator of torture and maltreatment of detainees during the martial law era.

PDU's special issue of June 7, 1978 was an example of the kind of reporting that the military did not like. That nine-page issue specifically identified certain officers like 1st Lt. Dencio Laurico, 2nd Lt. Pacis (first name not mentioned), Rolly Banta (rank not mentioned), Balao and Peralta (first names and ranks not mentioned) and Constable 1st Class Pat Ordona as the key officers involved in the torture of detainees who were rounded up in

1978: TRINING HERRERA was severely tortured by her military jailers.

April and May of that year. In the same issue, the *PDU* said that a civilian by the name of Ric (last name not mentioned) also took part in hitting the detainees. The publication also reported that 1st Lieutenant Matillano (first name not mentioned) was charged with the torture of Trinidad Herrera, leader of the homeless of Zone One Tondo in Manila. Herrera was a candidate of Laban in the Interim Batasang Pambansa elections of 1978.

The *PDU* likewise named the victims. The victims included Mario S. Cayabyab, 30, a former mechanical student at the FEATI University in Manila; his wife, Melvin Mendez, 31, a masteral student in social work at the UP; Eduardo Blanco, 23, a former high school student at Beata, Pandacan, Manila; Jose Duran, 25, a Fine Arts student at UP; Rogelio Dagar, 28, a helper electrician at Bago-Bantay, Quezon City; and Eduardo Hills, 25, a Journalism student at the Lyceum of the Philippines in Manila.

The victims told the *PDU* that beatings, water cure (water poured into the victim's nostrils with his or her face covered with a piece of cloth, usually a hand towel) electric shock (electric wires attached to thumbs, toes or genitals of the victims and activated by telephone cranks), hanging one of the victims upside down and subjecting the female victim to sexual indignities were the varied forms of torture they suffered.

'Torture Not Official Policy'

I took pains to narrate some gory details of the tortures suffered by victims named above to refute the facile assertions of Marcos and his Defense Minister, Enrile, that torture was not a policy of the government — implying therefore that widespread torture of detainees did not take place. Of course Marcos did not decree that torture was an official policy of the government. But, official policy or not, it was a fact that so many of our young people suffered brutal treatment in the hands of those in power during the martial law era.

Enrile did not only deny the use of torture by the military in local press interviews, he also claimed as much in a letter to the US Congress, then investigating the exposé of Primitivo Mijares. The Enrile letter said that "torture was more the exception than the rule" under the martial law regime of Marcos.

Liberation Theology

The military crackdown on the media activities of Catholic priests, nuns and lay people was intended to preempt the apparent restiveness of the members of the Catholic clergy from exploding into an all-out rebellion against the government. Some priests, like Fr. Frank Navarro in Surigao, Fr. Conrado Balweg in the Cordilleras, Fr. Jose Nacu in Baguio City, and Fr. Ed de la Torre in the Greater Manila area, were not only vocally critical of the government, they had joined armed groups actually rebelling against the government. In any event, the Marcos harassment of the Church personnel who were involved in the peaceful, as opposed to the violent, resistance failed to deter the growing nonviolent Opposition to the government.

For the ideologically inclined, it was an article of faith that Marcos was threatening Church activists — priests, nuns and laypeople alike — to prevent them from following the lead of South American priests who rebelled against their respective governments and were attracting support from the masses by their espousal of liberation theology. The theology, in effect, held that priests and the religious would be true to their vocations not only when they prayed with the people but especially when they worked with them in actively dismantling the oppressive structures of society. A Peruvian priest, Gustavo Gutierrez, who was reportedly the first to use the term *liberation theology* in 1973, became the guru of local priests, who believed that Christ's teachings called for "liberating the people of the world from poverty and oppression."

Aside from Gustavo Gutierrez, I think that the papal encyclicals, *Lumen Gentium* (1964), and *Populorum Progressio* (1967) and the resolutions of the South American bishops in Medellin, Colombia, (1968) fueled the entry of a good number of priests, nuns and laypeople of the Catholic Church in the country into the arena of poverty alleviation. Collectively, these church teachings held that the Catholic faithful, not only the bishops, had the responsibility of fulfilling the mission of the Church and of exercising its preferential option for the poor.

More directly, however, I attributed the radicalization of the domestic clergy to the fact that martial law had built a wall between the people and the government. Before martial rule was imposed, people could go to their local and national officials when oppressed by the powerful. Under martial rule, the access had been effectively diminished, especially when the oppressors came from the military sector. In its May 1984 issue, *Mother Jones*, a left-of-center magazine, published a brief explanation of my thesis:

> The ongoing pattern of harassment and injustice has come face to face with the Church. Filipinos who experience injustice and oppression can no longer go to their government. They go to their priest instead. The priest...gets emotional about the injustice. And when it happens over and over, he gets radicalized.

In the magazine's opinion, it was "the best explanation for the leftist tendencies of some clergy."

As a layman, I was disappointed that the leaders of the Catholic Church did not immediately seem to mind the replacement of the democratic system of government by an autocratic government that was imposed by martial law. It seemed to me then that they were doing a Pontius Pilate, washing their hands in a sterile wait-and-see attitude while the rights of thousands of the unlettered, the powerless and the poor for whom they were supposed to have a preferential option were being oppressed. The ambivalent attitude of the Church, I think, enabled martial law to last until 1986.

Other incidents also made 1976 a benchmark of sorts in the struggle against the martial law regime.

In that year, the government signed the onerous Bataan Nuclear Plant deal with Westinghouse.

Amendment No. 6

In October of the year, Marcos also ordered the holding of another referendum to amend the Constitution again. Specifically, the people were asked to answer whether or not they wanted:

(1) Martial law continued;
(2) Marcos to continue ruling by decree; and
(3) A provisional parliament created.

As expected, the Comelec reported that the people voted a consolidated (96%) in favor of Marcos's wishes. Without the people's realizing it, their supposed approval of the questions raised in the referendum made Marcos a super legislature. Even if a provisional parliament, the Interim Batasang Pambansa, would be created, Marcos still retained the power to continue ruling by decree — which could thrash the laws passed by it. This super amendment became known as the infamous Amendment No. 6.

The net effect of the numerous referenda that were held over several years from the proclamation of martial law in 1972 up to 1976, as the Civil Liberties Union put it succinctly, was that "President Marcos acquired greater and more absolute powers under the amendment than under martial rule."

Mijares Disappears

In January of 1977, Primitivo Mijares decided to test the sincerity of Marcos's offer to let him come home and serve his government again.

Boni Gillego tried to dissuade Mijares from going home. Boni advised Mijares that he was putting his life in extreme danger by going home. He believed there was no way Mijares could get back into Marcos's good graces. Mijares, however, thought otherwise. He decided to go back to Manila. But the closest he came to home was Guam. He was said to have disembarked in Guam from a commercial flight from the US. Thereafter, he disappeared and was not heard of again. Sadly, nobody — except Steve Psinakis — seriously sought to find out who was responsible for his disappearance or why and how he vanished without any trace. It was apparently just assumed that he received his just deserts from the dictatorship he had betrayed. Not too many knew that he also paid for his audacity in publicly criticizing Marcos with the life of his teenaged son, Luis, who was brutally murdered in Manila in May 1977.

Shortly before Mijares disappeared, two persons were seen in his company. Crisostomo Ibarra, according to Cesar Arellano, the MFP leader in the Midwest, USA, was a frequent companion of Mijares before he took the flight for home via Guam. The other was Querube Macalintal, who boarded the same plane that Mijares took to Guam.

Psinakis, who had prodded Mijares to testify in the US Congress against Marcos, lobbied the US government to prosecute certain Marcos agents, whom he suspected were responsible for Mijares's disappearance. He did not go far. The US government did not even start an investigation into the Mijares disappearance. It also did not decisively conclude its investigation into the Marcos government's attempt to bribe Mijares to dissuade him from testifying in the US Congress. The circumstance that led to the perceived whitewash of the case was reportedly the "close personal friendship" of the Marcoses with US President Reagan.

Ninoy Sentenced to Death

In the year, two major events exercised the Opposition. One was the sentencing of Ninoy Aquino to death by the military tribunal. The other was the escape of Serge Osmeña III and Geny Lopez, Jr., from the maximum security cells at Fort Bonifacio.

Ninoy had predicted that the military tribunal trying him would have no recourse than to sentence him to death. Still, when it happened, the shock of it hit us quite severely. His lawyer went to the Supreme Court to question the proceedings of the military tribunal that imposed the capital punishment on him.

Serge & Geny Escape

While the issue of Ninoy's death sentence was pending in the Supreme Court, Serge and Geny dealt a severe blow to the massive ego of Marcos. Three years earlier, the two had staged a hunger strike, which they aborted on the promise of Marcos that he would eventually release them. But, Marcos did not honor his promise. For a while, Serge and Geny suffered their solitary confinement in silence in their cells at Fort Bonifacio. And in the US, Lopez, the father, now and then gave agonizing statements to the US-based Philippine Media that he probably wouldn't see his son again before he died. Lopez was right. He died in 1975 about two years before his son, Geny and Serge escaped from their cells at Fort Bonifacio at 3 o'clock at dawn of October 1, 1977.

The Philippine News, published by Alex Esclamado, and other anti-Marcos US-based media banner headlined the great escape. Fort Bonifacio was the regime's premier military camp and the location of its maximum-security prison. Hence the news of their successful flight to Hong Kong and then to the US made the Marcos regime look silly. It provided grist for the rumor mills in Manila that the US was getting dissatisfied with his authoritarian ways and had thus assisted in making Osmeña's and Lopez's escape possible.

The two, however, had time and again publicly repeated that their successful escape was planned and implemented mainly by the efforts of their respective families and friends, and not by US agents covert or otherwise. The 1995 movie, *Escapo*, revealed the details of their flight. Serge made it clear that the filmmakers took liberties with the facts. Among other things, he said, the movie had a sequence in which a soldier shot at their speeding getaway car but, the truth is, that they got off without anyone noticing their having escaped until they were already on board a plane on their flight to freedom.

In December, Marcos asked the people in another referendum whether or not they wanted him to continue in office as both president and prime minister after the organization of the Interim Batasang Pambansa as provided for in Amendment No. 6 of the Constitution. Like a robot that was programmed to do the wish of its master, the Comelec announced that the people voted to grant Marcos's desires by a vote of 89.53%.

Chapter 16

Laban in the IBP Elections

In 1978, Marcos called for elections to the Interim Batasang Pambansa, his martial law parliament. He said the elections would be free and anyone qualified under the law was free to participate in it. Moreover, he also assured the people that free speech would be respected during the campaign.

I did not know immediately how to respond to this latest overture of Marcos. What I knew personally was that our leaders — including Macapagal, Tañada, Roxas, Diokno and Salonga — did not want to participate in the elections.

Salonga, in fact, convinced the Liberal Party stalwarts in Manila to follow his stand and boycott the elections. Some oppositionists, however, were eager to participate in the elections. Among them were Jaime Ferrer, Ramon Mitra, Jr., Charito Planas and Juan T. David. But by themselves, they knew that they could not mount a credible electoral challenge against the candidates of Marcos.

There was one man who could do that: Benigno "Ninoy" Aquino, whom most people saw as the best and most credible challenger of Marcos. Ninoy, however, was in jail in Fort Bonifacio. And his party, the LP, had through Salonga already made known its disinclination to join in the elections.

Ninoy Decides to Run

Ninoy, however, was a political maverick. He did not need much prodding to take up Marcos's dare. He saw that the IBP elections would provide a unique chance for him and those who did not like martial rule to speak out and bring the issues directly to the people. Hence, he announced forthwith that he was running for a seat in the Interim Batasang Pambansa for Metro Manila. While Ninoy saw that he would not lose anything by doing so, he, however, faced at least three major obstacles.

One, he was in jail. It was, thus, difficult for him to mobilize support of his candidacy. Since the media was controlled, even those of us who looked up to him as our leader, learned of his decision to run only by word of mouth from our mutual friends. Ninoy, of course, was not only a detainee; he was a death convict who had been sentenced by a military court on November 25, 1977 to die by firing squad.

Most people did not even know of Ninoy's courageous refusal to defend himself at his trial before the court martial organized by Marcos in 1973. He called the military tribunal a "kangaroo court" that would have no choice but to convict him at all costs. He said that no amount of legal argument could erase the fact that its members would do the bidding of their commander-in-chief, Marcos. It was a fact, he added, that Marcos had appointed them to their positions as colonels and generals. Ninoy sensed that his polemics would not dissuade the military officers from convicting him as Marcos wanted.

The second obstacle was that he did not have the support of the pillars of the Opposition. Former President Macapagal, for instance, did not want to participate in the Interim Batasang Pambansa elections. Neither did Senator Roxas, president of the Liberal Party, or Senator Salonga, who was more directly in contact with the rest of us in the Opposition at the time. Their common argument was that anyone running against the candidates of Marcos during martial law did not have any chance of winning. Worse, they said, that participating in the election would only legitimize his rogue regime.

The other problem was that Ninoy's candidacy put him in a direct collision course with Imelda Marcos, who had been proclaimed as the martial law administration's lead candidate for the IBP seats for Metro Manila. Hence, people saw that the contest in Metro Manila would be a bruising battle between Ninoy's supporters and the Marcos machinery which would do everything to make Imelda win.

The odds were plainly against him. People instinctively felt that Marcos would use all the tricks of the political game and the powers of his office to ensure Ninoy's defeat. Ninoy, however, believed he could give Marcos a good fight or, at least, a good thrashing during the campaign period where the sins of the "Conjugal Dictatorship" would be exposed in public forums and in a manner that had not been done since the declaration of martial rule.

Knowing that he was up against the forces of the government — not an ordinary but a martial rule government — Ninoy decided that the only way he could put up a credible campaign against the Marcoses was to organize a *kamikaze* team to run against Imelda's group for the IBP seats in Metro Manila. His candidates would have to give their all in the campaign against Marcos. He, therefore, gave personal attention to the choosing of his bets.

Ninoy's *Kamikaze* Slate

Despite the ever-present threat against their civil liberties and their lives, 20 kamikaze candidates agreed to run with Ninoy to challenge Imelda and her team in the Metro Manila elections for the Interim Batasang Pambansa. His drawing power was such that name politicians like Senators Francisco Rodrigo and Ernesto Maceda, and Jaime Ferrer, Alejandro Roces, Congressman Neptali Gonzales and a legend in the legal profession, Juan T. David, in addition to Manila politicians, Vice Mayor Felicisimo Cabigao and Councilors Primitivo de Leon and Cesar Lucero, readily joined his ticket.

Rodrigo was a byword in the ranks of the Opposition to the martial law regime. A former senator, he was one of those jailed with Aquino upon the declaration of martial rule. His peerless poems in Tagalog exposed the pretensions of the regime that the predominantly Tagalog-speaking people, in Metro Manila, fully enjoyed. He was reputedly so good in disputation that, in the Ateneo de Manila where he did his Bachelor of Arts degree, they called him "Soc" for Socrates, the Greek philosopher, a nickname that stuck not only in his college days but all the days of his political life as well.

Ferrer, a former Comelec head, was another martial law opposition politician whom Ninoy included in his slate. Ferrer had made a name for himself as the no-nonsense chair of the Comelec immediately before the imposition of martial rule. Ferrer had criticized the excessive spending of Marcos in the 1969 and 1971 elections. For speaking the truth, Ferrer was called "an ingrate" by Marcos and was replaced as Comelec Chair on May 28, 1973.

Maceda, an incumbent senator when martial law was proclaimed, had won under the banner of the Nacionalista Party headed by Marcos. He was, at one time, a member of the Marcos Cabinet. His wife, Marichu Vera Perez, said that Imelda was so jealous of Maceda's access to Marcos that she made it abundantly clear that he was no longer welcome in Malacañang.

Roces, an educator, was arguably the most articulate critic of the country's political and cultural scene. Born into the respected and wealthy Roces clan in Manila, he was a master in mixing deadly factual criticism of the Marcos regime with scathing humor that people found most entertaining.

Gonzales, a recognized legal authority, was professor of law and author of legal treatises. He was a dynamic pillar of the Opposition in the House of Representatives before Marcos shut it down upon the proclamation of martial law.

Ninoy also got moderate political activists like Tito Guingona, Charito Planas, Ernie Rondon and Noli T. Santos and UP student leader Jerry Barrican into his ticket.

Guingona, a dynamo in business, espoused ideas that defied the orthodoxy in capitalist Manila. He believed in propagating small businesses and protecting local industries from undue competition by foreign corporations. As a delegate to the Constitutional Convention of 1971, he fearlessly condemned Marcos for attempting to manipulate the work of the Convention. He was one of those arrested upon the proclamation of martial law.

Planas, an active civic leader, espoused the rights of women and other progressive causes. A lawyer, she was the executive secretary of the Integrated Bar of the country.

Rondon, a radio man, was known for his tirades against government wrongdoing. A pro-peasant activist, he came from the province of Nueva Ecija, where the insurgency of the Left had a strong following. Although he was not a communist, he expressed support for the causes espoused by the Left, like land reform and the dismantling of the US military bases.

Santos a young lawyer, educator and business entrepreneur, was an aggressive exponent of the "Filipino-First" business philosophy for the country.

Barrican, a prominent UP student leader, spoke for the rights of the youth. Articulate and personable, he was looked up to by the youth as a "progressive" and as a role model.

There were two concessions to the Left: Alex Boncayao and Trinidad Herrera. Boncayao was a labor leader and Herrera, a leader of the urban poor in Tondo, the poorest area in Manila. They had been separately arrested, detained and tortured by their jailors. Boncayao was made to sit on ice blocks for hours, and subjected to other brutalities as well. Herrera was subjected to sexual indignities that included electric shocks through wires wrapped around her thumbs and nipples.

Aside from recruiting known Manila oppositionists and activists of various stripes in his ticket, Ninoy wanted its composition to represent the regions of the country as well. Since Luzon and Metro Manila were already well represented, he got Napoleon Rama to represent the Visayas. A nationally known author of many *Free Press* articles critical of Marcos, Rama was among the first batch of journalists arrested by the military when martial law was declared. Marcos could not forgive Rama's mortal sin against him: he was the principal author of the most publicized Ban-Marcos resolution in the Constitutional Convention.

Ninoy also choose me for inclusion in his ticket, apparently to represent Mindanao. Call it luck or *suerte* in Tagalog or Visayan, but I did absolutely nothing to cause my being drafted in the Laban slate. At that time, I had no personal contact with Ninoy at all. My best guess was that he heard that I was one of those who had steadfastly opposed Marcos from Day 1 of the Constitutional Convention all the way up to the end of our sessions. In our family, it was my father-in-law, Dr. Justo de la Llana, who was most happy with the fact that I was included in the Laban ticket Although he sensed that it was going to be a steep uphill struggle to beat Marcos's ticket in Metro Manila, he also saw signs that I might one day be moving up in the hierarchy of the elective offices of the country. Unfortunately, he passed away even before the Interim Batasan elections were held.

Visits with Ninoy

Even as we were the candidates of Ninoy, our visits to him at Fort Bonifacio were severely restricted. We got to see him once as a group. After that, I do not recall any other visit to his cell where I was present as a candidate of Laban. But our wives were given permission to call on him. Of course, Marcos's propagandists gave our and our wives' separate visits to Ninoy a spin. They said it was a sign of Marcos's magnanimity.

Bing came away from the meeting of the wives of the Laban candidates with Ninoy completely sold to the idea of the justness of his cause. Ninoy, of course, had his way with ladies. For instance, he told Bing graciously that she "didn't look as fat" as she had been described to him. Naturally, she liked that compliment, but more fundamentally, Bing and the Laban women came home convinced that Ninoy was waging a crusade to save the nation from the Marcoses in which they too had a stake.

In the meantime, Ninoy adopted Laban both as the name of his political group and its battle cry in the looming political showdown with Imelda for the Batasang Pambansa seats in Metro Manila. As a Visayan-speaking native of Mindanao, I was not comfortable with the word. In the Visayas and in Mindanao, the word *"laban"* meant "to side with or to favor something." Soc Rodrigo had to explain to us that *laban* in Tagalog meant "fight," even as it was also the shortened name of the new Opposition party, *Lakas ng Bayan*, Power of the People. In the end, I realized that *"laban"* appropriately captured what we were doing. We were fighting the Marcos machinery electorally in Metro Manila where the *lingua franca* was Tagalog and simultaneously we were also subliminally egging the people to fight Marcos elsewhere in the country.

The Laban Campaign

In the Laban campaign, we hit Marcos and Imelda openly on the political stage throughout the metropolis. We were emboldened by the popular support we received as the campaign got into full swing. It was, however, not that encouraging at the start.

The first rally we had was held at a churchyard in Parañaque, the home turf of Ferrer. We chose Parañaque because Ferrer was known for his willingness to stand up to Marcos. He had a solid reputation for integrity and was known to have many followers from his guerilla days who were likewise not intimidated by Marcos or his goons.

Despite Ferrer's acknowledged drawing power, we found ourselves holding a rally in a churchyard on an improvised stage with a single flickering electric bulb to light up the place. On one pretext or another, the mayor did not give us a permit to hold the rally at the town plaza. But we knew that the real reason was that the mayor wanted to show Marcos that he was his man in Parañaque.

Only a handful of people were in attendance, with one or two brave souls standing in front of the stage and some individuals furtively lurking in the shadows. They were afraid of being seen by the loyalists of Marcos or, worse, by the dreaded Metrocom, the Metropolitan Police Command, which had the meeting place under surveillance. I saw two marked Metrocom police cars parked ominously beside the churchyard.

1978: *WITH NINOY AQUINO locked up in his prison cell, we in his Laban party conducted a blistering campaign against the evils of martial rule.*

'Bomba'

The presence of military and police agents, however, failed to dampen our individual or collective attacks, *bomba* in Tagalog, against martial rule and the Marcoses. We hammered away at the Marcoses for human rights violations, for corruption and militarizing the governance of the nation.

We cited specific instances of wanton misuse of public funds in projects like the Bataan Nuclear Plant, which was built on of an earthquake fault line and had several construction defects. We also denounced the human rights abuses of the martial law government, like the tortures of detainees. We cited as an example, Liliosa Hilao, who was found hanging in her cell in Camp Crame, ostensibly a suicide but, as the evidence showed, a victim of foul play and rape by her jailors.

We hit Imelda for her luxurious lifestyle, her unjustifiable use of public funds for a private event like the hosting of the Miss Universe Pageant, and her obvious lust for power in that she was not content at being named Metro Manila Governor by Marcos but also had to be appointed Minister of Human Settlements. As Minister of Human Settlements, her jurisdiction covered the country and made her the handler of international funds given to the country for the housing needs of the people.

Although the sparse crowd at the rally was mesmerized by the open and uninhibited manner by which we reproached the Marcoses, they were so unlike our vibrant people in the pre-martial law days who applauded, shouted and demonstrated their response in line with the mood of the speakers on the stage. In my view, the audience in the Parañaque rally was simply too scared to manifest their feelings. Since the imposition of martial law in 1972, they had not heard any criticism or verbal attacks against the dictatorship uttered in the terms we used to berate the Marcoses and publicly at that over a blaring sound system at the rally. While their passivity was understandable, it was certainly frustrating.

The timidity of the audience at our opening salvo against the Marcoses in the Parañaque churchyard reflected the paralyzing fear that martial rule worked upon our people. Up to that time, martial rule had created demigods of the Marcoses who could do no wrong and whose misdeeds, if any, could be mentioned only in whispers. We, therefore, could hardly blame the people if they were too afraid to express their resentments against the martial law regime openly. Indeed, even political leaders like former President Macapagal had tried to seek refuge in the US Embassy in Manila after writing a book critical of the regime in 1976. Incidentally, the US Embassy officials politely turned down his request for asylum.

In any event, in the Laban campaign we found out that the fear of the people to show their support for us was not the only major factor that we had to overcome. We also discovered that despite Marcos's assurances, the political playing field was not level at all. Marcos and his minions made things difficult for our campaign even to take off. It was, for instance, common for the mayors of the cities and municipalities in Metro Manila to deny us the use of the public plazas for our rallies as the mayor of Parañaque had done. It was also not unusual for electric power to be cut off in the places where we held our rallies, as in the municipality of San Juan, and for hooligans to make petty commotions to disrupt our meetings.

With Ninoy locked up in his cell, we tried our best to conduct a blistering campaign against the evils of martial rule even without him. In my case, I found the campaign more of a unique opportunity to highlight the ills that martial rule had inflicted upon the people rather than as a contest for a seat in the Interim Batasan. I found it gratifying that, as the campaign period progressed, the crowds were getting larger and more positively appreciative of the issues against martial rule than at its start. Since nobody was reported to have been arrested for his or her bias for Ninoy and the Laban slate, more people began to attend our rallies. With those encouraging signs, we believed that Ninoy, who was clearly the darling of the people even as he remained confined in Fort Bonifacio, would still come out a winner. Every time we mentioned the injustice of his incarceration, people heartily applauded. We interpreted the warmth of the people's response to mean that our message picturing Marcos as a tyrant who oppressed those who disagreed with him was getting across.

Ninoy's TV Appearance

Despite Marcos's announcement that rules of fair play would govern the electoral campaign, Ninoy was allowed to speak to the people only once in a nationally televised interview. It was conducted by Ron Nathanielz, a Marcos partisan, in March 1978. Nonetheless, in that one TV appearance, Ninoy captured the attention of the Metropolis and the nation. Everyone sat glued to the tube, listening to every word that he said. For once, the ever-crowded streets of Metro Manila were empty of people and vehicles as everyone stayed put, watching the televised interview in their homes, in restaurants or in hotels.

With that single TV interview, Ninoy enthralled the nation and captivated the viewers so palpably that Marcos and his Comelec felt that his wife could not win unless the elections were manipulated. Buoyed by his performance, we begun to entertain the thought that Rodrigo, Ferrer, Roces, Maceda, Gonzales and even Planas had good chances of landing seats in the Interim Batasan.

In my case, nobody — least of all I — believed that I had any chance of winning at all. I never believed that I could win, first, because my Tagalog was so atrocious that even the statements that I meant to be taken seriously sounded like jokes; and, second, because aside from my brief stint as a delegate to the Constitutional Convention, I had no political standing at all in Metro Manila.

Secret Weapon

While there were natural crowd drawers in the Laban ticket who held their own against the best that Marcos fielded in the campaign, the secret weapon of Ninoy and our Laban slate was no politician but his and Cory's seven-year-old daughter, Kris. She was so small, we often had to lift her to stand on a stool so that the audience could see her as she did her appeal before

1978: KRIS AQUINO and me at a Laban rally. Kris was Laban's secret weapon.

a microphone. Her brief message was simple and direct to the point. She told our audiences that Marcos had unjustly imprisoned her dad. The sight of a little girl pleading with the people in an angelic voice that only the truly innocent possessed to vote for her dad was, in my mind, worth more than the combined passionate rhetoric of the Laban candidates. Kris easily got the empathy of the crowd and her childlike appeal full of pathos filled many eyes with tears as she described how Marcos had mercilessly taken her father away from her, her mom and family.

For all his brilliance, Marcos did not quite know immediately how to respond to the inroads Kris was making for her father into the hearts of Metro Manilans as we intensified our campaign. Marcos could not very well imprison her. The people wouldn't stand for that — martial law or not. Neither could he afford to stage an incident where Kris could be hurt. The people would see through the ruse in the same manner that they saw through the stage-managed ambush of Enrile's car near Wack-Wack Golf Club that Marcos had used as the trigger for his declaration of martial rule. So Marcos did the next best thing he could think of without exacting an immediate backlash from the people. He mobilized the city and municipal mayors and the barangay officials of Metro Manila to go all out in support of Imelda and her ticket no matter what it took.

Noise Barrage

Anticipating massive cheating on Election Day, Laban leaders called for a Metro Manila-wide "noise barrage" on its eve, April 6, 1978. The noise barrage was meant to express the people's support for Ninoy Aquino and their outrage at what we saw was the impending manipulation of the polls. The people's response was nothing short of amazing. Indeed in living memory, I have never witnessed anything even remotely similar. From early evening up until midnight and in some places in Metro Manila even after midnight, people beat on pots and pans, rang church bells, honked cars and in general just made noise to rattle Marcos. Those who made noise after midnight took an added risk: all partisan activity was supposed to end by midnight of the day before the Election Day and engaging in any partisan political activity after the stroke of midnight was a criminal act. No matter. For a good number of Metro Manilans, at least on the eve of the election, they were no longer intimidated by Marcos's edicts. Even in Fairlane, a lower middle class subdivision in Marikina where I lived with my family, the ringing of bells and the honking of horns went on past midnight.

In that respect, the noise barrage achieved its purpose. The residents of Metro Manila made known their support for Ninoy, although, I think, it also alarmed Marcos so that he was all the more determined not to allow

1978: LABAN CAMPAIGN. The crowds grew bigger as the campaign began to take off. Here I address a huge crowd at a district rally in Metro-Manila.

Ninoy's victory by any means. Happily, even he did not know what was happening in our ranks in Laban so he could not exploit one circumstance that threatened to break Laban apart.

Within the week of Election Day, some supporters of Laban who said they represented the Left asked me, Charito Planas, Ernie Rondon, Juan T. David and some other candidates to officially withdraw from the race. They said there was no way we could win and if we continued with our candidacies, we would only legitimize the regime. I countered that they should come up with better reasons than what they proferred because, before we filed our certificates of candidacy, we already knew that we could not win. They then threatened to withdraw their support for us. I replied that, under the circumstances, I still could not go along with their suggestion without the people suspecting that we had been intimidated or, worse, bought by the Marcoses. As to the threat of their withdrawing support, I said there was nothing we could do about it. My colleagues aired pretty much the same views as mine. In the end, none of us withdrew from the race. I must admit, however, that there was no way I could verify whether or not the Left actually deserted us.

Election Day

On the day of the election, goons associated with KBL mayors manhandled our watchers and chased supporters out of school building precincts while the votes were being counted. In some instances, the hoodlums also snatched genuine ballot boxes and substituted them with pre-filled fake ballots for the KBL candidates. The cheating and the manipulation of the election were so massive and evident that the Catholic Bishops Conference called it an outright sham and not reflective of the people's will.

Senator Tañada, the campaign manager of Laban, officially wrote the Comelec on April 7, 1978, complaining against "election irregularities on a massive scale in Makati, Pasay City, Las Piñas, Pateros, Mandaluyong and Valenzuela *so far* ... which have made a mockery out of this election." Two days later, Tañada led a march against the fraudulent elections. The details of the march are set out in the next chapter.

Tañada assisted the Association of Major Religious Superiors document the anomalies perpetrated by KBL partisans in "A Report on the Anomalies and Irregularities in the Elections in Metro Manila." The report was dated September 21, 1978.

The 34-page single-spaced mimeographed AMRS report summarized the complaint of Laban and other election observers that:

> (1) Laban watchers were not allowed to enter the voting centers assigned to them and election Committees refused to open the ballot boxes, empty them and exhibit their contents to the public as required by the Election Code;

> (2) Laban campaign leaders and coordinators were arrested and detained on false charges, among them Councilor Cesar Alzona, Laban chairman of Makati (who was arrested by KBL Mayor Nemesio Yabut), and Amado Avecilla, Laban chairman of Pateros;

> (3) Laban voters and workers were threatened and made to open their ballots and change their votes in favor of the KBL. Those who refused were either chased out of the voting precincts or, worse, beaten up by KBL leaders and *tanods* (barangay police);

> (4) Teachers who were manning the voting booths were provided with 50 to 150 pre-filled ballot boxes; and

> (5) Flying voters were unloaded in Quezon City by busloads, mostly by Metro Manila Transit buses (run by the government under the supervision of Imelda Marcos, as governor of Metro Manila).

The report also quoted an open letter dated May 25, 1978 addressed to Education Minister Juan Manuel, his assistants and the Metro Manila Public School Teachers by 121 parents. Among other things, the open letter said:

> Today, we bow our heads in shame. It is no secret to you that several days before election-day on April 7, 1978, our public school teachers, supervisors and principals in

Metro Manila were given bribe money." In Manila, P200 was given to every school teacher, P500 to every principal, and P800 to every supervisor. The April 7 election was, the parents concluded, "the dirtiest election in our whole lifetime.

Marcos, nevertheless, had the Comelec, headed by his loyal henchman, Leonardo Perez of Nueva Vizcaya, proclaim Imelda and her entire ticket as the winners in the IBP election for Metro Manila. People were aghast at such an arrogant display of power. Nobody believed that Ninoy could be edged out of the 21 winning candidates by the likes of Pablo Floro, whose main claim to fame was that he was the principal stockholder of Crispa, a manufacturer of men's underwear, and owner of the Crispa basketball team, or by Alejandro Fider, or, indeed, even by Imelda herself.

The Comelec count had Ninoy leading the Laban candidates with 1.2 million votes as against Imelda's 1.7 million. While the count was spurious, to say the least, I kidded Tito Guingona, Ernie Rondon and Noli Santos that I scored higher than they in the election with 948,725 votes credited to me.

Despite the blatant and unscrupulous manner by which the KBL's massive electoral cheating was perpetrated in Metro Manila, the people did not appear ready to end martial rule. The time would come eight years later in 1986 and the trigger for the national effort to oust Marcos was not the sham Interim Batasan elections in 1978 but the assassination of Ninoy at the Manila International Airport in 1983. The murder, however, was still five years away into the future.

Fissures in KBL Ranks

In the meantime, Marcos tried to consolidate power as cracks began to show in the ranks of the Kilusan ng Bagong Lipunan (KBL). Marcos had intended the KBL to be the monolithic political party that would embrace all political personalities wanting to place themselves under his wings while martial rule tried to keep everyone else under leash.

He had every reason to mend his political fences because, aside from the mighty challenge that Laban gave to Imelda and the KBL in Metro Manila, Cagayan de Oro's charismatic and highly articulate political leader, Reuben Canoy, former Cabinet Deputy Minister of Information of Marcos and Cagayan de Oro mayor, won a seat in the IBP elections for Northern Mindanao. He bagged the seat without the blessings of the KBL and *against* the wishes of Emmanuel Pelaez, Marcos's chosen leader of the region. There was also an upset in Central Visayas where the entire 13-man Panaghiusa slate, led by Cebu candidates Natalio Bacalso, Fr. Jorge Kintanar, Felimon Fernandez and Hilario Davide, Jr., won handily over their KBL opponents, among who were name politicians like Eduardo Gullas, Lito Osmeña, Ramon Durano III and Tony Cuenco.

Cuenco was the odd-man in the KBL slate. Prior to the declaration of martial law, he was a known friend and supporter of Ninoy. Thus, his KBL party mates were wary of him and his former friends in the anti-Marcos groups in Central Visayas eyed him with suspicion. It was no wonder that he did not fare well in the IBP elections. While those factors debilitated Tony's bid, they did not apply to the rest of the KBL slate who were carefully chosen by Marcos and who received his full personal and financial support and that of the government. The reason why they lost was simple. The people were no longer pleased with martial rule and they voted for what they saw was the Opposition group in Central Visayas. Also, as fate would have it, the cheating machinery of the KBL and the Comelec malfunctioned. Pre-filled ballots and other fraudulent election paraphernalia intended for Cebu wound up in the other parts of the Visayas and were, therefore, unusable.

Chapter 17

My Second Arrest

1978: *IN CONFINEMENT, I see that "iron bars did not a prison make."*

Not surprisingly, the loudest and best-organized protest against the rigged elections came from Laban in Metro Manila. On April 7, Election Day, we saw on TV and heard on radio that Laban was routed by the KBL in all Metro Manila precincts, except in Jimmy Ferrer's home ground, Parañaque. Our leaders called for a meeting on April 8, during which we discussed what we should do. Some of our co-candidates cautioned against rushing into any activity that might provoke the worst response from Marcos. I argued that it would not look good for us as leaders to keep our heads low while the heads of our followers were being bashed. I said we had no right to claim the leadership of Laban unless we could show that we were not about to take the electoral abuses of Marcos sitting down. Soc Rodrigo, Tito Guingona and Ernie Rondon articulated similar views, which our leader Senator Tañada supported wholeheartedly. With Tañada in our corner, it was agreed that we would stage a protest march the following day.

Laban's Protest March

However, on April 9, out of 20 Laban candidates (Ninoy excluded because he was still in detention), only four of us, Soc, Tito, Ernie and I, joined the march that started at 2:10 p.m. I was disappointed that our other colleagues — Gonzales, David, Barrican, Cabigao, Ferrer, De Leon, Lucero, Maceda, Mitra, Martinez, Rama, Roces, Boncayao, Herrera, Planas and Santos — did not join us. In mitigation, I also knew that the military, especially the intelligence community was heated up against us Laban candidates, especially those whom they believed were associated with leftist organizations, like Boncayao, Herrera and Barrican. Thus discretion must have induced our party mates to think that the planned protest march would not amount to anything but create more problems for them.

Anyway, with Tañada leading and some 3,000 students making up the main body of the marchers, I put aside my disappointments and concentrated on the job at hand, which was to help arouse the anger of the people against Marcos and the Comelec for the recently held farcical IBP elections. At the scheduled hour, we filed defiantly out of the campus of St. Theresa's College, Quezon City, and proceeded towards Intramuros, Manila, where the Manila Cathedral and the Comelec headquarters were located. A group of students bearing two coffins symbolizing the death of democracy and the abuses of martial rule formed the vanguard of the march. Tañada, Soc, Tito, Ernie, Joker Arroyo and I marched immediately behind the coffins, while the rest of the protesters followed us.

I saw people at both sides of Quezon Avenue watching our protest march with quizzical looks on their faces. The elections were over only two days before and Marcos appeared even more entrenched than before. Ever the fighter, Tañada led us in shouting "Laban!" as we flashed the "L" sign with our thumbs and forefingers extended. Joker Arroyo, living up to his name, now and then let out a nervous guffaw and pointed to the incongruity of the occasion: we, the marchers, shouting our heads off with our anti-Marcos slogans and the onlookers betraying no sign at all that they understood what we were up to. Nonetheless, we went on with the march, putting up a brave front, stalling the traffic and creating a racket to attract the attention of the people.

Marchers Arrested

We had hardly gone a kilometer from our starting point when we were startled by a loud voice that said, "Stop! You are under arrest." Instinctively, those of us at the front of the march locked arms, *kapit bisig* in Tagalog, and looked toward the origin of the voice. We saw a uniformed police officer with

1978: TAÑADA, DEFIANT even under arrest, is flanked by Ruth Guingona and me partly covered by his arm. Joker Arroyo sits next to me and Soc Rodrigo is at the far right.

a bullhorn standing in front of a phalanx of heavily armed policemen. In an instant, we heard Tañada's voice loud and clear ask in lawyerly fashion, "What for?" The officer replied, "For marching without a permit." I breathed a sigh of relief at the response and told Ernie Rondon, "That's good news. We can get out of this problem in a jiffy." I was not able to explain what I meant to Ernie for the reason that we were being bundled up by the police into a police van (a Ford Fierra). Furthermore, there was a general commotion as thousands of feet scampered from our ranks into several directions to avoid arrest.

Incidentally, we later learned that the police officer who ordered us arrested was Police Col. Narciso Cabrera. His next in command was Police Maj. Jose de Jesus. Their names and positions were enumerated in the affidavit of Police Col. Elpidio Clemente y San Jose of the Northern Police District, dated April 9, 1978. The affidavit formed a part of the documents supporting the criminal charges that were prepared against us.

Now, even as he clambered into the police van, Tañada kept flashing the "L" sign and shouting "Laban!" to curious onlookers, who were watching from a safe distance on both sides of the avenue. Soc, Joker, Ernie and I followed Tañada into the van. Tito was about to board the van but, as Joker recounted later, he had difficulty doing so because Ruth, his wife, materialized at his side, grabbed him by the waist and would not let go of him. The arresting police then shoved both Tito and Ruth into the van. That was how, according to Joker, it came to pass that Ruth had to spend some days in detention with her husband at the Bicutan Rehabilitation Center, a military camp in Taguig, Metro Manila. The camp was where we landed on the night of our aborted march to the Manila Cathedral and to the Comelec. As for Joker, he tried to evade arrest by telling the police that he was merely the lawyer of the Laban candidates and, therefore, he should not be arrested with his clients. The police officers only stared at him and motioned that he should go up the van by himself or else. To my delight, he did.

The reason for our arrest, marching without a permit, according to Cabrera, the police officer who accosted us at the railroad crossing, was punishable only by a fine. That was why I told Ernie that we could get out of police custody in no time at all. But, when we got to the Western Police District Headquarters on UN Avenue in Manila, I sensed that the matter was no longer that simple. While we were waiting for the police to book us, I noticed a police officer carrying a pistol pass us by. He told another cop seated at a table in front of us in a voice loud enough for us to hear that the gun had been confiscated from one of the marchers. That was an ominous development.

The confiscation of a gun from a political demonstrator had grave implications not only for the possessor but also for his companions and even for the organizers. With that gun, I surmised that the police officers were laying the groundwork to upgrade our offence from a mere infraction of an ordinance (marching without a permit) to a more serious violation of criminal law that under the circumstances could be illegal assembly aggravated by the possession of a probably unlicensed firearm. The leaders of the march and the marchers could then be subjected to years of imprisonment, if not to the death penalty under the high mobility of martial law penalties that depended on the whims of Marcos.

In any case, at the WPD headquarters, I gave up hope that our peaceful march would be a walk in the park. As night fell, we were brought to the Judge Advocate's Office at the Metrocom Headquarters in Camp Crame where, as I guessed, we were booked for illegal assembly. From there, we were taken to Camp Aguinaldo, where we learned informally that we would also be charged with subversion, an offense that carried the death penalty.

Before 9 p.m., we were brought to and confined in separate cells in a building in the Bicutan camp. My cell (No. 11) was dingy and had only a small slatted window near the ceiling that was meant to be an air vent. King Rodrigo, son of Soc, was placed in Cell No. 12; Rondon in 13; Ruth Guingona in 14; her husband, Tito, in 15; Tañada in 16; Rodrigo in 17; and Arroyo in 18.

My cell had a faucet but no running water the lack of which was a normal feature of prison cells in the country. It also had no working toilet facilities. Only a broken pipe protruded about an inch from the floor, a forlorn remnant of what formerly was a flush toilet. I was told that, the day before our arrest, the inmates of what was now my cell had rioted and among the things they smashed was the toilet. The rioting inmates were transferred to individual cells elsewhere and I was then put in their cell.

It was through the remains of the sewage pipe on the floor that I relieved myself in the days of my confinement in the cell. I found it all so true that necessity is the mother of innovation, although at times modesty exacted its toll from me so that some of the more delicate acts were done under cover of darkness that night brings.

Serenade by Political Detainees

One of the things that surprised me was that, even as I was — and still am — a very light sleeper, in Bicutan I slept soundly from about 1 a.m. to the dawn of the day of our arrest.

It was at the break of dawn, perhaps about 4 a.m., that I dreamt I was hearing the haunting refrain of *"Bayan Ko"* or *"My Country"* being played on a flute and rough voices singing the lyrics and drowning the melodious magic of the song. The song, composed by Constancio de Guzman in 1928, had become the unofficial battle hymn of martial law dissenters. Its lyrics, written by Jose Corazon de Jesus to celebrate the unquenchable thirst of a caged bird to fly free of its gilded coop, never failed to evoke in us sentimental feelings of love of country and hope for a better tomorrow for our martial rule-oppressed people.

The voices sounded so insistent and so real that I sat up to listen. After a while, I realized that I was not dreaming at all. Indeed, some people were singing our song and were in fact shouting *"Mabuhay...Long live..."* Tañada, Rodrigo, Guingona, Rondon, Arroyo and me, Nene Pimentel!

I stood on a stool to peer through the slats of the small opening near the ceiling to locate where the singing was coming from. It was still a little dark, but I could see that a crowd had gathered to serenade us beside the wall of our detention building. I learned later that the serenaders were inmates of the compound next to ours. They were also political detainees, the "communists," the guards told us. But communists or not, the plaintive melody of the song transported me from the harsh realities of prison to some beatific heaven of sorts for at least some blissful moments.

Soon, the breaking rays of the sun brought home to me the stark reality that I was a detainee. But like the caged bird in the *"Bayan Ko"* song, I pined for freedom.

Among ourselves, as new detainees, we tried to share each other's joys and problems. Whenever we felt that someone needed consolation or just friendly attention, we readily gave it.

At first, I did not know that the Jesuit activist, Fr. Archie Intengan, had been arrested with us. It turned out that he had led most of the youth demonstrators to join our march on that fateful day. I had not met Intengan before then, but I found his detention with us most providential because he provided us with the spiritual guidance that we needed in those trying times. There were instances though, when I thought he needed our consolation more than we needed his compassion.

A few days after our arrest, Tañada was ordered released. We were elated by the news, but the senator was not. He had not asked Marcos or anyone that he be freed, he said. Rumors had it that Marcos was apprehensive that, since Tañada was quite advanced in age, he just might suffer a stroke or a heart attack and die in prison. Apparently, Marcos thought that the risk was not worth taking. Thus, the order to release the senator. But like a mule, Tañada did not want to be led out of prison against his will. He said that he was not leaving until all of us were released. It took all of our collective persuasive powers to convince the "Old Man," as we fondly called him, that it was to our common advantage that he should obey the release order. We said that he would be of greater service to the cause of freedom and democracy out of rather than in prison.

In a lighter vein, Soc told Tañada that he could always visit us, bring food and smuggle whiskey or wine for us to drink. Tito found the suggestion "critical" and added with a wink that Tañada should make sure that when he brought a bottle, it should get to us, the intended beneficiaries. Tito's caveat was meant to remind Tañada not to cause a repeat of our frustration when Diokno visited us sometime ago. Diokno brought an expensive bottle of whisky for us. Unfortunately, it turned out that he was clumsier handling a bottle of whisky than handling a court case. He was handing over the bottle to us when he dropped it on the cement floor even before it touched our hands. Our mouths simultaneously formed a big "O" when the bottle broke into shards and its "spiritual" contents spilled on the floor.

With the release of Senator Tañada, Soc became our *de facto* leader. Soc, whom Ninoy called "monsignor" because of his prayerful ways, would lead us in saying the Rosary or serving Mass that our fellow detainee, Fr. Intengan, celebrated in our detention quarters.

Days later, we were transferred to the second floor of a newly constructed two-story detention center. The place had better appointments and was more comfortable than our previous confinement place. We each had a room that had no bars, only curtains. That meant that we could mingle freely with one another and go up and down from one floor to the other without inhibition unless the guards padlocked the door between the two floors. More importantly, we could now enjoy visits from our families, including what is known in prison circles as "conjugal visits."

In any event, as soon as we were transferred to our new quarters, we, the Rodrigos, Tito, Ernie, Joker, Fr. Intengan and I, adopted some rules to govern the routine of our lives as martial law detainees. Ernie would do the dishwashing. I would cook breakfast. The only thing I really was capable of doing was to make Eggs Benedict, hard-boiled eggs, fried eggs sunny-side up or scrambled eggs. I also knew how to cook rice and boil water or heat whatever needed to be heated. Tito would be our exercise master. He was our skipping-rope expert. Joker would take care of the common space that served as our dining and recreation room; King Rodrigo, the toilets; Soc Rodrigo, the singing; and Fr. Archie, the praying for our early release from our military prison and for our eternal liberation. It was, I thought, a fairly good division of labor.

Although our new quarters were arguably better than the other cells we had previously occupied as detainees, we never allowed the relative comfort that we now enjoyed to dull our desire to be free. Our humdrum existence in our new quarters, which we tried to break by reading, exercise, prayers and jokes, continued for a few more weeks.

As the days of our confinement lengthened, we began to realize that we were more fortunate than some detainees who were subjected to far more inhuman treatment than we. Indeed, on some nights, I heard the muffled moans of detainees being tortured on the ground floor of the building in which we were confined. In fact, one early evening, I wandered down to the ground floor and opened the door of a room. I saw three men in civilian clothes trying to push another man out of the window. They stopped when I chanced upon their act. It must have been God's divine intervention that caused me to open that door because it probably saved that man's life. Prior to that incident, we heard of prisoners being pushed out of their cells and shot, ostensibly in the act of escaping.

Communist Leader with Us

Soon we found out that our quarters were not for our exclusive use alone. A known communist leader, Fidel Agcaoili, was given a room on the same floor assigned to us. The arrangement, disconcerted us. The military had tagged Agcaoili as the head of the Communist Party of the Philippines' Finance Committee, which purchased the M/V *Karagatan*, a vessel that was reportedly used for gunrunning of firearms purchased from China for the NPA rebels. The domestic press widely reported that the vessel was intercepted by government troops in Palanan, Isabela in July 1972. A firefight ensued and four government soldiers were killed. The military had also identified Agcaoili as the person responsible for the acquisition of another vessel, M/V *Doña Andrea*, which was used by the CCP/NPA in the 1974 aborted landing of firearms in La Union and Pangasinan, according to official documents copies of which I obtained later.

We interpreted Agcaoili's being jailed with us to mean that the military intelligence services sought to validate a thesis that we, in the peaceful Opposition, had links with the violent Left.

Since we assumed that the military had bugged our new quarters to monitor our conversations with Agcaoili, we took it upon ourselves to be very careful about what we discussed with him. In fairness, he never tried to win us over to his cause and neither did we try to bring him over to ours.

1978: THE BICUTAN GROUP. (Left to right), standing: Fr. Archie Integan, SJ, and Teofisto Guingona. Seated: Joker Arroyo, Francisco Rodrigo, Ernesto Rondon, Fidel Agcaoili and me.

Our detention did not deter us from kidding one another. We made jokes of all kinds to lighten up the day. The butt of most of the jokes was Tito because his wife Ruth was also detained with him in his cell. We kidded him no end that, even in his defiance of Marcos, he made sure he had his *baon*, emergency provision, with him. Incidentally, the Guingonas had the most number of family members in detention at the time, namely Tito, Ruth and Toti, their son, who was among the three thousand youths who followed us in that march. Second was Soc, who was detained with his son, King. Tañada also had a son detained by the military, but he was not held with us in Bicutan.

We also got encouraging words from our friends outside the prison walls. One nun, Sister Iluminada, a co-worker in Nassa, wrote a compassionate letter dated April 26 to us. While the letter was addressed to me, its contents were meant for all those who marched with us. Edited for brevity, the letter said:

> Only heroes can do what you have done. We are proud of you.
> I pray for your early release and for much courage. You are carrying the burden for many Filipinos who crave for justice.

In early June, Fr. Archie was released and placed under the custody of Fr. Jose A. Cruz, then president of Ateneo de Manila University. In a note that he addressed to Soc, Tito and Ruth, Ernie, Joker, Agcaoili and me dated June 4,

1978, Archie thanked us for the compassion we showed him during our detention. He wrote:

> I wish to express my deepest appreciation for your solid support during my moments of silent but obvious crisis. I am not ungrateful, but you might have been surprised at my relative silence when you were cheering this morning. The reason was that I was very touched, and should I have attempted to speak one word of thanksgiving, I would probably have wept. There is nothing wrong with weeping for joy, but our cultural values have made it embarrassing. From the bottom of my heart, thank you. The Holy Spirit indeed works in you, as seen in your kindness and concern for others even when you were no longer directly at stake.

Even as Intengan went back to teaching at the Ateneo, he could not but empathize with the people whom he saw were continually being oppressed by the Marcos regime. He was himself accused by the controlled media as a leader of a subversive organization, the April 6 Liberation Movement. The movement was, according to the martial law authorities, responsible for the bombings and the arsons directed at selected government and private buildings in Metro Manila.

In the second week of October 1980, Intengan disappeared from Manila. We learned later that he had gone to Sabah, Malaysia, where he wound up at a camp of rebels fighting the Marcos regime. That was the last time during martial law that we, his erstwhile colleagues, in the military facility in Bicutan heard of him.

While in detention, outwardly, we the Laban detainees in Bicutan, maintained our cheery disposition. We tried to show all our visitors, including our families, that we were bearing up well in our incarceration. The fact, however, was that we suffered inwardly not only from martial-law-induced tensions but also from politically generated ones.

Four days after our detention at Bicutan, a general, Hamilton Dimaya, assisted by two colonels, ordered us to go the gymnasium of the prison camp to hear the nature of the case they would file against us. I thought that the case would only be for one count of illegal assembly, as we had been informed on the night of our arrest at the Metrocom Judge Advocate General's Office in Camp Crame on our way to Camp Bicutan. I was wrong. When they read the charge sheet against us, I was simply flabbergasted. In my notes, I wrote:

> Fantastic! They're charging us with all the crimes in the book! Sedition, rebellion, subversion, illegal possession of firearms, rioting, election frauds, violence, threats, coercion, libeling the Republic, obstructing traffic, and illegal assembly. But since there was nothing much we could do about it at the time, we decided to just grin and bear it.

The criminal cases that the military officers said they would file against us were not the only concerns we had in Bicutan. We were also faced by questions as to whether or not Tañada should negotiate with Marcos on our behalf and whether or not Laban should convert itself into a political party.

Before Tañada was released, we discussed the matter of whether he should talk with Marcos regarding our predicament. Juan T. David, our colleague in Laban and in the Constitutional Convention, first broached the possibility of bringing the issue up to Marcos. He was of the opinion that Marcos could very well issue an amnesty proclamation to cause our release soonest. On that issue, we were split. Joker Arroyo and I expressed our views against it.

Roxas Warns Laban

Partisan political issues also intruded into our lives even as detainees. On at least two occasions Senator Roxas, LP president, visited us and he brought out his misgivings over reports that the leaders of Laban, under which Soc Rodrigo, Tito Guingona, Ernie Rondon and I had run in the recent Interim Batasang Pambansa elections, were thinking of converting it into a regular political party. When we joined Laban as candidates in the 1978 Interim Batasang Pambansa elections, it was merely a coalition of political personalities, not a political party. Roxas, as the LP president, interposed no objection to the formation of Laban to participate in the IBP elections. But now, he wanted the LP formally out of the coalition if Laban would convert itself into a political party. He said if Laban became a political party, he would field LP candidates in future elections that Marcos would call. That development sadly would divide the Opposition, he threatened.

We had no choice but to hear Roxas unload his misgivings. At the time, there was really no serious thought of organizing Laban as a political party. Nobody verbalized any opposition to the Roxas warning and we, sort of, allowed the issue to pass into history as we proceeded to enjoy the savory meal that he provided for us on that day.

Weeks later, we were told to pack up and leave. Without warning, we heard the good news: we were all going to be released. Except Agcaoili. Although we felt genuinely sorry for him, there was nothing we could do about it. And whether we agreed with his politics or not, he had become a part of our group and we felt sorry that we could not take him out of Bicutan with us. It was not until six years later, on October 26, 1984, to be exact , that we learned from a report in *Ang Tinig, The Voice,* a clandestine newsletter, that Agcoaili was given his temporary release papers after he had spent more than 10 years in confinement. In our case, we were jubilant that we could now get out of the military prison in Bicutan and rejoin our families.

No official reasons were given for our release. We were just told that the military doctors would give us physical examinations any time. The "physical" was the military's insurance that we would not file charges for torture or physical abuse once we got out of prison. After the doctors were through with the physical, they made us sign statements that we were not harmed in any way and that we had nothing to complain about the way they treated us in prison. I readily signed because that was the truth. Indeed, I had not been subjected to any direct physical maltreatment by my jailors. And I also eagerly wanted to get out of the military prison soonest.

Inde Recalls Bicutan Days

Among the silver linings of the months that I spent in Bicutan were the days that my youngest daughter, Inde, spent with me there. She wrote about the experience — she was eight years old then — in a brief first hand account that got published in the yearbook of the Fairlane Neighborhood Association for 1979.

Her article, "My Life in Bicutan," grammatical errors and all somehow captured our time in the military facility:

> I lived there three weeks. I was with Soc Rodrigo, Tito Guingona, Joker Arroyo, Father Intengan, Fidel Agcaoili, Ernie Rondon and my father, Nene Pimentel. At first I was sad because my father was a prisoner. I even cry when I first saw him but he embraced me and told me not to cry. Then when I was allowed to sleep there I began enjoying myself there.
>
> I was playing with Joseph, the son of Tito Fidel, and with Eric, the son of Tito Fidel, too. Every 5:00 or 4:00 o'clock in the afternoon, Eric, Joseph, Tito Fidel and me, we go out of the building and go to the other building. Tito Fidel was playing basketball there.
>
> We saw people with tattoo and I was talking with them but I don't know their names. But they don't know my name too. I was afraid because I thought they were bad but they were very good to me, Eric and Joseph....Someone who has a tattoo gave us a bird. We kept the bird. We found an extra box and a barbecue stick for a bird to sit on. Fr. Intengan said we don't have any food to feed the bird so we gave the bird to our friend, Bob. But Bob has a friend, girl. They played with the bird and the bird flew. Afterwards, the girl stepped on the bird because she did not see it. And the bird died. Eric, Joseph and me, we felt sad.
>
> If it's Sunday or Saturday, my father go out with Fr. Intengan or to the others to say Mass and because I wake up late. Tito Fidel or sometimes Tito Joker is the one who makes my breakfast.

Joker, however, was not exactly a good *yaya* or nanny, as Inde found out one night. Since she loved tomatoes, Joker piled up tomatoes on her plate. In her words:

> He kept bringing and bringing [tomatoes]. One night I ate tomatoes and I drank water, I began to vomit, and I went to the bathroom and I drank tea....

> At night we pray the Rosary. After we pray the Rosary, Lolo Soc Rodrigo speak Spanish. I can't understand so I just played with Joseph and then I sleep. Sometimes Lolo Soc will teach us a song in Spanish. The title is Dios *Te Salve*. Eric was singing a sour note so everybody laughed.
>
> My brother Jac and sisters visited us and I wanted to go home already. But Tito Joker was joking me. He said that I am not yet going home because I don't have my papers yet. And I said that I'm not a prisoner.
>
> Then I cried because I wanted to go home but my father do not have any body to sleep with. But my father said that it is not important to have somebody to sleep with.
>
> Then, my two brothers Koko and Jac and my three sisters and my mother got all the things of my father because my father was going to be released the next day. We got the pillow and mat and the things that I brought. My father gave the pillow and mat to the poor prisoners. We got the books that Ninoy Aquino let us borrow.
>
> Then my father was released. I was very happy because he was already released.

While no official reason was given for our release, we surmised that Marcos wanted to score points with Jimmy Carter, the new President of the US. Carter made human rights as a major plank of his foreign policy. Countries with bad human rights records would be hard pressed to receive US aid. Walter Mondale, Carter's Vice President, was in Manila the week of our release. He left the day before our release was announced.

Whether or not our release from Bicutan was the result of US policy on human rights, it really did not matter to me. Indeed, there were adverse comments about the uselessness of Carter's human rights policy. Maybe, the policy should have been pursued more vigorously to secure the release of other detainees, rather than just us. But, in my case, I was just happy to get out of prison and be reunited with family and friends. I also wanted to resume earning a living for my family.

While FEU and San Beda asked me to resume teaching, my heart was no longer in it. Neither did I want to go back to Calderon's companies because I knew he was leaving for the US. So I made do with whatever came my way as a lawyer for the poor. My friend and colleague in the Constitutional Convention, Emmanuel Santos, generously provided me with an office building he rented along Roxas Boulevard in Manila.

Karpov vs Korchnoi

Meanwhile, from July to October 1978, Marcos treated the people to another diversionary entertainment. Despite my dislike for Marcos-sponsored spectacles, I followed this one rather closely. It was the 13th World Chess Championship that was held in Baguio City. Anatoly Karpov and Viktor Korchnoi battled it out in what the *Philippine Panorama*, in its December 31, 1978 issue, called "the longest, rowdiest and most exciting world chess championship match in history." Karpov won the title which he deserved, but the cost of the games to the people was a little prohibitive considering the overall poverty of the nation. The Marcos government gave $350,000 to Karpov and $200,000 to Korchnoi.

The scandalous prize money had hardy left the vaults of the government when Marcos's think tank schemed to get a Fischer-Karpov match held in the country with prizes at least triple the bonanza given to Karpov and Korchnoi. Robert Fischer, an American, was at the time the acknowledged but freakish world chess champion. Matching him, an American, with Karpov, a Russian, at the height of the Cold War would have been a world sports event. Thankfully, the match did not materialize. Had it been held in the country, Marcos would not have hesitated to donate several millions of dollars in prize money for the games.

Part 6

The Opposition Dilemma

1979*: VISIT TO NINOY AQUINO at his house in Times Street Quezon City when he was given a furlough from prison on October 10. (Left to right): Me, Romy Capulong, Soc Rodrigo, Lorenzo Tañada, Pepe Diokno, Raul Gonzalez, Ninoy, Joker Arroyo, Sed Ordoñez, Nep Gonzales and Jovy Salonga.*

Chapter 18:

Hopes Dim

As 1979 began, I could sense that hopes for revitalizing the peaceful resistance to the martial rule regime were beginning to dim. In February even the members of the Senate — which Marcos closed when he proclaimed martial law — felt Marcos had become so powerful that they could do nothing better than to petition him in respectful terms to release their colleague, Ninoy Aquino, from military confinement.

Their three-paragraph letter to Marcos said:

> Dear Mr. President:
>
> As former Senators of the Republic and as plain citizens of this land, we respectfully request the immediate release of former senator Benigno S. Aquino, Jr., who as of this date, has been imprisoned in a military camp for 2,345 days or almost six years and a half, since the proclamation of martial law.
>
> We earnestly feel that his release is warranted by considerations of humanity and fairness not only to him but also to his long-suffering family.
>
> Your kind consideration of this request will go a long way towards restoring goodwill among many people, and will be appreciated by all of us.

The letter was signed by former Senate President Gil J. Puyat and 16 other senators: Jose J. Roy, Ambrosio Padilla, Rene Espina, Helena Z. Benitez, Ramon Mitra, Jr., Jovito R. Salonga, Lorenzo M. Tañada, Francisco Rodrigo, Maria Kalaw Katigbak, Eddie U. Ilarde, Jose Diokno, Salvador Laurel, Eva Estrada Kalaw, Gerry Roxas, Lorenzo Sumulong and Magnolia Antonino.

As a Mindanaonon, I was a little upset that I did not see the names of Emmanuel Pelaez and Alejandro Almendras in the petition. They probably had good reasons for not signing it. Nonetheless, I thought that they missed a good opportunity to strike a blow for freedom, not only for Ninoy but also for the entire country.

Marcos paid no heed to the letter of the senators. He was busy consolidating support for his regime, not only domestically but also internationally. Upon his invitation, the United Nations Committee on Trade and Development (Unctad) held its May meeting in Manila, the first-ever in the country. It was another psychological boost to Marcos's claim of the legitimacy of his regime. UN Secretary General Kurt Waldheim and World Bank President

Robert McNamara attended the conference. So did Andrew Young, the US Ambassador to the UN. The conference was given wide publicity in the domestic and international press.

Consultations in Geneva

Shortly after the announcement that Unctad would hold its meeting in Manila, the World Council of Churches, invited Nassa to send some participants to Geneva to brief the council about the status of poverty and human rights in the country under the conditions of martial law. Msgr. Ralph Salazar, who was our head at the Justice and Peace Committee in Nassa, asked me to participate in the Geneva conference.

My problem was that I had lost my passport. Had the circumstances been normal, it would have been fairly easy for me to get a new passport from the Ministry of Foreign Affairs. But the times were abnormal. In addition to the usual requirements imposed by the Ministry of Foreign Affairs, there was a Travel Committee that screened applications for passports and for travel abroad. As the chair of the Committee, Gen. Fabian Ver, the Chief of Staff of the Armed Forces, had a lot to say whether or not anyone got his or her passport. Ver's approval was a requisite before the Travel Committee would grant the application for leave to travel.

The process of securing a travel permit for those who had previously been detained was so rigorous that getting it was a cause for rejoicing. A note sent to me by Juan L. Mercado, a noted journalist and a martial law detainee, expressed the relief that one felt upon receiving the valued travel permit. He said:

> The government has finally given me an exit permit to leave the country with my family.
>
> I am joining the Food and Agriculture Organization of the United Nations in Bangkok.
>
> Leaving one's country and friends, I have discovered, is not a painless process. And there are the hundred-and-one details of settling down in a foreign city.
>
> My family and I thank you for the courtesies and kindness you have shown us in the past. We hope to see you again soon. In the meantime, our prayers and *paalam*, good-bye.

I personally went through the painful process that Mercado intimated in his note to me by formally applying for the renewal of my passport. It did not do me any good. For reasons that they kept to themselves, the MFA and the Travel Committee sat on my application for the renewal of my passport and for my eventual travel to Geneva. In exasperation, I sued them before the Supreme Court to compel the MFA to replace my lost passport and the Travel Committee to allow me to travel.

To my surprise, the Supreme Court dismissed my petition, which I thought was based on incontestable constitutional grounds. All citizens, I argued, were entitled to their passports and the right to travel was guaranteed by the Constitution. Probably, the Court resolved the issue in extreme caution as I had included Ver, then perceptually the military alter ego of Marcos, in my suit. But, to my even greater surprise, I got my passport and my permit to travel to Geneva. I was told later that somebody in the Supreme Court suggested to Ver that I had the legal right to demand the renewal of my passport and to travel abroad. It appeared then that the dismissal of my petition was premised on my getting my passport renewed and the issuance of my travel permit. Although it looked awkward, to say the least, it was what pragmatists would call "a win-win solution."

I was thus able to attend the WCC consultation meetings in Geneva. There, we discussed the problems of the massive poverty of the people, the endemic corruption in government, the ongoing militarization of Mindanao and the continuing human rights violations at home. I got the distinct impression from the discussions that the WCC was already helping alleviate the oppressive situation in the country. And, also perceptually, I thought that certain elements in the WCC looked with favor at the violent option chosen by the rebels against the martial law regime.

During the breaks in the consultation meetings, I took the streetcar to do the sights. I thoroughly enjoyed the city and its magnificent lake. I thought, however, that a developed Lake Lanao in Marawi City could give Geneva a run for its tourism-drawing potential.

After the conference, I left for home, but I had to make a stopover in Rome to get a connecting flight to Manila. Since my per diems were practically depleted by the time I got to Rome, I subsisted on hard-boiled eggs and water — happily only for a day and-a-half — while I waited for the flight home.

Days later, dreary-eyed from that first trip to Switzerland, I was browsing over some books in the University of the Philippines bookstore in Diliman, Quezon City, when the reality that I was back in Metro Manila jolted me. I suddenly realized that I had left my car without locking it. I rushed back to the parking lot. To my relief, the car was still there, however my attaché case was gone. The attaché case contained my passport, used plane tickets and other receipts that I needed to submit to Nassa to clear my accounts. Luckily, my kind superior at Nassa, Msgr. Salazar, accepted my explanation why I could not submit the papers to back up my expenses for the Geneva trip.

Unctad Conference, a 'Success'

The Unctad conference in Manila was, by the standards of the martial law regime, thoroughly successful. Marcos and Imelda proudly showed the monuments in stone that they had or were building for the "City of Man" — into which Imelda wanted to convert Manila. Imelda made sure the delegates were dined, wined and feted in the grandiose manner that she thought they were accustomed to, including servicing them with several brand-new government-imported Mercedes Benz limousines. There were some demonstrations against the lavish receptions that the Marcoses heaped on the Unctad delegates, but these were downplayed by the Manila media and were not noticed much by the people.

In fairness, the conference was not that useless to us as non-governmental organization activists or as citizens of a developing country like ours. Some positive measures were discussed. Among these were the need of permitting greater access for the developing countries to the markets of the developed world; transferring industries to developing countries, and reorienting the activities of transnational corporations. This last point was in line with the demands of many activist groups in the country that the multinationals should be concerned also with the needs of their host countries and not only with the exploitation of the resources of the latter for the profit of their stockholders.

Aquino US Heart Bypass

Perhaps the success of the Unctad conference in Manila or some other pragmatic consideration moved Marcos on May 8, 1980 to allow Ninoy Aquino to fly to the US for a heart bypass operation. The local media portrayed Imelda as the broker who made it all possible. She was supposed to have gotten Ninoy's assurance that he would come back to the country as soon as possible and that he would not get involved in political activities while he was in the US.

Salonga Under Fire

With Ninoy in the US, martial law authorities shifted their harassment of domestic political leaders of the Opposition to Salonga after a bomb exploded in a room at the YMCA on September 6, 1980. The room was occupied by a Filipino-American by the name of Victor Lovely. The explosion not only wounded Lovely almost fatally, but also injured a brother of his.

Military and police officers arrested Lovely and his brother on the day of the explosion, put them in isolation and eventually got Lovely to confess that he was a member of the Light-A-Fire Movement. The LAFM was a group that was organized to sow terror in Metro Manila and cause the destabilization of the Marcos regime. In his affidavit, Lovely implicated Salonga as one of the leaders of the movement. To buttress their case against him, the military produced a photograph of Lovely with Salonga and other people at a party hosted by Raul Daza in his home in Los Angeles, California. Daza, a former LP Congressman of Samar, had continued his oppositionist stance against martial rule in the US. The military's simplistic position was that the photograph proved Salonga's complicity in the bombing activities of Lovely.

The ASTA Bombing

The military stepped up their plot to get Salonga tied up with the bombing incidents in Metro Manila when another bomb exploded a few meters away from Marcos at the American Society of Travel Agents (ASTA) Conference at the Philippine International Convention Center on October 19, 1980.

Hours later, the *Bulletin Today* reported that Marcos identified Salonga along with three former senators who were now US-based, Aquino, Osmeña and Manglapus, as the brains behind the ASTA blast. It did not help the Opposition leaders that, days before the ASTA bombing, a pillar of the MFP in Chicago, Cesar Arellano, had issued a warning that conference participants should forego going to Manila because he feared for their safety. Arellano and his wife, Gloria, were then managing the highly successful Traveler International, Inc., a private tourism business, in Chicago.

While the other explosions in Metro Manila embarrassed Marcos, the ASTA bombing humiliated him the most. Marcos and his Minister of Tourism, Jose Aspiras, had assured the members of ASTA that Marcos was fully in control of the political situation in the country. Aspiras, in fact, had earlier dismissed Arellano's warnings as a part of the black propaganda that the dissidents in the US were mounting against the Marcos government. Moreover, since Marcos was the keynote speaker at the opening of the ASTA convention, it was assumed that security would be very tight to keep the affair safe for the more than a thousand delegates in attendance.

Marcos had just finished his keynote speech during which he assured the audience of the safe environment that his martial rule regime had created in the country. He was about to leave when a small bomb exploded some 15 meters away from where he was standing. Marcos was not hurt, but his ego was seriously bruised. Nobody died in the incident, although some 20 people were wounded superficially. But, to him, worse than the injuries the bombing had wrought on the participants of the ASTA conference was the clear message that anti-martial rule individuals had the capacity to harm him and his family directly.

The authorities had no clue as to the identity of the bomber. It took time before they were able to identify her as Doris Baffrey, a daughter of retired Commodore Santiago Noval, an Ilocano and a friend of Marcos. As an employee at the Philippine Consulate in New York, Baffrey did the ASTA conference organizers a favor by bringing in from the US metal detectors that they needed to secure the conference. It was, thus, fairly easy for her to enter the conference hall without inviting close scrutiny. Thus, she was able to place a bomb underneath one of the seats in the conference hall unnoticed.

When the authorities finally caught up with her, they locked her up in Camp Crame and formally charged her with illegal possession of explosives in May 1982. She spent four years and four months in prison before Marcos, through Regional Trial Court Judge Manuel Romillo of Pasay City, ordered her release. Human rights lawyers Joker Arroyo and Jejomar Binay provided her with legal advice.

The military, however, relentlessly pursued the other suspects in the Metro Manila bombings. They even picked up one young lawyer, Lutgardo Barbo, who was then the legal counsel of the Pepsi Cola Company in San Fernando, Pampanga. Barbo was arrested, the police explained, because they had recovered an address book from Lovely's YMCA room and Barbo's name was in it. The arresting team brought him to a safe house. There, they stripped him naked in a room where the air-conditioner was run full blast and poked his buttocks with the sharp end of a stick to prevent him from sleeping. They tried to compel Barbo under torture to name Salonga as a coconspirator of the LAFM. Barbo, even on the verge of breaking down, did not implicate Salonga for the simple reason that he really did not know if Salonga had any connection with the LAFM or with Lovely. As an aside,

Barbo told me years after the fact that one of those who stripped him naked was a gay military officer.

We in the Manila Opposition group found Marcos's and the military conclusions about Salonga's complicity downright ridiculous. The military, however, did not share our dismissive attitude. From our end, we were not especially concerned with Aquino, Osmeña and Manglapus because they were outside the country. We knew that if Marcos wanted them extradited, a thousand and one requirements had to be complied with before he could even get an order to investigate them seriously in the US mainland. We were worried about Salonga's health should he be detained by the military.

1980: TORTURE VICTIM, Lutgardo Barbo, a young lawyer implicated in the Light-A-Fire Movement.

In the event, the military pursued the charges against Salonga and arrested him even after he checked into a hospital for various ailments like chronic asthma and the wounds he had sustained at the Plaza Miranda bombing.

Salonga to Exile

Fortunately for Salonga, his reputation for sobriety and his good connections with religious groups here and abroad stood him in good stead. Despite Marcos's intense personal dislike for Salonga — Marcos called him "a petty, pompous and sanctimonious fraud" in his diary, perjorative adjectives that could very well have described the diary writer — he allowed him to leave for the US on March 25, 1981 for "humanitarian reasons." Marcos's order allowing Salonga to leave was based on a recommendation of Defense Minister Enrile, Salonga's fraternity brother at the University of the Philippines.

Salonga went into exile to the US and he stayed out of Marcos's reach until late January 1985 when he returned home. Even as he was in exile, the Marcos government pressed criminal charges of rebellion/subversion against him. It was only after Marcos fell from power in 1986, that the Supreme Court wrote finis to the harassment of Salonga in 1995. It ordered the dismissal of the case against Salonga for being based on hearsay evidence. That meant that Lovely's affidavit was insufficient in law to establish Salonga's culpability with the former's subversive activities. It was a belated but a welcome clearance for Salonga who had devoted his life fighting for what he believed was right and just for our people.

Chapter 19:

Light a Fire

Salonga and Barbo were not the only persons that Victor Lovely got into trouble with martial law. As an aggressive recruiter of people to the cause of ending Marcos's dictatorship by force, Lovely enlisted or tried to enlist other people in the endeavor. One person he tried to enlist in his violent crusade was lawyer Byron Bocar, whose practice was devoted to defending activists opposed to the martial rule regime.

Bocar and Lovely knew one another. They both came from the province of Samar and were "good friends." Bocar said:

> Jun [Lovely's nickname] asked me many times to join the violent plot to topple Marcos. He would phone me from the US to convince me that it was time now to destabilize Marcos. He suggested that I contact Salonga to confirm what he was telling me.

Although he considered Lovely "indiscreet" in his uninhibited use of long-distance calls to talk with him, Bocar nonetheless asked Salonga for an appointment, pursuant to Lovely's suggestion. He said that, after some time, he met Salonga at his house in Pasig. "But he was noncommittal and at most vague about any plan to oust Marcos by force," Bocar said. And he told Lovely about it.

Lovely, however, would not give up. Through another overseas call, he told Bocar that a person was going to visit him at his house in Quezon City. Indeed, a few days after the call, a man visited Bocar and introduced himself as Ed Olaguer.

Although Olaguer had already established his credentials as a man of good repute in the Makati business community, Bocar hardly knew him. At that time, Olaguer was an executive in IBM Philippines, a professor at the prestigious business school, the Asian Institute of Management, and a shareholder of the newspaper *Business Day*. Neither did Bocar know that Olaguer was a devotee of the Virgin Mary, which spoke volumes of the latter's conservative attitudes in matters of religion and his unshakable belief in the salvific hand of God, even in mundane matters.

Calibrated Plan

In their meeting, Olaguer told him about a calibrated plan to oust Marcos, first by economic pressures like boycotting establishments identified with the regime, then escalating the moves gradually to bombing and burning offices and businesses owned by the cronies of Marcos without injuring people, and finally to a selective targeting of people known to be pillars of support of his dictatorship.

At the meeting, Olaguer asked Bocar if he would be willing to drive a car and leave it at a busy intersection to cause a monstrous traffic jam. The naïve idea, although Olaguer did not call it that, was intended to get people mad at the government for failing to ensure a smooth traffic flow for starters. The people's anger, he said, would, then, escalate and turn violent as fast as the LAFM stepped up its arson activities in Metro Manila.

Bocar said that he "rejected Olaguer's overtures." He told him that he was limiting his acts of support for the Opposition to martial rule as a lawyer. His reluctance to join Olaguer's group did not forestall the violent incidents against the Marcos regime as outlined to him by the latter. But, when a bomb exploded in the YMCA room of Victor Lovely as narrated in the previous chapter, Bocar had to flee for his life. The reason was that the military was hot on his trail. They found his name in Lovely's address book like Barbo's and Bocar knew that Barbo was arrested by the military. He had no intention of surrendering to the military especially after he learned that Barbo was subjected to torture. Bocar successfully eluded arrest and saw Marcos fall from power in 1986.

In any case, bombings and arson, in quick succession, took place in several parts of Manila. A mysterious fire burned the Floating Casino; a bomb exploded in a store in Carriedo St. that took the life of an American tourist; and other bombs hit various places in Metro Manila.

Bombing Plan Goes Awry

At least, one bombing plan went awry. The LAFM, now abetted by the April 6 Movement, plotted to detonate some small explosives on some floors of the Rustan's Department Store. Gasty Ortigas and Gus Lagman were assigned to execute the plan on the 2nd floor of the store. Norberto Gonzales was designated to do the bombing of the 1st floor. They were under the supervision of Olaguer. But, when Ortigas and Lagman were about to set off the explosive on the 2nd floor, the unexpected happened. They saw their mutual friend, Rufo Colayco, enter the place obviously to do some shopping. Although Ortigas had a wig on, he knew that Colayco would recognize him and Lagman if he saw them. They hastily left the place. In the meantime, Gonzales, who was unaware of what happened on the 2nd floor, had problems following some of Olaguer's instructions. He likewise aborted his mission. As Olaguer said later on, it just was not written in heaven for the two floors of Rustan's to be bombed on the occasion.

Although the bombings and the burning of some public places were meant as an expression of the people's pent-up anger against the Marcos regime, they were also intended as a cover-up for a fantastic scheme to rescue Ninoy Aquino from his detention cell in Fort Bonifacio. Ninoy had been in confinement since 1972.

The plot was James Bond*ish* in that, according to Olaguer, it called for the renting of a house very near the Aquino residence on Times Street in Quezon City. From there, Otto Jimenez, Gaston Ortigas, Gus Lagman and Ed Olaguer would do the actual physical work of digging a tunnel to access Ninoy Aquino's bedroom or toilet. Steve Psinakis would supply the noiseless earth-drilling equipment from the US. The Aquinos would then fake a death or near-death in the family so that Marcos would allow Ninoy a brief home visit. The funds for the venture were to come from Al Yuchengco, a respected *taipan, a* successful Filipino-Chinese entrepreneur, and Ramon Diaz, former executive secretary of President Macapagal. Olaguer said that, in the end, "Ninoy Aquino thumbed it down. It was too dangerous for him and the members of his family who would be left behind to the mercies of Marcos."

Olaguer's Arrest

Before Olaguer could expand the operations of the LAFM, a military team headed by the feared Lt. Col. Rolando Abadilla and his assistant, Capt. Panfilo Lacson, arrested him on Christmas Eve, 1979. Despite his full trust in God's divine providence, Olaguer had his moments of apprehension that he would be "salvaged" by the dreaded duo. He made this assessment after the car into which he was pushed headed away from Camp Crame or Fort Bonifacio where political dissenters or rebels were usually detained.

In Olaguer's words, he was "manacled and trembling with fear at the back seat of the vehicle (for some) 45 minutes until the car's two-way radio crackled." Abadilla and Lacson were ordered by somebody to go to Camp Aguinaldo in Quezon City. But, even as Abadilla complied with the order, he heard Lacson curse under his breath that whoever gave the order was a *pakialamero,* meddler.

The meddler turned out to be Defense Minister Enrile. By ordering Abadilla to bring Olaguer to his office instead of elsewhere, Olaguer believed Enrile had "rescued" him from a fate, perhaps worse than death, in the hands of Abadilla and Lacson. Olaguer was pleasantly surprised by Minister Enrile's "extraordinary kindness" as the latter ordered all his subordinates within hearing distance of Abadilla and Lacson that Olaguer be treated well.

Nevertheless, Minister Enrile's benign treatment of Olaguer did not prevent the latter's prosecution and conviction for subversion by a Military Tribunal. On December 4, 1984, Olaguer was sentenced to death by electrocution with his co-accused, Otto Jimenez, Reynaldo Maclang and Ester Misa Jimenez. Also convicted in absentia were Raul Manglapus, Raul Daza, Charlie Avila and Steve Psinakis.

As a member of the Opposition, I saw the conviction of Olaguer as one

PEOPLE'S JOURNAL
Everybody's Newspaper

No.1
P1.50
Wednesday,
Dec. 5, 1984

DEATH TO 4 IN LIGHT-A-FIRE

A MILITARY court yesterday sentenced to death four leaders of the "Light-a-Fire" movement for their participation in the burning of big hotels and business firms in Metro Manila in 1979 in a bid to deestabilize the government.

Sentenced by Military Commission No. 34 to die in the electric chair were Eduardo B. Olaguer, Othoniel V. Jimenez, his wife Ester, and Renaldo Maclang.

Commission president Col. Higino Dacanay Jr. read the sentence in open court at the Judge Advocate General's Office in Camp Aguinaldo, Quezon City.

The court, however, acquitted two other accused — Rene J. Marciano and Mac Aceros — for lack of evidence.

The sentence was promulgated after five years of trial during which the accused led by Olaguer defied a court order for them to present counter-evidence and witnesses.

Dacanay pointed out that the court had been so lenient during the trial by giving the accused the opportunity to defend themselves.

Please turn to Page 2

jai-alai
8-2-1
P890.00

Eduardo Olaguer... shouts of "hallelujah" after the verdict.

1984: ED OLAGUER, leader of the Light-a-Fire Movement sits impassively after learning of the death penalty imposed on him, and his co-accused Otto Jimenez, Ester Jimenez and Rey Maclang.

more proof of the oppressive character of the martial rule regime. Yet, under the circumstances, I also knew that it would have been extremely difficult to justify any other outcome in his trial for the simple reason that Olaguer admitted he had taken up arms against the Marcos regime. He did so, he said, because it was an act of conscience and because he found no other means to end the regime's oppressive conduct towards our people than by force.

When I read a copy of Olaguer's statement which he had prepared but had not been allowed to deliver before the military tribunal, I thought that he was plain crazy. He actually sounded as if he welcomed his prosecution and conviction. On deeper reflection, however, I found his stand reminiscent of the Christian martyrs of old who chose death rather than renounce their faith in God. Olaguer was clearly a product of the 1599 *ratio studiorum* of St. Ignatius de Loyola. In his search for freedom for our people, he tried to meld the scholastic philosophy of the Jesuits with the principles of "The Art of War," the oldest military treatise in the world, articulated more than 2,400 years ago by

Sun Tzu, a universally recognized military strategist even today. That was where he got into trouble with martial law authorities. Or, as his friend, Otto Jimenez would say, "that was where martial law got into trouble with Olaguer."

Although he might not qualify to be a saint because of what he did, I believed that Ed Olaguer stood tall in the ranks of the Opposition. He was, in my opinion, made of the same heroic mold as Chief Justice Jose Abad Santos. The Chief Justice was left by President Manuel L. Quezon to head the government in the country, while Quezon and Vice President Sergio Osmeña went into exile to the US mainland during World War II. Abad Santos was arrested by Japanese soldiers in Malabang, Lanao. The Japanese military tried to persuade him to collaborate with them and join the puppet government that they were establishing in the country. Rather than collaborate, Abad Santos refused, for which reason the Japanese executed him.

Unlike Abad Santos, Olaguer did not die by firing squad, as ordered by the Military Tribunal. He was saved by God's design, he believed. God's will came in the form of an order by Marcos that stayed Ed's execution. In early 1986, Marcos ordered that he be allowed to go to the US for a cardiac operation. The US embassy, however, did not give Olaguer a visa. Thus, he stayed in the country and saw the downfall of Marcos a month or so later.

Chapter 20:

Boycott or Run?

As 1979 gave way to 1980, our Opposition group in Manila was reduced to meeting clandestinely and issuing occasional statements critical of the Marcos regime. At the time, Marcos seemed so entrenched in his dictatorship and so sure of his hold on power that he called for local elections in January 1980.

Marcos's call again placed the Opposition leaders in a quandary as to whether we should participate or not.

Leaders Prefer Boycott

Like their stand in previous elections called by Marcos, most of our leaders including Macapagal, Roxas, Diokno, Salonga, Manglapus, Chino Roces and — this time, including — Ninoy Aquino did not want to participate in the elections. Their basic argument was that to do so would legitimize the Marcos regime.

Likewise, in their opinion, the 1978 elections — in which some opposition groups, notably *Laban*, took part — resulted in the election of the Interim Batasang Pambansa, which turned out to be a rubber stamp that did what it was told by the Marcoses. As a mouthpiece of Marcos, it was "a most expensive one", Reuben Canoy told *Who Magazine* in its August 8, 1981 issue. He said that it took from P50 million to P60 million a year to maintain the IBP. In withering sarcasm, Canoy filed a satirical resolution in the IBP requesting Marcos, the Prime Minister, to ask Marcos, the President, to dissolve the Batasan so that new elections could be called.

The disinclination of the leaders of the Opposition in Manila to participate in any elections called by Marcos notwithstanding, some of us wanted to take his election dare at face value. Former Rep. Rogaciano Mercado of Bulacan wanted to participate. I also wanted to join the local election as an oppositionist in Cagayan de Oro. In my opinion, our participation in the local elections could not but prove beneficial for the cause of the Opposition.

Even if we were not given any chance to win in the local elections, which were the first in eight years since martial law was imposed, I argued that we could still use the period of the campaign to bring to the people's attention the abuses and the corruption of the Marcos regime — something that we could not do if we did not contest the elections or if there were no elections. And, if we won the elections, we could continue the Opposition cause in public office, which, to my mind, would definitely be an advantage.

While some of the major lights of our group in Manila had left for the US, other respected Opposition leaders remained in the country. We still had with us the likes of Senators Lorenzo Tañada, Soc Rodrigo, Pepe Diokno and Eva Estrada Kalaw. Chino Roces and lesser-known but equally dedicated patriots like Maria Feria and Luis Jose, who were identified with Raul Manglapus. In Manglapus's absence, Maring Feria and Jose took care of his affairs openly without any attempt at dissembling their connection with him. The two also helped other oppositionists who were harassed by the Marcos government in innumerable ways.

There was also former President Diosdado Macapagal who kept our Opposition spirits alive by his exhortations that the end of Marcos was near. Somehow, he believed Marcos was physically ill and would die soon. When I told him Marcos looked fit as a fiddle with his barbells in a photo then recently released by Malacañang, Macapagal said to me, "You know, Nene, a person's health is not proven by his outside looks. Marcos is ailing from the inside." Macapagal sounded prophetic. Marcos was, in fact, afflicted with systemic *lupus erymathosus,* an ailment that would lead to his death some years later in Hawaii.

My reservations about his motives notwithstanding, Macapagal kindly advised me not to go home to Cagayan de Oro. I wanted to help Reuben Canoy organize an Opposition group there, but Macapagal warned that it was easier for the military to get rid of me there than in Manila.

Despite the enormous problems facing us — dwindling leadership pool, no financial support, no visible popular backing — we determined to keep on with the peaceful struggle against the Marcos regime. Every week, we would meet at houses of friends to discuss what courses of action we could take to undermine the Marcos government. But his announcement that he would call local elections in 1980 once again threatened to split our already emaciated Opposition group.

NUL Compromise

Eventually, we arrived at a compromise. Those who wanted to join the elections could do so, but not as candidates of the Liberal Party, the major Opposition party before martial rule was declared, but of a new party that would be created. Mercado accepted the compromise because he also did not approve of the absorption of his party, the Nacionalista Party, by the KBL.

In fine, the compromise required those of us who wanted to run for local offices to file our certificates of candidacy as members of the new Opposition party, the National Union for Liberation, and not as Liberals or Nacionalistas. The NUL was an offshoot of an earlier group, called the National Union for Democracy and Freedom, which was organized at the Tagaytay vacation home of Senator Tañada.

The NUDF, with Mercado as chair and me as its secretary general, was, in Macapagal's words, "the first United Opposition" in the country during the martial law years. In that capacity, I visited Opposition groups in the Visayas and Mindanao to get them allied with the NUDF, an umbrella political organization of parties opposed to the Marcos regime. Unfortunately, the persons I got in touch with in Cebu and in Negros Oriental were not that keen on teaming up with us. Even in Cagayan de Oro, I found out that Adaza and Canoy had already organized the Mindanao Alliance and they were not eager to join any so-called Opposition party that was national only in name but not in fact. In short, the general response was that the Opposition groups in the Visayas and in Mindanao would rather stay on as regional Opposition groups than ally themselves with the NUDF.

Because of time and financial constraints, I could not do a broader consultation with Opposition personalities in other parts of the country. I returned to Manila and made my report to the leaders of the NUDF. I also told them that I had decided to run for mayor of Cagayan de Oro. Since it was a decision that I made unilaterally and the party had no funds to speak of, there was nothing much that I could expect from the NUDF except its permission that I run as the candidate of the NUL, the political arm of the NUDF.

1957: CAMPAIGNING FOR CANDIDATES of the Progressive Party of the Philippines Vicente Araneta (for vice president) at right and Fulvio Pelaez (for senator) at the mic. With straw hats on, my friend Gume Arcadio and I stand to Fulvio's right.

1962: AS DEAN of the College of Law of Xavier University, I sit at the school graduation ceremonies with Fr. James McMahon, SJ, President of XU to my left and Archbishop James T.G. Hayes, DD, SJ, next to him. Back row, at left, Fr. William F. Masterson, SJ, dean of the College of Agriculture.

1962: CHRISTIAN FAMILY MOVEMENT Chapter in Cagayan de Oro. Seated (left to right): Lili Marfori, Fr. Cip Unson, SJ, Lisa and Cesar Wee Sit, Nanay Mameng and my father. Standing (left to right) Baging Arguelles, my wife Bing, Linda Arguelles, Dadi Cua, Endring Salcedo, me, Abeto Salcedo, Ed Marfori and Dino Cua.

E

1970: *ED AND LILI MARFORI launched my candidacy for delegate to the Constitutional Convention without "strings attached."*

1971: *PRE-CONVENTION MEETING. I am (in a light suit) on the 2nd row, 2nd from left. Rolando Piit, with side-burns (in dark suit) on the 3rd row.*

1971: *I PRESIDE. One of President Macapagal's gimmicks that we, delegates, liked was his allowing us to open the sessions of our plenary meetings. Here I stand at the Presiding Officer's rostrum on February 21 as the national anthem is sung after I banged the gavel calling the session to order.*

1971: *AT THE CONVENTION. Enjoying the banter on the language issue between me and Pablo Trillana (at the other mic) are (left to right) Merceditas Teodoro, Jose Mari Velez, Dick Gordon, Romy Capulong and Caling Lobregat, half-standing at my right.*

1971: AT THE CONVENTION. Discussing some points with President Diosdado Macapagal (7th from left). Also in the picture, (left to right) are Fidel Purisima, Alfredo Abueg, me, Tony Tupaz, Raul Manglapus, Cesar Serapio and Augusto Caesar Espiritu.

1972: *SHORTLY BEFORE MARCOS padlocked Congress, senators discuss issues. (Left to right), Mamintal Tamano, Ernie Maceda, Gerry Roxas, Magnolia Antonino, John Osmeña, Ninoy Aquino and Rene Espina.*

1972: AT THE COMMITTEE ON PRIVILEGES. Frustration is etched on the face of Chair Eduardo Sison over the repeated failure of Quintero to appear before the Committee.

G

1972: DISCUSSIONS AT THE CONSTITUTIONAL CONVENTION a few days before the declaration of martial law. Fidel Purisima (seated back to camera), Alfredo Abueg, me, Tony Tupaz, Arturo Pacificador, President Macapagal, Augusto Caesar Espiritu and Ramon Diaz.

1973: DELEGATE ELFREN SARTE, a generous soul! On one occasion while I was in military detention, rice was a critical need in the house. Without anybody asking or telling him about it, Elfren sent rice to the family.

1978: SPEAKING AT A LABAN RALLY where people gradually made known their support for Aquino and the Laban party.

1978: NEWLY RELEASED detainees (facing camera) (left to right) Soc Rodrigo and Archie Intengan, SJ, (with plate) and Ernie Rondon (4th from left) regale my neighbors in Fairlane with stories about our detention in Bicutan. Romy Reyes is 3rd from left; Dr. Mau Manuel is 2nd from right Celedonio Cruz at lower leftmost.

H

Part 7

Quest for Mayorship

1980: THAT'S ME *(in T-shirt) shaking hands with a supporter.*

Chapter 21:

The Campaign

On the evening of my return to Manila, in our home in Marikina, I told Bing of my decision to run for mayor in the January 1980 local elections. She asked why I would do such a thing. I told her that I did not want to be asked by the people of my home city at some future time, "Where were you when we needed you?"

Her next question was predictable. She asked, "What will you do for money?" Knowing that we had nothing, absolutely nothing, by way of funds for a political campaign, I simply told her, "I will not allow the lack of money to prevent me from offering the people of my home city a choice for the mayorship."

Thus, armed with more faith than with anything else and forgetting Macapagal's friendly advice on the risks that I faced in Cagayan de Oro, I decided to go home and run for mayor. It was a decision that was backed up by much prayer and reflection. It was also a major one that meant rearranging our lives again — like leaving the children, at least temporarily, in Manila and having Bing resign as the placement director of the Ateneo de Manila University, a position she was beginning to enjoy as a professional — all for a political try that was not promising at all.

When Bing told her immediate superior, Fr. Bienvenido Nebres, SJ, that I had decided to run for mayor of Cagayan de Oro and, therefore, she had to resign, Fr. Ben asked the inevitable question, "How much money do you have?" Bing replied in all candor that I was leaving momentarily for Cagayan de Oro with P2,000 in my pocket. Fr. Ben was too kind to laugh, but that was indeed the extent of our finances at that time.

After Marcos formally set the date of the local elections for January 30, 1980, I flew home to Cagayan de Oro.

Testing the Waters

In the city, I asked friends what they thought of my running for mayor against whoever Marcos would field as his candidate. At the time, the Marcos-favored candidate was the formidable Pedro Neri Roa, a former congressman and governor of Misamis Oriental and the incumbent appointed mayor of the city. Politically, the elective or appointive positions that Roa held, while impressive, were not his most overwhelming assets. More terrifying, politically speaking, were the fact that Roa was a multibillionaire logger-businessman and the rumors circulating in the city that Marcos would back him up all the way as his candidate for mayor.

Most of my friends said that I had no chance at all. Their brutally frank advice was: "Forget it. Wait for better times." But I was not about to give up simply because some friends did not see how I could win as an opposition candidate for mayor.

Organizing My Slate

I decided to personally knock on doors of people I believed could be induced to run with me. While I did not have money, I had certain ideas on how to develop the city that I believed should be given a try. Moreover, if they agreed to run with me, then together, I was certain we could trounce the Marcos electoral machinery locally.

I first asked Solona, the wife of Reuben Canoy, to run with me as my vice mayor. She tactfully declined. She said that she was not a politician and that it was enough for her family that Reuben was in politics as an Opposition member of the Interim Batasang Pambansa. I, then, offered the position to Guerrero Adaza, brother of Homobono. A pragmatic person, he also turned it down. He had a business, a lending firm that catered mainly to public school teachers, which he did not want to leave. I felt, however, that the more important reason why Adaza did not want to run with me was that Roa, our expected opponent, was not only perceived to be a Goliath in the politics of the city but was also the principal sponsor at his wedding.

The initial difficulties, notwithstanding, I was able to complete my slate for all the elective positions in the city. My ticket was really a hodgepodge of new names in Cagayan de Oro politics, but I considered their willingness to stand up to the Marcos regime and their social and economic backgrounds as the best assets we had to fight the administration.

The odds-makers, however, gave us no chance of winning at all. We had no money. We had no barangay captains lining up to endorse us. We had no political bigwigs to root for us, except Reuben Canoy, the IBP Opposition assemblyman of our region. Concordio Diel, the governor of Misamis Oriental, was a Marcos partisan. Pelaez was also a Marcos henchman. Worse, politically speaking, we had defined our campaign line categorically and publicly that, as a group, we were unequivocally opposed to the martial law regime. Our candidacies, then, appeared to be thoroughly quixotic. A lowly clerk in the office of a city judge said it all when we campaigned in the chambers of the judge with all the contempt she could muster, *"Wala kamoy pagdag-an!"* "You can't win!".

Although we did encounter the likes of the skittish clerk now and then, we also had rah-rah boys who thought that there was no way we could lose. One of the most enthusiastic was Guillermo Parrel, a former student leader and a political supporter of Roa, who agreed to run as a candidate for councilor in my slate. Weeks before I declared for the city's mayoralty, he told me I was destined to be mayor of the city and no circumstance could deny me that position except my own doubts. His opinion was backed by another friend, lawyer Fred Gapuz, and some individuals who supported my candidacy in the election for Constitutional Convention delegate in 1970.

Mercado's 'No Show'

Despite the taunts that were hurled against our ticket, I thought that my city slate was a good one. But choosing my vice mayoral candidate turned out to be a harrowing experience — not only because my original picks, Solona Canoy and Guerrero Adaza, turned me down — but more so because the person who had committed to run with me as my vice mayor disappeared hours before the deadline for the filing of our certificates of candidacy.

Dr. Santiago Mercado, Jr., a popular Eyes, Ears, Nose and Throat (EENT) specialist not only in the city but in Northern Mindanao as well, was our group's unanimous choice for vice mayor. He had another factor going for him. He was a nephew of Pelaez. In our group's collective estimate, if we got him to be my vice mayoral candidate, he could bring in pro-Pelaez votes for our slate. It would also be a political coup of sorts because it would demonstrate that the formidable Pelaez political machinery in the city was beginning to show cracks.

After a series of meetings, we got Mercado's commitment to be my vice mayor. With his word, we proceeded to fill up the seven seats for the city council. There we had less of a problem. In no time, we formed a full slate of councilors. Heading the list was lawyer Pablo Magtajas, who was a well-known labor leader. Lawyer Roderico Villaroya, student leader and entrepreneur Guillermo Parrel, lawyer Henry Bacal, civic leader Lourdes La Viña, and businessmen Jose Abbu and Ramon Yap completed the team.

We had our certificates of candidacy prepared for filing on the last day fixed by the election law. We had to do so just before midnight. Fred Gapuz and I asked all of our candidates to be at our house on Victoria Street at the latest by 9 p.m. By that time, everybody was there except our vice mayoral candidate, Mercado. We thought he would only be a little late but, by 10 p.m., he had not yet arrived. We called his house. There was no reply. We sent somebody to fetch him. He was not there. And nobody seemed to know where he was. We waited a little longer, but Mercado did not come.

It turned out that Pelaez had talked with him and his family and, invoking familial ties, pressured him to withdraw as our vice mayoral candidate. The pressure on Mercado and his family must have been so great that he not only did not file his certificate of candidacy, he also did not explain why.

In near panic, I asked Magtajas to be our vice mayoral candidate. He declined. He said he had agreed to run with me only as a candidate for councilor, not for vice mayor. Also, he said, his wife, Anita, would never agree to his running for vice mayor. He simply was not prepared for it.

As we were discussing who should replace Mercado, the clock was ticking closer to the deadline. If we could not find a substitute, we would have no vice mayoral candidate. I thought the void would give the Marcos candidates for the city a valid point to exploit during the campaign. An unfilled slot for the vice mayorship would be a bad thing because it would be seen as a sign of weakness in that we could not even complete our team. I refused to accept that as a possibility. By all means, I told our group that we must fill up the slot.

Finally, upon suggestion of Gapuz, our political strategist, I agreed that Magtajas should, indeed, be our candidate for vice mayor. But there was a big problem. Magtajas did not want to be it. Since time was running out, Gapuz quietly proposed to me that the certificate of candidacy of Magtajas be corrected to reflect that he was running for the office of vice mayor, not councilor. Since we could not get Magtajas to sign an amended certificate of candidacy, he said that we should just erase with correcting fluid the portion which said that Magtajas was running for "councilor" and replace it with the words "vice mayor." The change was done and was revealed to Magtajas after the fact. As expected, he remonstrated. But, with peer pressure collectively exerted on him, he eventually gave in and agreed to run for vice mayor. In his place for councilor, we chose Cecilio Pepito, Jr., a young lawyer, whose family was engaged in a flourishing fishing business in Puerto, a barangay east of the city.

With Ambing Magtajas as our vice mayor, the certificates were filed minutes before the midnight deadline by Jose Pepe Abbu and Jacob Montesa. Ambing was a particularly good choice. He was a recognized labor lawyer, a loving husband to Anita and a doting father to their brood of six children. On top of it all, he was a godly person who had implicit faith in the goodness of Divine Providence. In retrospect, I could not have chosen a better man than Ambing to be my running mate. In fact, when as mayor I was persecuted by Marcos, he stayed the course and was faithful to the ideals of our Opposition group in the city.

My team for the city council was also made up of good individuals who were certainly qualified to serve the people of the city. By that I mean that I saw no indications at the time that they would promote their personal interests over the welfare of the people.

My Rival

Although Pedro Neri Roa was the odds-on favorite of political pundits in the city as the KBL bet for mayor, such were the vagaries of political fortunes that Francisco X. Velez, a former city prosecutor, turned out to be the party's candidate. Velez was Pelaez's choice for mayor. Practical considerations should have favored Roa. As a former Congressman and

Governor of Misamis Oriental, he still had a well-oiled political machine in the city. And while he won those elective positions as a Pelaez man in earlier elections, lately, he was appointed — without the latter's intervention — mayor of the city by Marcos, an indication that he had access to the very center of power.

Roa, however, was an unabashed womanizer who saw nothing wrong with keeping mistresses for as long as he could support them and the children who were born of their liaisons. Moreover, he was a high school-dropout and rather inarticulate in matters of public governance. But what he lacked in formal schooling, he made up for in demonstrable common sense and business acumen that made him, at the time, probably the wealthiest man in Mindanao.

His perceived lack of morals or formal education was not the cause of Pelaez's discarding him in favor of Velez. He knew Roa's deficiencies when he backed him in the latter's two successful political outings. In reality, he had a personal gripe against Roa. He did not like Roa because, among other things, the latter never consulted him on anything when he was congressman and governor of Misamis Oriental and, even more recently, when he was the appointed mayor of Cagayan de Oro. In a word, Roa, once in power, tended to go his own way rather than follow Pelaez. To Pelaez, the failure of his political protégés to ask him his opinion on political matters was the most grievous sin that they could commit and for which there was no forgiveness. As a seasoned politician, he also sensed that if Roa won as mayor with Marcos's direct support, he would be marginalized in the politics of Cagayan de Oro, the center of his power base in Northern Mindanao.

Thus, Pelaez chose Velez as his candidate for mayor. Marcos went along with his decision because Pelaez was the KBL head of the region and, anyway, he also did not see any strong opposition contender looming in the horizon. We were, of course, most pleased with the Pelaez decision. Roa, after all, would have been a more menacing opponent.

The choice of Velez as the KBL candidate for mayor angered Roa privately. But he held his peace until the last week of the campaign period when he gave the order to his followers to vote for me. For fear of offending Marcos, however, Roa never publicly announced his support for me. What he did was to send his lawyer-confidant, Enriquito Beja, who was also my cousin, to inform me that his supporters would junk Velez and go all out for me — on the sly. Roa's support, though covert, lifted the spirits of our campaigners immensely.

People's Support

At the start of the campaign, I suggested that the members of our slate should contribute a few thousand pesos each to our election fund. Everybody agreed to do so. Nothing of the sort happened. I did not see money flow into our campaign kitty from our candidates or from any major contributor.

Miraculously, we survived. Ordinary folks made up for the lack of hefty contributions and for what we, as candidates, could not provide.

Santiago Balabag, a market meat vendor, was an outstanding example of the kind of grassroots support that we enjoyed. He supplied us with enough meat for viands from Day 1 until the last vote-counting day. Other individuals took care of our propaganda needs in the barangays, including paying for the poll watchers who kept vigil on the day of the election and the days when the votes were being counted. Still others paid for vehicles that provided mobility for our workers. Bing told me that, without the unfailing support of Balabag and of the other generous souls, we would have lost the election even before the first ballot was cast.

Our rallies usually covered three or four barangays a day. I made it a point to be present at every rally. Interim Batasan Assemblyman Reuben Canoy was the only politician with national stature who energized our campaign by joining us every now and then and by providing us with moral and material support.

Whenever the opportunity arose, we campaigned also for Bono Adaza, our gubernatorial candidate and his slate in some towns of Misamis Oriental. Adaza was the founder of the Mindanao Alliance, which also supported my candidacy as a "guest candidate" for mayor even though I had filed as a candidate of the National Union for Liberation. My being a candidate of the NUL and a guest candidate of the MA later caused me problems. It was used by the KBL candidate for mayor to file a protest against me on the ground of turncoatism. The protest nearly cost me the position.

The Issues

As oppositionists, we harped on the need to regain the freedoms of our people and to end martial law. We told the people that we did not need to be ruled by guns so that we could feed ourselves. We needed freedom under the rule of law to develop our full potential as a people.

Velez, on the other hand, merely echoed what Pelaez articulated. The city needed to have a pipeline to Marcos not even to develop but to survive, he said. Pelaez and Velez also made broad hints that our group was leftist (read, communistic) in orientation.

The party lines were clearly drawn in the campaign. I could sense from people's reactions in our sorties that they liked our position better than the KBL's. The idea that we should not obsequiously depend for our development on the martial law authorities, for instance, clicked with the public. The spontaneous applause that greeted our punch lines linking freedom and development in our rallies showed that people resented the repressions of their rights under martial rule. As we campaigned in the 80 barangays of the city, only in the barangay of Patag did we experience palpable hostility among the audience in our rally. The reason was that Patag was the Mindanao headquarters of the 4th Military Area. Apparently, the soldiers and their families who resided in the barangay were brainwashed to consider us as communists.

Since Velez was a *novatos*, a neophyte, in politics, Pelaez took up the cudgels for him, extolling his virtues and hitting us with every conceivable issue, true or false. Old-timers in the city observed that it was the first time in the history of Cagayan de Oro politics that Pelaez campaigned even in the barangays for his candidate.

I liked that. I mean Pelaez's taking the most prominent role in the campaign for Velez. Now I could hit him back with more reason than if Velez were left alone. In my view, Velez was better ignored than talked about. And the more Pelaez thrashed me on the campaign trail, the more people who had barely heard of me became curious as to who I really was.

Pelaez charged that I was a *pinko*, a communist lover, an impractical individual whose thoughts on development were only sound theoretically, and an opportunist who only came home to ask for the votes of the people.

I denied that I was a communist or a communist lover. I retorted that the label was obviously false because communism and freedom in my view were mutually repugnant and I was an all-out advocate of freedom for our people. I also said that ideas to develop a city can only be demonstrated empirically and that he would never know if they worked or not unless given a try. As for his imputation that I only came home to ask the city folks to vote for me, I remonstrated that he should be the last one to raise the issue. After all, when he first ran for congressman, he was a resident of Manila who never showed his face to the people of Misamis Oriental before the campaign began. In addition, I said — with political license — that he conveniently forgot to mention that I was forced to reside in Manila because, as a political prisoner, martial law authorities wanted to keep an eye on my movements.

In their *miting de avance* on the evening of January 28, 1980, Pelaez, who was the last speaker, threw a bombshell from which he thought I could not recover. The midnight of January 28 was the last day allowed by law for campaigning. In the context of the campaign, that meant that I would no longer have the chance to rebut him publicly, say, on a public stage. He quoted a purported Comelec ruling that supposedly disqualified me. *"Ayaw na ninyo botohi si Nene. Sayang lang ang boto ninyo!* Don't vote for Nene. You'd be wasting your votes."

Surreptitious Comelec Ruling

Pelaez's polemics were based on a surreptitious Comelec ruling dated January 28, 1982, two days before the local elections, that I was not qualified to run for mayor of Cagayan de Oro because I was allegedly a "turncoat." In layman's terms that meant that I changed political parties when I ran for mayor and had, therefore, violated the election law. The Comelec argument was that, although I was a National Union for Liberation candidate for mayor,

I had also registered as an official candidate of the Mindanao Alliance for the same office. Hence, in their view I was disqualified to run for mayor.

The timing of Pelaez's broadsides against me was designed to make it difficult for me to get legal redress. He made the disqualification order public in Cagayan de Oro close to midnight of the KBL *Miting de Avance* on January 28.

As fate would have it, Pelaez ended his speech approximately 15 minutes before the midnight legal deadline for campaigning. That Pelaez stopped before midnight was by itself miraculous. In the past political campaigns, he would keep the crowds dogging his campaign trail on their toes until the clock tolled the end of the campaign season.

In the event, we had roughly 15 minutes to rebut Pelaez publicly. There was no other way to do that than by radio or television. I rushed to the local television station owned by businessman Dante Sarraga, which was just two minutes away from my place in the city. Sarraga who wanted to project an image of neutrality for his station readily gave permission for me to broadcast my rebuttal of Pelaez. Even at that late hour, the station was still on air and many city residents were tuned to it for last minute political developments.

Going straight to the point, I told the people over Sarraga's TV that Pelaez was totally wrong. I was not disqualified. And although we were hobbled by time constraints, my lawyers Joker Arroyo, Lorenzo Tañada, Soc Rodrigo, Abraham F. Sarmiento, and Raul Gonzalez — had gone to the Supreme Court to stop the Comelec from disqualifying me. At that point, then, the Comelec order was not yet final and enforceable.

As if my rebuttal did not amount to anthing, the following day, January 29 and on the early morning of January 30, Election Day itself, Pelaez had the Comelec order rebroadcast over the radio stations sympathetic to the martial law administration. The message was that the city electorate would be wasting their ballots if they voted for me because I had already been disqualified by the Comelec.

Supreme Court Issues TRO

On the day before the elections, the Supreme Court issued a TRO against the Comelec order disqualifying me. Our problem, however, was how to get it to the attention of the voting public cn voting day itself. We solved it by having Fred Gapuz, fly to Manila on the eve of Election Day and return on the "red-eye" morning flight on Election Day, itself, with an official copy of the restraining order.

On the very hour of Fred's arrival, our supporters mimeographed thousands of flyers quoting the TRO to show that Pelaez had misinformed the people.

Fortunately, the voters of Cagayan de Oro refused to believe the KBL-Comelec propaganda that I had been disqualified. From the exit polls done on voters in the *poblacion*, the city center and from a sampling of rural barangay election precincts, I knew I was doing quite well. My Cagayan de Oro lawyers Fred Gapuz, Bonifacio Regalado, Rolando Galimpin, Jacob and Felipe Montesa reported that the exit polls even in faraway barangays indicated that I would win handily even on the basis alone of the individual votes cast for me as mayor. The block votes cast for Mindanao Alliance, they said, would only ensure that all the candidates of my city slate would win.

In this election, according to Comelec Rules, block voting was allowed. Voters by the thousands cast their votes for me not only as their individual choice but also as the Mindanao Alliance party candidate for mayor.

Enter the Gargoyle

The Comelec, however, would not leave me alone with my imminent victory. On January 29, 1980, the day before the elections, the Comelec publicly displayed its gargoylian features for the first time in the City in the person of Virgilio Garcillano, the Comelec Regional Director of Region X. His first menacing move was to circulate through the Cagayan de Oro press and to all members of the Board of Canvassers in the city a telegram that he had supposedly received from the Commission on Elections in Manila. The contents of the telegram, a copy of which my office obtained, follow:

> RUSH January 29, 1980
>   Regional Election Director
>   Virgilio Garcellano (sic)
> Cagayan de Oro City
>
>   Pursuant to restraining order of the Supreme Court in GR No. 52428 you are hereby instructed to desist from implementing COMELEC resolution No. 248 stop However resolution No. 247 stands and should be implemented pursuant to its dispositive part stop This supersedes all other previous instructions by wire or phone end Commission on Elections
>
> (SGD) LEONARDO B. PEREZ
>   Chairman

Aside from the fact that Perez did not even know how to spell the family name of his regional director correctly — he addressed his telegram to Garcellano, instead of Garcillano — I was bothered by the "however" clause of the telegram. The troubling clause read, "However resolution No. 247 stands and should be implemented pursuant to its dispositive part."

Using the clause as his basis, Garcillano in turn ordered the city Comelec officer:

As a consequence NO BLOCK VOTES for Mindanao Alliance will be credited to its candidates belonging to the City. This supersedes all previous news bulletins issued by this Office.

Certified correct.
ATTY. VIRGILIO O. GARCELLANO (sic)
Regional Director

If Garcillano himself had sent the telegram, he also did not know how to spell his family name because he used the Perez spelling: Garcellano. It might, however, have been sent in his name by a subordinate who did not care whether the family name of his superior was spelled with an "i" or an "e." For many of us who spoke the Visayan language, it did not really matter that much. We tended to pronounce Garcellano as Garcillano anyway.

The net effect of the Garcillano order was to nullify the votes cast in favor of the Mindanao Alliance in the City. That meant that the ballots that only mentioned the MA would not be counted in favor of our candidates individually. If we allowed the order to prevail, I would still win, but my lead over Velez would be considerably reduced and our candidates for councilors would be risking defeat. It would also considerably affect the chances of victory of our gubernatorial candidate, Homobono Adaza, in the city.

The Garcillano order changed the rules of the elections midstream in that, at the start of the election period, we were made to understand that "block votes" were valid and would be counted in favor individually of the candidates making up a particular slate. Now, the Garcillano order would prevent that.

We, therefore, instructed our watchers to do everything legally possible to prevent any attempt by the Citizens Election Committees at the voting precincts to disallow "block votes" cast in favor of MA candidates. Our efforts at preventing a miscarriage of justice at the polling place got a boost from a telegram released by the Office of the Election Registrar of Cagayan de Oro, lawyer Bernardita F. Cabacungan, at 4:55 p.m. of January 30, Election Day. The telegram sent to her by the Commission on Elections in Manila reversed Garcillano's instruction to invalidate votes intended for me and the block votes cast for our slate. The telegram, written in capital letters, to her follows:

RUSH
ELECTION REGISTRAR
CAGAYAN DE ORO CITY

IN VIEW REGISTRAR RESTRAINING ORDER OF SUPREME COURT IN GR NO.52428 AQUILINO Q PIMENTEL JR ET AL VS COMMISSION ON ELECTIONS ET

AL FROM ENFORCING COMELEC RESOLUTION DISQUALIFYING PETITIONERS IN SAID CASE BEFORE SUPREME COURT AS CANDIDATES FOR POSITION (sic) INVOLVED THAT CITY CMA YOU ARE HEREBY DIRECTED NO (sic) TO ENFORCE SAID COMELEC RESOLUTIONS CONTAINED IN OUR TEL TODAY TO YOU ON CONTENTS OF COMELEC RES OF 28 JANUARY 80 ITEM 8519 PCD 247 AND ITEM 8520 PDC 248 CMA UNTIL FURTHER NOTICE FROM COMMISSION ELECTIONS STOP WIRE RECEIPT AND COMPLIANCE IMMEDIATELY END LAW

COMMISSION ON ELECTION (sic)

Cabacungan added her own interpretative postscript to the telegram as follows:

NOTE: Instruction to all Citizens Election Committee Members:

Mindanao Alliance is now entitled to *Block Voting*, so if a voter writes MA — all candidates of Mindanao Alliance from governor down to city councilor is credited one vote each.
Atty. Bernardita F. Cabacungan

Election Registrar IV
Cagayan de Oro City

Cabacungan's telegram, although released late in the afternoon of Election Day, was a shot in the arm for me and my teammates, as well as for Adaza and our provincial candidates. It was now clear that votes for me as a mayoral candidate and the "block votes" for our ticket were to be counted.

In the face of Comelec Manila's apparent volte face, as manifested in its telegram to Cabacungan on January 29, Garcillano, as the Comelec's regional director, was faced with no alternative but to issue his instructions, also in a telegram, dated January 30, as follows:

To all Citizens Election Committee
Of Cagayan de Oro City
  Hereunder quoted is the telegram of the Law Department, Commission on Elections, Manila to the Election Registrar of Cagayan de Oro City,

QUOTE
RUSH
ELECTION REGISTRAR
CAGAYAN DE ORO CITY

IN VIEW REGISTRAR RESTRAINING ORDER OF SUPREME COURT IN GR NO. 52428 AQUILINO Q PIMENTEL JR ET AL VS COMMISSION ON ELECTIONS ET AL FROM ENFORCING COMELEC RESOLUTION DISQUALIFYING PETITIONERS IN SAID CASE BEFORE SUPREME COURT AS CANDIDATES FOR POSITION (sic) INVOLVED THAT CITY CMA YOU ARE HEREBY DIRECTED NO (sic) TO ENFORCE SAID COMELEC RESOLUTIONS CONTAINED IN OUR TEL TODAY TO YOU ON CONTENTS OF COMELEC RES OF 28 JANUARY 80 ITEM 8519 PCD 247 AND ITEM 8520 PDC 248 CMA UNTIL FURTHER NOTICE FROM COMMISSION ELECTIONS STOP WIRE RECEIPT AND COMPLIANCE IMMEDIATELY END LAW

COMMISSION ON ELECTION (sic)

UNQUOTE

Again, Garcillano put an addendum to the telegram as follows:

This supersedes all other orders. As a consequences (sic) votes for Mindanao Alliance will entitle MA candidates one vote each to include the City slate.

Compliance is here enjoined.

VIRGILIO O. GARCILLANO
Regional Election Director

This time, Garcillano had his name correctly spelled in the telegram to the City Election Registrar.

Garcillano, however, had his own agenda. Since the public school teachers who chaired the Board of Canvassers at the polling precincts apparently did not follow the first order of the Comelec disqualifying me from running for mayor, he decided to go from one polling place to another to personally stop the counting of the votes in my favor. Fortuitously, many of public school teachers chairing the counting in the precincts engaged him in arguments that delayed his movement considerably and prevented him from causing substantial damage to my mayoral bid.

Bing Checkmates Garcillano

By dusk of Election Day, Garcillano found himself at the polling center of Nazareth, a barangay with a huge voting population where I had a rather large following. Bing, accompanied by Lourdes La Viña, a candidate for councilor in my slate, decided to confront him there. She told him that she doubted that Comelec Manila had instructed him to nullify my votes because Supreme Court Justice Claudio Teehankee informed our Manila lawyers, Senator Tañada and Joker Arroyo, that the SC had vacated the Comelec order disqualifying me from race for mayor. She challenged

Garcillano to verify what she said by going with her and La Viña to the office of the provincial commander at Camp Alagar, where they could use its communications facilities to get in touch with Comelec Manila and with Justice Teehankee, Senator Tañada and Arroyo. She suggested they go to the provincial commander's office because, at that time, the PC/INP had the best available telephone service not only in the city but also in the whole country.

Surprisingly, Garcillano agreed to go with Bing and Inday La Viña to Camp Alagar, which was about 20 minutes away from Nazareth. At the camp, they were received by the provincial commander, Col. Triunfo Agustin. In the presence of Agustin, Bing complained that Garcillano had no authority to stop the counting and the canvassing of the votes for me because the Supreme Court had taken jurisdiction over the matter. To buttress her argument, she repeated to Agustin what she previously told Garcillano that Justice Teehankee assured our lawyers, Senator Tañada and Arroyo, that the Supreme Court had restrained the Comelec order voiding my candidacy.

To impress Agustin and Garcillano that she knew what she was talking about, Bing asked Agustin's permission, which he so kindly gave, to use his office telephone to call up Justice Teehankee, Tañada and Arroyo in Manila. Bing, of course, had no direct access to Teehankee, but the mere dropping of his name at that critical moment disarmed not only Agustin but also Garcillano. After all, even under conditions of martial law, Teehankee was a respected and prominent senior member of the Supreme Court. By dropping Teehankee's name, Bing implicitly impressed upon Agustin and Garcillano that, if the latter was allowed to continue with his unwarranted attempts to stop the counting of my votes, he (Garcillano) could very well be cited for contempt of the Supreme Court.

In the event, Bing, however, could not get through to Teehankee, in all likelihood because it was not only already getting late on the evening of Election-Day but also because it would have been unseemly for a Supreme Court justice to receive a telephone call from the wife of a litigant whose case was still pending before the tribunal. Thus, she did the next best thing and that was to get our lawyer, Joker Arroyo, on the line. Before Joker could say anything, Bing told him in rapid-fire fashion that Garcillano was stopping the canvassing of the mayor's votes in Cagayan de Oro. She suggested to him that the matter should immediately be brought to the attention of Justice Teehankee. She requested him to get back to her as soon as possible because she and Garcillano were discussing the issue at the office of the provincial commander, Colonel Agustin. Arroyo must have been surprised at Bing's loud suggestions, which were intended more for the ears of Colonel Agustin and Garcillano. As if Arroyo had said he would call back in a few minutes, Bing hung up and she and Inday La Viña engaged Agustin and Garcillano in another round of discussion that repeated over and over again the same arguments Bing had brought up earlier.

Killing time, Bing repeatedly stressed that the Comelec and Garcillano were in error in trying to stop the canvassing of votes for mayor and that it would be better if the matter were left to the judgment of the people. Garcillano, on the other hand, kept stressing that he was merely following the orders of his superiors in Manila. Back and forth the argument went. Outside Agustin's office, in the various polling places in the city, the canvassing of the votes continued. Before anyone in Agustin's office noticed, it was almost midnight and the canvassing was just about finished in the urban polling centers. The radio reports that filtered through in the office of Agustin confirmed that I was already leading my opponent 75%-25%. Bing had successfully checkmated Garcillano.

The Die is Cast

By 12 midnight the colonel, who was probably a closet supporter of mine, pulled out a bottle of whisky from one of his desk drawers. He toasted everyone with the words "the die is cast." Indeed, by that time, Garcillano could no longer stop the overwhelming trend in my favor.

Anyway, the counting and the canvassing of the votes in Cagayan de Oro eventually reached that stage where the next step was for Comelec to set the date for my and my slate's proclamation as the duly elected local officials of city. The proclamation did not follow as would normally have been the case. The delay was caused by a telegraphic request dated January 31 sent by KBL candidates Velez and Tiro to Comelec Manila that the canvass and the proclamation of the winning candidates for the city and the province be suspended.

Our lawyers in Manila quickly argued that there was no other recourse possible but for the Comelec to respect the verdict of the people. The people had voted for me as their duly elected city mayor and for Adaza as the duly elected governor of Misamis Oriental.

At the City Board of Canvassers, Election Registrar Bernardita Cabacungan as chairman and Schools Superintendent Teodoro P. Dano and Auditor Diosdado Ortiz as members, unanimously turned down Velez's request to suspend the canvass of the votes pending resolution of his complaint by the Manila Comelec. The board also resolved to "unanimously continue the canvass until ordered by the Commission on Election (sic), Manila to postpone or discontinue the same."

Tally of Votes

When the votes were counted on the evening of January 30, 1980, I trounced Velez by a huge margin: 75%-25%. In actual numbers, I routed him by more than 42,000 votes. In addition, my candidates for vice mayor and all my seven councilors were overwhelmingly elected. In fact, the seventh councilor in my slate, Jose "Pepe" Abbu, beat the top ranking KBL candidate for councilor, lawyer Adolfo Balinado, by more than 7,000 votes.

Our group's clean sweep in the City also gave our candidate for governor of the province, Homobono Adaza more than 35,000 votes over the KBL candidate, Judge Meynardo Tiro. The city votes sealed his victory over Tiro. And that led Adaza to tell Bing and me shortly after the counting of the votes that he owed his victory to Cagayan de Oro voters and that he was grateful to our group. Without the Cagayan de Oro votes, he could not have overcome the sizeable leads that Tiro had posted over him in many of the municipalities of the province. In fact, only one of his board member candidates, Teddy Cabeltes, won. But overall, our victory was actually a big one because Pelaez had been the undefeated political champion in the province of Misamis Oriental and the city of Cagayan de Oro since the 1950s. Until the local elections in 1980, whoever he chose as candidates invariably won.

Pelaez Era Ends

Our group did the unthinkable in Misamis Oriental and Cagayan de Oro politics. Our victories at the city and provincial levels ended the political dominance of Pelaez. The event was not lost on Marcos. Marcos adviser, Antonio Tupaz, told me that, for several weeks after the elections, Pelaez was the butt of jokes in Malacañang meetings. They kidded him no end that he could no longer hold his own against political pygmies like Canoy, Adaza and Pimentel. The jokes on Pelaez's loss were not meant simply to amuse either Pelaez or the joke-maker. The jokes had a more politically sinister agenda. They were meant to prod him to get out of the Marcos machinery so that others like Oging Navarro, a grizzled old political veteran of Surigao, or even Tupaz could replace him as Marcos's point man in Northern Mindanao. At the time, however, Pelaez did not leave the administration on account of the sick jokes that were thrown his way. He was, as Shakespeare would say "made of sterner stuff" that mere jokes could not move.

Personally, our victory in Cagayan de Oro and Misamis Oriental was a vindication of sorts for our family. In the 1950s when Pelaez first run for Congress, he promised my father in writing that he would support him at the next elections if the latter withdrew from the congressional race. My father did so. But the pledge was never redeemed. Our superstitious neighbors called our win over the Pelaez political superstructure in the 1980 elections as *gaba* or, loosely, karma.

With the breakup of Pelaez's political hegemony in Northern Mindanao, our overexcited partisans thought that the Canoy-Adaza-Pimentel triumvirate would now become the rallying point of people opposed to martial law not only in Mindanao but also throughout the country. There was reason for that sanguine hope because we had bested the Pelaez-led KBL in Cagayan de Oro, the regional capital, no less, of Region X, and, as a bonus, Adaza was now the governor of Misamis Oriental. Also, in the earlier Interim Batasang

Pambansa regional elections, Canoy was the only Opposition figure to come out victorious. No wonder our supporters drummed up our group's victory in Region X as the best record of all Opposition groups in the electoral exercise of 1980.

The spin that we had the best showing politically among all opposition groups was only slightly true because two other opposition candidates for city mayor in Mindanao also posted spectacular victories.

Cesar Climaco won over Maria Clara Lobregat, the KBL candidate in Zamboanga City. His vice mayor, Manuel Dalipe, and their candidates for councilor, except one, also made it.

Jesus Sanciangco likewise bested Fernando T. Bernad, the KBL candidate, in Ozamiz City. His vice mayor, Dr. Ben Fuentes, and their candidates for councilor, except two, won.

Zamboanga City, Ozamiz City and Cagayan de Oro City thus shared the honors of having booted out the KBL slates and replaced them with legitimate opposition groups in the 1980 polls.

The media hype over our victory in Cagayan de Oro and Misamis Oriental continued for a while. Events, however, showed that Reuben Canoy, Bono Adaza and I were not destined to be the fulcrum of opposition politics. Not in Cagayan de Oro or Northern Mindanao or anywhere.

The problems that I had with my erstwhile colleagues in the opposition struggle for freedom in our part of the country got even more complicated by Marcos's and the Comelec's entry into the fray in less than two years of my incumbency as mayor of Cagayan de Oro. The details of my fight to keep afloat politically are set out Chapters 23, 25 and 26.

Chapter 22

Early Days in City Hall

1981: *CONFERING WITH MY KEY SUPPORTERS as mayor. (Left to right): Edwin Padla, Anastacio Abas, Luding Matias, me, Vice Mayor Magtajas and Councilor Parrel.*

A fter I was elected but before I assumed the mayor's office, a classmate of mine at law school, lawyer Abeto D. Salcedo, visited me in my house to tell me that Pedro Roa sent me a brand new Toyota Cressida for my use. The car was parked beside the house and he was handing the keys over to me.

Since Roa supported me in my candidacy for mayor even if he dissembled it for fear of displeasing Marcos, he probably had the best of intentions when he tried to give me a car. The offer was tempting because, truth to tell, I only owned a battered van and the city government did not have a good car for my use as the new city mayor. But I did not wish to be beholden to anyone. Thus, I told Salcedo as tactfully as I could that, while I appreciated Roa's gesture, I really could not accept it. I said that I would use whatever vehicle was available at city hall or I might avail of an ordinance passed by the previous administration to buy a new vehicle for the incoming mayor.

Salcedo's face fell in grave disappointment at my words. He did not think that I would turn down Roa's offer. But I did and that sort of started my work as the city mayor on the wrong foot as Roa received the refusal with ill grace. He made his displeasure known not only to me but also to the people of the city some days after I formally assumed the mayorship.

Simple Rites

My inauguration as mayor was marked by a simple ceremony. Departing from the formal traditional oath-taking during which the incoming officials usually dressed in suits or in Barong Tagalog with people lined up as witnesses at a public plaza, I opted to have my and my party mates' oath-takings at a seaside resort in the barangay of Bonbon. While the place was called a resort, it actually only had the barest of facilities. I met the owner, Artemio Baal, in a summer ROTC training program when I was finishing my law course and he and I became friends.

My slate and I took our oaths of office clad in our daily informal wear before the oldest barangay captain of the city, Juan Vuelban. I think we started a precedent here because to my knowledge no elective city official ever took his or her oath of office before a barangay captain. City mayors usually took their oath before judges of the trial courts or justices of the Supreme Court or some such high dignitary.

The people of Cagayan de Oro, however, did not mind that I took my oath before a barangay official. More than a thousand simple folks, mostly from the barangays, witnessed the oath-taking and joined the festivities at the beach. The mood was one of jubilation and many guests articulated their elation that the newly elected city hall officials were not beholden to the martial rule government or to vested interests. Later, I was told that a renegade priest, Fr. Frank Navarro, who became the head of the New People's Army in the Surigao-Agusan area, was there to witness my accession to office. Among other things, his presence at the affair probably raised the perception of Marcos and his minions in the military that I was, if not a card-carrying communist, at least, a fellow traveler, either of which I most decidedly was not. Incidentally, at that time, a number of priests like Conrado Balweg, Serapion Agatep and Edicio de la Torre had joined the armed struggle against the government.

To set a more populist style to my mayorship, I often went to the City Hall in T-Shirt and denims. Tommy Pacana, one of my more articulate and perceptive confidants, once described a crumpled shirt I wore to the office as "if I had slept on it." It was an exaggeration but had a grain of truth to it in that I was never one to pay too much attention to how my shirts looked. On select occasions, I wore Barong Tagalog. Despite pictures that occasionally show me in coat-and-tie, I was never comfortable in that get-up because of the country's high humidity. Also I believed that formal attire tended to put an unnecessary barrier between my constituents and me. Moreover, since I had turned down Roa's offer of a car early on in my incumbency and did not avail of the appropriations passed by the previous city council to buy a new car for my use, I would walk — with a bag slung on my shoulder — from my house to the city hall a few blocks away. Or I would backride on the motorcycle of my compadre and boyhood friend, Cecilio Nagac, an employee of the City Health Office. Any man in coat-and-tie walking to City Hall or back-riding on a motorcycle – even if he was the mayor – would look ridiculous. I did not want to go to that extent even in the name of service to our people.

Only after friends counseled me against taking "unnecessary risks" — like hitching on motorcycles or walking in a city which was no longer the city of friendly people that I had grown up in — did I take to riding whatever city vehicle was available or private cars lent to me for short durations by well-meaning friends. It was not the best arrangement for me as the new city mayor, but it sufficed to meet the needs for mobility and security for the moment.

Ending Reliance on Goodwill

In a matter of days, we got Roa's angry response to my nonacceptance of the car that he had offered. He recalled the trucks he had lent the city to haul garbage when he was the mayor. The trucks were there when I took over the mayorship. His recall — done without notice — caused some problems for my administration as the city did not have the dump trucks to collect the garbage. Roa probably thought, as some of our mutual friends had suggested, that I would go hat-in-hand to his *Kilometro 5* hideout along the road to Lumbia Airport and beg him to reconsider.

I did not have any such intention. If there was anything that I wished to immediately rid the city government of, it was reliance on the goodwill of any individual, no matter how well-intentioned, to enable us to deliver basic services to our constituents. With the strong backing of the city council, my administration decided to make do with what we could lease for the moment. Eventually, I got the city council to approve an ordinance to buy our own fleet of garbage trucks, which we did in a manner not done before. The transaction is detailed in the annual report I made to the people of Cagayan de Oro in 1981 that is mentioned in Chapter 28 of this book.

The acquisition of our own dump trucks ended the city's dependence on Roa's lending us his trucks for garbage collection and disposal. It also meant that the political support he extended to my administration had ended. Unwittingly, I had started an open war — though undeclared — with the mighty

Roa political machine. The state of political animosity between Roa and me added to the problems of my administration of the city from 1980 to 1984. It finally broke out into an all-out political battle when he and I tangled over the position of assemblyman of the city in the 1984 Batasang Pambansa elections.

Trimming the Workforce

In the meantime, aside from attending to "political problems" and mending local political fences, I also started to trim down the city's workforce, which, I thought, at more than 2,000, was bloated. I thought that we could do with no more than a thousand employees. With the advice of City Administrator Mordino Cua, we did not renew many "casual" appointments — employees who had no civil service eligibilities and who were mostly political accommodations. We also started to serve the walking papers of those we could terminate without violating the civil service laws.

I was not even halfway through with my goal to halve the work force at city hall when I could not go on any longer. The tears of the family members of those who were targeted for dismissal as they pleaded that their husbands, wives, sons or daughters be spared because they were breadwinners took their toll on me. I realized that my idealistic intent to employ only those needed by the city was no longer attainable. I saw that in a Third World city like Cagayan de Oro, city hall — up to a point — had to fill the role of an employer also. Were we a developed country, we could always tell people to go find jobs with the private sector. Unfortunately, there were no such jobs available to our people. So the purge of the overstaffed city hall ground to a halt and was never revived.

To assure the people that I was determined to fulfill my campaign pledge to modernize the city, I announced the prioritization of the construction of infrastructure projects in my administration by tripling the budget for roads, bridges and the like. I also indicated my determination to uphold the Rule of Law for the benefit of the people, regardless of status or rank or whether or not they were Christians or Muslims or of whatever denomination.

Upholding People's Right

Within days of my assumption as mayor, I received a report that two Muslim ambulant vendors were picked up by armed men in the commercial area of the city one evening. I did not personally know the two vendors, but since they were abducted in the city, I felt that it was my duty to find out where they were, why they were picked up and by whom.

I went first to Camp Alagar, the Constabulary camp, and then to Camp Evangelista, the Armed Forces camp, to inquire from their commanders if the two were being held in their detention facilities. Both commanders denied that they had detained the vendors. I told them separately that, assuming they were not responsible for the abduction of the vendors, since under martial law they had full authority to implement the criminal laws of the nation, it was their obligation to help me find out who did it. Of course, I did not use those tactless words. But I did make it plain to them that they could not just wash their hands as if they had nothing to do with the maintenance of law and order in the city.

The commanders politely told me that they would investigate the matter. After I left the military camps, I did not hear or get a responsive report from them at all. A few days later, the leaders of the Muslim community thanked me for my intervention in behalf of their lost brethren even if nothing concrete came out of it. They said that the incident showed that, as the mayor of the city, I cared for the well-being of the residents without any bias. They also had a surprise for me. One of the two abducted vendors was with them.

The man told me a riveting story of how an honest-to-goodness business venture that he and his companion were doing turned into a nightmare that ended in the death of his companion. He said they were selling their wares — mostly trinkets and perfumes in small bottles — on Tiano Brothers Street near the Divisoria Plaza, the city center, one evening when armed men in fatigues pounced on them, herded them — into military jeeps and brought them to the Kabula Bridge at the boundary of Cagayan de Oro and Baungon, Bukidnon. On the way, they were told that they were members of Moro groups rebelling against the government, which they both denied. At the bridge, the armed men forced them out of the jeeps and made them run for their lives. The bridge was ill lit and the night was dark. The surviving vendor said that he jumped off the bridge, risking injury from the big boulders below, and luckily landed in the deeper part of the flowing river. He heard shots but was not hit. His companion, however, was never found again.

When I asked him if he wanted to file charges against his abductors, he said that prudence dictated that he had better go back to Marawi and try to start life anew. He was not too sure that he could get justice under martial law conditions. Although I did not hear from the man again, my intervention for him showed the city's Muslim community that I was willing to put my office on the line to uphold the rights of any person, if he or she was victimized by anyone in Cagayan de Oro. Incidentally, the goodwill that I established with the Muslims of the city enabled me to recover, within months of my incumbency, two children — a five-year-old girl and an eight-year-old boy — from Bukidnon who were kidnapped and brought to Lanao del Sur. In another instance, through the intercession of friends in the two Lanao provinces, another kidnap victim, the wife of a prominent physician in the city, returned home safe and sound.

My resolve to uphold the Rule of Law was tested again in a few months when Angel Quimpo, owner of the Cagayan de Oro Coliseum, a cockpit in the city, announced that he would hold cockfights on days not prescribed by law. He said that he was authorized by the Philippine Constabulary-Integrated National Police Regional Commander Pedro Zafra and Provincial Commander

Triunfo Agustin to do so. Although Quimpo was a friend (I was his counsel in the libel case that Pelaez had filed against him years back), I told him in so many words that he had better not try to do it, otherwise I would order the closure of his cockpit. It was a good thing that he did not.

Blacklisting Offenders

A month or so after my installation as mayor, for some reason the prices of basic commodities and school supplies spiraled in the city. To prevent speculators from taking advantage of the situation, I activated the Price Stabilization Council. I asked Councilor Guillermo Parrel to head it. Under Parrel's guidance, the PSC closed down some retail stores for overpricing and other price control violations. It was a graphic lesson for me that a local executive merely had to show by example that he or she intended to enforce laws and that would cause a favorable ripple effect in the community.

Early on in my incumbency, I also had to tell a lawyer friend, Pascual Bacor, that I was blacklisting a client of his for delivering a secondhand lathe machine to the city that we were buying as brand new. Furthermore, I told Bacor that the city was rescinding the contract. I thought I did the city right but, in the process, I lost the friendship of Bacor and other lawyers with whom he was associated. They probably felt that they had lost face with their client. I felt the rupture of my friendship with Bacor and his circle of lawyer associates keenly because, as a lawyer myself, I had more kinship with fellow lawyers than with other professionals. As a professional sector, the lawyers were, in fact, the mainstay of my campaign for mayor.

I also caused the investigation of the siphoning of gasoline from the tanks of city trucks and vehicles by some unscrupulous drivers and employees. We punished some of the petty thieves who were caught, but I suppose the practice continued when the heat of the drive against it cooled off.

There was one other practice that I wanted to institute in the city hall and that was for officials to return the unused per diems given them whenever they traveled on official business. I started to do it myself. Later, I discontinued it because I was told that there were no official accounts to which the unused per diems could be returned. It was funny, I thought, that the government did not have the mechanism to cope with situations of the kind I described. But that was the way it was. And I left it at that by following the path of least resistance.

The most difficult corruption-related problem that I encountered as mayor was caused by a lady who visited my office one day. From Manila, she wired my office to inform me that she was coming to see me about the city's intention to purchase heavy equipment. She identified herself as an assistant of Dr. Pacifico Marcos, brother of the President.

My secretary, Anastacio Abas, probably overwhelmed by the name of her employer, suggested that we should send a car to meet her at the airport. Since I sensed that there was something amiss about the lady's expressed interest over the city's desire to acquire heavy equipment, I told Tio Tato Abas not to waste government time and money just to make her feel important. In any case, I added that the city was so small she could not miss the city hall even if she wanted to.

When she arrived in my office, the lady looked like a Kabuki performer, heavily made up and weighed down by jewelry dangling from her ears, neck and arms. Without much preliminaries, she importuned me to change the winner of the bid so that another supplier would supply the city with the heavy equipment. Weeks before, the city had conducted a public bidding for the acquisition of a bulldozer, a grader, a back-hoe and dump trucks costing several millions of pesos. The money was to come from a loan that had already been approved by a government banking institution and had only to be released.

When I told her that I could not do as she had urged, she dropped the name of Dr. Marcos and told me that the latter could facilitate the release of our loan. I did not change my stand and tried to explain with all the tact I could muster that the law forbade my changing the winner of the bid.

In the event, we did not get our loan. We could not buy our heavy equipment. And we failed to construct the roads and bridges that we envisioned for the city. In fairness, I never knew whether Dr. Marcos sent the lady or if she tried to intervene in the transaction on her own volition. In hindsight, I have often wondered if I was wrong in rejecting the proffered intervention of the office of a Marcos kin. Since I could not arrive at a definitive conclusion on the issue, I invariably consoled myself with the thought that following the law and one's conscience no matter what the consequences, in the final analysis, makes the challenges of life worth taking.

There was one other thing that I tried to avoid in the four years of my tenure as mayor. I tried not to celebrate my birthday in the city. The only time I was forced to be at home on my birthday was when I was under house arrest. The reason I stuck to that odd practice was to prevent people, especially total strangers, from giving me gifts. Early on in my stint as mayor, Dr. Florencio Zablan, who was a consultant of the Kawasaki Sintering Plant in Villanueva, Misamis Oriental, came to my office to brief me on the workings of the plant. Before I became mayor, I had criticized the plant as a pollutant and continued to do so even when I was already in office. As he was leaving, Zablan asked: "By the way, Mayor, when is your birthday?" Bluntly, I told him, "Sorry, Dr. Zablan. My birthday is my private affair. I do not intend to share the matter with you."

In the magnitude of the problems of the nation and of the city, what I tried to do in the city hall might be deemed petty attempts to minimize, if not eliminate, corruption. But we had to begin someplace and, in my judgment, those were the immediately doable ones. Incidentally, the drive to combat corruption in the city — feeble as it might seem to others — cost me the support of my political allies and even family friends.

Chapter 23

Taking on the World Bank amidst Partisan Challenges

O ne of the biggest problems that faced me immediately upon my assumption of office in 1980 was the question of the SIR, the Slum Improvement Rehabilitation project of the World Bank and the National Housing Authority. From afar, the SIR project did not look as if it had anything to do with corruption. But, scrutinized closely, it was clear that the project tended to waste millions of local and national government funds. And wasting the money of government in my book was corruption by another name. Hence, I opposed it.

For starters, I found its acronym "SIR" sycophantic. I said openly that it was meant to butter up to Marcos, who was known as "Sir" to his adoring subordinates. It was the bane of the bureaucracy that programs or projects undertaken by a ministry or department of the government invariably carried the name of the President, his wife or some other member of the so-called First Family. In Cebu, there was a rather well-received program among the rural poor. It was called the Medical Assistance to Rural Communities and Other Sectors. Its acronym spelled Marcos and it was a way, as Syth Mydans of the *New York Times* later said, by which Marcos and his wife, Imelda, gained "the allegiance of the village people."

A day or two after I became mayor, I went to visit the SIR site in Macabalan, where the principal wharf of the city was located, to consult with the intended beneficiaries of the project. I found the program so expensive that it would, in my mind, ultimately benefit not the poor in Macabalan but the rich. The monthly amortizations that the NHA and the World Bank required of them were so high that they would eventually be forced to sell the lots to the well-to-do. Among other things, I found out that the filling materials needed to raise the foundations of the lots would cost the city government a fortune similar to the amounts needed to develop the residential lots of Makati, the prime municipality of the country. I said so publicly and that angered the NHA and the World Bank.

A Challenge to Tobias

In public statements, I challenged the NHA Administrator, Gen. Gaudencio Tobias, to "get down from his ivory tower" and talk with the beneficiaries of the SIR program in the city. The challenge brought General Tobias and his assistant, Col. Antonio Fernando, to see me in Cagayan de Oro. They tried to convince me to drop my opposition to the SIR project. They told me, in effect, that the project was a done deal and that there was nothing I could do about it. Also, they issued veiled threats that my opposing the project could very well fall into the category of "economic sabotage" for which I could be ousted from office and jailed. At that time, economic sabotage was considered a "heinous crime" for which life imprisonment was imposable as a penalty and which, under martial rule, could very well rise to death.

I told them to their faces that I could not see how they expected me to go along with the project. As the mayor of the city, I saw that the project would not benefit the intended beneficiaries, the poor in Macabalan, nor would it benefit the city because its terms clearly undermined the city's interests.

As of the date of our conference, I said that the intended beneficiaries of the SIR were paying between P5 to P20 a month as rent for the lots they were occupying. In the proposed payment scheme of the SIR, once the lots were awarded to them, they would have to pay between P120 to P150 monthly. Under the circumstances, I said that the SIR lots in Macabalan would wind up in the hands of the well-to-do, even if at first they were awarded to the poor. I added that the project would impoverish the city, which would have to shoulder US$8 million of its total cost of US$15 million. At that time, the city's annual budget was only equal to US$4 million. The Marcos government wanted the city to source the deficit from loans coming from the NHA. I vehemently objected to what I saw would create an unreasonable burden on our people.

Tobias refused to see the validity of our concerns. Simplistically, he thought that he could intimidate me into accepting the project by constantly repeating that since it was a martial rule project that was funded by the World Bank, my objections no longer merited any further consideration. Thus, he dismissed my apprehensions as irrelevant. Tobias, however, could not move the project forward on his own steam because it needed acceptance by the city.

Tougher by the Hour

I found our talk was getting tougher by the hour. Tobias, a general who commanded our expeditionary troops in Vietnam, probably thought that he could just issue orders to me as if I were one of his sergeants and expect to have those orders followed without question. I could see that he was irritated not only by me but also by my city administrator, Mordino Cua, who asked blunt questions that seemed to embarrass him.

Cua was used to giving lectures to members of the cooperative movement not only in the city but also throughout the country before he took the job of city administrator. Like Tobias who sounded as if he was barking orders to his platoon leaders even in ordinary conversations, Cua also carried the mannerisms of a teacher talking to his students. I saw that the two would never become friends, which was bad by itself, but worse for me because I was responsible for the acts of city hall, not Cua. Anyway, I resisted Tobias's importuning that I should support the SIR project in Macabalan.

Frustrated by my stand and the belligerent arguments of Cua, who thought that the onerous conditions the NHA and the World Bank imposed would eventually bankrupt us, Tobias and his staff left our discussions in a huff. Before they left, they insinuated that a World Bank Mission would be visiting the city. It was meant both as an advance notice of the event and a veiled warning that the SIR was not only Marcos's business, but also the World Bank's. Thus, I should tread carefully on the issue. That, however, I had no intention of doing.

Partisan Challenges

Before the World Bank Mission came to Cagayan de Oro, Marcos's supporters in the city maneuvered to have two lawyers, Abeto D. Salcedo and Enriquito Beja, appointed as members of the city council. Salcedo was a long-time friend, having been my classmate at the Xavier University College of Law. Beja's mother was an aunt of mine. He was also the same Beja who brokered Pedro Roa's support for my candidacy as mayor in the last days of the 1980 elections. Their appointments were issued through a Marcos assistant, who had a reputation for under-the-table transactions that he could get Marcos to approve.

I sensed that, by this move, Marcos's supporters wanted to dilute our control of the city council. All the elected members — the vice mayor and seven councilors — were members of our party. The appointments of Salcedo and Beja were obviously intended to enable Marcos to gain a foothold in the city council and cause a change in our attitude towards the SIR and to the martial law government.

When the appointments were announced, I told the people of the city that there was no way I would recognize their appointments. Anticipating that the two just might barge into the sessions of the city council, I asked Vice Mayor Magtajas and our councilors not to acknowledge their presence. I also said that, even if they forced their way into the sessions, I would not authorize the payment of their salaries.

Capitalizing on their connections with Malacañang, Salcedo and Beja threatened that I could get suspended if I persisted in my refusal to recognize them. I replied that I stood on strong legal grounds and I, therefore, saw no reason to back off. I was certain that Marcos had no legal basis to appoint Salcedo and Beja. The two were supposed to represent the farming and industrial sectors of the city. But I knew that the sectors were not that organized in the city. The two lawyers were neither in farming nor in any industry to represent the sectors validly in the city council. Moreover, I knew that Salcedo and Beja needed a resolution of the city council recommending their appointments before Marcos could appoint them. Unfortunately, for them, they did not have that council resolution.

World Bank Mission Visits

Since the legal odds were clearly against them, my fight against the appointments of Salcedo and Beja to the City Council came to a close. Their patron in Malacañang gave up his support for them. While I won this fight, I lost the friendship of my law classmate (Salcedo) and my cousin (Beja) and the political support of their clans. At the moment though, my sole interest was to protect the city from unwarranted intrusion by Marcos, even if he used my relatives and friends as wedges to get his hand into the affairs of city hall. Soon after the Salcedo and Beja flap calmed down, the World Bank Mission came to the city to discuss the SIR project with me.

To be fair, the SIR project had good intentions. It was meant to respond to the criticisms leveled against previous World Bank-funded projects where squatters were forcibly relocated to areas far from their habitual places of work. In the SIR project, the squatters would be resettled in rehabilitated areas close to their work places. Since the Macabalan SIR beneficiaries were principally stevedores who worked at the pier and lived near the area, the World Bank and the National Housing Authority decided that the best place to provide housing for them was right there beside the main wharf of the city.

Showdown Set

Anticipating that pressures from Malacañang and the World Bank would be brought to bear upon me, the city council passed a resolution backing my stand and asking the World Bank and the Marcos government, represented by the NHA, to allow the city to withdraw from the project. The stage was thus set for a showdown between me, on the one hand, and the Marcos government and the WB, on the other.

In an attempt to forestall the showdown, the World Bank sent a middle-level bank official, Caroline Sewell, to see me in Cagayan de Oro. She visited my office and tried to convince me that the terms and conditions of the project were reasonable and affordable by the beneficiaries.

I told her candidly that I did not see it that way. I mentioned to her that the beneficiaries and I were in constant consultations and I knew that they could not afford the amortization costs. The stevedores working at the pier without any fixed compensation or fixed hours of employment were the most exploited of workers. Moreover, I told Sewell that the SIR costs ascribed to the city would derail our capacity to service the needs of our city hospital, schools and other social services.

Sewell made a mistake of telling me that she could "produce any number of affidavits from the beneficiaries who would attest to their capacity to pay the amortizations." I dared her to do so and added rather harshly that, for every affidavit that she could get, I would "produce 20 counter-affidavits showing that the beneficiaries could not bear the costs of amortization."

Since our conversation was not going anywhere to address the impasse, she asked me to go to the NHA Head Office in Quezon City so that we could discuss the issue again. I flew to Manila and went to the NHA office on the appointed day and at the appointed hour. Sewell was not there. I waited for more than 30 minutes. Still she did not arrive. I decided to leave. As I took the stairway down from another end of the second floor, I saw Sewell taking the escalator up to the office where we were supposed to meet.

I did not go back to meet with her. I had this belief that a person needed to be on time for his or her appointments. One of the things that I was hated for at city hall was my insistence that employees come on time for work. Now and then, I would go to my office by 7 a.m. and make it a point to pass by other offices just to impress on the department heads and their employees that I wanted them to come early to work. Even when I was practicing law, I found it irritating for judges to keep us lawyers waiting for hours for our cases to be called. I think that it is one of the flaws — generally speaking — of our people that many of us do not observe time schedules. Many of my friends were embarrassed by my coming on time for appointments as the mayor of Cagayan de Oro while they ran late.

A couple once asked me to officiate at their civil wedding at 2:30 p.m. on a Saturday. I went to the site of the wedding at exactly 2 o'clock, 30 minutes earlier. I waited for almost an hour, but they failed to arrive. I informed their embarrassed parents that I was leaving and, if they wanted me to do the rites of the wedding, they should look me up in my office. There were also some instances when barangay officials asked me to attend barangay functions, for example, at 6 p.m. on a certain date. When I gave the assurance that I would be there exactly at 6 p.m., they would then request that I arrive at 8 p.m. because the people would only be there by that time.

When Sewell failed to come on time for our meeting, I decided to stick to my belief. I did not think that I should revise it just to accommodate her. I also wanted to send her a message that Filipino officials knew how to value time. I heard later that the World Bank was so incensed at Sewell's failure to meet with me that she was eventually retired. But true or not, my struggle against the SIR project in Macabalan was not ended just yet.

General Tobias did not appreciate my continuing objection to the SIR project. He maneuvered to have me ousted from the mayorship of the city. He recommended to Marcos that I be expelled from office, among other things, for economic sabotage. To cover the legal angles, he secured an opinion of Minister of Justice Ricardo C. Puno, which stated:

> The memorandum of agreement, dated April 23, 1979, between the National Housing Authority, represented by its general manager, Gaudencio Tobias, and the City of Cagayan de Oro, represented by its then mayor, Pedro Roa, (was) valid, binding and enforceable upon the incumbent city administration headed by Mayor Aquilino Pimentel....

For good measure, Minister Puno added that the city was "consequently in duty bound to comply with and implement the same...." Puno came to these conclusions without hearing my side.

The odds were stacked against me. Still, it took Marcos some time before he found a way to remove me from office without directly ordering it himself. The blow would come later in July 1981.

Martial Law 'Lifted'

Before the Comelec actually ordered my ouster from the City Hall, Marcos made a big fuss about his announced lifting of martial rule on January 17, 1981. The announcement did not fool us in the Opposition one bit.

We knew that despite words to the contrary, the fact was that Marcos retained his sweeping powers under Amendment No. 6 to make laws as a super-legislator of sorts. He also had the power to order the arrest of anyone for sedition, subversion or rebellion against the government and issue search and seizure warrants of any document or property used in the furtherance of crime. Additionally, Marcos could order the closure of media that the regime considered "subversive," an all-inclusive term that covered activities of any person that did not jibe with the goals of the so-called New Society. Thus, even if Marcos announced the formal cessation of martial law, in essence it was still in existence.

The Civil Liberties Union of the Philippines (CLUP) saw through the façade of Marcos's announcement and warned in a statement signed by Jose W. Diokno, Jose B.L. Reyes and J. Antonio Araneta on December 31, 1980, that "the same restrictions on individual freedoms that are the hallmarks of martial law will continue (even) after martial law shall have been 'lifted.'"

Secret Visit to Aquino

In March of 1981, Salvador Laurel — whom we familiarly called "Doy" — told me that Aquino wanted to see me in San Francisco. Laurel flattered me by saying that Aquino considered me "a thoroughbred" among the few leaders opposed to the martial rule.

I told Doy that, even if I wanted to, it was not that easy for me to leave. As a local public official, I had to secure the permission of Roño, the Minister of Local Government, before I could go abroad — and very likely it wouldn't be given. But he was insistent. So I told him I was willing to go, provided they could "smuggle" me out of the airport. He assured me that he would take care of it. True to his word, on the appointed day, his people escorted me from the moment I alighted from a taxicab all the way through Customs and Immigration, right up to the plane without any hitch at all.

I met Aquino at the house of Lupita Kashiwahara, his sister, in San Francisco. He looked hale and hearty after his heart bypass operation. There we talked about the situation in the country. I told him that the evils of martial rule were only gradually sinking into the minds of our people and that it would take a lot of "conscientization" before we could eradicate the common perception that Marcos was the only person capable of leading the nation.

He told me that some people — not necessarily the communists or the NPA — in the country were preparing to take the violent path against Marcos. That was the reason why he said he wanted to return home early to engage Marcos in a dialogue on how to restore democracy to the country.

I did not give Aquino an inkling of what was in my mind regarding the scenario of violence that he said could take place in the country sooner rather than later. What I argued against was his plan to come home. I told him that his coming home, at best, could only result in Marcos's putting him to jail again or, at worst, he could get killed "accidentally" or otherwise. My impression then was that, while Ninoy pretended to listen, he was determined to come back to the country.

While I was in San Francisco, I also met Steve Psinakis at his home where he told me that some Filipinos in the US were training in the Arizona or Nevada deserts to engage the Marcos regime in a violent confrontation unless he restored to our people their democratic rights.

I flew home as quietly as I had left. Nobody seemed to have missed me because I was gone only for a few days. By prearrangement with Doy's people, I again passed through Customs and Immigration without any problem. And Minister Roño was not in the least aware that I had gone out of the country without his permission.

All this while, the virus of clashing political ambitions stealthily gnawed at the bonds which originally bound Canoy, Adaza and me into a team that had potentially threatened the hold of the KBL in Northern Mindanao. A small weekly, *Ang Bag-ong Katarungan* or *The New Reason*, based in Cagayan de Oro, first revealed the dark clouds signaling the impending collapse of our team. It reported that:

> In September, political followers of both the KBL and the MA were shocked to hear that Assemblyman Reuben R. Canoy broke off his relation with the Opposition party because of "loss of confidence." He right away announced the development of a new party [the Social Democratic Party]. In the cold war between the two that followed, Gov. Homobono Adaza described the leaders who [were] forming a new party as men without ideologies and [who had] better jump into the lake.

Canoy, of course, did not jump into the lake as Adaza vociferously suggested. What he did was to ask me to join him in the formation of the SDP. Together, he said, we could isolate Adaza and marginalize him as an Opposition leader in Northern Mindanao. He also explained that Francisco Tatad, Marcos's former Minister of Public Information and his immediate superior in the martial law cabinet, would be one of the pillars of their new party.

Before our conversation, I already heard that he and Tatad were planning to package SDP into a credible Opposition party. At the mention of Tatad's name, I immediately begged off. I told him that I did not see how Tatad could qualify as an oppositionist even if, in his opinion, the latter had the clout to bring other name politicians into the new party and infuse funds into the party coffers.

I told him that Tatad would be a political liability, not an asset, because he was so closely associated with Marcos's proclamation of martial rule. It was Tatad, with his unsmiling visage and monotone, who midwifed the birth of martial law on television and over radio on September 23, 1972. And every day thereafter, for months on end, he justified the imposition of martial law.

I, therefore, tried mightily to dissuade Canoy from going ahead with his plans to organize a national party with Tatad. I wanted him to join us, in-stead, as a leader, of a new national party that we were organizing. I told him that, since we had no monetary resources or patronage to give our political followers, the only asset that we could offer our people was our credibility as members of the legitimate Opposition. I said I did not think Tatad had the credentials at that point to claim that he was a legitimate member of the Op-position even if he had resigned from the Marcos cabinet the year before.

Canoy, however, had made up his mind. He and Tatad presented their party to the public in Cebu some weeks ahead of the convention of the party we were organizing. They had about 50 people with them, but hardly anyone's name rang a bell as a genuine oppositionist.

In any event, Canoy took offense at my refusal to support his and Tatad's formation of the SDP. Since then, our relationship as former political allies worsened.

Months later, on February 26, 1982, a *Far Eastern Economic Review* report by Sheilah Ocampo captured the essence of our differences. She said:

> Canoy's alliance with Tatad cast doubts on the Opposition credibility of the SDP. Tatad, long identified with the KBL, left the Marcos camp in 1980. Tatad's later actions, particularly as campaign manager of the token candidate Alejo Santos in (the 1981) presidential election — in which Marcos won a further six-year term — left many questioning whether Tatad was a genuine Opposition man.

Ocampo identified me as one of those who entertained those doubts.

> Pimentel, together with Luis Jose [a political associate of Raul Manglapus], has now organized PDP and persuaded those who refused to join Canoy's SDP to support it.

Propaganda Battle Royale

After that initial political spat, other developments caused Canoy and me to drift farther apart. I went on to help build a new political group, the

Pilipino Democratic Party, which sort of made our political estrangement permanent.

In December of 1981, Canoy, Adaza and I treated the political *cognoscenti* to a battle royale of announcements of our individual intentions to form new political parties that would take on the mighty KBL nationally.

Canoy, made known his intention to launch the SDP in Cebu sometime within the month with or without my support. In my case, I announced that in February of 1982, we would formally organize the PDP in Cebu City. Not to be outdone, Adaza issued a thunderous response that his party, the Mindanao Alliance, was also going nationwide. For reasons that were never clear to me, he also declared his party's intention to secede from Unido (the United Democratic Opposition), the umbrella organization of the Opposition parties headed by Sen. Salvador Laurel. Adaza claimed that "Unido ... failed in its role as a strong and effective Opposition."

Doy Laurel, whose yeoman work had kept the disparate political groups within the ranks of the Unido, dismissed the Adaza threat as a plain impulsive outburst. The *Review* quoted Laurel as saying:

> [Adaza's outburst could perhaps] be attributed to the fact that somehow Adaza felt a bit left out. His fellow Mindanao Alliance colleagues like Assemblyman Reuben Canoy (who was later expelled from the party) and Cagayan de Oro Mayor Aquilino Pimentel were instrumental in the forming of the SDP and the PDP, respectively.

Adaza's Predicament

"Left out" did not quite describe Adaza's relationship with Canoy and me. Adaza was not exactly a passive player in the contest for the leadership role of the Opposition in our region. He was actively, and legitimately so, pursuing his own agenda to be the *Numero Uno* Opposition leader in Northern Mindanao.

As things developed, Adaza's public falling out with Canoy was triggered surprisingly by the Comelec order in July 1981 ousting me from office. I was in the US on an official trip when the Comelec promulgated its order that I was a "turncoat" in the 1980 elections. As such, the Comelec ruled that I did not have the mandate to continue serving as mayor, which ruling Canoy and Adaza both denounced. However, when the protests against my ouster started, "Adaza was conspicuously absent," according to the article, "Politics, Cagayan de Oro Style," written by Casiano Navarro, Jr., in the *Panorama* issue of July 25, 1982. In the article, Navarro said that "Adaza had left in a green Lear jet that took off from the local airport" for an unknown destination. Other media reports that neither Adaza's wife Margot nor his brother Rino knew where he was did not help ease the intramurals between Canoy and Adaza. In fact, all sorts of intrigues regarding Adaza's whereabouts, including a weird theory that he had been kidnapped, emerged.

The mystery was compounded by the fact that, shortly before the Comelec decision ousting me was issued, former Rep. Roque Ablan, Jr. of Ilocos Norte, a known political leader of Marcos, called on Adaza in Cagayan de Oro. Canoy used the Ablan visit as the launching pad for his attacks that secret agreements had been entered into by Adaza and Marcos through Ablan. He then announced his resignation from the MA on July 31, 1981 on the ostensible ground that decisions for their party were made by Adaza without proper consultation. At the time Canoy resigned from their party, nobody in Cagayan de Oro had any definite clue as to Adaza's whereabouts.

Adaza, however, found an ally in the widely read columnist Teodoro F. Valencia. Valencia wrote in the *Daily Express* on July 9 that the Adaza kidnapping rumor was silly. He said Adaza lodged at the Manila Intercontinental Hotel from June 27 up to July 1 before he enplaned for Tokyo.

On August 6, Adaza issued a statement that there was no mystery in his absence in the first few days of my ouster. He said he had merely flown to Tokyo, then on to the US, among other things, to look for investors to reduce the pollution of the Sintering Plant in Villanueva, Misamis Oriental, and to modernize the provincial telephone system. With that facile explanation, he announced Canoy's expulsion from the MA. While he was rather harsh in his treatment of Canoy, he was a little conciliatory towards me. He said I would merely be considered "on leave" from the MA, or words to that effect.

I was still out of the country when the war of words between Canoy and Adaza started to seriously roil the political waters in our region. In my absence, Vice Mayor Magtajas acted as the head of a conciliation committee that attempted to patch up their differences. When I got back to Cagayan de Oro, I sat down with them to help them reconcile. Initially, Canoy agreed to reconsider his resignation from the MA and Adaza concurred with the idea to organize a new national party that would use the MA "as its nucleus." Some detailed steps were suggested to bring about the organization of the new party, including consultations with our supporters, especially in Davao and Bukidnon. But, as fate would have it, the reconciliation efforts fell through, primarily because many of our allies in the two provinces did not want to be associated with Tatad, Canoy's colleague in the SDP, who was expected to play a significant role in the new party.

The media also had a hand in driving the three of us wider apart. An August 8, 1981 *WHO* magazine article, "Reuben Canoy Inside, Outside, and Against the Ruling Circle," written by Roberto Z. Coloma, carried a boxed statement that said:

> [The magazine] learned that Assemblyman Canoy [had] resigned from the Mindanao Alliance (MA) because of a controversial trip to Hong Kong, Japan and the US by MA leader Homobono Adaza, governor of Misamis Oriental....Adaza had apparently met with President Marcos before leaving the country without consulting his MA party members.

Two weeks later, another article written by Coloma for *WHO* of August 22, spoke of the Mindanao Alliance becoming stronger after the quarrel between Canoy and Adaza. The article, however, actually extolled me as the "single most important unifying element at this point." Coloma concluded that "the politics of an enlarged MA will most likely reflect the politics of Pimentel and his political allies." I really did not know what Coloma meant by his conclusion, but the more the media wrote of me as an important cog in the wheel of the unification of the Opposition, at least, in Northern Mindanao, the more Canoy and Adaza got enraged not only at each other but also at me.

On October 13, 1982, *WHO* featured Adaza in a story written by Alex Dacanay on the problems of the coconut industry. In his usual belligerent rhetoric, Adaza said that Interim Assemblyman Emmanuel Pelaez, whose family owned huge tracts of coconut land in Misamis Oriental, was a part of the privileged caste of our society. He called him a *cacique*, a word that described an oppressive landlord during the Spanish colonial past. In the same article, he told of Canoy's having taken campaign contribution money for the MA from Unicom, a corporation invested by Marcos with powers over the coconut industry that was run principally by Eduardo Cojuangco. The contribution was made possible, Adaza said, through Maria Clara Lobregat, a mutual friend of Canoy and Cojuangco.

Adaza's disclosure that Canoy received P100,000 from Cojuangco to fund the MA distressed us because, as members of the Opposition, we were wary of being associated in any manner with Cojuangco, a close ally of Marcos. His accusation questioned Canoy's credentials as a leader of the Opposition. In the same article, Adaza also sideswiped me by saying that Canoy had told him that he gave some amount of the Cojuangco contribution for our campaign in Cagayan de Oro.

I never really knew whether or not Canoy received campaign funds from Cojuangco. But I knew that Canoy helped our Cagayan de Oro campaign a lot. In fact, I thanked him and his kindly mother, who he said was the source of the P10,000 he gave to our group. In fairness, it must be said that Canoy and his wife, Solona, spent much more than the sum that Adaza said Canoy gave to us. In real terms, I think that the Canoys — on their own — spent no less than the equivalent of P200,000 to get our team elected. And, had the Canoys not helped us, it would have been much more difficult for us to have won all the elective positions in the city government in 1980.

During the campaign, Maria Clara Lobregat, a colleague in the Constitutional Convention, sent some P30,000 through Bobby Cericos, a mutual friend. I declined the contribution and had it returned with my verbal thanks. To be polite, I said that, at the time, I no longer had any need for such funds. The real reason, however, was that I did not want to receive any contribution from people associated with Marcos.

Like Humpty-Dumpty

Eventually, Canoy, Adaza and I split three ways: Canoy formed the Social Democratic Party with Tatad; Adaza stuck to his Mindanao Alliance Party, and I, along with other oppositionists mainly from Mindanao and the Visayas, organized the Pilipino Democratic Party (PDP). Our permanent separation from one another politically was a sad thing for me. As the most junior — in terms of political reach — among us, I hoped that we could project our Opposition group from Region X as the core of a new national political party to challenge the KBL for political supremacy. Unfortunately, like Humpty Dumpty, the dream came crashing down and nobody could ever put it together again.

1982: REUBEN CANOY (left) heir apparent to Maning Pelaez (right) as Mindanao's best bet for national leadership.

In any case, Cagayan de Oro — indeed Region X — had become too small for the three of us. Just as little Palestine was not big enough to allow the peaceful co-existence of Arabs, Jews and Christians, the three of us found that Northern Mindanao did not have space enough for our clashing political ambitions.

Before he won as mayor of Cagayan de Oro and later as a member of the Interim Batasang Pambansa representing Region X, Canoy was already a well-read and much-appreciated sober-minded columnist of a national newspaper, the *Philippines Herald*. He also had a hugely popular daily political commentary in Visayan in the Canoy-family owned radio station, DXCC, which reached the homes of many in Mindanao and some parts of the Visayas. He was, thus, acknowledged as a local boy who not only made good but also excelled in the field of journalism in its written and verbal forms. A graduate from the College of Law of Dumaguete's prestigious Silliman University, whose School of Journalism was a byword among would-be writers, he was looked up to by many of us as Pelaez's Mindanao successor in the arena of national politics.

As for Adaza, before he won as governor of Misamis Oriental, he was already recognized nationally as a gifted writer. As a law student in the University of the Philippines, he was once editor-in-chief of the *Philippine Collegian*, the university's official student publication. Although his stint as editor-in-chief was mired in controversy because he wrote some columns demeaning the national hero Jose Rizal, instead of diminishing his standing, it actually raised his stature to the level of a demigod among student-intellectuals throughout the country. With a strong legal background sharpened by an extensive law practice and backed up by the ability to write deadly prose and deliver rapier-sharp arguments at the drop of a hat, Adaza also bidded fair as

Misamis Oriental's prince-in-waiting for national political preeminence after Pelaez.

In my case, what went for me was the fact that I was the mayor of Cagayan de Oro, the prime city of Region X. Whether people liked it or not, as city mayor, I attracted attention because the city was the location of several regional offices of the national government and was the choice site of many conventions of civic and other organizations. Before I became mayor, I had been dean of the College of Law of my alma mater, Xavier University, for five years; an elected delegate to the Constitutional Convention; a corporate lawyer in Manila, specializing in mining; a law professor of Criminal Law, Civil Procedure and Evidence at the San Beda and Far Eastern University Colleges of Law; a litigation lawyer for Nassa; and, in general, a fairly active law practitioner who focused on the rights of destitute litigants. Adaza and I also had a common additional qualification — we were both former martial law detainees.

Howsoever anyone tried to analyze what led to our breakup, there was no denying that the politics of personal ambition or plain jockeying for the leadership of the Opposition in the region was a major factor. It was simply unfortunate, but also all so true.

Since there was no longer any way to keep our political team together, I decided that it was time to formally launch PDP, the party that people from all walks of life in Mindanao and the Visayas wanted to organize.

Chapter 24:

Rise of the PDP

A t this time the country was being rent asunder by rebel guns that chal lenged martial law. The situation appeared to confront the people with only two alternatives: support martial law or go for rebellion. A number of us — first in Mindanao and then in the Visayas — thought that we should offer our people a third peaceful, nonviolent choice. That was the basic conceptual framework that led to the birth of the PDP.

I got in touch with my former colleague in the Constitutional Convention, Samuel Occeña in Davao, and suggested that we get a political party organized to fight Marcos on the political front. Without a moment's hesitation, Occeña conscripted young activists in Davao City, among them Rey Magno Teves, Cris Lanorias, Cesar Ledesma, Lito Lorenzana, Zafiro Respicio and Cesar Decena. In no time, we had an organization that did pivotal party organizing work in that part of Southern Mindanao.

Our efforts at party building also had the support of Malaybalay oppositionists like young businessman Ernesto Tabios, lawyers Fred Aquino and Rube Gamolo, and community organizers Bebot de la Torre, Carlos Novavos and Eduardo Catane. Gregorio Tambog and Maida Padian of the indigenous peoples of Bukidnon also joined the effort. So did Greg Hontiveros of

1982: PDP ORIGINALS: Luis Jose, Boy Tabios and Sam Occeña.

Butuan; Jose Manuel Tan, Claro Garcia and Vicente Calejesan of Surigao; Mauro Bulawin, Jun Tenorio and Dr. Felicisimo Abellanosa of Iligan; Domocao Alonto, Jr. of Lanao; and cooperatives expert Mordino Cua of Cagayan de Oro.

In the Visayas, we got in touch with my high school classmate, Congressman Tony Cuenco, the popular radio commentator Inday Nita Daluz, Ribomapil Holganza, Paul Rodriguez, Nanay Juling Ouano and Gemma Sanchez, all of Cebu. We also recruited farmer leader Felix Rengel and his wife, Mary, Jorge

Cabalit and Manang Santas Castillo of Bohol; Indong Dilag and his brother Bong of Negros Occidental; Nonoy Mosqueda of Iloilo; Vic Inserto of Aklan; Antonio Medina of Masbate; lawyer Lee Zosa of Samar; former Vice Mayor Tente Quintero of Tacloban City; and Res Salvatierra of Leyte. They all agreed to form the nucleus of PDP in the region.

A good number of activists from the marginalized sectors of our society like farmer Andres Oquinlay, barangay leader Artemio Baal, jeepney driver Gregorio Bautista and landless organizer Felix Alzola also signed up. I justified their membership because I said they would be "the bones and the sinews" of the new party.

The intellectuals were not left out. They were needed to articulate the strategic policies and the tactical positions of the party. One such person who freely dispensed his wise advice to us in the formulation of the basic principles and the fundamental demands of the new party was Fr. Ben Nebres, SJ. He personally joined us in a crucial three-day seminar in an abandoned mining site of the Cuencos in the hinterland barangay of Mantalungon, Dalaguete, of the province of Cebu. There Fr. Ben helped refine the principles that found their way into the party platform.

In Luzon, we received the support of Sen. Lorenzo Tañada, who became the first honorary chair of the party, and Manila businessman Luis Jose, who also was elected as the party's first working chair. Former Comelec Chair Jaime Ferrer, former Delegate Ernesto Rondon, Manila businessman Tito Guingona, lawyer Jose Lina, *Kasapi* activists Alfredo Juntilla, Brigido Simon, Jr., Herman Laurel, Tina Montiel, Gabriel David, Jesus Cellano, Rafael Baskinas, Ricardo Magbitang, Fernando Martin, Jose Arinue, Ciriaco Sabilano, Jun Lee, Cely Lee, Rey Montano, Percival Palmes, Teresita Samson-Castillo, Jose Alcuaz and a Boy Tusok of Metro Manila readily joined the party. Lawyer Antonio Carpio of Camarines Sur, Ed Frivaldo of Sorsogon and Rey Princesa of the Bicol Saro also lent their assistance.

Cebu City Convention Site

We chose Cebu City as the site of the founding convention of PDP. The city had an unmatched historical value as the place where the first Filipino successful resistance to foreign imperialism occurred. Its central location in relation to the rest of the country was also a pragmatic consideration why it was chosen as the convention site. Delegates from Luzon, the other parts of the Visayas and Mindanao could come by boat and save on expenses.

Birth of the PDP

For the launching of the PDP, we limited the number of delegates to 150 for the entire country, or 50 for each of the main regions of Luzon, Visayas and Mindanao. Allocating 50 delegates only for each of the major regions for the first time placed the Visayas and Mindanao individually on par with Luzon in terms of the size of the delegations to a political convention. At the conventions of other political parties, Luzon always had more delegates. This time, the PDP's message was that as a party, it would insist that the Visayas and Mindanao be treated separately as the equals of Luzon.

Actually, there was a hidden motive to our announcements limiting the delegates to 150. I feared that, if we announced a bigger number and only a few attended, we would be embarrassed. We also wanted to impress upon the people of Cebu that we could muster a crowd bigger than the 50 or so who attended the founding of the Social Democratic Party of Canoy and Tatad in Cebu City in December 1981.

Moreover, since we had no party funds to speak of, we were concerned about the logistical requirements of the affair. Thus, we made it plain that those who wished to attend the party convention in Cebu would have to spend for their own transportation and accommodation.

At least four times the cap of 150 delegates or about 600 people attended the formal organization of the party. To our pleasant surprise, we did not incur any deficit in our finances because the delegates paid their fares and their hotel accommodations, and contributed to the expenses for the food at the convention.

Some problems threatened the organization of PDP. There were reports that Unido looked upon the organization of the PDP as a new political party with hostility. Happily, it did not turn out to be the case. In fact, Doy Laurel, Unido president, officially expressed its solidarity with the party's intention to confront the Marcos regime peacefully. We welcomed Doy as a brother in the struggle against Marcos. Also there were rumors that our convention would be disrupted by hoodlums in the employ of the KBL dirty-tricks department. No such thing happened.

Tañada, Honorary Chair

The proceedings at the founding convention went well. We did not encounter any major problems. There was a flap of some kind over the election by acclamation of Senator Tañada as the honorary chairman of the party. Samuel Occeña of Davao City dissented, fearing that "traditional politicians" — referring to Tañada's colleagues in the Manila-based political party, Laban — would use

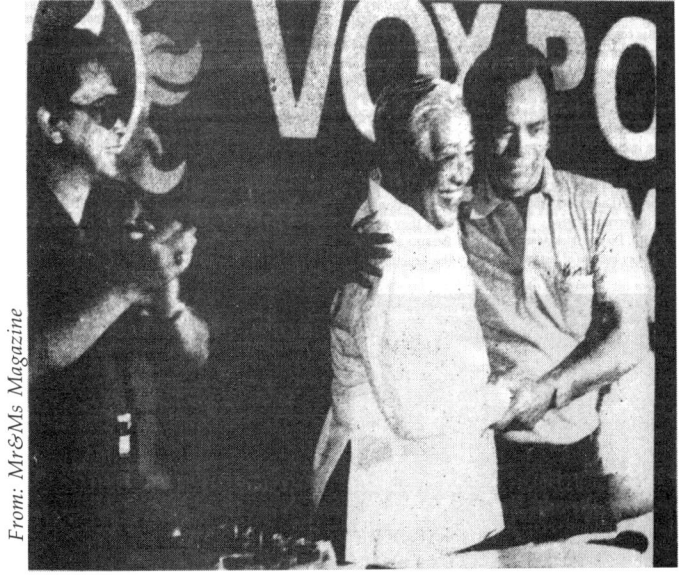

From: Mr&Ms Magazine

1982: PDP CONVENTION, I embrace Sen. Tañada as Antonio Cuenco, convention chairman, claps.

Tañada's chairmanship as the entry point for them to dominate the PDP. Overwhelming shouts of approval, however, drowned out his objections.

I welcomed Tañada's election by acclamation as our honorary chair. Rather than inhibiting the growth of the party, I saw it as an opportunity for PDP to become a national party. While we already had some members in Luzon at the time, the party's presence was hardly felt there. But Tañada's party, Laban, was already a byword in Luzon because it fought Marcos in the Interim Batasan elections of 1978. Although we — I was a candidate of Laban in that political exercise — lost, we gave such a terrific performance as a team that Laban enjoyed a high credibility rating among the people as a genuine Opposition party. Months later, PDP and Laban coalesced. The circumstances that led to the coalition are described in the succeeding pages.

The Bridge Builder

In February of 1982, I delivered the keynote speech at the launching of the Pilipino Democratic Party (PDP) in Cebu City.

My keynote speech was titled "The Bridge Builder." The title was taken from a poem that spoke of an old man who safely crossed a swollen river but who "turned when he reached the other side, to build a bridge to span the tide." I found the poem so aptly descriptive of our experiences that led to the organization of the PDP. The PDP, I said, was building a bridge over the troublous waters of martial law so that the youth of our generation could one day cross over in safety to the land where freedom, justice and peace would reign supreme.

The Platform

I described the PDP as a nontraditional party. Its platform was not quite the same as the platforms of other parties. Among other things, it had a nationalist orientation that called for the primacy of the Filipino in his own land, the dismantling of the foreign military bases, the establishment of a federal system of government, the adoption of a parliamentary form of government, the creation of a citizen army, and some other "un-

1982: WE CONDUCT PDP seminars first in Mindanao and the Visayas, then later, in Luzon.

usual" fundamental principles like belief in God and in the dignity of the human being.

Also, I underscored the fact that even as the party was against taking the path of violence against Marcos, we would not condemn the groups that were violently interdicting the martial law forces in fields of battle. That failure to condemn the violent groups opposing martial law angered the Marcos regime. But the Marcos military still could not brand the PDP as an outlaw organization because we were certainly not one. In fact, peace was a fundamental value that all members adhered to as defined in our party's constitution and bylaws. However, neither could they count us as members of the "loyal Opposition" in the manner that they dealt with the other traditional parties like the Canoy-Tatad Social Democratic Party, Adaza's Mindanao Alliance or even the Pusyon Bisaya, which we harshly condemned as "shadows of the KBL" posing as Opposition groups.

The rather cruel characterization we hurled against those political groups naturally hurt the sensibilities of Reuben Canoy and Francisco Tatad of the Social Democratic Party, and Governor Adaza of the Mindanao Alliance.

Nonetheless, we were happy that *Bulletin Today* carried a front page story the following day that said "PDP urges change." The *Philippine News*, at the time the largest Filipino newspaper in the US, also headlined the founding of PDP in bold letters, "New Opposition Party Emerges," and in smaller letters, "Nationalism, Democratic Socialism to solve inequities of old and present system."

Much later, in the *Diliman Review*, A.R. Magno wrote a more welcome accolade. He said that, because the party had a deeper analysis of the problems of the nation than just an anti-Marcos line and since it was mass-based, "the PDP [was] more advanced than the other open Opposition groupings. He added that the party also appeared to be "the most credible, the most dynamic and the most ideologically and politically assertive."

Whenever my work as mayor allowed it I went with other dedicated party members around the country to spread the gospel of the party, tailed by either of the two of the police security officers: Eddie Lumagbas or Bebot Paza, who were assigned by the PC-INP to be my guards. We went by plane, boat, bus, jeepney or whatever means of transportation was available. Often, we noticed hostile surveillance by police or military vehicles. When we reached our destinations, we sometimes found that our scheduled meetings had been cancelled. But we kept on and, before the year 1982 was over, we had thousands of PDP recruits. What was amazing was we did all that even as we were operating under an atmosphere of fear and intimidation and with very minimal resources.

Solidarity Messages

We also received hundreds of solidarity messages, mostly verbal. One reassuring message I received shortly after the PDP launch in Cebu was a

1983: AT THE FIRST NATIONAL CONVENTION of the PDP-Laban coalition on February 5 and 6, in Cagayan de Oro, I address the participants. At far left is Tito Guingona.

handwritten letter from Fr. Victor Helly, SJ, whose acquaintance I had made at Xavier University. Fr. Vic, who had earlier acquired Filipino citizenship, said that he was "excited" by the keynote address I made. He found it "idealistic, yet tempered with a clear-sighted, down-to-earth realism and pragmatism."

He also said:

> [I have been] very depressed about the situation in the country, particularly by what I know of the militarization in Mindanao. Still I see and feel at least a glimmer of hope, born of the realization that there are people who are realistic about the present situation and yet are desirous of working together in peaceful ways for change.

The kind thoughts of Fr. Helly strengthened my belief that the PDP was on the right track in seeking the dismantling of the Marcos regime through the ways of peace. His letter also emboldened our party mates to eschew violence and do everything to end the brutal martial law regime by peaceful means.

PDP-Laban Coalition

By July 1982, Laban, the party that put up candidates against Marcos, Imelda and the KBL in the Metro Manila IBP elections of 1978, coalesced with PDP. The coalesced parties became known as PDP-Laban. With the coalition, we became a national party.

Not every member of PDP was happy with the coalition. Some original PDP members like Sammy Occeña and Rey Teves of Davao and Felix Rengel of Bohol voiced their reservations. They argued that people like Cory's brother, Peping Cojuangco, Jr., Ramon Mitra, Jr., Tito Guingona, Augusto Sanchez, Jejomar Binay and Rene Saguisag and other stalwarts of Laban should not be conferred the status of legitimate members of the coalition without their undergoing the prescribed party membership seminars. The argument was popular with the Mindanao and Visayas members of the PDP. Not that the issue was raised for the first time. In fact, much earlier, the party, egged on by "purists," also denied membership to Raul Manglapus, the MFP anti-Marcos leader in the US, when his name was proposed. Still, I could not help but suspect that the main reason was "insecurity" in us *provincianos* that, in the inevitable party intramurals, we would be sidelined by the Laban bigwigs of Metro Manila.

Those of us, who favored the coalition, however, vastly outnumbered the few who did not. The PDP-Laban coalition then took root among the rank and file of the party throughout the country. I saw the coalition as a shortcut to the PDP's achieving national credentials as a political party. Also, I thought that we could take a chance with Laban, after all it was led by people whose purity of purpose and indomitable courage like Tañada and Ninoy Aquino were beyond question.

In Laban, consultations were held not only among its leaders in Manila but also, and more importantly, with Ninoy who was in Boston, Massachusetts. As a member of Laban and a founding leader of PDP, I saw the need to talk with him in the US.

Meeting in Boston

I flew to Boston to consult with Ninoy in his and Cory's family home. This time, Bing was with me. Ninoy met us at the airport. He seemed to have fully recovered from the heart bypass he had undergone. Before I could protest, he lifted our heavy luggage with ease and placed it in the trunk of his car and drove us to their place.

1982: I SEE NINOY in Boston to discuss the PDP-Laban coalition issues.

1982: *CORY BETWEEN ME and Ninoy in Boston*

There Ninoy and I talked about the political situation back home, while Bing helped Cory with the dishes. He was particularly interested to know how the people now viewed martial rule. I said that from the surface, there was no perceptible change yet in the people's attitude. I added that I could sense people were merely waiting for an opportune time to show how they truly felt about Marcos and the abuses of his regime. Then he spoke of the thing that was closest to his heart.

He wanted to go home soonest. He was getting impatient about having to stay away from the country for so long without any definite plans of coming home. He wanted a chance to see Marcos and suggest to him the way the country could get back its basic freedoms without our having to engage him in a violent upheaval. Basically, I repeated what I had told him a year or so ago when we met in San Francisco that there was not much he could gain by coming home. Marcos, I said would simply send him back in jail, put him under house arrest — or worst — have him killed.

When I brought up the proposed coalition of PDP and Laban, Ninoy said the proposed merger — he used the word "merger" not "coalition" — was not practical. He argued that Laban was an umbrella organization, while PDP was a party. Besides, there were Laban members who were not inclined to join the merger. If the merger took place, it would mean losing those who did not wish to join. I merely listened to what he said and assured him I would transmit his observations to the members of Laban when I got home.

What Bing remembered most during our two-day stay with the Aquinos was the constant ringing of their house phone with calls coming from the Philippines. Indeed, Ninoy's political leaders and friends incessantly contacted him to give him information or to ask him for guidance on what to do next about the problem of martial law in the country.

In our all-too-short stay with them, Cory was a most gracious host. In fact, she served us coffee while her husband and I talked politics. Little did I know that the following year, Ninoy would be dead by an assassin's bullet, and, in four years, Cory would be president of the country.

When I got back to Manila I joined a special meeting of Laban called by Tañada to discuss the proposed coalition of PDP with Laban. I reported to the conferees what Ninoy had said. Despite Ninoy's reservations, Tañada decided to go through with the coalition. Laban members Ernie Rondon, Ramon Mitra, Tito Guingona, Alejandro Roces, Jojo Binay, Rene Saguisag, Joker Arroyo and Bobbit Sanchez supported Tañada.

Timerman's Risqué Phrase

After the coalition, the PDP-Laban really went places in its peaceful challenge to the martial law regime. There were so many invitations for me to speak about PDP-Laban that I could accommodate only a few. My audiences invariably wanted me to amplify what the party was all about. Mainly, I dwelt on the theme that the party was dedicated to peaceful change.

There was one major speech that I delivered before the Cagayan de Oro Press Club on the occasion of the first celebration of Press Freedom Week on May 24, 1982. (As mayor, I issued an executive order to observe Press Freedom Week in the city every last week of May. It was my way of encouraging the media in Cagayan de Oro to exercise the freedom of the press in the city while the martial law regime suppressed this freedom in other parts of the country.)

In my speech, I spoke of the danger of the nation falling into "the eroticism of violence." I borrowed the rather risqué phrase from Jacobo Timerman, the famous Argentinian author and martial law detainee, who wrote the book, *Prisoner Without a Name, Cell Without a Number.*

I quoted liberally from a passage in Timerman's book in which he warned:

> Only nations capable of creating a political environment that embraces multiple political solutions for any situation are able to escape Argentina's violence. No one is immune to episodes of violence and terrorism; yet it should be possible at least to avoid a situation in which terrorism and violence are the sole creative potential, the sole imaginative, emotional erotic expression of a nation.

I cited him at length to lay the basis for my conclusion that, while it was not safe to condemn the extrajudicial killings in the country, we had to do it. I said:

> To sit idly by is to be as guilty as the perpetrators of the violence which if left unchecked would destroy and make a mockery of all the things we hold dear like the sanctity of life, the values of freedom, peace and justice.

The Path of Peace

I delivered another speech along the same vein before the Metro Manila conference of the Ministers of the Methodist Church at their cathedral in Manila. I told the ministers about the need for churchmen to condemn "government abuses, corruption and continuing deprivation of the fundamental rights of the people." The denunciation, I said, "was not only proper but was demanded by their state of life." I thought that the reminder was timely because even then I saw a tendency to mute public criticisms against government misdeeds. I also informed them that:

> PDP-Laban would seek a radical transformation of Philippine society by reposing power in the hands of the people economically, politically and culturally along the lines of nationalism, socialism, democracy and humanism.

In Cagayan de Oro and other places, I spoke of the need to provide alternatives to our people, who were being made to choose between supporting the martial law or abetting the rebellion against it. I said the choices were not only limited to the two violent alternatives. I spoke against "militarization" which could establish the peace of the cemetery and the order of the graveyard, recalling what Tacitus said of the Roman legions who "made a desolation and called it peace" in his account of their pacification campaigns. I also quoted Bishop Francisco Claver, SJ, of Bukidnon, who said that, while the option for peace, for nonviolence was not a popular one in the country, it was the only way we could face up to the evils of present day society and try to lessen, if not eliminate them.

I identified the third choice as the path of peace that was now more clearly defined in the platform of the PDP-Laban.

Pope Eases Bickerings

A little over a year after my election as mayor of Cagayan de Oro, Pope John Paul II visited the country to beatify Lorenzo Ruiz, the first Filipino to be so honored by the Vatican. The rites were done in the Luneta in the presence of millions of the faithful. His visit gave pause to our local political bickerings. Marcos and Imelda, however, saw the potential of the papal visit to neutralize the growing resistance of certain Church men and women to the martial law regime and to convert their opposition into subservience.

That was obvious in the way Marcos and Imelda tried to assume a more prominent role during the beatification ceremonies. This story is second hand, but it could very well have taken place. Marcos's operators reportedly suggested that on the stage at the Luneta rites, the chairs for Marcos and Imelda be placed on the same line as the Pope's facing the crowd of worshipers. Papal protocol, I understand, politely declined and had its way because the news photos showed Marcos's and Imelda's chairs a step or two behind the Pope's.

In the event, the Marcoses tried to squeeze whatever political juice they could from the Pope's every move while in the country. That was why Imelda took private jets to be at the airports of Cebu and Davao and lead the throngs of greeters when the Pope arrived for his pastoral visits there. She also wanted to project the image that, even as she was the wife of the President, as a faithful daughter of the Church, she was willing to go to any length to make the Pope's visit as safe and comfortable as possible.

The Marcoses likewise invited the Pope to Malacañang for a dialogue with the President in the hope of turning the papal visit into a PR plus for the martial law regime. To our delight, the Pope stood his ground and told Marcos in so many words that human rights must be respected. According to the *Panorama* of January 10, 1982, the Pope said:

> Any conflict between state security and the basic rights of the citizens must be resolved according to the fundamental principle that social organization exists only for the service of man and or the protection of his dignity and it cannot claim to serve the common good when rights are not safeguarded.

But, true to his conservative papacy, the Pope also told the clergy that they were priests and not political leaders.

There was reason for the papal admonition. Many among the clergy and the religious were getting radicalized by the abuses of the Marcos regime. Scores of priests and nuns were turning into active rebel supporters or rebels themselves, and a number were arrested or killed, a phenomenon that the country had not seen since the likes of the priests, Jose Burgos, Mariano Gomez and Jacinto Zamora were garroted on February 17, 1873 by the Spanish colonial government for alleged subversion. The military crackdown on activist priests and nuns widened the rift between the Church and the State represented by the Marcos regime.

After the Pope left for the Vatican, we were faced again by our parochial political concerns. By 1982, the *WHO* magazine analyses of the causes of the breaking up of the "political triumvirate of Canoy, Adaza and Pimentel" had become standard. An article authored by Ding Marcelo in the *Panorama* of March 21 concluded:

The legal Opposition today remains divided and fragmented as ever. The oppositionists are united by their common desire to put an end to President Marcos's regime but divided by the debilitating evils of ambition, distrust and suspicion.

The article further noted:

In the case of the Mindanao Alliance, the once monolithic Opposition group, a shining symbol of triumph amid adversity after this puny regional political party took on the giant Kilusang Bagong Lipunan and won, is now fighting for its survival. Its three outspoken and charismatic leaders — Assemblyman Reuben Canoy, Misamis Oriental Governor Homobono Adaza and Cagayan de Oro City Mayor Aquilino Pimentel — have gone separate ways. The reason: each accused the other of being a tool of Malacañang. Already divided by their own ambitions, party stalwarts are now fragmented by distrust and beclouded by questions of loyalty.

Actually, it was Canoy and Adaza who raised the issue of who between the two of them was playing footsy with Marcos. In my case, I simply tried to distance myself from Marcos as much as I could. I also expressed the view publicly that "whatever political differences Mr. Adaza and I have can be ironed out. I have never quarreled with him. Any arrangement between us can be arrived at if there is good faith and sincerity." My conciliatory position also applied to Canoy. The truth, however, was that the rift among the three of us had become impossible to contain.

Pelaez Ambush

The frays that I had with local politicians took some attention from my other concerns as mayor. But an incident in Quezon City in September 1982 certainly shook us up in Cagayan de Oro, as it did people all over the country. Interim Batasan Assemblyman and Minister of State for Foreign Affairs Emmanuel Pelaez, the political *niño bonito*, favorite son, of Misamis Oriental was ambushed near his home in Quezon City. He was wounded in the attempt, but his driver of 20 years, Arsenio Rogero, was killed.

At the hospital, Pelaez asked a senior police officer, Tomas Karingal, "General, what is happening to our country?" That famous quote became the byword of oppositionists whenever Marcos was caught with his finger in an anomaly or something went wrong in the country.

After the ambush, Pelaez renounced any political ambition for himself. He went into the propagation of Bible reading. Months later, I visited him at his office to tell him that I had a witness who was willing to identify the mastermind and the gunmen — there were two — who had tried to kill him. All that the witness wanted was some assistance to get out of the country. Pelaez told me that he had forgiven his assailants and would leave the matter to the Lord.

Before I called on him at his office, I insinuated to the media that the Pelaez ambush was related to the coconut-levy issue. At about the time of the assassination attempt, the issue of the use of the coconut levy was a hot topic. Pelaez wanted the money raised by the levy through various presidential decrees of Marcos to be given to the coconut farmers. The idea was vigorously resisted by powerful individuals who were counted among the "in-crowd" of Marcos. When the newsmen asked what made me think that the incident was linked to his moves to question the use of the coconut levy, I kidded them that the shells recovered from the crime scene were not .45 caliber shells but coconut shells.

It was a pity that Pelaez was no longer interested in ascertaining the identities of the culprits. Had he pursued the issue, some rather interesting names in the national political scene then and now and high-ranking military officials would have been revealed as the conspirators of the assassination plot.

Chapter 25

Farcical Presidential Election

On June 16, 1981, Marcos called for a presidential election, which turned out to be the most farcical in the country's annals. It would be the first presidential election since he declared martial rule in 1972, but the people greeted his announcement with derision rather than elation. The people knew that he called for the election simply to legitimize and perpetuate his absolute hold on power.

People didn't take the presidential election seriously and nobody of any political consequence wanted to run against him. Even Marcos, as a dictator, wanted the presidential election to have a patina of regularity. He and his political advisers then cajoled Alejo Santos of Bulacan to run against him. Our Region X Assemblyman Reuben Canoy, who would have been a better contender against Marcos, floated his name initially as an opposition candidate. But neither he nor Santos had the national political machinery needed for a presidential contest. Eventually, Canoy pulled out of the race. Bartolome Cabangbang of Bohol entered his name as the third candidate. His basic platform was considered a prank on the people. Cabangbang ran under a promise to make the Philippines the 51st State of the United States of America.

Adding to the national perception that the presidential election was a farce, Unido, the largest Opposition group, led by Sen. Doy Laurel, boycotted it. The Unido boycott statement lambasted the Comelec as incapable of supervising honest elections as it was "composed of men who [stood] ready to violate its duty of preserving the sanctity of the ballot upon orders of Mr. Marcos."

I supported the Unido boycott. To me, there was no credible Opposition candidate. Days before the elections, the Comelec qualified 13 candidates, but none, including Santos, had national name recognition or a national organization and, more importantly, no one had a credible platform. In a statement published by the *Panorama* on June 14, Sen. Pepe Diokno, a boycott proponent, said that "the biggest qualification of Santos for the presidency [was] that he was a former warden of the National Penitentiary." Diokno was a little off in that assessment. Santos was a former Secretary of National Defense. The problem was that nobody seemed to have heard of any outstanding achievement of his in that department either. The candidates who ran against Marcos, to use a media pun, were all "political toothpicks." Thus, the people considered the presidential election of 1981 as a bad joke that Marcos perpetrated against the nation.

Boycott Wins in Cagayan de Oro

In Cagayan de Oro, our boycott of the presidential election was a success. At the time, Cagayan de Oro had 151,333 registered voters. In the election, Marcos received 37,301 votes; Cabangbang, 4,561, and Santos, 3,381. Those who wrote "abstain" on their ballots totaled 48,030 and those who boycotted numbered 57,510. Those who marked their ballots "abstain" exceeded the votes received by Marcos by 10,729. And those who actually boycotted numbered 20,000 more than those who voted for Marcos.

Climaco Rams Comelec

More significantly, just weeks before the sham presidential election, Mayor Cesar Climaco of Zamboanga City produced solid evidence that the Comelec itself was a party to the manipulation of the April 7 plebiscite. Marcos used this plebiscite to justify the holding of the June 16 presidential election.

In a telegram to Marcos, which he copy furnished me, Climaco said that there was no point for the Opposition to participate in the elections. To prove his proposition, the bellicose mayor produced before the local media the falsified plebiscite returns and other fraudulent documents, which he had seized from a room in Hotel Lantaka in Zamboanga City on April 7. The exposé hardly made the national headlines. Only a few people then really knew how the Comelec had tampered with the April plebiscite to ensure that Marcos got his wishes to amend the Constitution to suit his ends.

Three days later, on April 10, Climaco filed charges of falsification of election returns against four Comelec employees, Roberto Baguio, Sofronio Manlapas, Jr., Regulas Palma and Ramon F. Dimen before the City Fiscal's Office of Zamboanga. The Comelec did nothing decisive about the complaints except to send a so-called task force composed of lawyers Silvestre Bello, assistant director for operations of the Comelec, and Francisco Santos of the Ministry of Justice. Bello and Santos merely suggested to Climaco that he should file a complaint under oath.

Climaco, as a lawyer, knew that there was no need for him to file any formal complaint before the task force. In fact, the sworn testimonies of witnesses to the crime had already been taken by the acting city prosecutor of Zamboanga, Jose Atanacio. The procedure that the task force lawyers wanted him to follow was simply a way of freezing action on his complaints.

Refusing to allow his complaints to be buried in the bureaucratic mess of the Comelec, Climaco bombarded Marcos and the Comelec with telegraphed demands that the matters be attended to. Nonetheless, it took two more years, before the Comelec formed another task force now composed of lawyers Felix Balalio, Comelec field supervisor, and Manuel Tatel, third assistant city prosecutor of Zamboanga. They were instructed to proceed with the investigation of Climaco's complaints on April 2, 1984. In contrast to the inaction of the first task force, the new one recommended the dismissal of the complaints on April 5, a record time of Comelec low-level official — but substantially flawed — efficiency. No further investigation was done.

Altogether, it took the Comelec Law Department another two years just to recommend the final dismissal of the complaints. The majority of the Comelec commissioners, with the exception of Commissioner Ramon Felipe, approved the recommmendation to dismiss the complaint. Among other things, Felipe bewailed the fact that the commission sat on the Climaco complaints for so long without acting on it.

People in general were so disgusted with the Comelec that a description that Palawan Opposition leader Ramon Mitra, Jr., wryly made stuck to it all throughout the Marcos regime. Mitra said that the Comelec "did not know how to count." This was a deadly indictment because one of its most crucial works was to count the results of elections.

In any event, Climaco proved to be a thorn that seemed permanently embedded in the gullet of the Comelec throughout his term as mayor of Zamboanga City. For instance, he did another exposé on the electoral irregularities in connection with the June 7, 1982, Regional Pampook Elections of Region IX. Again, Marcos and the Comelec simply ignored Climaco.

Incidentally, during the martial law era, Climaco was the only politician who successfully interspersed serious charges against Marcos with jocular asides that made his telegrams to Marcos hilarious. On one occasion, he sent a telegram to Marcos suggesting that Marcos should issue a decree mandating that, in the country, the word "aggrupation" should be considered a regular English word. The reason for his suggestion was that when he used "aggrupation" in an earlier telegram to Marcos, a crony of the President told him that the word did not exist. Never at a loss for a retort, Climaco said that the word "aggrupation" was first used by Marcos in a decree that enacted the Revised Election Code. Therefore, since Marcos made the original mistake, he should rectify it by issuing a decree mandating that "aggrupation" should now be accepted as an English word in the country.

Predictable Results

The warnings issued by the Unido, the CLUP and Climaco, notwithstanding, Marcos held the presidential election on June 16, 1981. The results were predictable. With no credible opposition candidate, the Comelec dutifully proclaimed him as the newly re-elected president with 18,309,360 votes or 91.4% of the support of the electorate. Alejo Santos, his supposedly closest rival, was credited with only 1,716,449 or 8.6% of the votes cast.

Marcos then claimed that, with a new "mandate" from the people, he had the authority to impose whatever he believed was needed to attain the objectives of the New Society. Among the steps that he took was to disable the members of the legitimate Opposition. I was one of those he targeted for removal from office.

Astutely, Marcos did not want to remove me directly himself. If there was one thing that he always endeavored to do during martial rule, it was to cover his tracks with the mantle of legality. In my case, he had the Comelec do the hatchet job. Dutifully, the Comelec officials dusted off a case that had been pending before it for the last 18 months since the local elections in 1980.

Chapter 26:

Turncoatism Surfaces Anew

B ut before the Comelec actually renewed its brazen assault on my right to continue serving the people of Cagayan de Oro as mayor, a number of significant events — less partisan than usual — got my attention.

NPA Emissaries

Within the year of my election as mayor, two men who I did not know personally came to visit me in my house.

I received them in my library where I usually talked with visitors in the house. I listened attentively to what they had to say. They told me that the New People's Army operating in Northern Mindanao wanted to establish a working relationship with me as the opposition mayor of Cagayan de Oro.

I told them that the proposed relationship would not be good either for them or for me. In so many words, I said that it would be bad for them because they would be dealing with me, a politician. I did not have to remind them that in their general view of electoral politics, politicians were to be treated like lepers, that is, shunned publicly. Neither did I have to remind them that they had, in fact, boycotted elections, including the local elections of 1980 where I was elected as mayor.

It would also be bad for me, I told them, because I would be giving the martial law government a valid excuse to run after me.

In effect, I suggested to them to leave me alone to do my job as best I could for the sake of the people who they also claimed they were working for. And if they could leave Cagayan de Oro in peace, that I said would be the best gift they could offer to our people. Then, we could, I proposed, "just live and let live."

To my delight, the two men took my negative response in good spirit. And to their credit, up to end of my tenure as mayor, the NPA did not break the peace in the city.

We shook hands when they left. I did not take their names down. Neither did I formally ask them who they were. I just sort of understood that they were supporters, if not actually regulars, of the NPA. One of them, I was subsequently informed, was from Tagoloan, a town in Misamis Oriental, that was less than 30 minutes away from the city.

Murder in Iligan City

Roughly 11 months after the elections, on December 5, 1980, shots shattered the early evening's calm in the nearby city of Iligan that took away the life of Demosthenes Dingcong, a correspondent of the *Bulletin Today*. Dingcong was shot dead inside his house in Iligan City, some 90 kilometers away from Cagayan de Oro. He had exposed the misuse of funds at the Mindanao State University in Marawi City. Four soldiers, Staff Sgt. Jaime Delgado, a bodyguard of Gov. Ali Dimaporo, and Cpls. Alberto Ilecho, Manuel Carabio and Joe Lumbag, were arrested weeks after the shooting but were subsequently released. Members of the Dingcong family told me that they never knew what ultimately happened to the murder case but, years later, Delgado, the principal suspect in the Dingcong killing, was accused and convicted of the murder of Gov. Francisco Abalos of Lanao del Norte.

In the aftermath of the Dingcong killing, I was warned not to show any sympathy to his family. Dingcong had offended Governor Dimaporo. And in the Lanao provinces, the governor had the status of deity. He was also the president of the Mindanao State University. Despite the advice of friends, I assailed the murder of Dingcong and went to attend his funeral in Iligan City. I was the only public official who joined his funeral cortege. Showing my face at his funeral was my personal message of solidarity with Dingcong's crusade even as his family were complete strangers to me. I was happy to see the bishop of Iligan, Fernando Capalla, leading the final rites for the slain newsman. Bishop Nanding, as his priests and parishioners fondly called him, lent the quiet dignity of his office as shepherd of his flock to protest against the violence engulfing his diocese.

Sister City, Lawndale

In January of 1981, I concluded a sister-city relationship with Lawndale, a suburban city of Los Angeles, California. Lawndale was actually a very small satellite city, smaller than the barangays of Carmen or Lapasan of Cagayan de Oro. By size, population or income, Lawndale was not on par with our city. But it had something going for it that prodded us to create that city partnership. Lawndale had one of the most socially concerned Filipino-Americans living there — Jimmy Cruz. Cruz actively worked for the sister-city agreement. He had a counterpart in Cagayan de Oro, his friend, Dr. Alex Magbag, a highly respected civic and sports leader.

Knowing that people, not other factors, made sister-city agreements succeed, I readily agreed to the twinning. I also wanted to test if Malacañang would allow me to travel to the US and, to my surprise, it did. So With Cruz and Magbag doing the spadework, the sister-city agreement between Cagayan de Oro and Lawndale came to pass. Lawndale sent thousands of books in English, Mathematics, Science and History, which I turned over to our city library. Lawndale City officials also warmly received many of our city residents who went to the US to celebrate *Tapok*, the gathering of Cagayanons in California. On our part, we received Lawndale Mayor Sarann Kruise and her party in a reciprocal visit and named a huge natural swimming pool in Taguanao after their city.

A political flap developed over that otherwise beneficial sister-city venture. Some self-styled nationalists among my political opponents called it a cop-out of my nationalist credentials because they said I was aligning myself with the Americans to shore up my supposedly declining political stock. The accusation was pure hogwash. I decided not to formally reply to them, except to say that, if they had any worthwhile city in the Soviet Union or China that they could recommend, all they had to do was tell me and I would not hesitate to sign a twinning agreement with it.

Within months of my visit to Lawndale, on July 23, 1981, the Comelec revived the turncoatism issue against me. I had been in office for more than a year and five months when the Comelec ruled that I was not qualified to be the mayor of the city on the ground that I was a "turncoat." The turncoatism issue reached the Interim Batasan where Assemblyman Marcial Pimentel of Camarines Norte spoke out in my defense. At that point, I had not yet met the assemblyman and had not bothered to trace our family tree but, because he was a ranking member of the KBL, he surprised me with his cogent arguments why the Comelec "should go slow in frustrating the people's will and mandate."

The KBL did not let Assemblyman Pimentel's polemics pass without rebuttal. Assemblyman Concordio Diel of Cagayan de Oro retorted in a statement that was published in the Daily *Express* of July 9, that it was our party, the PDP that "distorted the restraining order of the Supreme Court." Assemblyman Pelaez, the KBL Chair of Region X, echoed Diel's argument.

Cause: SIR Project

The "turncoatism" issue against me resurfaced for no other reason than my opposition to the World Bank-funded SIR project in Macabalan. Had I gone along with the SIR project, the issue would have been forgotten. But as fate would have it, I fought against the project. I did not want Marcos and the World Bank to foist upon the people of the city a project of dubious benefit to its beneficiaries and which would devastate the finances of the city. Publicly, I said that I would rather be booted out of office than bow to the impositions of the World Bank and Marcos.

Not surprisingly, Marcos took me on my dare with the Comelec as his surrogate. The Comelec declared that I was a "turncoat" who had no right to continue sitting as mayor. By getting rid of me as mayor, the martial law regime hoped that there would no longer be any obstacle to the implementation of the SIR project. I was, moreover, becoming a pesky thorn on the side of the KBL in Northern Mindanao. The fact that the people elected me with 75% of the votes and that the Comelec proclaimed me as mayor after which I had been discharging my duties as mayor for at least 18 months did not seem to bother the poll body.

Comelec Order Flawed

The Comelec order was clearly flawed, even from legal precedents alone which held that questions over qualifications of candidates in general were best resolved prior to, not after, the elections. Thus, aside from Vice Mayor Magtajas and the members of our city council, our political allies — Governor Adaza and IBP Assemblyman Canoy — deplored the arbitrary Comelec resolution. In public statements, Adaza said that his party's putting me up as its candidate for mayor was perfectly justified under the law. For dramatic effect, Canoy threatened to resign from the IBP if the "absurd" Comelec resolution was not reversed by the Supreme Court. Surprisingly, my ouster by order of the Comelec which they both condemned triggered the split between Canoy and Adaza as was shown in Chapter 23.

First People Power

For the moment, the unwarranted act of the Comelec also got the people of Cagayan de Oro exercised. They turned out by the thousands to protest my ouster in the streets of the city at the call of Vice Mayor Magtajas and our councilors. Councilors Parrel and Abbu actively mobilized the "warm

1981: *SOME 10,000 DEMONSTRATORS march from the Cathedral to the heart of the city to protest my ouster.*

bodies" for the demonstration. It was the first people power demonstration under martial law conditions that saw no less than 10,000 people marching in the streets and protesting a government (Comelec) order.

In Manila, the Unido organization, headed by Assemblyman Laurel, expressed its full support for me. Laurel said:

> There is no question that Mayor Pimentel is the overwhelming choice of the people of Cagayan de Oro City. But the Comelec, instead of using legal technicality to uphold the will of the people, has used it to frustrate and subvert the popular will.

The offending Comelec resolution ordered Velez to be seated in my stead. Since I had beaten Velez by 75% of the vote, Marcos saw the situation in the city for what it was: volatile. Craftily he issued an invitation for a meeting in Malacañang on July 13, 1981 of "the contending parties in the Cagayan de Oro electoral contest, to prevent tension and avoid further conflict while the case (was) pending in court." I was not able to attend the meeting because I was still in the US on an official trip.

In any event, the conference did not take place on July 13. It took place on July 16, at Malacañang, where Marcos ordered Velez not to take over as city mayor until a Supreme Court ruled on the issue of who was the rightfully elected mayor of the city. It was agreed that while waiting for the Supreme Court decision, my supporters would remove all propaganda materials and streamers — including a coffin that Councilor Parrel placed at the main entrance of the city hall to proclaim the "death of democracy" in Cagayan de Oro. They also agreed not to hold demonstrations so as not to further inflame the situation.

Vice Mayor Magtajas, Governor Adaza and Mayor Climaco of Zamboanga City represented me at the meeting. It was a good compromise for our side because it allowed me to continue as mayor and also for the administration because it defused the tensions in the city. As a result of the compromise, Canoy did not have to make good his threat to resign. I, therefore, came home in triumph having trashed the "turncoatism" issue, but I knew in my bones that there were more harassments coming my way from Marcos.

The people of the city got a favorable review from one of the major Manila dailies for the restraint in their reaction to my ouster by the Comelec. The *Bulletin Today* of July 15, 1981 editorialized the upholding of the "Rule of Law" by our constituents in the wake of my removal. The editorial said:

If Cagayan de Oro had not been blessed with an enlightened citizenry and articulate and enlightened political leaders, it would (not) have made a classic example for the application of the rule of law. For the rule of law means compliance with the law and its processes. Conversely, it means that the law should not be taken into one's own hands. But Cagayan de Oro, true to its name, is an essentially peaceful community and a progressive one at that. One proof is despite the election brouhaha set off by the Comelec decision nullifying the candidacy of Mr. Aquilino Pimentel, Jr., there have been protest demonstrations but no trouble.'

Chapter 27:

RCDP Seminar in Berkeley

In August 1981, along with 22 other city mayors, I attended a training seminar for some mayors sponsored by the Regional Cities Development Program of the USAID in California. Cesar Climaco of Zamboanga City and I were the only two non-Marcos mayors in the group. There were, however, five other mayors from Mindanao, aside from Climaco and me. They were Miguel Paderanga of Gingoog City; Omar Dianalan, Marawi City; Alfonso Tan, Tangub City; Germanico Carreon, Dapitan City; and Figurado Plaza, Butuan City.

The rest of the participating mayors came from various cities in Luzon and the Visayas. They were Feliberto Oliveros, Jr., Teodoro Arcenas, Gregorio Imperial, Jr., Carlos Solis, Pablo Lucero, Cipriano Manaois, Mario Tagarao, Jose Villanueva, Conrado Berberabe, Richard Gordon, Carlos del Castillo, Francisco Nepomuceno, Obdulia Cinco, Jose Aviles, Luis Herrera and Jose Montalvo.

The month-long seminar, which started on August 3, featured resource speakers who discussed substantial aspects of local governance at the Institute of Urban Planning and Regional Development and the Institute of Government Studies at the University of California in Berkeley. The UC Berkeley Campus was the hotbed of student activism in the 60s and 70s. Mayor Climaco with his long hair — uncut since the declaration of martial rule — and rugged build, roamed around the campus in his denims and T-shirt, easily blending into the activist environment of the university. He and I were the favorites of the anti-Marcos Filipinos living in the Bay Area who invited us to discuss the Philippine situation. In those forums, we took turns in lambasting the excesses of the Marcos government, especially in the field of human rights violations and official corruption.

The seminar also gave us an opportunity to visit select cities near Berkeley, which exposed us to different ways cities were managed in the US. Some cities had appointed city managers with varying degrees of power. In most cities, the city managers had more direct powers of governance than the elected city mayors. Although we did not like the idea, the thought that we could have city managers under our supervision and control was something that we appreciated. Our disinclination to adopt a system where city managers would have more powers than the city mayors was natural. In our case, as mayors, we were elected directly by the people and we were power figures in our own cities socially, politically and, in some instances, even economically.

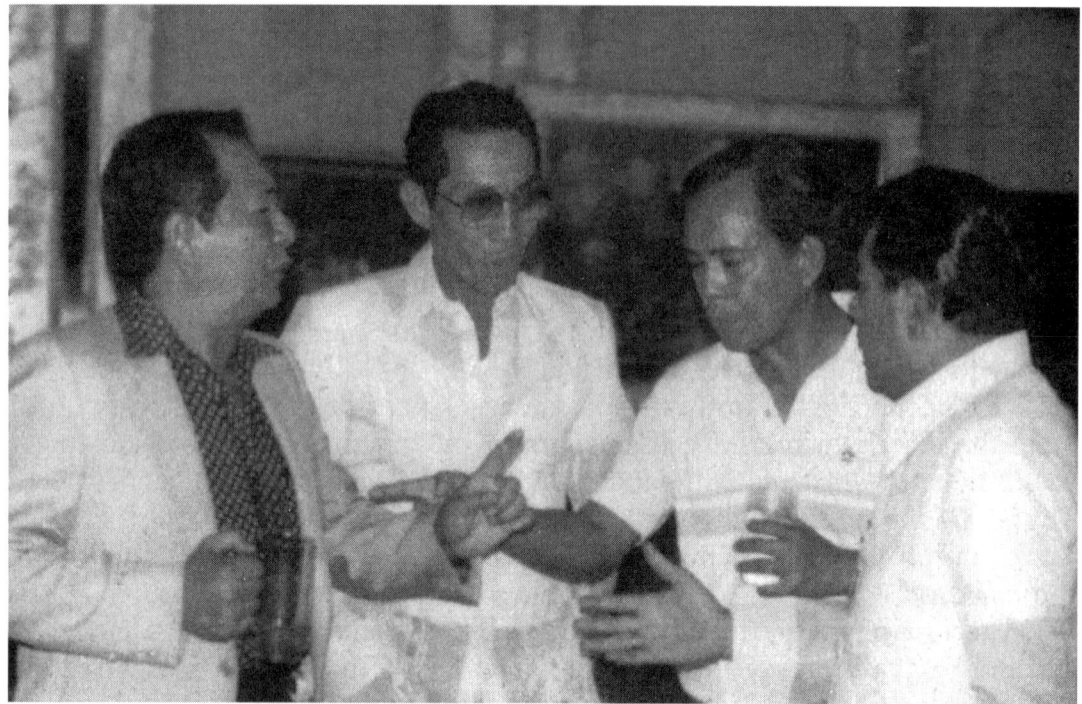

***1981**: WITH RCDP MAYORS. That's me 2ⁿᵈ from the right.*

From Berkeley, we flew to Washington, DC. There we did the sights: the White House, Congress, Supreme Court, Lincoln Memorial and a score of museums. At the Smithsonian, one of the world's best museums, Climaco startled not only us, his mayoral colleagues, but several other museum visitors, when in his usual loud voice (he was a little deaf), he asked an astronaut shown on a video clip walking on the moon what the latter was doing. He was clowning, of course. And we all had a hearty laugh over it.

Demos Against the Mayors

On our second day in DC, we had a memorable experience — the first for me — to be caught in the middle of a demonstration that was directed at the "junketing Marcos mayors," an ill-thought categorization that included Climaco and myself. We were on a bus en route to an official function in the US capital when a hostile crowd of Filipino demonstrators, led by Charito Planas, pressed in on both sides of the bus. Planas's eyes met mine, but she gave no indication that she knew me. In fact, the evening before, she and some of her friends met me and told me they would be demonstrating against us the following day. Now, they were there as Planas had promised, shouting obscenities in Tagalog and waving placards that hit our trip as a waste of public funds and a junket intended to strengthen Philippine-US relations under martial law conditions. They wanted the American government to know that, even there in the capital of the US, many Filipinos did not approve of the

Marcos government. Knowing that Climaco and I were not the objects of the demonstrators' ire, I sort of enjoyed the spectacle of the other mayors fidgeting in their seats, unable to do anything about it and being reduced to muttering curses against the "steak commandoes" in the US.

Our official trip to DC did not have much significance for me. The only thing that made the DC trip memorable was the forum organized by the Movement for a Free Philippines led by Manglapus. The affair was held in the house of Dave Valderama, a Filipino-American member of the legislature of Virginia. Valderama's home was filled with Filipino expatriates and their American friends. I had the fun of my life hitting the "conjugal dictatorship" of Marcos and Imelda and giving my audience some hope that, one day soon, democracy would be restored in the county.

Assessing the Seminar

At the end of the seminar, the Ministry of Local Government asked us to assess it. Local Government Undersecretary Salvador Socrates said our views would be included in a formal report that would be submitted to Marcos. I did not think that such an inconsequential report would ever reach Marcos's office but Socrates was tactfully reminding us to be gracious in our comment on the value of the seminar because Marcos would see it.

I tried to be as objective as possible in my assessment. I said that the seminar certainly "helped to sharpen the budgetary and urban planning skills of the participants." I added that it could have been made more relevant to the Philippine conditions had the mayors been allowed to share their own experiences in running their cities with the other participants. I added that I liked its main message that "consulting with the people in matters of planning for their benefit" was necessary for a successful integration of the views of city officials and their constituents.

In his assessment, however, the irrepressible Mayor Climaco said that it was providential that two groups of Filipino activists in America, one in Berkeley, California, and another in Washington, DC, demonstrated against the Philippine mayors. He recounted that the demonstrators shouted: *"Marcos mayors, tuta Marcos. Mayors, tuta — may araw rin kayo!* Marcos mayors, lap dogs of Marcos. Mayors, lap dogs — your day will come!" His report on the demonstrations was true.

In Berkeley, for instance, at the closing dinner tendered for us by our hosts, a group that styled itself as "the Filipinos of the Bay Area" sent a bunch of fortune cookies. The mayors identified with Marcos got fortune cookies with their names on it. The messages were not only insulting but also threatening. One message addressed to Mayor Richard Gordon of Olongapo read, "Your days are numbered."

Bearding the WB Lions

The RCDP seminar over, I flew home only to go back to DC in a few days to discuss the SIR issue with World Bank officials.

In my hotel the day before my meeting with the World Bank officials, an undistinguished looking person introduced himself to me as Walden Bello.

Although I had not met him before, I had read some of his articles on Third World economies that were mostly critical of the World Bank and IMF policies.

Bello asked if he could accompany me to my meetings with the World Bank officials. I said I did not see how that could be done. He suggested that he could come as my aide. Since I needed a witness to what I would discuss with World Bank officials, I agreed. I told him, however, that he should be prepared to be barred from the meetings if bank officials objected to his presence.

At the appointed hour, we went to the World Bank headquarters. Contrary to our apprehensions, Bello was allowed to accompany me without anybody asking who he was. In hindsight, it was a good thing that he went with me because he took notes of the discussion and later wrote about the meetings in the book, *Development Debacle: The World Bank in the Philippines*, that he co-authored with David Kinley and Elaine Elinson. The book was published in 1982.

At the World Bank, we had separate meetings with a number of officials who took turns in assailing my position against the SIR project. Collectively, their view was that my stand was prejudicial to the best interests of Cagayan de Oro. I stood my ground even as Inder K. Sud, head of the urban division for Asia and the Pacific, uttered a covert warning that, if I did not revise my stand, "World Bank money would be difficult to come by" for my city.

I gave Sud an answer he was not prepared for. In the presence of his staff members, I told him, if that was his opinion, then "you can keep your money, Sir." With that I left the bank offices, Bello trudging alongside me.

Minutes before that meeting with Sud, I met with Steven O'Brien, chief of the Philippine Division of the World Bank. From the outset of our conversation, I put O'Brien ill at ease by noting that from the way the bank officials were pushing for the project despite its apparent flaws, they probably wanted me ousted from the mayorship of my city. O'Brien lamely parried the thrust by saying that the bank officials did not indulge in matters of that sort. It probably was the very first time that World Bank officials were told to their faces by a Third World local official that their Slum Improvement Rehabilitation project in his city was not going to help the poor.

After the meeting, I braced myself for the worst. I had a feeling that Marcos and the World Bank were not through with me. For the moment though, I was personally satisfied that I had done the right thing for my city.

Marcos Tightens Media Control

While my relationship with the martial law regime was heating up, Marcos was also maneuvering to exercise more control over the media. In mid-July of 1981, Letty Jimenez-Magsanoc was removed as editor of a leading English language weekly magazine, *Panorama*. She wrote an article, "There Goes the New Society, Welcome the New Republic," in which she said, among other things, that Marcos "with all his powers was powerless before corruption and corruptors." Marcos did not like that. Furthermore, in the same article, she exposed the "corruption and dishonest counting of votes by the election commission" in the last presidential election. The Comelec did not like that either. To make Magsanoc understand the gravity of what she had done, Justice Minister Puno ruled that the story "incited or tended to incite its readers to sedition or rebellion." Although the lady was not haled to court, she was, however, forced to resign by the magazine's publisher, Gen. Hans Menzi, a crony of Marcos.

I read the Magsanoc article to find out why the regime was so offended. I found the reason. Aside from the biting observations that Marcos was unable to stem the tide of corruption, Magsanoc's description of his corrupt cronies as "smarter than others" got the goat, if not of Marcos himself, then of Imelda. Roughly two years before the Magsanoc article was published, the phrase "smarter than others" was in the title of a mimeographed 40-page pamphlet, *Some Are Smarter Than Others,* which detailed the corruption of the Marcos regime.

The pamphlet charged Marcos, Imelda and their cronies with amassing illegal fortunes at the expense of the people. It was often cited by newspapers not only in Asia but also in the US and Europe as a source document on the corruption of the Marcos regime. No wonder that the Marcoses took umbrage at the Magsanoc article.

The pamphlet was written by Ricardo Manapat, a member of *Kasapi* or *Kapisanan ng mga Sandigan ng Pilipinas,* roughly, the Organization of the Pillars of the Philippines, a progressive centrist youth organization that opposed the martial law regime. Manapat was aided in his research mostly by young people whom I met in our common struggle against Marcos. Among them were Rafael Cecilio, Margarita Valte, Karen Tañada, Rolando Montiel and Gerardo Esguerra. Their father figure in the venture was lawyer Luis Jose, who in 1982 became the working chair of our party, the PDP-Laban.

The removal of Magsanoc on such a flimsy excuse validated our view that Marcos had not really "lifted" martial law in January of the year. He still had vast powers in his hands and he used those powers whenever they came in handy to preserve his hold on government. Although I did not know Magsanoc, personally at the time, I admired what she said about Marcos and his government. I also thought that she did our province proud because Magsanoc's mother was from Misamis Oriental, my own home province. Her dismissal from the *Bulletin Today* was followed by the firing of other female writers from the same newspaper, namely Melinda Quintos de Jesus, Arlene Babst, Niñez Cacho Olivarez and Sylvia Mayuga. Their offense: writing mainly about freedom.

Part 8

Opposition in Cagayan de Oro

1983: *THE CLERGY with some 15,000 demonstrators protest my arrest.*

Chapter 28:

Developing the City

When I got home to Cagayan de Oro from my meetings with World Bank officials in Washington, DC, the SIR project was momentarily shelved. Subsequently, I got the approval of the city council to inaugurate our own housing project for the poor.

We expropriated a 14-hectare lot owned by the wealthy Tamparong family in Macanhan, in the barangay of Carmen, and subdivided it among the homeless in the city. A screening committee headed by City Administrator Cua chose the beneficiaries on the basis of need — in which the actual or near-poverty status of the beneficiary was the major factor, not their political connections. The lots were not given to them for free. They were required to pay a minuscule amount, something like P25 every month, and were prohibited from selling the land to other people. It was our attempt at social housing to show that the city government could do it better and more economically than the national government.

Unfortunately, because the city had not done any land banking before I became mayor, we had to expropriate land that we needed for the Macanhan socialized housing project and for other city public projects as well. In the process, I antagonized many of the city's landed families, whose lands were either subjected to actual or threatened expropriation by my administration. Also, early on in my term as mayor, in the barangay of Carmen, hundreds of squatters occupied wide stretches of private land owned by well-to-do friends of mine. The landowners expected me to drive the squatters out of their land. I told them that if they wanted to remove the squatters, they should go to court, not to the mayor's office. As a lawyer, I knew there were adequate recourses in law to protect the right of owners to their properties. Ultimately, the squatters were evicted and the land restored to their rightful owners. But my friendship with the wealthy landowners of the city never regained its original warmth. I had lost a lot of political capital.

Consultations

Anyway, I continued to implement our socialized housing program. For easier supervision, I had the Macanhan socialized housing project placed under the Office of Marginal Settlers (OMS) that Cua, the city administrator, had proposed. Among the first marching orders I gave to the employees assigned to the OMS was to go out to the rural and urban areas where the poor lived, organize them into viable livelihood groups, prioritize their needs which the city could address, and in general raise their level of hope for a better life.

The initial reaction of the poor whom our city hall workers were trying to reach out to was nothing short of hostile. They told our outreach workers to go home because, in their view, "government people were the same. They could not be trusted." I told our outreach workers to be patient and to persevere, because, while it was true that the government had indeed proven unworthy of the trust of the people, this time we were going to prove the people wrong. Over time, we earned the confidence of the poor through the efforts principally of Cua and two of his OMS subordinates, Laura Abejo and Nene Abonitalla.

Eventually, the people saw that my administration followed up our discussions with them with concrete action. We built the roads that the people wanted, put up the waterworks that they needed and lighted up the rural and urban areas that had no electricity. By the end of my first year in office, I could say that my administration delivered on most of our electoral promises, not only to the rural areas of the city but also to the *poblacion*. Even as people saw that changes for the better were taking place, as their mayor, I was not satisfied with our material accomplishments. I was dissatisfied because there was one thing that we as a people could not enjoy — freedom. I knew the people wanted that also but could not enjoy it because Marcos's vision for the country proposed bread first for the people before freedom. We eventually showed how wrong Marcos was. But that was still some six years after I became mayor.

1981: IN MY CONSULTATIONS with the people, members of the clergy like Archbishop Jesus Dosado, DD, and Francis Madigan, SJ, and nuns help articulate the people's priorities.

In the meantime, I kept on with my work and consulted with the people as often as I could. I had a six-year term and I thought that I might as well devote my time to serving the people of Cagayan de Oro as best I could. Consulting with the people took time and a lot of effort to get them to crystallize their priorities. Sometimes, I felt that I was just wasting time, especially when nothing concrete came at the end of a day's consultation. Nonetheless, I tried hard not to show my impatience. The alternative would have been for us to take the easy way out just by my ordering this or that project to be done without asking for the opinion of our constituents.

In fact, our city engineers often broadly hinted that there was no need to ask the people what they wanted done for their barangays because they already knew what the people needed. In the city engineers' view, if they saw a barangay road needed asphalting, they could immediately do that. They could also construct a water system or build a schoolhouse without asking for anyone's idea on how to do it. As engineers, they did not see the need to ask the people what their priorities were. They were of the opinion that government officials should do the prioritizing of the projects. That was not the way I looked at things.

I remember an instance when the flowers and fruits section of the city public market burned down. Before rebuilding the burnt section, instinctively I told the city engineers to go ask the vendors how they would like their stalls rebuilt. The engineers said that they did not need to consult the vendors. They already knew how to rebuild the fire-gutted area. To cut them off, I simply told them that, since I was the mayor and not they, they should just probably follow my instructions. They did.

Days later, the engineers told me it was good that they consulted the stall owners. When I asked them why, the engineers said the stall-owners wanted the partitions of their stalls to be made of chicken wire or some other porous material that would allow air to pass freely from one stall to another. In that way, they told the engineers, their goods could stay fresh longer in the absence of refrigeration.

The experience validated my theory that consulting with the people even if it consumed a lot of time was a good way of modernizing the city. On another occasion, I went to a barangay up in the hills and asked the people to list down their priorities of projects they wanted the city to do for them. I told them it was necessary to do so because they had so many needs that the city could not provide them all at the same time.

After much discussion, the barrio folks identified water as their foremost priority, followed by electricity and then a good road to enable them to travel to and from the city. I then praised them for doing their prioritizing well. I told them that potable water was most essential because, without it, they could not expect to see their children grow to adulthood since the threat of pollution in their stagnant water wells was ever present. I shared with them a report that I received that a farming family got seriously sick from drinking polluted water. The well from which they drank had accumulated toxic waste from pesticides and herbicides that were sprayed by light planes treating a nearby pineapple plantation. Incidentally, my stand against the indiscriminate use of pesticides and herbicides did not endear me to the American officials of the pineapple plantation, which at the time was the biggest employer of people in my city.

I lauded their next priority, electricity, because it was a vital need of modern living. Electricity, I said, would enable them to continue working at home and their children to read and do their homework at night. And lastly, I commended their prioritization of a road to link them to the city. Without good roads, they would be isolated from the city proper and they would have extreme difficulty in transporting their farm produce to the main markets of the city.

I tried to follow as best I could to deliver projects based on the priorities suggested by the barangay residents. By doing so, I felt that the projects we undertook had the backing of the people. I also sensed the people's joy that they were treated by city hall not as mere bystanders in the modernization of their areas but as actual participants in it.

Gerry Roxas Passes Away

Sometime in 1981, about a year after I was elected as mayor, news reached me that Sen. Gerry Roxas, one of our more reliable leaders of the Opposition, had died in the US after a liver operation. Roxas's death was a sad loss for me personally because he had treated me as a friend.

He appointed me the chair of the Liberal Party in the province of Misamis Oriental immediately before the presidential election of 1969. And, in the years between the imposition of martial rule and the time he had to leave for the US for his liver surgery, I worked with him in trying to keep the Liberal Party alive, particularly through the publication of the Liberal Party newsletter. Despite his class origins, he allowed the publication of a research paper that I wrote titled, "The Agrarian Reform in the Philippines: A Historico-Political View," in the August 21, 1978 issue of the newsletter. I also wrote another socially oriented article, "Housing the Poor: A Case of Government Neglect," in the newsletter in November 1978. Additionally, I penned other items critical of the martial law regime that might not have seen the light of day but which he allowed to be printed because of his inherent belief in the right of people to information and to a free discussion of ideas. Gerry Roxas was one Opposition leader who, aside from Aquino, would have been a good alternative to Marcos as the leader of the country.

Political Adversaries

In Cagayan de Oro, even as I was preoccupied with projects to modernize the city, I was also being harassed no end by our political adversaries. Several criminal charges were filed against me with the Ombudsman. A detractor even went to the extent of accusing my wife, Bing, of libel, just to add to our family problems. What ostensibly caused the filing of libel against Bing was her having uttered in my defense — in answer to questions raised by the media in Cagayan de Oro — that she thought that certain charges my detractor had brought against me were the product of a "disturbed mind." Bing had to defend herself in the office of the city fiscal of Iligan, in the nearby province of Lanao del Norte, where the preliminary investigation of the libel case was assigned.

Though the charges irritated me and hurt my children, I tried my best not to be distracted from my task of delivering the basic services that were due to our people in the city. Happily, Marcos's own Ombudsman, Justice Bernardo Fernandez, dismissed the graft accusations against me one after another for being without merit. The city fiscal of Iligan also threw out the libel case against Bing for lack of merit.

Psalm 35

I could only thank God that His grace kept me and my family intact in the face of harassments that came our way during those years. One of the prayers that gave me immense consolation during those difficult times was Psalm 35, where following David's lead, I asked the Lord to protect me from my enemies.

It was Fr. Joaquin Bernas, SJ, who, in a visit to my cell when I was under military detention, suggested that I read Psalm 35 of the Bible. When I did, I found the psalm all too relevant to my situation as a martial law detainee:

> Oppose, Lord, those who oppose me;
>> war upon those who make war upon me.
> Take up the shield and buckler; rise up in my defense.
> Brandish lance and battle-ax against my pursuers.
>> Say to my heart, "I am your salvation."
> Let those who seek my life be put to shame and disgrace.
>> Let those who plot evil against me be turned back and confounded....
> Without cause they set their snare for me;
>> without cause they dug a pit for me.
> Let ruin overtake them unawares;
>> let the snare they have set catch them;
>> let them fall into the pit they have dug.

State of the City, 1981

To inform the people formally about what I was doing for the city, I decided to give an annual report on my mayorship. I made the first report in February 1981. I called the report, the "State of the City Address." Even that innocent title did not escape the malediction of my political opponents who said that it manifested a hidden desire for me to be president. I ignored the carping of my detractors and did the report from year to year.

In the 1981 State of the City Address, I reported that my administration constructed seven barangay roads and paved 15 inner city roads. The construction and improvement of the roads cost the city some P3,870,308. I also said that we had improved drainage canals that cost P667,300. In addition, I related that the city had completed office buildings or built new facilities that cost P8,552,216. The city also got donations for five school buildings, aside from the school buildings that our administration built. The amounts in real terms were really not that impressive but, compared with the record of past city administrations I believed that we did quite well in our first year in office.

We also built water systems, mostly in the barangays far from the city. The water systems were built with the generous support of the USAID. And because I acknowledged publicly the assistance of the USAID in getting the water projects of the city implemented, I got criticized by my political adversaries who branded me as a stooge of the US. I, of course, hit back at my critics, saying they were motivated more by jealousy than by genuine love of country. To dramatize my point, I said that, if those people were sincerely minded about the development of our city, they should tell me if their friends in the Soviet Union or the Peoples' Republic of China had any assistance for cities like Cagayan de Oro and I would not hesitate to ask for it. While the repartee silenced them for a while, their hatred for me continued throughout the years of martial rule and beyond.

Although it happened some 22 years ago, I still recall the joy of the barangay people of San Simon over the water system that brought potable water literally to their doorsteps. Upon my request, US Ambassador Michael Armacost opened the valve of the water main pipe to inaugurate the system. In my remarks, I told Armacost — to his amusement — that the facility was first the modern water system that the people of San Simon had ever enjoyed from the time Magellan claimed to have discovered the Philippines in 1521.

The San Simon residents were so delighted that an American ambassador, in flesh and blood, visited their barangay that they tendered an impromptu barrio fiesta with the usual *lechon* or roast pig, *inihawng isda* or broiled fish, *bibingka* or rice cake, and other local delicacies for us. There was much laughter among the barangay folks when they saw Armacost gamely trying to drink coconut water directly from a freshly harvested coconut. His nose got in the way and that prevented him from enjoying *buko* juice *au naturel*. The barangay captain came to the rescue and gave the ambassador a glass, which enabled him to finish off the juice.

We also acquired four brand-new dump trucks for the city. The trucks were the first major purchase that the city entered into in my term as mayor. In buying the trucks, I did something that was out of the ordinary. I called all the prospective dump truck dealers to meet with me at city hall in an open meeting. At the meeting, in the presence of the Cagayan de Oro media, I told them that I wanted to make sure that no under the table deals were entered into with them by anyone connected with city hall. I told them bluntly that I did not want them to give any city hall official or employee any commission arising out of the purchase of the trucks. Instead of giving any one, including me, as mayor any commission, what I wanted them to do, was to deduct the amounts that they usually gave "for the boys" from the bid price. With the commissions deducted, I said that the bid prices would be lowered and the whole city would benefit from it and not the few corrupt officials who would otherwise profit from overpricing the trucks.

The purchase of the dump trucks was consummated and it was an honest-to-goodness transaction — no overpricing, no under-the-table deals. I was told later on that other local government officials in our region were called to explain by Manila authorities why the acquisition of their dump trucks which were of the same brand and model as the ones we bought cost their local governments much more than ours.

State of the City, 1982

In the 1982 State of the City Address, I reported that, with the support of Vice Mayor Magtajas, we continued the infrastructure development of the city. We constructed barangay roads such as the Pamalihi-Pagatpat road, Captain Vicente Roa Extension, Escobido Street in Puntod; the Kauswagan-Bayabas road; and paved the 15th and 26th streets in Nazareth. The road projects cost the city P2,107,000.

The Kauswagan-Bayabas road had the biggest impact at the time. Kauswagan and Bayabas were two of the more populous barangays of the city. But for a long time, all they had was an "all-weather road" that got dusty during the hot months and got muddy in the rainy season. Thus, the paving of their road made the residents of the two barangays extremely happy.

To implement my promise that I would relieve the people of the flood waters in major parts of the city, we dredged the Bitan-ag Creek, constructed a drainage canal along Escobido Street and installed box culverts in three barangays: two in Canitoan, one in Carmen and another one in Bulua. The drainage projects cost the city P1,139,290.

We also built water systems in the barangays of Tagpangi, Tablon, Migkiwan, Cugman and Pagatpat. The water systems cost the city P2,429,170.

Knowing that infrastructure like roads and bridges did not automatically translate into work for the women of the city, my administration constructed a needle-craft building in Iponan, a garlic production warehouse in Tagpangi and a goat-raising facility in Macasandig. We also extended a loan to the Tailors and Dressmakers Association of Lapasan, another huge barangay of the city. All told, the projects cost the city P511,414.

To help the unemployed women get productively occupied, Bing, assisted by Anita Magtajas, Anita Karagdag, Minda Soriano and Rosalinda Caragos, organized a livelihood foundation which they called the *Oro Kasandigan*.

We constructed a number of public buildings and facilities or completed the unfinished work of previous city administrations. I found it so wasteful of public funds for public buildings constructed by my predecessors to lie fallow. Thus, my administration completed the one-bay extension of the City Hall Annex Building, the Administrator's Office at Cogon Market, the detention cell in the Police Station in Carmen and the cementing and landscaping of the grounds of city hall. We also built an Integrated Bus Terminal Building in the barangay of Lapasan and a multi-purpose building in the barangay of Canitoan. In addition, we opened a new cemetery at Bolonsiri in the barangay of Camaman-an. The projects cost the city P4,607,930.

We also put up the perimeter fence of the elementary school of Barangay Puntod at the cost of P214,073. And, to show our concern for the women who did their laundry at the Cagayan de Oro river, we constructed two concrete stairways and landings at its edge at the cost of P72,985. At the time, women washing clothes at the river was still commonplace.

State of the City, 1983

In 1983, I reported in the State of the City Address that of the projects that we did for the year, the most contentious was the transfer of the cemetery from its old site at the side of Xavier University on the Archbishop James T.G. Hayes Street to Bolonsiri in Camaman-an. The cemetery had been there for as long as I could remember. It was already so full that new diggings for graves now and then turned out skeletons. It was obviously time to stop burying people there and to develop a new city cemetery.

While the transfer was so logical conceptually, it was hard to implement it in practice. The problem was that many people opposed the plan. Even the Catholic and the Aglipayan Churches, which owned a couple of hectares alongside the city cemetery, did not want the cemetery transferred. I went to see the Archbishop of Cagayan de Oro, Patrick Cronin, who was a dear friend, and the Bishop of the Aglipayan Church, Camilo Diel, who was now a close friend, and explained to them the necessity of moving the cemetery elsewhere. I told them that, if they agreed, they would get in the new Camaman-an cemetery twice the hectarage of their holdings in the present cemetery. They agreed with my suggestion, although to my regret, we were not able to put our pact in writing. So many events intruded into my life as city mayor that I was simply unable to formalize it in a legal document.

Anyway, with the tacit agreement of Archbishop Cronin and Bishop Diel, I got the city council to pass an ordinance expropriating a 22-hectare lot in Camaman-an, a few kilometers from the old cemetery, as the site of the new cemetery. It was my understanding that the holdings of the Catholic Church and the Aglipayan Church in the old cemetery would be transferred to the ownership of the city in exchange for new lots in the new. I also got the city council to set aside one-half hectare in the new Bolonsiri site to be used as a cemetery for Muslims.

I deemed it necessary to provide the Muslims with a cemetery of their own because I knew that whenever a Muslim died in Cagayan de Oro, the family concerned would — obliged by religious demands — transport the remains of their dead to Marawi City or other parts of Lanao del Norte or del Sur for burial. With a part of the new cemetery site reserved for their dead, the Moros of Cagayan de Oro no longer had to incur so much expense just to bury their dear departed in their home provinces. Their leaders publicly praised the city as the first non-Muslim city in Mindanao that provided a cemetery for their exclusive use.

Transferring the old cemetery to Bolonsiri was not the only thing that I wanted done. I also planned to transfer the remains of those buried there to the new one so that we could use the old site for new city development projects. That part of the plan to transfer the remains of those buried in the old cemetery proved even more problematic.

While the people generally agreed that we should stop using the old cemetery, they had this superstitious belief that excavating graves to transfer the remains of their dead to a new site would bring them bad luck, possibly including deaths in the family. Realizing the futility of arguing against that belief in words, I decided to show by example that their superstition was pure nonsense.

I had the remains of my grandfather Severo Pimentel, my mother Petra, my uncle Andro Quilinging, and Bing's grandmother Nanang, and sundry other relatives who were buried in the old cemetery, excavated and transferred forthwith to the new cemetery. When the people realized after several weeks had passed that I was still alive and that I meant business, they eventually followed suit. I had announced that if they did not voluntarily transfer their dead from the old cemetery, the city would do it for them and charge the expense to them.

I also said in my State of the City Address for 1983 that the new cemetery would be developed along the lines of the so-called memorial parks where the dead would be buried beneath the ground and no tombs would protrude above it. Only a cross or some such reminder would proclaim who was buried there. I wanted to eliminate the practice of people since time immemorial of building huge mausoleums or even *cabanas*, which were not intended primarily to house the dead but to indicate their social standing in the community. The ungodly message was that the larger and more imposing the tomb was, the wealthier its occupant.

I implemented the intent while I was the mayor, but after my incumbency, it ceased to be the rule. As the new cemetery took burials by the day, it also developed into an ugly site for the dead just like the cemetery of old where tombs of all sizes and shapes sprouted the way the surviving kin wanted them.

Foreseeing that the time would come when the new cemetery would be filled up, I also indicated in that State of the City Address that we should have a crematorium in the new cemetery. But the people were not prepared to accept the thought of having the remains of their loved ones burned to ashes. In an attempt to assuage their religious reservations, I told our people that I had consulted with local Catholic theologians and with the leaders of the Aglipayan Church and that their common response was that cremation was no longer taboo. I passed on the information to the people through the local media. Still, the people were not convinced that it was the right thing to do. I decided not to push the idea and just wait for better times.

In the meantime, I instructed Paz Regalado, my executive assistant, to plant shade trees in the burial grounds to spruce up the environment. Ms. Regalado, who had a green thumb, did a good job. The trees that she planted remain to this day as the only pleasant reminder of a plan laid askew by later city administrations.

To fulfill a campaign promise, I focused my attention on the city's infrastructure development. I had promised that if I got elected as mayor, I would modernize the city "without kneeling down before Marcos." Fulfilling the promise was most difficult.

But Cagayan de Oro was, in a sense, lucky that, during the period of martial law when I was its mayor, there were any number of US foreign aid projects that I could avail of. I had already mentioned some USAID development projects that I unabashedly utilized to bring water or even electricity to our barangays. There was also the Regional Cities Development Project funded by the World Bank that enabled us to do other infrastructure plans.

We did a lot of tough bargaining with the RCDP team that came to Cagayan de Oro. Among other things, the RCDP team offered to fund the construction of two roads in the city for P20 million, a huge amount at the time. I countered that perhaps it would better if they lent us the P20 million to enable us to buy all the heavy equipment that we needed for the city. For much less than the amount, we could buy a complete set of heavy equipment needed for road constructions. Then, I said, we would construct not only the two roads they suggested but all the roads the city needed. They did not see it that way. Neither did we agree with their proposal. The P20 million part of the RCDP package was stricken of the list of funds intended for the city.

The RCDP team also suggested the modernization of the telephone system as a priority. Indeed, it was a priority for the city which had an outdated telephone "crankshaft" system then. But I had to make a choice between modernizing the telephone communications and constructing a drainage network that would rid major areas of the city of recurrent floods during the rainy season. I chose the latter. I told the RCDP team that I preferred a working drainage network to a modern telephone system whose units might be floating in floodwaters when the torrential rains came. Incidentally, I received some advice from the more practical-minded mayors, whose cities were also recipients of RCDP assistance, that it was a better policy for politicians to choose projects readily visible to the people, rather than those that were hidden underneath the thoroughfares of the city like drainage canals. I did not follow their advice and stuck to my decision that my city urgently needed a working drainage system more than a modern telephone system. Part of my reluctance to invest city money into the modernization of the telephone system stemmed from the fact that it was the province of Misamis Oriental that held the franchise of the telephone network servicing the city. And at that point, I knew that the province had no desire to relinquish its telephone service monopoly. For me to have agreed to the RCDP suggestion would have opened up another unfriendly front in my already uneasy relationship with Bono Adaza, the provincial governor.

Some of the RCDP mayors were also not above giving me free advice on how to make money on the side. They told me that, if I allowed illegal gambling in my city, I could get at least P40,000 a month, a princely sum in those days, considering that the mayor's pay was only P5,000 a month. It was one of those things that I really could not abide because I knew that receiving money from gambling sources was plain and simple bribery, a crime under the laws of the State.

Our experience with the RCDP was not all that problematic. One of the team members, Mac McClellan, considered me his friend — despite the nationalist reputation that I was gaining. He gave me what, he said, was his "most treasured" possession, a book, *The Oxford History of the American People.*

He was not the only American in Cagayan de Oro who saw that I fought tenaciously for our people's rights against all other interests, including those of the US, whenever those interests clashed with ours. There was also an idealistic young man, Henry Howard, an exchange student in Xavier University, who hero-worshipped me. When Marcos harassed me, on his own, Henry, called up members of the US Senate — Sen. Ted Kennedy, among others — who were known for their libertarian stance — and asked them to request Marcos to ease up on me. I was told that Kennedy responded positively to Howard's petition.

Playing 'Politics'

Apart from playing hard-ball Opposition politics, I actually also played practical politics when needed to alleviate a problem of the city. On one occasion, the remittance of money intended to augment the payroll of city hall employees was delayed by the national government. At that time, a sizeable portion of the payroll of city hall employees came from the national government coffers. Agitated and upset by the delay in the full payment of what was due them, the edgy employees were looking for a scapegoat. While I knew that legally they could not blame me for the delay of their salaries, I also knew that winning the verbal argument in issues involving the lives of people was hardly of any significance. Moreover, I also knew that they could not possibly blame Marcos who continued to hold martial law powers otherwise they risked being fired or arrested for doing so. So, the unspoken sentiment of the employees was that there was nobody else to blame but me for the simple reason that I was the mayor, the top official of the city.

Since I could not go to Marcos for help — that would have breached my campaign promise not to do so — I did the next best thing that came to my mind. I sought the assistance of Concordio Diel, former governor of Misamis Oriental and IBP member and concurrently undersecretary of the Ministry of Trade and Industry. I requested him to kindly help stem the anger and the hunger of the employees of city hall. I told him that, since he was representing Cagayan de Oro at the IBP, he could secure the release of the funds for their salaries. Diel heeded our plea. In weeks, the withheld funds were released and the problem of the unpaid salaries of the employees was solved. Happily, it did not happen again. And I did not have to bother Diel or any other KBL leader close to Marcos to solve a similar problem again or, for that matter, for anything else.

In any event, Diel was now a "political" friend. It was through him that I met Maricor T. de Villa and Margot Baterina, big names then of *Panorama Magazine* and Nelly Sindayen of *Time* magazine in Cagayan de Oro. My meeting with de Villa and Baterina got me rather good write-ups in the *Panorama* and, from Sindayen, a line or two in *Time*.

It must have been Diel's hyperbolic introduction of me to them as "the fightingest mayor" that got the lady journalists interested in me. They visited me at my house on Archbishop Hayes Street which they found "old...spacious and comfortable but devoid of luxury," as they said in the *Panorama* of July 25, 1982. They were surprised that I was "complacent about the threats"— at least 20 verbal and three written — that had come my way. I told them that I was fatalistic about life and death, and that I would rather get out of office than compromise the things that I believe in.

When they asked me if I had regrets "about entering one of the bloodiest arenas called politics," I told them that I did not regret it at all. What I regretted, I said, was that I lost some friends like Reuben Canoy and Homobono Adaza, and others who were initially with me but "whose demands for accommodation (mainly political) I had been unable to satisfy after I became mayor. We had come to a parting of ways. That was painful. But it had to be done."

Chapter 29

Military Woes

While my official relationships with the national civilian officials of the government like Diel and even Local Government Minister Roño were civil, my contacts, in general, with the military officers were not.

One of the more dramatic confrontations I had with a general took place on June 15, 1980, the first Independence Day celebration that I was participating in as city mayor. The city had its usual contingent taking part in the civic and military parade that was joined by civic groups, students, labor organizations and units of the Armed Forces under the command of the Regional Commander Gen. Pedro Zafra. I stood on the Bandstand, the reviewing platform, in Plaza Divisoria with General Zafra where we saluted the flags borne by the parade participants as they passed by.

I had met General Zafra before the Independence Day rites but I never took a liking for him. He looked to me like the Filipino ersatz version of a Prussian military officer who wanted to make civilians feel inferior to him because he was a general. Inevitably, his supercilious attitude collided with my firmly held view that, in Cagayan de Oro City, the mayor outranked any military officer, no matter how many stars they wore on their shoulders.

At the Independence Day rites, Zafra spoke before I did. Towards the end of his largely nonsensical speech, he categorized those who opposed martial rule as people who "were not fit to live." Naturally, that provocative statement of Zafra singed my ears or, as Visayans would put it, *namula ang akong dalunggan,* my ears turned red. And I determined not to let his statement go unchallenged.

When it was my turn to speak, I directed my opening lines to the general. I said:

> General Zafra has just labeled those opposed to martial rule as people who are unfit to live. The general has to be reminded that our national hero, Jose Rizal, had written that "there are no tyrants where there are no slaves."

I could not see how Zafra reacted because he was seated behind me, along with other VIPs. After the ceremonies, I was told that Zafra's face tensed at my unexpected put down of his martial rule rhetoric and that he subsequently threatened to have me arrested under the cover-all-crime of subversion.

I noticed, however, that the police units standing at parade-rest on the right side of the Bandstand were stirred — favorably, I think — by my remarks, while the military units on the left side did not quite know what to make of my public tirade against their highest-ranking officer, something unheard of under martial rule. But, judging from the spontaneous applause of the predominantly civilian crowd, the audience apparently approved of what I had said. I finished my speech with the recollection of the sacrifices of our heroes — national and local — that made our Independence Day worth celebrating.

Offending the Generals

I was barely in office for weeks and I had already alienated two generals: Tobias of the NHA and Zafra of the Regional Command of Region X, which embraced the provinces of Surigao del Sur, Surigao del Norte, Agusan del Norte, Agusan del Sur, Camiguin, Bukidnon and our city, Cagayan de Oro.

Subsequently, I also offended other generals. In quick succession, I think I also made enemies of the PC Chief Fidel V. Ramos; the 4th Military Area Commander, Gen. Emilio Luga, Jr.; and much later, the PC Regional Commander Ramon Banaglorioso.

A few weeks after I became the mayor of the city, General Ramos, then vice chief of staff of the Armed Forces and chief of the Constabulary, visited the PC/ INP Regional Command at Camp Alagar in Cagayan de Oro. Local politicians from other areas within the region trooped to meet with him on matters of law and order and perhaps to curry his favor. In my case, I went on discharging my duties as if he was not in town. That evening, I was drinking beer with some friends in Reuben and Solona Canoy's *Caprice* eatery (choosing the name *Caprice* for a restaurant was an inspired idea that only a literary couple like Reuben and Solona could have conceived of) when a police major approached our table and said, "Mayor, General Ramos wants to see you, Sir." I asked him where the general wanted to see me and he replied at Camp Alagar, the PC camp, a few kilometers away.

I told the major rather testily, "Major, please tell General Ramos that, if he wants to see me now, you know where to bring him." General Ramos, of course, did not come to see me and, without my meaning to, he probably felt insulted by my reply.

Shortly after the Ramos visit, there was a change of command of the 4th Military Area, which was based in Camp Evangelista. The 4th Military Area was then the top command post of the Armed Forces in Mindanao, prior to the creation of the Southern Command.

Gen. Emilio Luga, Jr., had taken his post as commander of the 4th Military Area a few days earlier and apparently he expected local officials to pay "courtesy" calls on him. That was exactly the message that Col. Jun Calub, a friend of mine, conveyed to me one day. In no uncertain terms, I told Calub I was not inclined to call on Luga. Perhaps, Luga could probably call on me as the mayor of the city. He never called on me and neither did I call on him. The general and I were never destined to meet one another personally. However,

Luga and I met through our subordinates. One day, as I was making the rounds of the city streets in the battered van assigned to the mayor's office, I saw a man, knife in hand, chasing someone. I told my driver to stop the van and ordered Eddie Lumagbas, my police security, to stop the knife-wielding man. EddieLu, a top martial arts policeman, who had won medals in international tae kwon do competitions, did not hesitate. He jumped out of the van as it screeched to a halt and, without pulling out his gun, collared the man and disarmed him in quick order. I instructed EddieLu to get the name and address of the man and bring the knife to city hall where the owner could retrieve it if the person he had threatened would not file charges. Incidentally, EddieLu was assigned to me by the PC officials of Camp Alagar, ostensibly as my security aide, but actually also as a spy to report on my "suspected subversive activities."

In the event, it turned out that the knife-wielder was a driver of Luga. Bystanders who witnessed the incident told me that a pedestrian, was almost run over by Luga's driver, who had Mrs. Luga for a passenger. The near-accident reportedly irked Luga's driver who pursued the offending pedestrian with a knife. Luckily for the driver, the pedestrian did not press charges. That was the closest contact I had with Luga who was subsequently transferred elsewhere. Thereafter I heard nothing about him.

I also had some difficult encounters with the regional commander of the PC/INP, Ramon Banaglorioso, on at least two occasions when I either ignored or defied his orders. The first had to do with the reception that the people wanted to give me upon my arrival in the city to begin my house arrest after confinement in the military jails in Cebu. The incident is described in Chapter 31. The other dealt with the matter of raiding warehouses in the city.

Price Controls

Our second test of wills with Banaglorioso took place when I defined the city policy on price controls. In the aftermath of Aquino's assassination, there was panic-buying in Manila and in the major urban centers of the country. Simplistically, Banaglorioso ordered the regional police to raid the warehouses of businessmen who, he suspected, were hoarding basic commodities. At that time, rice, sugar, soap, paper and other essential commodities were in short supply at the city's re-tail establishments.

I had earlier discussed with businessmen the issue of making basic commodi-ties available in the city. In a conference in my home where I was placed under house arrest, the businessmen agreed with my suggestion that they should sell basic commodities at reasonable prices in Divisoria, the main public plaza of the city. The selling of those items in Divisoria was intended to assure the people that basic necessities were available and that there was no need for them to engage in panic-buying. I made it plain to the businessmen that I would not tolerate hoarding and neither would I allow anyone to harass them. I saw Banaglorioso's order to raid their warehouses as an act of sabotage and I said so publicly.

Instead of rescinding his order, Banaglorioso told the Cagayan de Oro press that he "did not recognize the authority of Pimentel as the city chief executive." Thus, his threat to raid the warehouses of the city became more imminent.

In a sharp retort, I told the local media:

> It is a pity that Col. Ramon Banaglorioso allowed himself to be manipulated by my political opponents. While he may be a good soldier, it would do him well to stick to military matters and not dwell on political issues that are beyond his competence. For him to dabble in issues that are clearly political could only lead to tension and consequent disorder in the city.

Further, I said that his order was without legal basis. As the mayor of the city, I told the media that I was duty bound to protect the business people against harassment by anyone. I pointed out that, under existing laws, the implementation of price controls was placed in the hands of the Ministry of Trade and Industry and local officials.

Luckily, Banaglorioso did not implement his order to raid the *bodegas* or warehouses of the businessmen of Cagayan de Oro and I did not have to prove him wrong. For a while, there was relative civil peace between Camp Alagar under Banaglorioso and city hall with me as mayor.

The proprietors of grocery stores and supermarkets in the city were gratified by my stand. Accordingly, they informed me that their stores and warehouses were open to inspection by the Price Stabilization Council to show that they were not hoarding essential consumer items. Naturally, I thanked them for their support, which kept the prices of basic commodities at reasonable levels in the city all through the "crisis" period spawned by the assassination of Aquino.

A local weekly, the *Sunday Journal*, had an editorial, "Dialogue with Merchants Fruitful," in its issue of December 18, 1983. The editorial, written by lawyer Ronulfo Sabanal, said that, unlike Surigao City, Iligan City and Pagadian City, where certain basic commodities had disappeared from their markets, things were different in Cagayan de Oro. It said:

> Visitors to Cagayan de Oro City are pleasantly surprised to know that basic commodities are still available in the supermarkets and retail counters.
>
> What distinguishes Cagayan de Oro from other cities in Northern Mindanao is the sincere concern of the local government authorities for the consumers by continually meeting with supermarket and grocery owners, the National Sugar Trading Company, and the National Food Authority to seek out ways and means of providing enough staple items and having their prices at levels within the public reach.

Not all grocery stores and supermarkets, however, followed the regulations of the Price Stabilization Council. On the recommendation of Councilor Parrel as the head of the PSC, I closed down some establishments to show that we seriously meant to implement the law. Because the violators were members of the Filipino-Chinese Chamber of Commerce, I came under tremendous pressure to either set aside my order of closure or to shorten its period. I told the officers of the chamber that I could not possibly do that without our drive against profiteering losing steam. By refusing to compromise on the penalties that I imposed on erring business establishments, I think I gained the respect of most of my constituents in the city but lost the support of the more influential members of the chamber.

Gentlemen Officers

Overall, my relationship with the military in the city was not all that bad. I remember the kindly Col. Cesar Navarro of the Provincial Command of the PC. He dealt with me as the mayor of the city with a certain degree of professionalism. He did not exude the air of domineering authority that his other colleagues in the military showed to civilians. Perhaps, it was because he also came from Mindanao. He was a Surigaonon and spoke the same language I did.

Early on in my term as mayor, for instance, Marcos issued an order that all mayors should organize their own security units, which would be armed like a minute militia to provide security to the mayor and the operations of local governments. I did not do as Marcos ordered. Colonel Navarro was expected to make a report of compliance by all the mayors within his area of jurisdiction. I never knew whether or not he reported my noncompliance to Marcos. What I do know is that I never had any martial rule-related problems with the colonel. The colonel was so humane in his dealings with people that Bishop Francisco Claver of Bukidnon once told the colonel that, were it not for martial rule, they "could be friends."

Then there was Col. Roberto Lastimoso, who succeeded Navarro as the provincial commander of the PC in Misamis Oriental. Lastimoso also treated me with kindness and consideration within the limits of his authority. In a letter to him on September 23, 1983, I told Lastimoso that he was the only man in uniform, a full colonel and a provincial commander, "who had the courage, the tact and the humility to own responsibility and apologize for the misbehavior of some of (his) men, which could have been easily covered up or disowned (by him)." I was referring to the incident on the midnight of September 22 when a group of apparently drunk armed men in civilian clothes banged on the door of my house on the pretext that they were trying to verify if I had escaped from house arrest.

Bing had the presence of mind not to open the door. Through the peephole, she saw that a group of armed men in civilian clothes was making the racket at our door. She asked them who they were and somebody replied that they were soldiers from Camp Alagar who wanted to know where I was.

Bing told them that I had not escaped and added that, since they had posted guards at our house around the clock, they could verify from the guards that what she was saying was true. She added that she would not open the door and that she would "report the incident to their superior officers in Camp Alagar first thing in the following morning."

Surprisingly, the soldiers backed down. Bing, nonetheless, went to Camp Alagar the following morning and registered her complaint with Banaglorioso. Bing told him that she suspected the soldiers were drunk and that they were out to harm our family had she opened the door. The soldiers were under the command of a Maj. Filipino Amoguis, whose men had acquired a tough reputation for dealing with "suspected enemies of the State" and were members of a reputed liquidation squad called "Mad Dog." For good measure, Bing also said that, "as a tax payer, I pay your salary and, therefore, I expect your men to respect our rights." Incidentally, at the time of the incident, video tapes of the assassination of Aquino taken by a Japanese TV crew were circulating in Cagayan de Oro. We were informed that one of the reasons why the *Mad Dog* agents were trying to get into our house at 12:30 past midnight was that they wanted to confiscate my copy of it as an illegal propaganda item. Bing told Banaglorioso that our copy was no longer in our hands as it had been borrowed by friends and if they wanted to get a copy of it all they had to do was go to any video store and for sure they could get one.

When Lastimoso learned that Bing had complained to the Constabulary regional commander of Region X about it, he went to my house and apologized for the whole thing. He promised the incident wouldn't happen again and that he would look into the circumstances of it. I don't know if he did investigate it, but I was satisfied that the Constabulary provincial commander had taken the trouble of offering his apologies for the incident and had given assurances to me and my family that nothing of the sort would happen again.

Threatening Message

My relationship with the military would have settled down to a humdrum level were it not for the fact that, one day, I received an envelop addressed to "Mayor Pimentel" with a threatening message in it. When I opened it, I found a folded bond paper with the letterhead of Lt. Jefferson Soriano, an intelligence officer of the Constabulary Command in Camp Alagar. Squashed between the folded bond paper was a *lagong*, a big fly, with the message that that was how I would look after the sender was through with me. At about the same time, Governor Adaza revealed that he had also received a death threat written on the stationery of Soriano.

I sent a brief note to Soriano to tell him that, if the threatening letter did not come from him, he should look for the culprit who did it. Soriano came to my office to deny in belligerent tones that he was responsible for it. Knowing that there was nothing much I could do about it, I let the incident pass into my memory bank.

After Marcos was ousted in 1986, Cory Aquino appointed me Minister of Local Government. Among the ministry's functions was to run the National Police. Since Soriano was still in the active service as an officer of the National Police, I heard that he expressed the apprehension that his career was over because I was now his superior. Although he probably had reason to be worried, he was wrong in thinking I would take revenge on him just because I now had some authority over him as the civilian supervisor of the national police. I do not remember personally meeting Soriano when I was the minister or even after I moved on to other government positions. In fact, the next time I met Soriano, he had risen to become national police chief inspector, the civilian rank equivalent to the Army's brigadier general. I congratulated him and wished him well in his rising career.

Likewise, I had a brief hassle-free relationship with Col. Triunfo Agustin at the start of my incumbency as city mayor. He was later transferred to the main office of the national police. Agustin was the PC/INP commander who listened to my wife, Bing, complain against the unwarranted attempts of Comelec Director Virgilio Garcillano to illegally stop the canvassing of votes in our favor on the election night of 1980.

I also had a cordial relationship with Gen. Angelo Quedding who, at one point in my incumbency as mayor, was the commanding general of the 4th Infantry Division in Patag, Cagayan de Oro. General Quedding replied to a complaint that I filed sometime in mid-April 1981 against some soldiers who fired shots at the houses of civilians in the barangay of Tumpagon. He investigated the matter and wrote me that, among the culprits, there was only one man in military uniform but he was not enlisted with the 4th Infantry Division. The soldier, he said, was under the Cebu military command. The general assured me, however, that he had "asked the Cebu command to impose disciplinary sanctions on the soldier."

While the Quedding reply did not really address the issue of military abuse that I brought to his attention deeply enough, it was sufficient for my purposes at the time to let the military authorities know that abuses of men in uniform in Cagayan de Oro would be criticized by me publicly.

Quedding's action assuring me of redress for the grievances of civilians brought to his attention was in stark contrast with the action of Gen. Pedro Zafra, the regional commander of the Constabulary in Camp Alagar. In a complaint that lawyer Adolfo Balinado filed with my office against Lt. Leo de Guzman for the harassment of "*feria*, legal gambling, operators," which I endorsed to Zafra for investigation, the latter merely told me that de Guzman was enforcing the laws on gambling when he disallowed the games of bingo and *pula-puti* at the fair.

At one point in my stint as mayor, Gen. Madrino Muñoz commanded the 4th Infantry Division. I found him a decent man. He was, to my mind, "a true gentleman and an officer," to quote that self-serving assessment of some officers of themselves. I did not have any problems dealing with him.

Incidentally, in my actuations as mayor, I did not offend only certain high-ranking military officers. I also displeased Juliano Barcinas, the regional director of the Ministry of Local Government, who made the mistake of ordering me to report to him the subsidies that the office of the mayor was extending to the Cagayan de Oro City police. In a blunt reply that was completely devoid of tact and which probably made me his enemy forever, I said the report he was asking for was not forthcoming for the simple reason that I was not his subordinate.

Criminal Elements

Aside from the military, some criminal elements tried to make my life as mayor a little complicated. One of the bolder criminals, a certain Macarong, wrote me a letter demanding that I deliver to him P20,000 or else! I wrote an open letter to him that was published in the local press. I told him that his letter to me was misdirected. I did not have the kind of money that he was demanding and so I told him to send his extortionate letter to public officials who were making money at the expense of the people.

That was not all that I did with Macarong. With the assistance of my friends in the police department, we set up a trap to get him at the drop-off point he had indicated in his extortion letter. Obviously an amateur, he went to the place and tried to pick up the package that our police team had left. We got him without much problem and charged him in court. But he did not stay in the custody of the police for long. It turned out that he had powerful friends in the KBL hierarchy in the city. Instead of being detained in the city jail, he was entrusted to the custody of a local political figure, Claudio Aguilar, who had close ties with Marcos's political henchmen in the city. The next thing I heard was that Macarong escaped from his custody. With so many things preoccupying me, I did not have the time to pursue the case against Macarong or Aguilar, as his custodian.

Another hoodlum who claimed he was a Moro rebel commander spread talk among members of the Muslim community in Cagayan de Oro that he was on a mission to liquidate me. I had him picked up by my police security and brought to the house. There I asked him if he had indeed been hired to kill me. I told him that if it was true, that would be most unfortunate because if he succeeded, the Moros of Mindanao would lose a friend. I think he was so taken aback by my velvety approach that he denied that he had ever uttered the threat. He also swore even without the Koran that he would be my friend forever.

No Fireman

One of my major failings as mayor was my reluctance to join firemen whenever fire gutted homes or buildings in the city. I had this aversion to playing up to photographers and pretending to hold a hose with firemen dousing conflagrations with water. In my mind's eye, I saw scenes like that as outright ridiculous and I had no intention of ever being seen doing it. I did the extreme. I avoided going to any fire scene. Not a few people probably resented my absence, but I justified it publicly by saying that putting out fires was the job of the firemen who were no longer under the supervision or control of the mayor but under the PC/INP provincial command.

One day, a big mall owned by See Hong, a Chinese-Filipino in Carmen, a barangay across the Cagayan de Oro River from the poblacion, caught fire. I was informed by telephone that looters were swarming all over the place, taking what they could, even while the fire that was still raging in parts of the mall. While I was willing to leave the fire fighting to the firemen, I was not about to see looters adding to the misery of the mall owner. I went to the fire scene, climbed to the rafters from where I saw many looters scampering with their loot. Over the din, I shouted at them to stop.

Most of the looters either did not hear me or could not believe that it was the mayor shouting at them to stop. So I ordered my security escorts — I had two — to fire warning shots in the air. That restored some order, but not in the entire mall, which was a fairly large one. I had to request the nearest police station to send more policemen to restore order in the place. By the time the police reinforcements arrived, most of the looters were gone and the mall looked like it had been hit by a tornado, except that there were panels of wood and other materials still aflame. Without his understanding the constraints I was operating in, I felt certain that See, the owner did not forgive me for the arson that gutted his mall, even if it was beyond my control to prevent.

Chapter 30

My Third Arrest

Even as I was advocating peaceful change, the military was setting me up for the kill. By cajoling a supposed former NPA commander, who was allegedly captured and was then enjoying life as an "informer" of certain military officers in the Visayas, I was named in the rebel's affidavit as "a supporter of the communist insurgency and a supplier of arms of the NPA."

Carlito Sandag, a self-confessed former NPA commander in the Visayas, told his military captors that he had met me in my house in Cagayan de Oro in the company of our Cebu PDP-Laban leader, Ribomapil Holganza. He said that I reportedly told him to "keep up the good work" and that the NPA and our party were one in our objective "to overthrow the government."

On the basis of Sandag's affidavit, a team of military officers led by a Col. Lyle Paras arrested me in my house in Cagayan de Oro on April 17, 1983, a Sunday afternoon. Mateo Hernandez, a regional trial court judge of Bukidnon accompanied them. Why Hernandez was there, I never found out.

PCO for Me

Upon the insistence of my wife, Bing, the arresting team produced a copy of the warrant for my arrest and detention dated April 14 and signed by Marcos. It was in the form of a letter addressed to the Defense Minister Enrile.

The first of the two-paragraph letter stated:

> Pursuant to Proclamation No. 2045, dated January 17, 1981, and in view of substantial reports that MAYOR AQUILINO PIMENTEL, of Cagayan de Oro City, is engaged in acts inimical to public order and national security, the request for the issuance of a Presidential Commitment Order (PCO) against him is hereby approved.
>
> I, therefore, hereby order the arrest and detention of MAYOR AQUILINO PIMENTEL, to continue as long as demanded by the requirements of national security, and until released by me or by my duly authorized representative.

Unlike warrants of arrest issued by the courts, no specific criminal case involving me was mentioned in the PCO, but it bore the familiar illegible signature of Marcos and was certified on April 15 by Brig. Gen. Hamilton B. Dimaya, the Judge Advocate General. It also showed on its face the names and signatures of Col. Ramon Banaglorioso and Maj. Ruben Cabagnot of the

1983: ARRESTED AND TAKEN AWAY from my city to Cebu. That's me between the soldiers.

Camp Alagar Constabulary Command, with the annotation that they received the order at 1:45 p.m. (of April 17).

The day before Paras and the other officers came to arrest me, friends from Cebu warned me of my impending arrest. I kept the information to myself and went about doing my job as mayor.

On the morning of Sunday, April 17, I went to visit some projects in barangays near the city center where I lived. Ben Emata, one of the more enterprising newsmen of Cagayan de Oro, interviewed me at a project site and we discussed when the project would be finished and what the costs to the city would be.

Arresting Officers Arrive

I went home for lunch and, shortly thereafter, the arresting team from Cebu came knocking at the door of our house. I met them at the door and bade them to sit down and make themselves comfortable. When they formally informed me that they had come to arrest me, I did not ask them "Why or for what offense?" I made light of the situation by asking in Cebuano why they came to arrest me only now.

Since it was the third time I was arrested, Bing already knew what I needed. We packed a few shirts, pants, underwear, toiletries, some vitamins and a book to keep me company. Soon Butch Emata, my brother-in-law, and his wife, Tess, arrived to help monitor what the arresting team did in the house.

One military officer, a Maj. Jose Ayap, nervously urged Paras not to tarry, but to bring me as soon as possible to wherever they were supposed to do so. He probably thought that the longer they stayed in my house, the greater the danger that my followers might rescue me. The possibility, let alone, the probability, that my followers would stage a daredevil rescue operation to get me out of military custody did not exist at all. We were all committed to the Rule of Law and none of us during my entire incumbency as city mayor ever seriously suggested we should arm ourselves and prepare to wage war against the Marcos regime.

When Bing asked where Paras would bring me, he said that they were bringing me to Camp Alagar for the night. Bing was, therefore, of the impression that the arresting officers and I would spend the night in the camp before going to Cebu.

As I was saying my good-byes to my family, Vice Mayor Ambing Magtajas, Councilor Henry Bacal and other political colleagues arrived. We had very little time to talk because the arresting officers insisted that we leave immediately. I asked the vice mayor to kindly continue the projects that we had lined up for our city. My request must have sounded like my last will and testament to his ears that Ambing actually shed tears. I tried to put up a brave front, but deep down inside I was touched by the vice mayor's display of loyalty and love for me. Bing then called up other friends and supporters to tell them that I had been picked up again by military officers and was being brought to Camp Alagar where they could probably visit me.

But when Bing and our friends went to Camp Alagar later that afternoon, they were told I was not there. That stirred some panic among them and they scurried to Camp Evangelista, the seat of the 4th Infantry Division, the other military facility in the city where I might have been taken. But when they got to the camp, they found out that I was not there either. This heightened their sense of apprehension that something untoward had happened to me.

They did not know that I was brought directly to the Lumbia Airport where I was taken aboard a Nomad turboprop plane of the Armed Forces and flown to Cebu. It took almost an hour for the plane to reach Lahug airport in Cebu, but the flight was smooth and nothing out of the ordinary took place during the trip.

Bing eventually learned through friends that I had been taken on board a military plane that took off for Cebu 30 minutes earlier. She immediately made arrangements to follow me by ship that night to Cebu.

In Camp Sotero Cabahug

In Cebu, I was brought to Camp Sotero Cabahug, a military facility, which also housed detention prisoners in the Visayas. I was given a cell that measured roughly 4.5 x 6 x 9 feet all to myself. It had steel bars at the door and the ceiling. It was a cell for "hardened criminals." Thus, in a space of six hours from my arrest in Cagayan de Oro to our arrival in the camp, my military custodians transformed me from city mayor into a hardened criminal. I stayed

1983: NEW FRIENDS like Nanay Juling Ouano (right) lighten up my life in detention.

in this military prison for two months, after which I was transferred to a wider cell in Camp Sergio Osmeña.

Since I was not able to bring any thing for my bedding needs, I sent a note to my friend, Tony Cuenco, a pillar of the PDP-Laban in Cebu, to inform him I was detained at the camp and to kindly lend me a blanket, some pillows and a mosquito net. In no time, he visited me at the camp and brought me all the things I asked for and more. He also brought me the guarantee of his friendship and support, even at great personal risk to himself and his family.

The morning after, Bing, accompanied by our daughter Maripet, arrived from Cagayan de Oro. They brought messages of cheer and encouragement from hundreds of our friends and supporters from the city, and a few hundred pesos in small denominations that people pressed into Bing's hands as she boarded the ship for Cebu to be with me in that hour of need. One friend from Bukidnon, Boy Tabios, who had a business in Cebu, also sent foodstuff and other things to lighten up my life in detention.

A Pack of Lies

As my friends from Cebu had intimated in their phone calls to me in Cagayan de Oro, it turned out that, indeed, the immediate cause of my arrest was my having been implicated by Carlito Sandag in his rebel activities in Cebu. More specifically, he said that I was a financier and arms supplier of the NPA. He was now a witness for the government in exchange for his freedom. Sandag was reportedly cornered by the military in Cebu after an alleged shoot-out.

Sandag's statement was a pack of lies. Unfortunately, it was the kind of story that Marcos and his military wanted to hear about me and other Opposition leaders in general because it provided the "legal" reasons to shut us up by the simple expedience of arresting us immediately without need of court processes.

Actually, what I remember of Sandag was that he came to my house one afternoon in 1982 and asked for transportation or pocket money for him and his wife for their trip back to Cebu. His wife was not with him, but I remember giving him P100 for the two of them. I could not have given him any encouragement for the NPA rebellion that he was supposedly waging because I was against the taking up of arms against the martial law government. Furthermore, I really did not know him well enough for me to recklessly endorse his supposed revolutionary plans. Neither could I have given him any arms because, the truth of the matter was that, upon the declaration of martial law I surrendered my only firearm — a rusty .38 caliber pistol that my friend, Ed Marfori, had given me. I had long wanted to dispose of it, but could not find an easier way than to give it to the military when martial law was declared. Even when I was already mayor, the only firearms around me were those carried by my police security. Otherwise, I absolutely possessed no firearms of any caliber or for any purpose.

In short, Sandag was peddling a tall tale. In fact, Interim Batasan Assembly-man Felimon Fernandez said that "it was probably induced by reward money of the sort that the Marcos government offered to those who would turn in rebels to the military."

To Marcos, Sandag's tale was enough justification to order my arrest by PCO. In fact, a few days after my arrest, Marcos told the national television, radio and print media that the military had "voluminous records" that showed my complicity with the communist rebels.

Making Headlines

The day after our arrival in Cebu, the Cebu daily papers headlined my arrest on charges of rebellion. My arrest was a big deal for the news-hungry media of Cebu. I found the enterprising Cebu media practitioners, who some-how interviewed me even in detention, quite innovative. Their interviews provided a great relief from the tedium of awaiting what was coming next in my life as a person accused of capital offenses.

The *Freeman*, a Cebu daily, had my picture being interviewed by a radio man on its front page on April 18 with the banner story: "Oro city mayor ar-rested, jailed" on charges of rebellion. Behind me in the photo was Rene Barrientos, former world welterweight boxing champion, a faithful aide through the days of my mayorship.

On the same day, Jesse E. L. Bacon II, staff member of the *Freeman*, had a story that had nothing to do with my arrest but with the proposed coalition of three Opposition parties I was supposed to have disclosed to him. I probably did talk about the possibility that PDP, Laban and Unido could coalesce. But, as Bacon reported it, after he interviewed me inside my cell at Camp Sotero Cabahug, it sounded like it was already a done deal.

The morning after, the *Bulletin Today*, had a front page boxed story by Casiano Navarro Jr., that headlined "Oro Mayor arrested." The *Bulletin* item said that it was the third time I had been picked up by the military since the imposition of martial law in 1972. The other newspapers like the *Daily Express*, the *Metro Manila Times* and the *Times Journal* also had front-page stories about my arrest on April 18. The *Times Journal* described the situation in Cagayan de Oro as "tense."

Looking back, it was nothing short of providential that I was confined in a military jail in Cebu rather than anywhere else. I could have been detained in Camp Crame or Bicutan where restrictions on the activities of detainees and their access of media were more severe. And, since I was facing criminal charges that could bring me the death penalty, had I been incarcerated anywhere else, conversations with newsmen would not have been possible at all. I found it a little funny that there I was in a Cebu military cell talking with a Cebu newsman not about the criminal cases that I faced but about our organizing a political coalition to challenge Marcos in elections!

Basically what Bacon wrote of my interview for the *Freeman* was right. He did get into my cell and asked me questions about the possibility of the formation of a new coalition of three Opposition parties and their adoption of a common platform. I said the possibility was always there of the three parties coalescing and adopting a nationalist platform that would protect the country against the abuses of multinationals and cause the removal of foreign military bases in the country.

As for the Sandag allegations, since they were complete fabrications, I believed that they would be thrown out of court forthwith, once the trial started. In any event, my detention in Cebu — first at the Camp Sotero Cabahug and later at the Camp Sergio Osmeña — was so unlike my other detentions in the sense that the Cebu media would not be denied their chance to interview me in person or by phone when the mood hit them. I was surprised that the military in Cebu City were not that strict about media interacting with their detainees. So, throughout my stay in the military detention camps in Cebu, my incarceration was a media event. I felt like the turtle in Aesop's fables, which happily accepted its fate when its enemies threw it into the water to drown.

Waiving Preliminary Investigation

On April 18, I waived my right to a preliminary investigation of Sandag's charges. That meant that I was not going to submit any witness or statement to the office of the city fiscal of Cebu to contradict Sandag's allegation. It was a move that my lawyers and I agreed upon. I would dispute Sandag's allegations when the trial commenced before the Court of First Instance. As if it were such a big deal, the *Freeman* in Cebu bannered the story on April 19. Surprisingly, the waiver also hit the front pages of the Manila dailies.

On the same day, Tañada and Laurel issued, in behalf of the Unido-PDP-Laban Coalition, a joint press statement strongly deploring my "arbitrary arrest...under an unconstitutional Presidential Commitment Order." The statement said:

> [This is not the first time that] the Marcos regime has tried to immobilize a worthy Opposition leader. This arrest confirms the widespread belief that martial law was never really lifted. It likewise confirms that Mr. Marcos was not sincere when he said he wants to see "a strong legitimate Opposition" in the country.

In Cagayan de Oro, also on April 19, Archbishop Patrick Cronin, an Irishman, who had served as a missionary in many parts of Mindanao, led a concelebrated Mass with Bishop Christian Noel and 42 Jesuit, Columban and secular priests to pray for my release. In his homily, the Archbishop, who was not known for getting involved in political issues previously, forcefully came out in my defense. He said:

> Many people, including myself, have known the mayor for many years, and every one who has known him can testify that he never engaged in acts inimical to public order and national security. We can proudly boast that Cagayan de Oro has been the most peaceful city in Mindanao. Is this not something to be proud of? To whom under God do we owe this great and happy condition but our beloved mayor? Justice has been defined as a virtue that inclines us to give everyone his right. When someone's right is violated, there is injustice. In the case of Mayor Pimentel, we believe that in his detention, there has been a violation of his right, his right to be free. Peace is the fruit of justice. If justice is granted to Mayor Pimentel, then peace is secure in this city.

Supreme Accolade from Cronin

The Archbishop later formally petitioned Marcos for my immediate release. Cronin said he did not believe Sandag's charges had any basis at all. He vouched for my being "a good man and a man of peace." And he said so in other homilies that he delivered in Masses that were offered for my release. Coming from a man of God who had nothing personal to gain from my release, Archbishop Cronin's assessment of my person was a supreme accolade for me.

1983: TWO OF MY STAUNCH SUPPORTERS in the struggle for freedom: Archbishop Patrick Cronin and my father.

I could not thank the Archbishop enough for what he did because, truthfully, I was not a big contributor to the church in the city with whom the head of an archdiocese could easily identify. I had no business enterprise for him to bless. I did not even particularly remember his birthday as an occasion for me to visit with him and offer "tithes" to the Church.

The only thing that went for me as far as my Church was concerned was that I was a regular Mass goer, who gave a few pesos when the collection plate passed by, and an occasional penitent at the confessional box. Bing and I were also active members of the Christian Family Movement in the city and, in my case, I was a so-so member of the Knights of Columbus. Other than that, I was not the kind of Catholic layman who devoted most of his waking hours to the Church and of whom its leaders would normally be fond. While I would have wanted to contribute more to my Church, I could not because Bing and I earned just about enough to support the expanding needs of our growing brood of six children, who by time were all of school age.

Nonetheless, the Archbishop's concern over my arrest and detention was not totally unexpected. Way back, on January 6, 1974, the Archbishop wrote me a letter thanking me for a fruitcake that Bing sent to him on New Year's day. In that letter, he revealed his sentiments about what was happening to Cagayan de Oro and the nation as a result of the imposition of martial rule two years back. He said:

> Cagayan [de Oro] is very peaceful. Many people are poor and suffering because the minimum wage — in spite of the high prices — is only eight pesos. The New Society is a paradise — but for millionaires and capitalists only who grow rich by the sweated labor of the poor. Still the future is bright — and I am confident that a better tomorrow is waiting for the common *tao* [man] of the Philippines. There seems to be considerable progress but we must work to get it down to the poor man.

Visits from the Clergy

Archbishop Cronin's appeal for my release was supported by Fr. Jose Villamil, the parish priest of the San Agustin parish, where I usually went to church. Like the Archbishop, Fr. Villamil also did not benefit materially from our friendship. But he also said that, from the kind of life I led, he did not believe Sandag's accusation had any grain of truth.

The Archbishop and some priests of the archdiocese did not limit their support for me to the offering of prayers to God and the sending of petitions to Marcos for my release. Cronin and some priests of Cagayan de Oro also visited me at my cell in the Cebu military facility. The Archbishop came suitably attired in his bishop's regalia. I met him at the reception room of the military camp commander. He told me of the continuing support that the people of Cagayan de Oro had for me. He asked how the military was treating me. I told him that there was not much I could really complain about the way I was being treated in detention, except for the fact that my detention was plain and simply arbitrary. I thanked him for his assurances of his and the archdiocese's support for me.

As he was about to leave, the Archbishop pressed into my hand some money that he said I could use for my needs in jail. I respectfully declined to receive it and told the Archbishop that my needs in jail were very simple and were taken care of by friends in Cebu and that there was no need for him to be concerned about my personal needs. Later, I was told that my priest friends found a way to help my family in Cagayan de Oro directly, instead of coursing their assistance through me, personally, in prison.

Cronin's petition for my release was weighty enough to elicit a reply from Marcos. The *Freeman* on April 20 carried the banner story, "Archbishop's Appeal Rejected: FM says evidence strong v. Pimentel." Briefly, the item quoted Marcos as having said in a telegram to the Archbishop that "Mayor Aquilino Pimentel Jr....was arrested and charged with rebellion on the basis of 'very strong evidence' that he provided arms, funds and sanctuary to subversive elements."

In Manila, the *Bulletin Today* on April 20, also did a banner story on Marcos's reply to Cronin: "Pimentel is linked to arms, fund doles." The military, Marcos said, had "voluminous records of the mayor's activities supporting the charges of rebellion and of inciting to rebellion." Marcos, therefore, told Cronin that he could not accommodate the latter's request for my release.

Marcos's statement that the military had "voluminous and strong evidence" against me was a virtual guilty verdict for me, considering that martial law edicts governing public order detainees like me were still in place. Nonetheless, because there was no truth to the charges, I did not waver in my belief that the Lord God would not allow a miscarriage of justice in my case. I was thoroughly convinced that, despite the odds, I would get out of the situation unscathed.

Protests in Cagayan de Oro

In Cagayan de Oro, the PDP-Laban organization led by Vice Mayor Magtajas immediately engaged in agitprop protests. Black streamers denouncing my arrest and announcing the "death of democracy" were unfurled at the top of the city hall. At its main entrance, a replica of my cell at the Metrodiscom camp in Cebu was displayed. Black streamers were also flown at Xavier University and Lourdes College, two Catholic schools in the city, where our children began their formal studies. When Maj. Ruben Cabagnot, the assistant provincial commander of the Constabulary in Misamis Oriental, asked Vice Mayor Magtajas to remove the streamers, the latter told him that only the courts could order their removal.

On April 23, approximately 15,000 Cagayanons marched from the St. Augustine Cathedral grounds to the bandstand in the heart of the city, where a rally was held to protest my incarceration in Cebu. Speakers from many parts of the country highlighted the illegality of my incarceration.

Antonio Cuenco, PDP-Laban chairman for the Visayas, called my arrest a "desperate effort of Marcos to illegally quell peaceful dissent." He also read a handwritten note from me that asked my followers in Cagayan de Oro to stay calm and keep their protests peaceful.

Luis Jose, the working national chairman of the party, recounted that he heard of my arrest from an overseas call by Raul Manglapus and Ninoy Aquino, who both expressed concern about my safety and well-being in the hands of Marcos's military. Carried by the emotions of the moment, Jose could be forgiven his over-statement that "Nene is the man of all Filipinos. He is the man of the nation." He also told the demonstrators that UP and Ateneo de Manila students held a prayer rally for my release that was attended by more than 2,000 students. He said that other prayer rallies were also held in many parts of Manila.

Other visiting speakers included Ernesto Tabios of Bukidnon, Orlando Fua of Siquijor and Danny Gonzales of Cebu. But the most stirring of them all was Zafiro Respicio, chairman of PDP-Laban Davao. He said:

> Mr. Marcos can arrest as many Pimentels as he can, but he cannot guard or coerce or cow the people because, for every Pimentel that goes to jail, thousands more will fight and say to Mr. Marcos, we do not like the way you run the government and, therefore, you should get out of office.

In the rally, a song, *"Pag-ibig sa Bayan"* or "Love of Country" that Bing had composed, drove many of the participants to tears. It was interpreted by the City Sanggunian Choir, under the baton of the award-winning pianist and conductor Lino Abrio, a native of the city.

Prayer rallies and protest marches demanding my release were also held in other towns in Mindanao. In the Malaybalay rally, among other speakers, Bishop Francisco Claver, SJ, decried the injustice of my arrest. In Davao and in Cebu as well as in Manila, similar mass actions were staged to show Marcos that the decision to arrest me was ill considered. Nationwide, some 50,000 people signed a petition for my release.

Jesuits Petition Marcos

On June 27, the Jesuits likewise addressed a petition to Marcos for my immediate release. The Jesuit signatories, some of whom were my teachers, told Marcos that they knew me as a student, then later as the dean of the College of Law of Xavier University, and as a layman active in the Christian apostolate.

Sounding like they were delivering a premature eulogy at my wake, they vouched for me as an upright man. They said, "Nene Pimentel stands out as an articulate nationalist, a lover of freedom and a man of peace." They saw me as a "believer in the modest style of life" who never used my office to enrich myself or my family."

In a direct challenge to the accusation that I had committed rebellion, the Jesuits underscored the fact that the party I helped found, the PDP, had for its main tenets nonviolence and achieving political changes through the processes of law, never through lawlessness. The Jesuits ended their letter with an appeal for my immediate release because it was "their belief that in a situation of increasing violence, a man of peace should not be put behind bars."

1983: *THE PEOPLE keep their protests peaceful.*

The signatories included virtually all the Jesuits in the country at the time. I include their names in this book as a belated acknowledgment of my gratitude to them for putting their lives on line for me during those difficult days. They were: Jose Arcilla, Catalino Arevalo, Guido Arguellas, A. Balchand, Soleto Barona, Pablo Bartolome, Joaquin Bernas, Jose Blanco, Raul Bonoan, Arturo Borja, Eladio Borja, Rafael Borromeo, Ted Butalid, Pio de Castro, Percy Chaves, Francis Cody, Antonio Cuna, Nicasio Cruz, F.R. Cuerquis, Vincent Cullen, Francisco Demetrio, J. Embile, Bishop Federico Escaler, Jesus Fernandez, Nap Franco, Ted Gonzales, Vitaliano Gorospe, L. Ma. Guerrero, Nil Guillemette, F. de Guzman, Victor J. Helly, George Hofileña, E. P. Hontiveros, R. Javellana, Ernesto Javier, William Kreutz, Victor Labao, Antonio Ledesma, J. de Leon, Randolph Lumabao, Ando Macalinao; N. Maceda, Francis Madigan, Danny Madrazon, Jojo Magadia, V. Marasigan, William F. Masterson, Oscar Millar, William Molley, Bienvenido Nebres, Timothy Ngodcho, Al Nudas, James J. O' Brien, Joseph O'Brien, Paul Brunner, Rene Ocampo, R. C. Ocampo, James O'Donnell, Antonio Olaguer, Salvador Orara, Jose Pais, James B. Reuter, Jose Raviolo, William Schmitt, John N. Schumacher, Jemy See, Pedro Sevilla, Paul Sheehan, Lito Silverio, Sim Sumpayco, Reuben Tanseco, Ramon Prudencio Toledo, Alvin Valerio, Mariano Varela and Walter Ysaac.

Bartholomew Lahiff, a Jesuit historian at the Ateneo de Manila University, sent his own letter of support to me. Though originally an American citizen,

Lahiff like Fr. Victor Helly, SJ, acquired Filipino citizenship by naturalization and he felt free to express his condemnation of my arrest. He said that he suspected that envy caused my arrest "because you have remained independent in the only meaning of the word." To console me, he also said:

> One day your grandchildren will proudly say of you, "Yes, he was my father's father." What better heritage could a man leave to his heirs? And what could make a man prouder than that?

At the time the letter was written, I hardly knew Fr. Lahiff. And, to my shame, I do not even know if I thanked him for his kind words. I hope my negligence in that respect will be mitigated by my saying in this book, "Thank you, Father Bart." My thanks also go to many others like Ding Lichauco, a friend of Fr. Fritz Araneta, SJ, and Fr. William Nicholson, SJ, who also extended their munificent support to me and my family in those troubled times.

In My Defense

In addition to the political and religious groups, the *Bulletin Today* of April 20, reported that civic organizations like the Jaycees, the Rotary and Lions Clubs also petitioned Marcos for my release. Some columnists of the major dailies like Apolonio Batalla, Melinda Q. de Jesus and Arlene Babst took up the cudgels for me.

Batalla said that, while the charges of rebellion against me may be "well-founded," he believed otherwise. He said:

> A public official who is not rich, goes around in sneakers and T-shirt, strives for the improvement of his community, and speaks out his mind, cannot but be popular. He is of the masses. We do not say that he is a hero. But it seems that like heroes he has to pay a penalty.

De Jesus was bothered by the "silence about recent developments," meaning more precisely, my arrest. So she wrote in her column of May 9, "Now that Mayor Aquilino Pimentel of Cagayan de Oro has been charged with rebellion, it might [be] fair to have run some background on him." She spoke of me as having won 75% of the vote in my city and of having founded the PDP-Laban. She described me as having "remained a simple man without the usual perquisites of public office (and) that the testimonies of those who have known him as a lawyer and politician attest to his idealism, commitment to his constituents, and his adherence to the ways of peace."

Babst on the other hand wrote a titillating article that asked, "Who cares if Nene Pimentel was arrested?" Answering her rhetorical question, the lady said:

I don't care if Cagayan de Oro Mayor Aquilino "Nene" Pimentel was arrested.
I don't even care that he is facing charges of "rebellion" etc. I still think he is
one Filipino leader whom Filipinos really like, respect and trust.

She then recounted how she met me a year earlier at a women's media forum
after which she drove me to the National Press Club. Of that brief meeting, she
wrote that I was "the kind you'd never think would wind up leader to thousands
of Filipinos." Babst also quoted an unnamed colleague of hers who reportedly said,
"I like him so much because he has no charisma at all. He's just real."

She ended her column saying:

> Nene Pimentel is in jail again — I want to ask him, who does he think he
> is getting jailed so often, Gandhi? So who cares if Nene Pimentel was
> arrested? A lot of people do. People in Cagayan de Oro, Cebu, Manila. We
> do. We care a lot that Nene Pimentel has been arrested.

International Petitions, Too

Petitions for my release were also circulating abroad. I received copies of
mimeographed statements — sometimes with only one paragraph — from
members of Amnesty International as far as Europe asking Marcos for my
release.

The Mennonite Central Committee based in Washington, DC, also got
involved through a letter dated April 27, 1983, that its Assistant Director, Earl
S. Martin, addressed to George Schultz, US Secretary of State.

Martin told Schultz, "Developments in the Philippines in recent months
raise troubling questions about the nature of the government there and the
relationship of our government to the Philippines. While it may be inappro-
priate to suggest any causal relationship, we are disturbed to observe a significant deterioration of human rights matters in the Philippines since the visit
of President Ferdinand Marcos to this country last September."

Martin cited three cases to illustrate what he meant: (1) the abduction of
Karl Gaspar by unknown men only to surface later in military custody. Gaspar,
Martin said, was a leading church lay leader in the island of Mindanao; (2)
the deliberate attempt by military authorities to intimidate journalists by the
libel charges against Ma. Ceres Doyo and Domini Torrevillas-Suarez, both
writers for *Panorama Magazine*; and (3) my arrest and detention by military
authorities.

The Mennonite leader told Schultz:

> [Pimentel], a Jesuit-trained man who grieves at the growing violence in
> Philippine society, is instrumental in forming the Philippine Democratic
> Party (PDP) which seeks to bring about change in peaceful ways.

I never knew if Schultz ever replied to Martin. But it certainly boosted my morale to know that people who were not that close to me or even complete strangers brought up the problem of my arbitrary arrest and detention to the attention of high US government circles.

Bing at the MFP

Willy Crucillo, who was then based in New York, also informed Bing in a letter dated July 22, that various chapters of the Movement for a Free Philippines in Washington, DC, New York and Chicago had launched in mid-July their own "Free Pimentel Campaigns."

Then, in August 1983, upon the invitation of Cesar Arellano, the chair of the MFP regional organization in the Midwest, Bing attended and spoke at a gathering of MFP leaders at Roadway Inn-O'Hare in Chicago. With the special participation of Senator Diokno, who came from Manila, other concerned Filipinos from the US and Canada lent their presence to the occasion. They included old friends and new ones in the peaceful struggle to oust Marcos, namely: Gloria Arellano, Steve Psinakis, Gil Ramos, Bonifacio Gillego, Dr. Arturo Taca, Dr. Renato Roxas, Tomas Gomez and Charlie Avila.

Bing spoke of PDP-Laban's providing hope for the people and supporting peaceful demonstrations against the dictatorship. She also made a pitch for MFP support not only for the party's long-term struggle for the liberation of our people but for my release from detention.

1983: BING APPEALS TO MFP in Chicago to support calls for my release.

Even in detention, I sensed that the message of peace that I pounded on repeatedly in many forums appeared to have sunk into the consciousness of people. The theme of my being a man of peace who was searching for peaceful means to end martial rule permeated all the petitions that were sent to Marcos and the letters of support that I received.

But Marcos was unmoved by it all. He told the media that I had been under surveillance by the military for a long time and that the "evidence against (me) was strong." He, therefore, said it was now up to the court to decide what to do with me.

He was engaging in doublespeak. In the very PCO that he issued for my arrest, he ordered my detention "until released by me or by my duly authorized representative." Therefore, the issue of what to do with me was really in Marcos's hands. Nonetheless, my lawyers did everything to exhaust the judicial remedies available to me.

Petition for Bail

At the Cebu Court, the most significant movement in my case was the hearing of the petition for my bail. Although the crime of rebellion and whatever else the prosecution had filed against me were non-bailable for being capital offenses, my lawyers maintained that, since the evidence of guilt was not strong, even hardly existent, I was entitled to bail.

The hearings on the bail petition took place in the *sala* of Judge Francisco Burgos of the Cebu Court of First Instance. I had a top-flight corps of practicing lawyers to represent me. They were: Joker Arroyo, Senator Laurel, Senator Diokno, Juan T. David, Rep. Tony Cuenco, Rene Saguisag, Assemblyman Felimon Fernandez and Tito Guingona.

1983: CONSULTING WITH ONE of my top-flight lawyers, Juan T. David, in my cell in Cebu City.

Handling the prosecution, which opposed my bail petition were Brig. Gen. Hamilton Dimaya of the office of the Judge Advocate General of the Armed Forces and Cebu City Fiscal Jufelinito Pareja. Dimaya pulled rank to be the head prosecutor of my case but he was a lightweight as a law practitioner. He was no match for any of my counsel in terms of experience in legal practice. But the moves that he made and the comments he released to the media got more mileage than those of my lawyers.

In the end, Judge Burgos denied my motion for bail on the ground that I had been arrested by means of a presidential commitment order and, in his view, only the President could order my release.

My lawyers refused to take Burgos's order denying me bail at face value. They filed a motion for Burgos to reconsider his order. In the meantime, military propaganda made it appear that I had air conditioning in my new cell at Camp Sergio Osmeña, which was not true. But there was virtually nothing we could do to correct the statement issued by the office of Gen. Alfredo Olano, the camp commander.

Back in Cagayan de Oro, to support the criminal charges against me, some military intelligence agents attempted to gather perjured testimony that I was, at least, a rebel fund-raiser. I did not know about it until our City Councilor Roderico Villaroya disclosed the fantastic plot to the media. He said the military agents wanted Pierre Welemberg, a foreign consultant of the World Bank assigned to the city, to provide false information that he had given me money to support the rebels, ostensibly upon my request. Welemberg, however, refused to have anything to do with the false accusation. He flatly denied, in an item in the *Metro Manila Times* of May 6, 1983, that he had "given a single dime to Pimentel as aid for the subversives.

Vice Mayor & Councilors Arrested

A side issue developed while my lawyers were busy arguing my bail petition. Upon orders of Judge Burgos, military officers in Cagayan de Oro led by Col. Triunfo Agustin, Maj. Ruben Cabagnot and Maj. Filipino Amoguis, assisted Maj. Luis Kintanar of the Cebu PC regional command to serve warrants of arrest on Acting Mayor Magtajas and Councilors Guillermo Parrel, Roderico Villaroya, Jose Abbu, Henry Bacal and Cecilio Pepito, Jr. The arrests were effected on May 10. General Dimaya had Magtajas and the councilors arrested for contempt of court on the ground that, in Cagayan de Oro, they criticized my incarceration, which was sub-judice in the Cebu Court of Judge Burgos. In layman's terms, Dimaya's argument was that my case was under judicial consideration and therefore Magtajas and our councilors had no right to discuss it outside the courtroom of the judge.

My lawyers and I believed that Burgos acted arbitrarily in ordering the arrest of Magtajas and the councilors. Normally, in motions to cite for contempt, the courts would not immediately order the arrest of the persons being cited for contempt if they did not do the contumacious act in the presence of the judge. They would simply be cited for contempt or given a chance to explain why they should not be held in contempt of court and punished accordingly. If done in the presence of the judge, the rule was that the persons concerned could be directly cited for contempt and punished accordingly, more or less in summary fashion.

Magtajas and the councilors, however, did not commit any act of contempt of court inside its premises or in the presence of Judge Burgos. In other words, if Magtajas and the others were guilty of anything contemptuous of the court, it would be in the category of an indirect contempt, meaning that the act was done far away from the sight and hearing of the judge. Burgos, however, apparently acted under pressure from the military so that, instead of merely citing Magtajas and the councilors for contempt of court and asking them to explain their side, he ordered their immediate arrest.

Certainly the arrest of Magtajas and the councilors upset me, but I saw a deeper motive behind their arrests. Their arrests, if unchallenged, would have created vacancies in the office of the mayor, the vice mayor and the city council, which would then have enabled Marcos to fill them up with his own people.

Seasonably, Congressman Cuenco and Joker Arroyo brought the matter to the Supreme Court, which again came to the rescue of the beleaguered officials of Cagayan de Oro. In no time, to its credit, the Supreme Court issued a temporary restraining order against the Burgos order of arrest. It ordered Burgos to appear before the Supreme Court and explain why he issued the controversial ruling and not to proceed in any manner regarding the matter until ordered by the high court.

Commenting on the action of the high tribunal, the *Philippine Sunday Express* of May 15, 1983, said in an editorial, "The Supreme Court deserves congratulations for its speedy action in ordering the release of the acting mayor and six councilors of Cagayan de Oro City who were ordered arrested earlier for alleged indirect contempt." What was more pleasant to my eyes were the lines that said, "Cagayan de Oro is relatively one of the more peaceful places in Mindanao. Everything must be done to keep it that way." The editorial was a big surprise, coming as it did from a newspaper that was considered the major mouthpiece of the martial law regime. Its admission that Cagayan de Oro was "one of the more peaceful places in Mindanao" to some extent debunked the charges that as its mayor I was involved in rebellion against the government.

Cebuanos Protest Our Detention

My PDP-Laban party mates in Cebu also rode on the rather free atmosphere there. Not only did they organize a rally in my favor, they also kept the Cebu media up to date on the developments in my case.

Within days, Tony Cuenco and Inday Nita Daluz organized a protest rally on April 30 at Fuente Osmeña, the rough equivalent of Plaza Miranda in Manila, against my detention and the detention of PDP-Laban Cebu stalwarts, Ribomapil Holganza and his son Joeyboy, and Dr. Felimon Alberca.

In a news item written by Danny M. Gonzales, Tony Cuenco identified the PDP-Laban leaders who joined the protest rally as: Zafiro Respicio of Davao; Ernesto Tabios of Bukidnon; Vicente Callejesan of Surigao City; Santas Castillo, Felix Rengel

1983: GWEN, MARIPET AND TERELOU greet Bing and me a happy anniversary in my cell at camp Sotero Cabahug, Cebu City.

and Timmy Cabatos of Bohol; Tente Quintero, Res Salvatierra, Wally Banzon and Eddie Espina of Leyte; Rene Espiritu of Bacolod; and Orlando Fua of Siquijor.

A Cebu newspaper said the rally drew about 2,000, a figure that was at least three times lower than the actual number of rally participants. In any event, I was gratified that even in Cebu, which was not my hometown, thousands of people demonstrated for my and my PDP-Laban colleagues' freedom at the risk of their lives, limbs and liberty.

Wedding Anniversary in Jail

Aside from the political events that swirled around my detention in Cebu, Camp Sotero Cabahug also became the improbable site of our 23rd wedding anniversary on April 30. A concelebrated Mass was offered by Fr. Ernesto Javier,

1983: FR. ERNESTO JAVIER, SJ, FR. OSCAR MILLAR, SJ, and other priests concelebrate mass for our 23rd wedding anniversary on April 30, inside my cell at Camp Sotero Cabahug, Cebu City.

SJ, Fr. Oscar Millar, SJ, and other priest friends inside my cell for Bing and me. We had simple fare for our guests provided by friends in Cebu, particularly by Tony Cuenco, Inday Nita Daluz, Inday Holganza, Nanay Juling Ouano, Norma Guardiana and her daughter Athenes, Gemma Sanchez and other intrepid souls who dared to identify with us even in those difficult days.

My notes record that on the occasion, I wrote Bing a three-page letter in Visayan. Essentially, I said:

> [We can] offer the sacrifice of my unjust incarceration to hasten the day of the liberation of our people. Despite the many trials in our life, we still have so many things to be thankful for to the Lord, especially because there are so many people who identify with our cause and who are helping us beyond measure. There is no other way for me to reciprocate their love except by offering my life to the cause of freedom, justice and peace for the people.

Romantically, I ended the note with assurances of my undying love for her.

Aside from the prayers of my lay and religious friends that kept my spirit soaring beyond the confines of my cell in Cebu, my supporters from Cagayan de Oro also boosted my hopes that my travails would end well for me and my family.

By the hundreds, they took the boat, MV Trans-Asia, every-weekend to visit me in the Camp. They would board the ship on Friday evenings, arrive in Cebu Saturday mornings. They would see me during the visiting hours of the day, leave for home Saturday evenings and be back in Cagayan de Oro Sunday mornings. The shipping company got into the act by offering generous discounts to those who were going to Cebu from Cagayan de Oro to visit me. I kidded friends that I had now "become a tourist attraction."

Chapter 31:

House Arrest

After three months and 11 days in detention, Marcos finally agreed on July 25, 1983, not to free me really, but to place me under house arrest in Cagayan de Oro. He did it as a concession to Cardinal Sin, who brought the matter to his attention upon the request of Archbishop Cronin. Bing and our elder son, Koko, went to the Cardinal to personally ask for his intercession.

Despite Marcos's clear order for the military to bring me back to Cagayan de Oro so that I could serve my detention under house arrest, the Cebu military, however, had other thoughts. They did not want me out of their custody just like that. So, minutes before the order of Marcos could be implemented, the Cebu military served another warrant for my arrest on some vague charges of my being a public order violator. It was, of course, a pure act of harassment.

Bing had to make a lot of fuss about it before the military authorities eventually softened their hard line. They then told us that they were ready to bring me back to Cagayan de Oro if I agreed to fly on a military plane. Knowing the sad state of repairs of military planes, Bing said we would rather take a Philippine Air Lines plane and pay for our fares than have a free ride in a flying coffin. The officers, however, would have none of that proposal. It was either we flew by military plane or our trip home would be delayed.

The matter of how we would be going home became a bone of contention between Bing and the military officers for some hours. After repeatedly ventilating their and our sides of the issue, the reason why the military officers did not want us to take PAL emerged. They were apprehensive that thousands of my supporters would welcome me at the Cagayan de Oro airport and give me a hero's welcome.

Bing then suggested that they should allow us to take the boat from Cebu to Cagayan de Oro. Since the boat departing Cebu at night would arrive in the city at dawn the following day, she said it would be less likely that huge crowds of well wishers would meet me at the pier. In the end, the military approved Bing's suggestion.

Candlelight Welcome

That night, Bing and I took the boat home. Little did I — and much less the military — know that upon arrival at the Macabalan pier at early dawn of July 26, 1983, there would be a candlelight welcome by at least a thousand of my supporters who would not be denied their expression of love for me.

The day before, the regional commander of the Police, Colonel Banaglorioso, directed the police and the military in the city not to allow public demonstrations in my support. His instructions also barred my participation in the *Te Deum*, a Catholic ritual of giving thanks to God, at the St. Augustine's Cathedral, which my supporters had prepared.

Hundreds of my supporters led by Vice Mayor Magtajas, however, ignored Banaglorioso's order. The soft glow of more than a thousand candles illuminating the Macabalan wharf at the crack of dawn was the most ethereal sight I had seen in my life. The emotional content of the situation was heightened by the stirring melody of *"Bayan Ko"* sung with passion by more than a thousand voices.

Te Deum at the Cathedral

Despite Banaglorioso's order to escort me directly from the ship to my house, the military officers could not do so without inviting trouble. They could not even restrain my welcomers from boarding the ship en masse. Hundreds of welcoming arms hugged me as if they had missed me for so long. Before disembarking from the ship, Bing, Vice Mayor Magtajas, Councilors Parrel, Pepito and Abbu and a handful of my core political leaders negotiated with Banaglorioso's deputies that I should be allowed to drop by the St. Augustine's Cathedral to attend the *Te Deum.*

1983: BING FLANKED BY me and Teresa (center front row) pray at the Te Deum organized by my supporters in thanksgiving for my safe return.

1983: WE ACKNOWLEDGE *people's applause inside St. Augustine's Cathedral.*

Banaglorioso's subordinates said "No" by simply repeating what their orders were. Magtajas, however, pleaded with the officers and pointed to the growing crowd impatiently waiting for me to disembark. He insinuated that our supporters would be gravely "disappointed" if I was not allowed to pray at the cathedral. Banaglorioso's subordinates then called him up to explain the situation "on the ground." Apparently, Banaglorioso saw the risks of denying our request to attend the *Te Deum* and he finally agreed to allow me to go to the cathedral, but on the condition — which I accepted — that I should not speak before the people attending the prayers. Before long, Bing and I were in St. Augustine's, which was filled up by our supporters.

The *Te Deum* passed without any untoward incident. Archbishop Cronin, Fr. Villamil and a handful of other priests led the prayers, after which Bing spoke on my behalf. She thanked the Archbishop, the clergy, nuns and the congregation for their unceasing support and confidence in me as their mayor.

I was extremely happy with the presence of Archbishop Cronin at the *Te Deum*. I did not know that he was going to be there to thank God for my safe return to the city. After the rites, the soldiers brought me to my house to begin my house arrest that lasted for roughly six months.

In the course of those six months, some intrepid souls visited me and made the tedium of confinement somewhat easier for me to bear. One of those who surprisingly braved possible repercussions on his career as a Marcos bureaucrat was Roilo Golez. He was then the postmaster general. He dropped in the house and made small talk with me. Even the local KBL stalwart, Interim Batasan Assemblyman Concordio Diel also paid me a visit. I was, of course, honored by their visits. Movie stars like Tirso Cruz, Bembol Roco, Mark Gil and Rez Cortez also popped in to say hello to me. The film actors had a basketball exhibition in Cagayan de Oro and out of curiosity they asked the guards at my house if they "could see Mayor Pimentel in person". The guards, probably spellbound by sight of the movie stars readily allowed them into the house to see me. Their visit was a welcome respite from the routinary boredom of my house-arrest.

There was also Ducky Paredes who wrote perceptive articles for *Panorama*. He visited me and picked my mind about what preoccupied me while under house arrest. The November 6, 1983 issue of the magazine published the interview titled, "'Nene' Pimentel: *Out of Prison But Not Yet Free*". In the article, I expressed my forebodings to Ducky that

> The trend in our country is ...the preservation of the caudillo-type of leadership that is the norm in Latin America.
>
> If we change Marcos with another politician (from) the elite ... there will hardly be any change in the life of the ordinary man ...
>
> The problems of a huge foreign debt, the flight of capital, the multinationals dividing the country into their own spheres of influence ... will not disappear even if Marcos goes out of the political scene tomorrow.

In the first few days of my house arrest, the military insisted that those who visited me must sign a visitor's log book. For a while, the guards strictly enforced the requirement. After a couple of days, they found the practice too tedious and too expensive – more log books would be needed - just to list down so many callers. So the military abandoned it.

One of those who took advantage of the relaxation of the log book listing requirement was a local *babaylan*, a witch doctor, by the name of Ramoncito Boyatac. He told me that he could perform voodoo rites to make life miserable for Marcos. For fun, I asked him to show me how. And he did. We repaired to a secluded corner in the yard of my house and in the presence of some friends he stuck a sharpened bamboo stick several times into the gullet of a stuffed toy that represented Marcos while muttering gibberish in *Binukid* or the Bukidnon dialect. Boyatac assured me that Marcos had no defense against his incantations.

My friends and I had a good laugh over it although I must confess I never discovered if Boyatac's voodoo was the cause of Marcos's lupus ery-themathosus that eventually felled him in his Hawaiian exile some years later.

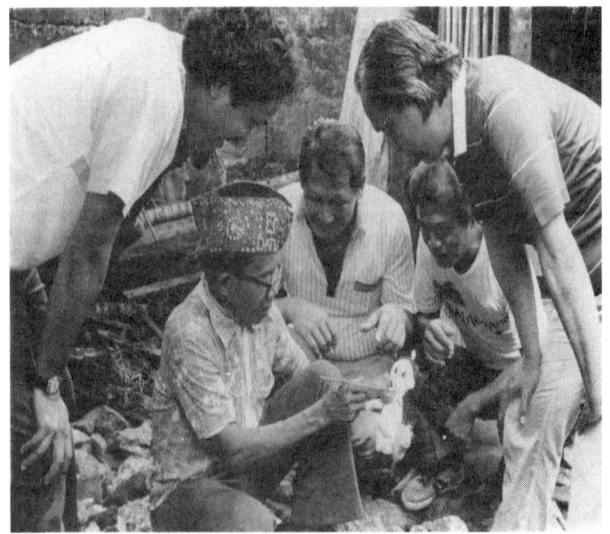

1983: FOR FUN, friends and I (at right) watch local Babaylan *or roughly, Witch Doctor, Ramoncito Boyatac, (with cap), perform voodoo rites to drive Marcos crazy.*

Chapter 32:

Resuming My Mayoral Duties

While I was imprisoned in Camp Sotero Cabahug, then later in Camp Sergio Osmeña in Cebu City, Vice Mayor Pablo Magtajas ran the affairs of our city efficiently and well. When I got back, I allowed things to settle down a bit for about two months. Then, on October 3, I formally notified the City Hall officials and Local Governments Minister Roño that I was reassuming the functions of the mayor on October 15. I had no problem with the ever-loyal Ambing Magtajas. He willingly gave way to me although he could have made things difficult for me because Minister Roño had designated him as acting mayor while I was detained in Cebu. When Roño came to town a few days earlier, Roño expressed reservations about my right to reassume my duties as mayor. He told the Cagayan de Oro Press Club that, since I was detained under house arrest and could not go to the office of the mayor, I could not legitimately discharge my duties as mayor.

I told the members of the COPC that Roño's "opinion had no basis in law." I dared the minister to show me any provision of law that required me to go to city hall before I could discharge my duties as mayor. "If such a provision of law exists, then I would desist from acting as the mayor of the city," I said.

Roño left town without rebutting my argument. I, therefore, resumed my functions as mayor on the day stated. I signed city hall documents and payrolls, and conducted consultations with the business community, civic clubs, non-government organizations and sundry city officials in my house. With the Roño flap out of the way, I discharged my duties as city mayor without any interruption, even though I was under house arrest until 1984 when I ran and was elected as the city's representative to the Batasang Pambansa, Marcos's so-called regular parliament.

Incidentally, I relinquished my chairmanship of the City School Board to the City Superintendent of Schools Teodoro Dano, believing that the latter as a professional educator knew the needs of public education much better than I, as a politician. With my full support, the School Board produced chairs, desks and blackboards for our students that were much cheaper than the ones that the Ministry of Education in Manila supplied to the school districts throughout the country. Thus, we ended our dependence on Manila for school chairs, desks and blackboards and saved thousands of pesos every year for the other needs of the city schools.

In Manila, my lawyers, Joker Arroyo and Lorenzo Tañada supported my resumption of office with legal memoranda that they filed with Roño and with the Defense Minister Enrile. Surprisingly, while Roño's position was that I could not reassume my post because I was under house arrest, Enrile had a different view. His military subordinates, Brig. Gen. Samuel M. Soriano, assistant secretary for Legal Affairs, and Brig. Gen. Jaime Alfonso, senior assistant secretary of the Defense Ministry, recommended that I should be allowed to resume my duties. Enrile endorsed the views of his subordinates to Marcos on December 16, 1983. By that time, I had already been functioning again as mayor without any legal hitch, except for one last attempt by my political adversaries headed by Governor Adaza to block my return to office.

Adaza Objects

In a letter to Roño on November 4, 1983, Adaza objected to my resumption of office. As if the city was under his supervision, which it was not, he complained, "For the past week, Cagayan de Oro has been in continuous confusion. The situation has been brought about by your previous designation of Vice Mayor Pablo Magtajas as acting mayor of the city and the recent assumption of office by Mayor Aquilino Pimentel, Jr., who is still under house arrest." He added, "Because of the present confusion, the city government employees and the residents are in a quandary as to who is the mayor of Cagayan de Oro." Gratuitously, he said, "Criminal elements are taking advantage of the situation."

The clincher in his letter, by which he wanted to prod Roño into action, was that the "city government...not to speak of the 22 cases of graft and corruption against Mayor Pimentel which are now pending resolution by the Tanodbayan — is swamped by more cases of graft and corruption which are mushrooming with increasing regularity with every passing day." Couched in standard Adaza agit-prop against me, to which I had gotten used, his opposition to my resuming my mayorship no longer bothered me. I did not even reply to it.

Roño, however, sent him a proforma one-page letter dated November 9, 1983, where he said that, in his view, my having been placed under house arrest was "a legal impediment [for me] to discharge [my] office." He appended a telegram dated July 29, addressed to Local Governments Regional Director Barcinas that ordered me "to desist from the performance of" my duties as mayor. I simply ignored Roño's directive and Adaza's fulminations and continued to do my duties as mayor.

Ombudsman Dismisses Charges

Aside from trying to block my resumption of the mayorship, my political adversaries also accelerated their efforts to put me in jail by having their subalterns file several criminal cases against me with the Ombudsman. Governor Adaza told a cousin of mine from Balingasag, a town some 50 kilometers from Cagayan de Oro, who — thinking that Adaza and I were still on good terms — had naively asked him when I could get out of the military jails in Cebu City. He told her that

Photo by Joe Gabor, with permission from *Panorama*

1983: *BING AND I to go to Mass under guard.*

she should not expect to see me again because I "would rot in jail." He cruelly added that since I was facing more than 22 charges of abuse of power and corruption, there was no way I could get out of prison.

Despite the verbal and legal provocations that my political adversaries heaped on me, I kept my peace. But I still had to defend myself as best I could against the unwarranted criminal charges. It helped that lawyers Joker Arroyo, Abe Sarmiento and Rene Saguisag acted as my counsel, while Bing and the children stormed the heavens with their prayers that God's mercy and justice would prevail and keep all of us safe from harm. Looking back, the trials I suffered as a public official caused needless irritation and anxiety to my family, especially my young daughters who felt unduly maligned by the cruel and baseless charges against me.

As things turned out, God answered our prayers. Marcos's Ombudsman, Justice Bernardo Fernandez, did not find a single graft and corruption charge against me worthy of credence. He dismissed them all for being without merit. The malicious criminal charges that the Ombudsman dismissed were different from the trumped-up cases that Marcos and his minions in the military concocted against me. It was the military charges that led to my incarceration at various times in the military prison camps in Luzon, the Visayas and Mindanao. I told friends jokingly that with those detentions, it was only I who could claim that I was a *national* political detainee during the martial law years.

Friends Affirm Faith

While my family and I endured all these travails, friends like Ed Marfori of Cagayan de Oro and Oscar F. Santos, a former delegate from Quezon, affirmed their faith in my innocence.

Marfori sent a letter to the editor of the *Times Journal* that was published in its issue of April 18, the day after my arrest in the city by the Cebu military. He told the newspaper that three of my detractors who were members of the city council could hardly be described as crusaders for good government. He enumerated what he said were their failings and invited the readers of the newspaper to come and visit the city to find out for themselves who was telling the truth. Coming from Ed who was apolitical in his attitude towards life, his public defense of me was, indeed, a boon to our morale as a family.

In the case of Oca Santos, he sent me an undated letter after he had read of the filing of several criminal charges against me. Santos said, "Even if they send you to jail a hundred years, still I won't believe you helped yourself with the people's money. You could not even buy me a decent meal when you come to Manila." He added:

> *Ako pa na walang-wala ang nagbabayad. Kaya huwag ka na pupunta dito kung wala kang pambayad sa turo-turo.* It was I who have nothing who had to pay for our meals. Please do not come here any more if you do not have money to pay for a simple meal. Still, more power!"

The Negros Nine

Even as Marcos said that he had already "lifted" martial law, activist priests and lay people in many areas of the country still suffered harassment by powerful elements using their connections with the authoritarian regime. The most notorious example of the persecution of priests and laymen was the case of the so-called "Negros Nine." From early 1983 to mid-1984, three priests, Niall O'Brien, Brian Gore and Vicente Dangan of the Diocese of Bacolod, and six lay Church workers were imprisoned on a concocted charge of murder for the killing of Kabankalan Mayor Pablo Sola and his bodyguards in 1983.

Actually, some pillars of the sugar industry of the province and their political allies got upset over their preaching of the social doctrines of the Church that told the sugar workers they were entitled to just wages and humane treatment. To make them stop their "political proselytizing", they were made the scapegoats for the murder of Sola and his security personnel.

For most of 1983, I was in detention for charges of subversion and rebellion, but upon my release from house arrest the following year, one of the things I immediately did was to visit the Negros Nine at the old Bacolod City jail. I met with them and expressed my solidarity with their cause. I saw that even the criminal inmates accorded them respect because they knew that they were innocent of the murder charges and were merely championing the rights of the poor sugar workers in Negros Occidental. They also got the unfailing support of the activist Bacolod Bishop Antonio Fortich and wide publicity in the international media. These two factors in addition to the unrelenting legal work of Juan Hagad and Archie Baribar led the Marcos regime to eventually dismiss the case, but not until the nine had spent 14 months in detention — six months in jail and eight months under house arrest,

While Gore and O'Brien deserved all the praise that their parishioners accorded them, Dangan and the six lay people deserved much more. Gore and O'Brien knew — and they said so — that Marcos and his military could not really harm them without inviting adverse international condemnation, but that Dangan and the six ordinary church workers were really at more peril. Ironically, as citizens of the country, they were in greater danger than the foreigners who were merely helping them get what was due to the sugar workers of Negros during the martial law years.

Chapter 33

The Aquino Assassination

Before I visited the Negros Nine, I heard that Ninoy Aquino was raring to return home from exile in the US. I told friends that Ninoy would be risking too much by coming home. Marcos did not want him home. Aquino home would cause too many headaches for Marcos. For one, the leaderless, peaceful Opposition would immediately acquire a leader. For another, even the violent Opposition would acquire an ally under the theory that the enemy (Aquino) of their enemy (Marcos) was their friend. Furthermore, the domestic media had published Imelda's and Defense Minister Enrile's statements that they did not want Ninoy to come home. They said he would put his life at extreme risk if he did so. In a famous quote that Newsweek published, Imelda said of Ninoy, "If he comes back, he's dead."

There was, however, no stopping Ninoy from coming home. Friends like Joe Calderon and Heherson Alvarez tried to reason with Ninoy but they could not budge him an inch from his decision. In their presence, he bade his wife Cory and their children good-bye in Boston, Massachusetts, and flew first to Taipeh and from there to Manila.

In a letter dated June 27, 1983, that Ninoy sent to our mutual friend, Tony Cuenco of Cebu, Ninoy said, among other things, that he felt "sorry to hear about Nene P but when I return I'll be able to take away some heat from him." When Ninoy enplaned for home, I was under house arrest in Cagayan de Oro.

Common Opposition Principles

I can only surmise that as a politician, Ninoy saw an opportunity to lead the Opposition groups in Manila who by June 12, 1983, had coalesced "to avert an armed conflict and civil war" in the country and fight for the restoration of freedom, justice and peace in the land. On that day, the coalesced political groups issued a "Declaration of Common Principles of the Allied Opposition."

The declaration covered a wide range of subjects. It included calls for the termination of foreign domination in the economic field, the removal of the foreign military bases, the inculcation of nationalist values in education, the need for morality and integrity in public service, the elimination of graft and corruption, the restoration of free and orderly elections, the recognition of the people's freedom of expression and the protection and enhancement of the culture of tribal Filipinos.

As regards the part of the declaration that dealt with graft and corruption, the signatories had in mind the anomalies that attended the grant of unconscionable fees to Herminio Disini, a relative of Marcos by affinity who brokered the government-Westinghouse deal on the BNPP.

The demand for the protection of the culture of tribal Filipinos arose from the perceived oppression of the Kalingas who opposed the construction of the Chico River Dam and of the Tiboli's, the native dwellers around Lake Sebu, Cotabato who were alarmed by the indiscrimate logging operations in the forests around the lake. As a Mindanaonon, I was gratified by the environmental aspects of the declaration because even at the time, serious alarms were raised over the denudation of the remaining forests of the island.

The news accounts of the day identified the signatories of the document as Tañada, on behalf of PDP-Laban; former Sen. Salvador Laurel of Unido; Abraham Sarmiento of the Liberal Party; former Speaker of the House of Representatives Jose B. Laurel, Jr., Nacionalista Party; former Sen. Eva Estrada Kalaw, National Organization of Women; former Rep. Rogaciano M. Mercado, National Union for Liberation; Gov. Homobono A. Adaza, Mindanao Alliance; Mayor Cesar Climaco, Concerned Citizens Aggrupment; Salvador Princesa, Bicol Saro; former Delegate Antonio Olmedo, Interim National Assembly Association; Valentino L. Legaspi, Unido-Central Visayas; Luis Mario M. General, Kabataang Pilipino; and Wilson Gamboa, Unido Hugpong.

The declaration was meant to be the basis for the unification of the groups opposed to martial rule which had diverse reasons for their opposition. But it did not really attain that purpose. Its failure to unify the opposition groups emerged days after the supposed signing of the declaration. The assumption then was that all the major personalities of PDP-Laban and Unido signed it. It turned out that Doy Laurel, the head of the Unido, did not. The 2005 book, *Doy Laurel*, written by his wife, Celia Diaz, documents Doy's decision not to sign it. And according to Doy, as quoted by Celia, neither did former Sen. Eva Estrada Kalaw of the Liberal Party sign it. The reason the two did not sign the declaration, Laurel said, was that it committed the signatories to demand the immediate removal of the US bases and to legalize the Communist Party.

Neither was I a signatory to the declaration, but not for the reasons advanced by Laurel. The declaration, in fact, had my full support. But it was Senator Tañada who signed it as the leader of our political group, the PDP-Laban.

As usual, the Marcos regime paid no heed to the declaration.

The Storm Begins

The next thing I heard about Ninoy was that he was assassinated at the tarmac of the Manila International Airport on August 21, 1983. I was then under house arrest and heard it over the radio. The report was sketchy and it was obvious to me that the controlled Manila media were not at all eager to report the details of the assassination. Nonetheless, before nightfall, I received several phone calls that built a fairly accurate picture of what happened.

Briefly, I learned that a group of soldiers had gone up the plane, grabbed Ninoy by the arm and escorted him down the ramp — all the while blocking him from the sight of his friends in the international media (who had accompanied him) and from the view of the other passengers. Then gunshots were heard. Moments later, a bloodied Ninoy lay sprawled on the tarmac. The military authorities announced that a lone NPA gunman had penetrated the security cordon around the arrival area and had shot him dead.

The government account that Ninoy was shot by a lone NPA gunman was pure fiction. I could only gasp in utter disbelief when I heard that official explanation. When I was asked by members of the Cagayan de Oro Press Club who I thought was responsible for the assassination, I said without equivocation that Marcos should be held responsible for it. I said Marcos was liable for Ninoy's assassination because he had assumed full powers of government and, therefore, the security of the life of his principal political opponent was in his hands.

It was not that easy to pin the blame on Marcos. Rumors — for which no verification was then possible — flew thick and fast that Marcos had just undergone a kidney transplant so that it was physically impossible for him to have had anything to do with the killing of Ninoy. The rumor mills, however, refused to dissociate Marcos from Ninoy Aquino's killing. If Marcos did not do it, it was widely believed that Imelda and Ver were the immediate culprits.

Martyr to Freedom

Later, I elaborated on my thoughts about the government statements on Aquino's killing. I told the Cagayan de Oro media that it was illogical to believe that the so-called assassin, Rolando Galman, did it. The pictures published in *Time*, *Newsweek* and *Asiaweek* showed Ninoy Aquino's body bathed in blood from a wound caused by a single bullet, while Galman's body, which was riddled by armalite bullets, did not ooze fresh blood. The comparison I made of a bloodied Aquino and the relatively bloodless body of Galman indicated that the latter had been killed earlier in another place and his body was just dumped on the tarmac to make it appear that he was cut down by armalite fire of the soldiers guarding the place.

The media asked if I had known that Ninoy was coming home. I told them that I knew about it some two years before his assassination. I said that I had tried to dissuade him because there was nothing to be gained from it. Marcos would, at worst, want him eliminated physically, or at best, disabled in jail. As fate would have it, he came home and got a bullet in the head.

Ninoy's death, I said, made him a "martyr to freedom, to justice and peace." I also predicted that his "blood, which [his] murderers spilled on Philippine soil, will infuse life and power into our democracy struggling to be reborn in our beloved land."

I made other statements on the murder to the local media. In one, I com-

1983: THE PUBLIC'S DISGUST over Aquino's assassination is manifested in huge rallies even in Cagayan de Oro.

pared Ninoy to the Spanish hero, El Cid. I said that the hundreds of thousands who passed by his bier at the Sto. Domingo Church in Quezon City and followed his casket to his final resting place for 13 hours under the hot sun evoked images of El Cid. Legend had it that El Cid — already dead — was propped up on his horse by his officers and his "presence" inspired his troops to drive the Moors out of Spain in the 9th century.

To show that the people of Cagayan de Oro disagreed with Marcos in his characterization of Ninoy as a villain, the city council passed a resolution naming the main building of city hall the Benigno S. Aquino Hall of Justice. The resolution was passed through the efforts of Vice Mayor Magtajas and the members of the city council, in particular Henry Bacal, Guillermo Parrel, Cecilio Pepito, Jr., Jose Pepe Abbu and Roderico Villaroya.

It was the first public building dedicated to Ninoy Aquino after his assassination. As I was under house arrest at the time, Vice Mayor Magtajas officiated at the formal ceremony naming of the building after the fallen leader of the Opposition. An estimated crowd of 20,000 in words of the *Sunday Journal* "braved the searing afternoon sun" to witness the rites. Magtajas said the monument was "but a feeble tribute to the courageous quest for justice, freedom and peace by the late Senator Aquino." Magtajas also told the Cagayan de Oro media that he would set aside a room in the Benigno S. Aquino Hall of Justice for any Aquino memorabilia available in the city for public viewing.

The honored guest of the occasion was the mother of Ninoy, Mrs. Aurora Aquino, who "tearfully recounted the loss of her famous son at the hands of an assassin." The people who attended the formal christening of the Benigno

S. Aquino Hall of Justice did not come only because of Doña Aurora. They also came to see and hear a battery of high-profile Opposition speakers like Sen. Doy Laurel, Rep. Tony Cuenco of Cebu, Zafiro Respicio of Davao City, Jun Alonto of Lanao del Sur and Antonio Carpio of Camarines Sur. My wife, Bing, spoke in my behalf, since my jailers prevented me from leaving the house. They only allowed me to visit the hall the day after its inauguration.

1983: MRS. AURORA AQUINO tearfully recounts the murder of her son Ninoy before a crowd of 20,000 in Cagayan de Oro. To her right, Tommy Pacana (with skull cap) and Manolo Tagarda (in Barong).

Q & A Pamphlet

To deflect the blame being pointed at him for the murder of Ninoy, Marcos's propaganda machines issued a pamphlet, *Questions and Answers About the Aquino Assassination,* without attributing its authorship to anyone. The main message of the pamphlet was that Galman killed Aquino as a part of a communist conspiracy. I condemned the pamphlet as a silly and cowardly publication to divert the attention of the people from the true circumstances of his assassination.

Ten days after the killing of Ninoy, PDP-Laban and Unido issued a joint statement under the signatures of their respective chairmen, Tony Cuenco and Doy Laurel. The statement pinned the blame on Marcos and called for his resignation. The statement said:

> We hold Mr. Marcos's one-man rule politically responsible for the cold-blooded murder of Sen. Benigno S. Aquino. This is the last straw.
>
> We also hold him responsible for the reign of greed and terror, the present economic mess, the general outrage of the people, and the complete loss of confidence in his unwanted regime.
>
> We, therefore, demand — in the national interest — that Marcos and his entire regime now step down in favor of a caretaker coalition government to be composed of the most respected citizens representing the major sectors of our society. National reconciliation and survival demand no less.

1983: BEFORE THE BENIGNO S. AQUINO HALL OF JUSTICE a day after its inauguration, (left to right): Brgy. Capt. Romeo Edadis, Councilor Guilly Parrel, Josefina Bacal, Luz Sabanal, Bing, Mrs. Aurora Aquino (Ninoy's mother), me, Maur Aquino (Ninoy's sister), Estela Garcia, Vice Mayor Ambing Magtajas and Councilor Henry Bacal.

Demonstrations & Prayer Rallies

In Manila, the public disgust over the murder of Aquino was manifested in massive public demonstrations. Smaller prayer rallies were also held in his honor. One of these prayer meetings was organized by the Marriage Encounter group at St. Francis Church, in Mandaluyong on October 1. It featured my son Koko, then a teenager, as a speaker.

I did not know about it until it was over. From the reports of my friends (biased sources, of course), the audience gave Koko a standing ovation. Koko shared that, before Aquino was killed, he was content with life for as long as he received his monthly allowance, but now he saw things differently. Koko said:

> [Ninoy's selflessness] made me realize my own selfishness.....Ninoy's death changed me....I want to tell Ninoy, *"Talagang hindi ka nag-iisa* (You are not alone)," for as long as my father is alive, the principles which you died for will continue to be defended. If they take my father, then I will continue to defend freedom and justice.

Ninoy's murder, however, also placed the Opposition in a bind. Ninoy came home to propose ways to prevent a bloodbath that he saw was coming to the country. One of his major proposals was to create a government of national reconciliation. Reconciliation with Marcos? That boggled our minds. Many of us did not want to have anything to do with Marcos, except to cause his ouster. The issue of national reconciliation and how to bring it about continued to weigh heavily in our minds all the way up to 1986 when Marcos held a snap presidential election. In order not to contradict Ninoy's peace effort directly, in answer to questions posed by the media, I merely said:

> There is no decision yet of the PDP-Laban here to support that call. We who have followed the politics of Ninoy as his allies in our common quest for democracy for our people know that violence is not the solution to the problems that beset the country. We also know that the unification and reconciliation of our people, which Ninoy had so ardently wished for, can only be based upon freedom, justice and peace.
>
> That democratic ideal, however, will continue to elude our people unless we have a national leadership that can command the respect and confidence of the people. Which is easier said than done because as of the moment, the country is reeling from a crisis of confidence in the national leadership occasioned by its inept handling of the mu·.der of Ninoy. Such a crisis would be cause enough for the resignation of people in responsible government circles in democratic countries. In our country, however, it would be height of naiveté to expect anyone to do so. As I see it, the national leadership needs no less than a miracle to pull it through this crisis. Trouble is, miracles happen only with God's direct assistance.

We in the Opposition did not see the miracle coming to pass in favor of Marcos. We wanted the miracle to push Marcos out of Malacañang.

The Fernando Commission

To blunt the growing public outcry that blamed him for the Aquino assassination, Marcos created a commission headed by Chief Justice Enrique Fernando to investigate the matter. The panel, aside from Fernando, was composed of elderly ex-jurists: Felix Antonio, 72; Guillermo Santos, 68; Julio Villamor, 81; and Ruperto Martin, 70. All of them, at one time or another in their public lives, were appointees of Marcos. Earlier, the respected former Chief Justice Roberto Concepcion and Jaime Cardinal Sin had both declined appointments to the Commission proffered by Marcos.

No wonder the Fernando Commission immediately drew fire from the people who did not believe that Fernando and, inferentially, the other members would be impartial investigators. In fact, some reputable citizens led by former Supreme Court Justice Cecilia Muñoz-Palma said, in a tactful public statement, that it was "not appropriate" for Fernando to chair the commission, as reported by the *Bulletin Today* on September 6.

The lawyers' group, Mabini, an acronym for the Movement for Brotherhood, Integrity and Nationalism, Inc., founded by Augusto Sanchez and Rene Saguisag, was less diplomatic. Mabini filed a petition with the Supreme Court to restrain Fernando from chairing the commission. Among other things, the petition pointed to Fernando's public display of subservience to President and Mrs. Marcos "even in political functions...[during which he] has been photographed holding an umbrella over the head of Mrs. Marcos,"*Mr&Ms* magazine reported in an early September 1983 issue.

The people's rejection of the Fernando Commission paralyzed it from taking any substantial action. After two inconsequential hearings, Fernando resigned on September 8. The other members of the commission followed suit. For a while, there was a lull in the investigation as Marcos pondered his next move. The move came after 15 days when Marcos tested the sentiment of the people by announcing that he would expand the membership of the commission to include some Opposition figures.

Among other Opposition leaders, Marcos thought of was Interim Batasan Assemblyman Filemon Fernandez of Cebu. Fernandez was a good choice. He had been speaking out openly against the excesses of the Marcos regime. I believed, however, that it would have been better if an independent commission — if that was at all possible under martial law conditions — could be formed.

In the event, Marcos created a new panel to investigate the Aquino assassination. The media named the new panel the Agrava Board, after its chair, the retired Court of Appeals Justice Corazon Juliano Agrava. The other members were Dante Santos, Luciano Salazar, Amado Dizon and Ernesto Herrera. Andres Narvasa, dean of the UST Faculty of Law, was named counsel of the board, and Mario Ongkiko, a legal eagle in his own right, as deputy counsel. After roughly 10 months of hearings, Agrava submitted her findings, the details of which are discussed elsewhere in the book.

In any case, before the Agrava Board was created, to my surprise, Marcos sent Jerry Barrican to Cagayan de Oro with a letter for me. I was genuinely astonished that Barrican had become an emissary for Marcos, because, when we were Laban candidates for the Batasan seats of Metro Manila, he was a radical firebrand, breathing damnation on anything that Marcos stood for. Thus, I found it odd that he was now a letter-carrier of Marcos. Also astonishing was his suggestion that we, in the Opposition, find a *modus vivendi* with Marcos. He likewise said that, since the Americans' top priority in the country was the retention of their military bases, it might be "best that they (be) given a fixed timetable to get out, say, until 1993 or thereabouts."

Marcos's letter, in effect, asked for my opinion as to how best he could have the assassination investigated in a manner that would be credible to the people. The letter suggested that the membership of the Fernando Commission could be widened to include Opposition leaders and other individuals known for their probity and independence.

Although Marcos did not say that he wanted me in the commission, I saw that he was trying to co-opt the Opposition so that he could tell the people that he was sincerely getting to the bottom of the Aquino assassination with our support. I was not inclined to play his game. I told Barrican bluntly that since Marcos created the problem, he should solve it. And I added that he could tell Marcos my reply verbally because I was not giving him a written answer.

Barrican took my rough response to Marcos on the chin. There was no sign that he was offended by what could be interpreted as an uncouth reply from a small-town official to the President of the Republic. In fact, before returning to Manila, he had lunch with me at our house, along with Vice Mayor Magtajas, Councilors Roddy Villaroya, Henry Bacal, Guilly Parrel and my cousin, lawyer Bonifacio P. Regalado. Over lunch, I mentioned casually to Barrican that national reconciliation was possible only if Marcos resigned and if based on freedom, justice and peace.

Chapter 34

Consulting with Opposition Leaders

Despite my rather curt verbal rejection of Marcos's overtures to me, in my political eye, I saw an opportunity for me to go to Manila by using the note he had sent to me through Barrican. With that in mind, I told, rather than asked, the highest-ranking police officer in Misamis Oriental, Colonel Banaglorioso, my jailer, that I was going to Manila on the afternoon of October 17, 1983. I insinuated that Marcos wanted to discuss the Aquino assassination with five people, including me.

It was a calculated move on my part and I presumed that Banaglorioso would not object because, the day before, the *Sunday Express* bannered the headline: "FM okays dialogue with Opposition panel." Since it was the *Express* that published the news, it was assumed that it spoke for Marcos. According to the newspaper, Marcos wanted to have dialogue with Jose W. Diokno, Jose B. Laurel, Jr., Francisco Tatad, Vicente Jayme, who was the chair of the Bishops-Businessmen Conference, and me. The news story said that we would first meet with Ministers Juan Ponce Enrile of National Defense; Blas Ople, Labor; Roberto Ongpin, Trade and Industry; Leonardo Perez, Political Affairs; and Fred J. Elizalde, president of the Chamber of Commerce and Industry before we talked with Marcos.

Thus, aside from Marcos's letter that Barrican hand-carried to me, I now had the *Express* news story to back up my claim for the urgency of my going to Manila. I told Banaglorioso that, before I could give my final reply to Marcos, I must be allowed to consult with my colleagues in the Opposition in Manila.

To my delight, Banaglorioso agreed to let me go to Manila escorted by Maj. Angelito Moreno and another police officer. I was surprised that he allowed my trip to Manila considering that, hours after the assassination of Aquino, the PC Command tripled the number of the soldiers assigned to guard me in my house. The official reason they gave Bing was that my life was in extreme danger as there were unidentified elements who were out to liquidate me at the slightest opportunity. Moreover, before I left for Manila, there were news reports that Diokno, Laurel, Tatad and I had denied that it was the Opposition that sought the dialogue with Marcos.

Diokno told the Opposition-friendly media that the proposed dialogue "bears all the earmarks of a Malacañang concoction." Former Speaker Jose B. Laurel, Jr., was even more direct, "That was a false announcement. I have not sought any meeting with Mr. Marcos nor with any of his subordinates."

To add to the confusion, I was quoted as having said that "I don't know anything about it" while I was still in Cagayan de Oro. The statement, however, was true because Marcos did not formally invite me to have a dialogue with him. The letter he sent through Barrican did not categorically invite me to meet with him. Neither did I authorize anyone to seek a dialogue with him.

After our denials, Tatad also denied having sought a dialogue with Marcos. Doy Laurel, brother of the Speaker, advised that Marcos should stop "inviting us through press releases."

In any case, Banaglorioso said he was allowing me to go to Manila. He asked only that, upon arrival in Manila, I should report first to Minister Enrile of National Defense and get my instructions from him on what I may or may not do while I was in Manila.

Meanwhile, we in the opposition praised a report that US President Reagan had canceled his planned visit to the country in November. We took the cancelation as a sign that the US government no longer saw Marcos as the only person capable of running the nation democratically. Earlier, we also learned that Cardinal Sin met with Reagan in Washington, DC, and had told him that, aside from the communist rebels, there was a moderate Opposition group in the country that was challenging Marcos's leadership in a peaceful manner.

Taza de Oro

The day after Banaglorioso granted me the permit, Bing and I flew to Manila with my two police escorts. Since it was already 5 p.m. when we arrived, I suggested to my guards that we drop in at Taza de Oro for coffee. We could report to Enrile and Ramos the following morning, I said. They agreed. As *provincianos*, the guards did not know that Taza de Oro was a favorite hangout of oppositionists, news people and idlers who love no menu better than cups of steaming coffee with liberal doses of gossip against the Marcos regime.

At the coffee shop, newsmen from Reuters, Agence France Press, the *Guardian* and DZMM interviewed me. I told them that the reason I came to Manila was to consult with fellow Opposition leaders on what we could do to continue Ninoy Aquino's desire for peaceful change.

It was almost 9 p.m. when we got to my house in Fairlane Subdivision, Marikina. Milling on the street in front of the house were several Metrocom police officers and other military men. They had apparently come in Metrocom cars and other unmarked vehicles in anticipation of my arrival. My neighbors were also there en masse to greet me. They had been alerted by Bing, who went directly to Fairlane from the airport, while I tarried at Taza de Oro. Ben and Baby Perez, Romy and Rosie Reyes, Danny and Emy Cua, Osie and Bella Villanueva, Mauro and Eli Manuel, Jess and Susie Velasco, Ed and Rose Mojar, Arman and Leoning Belen, Cito and Auring Buenviaje, Aster and Charing Perez, Frank and Pat Ogsimer, May and Baby Villanueva, Nick and Auring Partin, Fred and Sion Cruz, Odi and Luming Cagurangan, Fred and Lina

Mallari, and Tony and Lita Togonon turned the occasion into an unscheduled *bienvenida* party.

That night, we did the four things that Filipinos do best when they meet without any prearranged agenda: we recalled the good times we had together, drank our favorite beer, sang nostalgic songs, and ate our favorite food (*inihaw na isda*, fried chicken and *lechon*). On that happy occasion, we forgot about Marcos, martial rule and the problems of the nation, and just let go as simple human beings bound together by love for one another as neighbors in our small, tightly knit lower middle-class subdivision until half-past midnight. To this day, I cannot forget the fortitude of my neighbors in manifesting without fear their happiness over my coming "home" to Fairlane, even if it was only for a short while.

A Colonel Calls

Before I got to bed, I received a phone call from a certain Colonel Zulueta. He said that I should just stay home and not move around in Metro Manila to contact my fellow oppositionists. If that was the case, I said I would fly back to Cagayan de Oro the following day because I came to Manila precisely to get in touch with my fellow Opposition leaders to formulate our stand in the light of the Marcos's supposed desire to look deeply into the Aquino assassination. Sensing that I was not about to beg him for any favors, Zulueta modified his stand. He said that, in the morning, we should proceed as scheduled to see General Ramos and Secretary Enrile to find out if I could be allowed to contact my fellow Opposition leaders.

At 6:15 a.m., the following day, I cajoled my guards to let me pass by the house of the Laurels on Shaw Boulevard, Mandaluyong, before we went to see Ramos and Enrile. They agreed. I met with both Sen. Doy Laurel and former Speaker Pepito Laurel. They said that they did not like Marcos's ploy of first announcing that he wanted to meet with the Opposition leaders before they were formally invited, which is what Marcos did as far as they were concerned. They were, thus, disinclined to meet with Marcos.

Meeting with Ramos

From the Laurel house, we went to Ramos's office. We got there in no time at all, not only because I was ferried on board a Metrocom car, but also because another Metrocom car cleared the way for us, with an unmarked intelligence car taking the rear in our three-car convoy. At the appointed hour, 8:45 a.m., I was there facing the chief of the Philippine Constabulary. Bing joined me in this call on Ramos. Probably because of Bing's presence, Ramos was cordial and merely asked a few perfunctory questions. He already knew that the dialogue between Marcos and the Opposition leaders would not take place. The cancelation of the meeting had been published in the newspapers and aired over television and radio.

I told Ramos that I would like to stay in Manila for at least a week so I could touch base with the Manila-based Opposition leaders and find out what their views were on the current crisis spawned by the murder of Ninoy Aquino. Ramos said it was all right by him, but he suggested that I be placed under the custody of an Opposition leader while in Manila so that, in his words, they "could withdraw the Metrocom (and intelligence services) escorts." There were about 10 officers and men assigned to guard me. He added that we had to seek Enrile's approval before my request could be granted.

Face to Face with Enrile

Before 9:30 that morning, we were at the office of Minister Enrile at Camp Aguinaldo. Bing and I were ushered into Enrile's office right away. It was the first time we had met Enrile in person. I must say that he turned me off immediately. His reputation as Marcos's iron-fisted implementor of martial rule preceded our meeting and it was of common knowledge that I had no liking whatsoever for anyone who worked that closely with Marcos. Thus, my harsh impression of him.

But, even before martial rule was declared in 1972 — to be more precise, in the 1971 senatorial elections — I had already indicated to my fellow Convention Delegate Edgardo Angara of Aurora that I could not support Enrile's bid for the Senate. Angara, the lead partner of the Angara, Cruz, Concepcion, Regala and Abello Law Office, offered airplane tickets and some campaign funds in support of the Enrile candidacy to a select group of delegates, including me. I declined the offer, telling him I could not possibly work for Enrile's candidacy. I would feel uneasy, I said, if I accepted campaign funds for anyone whom I could not support. Angara took my explanation kindly and, I hoped, without any resentment against me.

Meeting Enrile in person for the first time, I got the impression of a person who exuded the air of omniscience and omnipotence — attributes that catechism taught me were God's alone. Indeed, at that time, Enrile was perceived by most everyone who followed political developments in the country to be the third person of the unholy trinity holding the levers of power in Malacañang: Marcos, Imelda and Enrile. Thus, at our first meeting, he struck me — he probably wanted me to believe that, too — as possessing godlike martial law powers over the lives of the people and the destiny of the nation.

I had barely warmed my seat when he launched into a nonstop 15-minute monologue about the responsibility of the Opposition to the nation and of the Opposition's need to unite and work with the Marcos government for the good of the nation. I did not quite understand his concern for the unity of the Opposition, but I kept quiet until he was done haranguing me on the futility of resisting martial law. As an afterthought, probably realizing that I must have been brought to his office for a purpose, like an immigration official of a foreign country, he barked out the questions why I had come to Manila and how long I intended to stay.

Briefly, I told him what I had mentioned to Ramos earlier that morning

1983: *AFTER THE SCOWLS, the smiles. Defense Minister Enrile cordial now after eliciting the reason for my trip to Manila. With us is General Ramos.*

and added that, if he allowed me a week's stay, it would suffice for my consultations with my fellow Opposition leaders in Metro Manila on what we could do to continue the peaceful objectives of Ninoy Aquino. As he did not respond immediately, I added that I also wanted to report to him a "massacre" of some 45 peasants in Barangay Sag-od, Las Navas, Northern Samar, on September 15, 1981, that up to that very day had not yet been conclusively investigated. There were reports even then that CHDF and goons associated with loggers in the island of Samar were the perpetrators of the massacre. Tersely, he replied that he would look into it.

I then shifted to speculations fanned by the controlled media that we, the leaders of the Opposition, could sit in the Marcos-created panel to investigate the Aquino murder. I said that, as far as I was concerned, since I was a prisoner (under house arrest), I found it awkward even to consider it. He cut me off by saying that Marcos had not really asked us in the Opposition for a dialogue on that issue. He said it was a certain Consul Ramirez who made a representation with Comelec Chair Leonardo Perez that we, in the Opposition, had sought to dialogue with Marcos (which was not true at all).

Nonetheless, I managed to say edgewise that, if a dialogue between Marcos and us in the Opposition would take place, my being a detainee might prove to be an embarrassment. I explained that, "If an agreement is reached between Marcos and us on any matter, people might suspect that I went along because, as a prisoner, I was acting under duress or, worse, because of self-interest." I was, of course, insinuating that my being held as a prisoner of martial rule was not for the good of anyone.

Catching the drift of my statement, Enrile said that "if these were times under martial law, I could do something about it, but now I could only refer it to higher authority" for action. His reference to his inability to do anything by himself to ease my situation as a prisoner under house arrest had to do with Marcos's having ostensibly lifted martial rule in 1981. I used the word ostensibly because, while martial rule was said to be no longer in existence, authoritarian rules that lodged absolute power in the hands of Marcos were still in place.

As my call was coming to a close and apparently for my listening pleasure, Enrile ordered Ramos to make sure that I was "allowed to move around Metro Manila and see whomsoever (I) wanted to see, but always under escort." He added ominously, "I don't want another incident" — most likely referring to the Aquino assassination. By giving that order to Ramos, Enrile disposed of Ramos's earlier suggestion that I should be placed under the custody of a Manila-based Opposition leader while I was making my visits to colleagues in the Opposition.

When it was time for us to leave, in a complete reversal of the cold reception he gave us when we entered his office, Enrile said that it was a good thing that Bing was with me. He told Bing that she "was my best security" against those who might wish to do me harm. Then, addressing me as if we were bosom friends, he said that I could see him anytime I got the chance to come to Manila. I wondered why Marcos's "Iron Fist" in the person of the Minister of National Defense was now using the "carrot-and-stick" approach in dealing with me. I simply smiled as we shook hands. I could not believe it but he smiled back. Bing and I then left with my armed guards.

Opposition Leaders' Views

When we left Enrile's office, I understood that I had until the 24th of October to do my consultations with the Metro Manila-based Opposition leaders. I made full use of the period allotted to me.

From the Defense Ministry, Bing left to do her family chores while I went see Senator Tañada. I explained to him that I was able to come to Manila by telling my military jailors in Cagayan de Oro that Marcos wanted to have a dialogue with us, the Opposition leaders. I told him about Marcos's letter to me that Barrican had personally hand-carried.

Tañada was of the opinion that Marcos should resign first before we have a dialogue with him. Sequentially, he said, a caretaker government should be formed, followed by the convening of the Constitutional Convention whose work would then be submitted to a plebiscite, first "informally" and later "formally"— terms we were not able to discuss more fully in the little time we had together.

Guingona, whom I saw next, supported Tañada's views on the resignation of Marcos first before any dialogue could be had with us in the Opposition. In all candor, I could not quite follow how their idea could be brought about. In my opinion, the proposal was good only as a bargaining chip, although, knowing Marcos, I thought it was a no brainer. In fact, I found the process so "iffy" as to be totally impractical. Why would Marcos agree to resign first and then hold a dialogue with us in the Opposition? If Marcos resigned, in what capacity would he be having a dialogue with us? The questions were left hanging in the air without any answers.

Joker Arroyo's Caveat

After my talk with Guingona, I went to see Joker Arroyo. He was acting as counsel for the accused in the *We Forum* cases at the Court of First Instance at the Quezon City Hall. The accused were all journalists writing for the *We Forum* daily that the redoubtable Jose Burgos published as a vehicle for uncensored news. In the courtroom, I saw lawyers Rene Saguisag, Tony Rosales and Sen. Ambrosio Padilla, who were Joker's co-counsel, and *We Forum* writers Ernesto Rodriguez, Armando Malay and Salvador Roxas Gonzales. (The cases were dropped by the government only in 1985, after the Supreme Court found the military raid on *We Forum* illegal and barred the use as evidence of the records or documents seized in the raid.)

While waiting for Joker Arroyo to finish his duties as counsel for the accused journalists, television reporters Rey Vidal and Jun Bautista, both of Channel 7, interviewed me on many issues. Vidal insinuated that I had come to Manila to beg Marcos for reinstatement as mayor of Cagayan de Oro. I told him that, before I came for this visit to Manila, I made sure that I had resumed my duties as the mayor of Cagayan de Oro. I precisely did not want it said by anyone that I got my seat as mayor back because I had bargained for it with Marcos. I told Vidal that, as far as I was concerned, I would never bargain with Marcos for any personal benefit.

Bautista asked me about Interior Minister Jose Roño's opinion that I could not legitimately assume my duties as mayor of Cagayan de Oro because I was under house arrest. I told him Roño's view was off tangent. There was no law, I said, that prohibited me from doing my duties at my house while I was under house arrest. And, since I had not been suspended, there was no legal inhibition to deter me from discharging my duties as mayor of Cagayan de Oro. That Roño did not cause my suspension even on imagined grounds remains a mystery to this very day. It could have been that Marcos and Roño did not want the people to suspect they were overdoing their harassment of me. In any event, it probably was written in the stars that, despite all the charges they were throwing at me, the martial law authorities could not, at that time anyway, find a plausible legal basis to suspend me.

Joe Burgos, publisher of *We Forum*, also interviewed me. Joe was a genuine believer in the freedom of the press. Despite the closure some weeks earlier of his newspaper by "goons" in uniform, he did not allow himself to be cowed by Marcos. Essentially, I repeated to him what I told Tañada and the other leaders of the Opposition about the purpose of my trip. I also denounced Marcos's harassment of the *We Forum* journalists even as he had supposedly already lifted martial law.

Later, I briefed Joker Arroyo in detail as to how and why I was able to come to Manila. Ever the cautious lawyer, Arroyo simply said I should be careful in dealing with Marcos directly.

Macapagal for Dialogue

After I talked with Joker Arroyo, I went to see former President Macapagal. We discussed the situation of the country and the status of the Opposition after the assassination of Aquino. Macapagal was of the opinion that we should not refuse a dialogue with Marcos if he should call for any such conversation with us. He advised that we should participate in the dialogue if only to find out just exactly what Marcos's thoughts were on the volatility of the country's situation.

Roces's Warning

The following day, I met with Chino Roces, the highly respected publisher of the *Manila Times*. Roces treated me to a spartan meal of broiled fish, rice and noodles, the kind that he was famous for among his friends. More important than the menu, however, were his views on the current situation of the country, especially because these coincided with mine. Like me, he did not believe that demanding that Marcos should resign as a precondition to having a dialogue with him was attainable at all. And, even if Marcos would agree to do so, he said it might be detrimental to the national interest unless a legal device was put in place "to cushion the fall of Marcos so that he does not drag the whole country into ruin with him."

Roces warned me that my life was in danger from military elements, leftist extremists and even from political enemies. He said rather prophetically that when I go back to Cagayan de Oro, political brickbats will be thrown my way because I would be "misunderstood." I told him that being misunderstood was the least of my worries because I was ever ready to stand up for the things I believed in. I said that I would not allow being misunderstood to deter me from doing what I thought needed to be done.

As Roces had predicted, a political hailstorm of sorts battered me even before I got home — surprisingly not by dyed-in-the-wool Marcos loyalists but by my erstwhile colleagues in the Opposition, notably Misamis Oriental Governor Adaza.

On October 31, Adaza lamented my going to Manila in a press release that he signed in the name of the Makabayang Alyansa-Mindanao Alliance. He said that I had betrayed "the interests of the people" and undermined "the cause of the Opposition" by "seeking a dialogue with Marcos." He went on to say that I did so "to save myself from the 22 charges of corruption that were pending before the Tanodbayan," which were, of course, completely untrue. Since he really did not know what I was doing in Manila, I ignored this latest diatribe from Adaza.

At some point, Canoy joined the fray. Although he was a little less acerbic than Adaza, both of them argued, among other things, that I was not a genuine Opposition leader, probably in the hope that my Opposition colleagues in Manila would shun me.

Celebrity Status

Nothing of that sort happened. In fact, I enjoyed a kind of celebrity status in the metropolis as shown by the warm reception my Opposition friends accorded me and the interest of the media in my visit to Manila. Television, radio and print media people hounded me from place to place asking for interviews. At one point, all the major local television networks — Channels 4, 7, 9 and 13 — along with some radio and print media journalists, interviewed me. They were all interested to know why I was in Manila and how my trip was going. Even the foreign media got into the act. I remember speaking to Guy Sacerdotti, Paul Quinn Judge and Teodoro Benigno, who was then writing for Agence France Press. A German TV crew also taped an interview with me.

In answer to their queries, I repeatedly told them I was in Manila to consult with my fellow Opposition leaders as to how best we can pursue the peaceful transition from Marcos's martial law government to a democratic one that Ninoy Aquino had advocated before he was assassinated. I emphasized I was not in Manila to cut a deal with Marcos for my personal or for anybody's benefit. I said I only contacted the Manila-based Opposition leaders and would continue to do so until I could return to Cagayan de Oro in a couple of days.

Nach in the Act

Even the US Embassy's political officer, Jim Nach, talked with me while I was in Manila. Nach saw me at the Philippine Columbian. He was interested in my views as to how I thought the Americans should act vis-a-vis the Marcos regime and the Opposition in the aftermath of the Aquino murder. I gave Nach an earful.

I told him that Marcos was finished. He no longer had the capacity to hold the nation together. At the time, I said, Marcos had lost total credibility. And credibility was important to any political leader. Marcos, therefore, could no longer exact compliance with his decrees, even with the threat of force or punishment.

As for the US, I told Nach that it would be better if the US did not continue giving support to Marcos. Otherwise, they'd get a good share of the hatred the people reserved for Marcos.

In my talks with Nach, it came out quite clearly that the Americans wanted to see the fragmented Opposition united because, at about this time, they already saw Marcos — in the unforgettable phrase of the *New York Times* — as a "ruinous burden." Unfortunately, every Opposition personality who had a ragtag band of political cheerleaders saw himself or herself as a viable challenger to Marcos.

Later, I got word that Doy Laurel had arranged a meeting for me with US Embassy people at the US Ambassador's residence in Forbes Park, Makati. I did not think it wise to have the meeting. I begged off and the meeting was canceled.

Cory's Moderate Views

Next on my visit list were Cory, Aquino's widow, and her brother Peping Cojuangco, Jr., both of whom I saw at the Cojuangco Building in Makati. Jose Yap, a close associate of Ninoy, was also there. The three of them surprised me with their moderate views on the ouster of Marcos. I thought that, because of the murder of Aquino, they would be for the ouster of Marcos by any means. Not so. They told me that they wanted a peaceful transition and that means, in their words, "giving Marcos a graceful exit."

Incidentally, as I was going to the Cojuangco Building, there was a massive rally in the heart of Makati. Tons of yellow confetti flew out of the town's major skyscrapers, cars were honking and people were flashing the "L" sign for "Laban," the battle cry of the Aquino-led Opposition candidates for the Interim Batasan in 1978.

The demonstrators were so openly anti-Marcos that my military escorts were afraid the Metrocom cars and the unmarked intelligence vehicle of our convoy would be stoned or subjected to violence by the pro-Aquino rallyists. My guards said that, if they saw any sign of hostility against them, they were prepared to shout that they were my escorts! In the event, no untoward incident marked my visits to Cory at the Cojuangco Building and to the other leaders of the Opposition.

Diokno's Advice

The following day, I met with Senator Diokno. He struck me as having toned down his "nationalist stand" vis-a-vis the American bases. He told me that as a matter of tactics, stressing the removal of the bases — which was the stand of my political party, PDP-Laban — would only "create more enemies for us." Diokno suggested that the Opposition focus first on the removal of Marcos, who should resign before we engage him in a dialogue. In that respect, his stand was similar to that of Tañada and Guingona, which I did not fully understand.

There were other lesser lights of the Opposition whose opinions I also sought. Lawyer Abe Sarmiento, former vice president of the Constitutional Convention, was one. He told me that he supported the Tañada and Diokno position that Marcos should resign first before we discuss other matters of national interest with him. I also talked with lawyer Raul Gonzalez, one of Ninoy Aquino's counsel at the latter's trial by a Military Commission. He was for engaging Marcos in a dialogue. He did not see anything wrong with my talking with Marcos and finding out what he really wanted.

Araneta: Marcos Resign

I also contacted the Jesuit priest, Francisco Araneta, the president of Xavier University in Cagayan de Oro when I was a college student. Araneta surprised me with his views that included calls for the resignation of Marcos and the removal of General Fabian Ver, Marcos's chief of staff of the Armed Forces. I told him that we should perhaps temper the options for the legitimate Opposition to those that were "attainable in reason."

Araneta insinuated that I might have been manipulated to come to Manila for Marcos's benefit. Although my ears burned at the unfounded insinuation, I replied as coolly as I could that he got it all wrong. I said my one and only purpose for coming to Manila was to consult with the leaders of the Opposition and find out from them firsthand what they thought we should do next after Aquino's assassination. I assured him I would not enter into any covert deals with Marcos. I also thanked him for the support that he had extended to me and my family at the start of my problems with Marcos.

On the remaining days of my Manila visit, I met separately with Rep. Tony Cuenco of Cebu, Jejomar Binay of Makati, Ramon Mitra, Jr., who was Aquino's contemporary before Marcos abolished the Senate, and Ceferino Padua, a delegate to the Constitutional Convention. They were all agreed that Marcos should be ousted from office. They were, however, not unanimous on the question of how we were supposed to depose him.

I also had a chance to meet with the Japanese delegation to an antinuclear conference that was held in Manila in the week of my visit. I told the delegation that I, too, was against the development of nuclear weapons in the country and the establishment of nuclear power plants in Bataan.

Visiting Ninoy's Tomb

In between my calls on the Opposition leaders, I paid a visit to the tomb of Ninoy Aquino and said a prayer for the repose of his soul. Bing, had represented me at his funeral since I could not get a permit to leave house arrest.

On my last night in Metro Manila, my neighbors hosted a *despedida* party for me at my house in Fairlane. I could join them only after 9 p.m., because of the calls that I had to do on my opposition colleagues, but they stayed until half-past 12 enjoying the remaining moments that I could be with them.

By 5 a.m. on October 24, Sean Olaer, a supporter from Cagayan de Oro, roused me from bed and drove me to Radio Veritas for an interview with Louie Tabing and Jose Orestain. At the station, we discussed what brought me to Manila and how things had turned out in the consultations I had with my colleagues in the Opposition. In essence, I told our listeners that the leaders of the Opposition were agreed on the need to get Marcos out of Malacañang and to do so peacefully. But we were not in agreement on how to proceed with the proposal to engage Marcos in a peaceful dialogue so that Ninoy Aquino's dreams for a peaceful transition would be realized.

After the Radio Veritas interview, I had breakfast with Sen. Eva Estrada Kalaw at 9 a.m. Over coffee and bread, we discussed possibilities of

From Malaya

1983: I PRAY at Ninoy's tomb

peaceful change from the martial law regime to a democratically elected government. Kalaw had another guest, Dr. Emmanuel Yap, a nationalist intellectual who suggested possible options for the Opposition.

At 11 a.m., we drove to the airport for the flight home. Arriving in Cagayan de Oro at 3 p.m., I was greeted at the airport by an enthusiastic crowd that included several Moro leaders like Dr. Jun Alonto, Abul Kayr Alonto and Joel de los Santos from Lanao, and Al Tillah from Sulu. They came not only to greet me but also to show the Marcos government that the young Moros of Mindanao did not like what they were doing to our people on the island. In a few minutes, I was back again in my home as a martial law detainee under house arrest.

Kompil Organized

I went home without any clear indications that the Opposition would come up with a viable candidate for the presidency against Marcos. I felt, however, that it was only a matter of time before the anti-Marcos groups would realize that it was to our advantage to field a single candidate for president, if and when Marcos called for presidential elections. Indeed, in early January of 1984, Lorenzo Tañada, Cory Aquino and businessman Jaime Ongpin, among others, organized the *Kongreso ng Mamamayang Pilipino* (Kompil) to help identify an Opposition presidential candidate against Marcos. Because I could not attend the Kompil conference, the organizers asked me to send a written statement of solidarity. I sent a one-page statement that compared Kompil to the puny David of the Bible who felled the mighty Goliath with one slingshot. I thought it was an apt allusion to the power of an aroused and oppressed people to rise above their weaknesses and break the chains of their bondage.

Kompil named 15 alternative leaders to Marcos. Among the more easily recognizable ones, politically speaking, were Lorenzo Tañada, Salvador Laurel of Unido, Ambrosio Padilla and Jovito Salonga of the Liberal Party. And just to show Marcos that the Opposition had a long bench of contenders for the presidency, Kompil also listed Rene Saguisag, Horacio Morales and me.

One issue that surfaced at the Kompil meeting was whether or not those who opposed Marcos should boycott the Batasan Elections that were set for May.

Butz Aquino, brother of Ninoy, and a major organizer of Kompil, told the media the day following the conference that the delegates did not reach a consensus on the matter. Some 20% of the delegates opted for boycott, while 37% chose to participate, the *Metro Manila Times* reported. The others attached several conditions to their options that made their intentions unclear.

National Day of Sorrow

About a month after the Aquino assassination, Marcos declared September 21, 1983, as a national thanksgiving day to commemorate his proclamation of martial law 11 years earlier. I deplored the incongruity of having to thank anyone for martial law which did not do the country any good. Rhetorically I asked in an article that was published in a local newspaper, "What's there to be thankful for on National Thanksgiving Day?" I argued that "instead of saving the Republic, martial law destroyed it, and...instead of reforming Philippine society, martial rule deformed it."

I also lamented the fact that, even economically, the country did not gain from the declaration of martial rule. Instead of working out an economic miracle, I said that the martial rule strategy had brought an economic debacle to the country and our people. A Makati Business Club assessment of the economy supported my observation. The businessmen said, "The rising GNP per capita has not trickled down to the mass of the people, close to half of which live below the poverty line." I rubbed in the acerbic assessment, saying:

> The trade off between bread and freedom that martial rule promised did not work out because, while we certainly lost our freedoms as a consequence of the imposition of martial rule, we hardly earned more money to buy more bread for our tables.

I concluded that there was nothing for the people to thank martial law for. The Republic was lost. Our freedoms were lost. And the people were hungry. There was anger, not gratitude, in their hearts. The millions of people who braved the heat and the rain to express their solidarity with Aquino at his funeral were ample proof of their frustration against the martial law regime.

In Manila, at Liwasang Bonifacio, thousands of people attended the commemoration of the "National Day of Sorrow" on September 21, 1983 where they signed a Manifesto of Freedom, Democracy and Sovereignty. It was a bold statement that decried not only the excesses of martial law, but also the "denigration of (the nation's) sovereignty that was abetted by the US government."

The signatories were a mix bag of staunch martial law oppositionists and the conscienticized religious and politica! ideologues. Among them were Aquino's widow Cory, former President Macapagal, former Senators Tañada, Doy Laurel and Diokno, former House Speaker Pepito Laurel, former Delegate Abraham Sarmiento, former Rep. Tony Cuenco and Butz Aquino. Some priests also signed, among them Rudy Romano of Cebu and Jose P. Dizon of the National Priests and Religious Union. So did nuns like Sister Christine Tan of the Ecumenical Center for Social Concern, Sister Vincent of the *Kapisanan ng mga Madre sa Kamaynilaan*, Association of Sisters of Metro Manila, and Sister Mary Soledad of the Press Freedom Committee. Constitutional Convention Delegates Dominador Carillo, Augusto Sanchez and Ernesto Lichauco also signed the manifesto.

The radical fringe of the Marcos Opposition was represented in the manifesto by Elmer Mercado and J. Virgilio Bautista of the League of Filipino Students, Leandro Alejandro of the UP Student Council and Loreta Ann P. Rosales of the Association of Concerned Teachers.

Part 9

Going to the Batasan

1984: TAKING MY OATH AS AN ASSEMBLYMAN in the Batasang Pambansa before Barangay Captain Atilano Labuntog of Lapasan, Cagayan de Oro City. My youngest daughter, Inde, stands by my side.

Chapter 35

The Batasan Elections

By this time, the people's outrage against the unconscionable killing of Aquino was building up nationwide. One of the ways Marcos thought of to defuse the mounting demands for his resignation was to call for elections in May 1984 to the unicameral legislative body that was created in the 1973 Constitution. The elections would be supervised by the Comelec.

I had grave doubts about the electoral body's ability to conduct the elections impartially. Earlier, Mayor Climaco of Zamboanga City assailed the Comelec's incapacity to conduct clean elections citing his experience in his city. I added my own data that some 30 ballot boxes had been hijacked by armed men in Misamis Oriental and Cagayan de Oro in the Comelec-supervised plebiscite on January 27, 1984. Like Climaco's, my position was that the Comelec had proven itself to be an unreliable arbiter of the people's electoral will. My view was that it should be revamped so that only individuals known for their wisdom, probity and independence of mind would be appointed as commissioners.

Our misgivings, notwithstanding, Marcos pushed for the May 14, 1984 Batasang Pambansa elections and used psywar tactics on the people to make them vote for his candidates in the elections. He had soldiers in active duty conduct "surveys" on the "voting trends" in the nation. The survey questions in Northern Mindanao included two that specifically zeroed in on me. One survey question asked who between "the KBL candidate, Pedro N. Roa, and the PDP-Laban candidate, Mayor Pimentel" would win? Another asked "what groups/organizations [were] supporting Pimentel?"

I found the latter question most objectionable because survey respondents who did not like me could allege that I was being supported by armed groups espousing violence against the government. From that bare allegation, the military authorities could tag me as a "danger to the security of the State." Marcos could then issue a detention or commitment order to send me indefinitely to a military prison.

In the event, no such thing happened. And, regardless of the perceived odds, I launched my candidacy for a seat in the Batasang Pambansa from my residence, where Marcos had placed me under house arrest since mid-1983.

Since I was prevented from campaigning freely for the Batasan, I addressed my supporters in rallies organized in front of our house on Archbishop Hayes Street. Cory Aquino came for one such rally and she proclaimed me as her candidate

1984: *CORY PROCLAIMS ME her candidate for the Batasang Pambansa at the doorstep of my house in Cagayan de Oro. I was under "house arrest".*

for the Batasan. On other occasions, Tingting Cojuangco, wife of Cory's brother Peping, and Lorna Verano Yap of Surigao, also came and endorsed me for the Batasan. Technically, I did not violate the restrictions of my house arrest because I did not step outside my house without permission from my military jailers.

I was up against the might of the Marcos regime and the money of my main opponent, Pedro Neri Roa, former congressman and governor of Misamis Oriental and erstwhile mayor of Cagayan de Oro. And because he bore the Roa and the Neri names that were identified with the elite of the city, the odds against my winning were great. But the city voters thought otherwise. They voted for me instead of Roa by a margin of over 4,000 votes.

Support from the Pelaez Camp

In this electoral contest, the followers of Pelaez, whose numbers had shrunk to a sentimental few due to changing political fortunes, threw their support behind me. It was a big psychological boost that I used in my election campaign. I said that even my former political adversaries identified with the Pelaez camp were now behind me in the campaign.

Pelaez's support for me had nothing to do with my qualifications for lawmaking being better than Roa's. Pelaez disliked Roa more than he liked me. His dislike for Roa stemmed from the fact that Roa tended to act independently of him. That was exactly the same reason why he backed Velez instead of Roa in the local elections of 1980.

Roa could chart a political course of action independently of Pelaez because he was wealthy in his own right and he had direct access to Marcos, the source of all government power and money during martial law. In Pelaez's view, if Roa became a member of the Batasang Pambansa, Roa could maneuver to exclude him from having easy access to Marcos.

Roa's money and the combined backing for him of the Marcos machinery, the military and the Comelec nearly cost me the elections. The results of the precincts for the voters of Carmen Hill were typical of the rest of the city. I had expected to beat Roa by a margin of at least 4-1 in Carmen Hill. I barely led him by 200 votes there.

The voting results in Carmen Hill demonstrated the power of money. As mayor, I delivered the basic needs to Carmen Hill residents. When they asked for an access road, I had one made. When they asked for electricity, I facilitated the connection. When they asked for water, I had a water system installed for them. When they asked for a school building, I had one constructed for them. Thus, I had reason to believe that I would crush Roa there to within an inch of his political life.

But when the votes were counted, I beat Roa there, but barely. Carmen Hill drove a practical lesson in politics to me. I found out that, while it was still possible to win, it was extremely difficult to survive a challenge from a well-heeled contender even if, as an incumbent, I had delivered the basic services required by our people.

I also discovered the rhetoric that some priests and naive politicians like me often used in the face of money politics — *"Dawata ang kuarta, iboto ang konsensiya; Get the money, vote your conscience"* — did not actually work among the poor and the unlettered voters who were the major targets of vote-buying. On the contrary, the slogan tempted them to accept the money as if it was the normal thing to do. Culturally, however, the fear of *gaba*, karma, that threatens with damnation people who renege on their commitments after accepting favors would haunt those with scrupulous consciences. That apparently was what bothered two elderly women who came to see me at about noon of Election Day. They were in tears. Since they were family friends, I asked them what they were crying about. They confessed that they had received P100 each to vote for Roa. At the polling place, they said, it took a lot of soul-searching before they decided to vote for me anyway. The tears they shed in my presence were, thus, induced by their fear of *gaba*.

With the ill-thought slogan, *"Dawata ang kuarta, iboto ang konsensiya"*, ringing in their ears, I believed, many voters — with pliable consciences — who got paid P100 to vote for my opponent stayed bought out of fear of *gaba*.

Culture of Violence

While the elections in Cagayan de Oro were generally peaceful, the political rhetoric was not only dirty, but also bordered on the violent. My political opponents were not above inventing stories to inflame the voters' passions against me. For instance, they pictured my old, two-story wooden house in Marikina — which Bing and I had bought in 1973, seven years before I became mayor in 1980 — as a mansion with a swimming pool, the product of corruption. They also raised anew the false allegation that I had acquired a mansion in California. Of course, I did not have a house, much less a mansion, in the US or any other part of the globe, except the modest house in Marikina and the old family home in Cagayan de Oro. And neither had a swimming pool.

While there were no incidents of outright election-related violence in the thickly populated parts of the city, the culture of violence that martial law had spawned crept inexorably into Misamis Oriental. In Gingoog City, approximately 100 kilometers east of Cagayan de Oro, Renato Bucag, a stalwart of PDP-Laban, his wife Melchora and their 11-year-old son Reneboy were killed in their farmhouse on May 1. They were shot, hacked and mutilated to death by four armed men who were members of the dreaded Civilian Home Defense Forces (CHDF).

I learned about the massacre of the Bucag family via a long distance call from our PDP-Laban candidate for the Batasang Pambansa in Misamis Oriental, Arturo Lugod. I was distraught over the tragedy, especially because Bucag was a personal friend and a reliable political leader.

The massacre of the Bucag family was so heinous that Cagayan de Oro's Archbishop, Patrick Cronin, wrote Marcos on May 28, 1984 to plead that he should do something about it immediately. Cronin said, "Surely a murder so savage as this and so completely un-Filipino calls for the immediate punishment of the perpetrators." The Archbishop also informed Marcos that, "within this year, we have had some cruelly shocking murders in this Province. A whole family of seven was massacred in Barrio Rosario, Tagoloan, and more recently in Midkiwan, Cagayan de Oro, a family of six were murdered." Cronin ended his letter with a plea: "Kindly help us, Mr. President, a word from you will activate all the Law Enforcement Agencies of the Province to seek out the criminals responsible for these murders, and punish them for their great crimes."

At this time, the military often used the CHDF in the fight against the communist rebels in the rural areas. The conscription of the CHDF had an adverse impact on the early solution of the Bucag family massacre because the main suspect of the killing was Felipe Galarion, a member of the CHDF and a political henchman of Mayor Miguel Paderanga of Gingoog City.

I condemned the massacre as best as I could over the media and called on the authorities to arrest Galarion and the other principal suspects, Manuel and Julito Ampo, Cesar Sabit and Eddie Torion. An eyewitness, Arthur Marban, executed an affidavit identifying Galarion and his companions as the perpetrators of the massacre. The affidavit was submitted to the investigating authorities. With my assistance, Dr. Helen Bucag-Canoy filed murder charges against Galarion and his group of killers.

Sad to say, the authorities feigned ignorance of the complicity of Galarion and the other accused. And, on the dates set for the preliminary investigation

Photo courtesy of Manila Bulletin

1984: TONY CUENCO, DR. HELEN BUCAG CANOY and I hold a press conference to condemn the Bucag family's massacre in Gingoog City and call on authorities to arrest their killers.

of the case, Galarion and the other suspects could not be found. My friend Tony Cuenco and I helped Dr. Bucag-Canoy publicize the killings by arranging a press conference for her. By that time, Tony and I were already Assemblymen-elect to the Batasan. Although I had seen ghastly photographs of victims of violence, I was not prepared for the pictures she presented to the media. I was particularly appalled at the manifest cruelty to which the killers subjected Reneboy who had gaping wounds on his thighs and neck. They had also ripped open his abdomen.

Efforts to have Galarion arrested were frustrated time and again by CHDF officials who told the warrant servers that he could not be found. It was relatively easy for him to evade the process servers because he was not only an "asset" to the military, he was also notoriously known as a henchman of the Gingoog mayor. It took a long time before Galarion was collared by the law and brought before the bar of justice where he was finally sentenced to *reclusion perpetua* or life imprisonment. Liberty, a surviving daughter of Bucag, informed us years later that the cases against the other accused "were dismissed because the witnesses were killed."

Comelec's Bullying Tactics

While the Cagayan de Oro Batasan election appeared peaceful and orderly on the surface, its concluding days were marred by the bullying tactics of the Comelec, which had become my nemesis. On May 14, Comelec Manila sent an ominous telegram to the City Election Registrar. The telegram told the Cagayan de Oro Election Registrar, Bernardita Cabacungan, that:

(1) They received several complaints that the results of the vote in Cagayan de Oro were being manipulated before the Canvassing Boards could do their job;

(2) Operation Quick Count [a duly accredited non-government body to help the Comelec do a fast count] was announcing who was winning in the Batasan election in the city;

(3) The Election Registrar should not allow any unauthorized person to interfere with the proceedings; and

(4) She should wire back her having received the basic Comelec telegram and her compliance with it.

Comelec Manila was, in effect, charging me with tampering with the results of the elections. Since the Comelec publicized the telegram, I told the Cagayan de Oro Press Club that I did not and could have not done any cheating. I was under house arrest until a few days before the election. Additionally, as the opposition candidate, I was up against the richest man in Mindanao who had the backing of Marcos, the military and the Comelec. Later, in November 1984, when the question of my election reached the Batasan, I clarified who cheated whom.

For the moment, the Comelec desisted from preventing my proclamation. Hence, I was one of the 59 Opposition candidates certified by the Comelec to have won over Marcos's bets nationwide. In a legislative assembly of 200 members, 59 Opposition solons were a sizeable group.

Thistles on the Road

My road to the Batasan was not strewn with roses. Just as the Comelec laid legal thistles to spike my way to the office of mayor of Cagayan de Oro in 1980, the Comelec installed legal — illegal really — barbed wires to block my path to the Batasan.

From the start of the electoral period, I campaigned under a handicap as Marcos had placed me under house arrest. It was only a few days before Election Day that Marcos ordered the lifting of my house arrest restrictions. The lifting did not come merely from the good graces of Marcos. As a practical politician, he knew that it would be a monumental embarrassment to the administration if I won despite my house arrest. News reports during the period indicated that the KBL bets for the Batasan in Misamis Oriental and in the other provinces of Region X would be adversely affected by my continued house arrest. I naturally depicted myself as the underdog in the race for the Batasan and, through the media, exploited my house arrest as a sign that Marcos was oppressing me because I was a vocal oppositionist. The propaganda worked. Marcos lifted the restrictions on my movement, as mentioned above.

Attending *Mitings de Avance*

Once freed from house arrest, I campaigned briefly in the city where I was hailed like Flash Elorde, coming home as a hero, fresh from a world championship boxing bout. Thereafter, I accepted invitations to the *mitings de avance*, the winding up rallies, of my Opposition colleagues in other places.

I attended one very memorable *miting de avance* in the town of San Jose, the capital of Antique, the proclaimed bailiwick of a dyed-in-the-wool Marcos man, Arturo Pacificador. I did not go there for Pacificador. I went with Eva Kalaw to pro-

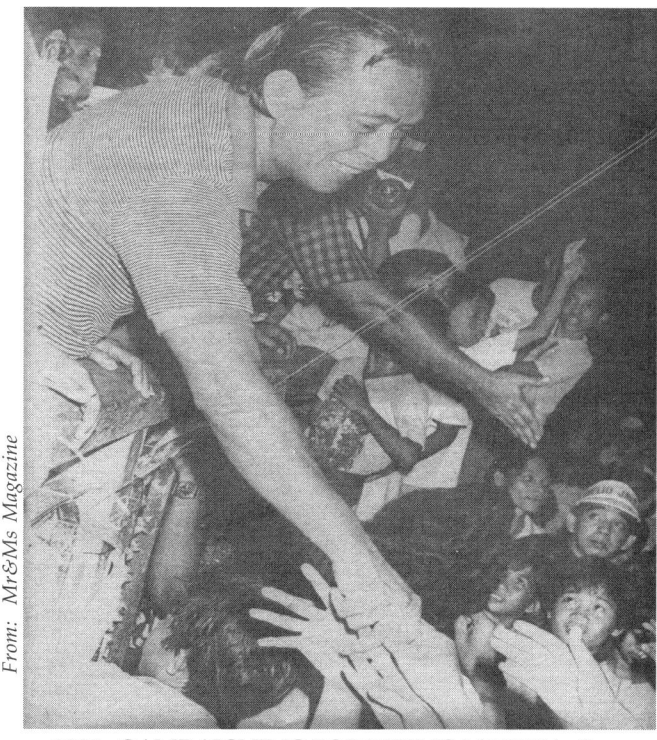

From: Mr&Ms Magazine

1984: CAMPAIGNING FOR EVELIO JAVIER in San Jose, Antique.

claim Evelio Javier as the Opposition's candidate. The town plaza was filled to the brim with people, indicating Javier's broad-based popularity. Our endorsement, however, was not enough to get Javier elected, and Pacificador "won the election" in Antique. Javier protested against the use of the evil electoral trinity of guns, gold and goons, but failed to legally establish his victory over Pacificador.

Two years later, Javier was shot dead in the course of the 1986 presidential contest between Marcos and Cory Aquino. Javier, our point man in Antique, had supported Cory in the province — as it turned out, at the expense of his life.

I also spoke in some *mitings de avance* in Metro Manila and other parts of the Visayas, endorsing our candidates to the Batasan. The endorsements were good mainly for their psychological, not political, value. I had no political clout in those places, but my presence elicited enthusiastic responses from the opposition crowds because I was a live exhibit of Marcos's oppression, having just emerged from imprisonment. The people lapped up my denunciations of the corruption, oppression and human rights violations of the martial law regime. In a Unido proclamation rally in Quezon City in April 1984, the crowd, according to Art Borjal of the *Metro Manila Times*, "refused to let [Pimentel] stop speaking despite the late hour."

Request for DOP Denied

Shortly before the May 14 elections, I returned to Cagayan de Oro to pep up my supporters and to vote. But my political opponents were not about to let the elections transpire without exhausting their legal — illegal would be a more appropriate term — maneuvers to prevent me from winning. In fact, months before the elections, my party, the PDP-Laban, sought Comelec accreditation as the dominant opposition party (DOP) in Cagayan de Oro City. The Comelec, however, denied our request and instead accredited the Mindanao Alliance.

The denial of our request deprived us of representation in the City Board of Canvassers. Only the KBL, with Roa as its candidate for mayor, and the Mindanao Alliance, with Guerrero Adaza, brother of Homobono, as its candidate had representatives on the Board of Canvassers. Guerrero Adaza, who received only 2,472 votes out of nearly 115,000 votes cast, was clearly a nuisance candidate.

While Guerrero Adaza's candidacy appeared to be on the level, I believe he ran for two interrelated reasons: to provide the Comelec with an excuse to deny my party's accreditation as the DOP in the city and to provide a cover for the assistance that his candidacy extended — wittingly or unwittingly — to Roa's bid. At the time, the Mindanao Alliance had no substantial presence as a party in the city. Outside of the KBL, the single best-organized political party in the city was certainly the PDP-Laban.

Looking back with dispassionate eyes, I saw that the Mindanao Alliance had every reason to fight us in Cagayan de Oro. After all, PDP-Laban had fielded Gingoog Mayor Arturo Lugod and Cagayan de Oro Councilor Constantino Jaraula as our candidates for the Batasan seats for Misamis Oriental. They lost to Governor Adaza and IBP Assemblyman Concordio Diel. Ultimately, it was not the Mindanao Alliance's fault that we did not get the DOP accreditation. It was the Comelec's doing.

The Comelec did not stop at denying us DOP status to make it more difficult for me to win. Without providing a valid reason and without giving us notice, shortly before the board convened to canvass the election results, Comelec Manila's Assistant Director of Operations Silvestre Bello, Jr., through Comelec Regional Director Virgilio Garcillano, relieved lawyer Bernardita F. Cabacungan, the City Election Registrar, as chair of the City Board of Canvassers. She was replaced by Comelec Regional Legal Officer Jose B. Amarga. I thought that Cabacungan was a fairly decent Comelec officer, but her superiors apparently believed otherwise. No doubt, she was a victim of Comelec intrigue and machination.

At the canvassing of the results of the election for the city's lone district seat for the Batasan, the KBL representative on the Board of Canvassers raised innumerable objections to the proceedings of the board. Despite these maneuvers, the Board of Canvassers proclaimed me as the winner in Cagayan de Oro on May 16 with 63,784 votes. Roa, the KBL candidate, received 59,102 votes.

Chapter 36

Election Results

Our victories gave the Opposition impressive gains in the more politically significant regions. In the National Capital Region (NCR), we captured 15 out of 21 seats. The importance of the victory of our colleagues in Metro Manila was something that no amount of political spin from the KBL could explain away. The seats of the major government offices were located in Manila, Quezon City and their environs.

In Manila, our candidates Jose Atienza Jr., Carlos Fernandez, Eva Estrada Kalaw, Gemiliano Lopez, Jr., and Gonzalo Puyat II edged out all their KBL opponents, except for Arturo Tolentino, who barely managed to get the sixth and last slot of the city. In Quezon City, Orlando Mercado, Cecilia Muñoz-Palma and Alberto Romulo shut out the KBL bets, but for Ismael Mathay, Jr., who got the fourth and last seat of the city. In Caloocan, Antonio Martinez and Virgilio Robles took the two Batasan seats of the city, and in Pasig and Marikina, Emilio de la Paz, Jr., and Augusto Sanchez blacked out the KBL in the two towns.

The story was the same in the three single-seat constituencies of Las Piñas and Parañaque; Malabon, Navotas and Valenzuela; and San Juan and Mandaluyong, where our candidates Jaime N. Ferrer, Manuel Domingo and Neptali Gonzales respectively bested the KBL candidates.

In Luzon

In Region I, long considered a Marcos bailiwick, three of our candidates made it. Demetrio Demetria and Fabian Sison, bagged two of the six seats of Pangasinan, and our candidate Honorato Aquino captured the lone district seat for the City of Baguio, a major feat.

In Region III, our candidates also did remarkably well. In Pampanga, Rafael Lazatin, Emigdio Lingad and Juanita Nepomuceno got three of the four seats. In Bulacan, Rogaciano Mercado landed one of the four slots of the province.

In Region IV, our candidates, Cesar Bolaños, Bienvenido Marquez Jr., Hjalmar Quintana and Oscar Santos took all four seats of Quezon province in a super rout of the KBL. In Batangas, our candidates Jose B. Laurel, Jr., Hernando Perez and Rafael Recto won three of the four seats. In Rizal, Francisco Sumulong and Emigdio Tanjuatco, Jr. won the two seats of the province, a knockout performance. In Mindoro Oriental, our bet Rolleo Ignacio overcame his KBL rivals for one of the two seats. And our candidates, Natalio Beltran, Jr., and Ramon V. Mitra, Jr., trounced the KBL bets in Romblon and Palawan.

In Region V, the Bicol area, the Opposition also delivered outstanding performances. In Camarines Sur, Ciriaco Alfelor, Rolando Andaya, Edmundo Cea and Luis Villafuerte booted out their KBL rivals to take all four seats of the province. In Albay, our candidates Pedro M. Marcellana, Jr., and Victor Ziga prevailed in two of three seats. In Camarines Norte, our bet Roy Padilla won the single seat of the province. And, in Masbate, our candidate Jolly Fernandez came out ahead in the race for the two provincial seats, besting Venancio Yaneza, one of Marcos's most-trusted lieutenants, who won the other seat.

In the Visayas

In Region VI, the Opposition made some inroads. Our candidate Rafael Legaspi took the lone seat of Aklan. In Iloilo, our candidates Fermin Caram, Jr. and Arthur Defensor got two seats out of five, and in Negros Occidental, our bet Wilson Gamboa topped the race for seven seats, although he was the sole Opposition winner there.

In Region VII, three of our candidates made it in Cebu. Antonio Cuenco and Marcelo Fernan, won the two seats of the prime city of Cebu. In the province of Cebu, our candidate Nenita Cortez-Daluz landed one of the six slots. Their victories were a major blow to the KBL because Cebu City and Cebu Province were deemed Marcos territory — courtesy of Ramon Durano who engineered Cebu's switch from the Osmeñas to Marcos in the 1969 presidential election.

In Mindanao

In Region IX, the Opposition made a spectacular showing. In Zamboanga City, Cesar Climaco bested KBL candidate Maria Clara Lobregat and four others for the lone district seat. His votes totaled more than the combined votes of his five opponents. It was a terrific showing for Climaco because Lobregat was one of the KBL's pillars in the region and was widely known to be a close confidante of Marcos. In Basilan, our candidate Candu Muarip won its lone seat. In Zamboanga del Sur, Isidoro Real, Jr., landed one of three slots for the province.

In Region X, the Opposition did quite well only in our province and the city. In Misamis Oriental, Homobono Adaza won one of two seats. In Cagayan de Oro City, I won the lone district seat.

In Region XI, the Opposition posted one of our best victories. In South Cotabato, our bets, Rufino Bañas, Rogelio Garcia and Hilario de Pedro, prevailed over their KBL rivals. In Davao del Norte, our candidate Rolando Marcial got one of three seats, while in Davao del Sur, our man Douglas Cagas topped the contest for the province's two seats. The other winner was a KBL political icon, former Sen. Alejandro Almendras. And in Davao City, our candidate, Zafiro Respicio, shared the honors with a KBL candidate who got the other seat.

Opposition Blanked in Three Regions

Three regions — II, VIII and XII — however, blanked the Opposition. Region II had 11 seats; Region VIII had 10 seats; and Region XII, composed of the predominantly Moro provinces in mainland Mindanao, 9 seats. Marcos had these 30 Batasan seats of the three regions securely in his pocket. We dismissed the KBL win there as the result of "command votes," instead of an expression of the will of the people, a failure attributable to the Comelec. Had the Comelec neutralized the warlords there, the people's will would have prevailed. Still, we were prepared to tackle in the Batasan the minions of Marcos coming from the three regions or wherever. At the national legislature, we hoped that the Rule of Law would prevail over the Rule of the Gun, which had brought some of our colleagues to its halls.

Boycott Movement's Effect

The Opposition contenders in the May 14 elections had Marcos's KBL candidates as our major opponents. But the Boycott Movement, in general, also took away some support from the Opposition candidates. The Boycott Movement was led by some of the most credible names in the country: former Senators Lorenzo Tañada, Jovito Salonga, Jose Diokno and Raul Manglapus and lawyers Joker Arroyo, Abraham Sarmiento, Haydee Yorac and Rene Saguisag. Former President Diosdado Macapagal was also a known advocate of the Boycott Movement.

In April, a month before the May elections, boycott leaders Tañada, Butz Aquino, Diokno and Manglapus, among others, met in Hong Kong and formed a committee to provide a transition government once Marcos was removed from power.

The impact of the Hong Kong meeting was more symbolic than substantial on the Opposition's struggle against martial rule. It merely showed that the boycott leaders were dead serious in shunning the elections. It also suggested that the boycott leaders felt that the end of the Marcos era was near.

In any case, the Boycott Movement in Cagayan de Oro exempted me from its drive. Senator Tañada maintained that I should be allowed to participate in the elections. He predicted — accurately — that Marcos would never bring me to trial in the rebellion case filed against me in Cebu and only through the election could I prove my innocence.

In Quezon City, Salvador P. Lopez — former Foreign Affairs Secretary, former UP president, professor and journalist — had agreed to run as an Opposition candidate for the Batasan. But a month after announcing his candidacy, he withdrew because he was convinced by the boycott rhetoric. Had he stayed on as a candidate, he would have made it, considering the tremendous showing of the Opposition candidates who won three out of the four seats for Quezon City without him.

'Beyond Our Wildest Imagination'

Unido President Salvador Laurel summed it all up beautifully when he told the *Panorama Sunday Magazine* that the results of the elections were "beyond our wildest imagination."

Sheila S. Coronel wrote a post mortem on the Batasan elections in *Panorama's* May 27, 1984 issue that accurately assessed the reason why many opposition candidates won over their KBL rivals. Our victories were the consequence "not so much of political parties or individuals, but of a courageous and vigilant people," she said. The article pointed out:

> [Metro Manila] residents remained in the polling centers to guard the counting of the ballots. Many stayed on to escort the ballot boxes to the canvassing places. In Mandaluyong, Makati and Pasay [cities in Metro Manila], where cases of ballot box snatching and ballots-switching were reported, people spontaneously massed in protest in front of the municipal halls....In Mandaluyong and Makati...citizens held torches aloft, keeping vigil.

The Smoking Gun

The description of a vigilant and courageous people spelling victory for their candidates also applied to, among many localities, Batangas, Quezon City, Quezon Province, Cebu City and Cagayan de Oro. In my city, for instance, the people not only stood ready to pounce on any would-be manipulator of the votes during the counting, but they also put a round-the-clock security cordon around the storeroom of the city treasurer where the ballot boxes along with their contents were deposited after the count was done. In addition, and this irked the Comelec, the people put a live electric wire at the door of the storeroom to prevent unwarranted access to the ballot boxes. Guarding the votes even against the Comelec was warranted because of the notoriety of Comelec officials and personnel in terms of corruption, inefficiency or plain bias.

As an example of one such Comelec deficiency in ensuring the integrity of the election process, Vicente Gerochi, Jr., then the manager of Election and Barangay Affairs Department of the Comelec, sent a telegram to the Provincial Election Supervisor of Naga City on May 8, 1984. The telegram said.

> In view error committed in allocation of official ballots for municipalities of Camaligan and Goa, you are hereby directed to instruct Provincial Treasurer to hold excess ballots of 81,000 for Camaligan and 96,000 for Goa. In the event the distribution [of] the official ballots already effected by Provincial Treasurer to direct the municipal treasurer to return immediately the stated excess ballots to office of Provincial Treasurer. Report to Election and Barangay Affairs Dept your compliance herewith. End.

If there was a smoking gun that showed the Comelec's laxity in the observance of rudimentary procedures to prevent misuse of ballots, this was it. Time and again, as politicians, many of us in the Opposition verbalized our concern that excess ballots were sent to places where these would be used to pad the votes of the candidates backed by the administration. But, more often than not, we were not able to produce solid evidence of such wrongdoing. Gerochi's telegram, a copy of which wound up in my possession, validated those complaints.

The Gerochi action was made possible only because Comelec Commissioner Ramon Felipe, Jr. supported him. With Felipe supporting him, Gerochi was emboldened to do what he did to help cleanse the electoral process, at least in the home region of Felipe.

In addition to the people's vigilance, legitimate issues, too, carried the day for the Opposition candidates. During the campaign, we capitalized on the still unresolved murder of Aquino and the worsening economic situation.

Roa's Petitions

In the two days following the elections, Roa filed three petitions with the Comelec, initially to prohibit the City Board of Canvassers from proclaiming me the winner and, later, to annul such proclamation. Surprisingly, all three petitions suffered from a basic defect: the petitions did not include me as a party to the proceedings.

On May 19, 1984, Roa filed a fourth petition to "declare *void ab initio* [the] Proclamation of 'Nene Pimentel.'" This time, I was already included as a party respondent. By Divine Providence, however, the fourth petition, sent by registered mail, was not received by the Comelec Office in Intramuros, Manila. These egregious blunders by Roa's counsel added to their problems when the matter reached the Supreme Court.

In the Roa effort to dislodge me from the Batasan, I was not given a chance to respond by the Comelec. One reason was that I was not "impleaded" in the cases filed against me with the Second Division of the Comelec. That was why, on May 22, when the Second Division of the Comelec set the pre-proclamation case against me, I had no lawyer to represent me at the Comelec office.

By sheer serendipity, Raul Gonzalez, a friend, was in the Comelec office at the time for a client and, when he learned that the Comelec was hearing a case against me in my absence, he entered *pro tanto*, for the time being, his appearance as my lawyer. Had Gonzalez not done so, the Comelec could have fast tracked my ouster from the Batasan. Gonzalez's appearance compelled the Comelec Division to notify me formally of the proceedings.

On May 30, my lawyer, Joker Arroyo, filed a motion to dismiss Roa's case against me on the ground that I had not been impleaded formally as a party. It took the Second Division 20 days to act on the issue. In its June 20 decision, the division did not dismiss the cases. Instead, among other things, it ordered City Board of Canvassers Chairman Jose Amarga, Jr. to bring the contested election documents to Manila.

Massacres Denounced

Meanwhile, even as my election to the Batasan hung in the balance, I continued to hit the Marcos administration whenever the occasion arose. It was my way of keeping alive the more fundamental struggle for the freedom of our people and for the early termination of the martial law regime. It helped that my statements were considered fit for the front pages of national newspapers.

On June 3, 1984, the *Bulletin Today* featured my denunciations of the slow probe of the Sibalom, Antique, ambuscade that resulted in the killing of some followers of our opposition leader, Evelio Javier. The newspaper also printed on June 4, my condemnation of the continuing "salvaging" of noncombatants by some soldiers. On June 8, Eggy Apostol's *Mr&Ms* magazine published my call for justice in the Bucag family's massacre in Gingoog City.

Those months were filled with sadness for me because, apart from the killing of the Bucags, I also learned that my friend and Constitutional Convention colleague Ernie Rondon, who had escaped to the US, died of a heart attack on June 7 in San Francisco, California. He left behind his widow Thelma and three young daughters.

Lawyers Respond to Comelec

On June 26, my lawyers told the Comelec Second Division that the 53 election returns questioned by Roa were not enough to change the results of the elections. They said that, even if Roa succeeded in nullifying the votes in the questioned 53 election returns, I would still come out the winner. They, however, failed to move the Second Division to act in our favor.

After numerous preliminary legal skirmishes between Roa's lawyers and mine, the Second Division reiterated on July 10 its ruling that Amarga should bring the contested election documents to Manila. We resisted the order because we did not trust the Comelec and also because we believed that only the Comelec en banc, not a division, had the authority to decide controversies involving members of the Batasan. Subsequently, the division denied our move for it to reconsider its ruling. As a result, I brought the matter to the Supreme Court for resolution on July 30.

Notwithstanding the innumerable maneuvers of my political opponents, I managed to make it to the Batasan as the representative of Cagayan de Oro when the Batasan began its sessions on July 23, 1984.

Batasan Opening Day

The Batasan opened its session on July 23, 1984. At 5:30 that morning, I was already awake and I prepared to go to the Batasan from our house in Marikina. Bing was in Cagayan de Oro supervising the shipment of our belongings to Marikina. Since neither she nor any of our children could go with me, my mother-in-law, Remedios de la Llana, and my brother-in-law, Judge Himerio B. Garcia, accompanied me to the opening ceremonies.

PDP Demonstrators

At the junction of the highway and the road leading to the Batasan, we saw a small band of demonstrators composed of PDP-Laban supporters, members of the National Organization of Women (NOW), the Association of Women for Action and Reforms (Aware), and the Alliance of Multi-sectoral Associations (AMA). Led by lawyer Jose Lina, a PDP-Laban activist, they tried to accompany their favorite assemblymen to the Batasan but were barred by helmeted and truncheon-wielding troopers who were backed by fire trucks and armed men lolling under whatever shade was available to avoid the morning sun. To make use of their time "productively," the demonstrators shouted anti-US/Marcos slogans and invectives against the military in general.

We arrived at the Batasan at 9:30 a.m, with 30 minutes to spare before the formal opening of its first session. As I was about to enter the Batasan lobby, a security guard wanted to frisk me. I noticed he did not frisk the others who preceded me. So I told him he had no right to frisk me not because I had any concealed weapon in my body but because, as a member of the Batasan, I considered it our home and no guard under our employ had the right to subject me to any body search. He relented and that ended what could have been a more unpleasant episode.

In the cavernous hall of the Batasan, the first sight that greeted me was this enormous flag attached to the wall behind the Speaker's rostrum. It was so big, I thought, to save on flags, it could very well be used to drape all the coffins of the KBL members of the Batasan should they die together in one fell swoop. According to architect Cesar Guevarra, the flag measured 6 x 11 meters.

'Rightists' and 'Leftists'

For the first session, there was no prearranged seating for us. The only rule was the KBL members were to be seated to the right of the Speaker's rostrum and the Opposition to the left. Inevitably, we joked that the KBL members were the "rightists" and we in the Opposition the "leftists" in the national legislature. Some of us from Mindanao, like Zafiro Respicio, Douglas Cagas and I, were used to being tagged as "leftists" by Marcos and his military. They had, through the years of martial law, pictured us a communists, which we certainly were not. We were, at most, left of center.

Neither could other members of the Opposition be considered leftists. Not Jose B. Laurel, Jr., of Batangas; Eva Estrada Kalaw and Gonzalo Puyat II of Manila; Neptali Gonzales of San Juan and Mandaluyong, Metro Manila; Marcelo Fernan of Cebu City; and Ramon Mitra, Jr., of Palawan. The only one among us who might have enjoyed being labeled a "leftist" was Rogaciano Mercado of Bulacan. Mercado, in his youth, was a founding member of the pre-martial rule Movement for the Advancement of Nationalism (MAN), which was subsequently outlawed by the government.

The Agenda

The main items on the agenda were the election of the Speaker of the Batasan in the morning and the "State of the Nation Address" by Marcos in the afternoon.

Antonio de Guzman, the Secretary General of the House, acted as the temporary presiding officer. After the roll call, I rose to ask why our colleague, Assemblyman Cesar Climaco's name was not called. De Guzman explained that "Climaco had not taken the oath required of incoming assemblymen." He had chosen to stay on as mayor of Zamboanga City, although he had won the Batasan elections in his city.

Yñiguez Nominated by KBL

In the morning session, we elected the officials of the Batasan. The KBL majority had Foreign Minister Arturo Tolentino, Fernando Veloso, Winceslao Lagumbay and Ali Dimaporo nominate Assemblyman Nicanor Yñiguez of Southern Leyte for Speaker of the House.

Tolentino perfunctorily nominated Yñiguez. He merely chronicled the long career path Yñiguez had carved in public service. Yñiguez, Tolentino said, had the best qualities to "guide the deliberations of the Chamber" in a manner that would prevent "pent-up emotions of the members of the Batasan from rising up to dangerous levels." Veloso and Lagumbay largely echoed Tolentino's appraisal of Yñiguez's humane guiding hand that he would show as Speaker. Dimaporo, on the other hand, emphasized Yñiguez's sympathy for the aspirations of Mindanao.

Laurel Nominated by Opposition

The Opposition chose Eva Estrada Kalaw, Homobono Adaza and me to nominate Assemblyman Jose B. Laurel, Jr., as our candidate for Speaker. We did not have the numbers to elect Laurel. Nonetheless, parliamentary practice in the country demanded that we put up our candidate to challenge the majority's candidate. By tradition, the reward for making the hopeless challenge was that the challenger would automatically become the Minority Leader.

Without intending it, Kalaw provided a funny respite from the tedium of listening to the boring nominating speeches. She failed to mention the name of Laurel as our candidate in her three-paragraph nominating speech and had to take the floor again to rectify the omission. Everybody had a good laugh at the *faux fax*. But she was boisterously applauded when she said, "I took for granted the Honorable Jose 'Pepito' B. Laurel Jr., distinguished son of a distinguished father and a distinguished family, was the nominee of the Opposition for Speaker of this House."

After Kalaw, it was my turn to nominate Laurel. I underscored his well-known quality as a man of courage, who spoke his mind regardless of the consequences. I hammered on that theme because the Interim Batasang Pambansa, the immediate predecessor of our Batasan, had the ill repute of being an expensive rubber stamp of Marcos. I, therefore, emphasized, "If there is anything that this Batasan will suffer from unless we corrected the defect immediately, it is the fact that some people would think that we will continue to be a rubber stamp of somebody out there."

Judging from the warm applause from the ranks of the Batasan members and the audience in the gallery, the theme seemed to have resonated well. Another round of applause greeted my assertion that:

> If the Batasan wants to be relevant in our struggle for the liberation of our people from economic bondage, from all kinds of repression, it is necessary that we must have a man who is able to stand up and say so without fear of pressure from anyone. This person happens to be Speaker Pepito Laurel.

In his nominating speech for Laurel, Adaza waxed poetic. He paid tribute to Laurel as a person who could not be bought and who would stand up for the sake of truth and honor even if he would have to suffer long and fast for it.

Caucus of Independents' Nominee

Our claim to being *the* Opposition group in the Batasan was contested by a third bloc. We did not take kindly to them. We thought that they were like the bats in the mythical battle between the birds and the beasts at the dawn of history. The bats preferred to hang upside down on tree branches, waiting for signs which side victory would favor before they took a stand.

Members of this bloc were loud in their protestations that they were neither KBL (at least in their self-appraisal) nor Opposition. They called themselves the

"Caucus of Independents." This bloc also contended for the Speakership. In fairness, they had some good people in their bloc.

Edelmiro Amante of Agusan del Norte, Romeo Jalosjos of Zamboanga del Norte and Enrique Belo of Capiz went through the motions of nominating their candidate for Speaker, Assemblyman Rafael Palmares of Iloilo. They said that the Palmares's chief virtue was that he would be an instrument of reconciliation.

Yñiguez Becomes Speaker

It was a foregone conclusion that the KBL nominee, Yñiguez, would be the choice of the overwhelming majority. The results validated the assessment: Yñiguez received 111 votes; Laurel, 56; and Palmares, 8. There were three who did not vote: Roberto Ongpin, Leonardo Perez and Yñiguez.

Yñiguez was thought to be the unanimous choice of the KBL members. He was not. The main thing going for him was that he was Marcos's choice. They were classmates in law school. And, as a native of Leyte, he was a province-mate of Imelda and perceived to be her close confidant.

Unknown to the public at large, Rodolfo Albano, a KBL assemblyman from Isabela, had actively sought his party mates' support for his own bid to become Speaker. Albano relied on what he saw was his plus factor: his Ilocano regional roots that were like Marcos's and negatively on the fact that, if Yñiguez were elected Speaker, then the two top posts in the Batasan would come from the same region, Samar-Leyte, because Jose Roño, Minister of Local Governments, was already being touted as the Batasan Majority Leader.

Albano's supporters from the Ilocos provinces and the Cagayan Valley issued press releases proclaiming his virtues, which, they said, made him fit for the position of Speaker. But that was as far as they went. As pragmatic politicians, they saw that Yñiguez's election as Speaker by the KBL majority was already a done deal. In the end, Albano withdrew his bid for the Speakership and settled for the post of Assistant Majority Leader.

In his brief acceptance speech, Yñiguez predicted that the Batasan "will be remembered as a dynamic and achieving parliament." It was not going to be so. The continued concentration of power in the hands of Marcos, I think, contributed to the paucity of achievement of the Batasan. Most KBL members could not, on their own, propose bills and get them calendared, debated and approved without getting the clearance and support of Marcos. The Coalesced Opposition, however, showed by words and deeds in the Batasan that we were prepared to stand up for the national interest.

Laurel Is Minority Leader

Having received the next highest number of votes for the Speakership, Jose Laurel became, by parliamentary practice, the Minority Leader. Along with Edmundo Cea of Camarines Sur and Neptali Gonzales of Mandaluyong and San Juan, Metro Manila, I was chosen as one of three Assistant Minority Leaders.

Playing a supporting role to Pepito Laurel was all right by me. He was not only a seasoned political leader. He was also a veteran lawmaker, having held the highest position of leadership in the House of Representatives for some time before martial law was proclaimed. As a Laurel, his name was a byword in the country. He enjoyed the support of the non-Marcos members of the Batasang Pambansa.

Laurel Deputizes Me

Laurel trusted me enough to authorize me in writing to be his representative in seven rather important committees of the Batasan. Under that arrangement, I represented him in the Committees of National Security, Revision of Laws, Public Works, Justice, Labor, Local Government, and Muslim Affairs. Considering that we were operating under martial law circumstances, individually, the committees acquired tremendous relevance to the duties we were discharging.

The Committee on National Security had jurisdiction over matters affecting the security of the State. If Marcos and his military had their way, everything was invested with matters involving national security. Thus, the presence of the Opposition in the discussion of bills, resolutions or privilege speeches referred to it tended to inhibit the KBL members from doing as they pleased.

The Committee on Revision of Laws covered bills amending or repealing decrees or orders of Marcos. On top of those offending decrees or orders, there was Amendment No. 6 of the martial law Constitution, which we in the Opposition all wanted to repeal. Without the Opposition in the committee, amending or repealing those enactments would not even be considered.

The Committee on Justice mainly had to do with matters affecting law enforcement and the rights of people, and how the courts arbitrated conflicts among litigants or between the government and the people. Increasingly, the people were now demanding the right to peaceably assemble for the redress of their grievances. Without Opposition representation in the committee, nobody would speak out for those concerns.

The Committee on Labor dealt with labor problems and these were legion, considering the nebulous relationship between labor and capital that under martial rule was increasingly becoming mostly multinational. Labor organizations were straining against the leash of martial rule restrictions and demanded more leeway to organize freely so that they could bargain more effectively with companies for better working conditions and better pay. Again, without the Opposition in the committee, there would be less opportunity for the demands of free labor to be ventilated there.

The Committee on Local Government, by its very name, took cognizance of matters involving provinces, cities, municipalities and the barangay. What we in the Opposition were concerned with was to prevent their being used as instruments of martial rule to further the enslavement of our people. At the same time, we also wanted the local government units to have more powers to enable them to be devices of development.

While last in the list of the committees that Laurel wanted me to oversee in his behalf, the Committee on Muslim Affairs was most relevant to the life of the nation under the circumstances. It was the Moros of Mindanao who mounted the most credible, though violent, resistance to the martial law regime. The Moros were represented in the Batasan, but they needed the help of non-Moro members to air their grievances more credibly in the Batasan. Since the Moro rebellion was still going on, the necessity of proposing initiatives for peace in Mindanao acquired critical importance. It was in that light that I asked Laurel for the privilege of representing him in the committee.

In addition to these committees, I was also a member of the Rules Committee, an important one, because it prioritized the bills or resolutions to be discussed on the floor.

As an Assistant Minority Leader, it was part of my work to get our colleagues in the Opposition assigned to committees of their choices. That entailed a lot of time and effort as we had to haggle even with our own members to accept our recommendees to the committees when their choices collided with the majority's. As an Assistant Minority Leader, I learned, among other things, that even the sequence of listing our nominees to the committees mattered.

Those whose names were first in the list of recommendees had seniority in the committees. Hence, upon the request of our members, time and again, we had to change the sequence of the names of our Opposition nominees to the committees. It was also a part of my duties to spot and assign the best among our Opposition colleagues to interpellate the sponsors of the national appropriations act then under consideration. And, whenever a member of our group wished to speak on any matter, I had to request the Speaker to recognize him or her.

More than anything else, as an Assistant Minority Leader, I learned the importance of patience in dealing with our colleagues, particularly those of the Opposition. Most of the Batasan oppositionists were not the pliant type. They needed to be convinced of the reasonableness of a proposition before they would support it. Thus, even if at times they tended to be somewhat overbearing or unreasonable, those of us who were their chosen leaders had to use tactful ways of dealing with their concerns as these arose.

Other Officials

After the election of the Speaker, the assembly elected without any Opposition the following officials: Salipada Pendatun of Maguindanao as Speaker Pro-Tempore; Antonio de Guzman, Secretary General; and Cesar Pobre, Sergeant-at-Arms.

Pendatun was a good choice for Speaker Pro-Tempore. He was a former congressman of Maguindanao and senator of the nation. A former guerilla leader during the Japanese war, he was respected by the people of Mindanao. In my view, were it not for the general bias of Christians against Muslims, Pendatun could have been elected Speaker of the Batasan.

De Guzman was a clear favorite among members of the Batasan who crossed party lines to unanimously elect him Secretary General. Days before the sessions begun, he went out of his way to befriend all members of the Batasan. He thus projected the image of a professional official who would do the job of Secretary General without partisan bias. Although he was closely identified with Marcos in the Constitutional Convention during which he represented La Union, de Guzman succeeded in minimizing the stigma of being a *tuta* of Marcos. I even saw him kiss the hand of the leader of the Batasan Opposition, former Speaker Jose Laurel. The act sent a message to all of us that de Guzman would be every Batasan member's Secretary General. To his credit, he lived up to the billing well enough, considering the circumstances.

Welcoming Committee for Marcos

Since Marcos was scheduled to deliver his "State of the Nation Address" to the Batasan that afternoon, the Speaker, in line with parliamentary practice, appointed a committee of seven members to formally inform Marcos that, at 5 p.m., the Batasan would be ready to hear his address. The appointments to the committee were more or less a pro forma act.

A hitch developed, however, when Opposition Assemblyman Antonio Cuenco, PDP-Laban, of Cebu City, rejected his appointment. In a barbed statement that earned a round of applause from our colleagues and the audience in the gallery, Cuenco declined his designation as a member of the welcoming committee. He told Yñiguez:

> [While I am] honored to be appointed as a member of the committee to inform the President...I beg to be excused, Mr. Speaker. I have another engagement this afternoon, which is more important.

That was how the Batasan recorded what he said. Cuenco had a slightly different recollection. He told me that what he said was that he had "more important things to do" than escort Marcos to the session hall.

In any case, that was the first time the Speaker heard any member of the legislature refuse in such pointed terms his appointment to the Batasan welcoming committee for the President. The welcoming committee was one of those archaic parliamentary devices handed down by custom from the country's legislatures of old to the Batasan.

Cuenco probably did not realize it then that his refusal had serious implications in that he had, in fact, thrown down the gauntlet for Marcos and his cohorts to pick up. In effect, he told Marcos and the KBL, "From now on, we won't pander anymore to your wishes because we have more important things to do."

The "more important things" that we in the Opposition had to do referred to our collective desire to end the Marcos one-man rule. Specifically, as members of the Batasan, we were determined to repeal the repressive decrees of Marcos and work to restore the Rule of Law, uphold human rights and redeem the basic liberties of our people from the clutches of martial rule.

In the event, the Speaker replaced Cuenco with another legislator. Thereafter, the session was suspended until 5 p.m. when Marcos would deliver his State of the Nation address. I was not there when Marcos arrived because I chose to join the demonstrations at the Liwasang Bonifacio in Manila.

Marcos's Address

I read from the record of the Batasan that after the short welcome ceremonies, the Speaker introduced Marcos with the standard one-liner, "Ladies and Gentlemen, His Excellency, the President of the Republic of the Philippines, Ferdinand E. Marcos."

Marcos spoke for roughly 55 minutes. He talked of an alleged economic turnaround and the stability of the nation. The Coalesced Opposition received his misplaced optimism with skepticism. Surprisingly, administration partisans responded with only lukewarm applause. The loudest applause he received was when the Speaker introduced him. Thereafter, no applause punctuated his speech until the last six minutes when he extemporized on his desire to consult the Batasan on the use of his powers under Amendment 6 of the Constitution and when he made his call for sobriety on the part of members of the Opposition.

Parliamentary practice did not allow Batasan members to interpellate Marcos, but we in the Coalesced Opposition would not be denied our assessment of Marcos's speech. As reported by *Veritas* magazine, Ramon Mitra, Jr., dismissed the speech by summarizing the true state of the nation in four sentences:

> It is in a mess. It is bankrupt. It is in fear of secret marshals. Its leaders have lost credibility and can no longer govern.

Orlando Mercado said of Marcos's speech, "I cried twice today. The first time at Liwasang Bonifacio where I was teargassed, and the second when I heard the President's speech. It was very sad."

In my case, I told the media that I joined the demonstration at Liwasang Bonifacio on the afternoon when Marcos spoke at the Batasan. I said that, in the morning ceremonies, I saw the military and police preventing people from coming near the Batasan. "The Batasan is supposed to be the lawmaking body of the people. If they are not allowed to watch the proceedings, how can the Batasan be relevant to the aspirations of the people?" I asked.

Incidentally, we now formally called ourselves the Coalesced Opposition because our members came from many parties and wore different political stripes.

Chapter 38

Electing the Prime Minister

On July 30, 1984, KBL Majority Floor Leader Jose Roño moved for the election of Cesar Virata as Prime Minister. The KBL majority in the Batasan thought that the nomination of Virata would be followed as a matter of course by his election as Prime Minister. They did not want any prolonged debate on Virata's qualifications for the post. In so many words, they said that it was the prerogative of the KBL to choose whomever they wanted to be the Prime Minister. The pseudo-Opposition group of Palmares supported the KBL position.

The Coalesced Opposition did not see it that way. We believed that the qualifications of Virata and his plans for the nation had to be disclosed and debated on the floor of the Batasan in furtherance of the right of the people to know. And we demanded the right to be heard on the matter.

Luis Villafuerte and Edmundo Cea took the lead in denouncing the KBL maneuver. They argued that, if the Batasan as a whole had to vote for the Prime Minister, it stood to reason that the nominee's qualifications should be discussed before the voting. The Speaker, however, upon the urging of Leonardo Perez and Rodolfo Albano, ruled that the objections of the Opposition were out of order and he instructed the Secretary General to proceed with the roll-call vote.

Following Villafuerte's and Cea's line, Neptali Gonzales, Homobono Adaza, Ramon Mitra, Jr., and I repeatedly asked for recognition from the Speaker to allow us to define our position on the ruling of the chair that the election of the Prime Minister was not debatable. The session became rather rowdy because the crowd in the gallery often manifested their support for the stand of the Opposition by applauding us and booing the KBL lawmakers.

The Mace Is Used

It came to a point when, for the first time in the session of the Batasan, the Speaker ordered the Sergeant-at-Arms to bring the Mace of the Batasan before some of us members of the Opposition to restore order. In the olden days, the mace, a weapon with a heavy head on a solid shaft, was used to bludgeon opponents. The mace survived as a symbol of authority in legislative bodies and was used as such to symbolically bludgeon unruly members to behave properly.

Six of us — Cea, Villafuerte, Gonzales, Adaza, Mitra and I — refused to simply stand down at the Speaker's order. But the Batasan record showed that only two members were confronted with the Mace: "The Sergeant-at-Arms went down from the rostrum carrying the Mace, and placed it first in front of the Honorable Pimentel and the Honorable Adaza." The *Bulletin Today*, however, reported the following day that it was not us but Cea whom the Speaker disciplined with the use of the Mace.

Hard-line Against Virata

In any event, it was not our confrontation with the Mace that deterred us from further questioning Virata's qualifications. Rather, it was the sense of the futility of further raising our objections because our colleagues had started to explain their votes on the issue.

The Speaker's use of the Mace to restore order drew a withering comment from Jose Laurel, Jr., the Minority Leader. Laurel, however, did not condemn the arbitrary use of the Mace immediately. He did so shortly after Virata was voted Prime Minister, but before Virata took his oath. Laurel, a three-term Speaker of the House of Representatives, recounted that he had "never used the [earthy Tagalog expletive deleted] Mace to silence any member of Congress." He received a loud ovation from the Batasan Opposition and from the gallery.

Mitra seconded Laurel's observation. Mitra, a former congressman and senator, said he was "saddened...that the Mace had to be brought down to quell the Opposition who wanted merely to be heard on the question (of Virata's nomination as Prime Minister)."

While the KBL majority successfully prevented us from debating the merits of Virata's nomination prior to the vote, they could not stop us from explaining why we were voting against it. Giving vent to our pent-up emotions, we literally threw the book at Virata when we aired our objections to his nomination.

The first oppositionist to vote "No" to Virata was Douglas Cagas, PDP-Laban, of Davao. He told the Batasan that Virata did not deserve his vote because "he has not been true and faithful to his oath of office." The statement was greeted by a wild burst of applause from the gallery that so offended the Speaker that he threatened to expel the unruly audience from the halls of the Batasan. Thereafter, Cagas proceeded to castigate Virata for being "an active collaborator in the desecration...of the Constitution." In a blistering finale to his condemnation of Virata, Cagas said:

> Finally, Mr. Speaker, instead of consecrating himself to the service of the nation, he has consecrated himself to the service of one man in Malacañang, and of the IMF and other foreign masters.

Tony Cuenco, PDP-Laban, of Cebu City, followed the line of Cagas when he explained why he would not vote for Virata. He said:

> The decision to pervert the borrowing policies into the biggest swindle of public funds in the history of the nation can only be laid at the doors of his leadership. Virata and the technocrats of the government lent their credentials,

their international connections, and prestige to deodorize this crude and corrupt regime.

Nenita Cortez-Daluz, PDP-Laban, of Cebu Province, hit Virata for allowing himself to be a "tool of the multinationals whose interests are definitely anti-people." Virata's economic policies, she said, "have plunged our country into its worst economic crisis....Our country needs a prime minister who really is for the welfare of the people and who can say 'No' even to a tyrant."

Some members of our group wanted to be more diplomatic and they expressed their "No" votes to Virata by citing his "economic policies (as) causing more problems to the nation."

Speaking in Tagalog, Manuel Domingo voted against Virata because our country was in dire straits and our people were without adequate sources of livelihood. Virata, he said, "had not explained the reasons for the problems of the nation." He said he feared that, if Virata were given the chance to be Prime Minister, our country would suffer even more.

Marcelo Fernan also voted against Virata because as "a technocrat," he brought "our nation to the brink of economic disaster. "

Jaime Ferrer, PDP-Laban, of Las Piñas-Parañaque, said:

> It is not enough [for] a public official [to] have ability and integrity. More important than that is for a public official to have the moral courage to fight for his conviction and to resign from his position if necessary.

Ferrer's comment was an allusion to Virata's inability to say "No" to Marcos.

Although he tried to be circumspect in explaining his vote against Virata, Neptali Gonzales compared him with Friederich Eichman, Hitler's man-Friday. Like Eichman, Gonzales said, Virata was "nothing but an efficient bureaucrat" who had a moral choice, but chose to be "a participant in the formulation and implementation of the economic policies that led our country to disaster and ruin."

Cecilia Muñoz-Palma said she could not vote for Virata because she did not want to be a party "to the perpetuation of the political and economic crises and disaster now facing our country and the perpetuation of (Marcos's) one-man rule."

Zafiro Respicio, PDP-Laban, of Davao City, in voting "No" to Virata's nomination, accused him of "subservience to the World Bank and the IMF" and of being unable to "stand up against the dictatorship and who has shown his blind obedience to President Marcos."

Francisco Sumulong and Emigdio Tanjuatco, Jr., both PDP-Laban of Rizal echoed the contention that Virata blindly followed Marcos. Tanjuatco also faulted Virata for his "inability to stop the indiscriminate and unabated dispersal and teargassing of peaceful demonstrations."

In my case, I voted against Virata because I found him guilty of malfeasance and misfeasance "as an active co-conspirator in the overborrowing of funds from the World Bank and the IMF which led to greater hardships among our people."

The accusations against Virata were as varied as they were bitter. In a brief statement that he made on the floor after the debates on his qualifications for the position of Prime Minister, Virata let out that the accusation that he was a traitor to the country hurt him the most. Efren Danao of *Veritas* (August 5-11, 1984) quoted him as saying, "Many things had been said here tonight, but the most serious and most painful was that I have been disloyal to the Republic and the people."

Chapter 39:

Opposition Resolutions

I n our regular sessions, we filed resolutions that flew directly in the face of the martial law regime. Resolution No. 1 was Mitra's brainchild. Mitra asked the Batasan to express its sense (which was too much to expect) that the International Monetary Fund's approval of the application of the government for a standby credit loan of $600 million should be conditioned on the removal and replacement of all the current economic and monetary planners and managers. It was Mitra's way of telling Marcos and the IMF that Central Bank Gov. Jose Fernandez and Finance Minister Roberto Ongpin, among others, should be removed from office as the people did not see them doing anything good for the nation.

1984: *SPEAKER NICANOR YÑIGUEZ (leftmost) with some members of the Opposition in the Batasan. (Left to right): Luis Villafuerte, Francisco Sumulong, me, Natalio Beltran, Jr., and Arthur Defensor.*

In Resolution No. 2, five of us, Luis Villafuerte, Antonio Cuenco, Homobono Adaza, Hjalmar Quintana and I, demanded that the Prime Minister should explain the causes of the economic crisis besetting the country and offer solutions to it. We wanted the martial law administration to come up with details as to why the country was suffering from its clutches.

Repeal Amendment No. 6

Along with 37 of our colleagues, I signed Alberto Romulo's initiative entitled Resolution No. 4 to cause the repeal of Amendment No. 6. The other signatories were: Ciriaco Alfelor, Jose Atienza, Jr., Natalio Beltran, Jr., Rufino Bañas, Douglas Cagas, Fermin Caram, Jr., Antonio Cuenco, Nenita Cortez-Daluz, Manuel Domingo, Carlos Fernandez, Jolly Fernandez, Jaime Ferrer, Wilson Gamboa, Rogelio Garcia, Rolleo Ignacio, Eva Estrada Kalaw, Rafael Lazatin, Honorato Aquino, Rafael Legaspi, Gemiliano Lopez, Jr., Rolando Marcial, Bienvenido Marquez, Jr., Antonio Martinez, Homobono Adaza, Orlando Mercado, Ramon Mitra, Jr., Roy Padilla, Cesar Bolaños, Candu Muarip, Demetrio Demetria, Juanita Nepomuceno, Hjalmar Quintana, Hilario de Pedro, Rafael Recto, Zafiro Respicio and Virgilio Robles.

A select group of PDP-Laban members followed up the intent of Resolution No. 4 by filing Resolution No. 8 that also called for the repeal of Amendment No. 6. Emigdio Tanjuatco, Jr., Rogelio Garcia, Douglas Cagas, Zafiro Respicio, Emigdio Lingad, Augusto Sanchez, Jaime Ferrer, Nenita Cortez-Daluz, Antonio Cuenco and I authored the resolution. We likewise supported Resolution No. 23 authored by Isidoro Real, Jr., and Parliamentary Bill No. 237 initiated by Cecilia Muñoz-Palma which also demanded the repeal of Amendment No. 6.

Impeachment Rules

One of the things that we in the Coalesced Opposition wanted was the re-institution of the power of the legislature to impeach Marcos and other impeachable officials like the Comelec commissioners. But we noticed early on in the discussion of the proposed rules to govern the impeachment process in the Committee on Justice, Human Rights and Good Governance that the KBL majority wanted to make it difficult for anyone to start impeachment proceedings. During discussions at the committee level, we made our stand clear that we could not go along with the intent of the majority.

On August 7, the KBL majority in the Committee on Justice, Human Rights and Good Government, headed by Solicitor General Estelito Mendoza, a minister in Marcos's cabinet, submitted Committee Report No. 1, the proposed rules to govern impeachment proceedings. Seven of us Coalesced Opposition members of the committee, Muñoz-Palma, Orlando Mercado, Fernan, Caram Jr., Hernando Perez, Cuenco and I dissented from the report. We were joined by Rustico de los Reyes, Jr., of the Caucus of Independents. The committee split along party lines: 10 KBL members in

1984: *AT THE BATASAN, I explain why Amendment No. 6 should be repealed as Hjalmar Quintana (right) listens.*

favor, 7 Coalesced Opposition and one Caucus of Independents members against.

When we debated Mendoza's report on the floor of the Batasan on August 15, Atienza moved to send the report back to the committee for further consideration. While the motion was in accord with parliamentary rules, it had rarely been invoked because, culturally, among our highly sensitive people, a motion of that kind could be construed as a slap on the face for the chair and the majority members of his committee.

Anyway, several members of the Coalesced Opposition took turns in lambasting the committee report. Some like Romulo and Muñoz-Palma anchored their arguments on the failure of the committee to uphold the constitutional requirements for the initiation of impeachment proceedings.

Marcos Defender

I supported the Atienza motion and, in a direct reference to Estelito Mendoza, I said that he was suffering from a "crisis of identity." The rules, as proposed by Mendoza, I explained, were intended more "to interdict" than to facilitate the right of the people to impeach the President. That was surprising because the *Interim Batasang Pambansa*, the predecessor of our supposedly regular Batasan, adopted impeachment rules that were more "forthright in the recognition and protection of the right of the people to file impeachment complaints" than those proposed by

Mendoza.

I added that, in diluting the right of the people to file impeachment cases in the very rules under discussion, Mendoza was "playing the role of Solicitor General, the lawyer of the President and the defender of the actuations of impeachable officials, instead of being a member of the Batasan, whose primary loyalty is to the people and not to one man or to a group of men holding the reins of power today."

Mendoza's Belated Response

There were other adverse comments from our group on the proposed impeachment rules. Mendoza appeared to take them all with grace. Fifteen days later, however, he stood up on the floor after the debates on *his* proposed rules were over to reply belatedly to my comments. Some people must have told him that, unless rebutted on the floor, my remarks, which pictured him as a "microphone" of Marcos, would be taken as true.

Thus, he rose on a question of personal privilege. He said my remarks were "most unkind, grossly unfounded and...grievously offend that which is priceless to every man — honor." To some extent, he was right when he said that my description of him was "most unkind" because it was meant to draw blood, at least figuratively. But for him to describe what I said of his proposed rules as "grossly unfounded" was misplaced. In that respect, my comment was based on fact that only the blind followers of Marcos could not see.

Mendoza also said it was "sad when a member of the Batasan denied to a colleague the fidelity to the Constitution and the loyalty to the Republic and our people, which I am certain motivates every member of the Assembly...." That statement betrayed what disturbed Mendoza the most. He was clearly upset by my charge that he suffered "from a crisis of identity" in proposing the rules of impeachment, which looked to me as if they were intended more to protect the President than to provide for ways to make him accountable to the people. He said that, while it was true that he was the Solicitor General, the Minister of Justice, and a member of the Batasan, he was faithful to the country's "Constitution and its laws." Mendoza insisted that every member of the Batasan was presumed to be a loyal Filipino who acted in good faith in the discharge of his duties.

Interpellating Mendoza, I said that to presume that every one acted as "a loyal Filipino" was misplaced. Under the circumstances, I said:

> The motivations of everyone in this Assembly are open to question. The country is in difficult straits and, if we always presumed good faith on the part of everyone, it would be hard to say whether the country is being run for good or ill.

I criticized his committee report as being "tilted against the right of the citizen and the right of the people to file impeachment proceedings against those who may have violated the Constitution."

Mendoza replied that Marcos did not need any protection from anyone from the dangers of impeachment. On that point and, at the time he made it, he was absolutely right. Marcos was so powerful that the idea that he could be successfully impeached never crossed our collective minds even as members of the Opposition. Months later, however, the Opposition did try to impeach Marcos. But, during our discussion, Mendoza claimed that the rules covered other impeachable officers like those of the Supreme Court, the Comelec and the Commission on Audit.

When I insisted that a reading of the rules led to no other conclusion but that they were also "designed primarily to prevent even the mere filing of impeachment proceedings against all constitutionally impeachable officers," Mendoza sought cover in a technicality. He said, "The time to debate the rules is past" and "there is no point in discussing the matter further." I replied that the matter had also crossed my mind, but I wondered for the record why Mendoza took "so long to raise the point." He let the matter pass and that ended our somewhat bitter exchange.

When the Atienza motion to recommit the Mendoza report back to his committee was put to a vote, the KBL majority rejected the motion by a vote of 102-51. The members of the Caucus of Independents led by Palmares voted along with the KBL.

PDP-Laban Issues

Soon after the opening of the session of the Batasan, the KBL majority began to feel the collective verbal firepower of the Coalesced Opposition.

As members of the Coalesced Opposition, our PDP-Laban legislators were active not only in committee work but also on the floor of the Batasan. We spoke on issues and sundry matters that affected our constituencies.

For instance, Tony Cuenco, PDP-Laban, of Cebu City, criticized the exemption given to the Philippine Games and Amusement Corporation (Pagcor) from public audit. He said that the billions of pesos earned by Pagcor casinos in Manila, Baguio, Angeles, Olongapo, Cebu, Iloilo, Bacolod, Davao and Zamboanga were not subjected to audit by the government. As a result, he said, nobody knew what the real income of Pagcor was and the uncertainty affected the share of local governments and other entities in the Pagcor revenue. He, therefore, asked that the Batasan should compel Pagcor's inclusion in the entities to be audited by the government.

Douglas Cagas, PDP-Laban, of Davao del Sur, also deplored in a privilege speech the rampaging lawlessness and extrajudicial killings taking place in many parts of Mindanao.

Other members of the Coalesced Opposition also hit Marcos and his government whenever the opportunity arose.

Chapter 40

Nuclear Plant &
Other Controversies

There was another basic issue that we brought up on the floor of the Batasan against the Marcos regime. It had to do with the Bataan Nuclear Plant. I spoke against it on August 27, 1984.

In my speech, I discussed some major concerns originally raised by Senator Tañada and some anti-nuclear groups. Among these were:

(1) The Westinghouse designs of the nuclear plant in Bataan needed fundamental changes and additional safeguards;

(2) The unresolved issue of where to dispose of the nuclear wastes of the power plants once these were in operation;

(3) The perils connected with the location of the proposed nuclear plants; and

(4) The questionable pricing schemes that the government was entering into with Westinghouse.

Silent on Disini

Most of the concerns I raised were included in the findings of the three-man commission that Marcos created on June 15, 1979 to investigate the issues concerning the Bataan Nuclear Plant. The commission was chaired by Ricardo Puno. One thing that the commission did not deal with was the issue of corruption that we charged tainted the transaction between the government and Westinghouse. Not surprisingly, it was silent on the participation of Herminio Disini. Disini was reportedly a golfing crony of Marcos and was a relative by affinity of Imelda.

To substantiate the claim that the BNP was unsafe, I quoted Dr. Zoilo Bartolome, the late Commissioner of the Philippine Atomic Energy Commission (PAEC). Bartolome had earlier found certain defects in the construction of the nuclear facility, among which, were "a crack on the main floor of the plant, defective cable installations and damaged steam pipes." The defects, singly or collectively, could cause the nuclear facility to malfunction and create a major catastrophe in Bataan and its environs all the way to Metro Manila and Central Luzon. I also adverted to the threat of nuclear radiation that nuclear power plants in general pose to the health and well-being of people.

The matter of how the nuclear wastes were to be disposed, I suggested, also had to be clearly specified. There was no such provision in the government plan for the construction of the BNP. Neither the PAEC nor the National

Power Corporation (NPC) or any other agency of the government, I said, had assured the people that it had an adequate, inexpensive and safe nuclear-waste disposal system. Nuclear wastes were lethal for up to hundreds of years and talk that the wastes would be shipped to Palawan did not help the people's unease.

Earthquake Fault Line

I also pointed out that it was folly for the government to locate the Nuclear Plant in Bataan at a site that was "crisscrossed by major earthquake faults and surrounded by at least four volcanoes." Jorge Emmanuel, coordinator of the Campaign for a Nuclear-Free Philippines, identified the volcanoes as Mt. Natib, Mt. Banahaw, Mt. San Cristobal and Mt. Taal.

I likewise adverted to the "financial finagling" that attended the nuclear power plant deal. In early 1974, the government opened bids for the construction of two nuclear power plants. I recounted that two offers were made to build the nuclear plants: one from General Electric with details and specifications for $700 million, and the other from Westinghouse for only $500 million but without specifications or cost justification." In June 1974, the National Power Corporation approved Westinghouse's letter of intent to build the two nuclear power plants for $500 million. Then, in March 1975, without the conditions being made public, Westinghouse formally raised its price from $500 million to $1.2 billion for two power plants. Two months later, in May 1975, the US Export and Import Bank informed US Ambassador William Sullivan that the two plants cost $1.6 billion, not $1.2 billion.

In my speech in 1984, I referred to the "unusual and rapid increase in the pricing of the project from the original proposal of $500 million for two nuclear reactors to $1.1 billion for one reactor." That, I suggested, might be explained by the "shadowy participation of a certain Herminio Disini, a relative of the First Couple, who was reportedly paid a handsome amount estimated at a low $4 million to an outrageous $35 million in various fees for activities connected with the nuclear plant transaction."

Monfort's Interpelation

In his interpellation, Narciso Monfort wanted proof of Disini's involvement in the transaction between the government and the Westinghouse on the BNP. I replied that, based on reports by the Coalition for a Nuclear-Free Philippines, Disini was reportedly paid an amount of $4 million as fees.

To belittle the revelation that Disini, the first-cousin in-law of the First Lady, was paid such an amount in "fees," Monfort said the "$4 million (was) just peanuts" to a person of Disini's category.

In amateurishly attempting to defend Disini and Imelda, Monfort made what lawyers call "a negative pregnant" admission. He issued a denial that something did not happen but somehow admitted that it did. To lure him into digging the hole (into which he was putting Disini directly and Imelda

1984: BATAAN NUCLEAR POWER PLANT.

indirectly) deeper by his naive interventions, I asked Monfort how much he thought Mr. Disini received. The question drew laughter from the floor and the gallery.

Monfort avoided the legal pitfall by insisting that all he wanted was for me to produce proof of Disini's actual commissions. At that point, I did not have the documents to prove the exact amount of his so-called fees. But circulating in Manila at the time were many reports indicating that Disini had been paid an unconscionable amount in undeserved "fees." (20 years later, in July 2004, long after Marcos was deposed, Disini was charged in the Sandiganbayan for taking an $18 million bribe for securing the government approval of the BNP contract.)

Virata's Admission

In reply to Monfort's query, I referred him to an earlier debate between Hernando Perez and Virata on August 9, 1984, when Virata admitted that a commission had been given to Disini. Virata, however, denied knowing the "exact relationship" of Disini by blood or affinity with any high-ranking official of the government or the amount given to Disini. Virata's replies drew disdainful laughter from the gallery.

In an attempt to make light of the perils of nuclear power plants, Monfort, a doctor of medicine, made the idiotic suggestion that "smoking is more dangerous than radiation because it directly affects the lungs of the person smoking." The comparison was clearly invidious and I replied that the person who smokes "has the satisfaction of smoking voluntarily, but [a malfunctioning nuclear power plant] will...incinerate [all of us] without our consent."

After Monfort, Estelito Mendoza, asked me to substantiate my claim that, in general, nuclear power plants were unsafe and that the BNP, in particular, was defective.

Dangerous Defects

In reply, I cited the opinions of Dr. Roger Posadas of the University of the Philippines and Dr. Robert Pollard, an American nuclear scientist, who made an assessment of the BNP, as well as a study called the Nuclear Power Safety Report for 1981. Pollard's study spoke of some 4,000 nuclear power reactors "breaking down with regularity," which, among other things, was the reason why the United States has stopped constructing nuclear plant reactors. As for the details on how unsafe the BNP was, I said the Puno Commission held in no uncertain terms that the BNP had so many defects, which have not been corrected to date.

No matter how authoritative my answers were, they were not sufficient to sway the likes of Monfort or Mendoza. Nonetheless, I had to go through the motions of responding to their questions as best I could, not for the sake of satisfying them but to inform the people in general.

Contract Kept Secret

In my answers to the interpellators, I put on record that the Opposition had not been given a copy of the contract covering the Bataan Nuclear Plant, despite our recent demands and those of Senator Tañada and concerned private organizations years earlier. Obviously, the government did not wish to share the vital document with us because it would have provided us with more ammunition to question not only the legality but also the necessity and the wisdom of constructing the BNP.

The Marcos government clearly wanted to sweep the BNP problem under the rug, as it were. But the Batasan Opposition did not want the issue to simply disappear from public awareness.

Generic Defects

Two days later, on August 29, Rafael Recto followed up with another denunciation of the BNP. He questioned the ability of Westinghouse to run the BNP efficiently and well. He said that "all Westinghouse reactors have the same generic deficiencies," indicating that the BNP had inherent defects. Recto cited a Pollard report that the Westinghouse reactors had 133 generic defects.

The Batangas assemblyman underscored the dangers posed by the malfunctioning of a nuclear power plant by citing a study made by Professor Norman Rasmussen of the Massachusetts Institute of Technology. Rasmussen concluded:

An unimaginable approximate accident at a nuclear plant facility could cause 3,300 fatalities, 45,000 latent cancer victims, 5,100 generic defects on the first generation of victims and the contamination of at least 3,200 square miles of land and an estimable damage to property running into billions of dollars.

More specifically, Recto asserted that, "Westinghouse has the worst record in the United States of especially significant mishaps....And, also in the Americas, Westinghouse has the worst record again of the highest number of mishaps per plant."

Unnecessary Expenses, Perks

Six days after Recto's privilege speech, on September 4, Cagas took the floor to assail the unnecessary expenses that were charged to the costs of constructing the BNP. Cagas pointed out that "part of the huge $2.1 billion expense of the nuclear plant construction was used (to build) a 50-room motel with disco, betamax facilities, wall-to-wall carpeting, and 90 bungalow units worth P320,000 to P500,000 each" for the use of "68 Westinghouse employees and their families, 12 subcontractors and foreigners, and 10 Napocor managers."

Cagas also deplored the perks and privileges extended to favored personnel in the construction of the BNP. Specifically, he said that two American-type schools with American curricula taught by American teachers were provided the children of Westinghouse personnel. In addition, the Davao del Sur assemblyman revealed that, aside from recreational facilities within the premises of the BNP, "luxury cars like Toyota Crowns and Opel Rekords and two helicopters were placed at the disposal of Westinghouse executives."

When Budget Minister Alba took the floor to defend parts of the appropriation of the Ministry of Energy, Cagas continued his tirade that the BNP was unsafe, unreliable and too expensive. To buttress his argument, he cited the Puno Report and the admission of Energy Minister Geronimo Velasco, published in the August 24 issue of *Mr&Ms*, that "if the government had its way, it would gladly dispose of [the BNP] because of all the problems and the headaches that the controversial project has caused."

Alba tried to dodge the question by suggesting that the matter of the safety of the BNP be posed to Velasco at the Question Hour scheduled within the week. Cagas deftly replied that he wanted to discuss "the items in the Budget with reference to the additional costs for the construction" of the BNP. Specifically, he reiterated that Alba should provide justification of the construction of the motel, disco houses, bungalows, the special schools, recreational facilities, the luxurious cars and the helicopters "for the use of the top executives (of Westinghouse) and to ensure the arrival of the newspapers daily" that pushed the costs of the BNP up to $2.1 billion. And, as if Cagas did not feel Alba's embarrassment at his failure to give the answers, the former asked the latter in so many words if a part of the $2.1 billion costs of the BNP went to Disini as commission.

Alba had no credible reply to Cagas's questions except to reiterate that the issues should be addressed to Velasco during the Question Hour.

Marcos Turns 67

On September 11, 1984, Marcos's 67th birthday, the Batasan Opposition members had a field day satirically wishing him a happy birthday. Alberto Romulo and Hjalmar Quintana said that Marcos should "stop exercising his powers under Amendment No. 6."

Mitra and I expressed similar sentiments when we told *Veritas* that Marcos should resign. Mitra said Marcos had served the nation for too long. In my case, I wished "the President well, that is why I believe he should resign — it is good for his health, it is good for the country."

Ten days later, on September 21, the police and the military violently dispersed a peaceful demonstration against the martial law regime at the Mendiola Bridge near Malacañang. Earlier, Marcos proclaimed September 21 as a day to be celebrated. We in the Opposition, however, did not see the day as something to be commemorated. We saw it as a day to be rued.

On that day, thousands of marchers joined a peaceful rally that would have culminated at the top of the Mendiola Bridge with a program calling for the peaceful dismantling of the martial law regime. The bridge, however, was no ordinary span. It provided access to Malacañang, the Presidential Palace, a few hundred meters away. The authorities were wary of demonstrators coming too close to the seat of the martial law government.

The demonstrators started their march from Liwasang Bonifacio in an orderly manner, but, at the foot of the bridge, barbed-wire barricades blocked their way. Beyond the wires, tanks mounted with machine guns stood ready to crush any attempt by the demonstrators to enter the prohibited zone. Because the demonstrators could not go beyond the barbed wire barricades, their leaders, Sen. Lorenzo Tañada, Sen. Ambrosio Padilla, Chino Roces, Joker Arroyo, Butz Aquino, Tito Guingona, Rene Saguisag and Sister Marianni, assisted by members of the Batasan, Augusto Sanchez, Alberto Romulo and Cecilia Muñoz-Palma, stopped at the foot of the bridge and began their harangue against the Marcos regime.

As the afternoon hours passed into the night, tension began to build up between the demonstrators on one side and the police and military contingents keeping watch on the other side. Butz Aquino negotiated with Police Gen. Narciso Cabrera to allow the demonstrators to reach the top of the bridge, but Cabrera would have none of it. The demonstrators then continued their program, berating the martial law government at the foot of the bridge.

Tear Gas, Water Cannons & Plastic Bullets

Sixteen hours later, at 6:30 in the morning of September 22, the order to disperse the demonstrators came. The demonstrators refused to budge. Police and military elements fired teargas canisters and the fire department used water cannons to forcibly disperse the crowd. Police then used their truncheons on the demonstrators who were not fast enough to elude them and the military fired plastic bullets into the fleeing crowd. Many were hurt, among them PDP-Laban youth leaders Vic Baltazar and Rey Miranda, who suffered head and body injuries.

Baltazar and Miranda recounted to us, their elders in the party, how, in the midst of all the brutality by men in uniform at the height of the dispersal operations, the innate goodness of other policemen also surfaced. These policemen personally protected them from further harm. The cops stopped their colleagues from beating up Baltazar and Miranda and urged them to run for their lives.

On September 26, I condemned the unwarranted brutal dispersal of the September 21 rally and moved that the Batasan conduct an investigation of the incident during which "scores of our youth and elderly citizens were maimed, mauled and manhandled by certain members of the police and the military."

A Blow for Freedom

The Batasan approved the motion to investigate the incident. To my pleasant surprise, the Committee on Justice, Human Rights and Good Government immediately conducted a probe. It decided to investigate the heavy-handed dispersal not only of the September 21 demonstration but also of the September 27 rally at the Welcome Rotunda in Quezon City. Senators Lorenzo Tañada, Ambrosio Padilla and Tecla San Andres Ziga, and Butz Aquino, Tingting Cojuangco and Fernando Campos, among others, gave testimony that led to an unexpected report of the committee.

The committee made a report, Resolution No. 162, which astounded all of us in the Opposition and which the Batasan even more amazingly approved in plenary session. The report declared that the right of the people to stage peaceful demonstrators even without permits was legitimate and it condemned the brutal police response to the September 21 demonstration. It was a singular achievement in that, under martial law conditions, incredibly the Batasan unanimously struck a blow for freedom.

'Intelligence Funds'

On October 1,1984, I explained on the floor of the Batasan why Cabinet Bill No. 1, the National Budget for 1985, did not merit our support. I decried that the proposed budget "builds a national network of spies."

Citing specifics, I pointed out that the budget set aside P420 million for "spying and investigative purposes" of various intelligence agencies. The amount was larger than the individual budgets of the Batasan (P200 million), the Ministry of Agrarian Reform (P249 million), the Ministry of Social Services and Development (P358 million), the Ministry of Energy (P81 million) or the Tanodbayan (409 million).

Several ministries like Finance, Health, Tourism, and Trade and Industry, and the Commissions on Civil Service and Audit also had "intelligence funds" allocated in their budgets. I did not believe they should have been provided with intelligence funds. That they were vested with intelligence funds indicated there was a "creeping militarization" that threatened to envelop the country.

As a result of the "misallocation of [the country's] scarce resources," I said that government hospitals like the National Orthopedic could not provide adequately for the needs of its patients who clogged "every available square inch of space in the wards and in the corridors." I also reported that I saw "makeshift beddings and broken-leg pulleys and paint peeling off the hospital walls." And, in Cagayan de Oro, several public schools suffered from a "dearth of laboratory equipment like ordinary microscopes, test tubes and burners."

In his speech against the approval of the budget, Cuenco called the General Appropriations Bill a "Trojan horse containing the evils of deception and monstrous deficits" that would work hardships on the people. He specifically decried the "lion's share" of P7.9 billion or 13.25% of the budget that went to the National Defense Ministry and the "lump-sum funds in the amount of P33.7 billion." By putting such a huge amount in lump-sum appropriations, the Batasan countenanced "profligacy and waste," he said.

In the end, the KBL majority had their way. By sheer force of numbers, they barreled through the debate and approved the national budget by a vote of 98 to 50.

Reagan's Gaffe

In the month of October, I kept indoctrinating the people on the merits of restoring democratic space to the country and on the evils of the martial law regime. I also had occasion to hit US President Ronald Reagan for his statement that Marcos was the "only alternative to a communist takeover of the country."

Reagan made the assertion in a debate with the Democratic Party candidate for US President, Walter Mondale. In a statement that made the pages of the *San Francisco Examiner* on October 26, I said:

> If Mr. Reagan is not totally isolated from reality and living in the simplistic movie world of his past, he should know that the overwhelming majority of those who oppose the dictatorship are not communists.

Three days later, on October 29, I spoke before the Management Association of the Philippines where I suggested that the "parliamentary struggle will succeed only if we were willing to pay the price for it." I justified our participation in the electoral exercises that Marcos called by pointing out that "progressively we have put into public offices more and more non-administration candidates."

As examples, I said, in 1978 only 15 non-KBL assemblymen were elected to the Interim Batasang Pambansa: 13 Pusyon Bisaya assemblymen representing Central Visayas, one assemblyman representing Northern Mindanao and one Konsensiya ng Bayan representative from Region IX. In the local elections of 1980, Opposition candidates won as mayors in Zamboanga City (Climaco), Ozamiz City (Sanciangco) and Cagayan de Oro City (I). There were also non-KBL mayors and several vice mayors and councilors who won, particularly in Davao City and Cotabato City. Three non-KBL governors also won in Batangas, Eastern Samar and Misamis Oriental. Then, in the regular Batasan elections, 59 seats went to the Opposition.

Effective Opposition

In my view, the record of the Batasan Opposition clearly refuted the criticisms of ineffectiveness and uselessness that were leveled against us. The Opposition made its presence felt rather strongly even within the constraints of the power setup.

Virata, for instance, literally had to go through the eye of the needle when he was up for election as Prime Minister. The defects and the corruption that attended the deal on the Bataan Nuclear Power Plant with Westinghouse were unearthed and scrutinized with a fine-toothed comb. So were the attempts of Estelito Mendoza to present a set of psuedo impeachment rules that were designed to prevent rather than ease the initiation of impeachment proceedings against Marcos and other impeachable officials. And the proposed national budget for 1985 was subjected to thorough discussions only because the Opposition insisted on it. During the debates on the budget, Marcos's issuances of antedated decrees were uncovered and denounced by Opposition members. Also, the Opposition demonstrated that disproportionate amounts of public funds were allocated to the Office of the President in "lump-sum" items to enable him to use the funds as he pleased and to fund the intelligence services of the Armed Forces, the police and other civilian agencies.

For the first time since martial law was declared in 1972, the abuses and anomalies of government were now openly discussed and debated in the Batasan, a public government forum.

Earlier, I reiterated before a Makati Rotary Club the theme of hope in the parliamentary struggle that I had espoused since the advent of martial rule. Even as the KBL dominated the Batasan with 111 elective members and three appointive ones and 11 allies in the so-called Caucus of Independents, I said that the Opposition in the Batasan had reason to be proud. Particularly, I cited the fact that upon the insistence of the Opposition, we got the KBL majority to approve Batas Pambansa Blg. 880 that upheld the right of the people to assemble peaceably for redress of their grievances.

I shared with the Rotarians specific examples of Marcos's abuses in the budgetary process, his administration's anomalies in the Bataan Nuclear Power Plant deal, and the suppression of the rights of the people in Mindanao — all of which were exposed by the Opposition in the Batasan.

The Southern Conference

While I was deeply engrossed in revealing the anomalies of the martial law regime, as a Mindanaonon, I also felt the need of getting our representatives from Mindanao to band together, cross party lines and work for the good of our people on the island and its environs. I first suggested the idea to my party mates in PDP-Laban.

After I got their go-signal, I broached the idea to, among others, Batasan Deputy Speaker Salipada Pendatun of Maguindanao, Alejandro Almendras of Davao del Sur, Edelmiro Amante of Agusan del Norte, Candu Muarip of Basilan and Tomas Baga, Jr., of North Cotabato. When the idea was approved, I drafted a press statement dated August 16, 1984, for the signature of Pendatun, announcing the creation of the Southern Conference and urging all members of the Batasan from Mindanao, Basilan, Tawi-Tawi and Sulu to rally behind it.

In the press statement released by his office, Pendatun said:

> The Southern Conference may be the only way to enable our constituents to catch up with the rest of the country in terms of development.

The Manifesto

Then I helped draft the "Manifesto of the Southern Conference." It was a brief statement that acknowledged the "multifarious problems besetting Mindanao, Basilan, Sulu and Tawi-Tawi" and that our part of the country has "historically lagged behind the rest of the Republic in terms of national development." As a consequence, we, the signatories, bound ourselves "to work together without regard to party lines and to support proposals that in our judgment will promote the best interest of our people."

The Signatories

Apart from Pendatun, 38 members of the Batasan from Mindanao signed the manifesto. From Region IX, those who signed were Vicente Cerilles; Bienvenido Ebarle, Isidoro Real, Jr., and Romeo Jalosjos of Zamboanga del Sur; Guardson Lood, Zamboanga del Norte; Hussin T. Loong, Sulu; Candu Muarip, Basilan; and Celso J. Palma, Tawi-Tawi.

From Region X, those who affixed their signatures on the manifesto were: Constantino Navarro of Surigao del Norte; Homobono Adaza and Concordio Diel, Misamis Oriental; Edelmiro Amante, Agusan del Norte; Lorenzo Dinlayan and Jose Zubiri, Jr., Bukidnon; Jose Paul Neri, Camiguin; Democrito Plaza, Agusan del Sur; Henry Regalado, Misamis Occidental; and I, Cagayan de Oro City.

From Region XI, the following members gave their support to it: Rogelio Sarmiento, Rolando Marcial and Rodolfo del Rosario of Davao del Norte; Zafiro Respicio and Manuel Garcia, Davao City; Douglas Cagas and Alejandro Almendras, Davao del Sur; Rufino Bañas, Hilario de Pedro and Rogelio Garcia, South Cotabato; Merced Edith Rabat, Davao Oriental; and Higino Llaguno Jr., Surigao del Sur.

From Region XII, the following assemblymen backed it up: Tomas Baga Jr. and Carlos Cajelo of North Cotabato; Camilo Cabili of Iligan City; Simeon Datumanong, Maguindanao; Omar Dianalan and Macacuna Dimaporo, Lanao del Sur; Abdullah Dimaporo, Lanao del Norte; and Benjamin Duque, Sultan Kudarat

Although the Southern Conference did not accomplish much for Mindanao during our stint in the Batasan, it sent a message to our colleagues that we, the members from Mindanao, at the very least, did not like what we perceived was a historical discriminatory treatment that had been accorded to our part of the country.

Muslim-Christian Dialogue

In my capacity as an Assistant Minority Leader, I represented Laurel in the meetings of the Committee on Muslim Affairs. I did that and more. Since my party, the PDP-Laban was seriously concerned with addressing the Moro problem in Mindanao, I was deeply involved in promoting Muslim-Christian dialogues not only in the Batasan but in other forums as well.

One such forum that we organized was the Muslim-Christian Dialogue held at the Communication Foundation for Asia in Manila on October 6. I gave the keynote address, in which I underscored "the need to remove the walls that separate Muslims from Christians and to create a society of Muslim and Christian equals" in Mindanao, particularly, and in the country, in general.

The participants in the dialogue headed by Dr. Ahmad Alonto of Marawi City and Bishop Antonino Nepomuceno, OMI, knew whereof I spoke. They knew, for instance, that Jolo, that once beautiful site of Muslim culture, had been leveled to the ground by the military in 1974 to recover the town from MNLF rebels. The military operation radicalized many a Moro intellectual. Parouk Hussin, a doctor of medicine, who did postgraduate work in the Scandinavian countries, for instance, was in his clinic when bombs that hit his place almost killed him and completely destroyed his brand new car. Among other reasons, the indiscriminate attacks on civilian homes drove Dr. Hussin into the folds of the MNLF.

I also emphasized that, in terms of economic development, the Moro areas of Mindanao had "least priority in the concerns of the government compared to the rest of the land." And that consciously or unconsciously, we, the Christian majority, had not been sensitive to the uniqueness of the culture of the Muslims as a people. It was my position that the Christian majority must help create the environment whereby the Muslim culture could be preserved and enhanced within the context of the Republic.

1984: MUSLIMS express their gratitude for my support for their just aspirations including the adoption of the federal system of government.

Solutions to the Mindanao Problem

The immediate solution, I suggested, was to prevent the escalation of the bloody upheaval engulfing the island of Mindanao and, eventually, to adopt the federal system of government where a Bangsamoro federal state may be created.

My proposal found articulate supporters in lawyer Saidamen Pangarungan and Dr. Ahmad Alonto, both of whom were Moro leaders. They discussed the beneficial ramifications of Muslim Autonomy and the Federal System respectively, in the search for peace in Mindanao.

Towards the end of the dialogue, in a stirring appeal, Bishop Nepomuceno called upon "the Moros and the Christians of Mindanao to join hands in the liberation of our peoples from ignorance that had led to violence and from the manipulation of neo-colonial powers under the oppressive Marcos dictatorship."

Chapter 41

Ouster from the Batasan

Outside the Batasan, the machinations of the Comelec against me came to a head on August 7, 1984. I was discharging my duties as a member of the Batasan when the Comelec threatened to cite me for contempt for defying its orders relative to the case that Roa filed against me. If the Comelec Commissioners thought I would back down because of their threat, they were sadly mistaken.

Previously, as mayor of Cagayan de Oro, I had some experience tilting against the Comelec. I knew that the Comelec, an apodictically discredited government agency, was now a pliant tool in the hands of my political opponents who were allied with Marcos and that it suffered from certain vulnerabilities. For one thing, I believed that the Comelec read the law upside down and I had the law behind me.

In this controversy, a Comelec division of three commissioners tried to assume jurisdiction over the case against me soon after I was proclaimed by the City Board of Canvassers as the duly elected representative of Cagayan de Oro to the Batasan in 1984. Under the law, a Comelec division could not undo that proclamation by means of a summary proceeding. In such a proceeding, they would merely do a pro-forma review of some questioned election papers and they would then use the results to nullify my proclamation.

If Roa really wanted to contest my election, he should have filed an election protest after my proclamation. That was what the law required. But he did not do that because he would have to produce witnesses and documents to support his protest and I would have the right to cross-examine his witnesses and dispute his documents formally. Then, I would also have the right to present my own witnesses and documents to refute his complaint. The proceedings would take months, if not years, to conclude.

But with the complicity of the members of the Comelec Division composed of Victorino Savellano, Jaime Opinion and Froilan Bacungan, Roa secured an order directing me to submit to the jurisdiction of the Comelec. I refused. Thus, the Comelec threatened to cite me for contempt. Incidentally, Opinion was a colleague of mine in the Constitutional Convention. He was a known Marcos man and was, in fact, rewarded by Marcos with a plum post at the Comelec.

1984: SOON AFTER THIS speaking engagement, I was ousted from the Batasan.

Bullfight

I saw the Comelec threat to cite me for contempt as a bull sees the red cape of a *matador* in a bullfight arena. I charged headlong at it knowing that, if the Comelec had a legal forum to which they wanted to hale me for contempt, I also had the bully pulpit of the Batasan to hail the Comelec before the bar of public opinion. I ventilated my grievances against the Comelec by way of a privilege speech on the floor of the Batasan. I did not ask for concessions from the members of the Comelec Division of Savellano, Opinion and Bacungan.

I took a dig at the three commissioners. By combining the first letters of their family names, I called the Comelec Division the "SOB" team. I certainly did not mind if the people who heard me thought that the initials SOB were meant to describe their respective pedigrees from their mothers' side. Because of their blatant disregard of the Rule of Law, I believed that they deserved the appellation in whatever sense the people thought it apt.

The SOB division ordered that the contested election documents be brought to Manila for their review. I said that it would be better for the SOB team to "go to Cagayan de Oro City and do (their) inspection of the returns...under the glare of the public eye of the people of the city and not in the dark and devious corridors of the Comelec in Manila." I was convinced that, if the election documents were brought to Manila and submitted to the

SOB division, we could no longer be sure of their integrity.

In fairness, shortly after this initial skirmish between the Comelec SOB division and me, Bacungan inhibited himself for unspecified reasons. *Veritas* in its November 11 issue quoted Comelec Chairman Santiago as saying that Bacungan inhibited himself voluntarily "because of his personal relationship with Pimentel." At the time, I neither had a personal nor an official relationship with Bacungan, aside from his being a Comelec commissioner. Santiago, as usual, engaged in double-speak for which Comelec officials were notorious. In any case, Bacungan was replaced by Commissioner Noli Sagadraca.

Without circumlocution, I said in my speech that the people of Cagayan de Oro decided to protect the votes cast in the Batasan elections because of the "dubious track record of the present Comelec." I also pointed to the Comelec as "the seat of subversion" in the country. Those were, as Western novelist Zane Grey would say, "fighting words." It was the first time in recent memory that the Comelec was excoriated in those terms and in a public and official manner.

Arturo Borjal of the *Metro Manila Times* wrote in his column of September 20:

> There is a very bitter word war between the camps of Aquilino Pimentel, Jr., and Pedro "Oloy" Roa. The whole town is sitting on pins and needles awaiting the judgment of the Supreme Court on the true winner of the Cagayan de Oro Batasan election. The Roa camp claims Oloy won by 87 votes. But the unsinkable Nene Pimentel says the latest figures from the Supreme Court show him leading by more than 5,000.

The recount in the Supreme Court eventually showed that my claim was closer to the truth. But for the moment, my tirades against the Comelec riled the commissioners immensely. On October 24, the Comelec division nullified the votes in my favor coming from several precincts in Cagayan de Oro. The nullification altered the results of the election. Instead of my winning over Roa by almost 5,000 votes, he now led me by 1,500 votes. The Comelec declared that Roa was the duly elected member of the Batasan for the city. It also ordered that a copy of the ruling be furnished to the Secretary General of the Batasan. With that move, the Comelec ousted me from the Batasan.

Surprisingly, the *San Francisco Examiner* noted my "ouster from [my] Parliament seat...by the Philippine Commission on Elections, a board appointed by and, opponents say, manipulated by Marcos."

At that time, my colleagues in the Opposition could not do anything for me because the Batasan was still in recess. The release of the decision appeared to have been timed to fall within the period of our recess so that neither my Opposition colleagues nor I could hit back the Comelec on the floor of the Batasan.

Agrava Hogs Attention

Moreover, on the day of my ouster, the Agrava report on the Aquino assassination hogged the headlines of the newspapers. The day before, on October 23, 1984, Corazon Agrava made a move that surprised legal circles. Without waiting for the report of her colleagues in the Board, she submitted her own findings to Marcos. She concluded that, of the 31 members of the Armed Forces charged with the killing of Aquino, only Gen. Luther Custodio, chief of the Aviation Security Command, and six enlisted men were liable for the assassination. She exonerated Gen. Fabian Ver, chief of the Armed Forces, Gen. Prospero Olivas, chief of the Metrocom, and most of the enlisted military personnel. She gave her recommendations to Marcos, obviously to please him and, in the process, she created the impression that it was the board's verdict. The fact that it was issued by Agrava did not make it the Board's report. It was still a minority or dissenting report by only one member of the Board, even if she was its chair. I found Agrava's act rather unusual because a minority report of a judicial or a quasi-judicial body like the Agrava Board was not normally issued ahead of the majority report. But times were not normal. Marcos appeared to be securely in power and ample rewards awaited those who pleased him.

Marcos praised the Agrava report to the high heavens and even as he knew that it was just the opinion of one person and not of the Board, he immediately proclaimed the acquittal of Generals Ver and Olivas. He went along with her charade because her stand hewed closely to his scenario. He never wanted Ver to be associated in any manner with the killing of Aquino. Ver was too close to him, not only officially but also personally, to be indicted without Marcos's getting implicated, even indirectly in the assassination. Marcos added that he was reinstating Ver and Olivas to their military posts from which they had gone on leave.

The Agrava report did not sit well with the public. People did not believe that Galman had shot and killed Aquino. Most believed that the soldiers who boarded the plane and escorted Aquino down were responsible for his murder. Following the handing of the Agrava minority report to Marcos, people took to the streets to criticize Agrava. The news and media commentaries for several days pilloried her and, rightly so, for her lapse of judgment.

The Majority Report

By and large, the uninformed public did not know that the report was only Agrava's and not the Board's. The four members of the Board issued their majority report a day after Agrava's. The four, Dante Santos, Luciano Salazar, Amado Dizon and Ernesto Herrera contradicted the findings of Agrava. They found the three generals, namely Ver, Olivas and Custodio, and the 22 military personnel guilty of a conspiracy to kill Aquino. They recommended their prosecution according to law.

When the four board members submitted their majority report, they were made to cool their heels in the office of Information Minister Gregorio Cendaña for over an hour until Marcos received them. Unlike his usual cool-under-fire posture, this time, Marcos was agitated. Herrera recalled that they had barely sat down, after Dante Santos turned over their report to him, when Marcos told them, "I hope you can live with your consciences with what you have done." With that curt statement, Herrera said, "Marcos turned his back on us and left."

Herrera told me that when the members of the board were individually preparing their respective opinions, his draft report recommended the indictment of Generals Ver, Olivas, Custodio and the other military personnel under investigation. Over time, he was joined by Santos, Dizon and Salazar. Once their position had jelled, he asked Agrava to support it to make their opinion unanimous. She demurred. On the contrary, she wanted Herrera to sign the report that she would submit to Marcos. In a famous line, Herrera told her, "I would rather commit suicide than sign that version." The quote fitted newspaper descriptions of Herrera as being "brash" and the one who asked the "sharpest questions." To Marcos sympathizers, these made him appear *bastos* or uncouth. The split between Agrava and the four commissioners became irremediable. Agrava, as chair, was left with her solitary opinion, and the four members of the board stuck to their majority view.

Herrera also said that, while he was crafting his opinion, he was under constant pressure by Col. Galileo Kintanar, the head of the Military Intelligence Group in Manila. Kintanar continually visited his office to suggest that he should follow the line of the military, which wanted to exclude Ver but include Eduardo Cojuangco as a co-conspirator in the murder of Aquino. Herrera refused both suggestions and told Kintanar that, if he had the evidence on Cojuangco, he should produce it before the board to lay the basis for his inclusion as an indictee.

Incidentally, Herrera confirmed an interesting sidelight in the Agrava Board investigation. During a session of the Board, it was discovered that a junior officer, Angelo Reyes, had a gun secretly tucked into one of his boots. Reyes was cited for contempt but was allowed to explain his act. Reyes claimed that he had simply forgotten about the gun when he went inside the hearing room. Agrava's grandmotherly instincts prevailed over those of the other members of the board. She did not wish to make a big fuss about it and they went along with her stand that the matter be considered closed.

With the majority report of Herrera, Dizon, Santos and Salazar recommending the indictments of Ver, Olivas, Custodio and the other military personnel, Marcos had no choice but to take the next step. He had to refer the matter for prosecution. But to what office? Normally, he should have forwarded it to the prosecutor who had jurisdiction over the place, the Manila International Airport, where Aquino was assassinated. That would have been the Office of the City Fiscal (Prosecutor) of Pasay City. Marcos, however, chose to refer the matter to the Tanodbayan (Ombudsman), which drew a lot of criticisms from those who doubted the impartiality of the Tanodbayan. Nonetheless, what Marcos had done, he did not want to undo.

In fairness, after conducting its assessment of the evidence against Ver, Olivas and the others, Tanodbayan Bernardo Fernandez filed the case for the murder of Aquino against the three generals and the other military personnel with the *Sandiganbayan* (the Criminal Court). While awaiting trial, Ver, Olivas and Custodio had to go on leave from their respective positions in the Armed Forces.

Sandigan Justices Manuel Pamaran, Augusto Amores and Bienvenido Vera Cruz tried the case. On December 2, 1985, the Pamaran court acquitted Ver and the other accused. They basically followed the lead of the military investigators that it was Galman and the communists who plotted and killed Aquino. In general, the people derided the acquittal as laughable. Enrique P. Syquia, president of the Catholic Lawyers Guild and one time head of the Philippine Bar Association, who participated in the investigation as an accredited lawyer, summed up the people's view succinctly: "Galman didn't shoot Ninoy."

Lawyers Go to Supreme Court

In the meantime, on October 25, my lawyers, Sen. Lorenzo Tañada, Joker Arroyo, Rene Saguisag and Eduardo Araullo, assisted by Rodrigo Melchor and Jacob Montesa, went to the Supreme Court to question the erroneous Comelec move ousting me from the Batasan. We hoped that we could get a fast relief against the blatant abuse of the Comelec in unseating me in favor of Roa without the latter's filing a formal election protest. Our hopes were dashed six days later when, on October 31, the Court strangely issued a temporary

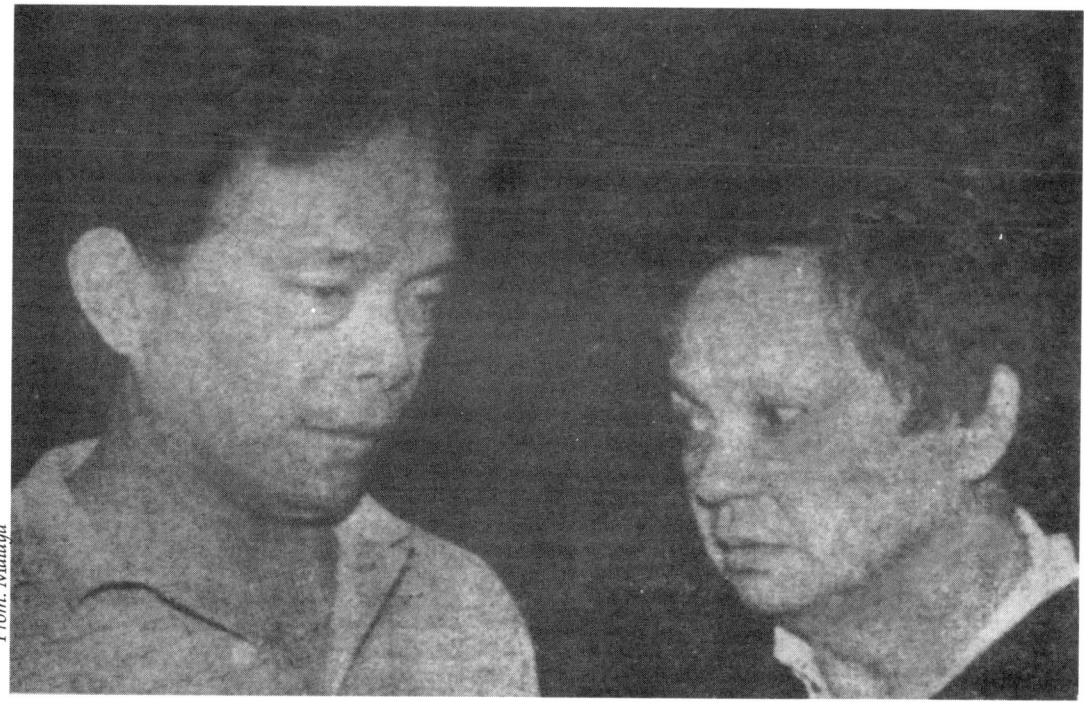

From: Malaya

1984: I CONFER WITH MY COUNSEL, Joker Arroyo, at the Supreme Court

restraining order prohibiting *both* Roa and me from assuming the position of member of the Batasan until further orders.

I was baffled by the development. I was the aggrieved party and I went to the Supreme Court to ask it to preserve the status quo, that is, for the Court to allow me to continue as a member of the Batasan while the issues that Roa brought would be litigated before the Comelec. In any event, since both Roa and I were not satisfied with the order of the High Court, our individual lawyers filed a flurry of motions to advance our respective sides.

Colleagues Manifest Support

On November 5, 1984, the Batasan resumed its session. There, my Opposition colleagues manifested their full support for me in my electoral fight with Roa.

At the opening session, the Secretary General did not read my name during the roll call. Assemblyman Cuenco of Cebu City stood up and blamed the Speaker for it.

The Speaker tried to defuse the situation by informing the Batasan that the omission of my name from the roll call was based on an order issued by the Supreme Court. The order said that it was "temporarily restraining Pimentel and Pedro N. Roa from discharging the functions of a member of the Batasang Pambansa for Cagayan de Oro until further orders from the court."

The Speaker emphasized, "It does not mean that the name of Mr. Pimentel is stricken off the record of Batasan."

Assemblyman Jose Atienza, Jr. of Manila then suggested a compromise.

> We could probably just include his name in the roll and mark it properly that he is the subject of a Supreme Court restraining order. The same way as we are marking our absences here: one star when we appear after the roll call; two stars when we are on official mission; three stars when we officially notify the Batasan of our absences; four stars when we are absent. Maybe we can give five stars to a gentleman as diligent a member of this Body like Nene Pimentel.

Speaker Yñiguez absentmindedly replied that "the name of Honorable Roa was not stricken off the record." Atienza had to remind him that he was talking about me, not about Roa.

Atienza's Argument

In a Batasan that had so many lawyers, the cogent legal arguments of a nonlawyer like Atienza caught the attention of his hearers. Atienza underscored the fact that the Batasan was not ordered by the Supreme Court to oust me. The worst that could be said of the High Court was that it restrained me — and Roa — from "discharging" the duties of a member of the Batasan. And the burden of his thesis was that keeping me in the roll of members did not constitute "discharging" the duties of an assemblyman.

The specific merit of Atienza's position was that he did not only argue that expunging my name from the list of members was highly questionable, he also offered a way out for the Batasan: keep my name in the roll of members but put a mark, an asterisk or several asterisks, to indicate that I was under a restraining order of the Supreme Court.

I was not in the Batasan when my colleagues in the Opposition took turns in hitting the order to exclude me from the roll of members. Judging from their interventions, as these appear in the Record of the Batasan, I can only say that I had a first-rate team of defenders. Among them, aside from Cuenco and Atienza were Marcelo Fernan, Arthur Defensor, Isidoro Real, Jr., Neptali Gonzales, Gonzalo Puyat II and Luis Villafuerte.

Cuenco's Summation

Tony Cuenco was particularly scathing in his tirade against the Speaker's order. He said:

> Indeed, what has unfolded is a blatant show of double standards. According to the administration, what is good for the goose is not necessarily good for the gander. What we have seen so far is part of a grand design to silence one of the foremost critics of the President and his regime and who is a living champion of the people's rights. If we do not signal our objection to this scheme, then we would be privy to an unwarranted and naked disregard of the people's will. If we do not voice our protests to this high-handed assault against the cause of democracy in this country, then there could be no hope in this Batasan.

Cuenco also quoted Jesus Bigornia, a columnist of the *Bulletin Today:*

> The proverbial cat is out on the loose. Loosed with obvious premeditation by the Supreme Court, neither cajolery nor tantrums of the Commission on Elections (Comelec) can lure it back into the bag. By hurriedly unseating Assemblyman Aquilino Pimentel and declaring former Rep. Pedro Roa the duly elected assemblyman from Cagayan de Oro City, the Comelec's Second Division opened itself to suspicion of violating Article XII, Section 3 of the Constitution. The Second Division had stunned bench and bar circles by ignoring the clear and express requirement for the Comelec en banc to hear and decide election contests involving Members of the Batasang Pambansa.
>
> In its resolution en banc dated October 31, the Supreme Court unanimously agreed eight days before promulgation to order the Comelec to dismiss Roa's pre-proclamation protest against Pimentel. It [takes] some time for the High Court resolution to be typed, finalized, signed and released. In the meantime, the Comelec's Second Division released its own decision

proclaiming Roa winner in last May 14 polling and declaring Pimentel
unseated from the Batasang Pambansa, preempting the High Tribunal's
adverse decision.

For this reason, Associate Justice Claudio Teehankee branded the
controversial Comelec decision an "AMBUSCADE" of the then impending
Supreme Court resolution. For, if the preproclamation protest of Roa had
been thrown out as already agreed upon by the magistrates of the High
Tribunal, there would have been no case for the Comelec's Second Division
to decide. Two questions are now being asked in Supreme Court circles:
(1) who tipped the Comelec on an impending Supreme Court resolution
on the Roa\Pimentel case; and (2) why should Pimentel now be penalized
by the High Tribunal's restraining order?

Cuenco's speech, in my view, was a brilliant summation of the hard facts
and relevant precedents of the issue that he marshaled to show that the removal of my name from the roster of members of the Batasan was unwarranted. He cited cases where the Supreme Court ordered the suspension of a
member of the Bar, but retained his or her name in the roll of lawyers until
final decision. He referred to administrative resolutions where public officials were suspended without being ousted. He pointed to the Narciso Umali
case in 1950 where the House of Representatives did not delete the name of a
member who was convicted of sedition until after the finality of the case.

To assure our colleagues in the Batasan that I would follow the Rule of
Law, Cuenco read my letter to him dated November 12, 1984. I wrote:

> Dear Tony,
>
> Regarding our conversation about my plans re...the Supreme Court
> case against the Comelec, please know that:
>
>   1. I intend to refrain from attending the sessions of the Batasan
>   before the issues in the case are resolved particularly on the
>   matter of my sitting in the Batasan; and
>   2. I am questioning the decision of the court barring me from
>   discharging my duties as Cagayan de Oro representative in
>   the meantime.
>
> Kindly thank our colleagues who have espoused our cause on the
> floor of the Batasan.
>
>   Best regards.
>   Nene Pimentel

Cuenco also raised the specter that expunging my name from the roll
pending a decision of the Supreme Court could backfire on the members of
the KBL in the Batasan who also had pre-proclamation controversies that were
still being tried.

Neptali Gonzales amplified Cuenco's argument, stressing that:

> Mr. Pimentel is aware of the terms of the temporary restraining order. He is an adherent of the rule of law; it is to the Supreme Court where he turned for the enforcement of his rights and the will of his constituents. He has not shown up since the restraining order was issued; he has not made any attempt to discharge the duties and functions of a Member of the Batasang Pambansa in obedience to or in compliance with the temporary restraining order. He is responsible enough not to disobey it; otherwise, he makes himself open to charges of contempt for violating the terms of the temporary restraining order.

Some KBL Assemblymen tried to refute the arguments of my colleagues in my favor, but their reasons were far from convincing.

Finally, after consuming 110 pages of the Record of the Batasan, First Session, 1984-1985, spanning five days of debates, the issue of whether or not my name would be retained in the roster of members of the Batasan was settled. The amendment proposed by Villafuerte that Atienza and Defensor seconded early on in the debate to simply put an asterisk beside my name to connote that I was under a restraining order by the Supreme Court was accepted by Cuenco. The compromise gave the KBL leadership a graceful way out of the problem.

A Pleasant Surprise

One pleasant development in the prolonged debates on whether or not my name should be retained in the Roll of the Batasan was the intervention of Bono Adaza. He supported Cuenco's stand that my name should not be expunged.

The chief value of Adaza's participation was that he spoke on the issue at all. Like a Vietcong ambuscade that upset many a well-laid plan of the American troops in the Vietnam war, he used the element of surprise to catch not only the KBL Batasan members off-guard but also the Opposition in general. Not too many of our colleagues believed that he would take the floor to defend a proposition that would benefit me. Nonetheless, he did.

Although Adaza and I had previously exchanged bitter words over political issues, his family and mine were friends before politics complicated our relationship. In fact, when the volcano Hibok-Hibok in Camiguin had a major eruption in the 1950s, my father and mother gave their family temporary refuge in our modest home in Cagayan de Oro. Also, Bing was a principal sponsor at the baptism of his and Margot's first born, Aileen.

I was, therefore, not too surprised when Adaza stood up to defend a legal proposition, not necessarily me as a person, that the Speaker was wrong in expunging my name from the roll of Batasan members. I had known him as a fierce exponent of law in our days as legal practitioners in Cagayan de Oro and as neophyte executives in local governments, he as the governor of Misamis Oriental and I as the mayor of Cagayan de Oro.

The KBL had the last word in the debate. Assemblyman Dinlayan of Bukidnon spoke after Adaza. But like an off-tune soloist in a concert that was ending well without him, Dinlayan's chanting of the Speaker's already overused and untenable position aggravated the KBL stand on the issue.

Climaco Murdered

After the decision to retain my name in the Batasan roll of members was made, a piece of sad news reached the Batasan that Zamboanga City Mayor Cesar Climaco had been murdered that very day. In a fitting tribute to the memory of the man, the Batasan immediately calendared for discussion Resolution No. 217 condemning the assassination of Mayor Cesar Climaco. The resolution also sought the creation of an ad hoc committee to investigate his assassination.

Many of our colleagues took turns in extolling the virtues of the fallen mayor of Zamboanga City. It was left, however, to Assemblyman Quintana to give a portrait of Climaco as a human being, a caring public official, guileless and absolutely devoted to his constituents. Quintana's speech, which sounded more appealing in Tagalog, is translated roughly as follows:

> On August 25, 1984, Mayor Cesar Climaco met me at the Zamboanga City Airport. When he saw me, he grabbed my hand-carried bag to carry it himself. I told him, "Mayor, that does not seem right."
>
> "Hjalmar," he said, "your are my visitor."
>
> I was his visitor during the inauguration of the miniature monument of the late Ninoy Aquino in his favorite park, Abong Abong, in Zamboanga City.
>
> When we got to his house, we ate dinner, then we walked around. His driver accompanied us. Neither Mayor Climaco nor his driver was armed.... We went around the city of Zamboanga.
>
> We went to Abong Abong. We saw a group of young people, young boy scouts and girl scouts. When they saw Cesar Climaco, they stood up and sang "*Ay, si Cesar, ay, si Cesar, ay si Cesar Climaco; esta viejo pero pogi, ay, si Cesar Climaco.* Look at Cesar, look at Cesar, look at Cesar Climaco; he is old, but still handsome. Look at Cesar Climaco."
>
> [Then] we went to the Grave of the Unknown Soldiers, which Cesar also constructed in Abong Abong. And then he asked the veterans, whom we saw there. "Have you eaten?" They said, "Not yet, Mayor."
>
> We went back to his house, got *suman*, a sticky rice dish, and went back to Abong Abong. Like a child, Cesar Climaco distributed the *suman*, himself. I asked him, "Mayor, why distribute the *suman* yourself?"
>
> He said what he was doing was but a small token of service that he was rendering to the veterans, many of whom had died for the country. He considered it "an honor to serve the veterans."

After the speeches, the Batasan unanimously approved Resolution No. 217.

Because I was out of the Batasan, I could not put in a word of praise for my friend, Cesar Climaco, in the halls of the assembly. The family of the late mayor, however, asked me to be a special guest at his burial. I went to his interment. The truth is that, even if I had not been asked to pay my last respects to Cesar, I would have done so willingly.

Cebu Indignation Rally

On my way to Zamboanga City, I dropped by Cebu City where I joined an indignation rally spearheaded by PDP-Laban leaders, Tony Cuenco and Nenita Cortez-Daluz that protested the killing of Climaco and the militarization of the country. The rally drew more than 10,000 marchers according to the *Freeman*, a Cebu City daily.

While in Cebu City, the Cebu Breakfast Club had me as a guest speaker on the morning of November 17 where I discussed the necessity of removing the US military bases. The main reason, I said, was that the bases propped up the Marcos dictatorship as instruments of the further oppression of the people, instead of being used to protect and enhance our freedoms and liberties. The *Freeman* further reported that I did so in the presence of the American Consul in Cebu, Stanley Ifshin. It did not really matter to me whether Ifshin or any other US embassy official or personnel was there. The issue had to be discussed openly so that the people would know whether it was good or bad to retain or remove the bases. There was no need in my mind to keep our stand secret, even from the Americans. During the day, in interviews with the *Republic News* daily and the radio station DYRF, I said that the country could not recover from its "economic crisis under Marcos. Having lost their confidence in Marcos, the people could not be expected to rally behind him."

I got to Zamboanga City on November 19 to condole with Climaco's family. I felt a personal sense of loss, not only because he had been a colleague in the Batasan, but also because he and I were two of the three elected Opposition mayors in Mindanao in the 1980 local elections. And he and I were bound by a common vision to serve our people faithfully and see democracy and freedom restored to the country.

I had enjoyable memories of him when we went to a conference of city mayors in the US early on in our incumbency and when he visited me in Cagayan de Oro. When I met him at the Cagayan de Oro airport, he immediately pulled a joke on me. I saw him carrying a tote bag that did not look heavy by the way he handled it. In consideration of his age, I offered to carry the bag. He willingly gave it to me. As I took it from him, I almost lost my balance. The bag was very heavy. He had his barbells in it! He let out a loud guffaw that I did not find amusing. When I recovered my bearings, I carried

1983: HAPPIER TIMES WITH MAYOR Cesar Climaco during his visit to Cagayan de Oro. I introduce my daughter Teresa to him. He half seriously tells Teresa, "Thank God, you look like your Nanay!"

the bag as if it were the easiest thing to do to show him that I, too, could carry the heavy load as nonchalantly as he.

Susan de los Reyes, one of the late mayor's closest confidants and the No. 1 councilor of Zamboanga City at the time, recalled that I had given — in her words — "a moving eulogy" at Climaco's graveside which challenged those he had left behind "to uphold his ideals and to intensify the struggle for the freedom of our people."

In Zamboanga, I also gave a statement to the media. *Veritas* quoted me as saying that the "climate of fear" enveloping Zamboanga engendered by the blatant killing of Climaco was aggravated by the fact that the military had absolute control of Zamboanga City.

Following Climaco's murder, the military spoke of several "leads" on the identity of his killer or killers. One of the suspects, Rizal Alih, was a police officer in the city. The motive, the military intelligence said, was that Alih reportedly suspected the mayor of having engineered the shooting of Alih's brother. When I was interviewed by Virgilio S. Labrador and Efren Danao of *Veritas*, I said that Alih was Zamboanga's Galman, a reference to the fall guy whom military officials had tagged as the killer of Ninoy Aquino.

In a conversation I earlier had with Alih, he recounted an incident that convinced me he could not have killed Climaco. He said that, shortly before the mayor was assassinated, his brother, Lt. Abdul Rassad Alih, was shot near the mayor's house. When he rushed to the scene of the shooting, he came upon the mayor, all by himself, ministering to his brother. Alih said:

> If I thought that the mayor had a hand in killing my brother, I would have immediately taken revenge. That I did not was proof that I did not blame the mayor at all for what happened to my brother. In fact, I considered his trying to help my brother, at the crucial moment, an act that merited my eternal gratitude.

Batasan Reintroduces My Name

Some days before the burial of Climaco, at the Batasan session of November 14, my name appeared with asterisks in the roster of members in this wise: "Pimentel**." A footnote at the bottom of the page of the list explained the asteriks: "Under restraining order issued by the Supreme Court in the case of Pimentel vs. Comelec, KBL and Roa, GR No. 68113."

I saw the reintroduction of my name in the list of members of the Batasan as a good omen that I would soon be back in the legislative body. In the meantime, I continued to speak out on the problems of the nation.

In an interview, I told Sheila Coronel of the *Philippine Panorama*, that the Comelec acted "with unseemly haste" — probably to steal the thunder from the dissenting opinion of the four members of the Agrava Board who submitted their findings on the day I was ousted. In the interview published on November 11, Coronel pictured me as "brave and confident, cool for a man so beleaguered and every inch the political animal." She had interviewed me as the mayor of Cagayan de Oro before my election to the Batasan and she wrote that I was a "more skillful interview subject now than two years ago" and despite my ouster, I was also "more sure" of myself and of my political role.

The reason why I was "cool for a man so beleaguered" — and this Coronel did not know — was that I was not overly attached to the office Roa and I were fighting over. I was concerned about the truth. And my position was simple: if the people of Cagayan de Oro voted for me, then I should sit as their representative at the Batasan. If not, then Roa should represent the city, not I.

Coronel quoted an unnamed Batasan Opposition member as having said that "Nene is a very outspoken oppositionist and, among us, one of the most acceptable to the parliament of the streets." The unnamed source added that "among us, he is one of those with political ambitions beyond being assemblyman and so they ... wanted him out."

The decision of the Comelec was unprecedented in that, among other things, "it was the first one [that caused] the ouster of a person already exercising his functions as assemblyman." Although unprecedented in that respect, the record of the Comelec Division led by Commissioner Savellano also showed that it had consistently "voted in favor of KBL candidates in the cases of *Javier vs. Pacificador* (Antique); *Yap vs. Sawit* (Tarlac); and *Padilla vs. Perez* (Nueve Ecija)."

Savellano admitted in the Coronel article that "the decision was unpopular." Coronel said, "In fact, most people greeted the news of Pimentel's ouster with disbelief."

MFP Protests Ouster

Meanwhile even in the US, my ouster from the Batasan caught the attention of Filipino expatriates. Cesar Arellano, US Midwest Chairman of the Movement for a Free Philippines, wired his protest in behalf of the MFP against my ouster to the Supreme Court. Arellano also sent telegrams to US members of Congress and the State Department asking them to look into the matter of my ouster.

A typical answer to Arellano's crusade to get the attention of the US Congress to my ouster came from Congressman Sidney Yates. Yates wired him back:

> I share your concern about what is happening in the Philippines under the Marcos government. You may be sure that I will pay very careful attention to the administration's budget request for the Philippines when it is considered by the Foreign Operations Subcommittee in the new Congress.

Faith in the Supreme Court

Despite my setback at the hands of the Supreme Court, I believed that, in time, the court would rectify its error. After all, it had, time and again, come to my rescue in many a legal battle that I fought during the Marcos years. In late November 1984, for instance, I won a signal legal victory in the rebellion case in Cebu filed against me when I was still mayor of Cagayan de Oro. The Supreme Court ruled that I should be excluded from the amendments to the charges of rebellion that were filed originally against Ribomapil Holganza, his son Joey and Dr. Filemon Alberca of Cebu and four others. This was the case that led first to my incarceration in the military jails in Cebu and then later to my house arrest in Cagayan de Oro.

The ruling was published in the *Bulletin Today* of November 24, 1984 with the headline, "SC excludes Pimentel in rebellion charges." The Supreme Court ruled:

> The inclusion of Pimentel as an additional accused to be tried jointly with his alleged co-conspirators in the rebellion case prejudices the original seven accused as they will be held liable not only for their acts but also for the acts of Pimentel in the same way that accused Pimentel would become equally liable for the acts of those originally accused.

The ruling disposed of the rebellion case as far as I was concerned. The prosecution apparently did not ask for a reconsideration of the ruling and that sort of ended the rebellion case against me.

Sideshow to Batasan Case

Earlier, on November 7, the national daily, *Malaya* reported an interesting sideshow to my Batasan election problems. In a headline, the *Malaya* said, "Comelec man exposes P50,000 bribe try" in connection with the charges that Roa filed against me. When I read the headline, I thought that a Comelec man was charging me with bribing him. The news item, however, clarified that it was Roa's camp that attempted to bribe the Comelec official.

The Comelec man was none other than the legal officer of Comelec Region X, Jose Amarga, the person whom Comelec Manila designated as the chair of the City Board of Canvassers in lieu of Bernardita Cabacungan, the City Election Officer. Amarga said that a prominent lawyer supporter of Roa offered to bribe him with P50,000 to alter the canvass results of the elections. In his statement, Amarga said that, had he agreed, "two other Comelec people from Manila" would facilitate the handling, and, inferentially, the "doctoring" of the certificates of canvass that would then be used to unseat me from the Batasan. The funny thing was that Amarga was Comelec Regional Director Garcillano's choice to replace City Election Registrar Cabacungan because she was suspected of being a closet supporter of mine. The truth was that Cabacungan was, at that time, closer as a friend to Homobono Adaza than to me. When asked by media friends what I thought of the episode, I said in Visayan, *"Nagaba-an sila!* They got their just deserts!"

The Roa supporter mentioned in the news item sued Amarga for libel in

Manila instead of in Cagayan de Oro to make things more difficult for him. In the face of the flagrant harassment of Amarga, I felt that I should help him somehow. The most practical way was to provide him with legal assistance. I asked my friend, Francis Garchitorena, to represent Amarga as his counsel. Francis did such a good job at it that Fiscal Emilio Bernabe, Jr., of Manila dismissed the case against Amarga on June 17, 1985, for lack of jurisdiction.

At the time, the bribery story was more newsworthy than the other things that my political rivals were doing to prevent my assumption of the position as the representative of the City to the Batasan. But, at bottom, my opponents had one major tactical objective: to bring the questioned ballots to the Supreme Court pursuant to its resolutions of October 31 and December 19, 1984.

Ballot Boxes to Manila

Despite the two orders of the Supreme Court, there was no movement in the case until after the Christmas season was over. Unfortunately, in the Philippines — the only Christian country in Southeast Asia — even the demands for speedy justice in my case took a back seat when the Christmas holiday spirit consumed the attention of the people in or out of the government.

It was only on January 14, 1985, almost a month after the Supreme Court order dated December 19, 1984, that an Air Force C130 plane finally lifted off from Cagayan de Oro for Manila with the ballot boxes. Our PDP-Laban supporters, led by Jacob Montesa, Willy Cuenca and Pepe Abbu, hanging on to straps inside the belly of the mammoth military cargo plane, stood by four 8'x4' marine plywood containers holding the questioned ballot boxes for the 90-minute flight to Manila.

Upon arrival at the Villamor Air Base, they were met by PDP-Laban volunteers, mainly from Parañaque. Party leaders Elfren Cruz, Toti Ferrer, Pepe Sarmiento, Bening Allanigue and several other PDP-Laban party mates from Manila, Quezon City and nearby places were on hand to provide security arrangements for the transportation of the ballot boxes from the air base to the Supreme Court.

Elfren Cruz described what he saw:

> I was surprised when the tailgate of the C130 opened to see PDP-Laban members from Cagayan de Oro sitting on top of the ballot boxes. That was how dedicated they were. It was there that I met Jacob Montesa, Willy Cuenca, Pepe Abbu, Steve Picut, Suzing Abueme, Emerald Platino and Raul Sabuero, volunteer supporters of Nene Pimentel from his city.

The recount of the votes at the Supreme Court required that, in addition to my lawyers, I had to organize my own team of revisors, provide their per diems, their meals and transportation. I also needed round-the-clock security teams to physically guard the premises of the Court where the ballot boxes were kept. I must say that my security teams did an excellent job of ensuring the integrity of the questioned documents and preventing access of unauthorized personnel to the questioned ballot boxes.

Rain or shine they kept vigil in the premises of the Supreme Court to watch over the ballot boxes, much like the guards who keep a sleepless eye over the Crown Jewels of England. I would say our volunteers did the Queen's Royal Guards one better because, while some of our volunteers stood guard, others slept on bare mats right next to the padlocked room where the ballot boxes were kept in the Supreme Court. They did this tedious chore without letup from January to November 1985 when the case was resolved with finality.

Among the members of PDP-Laban in Metro Manila who secured the ballot boxes in the Supreme Court were Bert Roa, Arthur Esplana, Freddie Geronimo, Rolly Flores, Mauricio Austria, Mario Gines, Chingching Marcelino, Alfredo Rogelio, Bobby de Mesa, Junior de Mesa, Danny Macasado, Donato Estacio, Ising Garcia, Wilfredo Baro, Efren Aquino, Emer Sta. Ana, Rolly Aquino, Wilfredo Reyes, Arsenio Espiritu, Oscar Novales, Romy Soriano, Raul Santiago, Doming Santos, Rudy Arcega, Rolly del Rosario, Ernesto Teparel, Wilfredo Parro, Clodualdo Carrasco, Hector Aviles, Jessie Guevarra, Pines Gamboa, Garrie Legaspi, William Galvan, Jaja Banga, Butz Suarez, Cery Sabilano, Art Bulquirin, Mary Ann Sartorio, Butz Guidote, Cris Samson, Arnel Antonio, Norman Borja, Bernie Osorio, Boy Lopez, lawyer Art Amansic Leonardo, Chito Sombilon and Dr. Narip Cruz.

On January 22, 1985, the Supreme Court started to examine the originals of the disputed election returns and compare them with the other copies in the possession of other officials and persons.

Rallying the People

While waiting for the Supreme Court to decide my case against Roa, I devoted my time to building up the PDP-Laban, spreading the gospel of freedom, justice and peace and prophesying the imminent collapse of the martial law regime. I was in several places in Luzon, the Visayas and Mindanao in a matter of days most of the time rallying the people against the Marcos regime.

In my talks before mass audiences or social clubs, I never failed to mention that, contrary to the Marcos promises in 1972 of a better tomorrow for our people, he had impoverished the nation and ruined its democratic moorings. Additionally, he plunged the nation into a cycle of violence from which there seemed to be no redress unless he was evicted from power.

One of the things for which Marcos could rightfully be blamed, I invariably said, was the fact that senseless salvagings, extralegal executions or outright state murders, under his regime had caused the deaths of the best and the brightest of the land. Among the ones that I often cited as examples were Ninoy Aquino, Cesar Climaco, Macliing Dulag (tribal leader of the Kalingas who opposed the construction of the Chico River Dam), Dr. Roberto de la Paz,

Fr. Tulio Favali, Fr. Alberto Romero, Fr. Nilo Valerio, Fr. Godofredo Alingal, Fr. Zacarias Agatep, Edgar Jopson, Alex Orcullo, Jacobo Amatong, Renato Bucag and Fr. Rudy Romano.

There were also scores of nameless people who were executed by the so-called "secret marshals" — 1,000 of them — that Marcos fielded in Metro Manila. The marshals were supposed to flush out and do away with bad people as their historical namesakes did in the Wild West saga of American history. And they did so with gusto. A report we in the Opposition received indicated that they killed more than 40 people in a little over a week. In one incident they killed someone from my home province, Misamis Oriental. The poor fellow was scheduled to leave for a job in the Middle East when he was fatally shot while drinking beer on a sidewalk with some friends by secret marshals on the eve of his departure. There were other unfortunate victims. Sadly at the time, we had no adequate redress for them. In any case, the secret marshals were disbanded quietly, as a result, among other things, of the outcry — in and outside the Batasan — that we made against the perils they posed against our own people.

Malaysian Intrusion

While our attention was focused on human rights violations, a serious intrusion into our sovereign territory took place. Malaysian troops attacked populated areas in Maddanas Island in the province of Tawi-Tawi on September 26, 1985. The attacking troops killed 53 people according to Brig. Gen. Carlos B. Aguilar, commander of the Western Mindanao Constabulary and Police Command.

The Aguilar report said the Malaysian attack was in retaliation to a raid that pirates from Sulu had conducted in the coastal town of Lahad Datu in Sabah three days earlier. The pirates robbed a bank and killed five Malaysians.

I thought that the Marcos government would react forcefully to the punitive action that the Malaysian government conducted within our national territory, but it did not. Prudence, I suppose, dictated the weak government response. The Marcos presidency was under siege by demonstrations and labor strikes at home. Even if he wanted to, he was not in a position to mobilize the nation for a confrontation with Malaysia. Defense Minister Enrile meekly shrugged off the incident as being "more of a diplomatic than a security problem." Frankly, I did not see how the incident that took the lives of 53 Filipinos could merely be a "diplomatic problem." But that was how he saw it and he was the Minister of National Defense. Accordingly, the controlled media in Manila largely ignored it.

LAWYER EXTRAORDINARY and political strategist, Fred Gapuz.

1980: ME AND BONO ADAZA in better times.

SELF-TAUGHT PAINTER MULAWAN gives me paintings that depict our struggle for freedom in Cagayan de Oro.

1981: LAWNDALE OFFICIALS show Bing (in yellow dress) and me (in Barong Tagalog) the "Oro Lane" which they named in honor of Cagayan de Oro.

I

1981: A RARE MOMENT *in the* Mayor's office. The cameraman catches me all by myself

1982: BING AND I *pose with Ninoy. Picture was taken by Cory at their house in Boston.*

1983: 2ND *NATIONAL CONVENTION OF PDP in Cagayan de Oro. (Left to right):* Fr. Francisco Demetrio, SJ, me, Anding Roces, Tony Cuenco and Tito Guingona.

1983: COMING HOME *from Cebu jails I (with lei) am mobbed by welcomers.*

1983: A HUGE DELEGATION of PDP-Laban members go to the Manila International Airport to welcome Ninoy home on August 21, 1983.

1983: AT NINOY'S BURIAL, PDP-Laban members join the 13-hour procession.

1983: DODONG HOLGANZA is allowed to visit me at my cell. His acquaintance with an alleged New People's Army commander led to my detention in Cebu.

1983: INDAY NITA DALUZ (center) visits me in Camp Sotero Cabahug in Cebu City, Bing to her left.

1983: *COUNCILOR GUILLY PARREL plans people power protest in Cagayan de Oro against my arrest with Rene Barrientos (left) and Jun de Gracia (right).*

1983: *LABAN MEMBERS protest violation of human rights, ejection of slum dwellers and military abuses. They also call for the adoption of the Federal System of government.*

1984: *SPEAKER PRO-TEMPORE SALIPADA Pendatum warmly greets me on a visit to the Batasan while I await the Supreme Court order to restore me to my seat. Smiling (at the center) is Celing Fernan.*

1985: *I EXPLAIN the volatile situation in the country to US audiences after the Aquino assassination.*

1986: *PDP-LABAN participate in the proclamation rally of Cory Aquino as the candidate of the Opposition against Marcos.*

Part 10

The Opposition's Platform & Other Issues

1985: *I LEAVE FOR THE US to address the Council of Foreign Relations. At my back (left) Joey Lina and on my right, Bebot Paza, the security officer assigned to me by the PNP.*

Chapter 42:

CFR Invitation

While waiting for the wheels of justice to turn again in my case against Roa and the Comelec, I received an unexpected invitation to speak before the Council on Foreign Relations (CFR) in New York and its affiliates in the US. The invitation to discuss the country's situation in a no-holds barred dialogue was extended by Walter Levy, an official of the CFR, through Paul Kriesberg. The invitation also included a series of high-level discussions with Canadian, French and Belgian officials that took all of January 11 to March 1, 1985.

I was flattered by the invitation, especially after I was told that notable persons who had addressed the councils in the last two years included Prime Minister Zhao Ziyang of China, President Robert Mugabe of Zimbabwe, Prime Minister Robert Muldoon of New Zealand and President Daniel Ortega of Nicaragua. Kriesberg also assured me that the council would organize audiences for me in the major cities of the US, as well as in Canada and Europe. What made the invitation even more enticing — considering my tight financial situation — was the fact that it would be an all-expense-paid trip.

I accepted the invitation, but I told Kriesberg I had a problem. My passport had to be renewed. He suggested that I work on it and he proposed that I leave by the first week of January 1985.

Passport Hassle & Airport Scare

I applied to have my passport renewed seasonably, but the bureaucrats at Malacañang and the Ministry of Foreign Affairs gave me the runaround so that, a day prior to my scheduled departure on January 11, the question of whether or not I would get my passport was still unresolved.

Felicitously, on the morning of January 11, an official of the US embassy alerted me to be ready to fly at a moment's notice. I was told that the chair of Chase Manhattan Bank in New York, David Rockefeller, had requested Marcos by phone to allow me to leave for my CFR speeches. Marcos, apparently, gave that permission because my passport was renewed and delivered posthaste to me at Taza de Oro, the coffee shop hangout of Opposition personalities in Manila.

The US Embassy official then escorted me to the airport for the flight to New York. That was my first personal experience on how Uncle Sam could get his way in this country whenever he wanted to flex muscle for whatever cause.

I was already at the pre-departure area when I had another scare that my trip would be aborted. A Reuters correspondent phoned to ask if I knew that a new case for rebellion had been filed against me that morning. I did not know it and told him so. He then gave me the court case number. Luckily, no warrant of arrest was served on me at the airport and I was able to go on with the trip.

The delayed renewal of my passport and the filing of a new case of rebellion against me were not the only problems that bugged the CFR invitation to me. There were also the nasty rumors spread by my critics.

Malicious Carpings

They circulated stories that I had become an "Amboy," a derisive term for somebody who would do anything to please Mother America, or worse, a stool pigeon of the CIA or some such canard. I did not pay too much attention to the malicious carpings because they were so manifestly untrue.

I was, however, bothered more by the opinion of Alfonso P. Policarpio who wrote for *Malaya*. Policarpio's December 13, 1984 column had this titillating headline, "Reagan invites Nene Pimentel to his inaugural." There was no truth to it. Reagan did not invite me to the US; the Council on Foreign Relations did. But the column provided my critics with the ammunition to question my credentials as an oppositionist who would take no dictation even from the US.

Preparing for the Trip

While waiting for my passport to be renewed, friends in Manila excitedly helped me prepare for the trip. Some had a tuxedo tailored for me, others gifted me with two new pairs of shoes — one for formal and another for informal affairs. Still others gave vitamins, toiletries and knickknacks. Another bunch of friends taught me table manners. They accurately guessed that, since I was a *provinciano,* I would have difficulty choosing which fork or spoon to use in multi-course official luncheons or dinners to which I would inevitably be invited. Getting used to a three-piece suit was no problem, especially in the freezing weather that greeted me in New York, Washington and Canada. But, despite the last minute teach-ins on table manners, an awkward incident took place during a formal dinner tendered in my honor in Philadelphia, as we shall see several pages hence.

Phone Call to Bing

In this trip, my port of entry was New York. On the evening of January 11, I breezed through Customs and Immigration, courtesy of my host. Upon arrival at my hotel, I called up Bing to let her know I had arrived safely. I also inquired if it was true that a new rebellion charge had been filed against me. She replied in the affirmative and said the Manila press had reported that I left for the US shortly after the rebellion charge was filed.

Bing added that a warrant for my arrest had already been issued. I was thus forewarned that I would be arrested upon my return home. At that point though, the thought of my being arrested when I got back did not quite faze me. I focused my energies on analyzing the concerns of the audiences I would be addressing and how I could adequately depict the oppressions that martial law has brought upon our people.

Since I had a couple of days before the formal start of my schedules on January 15, I met with a number of friends in my free time.

Among my first visitors the day following my arrival were my former colleagues at the Constitutional Convention, Jose Calderon and Bonifacio Gillego. Manong Pepe Calderon was the chairman and president of the mining companies that I had worked with soon after my release from my first incarceration under martial law in 1973. He took me to dinner at a seaside resort way out of the city of New York. There we talked about the political situation in the country. I told him and his companions why the CFR invited me and that the Opposition groups in Manila would present one candidate against Marcos in the event of a presidential election.

In the next few days, I met with other individuals whose common denominator was their desire to rid the country of Marcos. I told them my assessment of the situation in the country and of my belief that Marcos was not going to last long especially in the light of his responsibility for the murder of Aquino the year before.

CFR Luncheon in New York

At the CFR luncheon meeting on January 15 at the Pratt House on 58 East 88th Street, New York, I was introduced by former US Ambassador to the Philippines William H. Sullivan, the president of the American Assembly. The CFR meeting was off the record and there was not much that I remembered of what Sullivan said of me except that he acknowledged that I was one of those who were sincerely seeking the end of the Marcos regime by peaceful means.

In my talk, I directly addressed the issue of who would succeed Marcos. The matter was of grave concern to the American government and public. The reason was that Marcos made a lot of people, especially foreigners, believe that nobody could succeed him because he was indispensable. Only he could keep the Republic stable for the requirements of international trade, safe for investments and hold the communists at bay. If there was a dearth of leadership material in the country, I said, nobody else was to blame but Marcos. He had imprisoned many potential leaders of the country, harassed those who opposed him and was responsible for the killing of Aquino. His assertion that nobody could stand up to him in an electoral contest for the presidency was merely a propaganda ploy that he was constantly exploiting for the gullible to swallow.

I told them of the Convenor Group composed of Cory, Aquino's widow, Sen. Lorenzo Tañada and businessman Jaime Ongpin. They had drawn up proposals for choosing the standard bearer to oppose Marcos for the presidency and had identified some alternatives to Marcos. The Convenor Group, I said, also proposed to remove the US bases from the Philippines. I explained:

> The Convenor group took this position because Marcos is using the bases to wangle economic and military concessions from the US. In effect, Marcos is manipulating the presence of the US bases in the country to wring US support for his oppressive policies. The bases are the funnels through which US economic aid and military support are poured into the country. The bases are therefore prejudicing our people instead of helping them. The bases were supposed to be bastions for the protection of the people's freedom and democratic way of life. Now, under Marcos, they are used to further enslave our people.

Although I sensed that the audience did not exactly like what I said, I believed it was important for the Americans to know that we viewed the bases in a light different from theirs.

I also discussed the proposal of the Convenor Group to legalize the Communist Party. I said:

> It is better to allow various ideologies to compete freely in the marketplace of ideas than to suppress them and compel them to seek their place in society by the use of the gun. Because of Marcos's dictatorial policies, he is the No. 1 recruiter for the New People's Army, the military arm of the Communist Party in the Philippines. It is the view of the Convenor Group that legalizing the Communist Party will remove a vital propaganda prop for the active rebellion of the NPA.

Bodyguard

Aside from Sullivan, I also had a chance to interact with Walter Levy, the principal sponsor of my trip; Winston Lord, the president of the New York CFR; and David Chapman, who took charge of my itinerary. Chapman assigned an "interpreter" to accompany me to the major cities in my speaking tour. It was odd that he thought I needed an interpreter when he knew that I spoke English indeed with an accent but well enough to communicate my thoughts. I realized later on that the "interpreter," George Lambert, was actually assigned by the CFR as my bodyguard. He looked the role. He was my idea of a "special forces" agent — quiet, well built, someone who could kill with his bare hands and very knowledgeable about outdoor life. The New York CFR probably suspected I was under threat by Marcos partisans and thought it best that Lambert be at my side during most of my public appearances at the forums the CFR organized.

Call on Fordham President

In between my formal engagements, I had a pleasant call on Fr. Joseph O'Hare, SJ, president of Fordham University, at his office at the Lincoln Center. As a young Jesuit, O'Hare had been assigned to the Philippines. I had a lot to tell him about the support that the Jesuits had extended to me, even as Marcos was persecuting me. I told him of the all-out assistance given me and my family by Fr. Ernesto Javier, SJ, president of Xavier University in Cagayan de Oro, Fr. Francisco Araneta, SJ, and other Jesuits back home. I also mentioned to him the kindness of Fr. Jack Ryan, SJ, who was based in New York at the time. I was extremely happy when Ryan had lunch with me on January 13. I thanked him profusely for the assistance he had extended through a Cagayan de Oro-based Jesuit, Fr. John Gordon, which made life for my family a little more bearable.

Chance Meetings

I also had chance encounters with some of my political friends who were also in New York. Among them were former Senators Jovito Salonga and Salvador Laurel.

I had a brief talk with Jovy Salonga at the La Guardia Airport on January 13. He expressed pessimism over the chances of the Opposition in any election called by Marcos. Of those mentioned by the Convenor Group, he said that he would like to support Diokno or me for the presidency. His remarks about his intent to support Diokno surprised me because Salonga and Diokno were not known to be the best of friends. In fact, their rivalry, which began when they both topped the bar examinations in 1944 with the same score, was of common knowledge. I also knew, however, that Salonga was capable of suppressing his own personal ambitions and giving way to other people. I therefore gave his comment about supporting Diokno the weight that it deserved.

As to his generous reference to the possibility of his endorsing me, I took it for what it was — a manifestation of his gentle nature, which in all likelihood was merely meant to assure me that I was also in his thoughts. In any case, soon after our chance meeting at La Guardia, Salonga went home to a reception at the Manila International Airport that was accorded to dignitaries like him. *Time* magazine in its issue of February 4, 1985 said:

> The government had taken some of the drama from his arrival, first by dropping the subversion charges against him only two days before his homecoming, and then by inviting Salonga's family to participate with the military and other civilians in enforcing tight security precautions at the airport.

In the case of Doy Laurel, I met him at Judy Araneta's Park Avenue apartment. He was trying to get Judy's support for his presidential bid. As an heir of the affluent sugar-landed Aranetas of Manila and Negros Occidental, Judy had a power base of her own, aside from the fact that she was the widow of Gerry Roxas, who immediately prior to the declaration of martial rule was the minority leader of the Philippine Senate.

As Doy and Judy were knowledgeable about the situation back home, we did not discuss the problems we all faced at the hands of the Marcos regime. I merely recounted to them briefly why I was in the US and how I got there. Since I heard that Judy's son Mar was being groomed to run for governor in their home province, I suggested that he should be prepared to live in the province and not be an absentee governor who would stay in Manila most of the time.

Coordinating Council

The day after my speech at the CFR, I met with the Coordinating Council of the anti-Marcos groups in New York at the house of Amador Muriel. There I met Primitivo de Leon, who was a colleague from the Laban group that fought Imelda Marcos in the 1978 *Interim Batasan* elections in Manila. He left for the US soon after the Comelec fraudulently proclaimed Imelda and her group as the winners of the electoral race. I also met Manuel Maravilla and Dr. Orlando Apiado, longtime residents of New York, and Abraham Friedman, an American Jew who generously supported the Movement for a Free Philippines. Friedman was a survivor of the Holocaust in Europe. He lost his parents and siblings in that most horrible episode in European history. He told me that the tragic loss of his family at the hands of Hitler's murderous band of Nazis led him to support the cause of his Filipino friends in New York against the Marcos dictatorship. He believed that all dictators were bad.

I found it sad, though, that the Opposition groups in the US were just as fragmented as the parties at home. By that I meant that the Opposition groups in the East Coast tended to rally behind their individual leaders such as Primitivo de Leon, Poch Macaranas, Norman Madrid, Manuel Maravilla, Willy Crucillo, Joey Ortiz, Boni Gillego, Romy Capulong, King Rodrigo, Jr., Orly Apiado and Sonny Alvarez, instead of banding themselves together as one organization. And in the West Coast, as we shall see, the Opposition groups also followed different leaders.

Incidentally, Sonny Alvarez facilitated my meeting with Rafael Salas, a top UN bureaucrat, who was among those listed by the Convenor Group as a possible presidential candidate against Marcos. It was the first time I met Salas. Before his stint at the UN, he was already a highly respected technocrat in the Philippines.

In our meeting, Salas told me that the Convenor Group nominees for the presidency should be limited to those who had stayed in the country all the years of martial law. I understood that remark to mean that he was disqualifying Manglapus, Salonga and himself. He assured me, however, that he would support whoever was chosen to run against Marcos for the presidency.

Of the appointments made for me in New York, I canceled only one. It was an appointment with an assistant of New York Mayor Edward Koch. I did not think that the assistant of the New York mayor had anything important to discuss with me.

In addition to the New York CFR, my host lined up eight other forums in the US for me to address. These were the Washington, DC, Council on Foreign Relations; the Philadelphia Committee on Foreign Relations; the Boston Committee on Foreign Relations; the Worcester Club of Massachusetts; the Chicago Asian Americans Association; the Chicago City Council; the St. Louis Committee on Foreign Relations; and the World Affairs Council in San Francisco. My speeches hewed closely to the theme I had expounded before the New York CFR.

DC CFR

At the Washington, DC, Council on Foreign Relations, I had the pleasure of being introduced by former Ambassador David Newsom, then associate dean and director of the Institute for the Study of Diplomacy, School of Foreign Service, Georgetown University. Basically, I articulated views similar to those I expressed before the NY CFR.

I must say that my host had carefully organized critical audiences for me to address and had set up meetings for me with US government officials, bankers and business people with great responsibilities over political, economic and military developments in our country.

Foreign Debt

My appointments, for instance, included meetings not only with officials of the World Bank and the International Monetary Fund but also of other banks with which our country had dealings. The bankers were worried not about the impending fall of Marcos but what would happen to the monies they had lent to the country once he was ousted.

The first World Bank official I met with was Attila Karaosmanoglu, vice president for East Asia and the Pacific Region. I discussed with him what I saw was the danger of pumping in so much World Bank money into the country on what might be ill-conceived projects. I pointed to the problem of prices overshooting estimates for projects that had been prepared before the Aquino assassination. I suggested that the World Bank should be a little flexible in its expectations that what Marcos borrowed should be paid back to the last centavo. I floated the idea that the bank and the post-Marcos government should discuss what to do with loans whose proceeds went to the pockets of the cronies of Marcos and not to the promotion of the welfare of the people.

Karaosmanoglu assured me that although the World Bank had to deal with Marcos because he was the president, it would always include in its decisions what was best for the people of the country.

I also talked with Richard Erb, deputy managing director of the International Monetary Fund at the IMF building. We discussed the foreign loans of the country and the difficulties we were encountering in paying off the loans. Erb's view was that unilaterally abrogating the loan contracts would be bad for the credit standing of the country but the restructuring of loans with the concurrence of lending countries could be done.

Earlier in New York, on January 16 at the Federal Reserve Bank building, I discussed the possible scenario of how the post-Marcos government could deal with the loans obtained during martial rule. I also talked about the same concerns with the officials of the Asia Society at the Waldorf Astoria on January 17. The bankers and the businessmen were worried that, in the event a new government took over from Marcos, the huge foreign debt incurred by Marcos would not be paid. I told them:

> The Opposition will not renege on our loan commitments, but we will certainly work for better and more humane terms than the *conditionalities* attached to the original loans or to the restructured loans that Marcos and Virata had obtained from the World Bank/IMF. These loans were causing unspeakable hardships upon our people.
>
> In the Batasan, we are investigating the anomalous use of loan monies, as in the case of the $25 million loan of the Asian Reliability Co., Inc. The ARCI loan scandal was grist for the rumor mills in Manila, which linked Imelda's deputy at the Ministry of Human Settlements, Jose Conrado Benitez, to the anomaly.

A representative of the Manufacturers-Hanover Bank, the lender of the questioned ARCI loan, was among the bankers present at the meeting.

What I did not tell them was that, at the Batasan, Opposition Assemblyman Hernando Perez had made mincemeat of Benitez's attempt to exculpate himself from the mess. From the time Perez called the housing project a *Kubeta* Village or Toilet Village, the demeaning phrase attached to Benitez as the person principally responsible for the mess. Moreover, it did not help his cause that his wife, the chief financial officer of ARCI, was involved in the messy affair in which government agencies guaranteed the corporation's $25 million loan.

Meeting Top Bureaucrats

On January 22, I met with Gaston Sigur of the National Security Council at Room 202 of the Old Executive Office Building on Pennsylvania Avenue. I also had serious discussions with some of the most experienced bureaucrats at the State and Defense Departments like John Maisto, who manned the Philippine Desk at the State Department; Paul Wolfowitz, assistant secretary of state for East Asian and Pacific Affairs; John Monjo, deputy assistant secretary of state for Asia Pacific Affairs; Michael Armacost, undersecretary of state for Political Affairs; Richard Armitage, assistant secretary of Defense; and Morton Abramovitch, chief intelligence officer of the Pentagon (or so I was told). I warned them that:

> The continuing support for the Marcos dictatorship by the US government, particularly in terms of military aid, lent currency to the impression that the interests of the US are now identical to the interests of the Marcos's authoritarian regime. Marcos is using the bases as a pawn to ensure the flow of US economic and military support to his regime.
>
> The bases then ought to be phased out when the lease agreements expire in 1991, not thrown out tomorrow. We are concerned about the welfare of the 30,000 or so workers in the bases. To immediately terminate the bases agreement would result in a social problem that would be caused by the displacement of the bases workers.

On their part, the US officials emphasized that, while the US would continue giving military support to Marcos, there would be conditions to be fulfilled before the funds would be released, like purging the ranks of the military of misfits. I replied that it would not do to isolate the problem of the military from the problem posed by the authoritarian structure of government. The US would, in effect, still prop up Marcos by using the military bases as the conduit for that support.

Armitage told me that the US was "behaving properly towards the Marcos government." He said that to describe the US posture as "distancing" itself from the Marcos regime was incorrect.

Regarding my fears of a military coup in the country, the officials I met said that the US would not support any move that would subvert the constitutional process on presidential succession.

Pentagon Bull Session

At a Pentagon meeting, I was asked to sit on a chair in the pit of a hall that had elevated tiers of seats forming a semicircle like a modified Roman amphitheater. My US Defense interrogators occupied the higher-level seats, so that they looked down on me while I had to look up to them in the course of our conversation. Despite the superior-and-inferior sitting arrangement, I made my stance plain to them:

> I did not come to ask you to assist the Opposition in toppling Marcos. Rather, I ask you to refrain from assisting Marcos because, without your assistance, we can deal with him ourselves and rid the country of his dictatorship.

The communist insurgents in the country, while irksome, do not have the capability of toppling the government in the immediate future. But if democracy is not restored to the country soon, then I fear that a violent upheaval could very well ensue within the next five years. The communist rebels have increased considerably since 1972. The longer Marcos stays in power, the sooner the violent scenario could take place. The Marcos administration is on the verge of collapse. There is no basis for the facile claim that only he can save the nation from the communists. There are hundreds of qualified Filipinos who could take over from him.

I repeated the message that the Convenor Group, led by Cory Aquino, Tañada and Ongpin, had identified possible leaders of the country after Marcos who were not only competent but were also definitely not communists.

Heated Talks

The stand of the Convenor Group and the PDP-Laban that I endorsed before the private groups and the US officials previously mentioned did not ease the apprehensions of the Americans. At the Worcester Club, for instance, former US service men among the audience were so upset by what I said that I could hear rumblings from them even while I was still discussing the issue. They were probably inhibited from booing me only because I was their guest.

I had a similar experience in the meeting I had with Senators William Cohen of Maine and Frank H. Murkowski of Alaska and their staff members on the afternoon of January 23. The meeting did not go well. We had a heated exchange on the issue of the removal of the US bases, even though I said that we were not proposing the immediate termination but rather the phase out of the bases agreement. Cohen and Murkowski had their own inflexible stand on the need for the maintenance of the US bases and I had my position which I was in no mood to alter just because they thought that it was folly and rank ingratitude for us to call for the abrogation of the bases treaty at all. I had to tell them that I did not come to their country to ask for help, not even to get rid of Marcos. We will survive, I said, and we will dispose of Marcos if only the US would not support the Marcos regime.

Solarz, an American First

At this time, Congressman Stephen Solarz was seen by us who opposed Marcos as a pillar of support for our cause. Indeed, he was. But, when I discussed the bases issue with him, I saw that his position was the same as that of the other US officials. He wanted the bases retained. Probably because of the pronounced anti-bases stand of the Convenor Group and PDP-Laban, one of his aides suggested to him in my presence that perhaps the best candidate they could support was Salvador Laurel. Doy Laurel did not agree with the Convenor Group's platform on the phasing out of the bases.

I also had a conference with Senate Foreign Relations Committee staff members led by Fred Brown and Carl Ford at Room 446, Dirksen Senate Office Building. Brown and Ford usually represented the Republican and the Democratic parties respectively in conferences on foreign policy issues. Basically, I articulated the same views on the state of the insurgency in the country, the Opposition's stand on the removal of the US bases and the post Marcos scenario as spelled out in the platform of the Convenor Group.

Brown and Ford did not dispute any of my interpretation of the unfolding events in the country. They were more interested in hearing me out than in arguing for or against my stand on the issues that concerned them. In that respect, I think that they were good bureaucrats who did their work drawing out insights from me on the issues of the day concerning the county rather than their trying to proselytize me with their preconceived notions of what our relationship with their country should be.

Human Rights

The breaks in my official schedule afforded me time to meet with other sectors including anti-Marcos personalities and groups in the US.

For instance, I discussed the issue of human rights with two concerned Americans, namely Jonathan Fine, president of the American Committee for Human Rights, and Richard Hoolbrooke, former deputy assistant secretary of state for Asian and Pacific Affairs of the Carter administration.

I told Fine about the deteriorating condition of human rights in the country. Specifically, I drew his attention to the case of Ribomapil Holganza, his son Joey and Dr. Filemon Alberca, whose detention since 1983 without any end in sight was a clear case of violation of human rights. He promised to look into it. The Holganzas and Alberca were charged in the same rebellion case that caused my incarceration in the Cebu military jails in that year.

Hoolbrooke was pleased to hear my assessment that Carter's human rights policy — though implemented halfheartedly — had a positive impact in the Philippines. As an example, I cited the release from indefinite detention of Tondo urban poor leader, Trinidad Herrera, after the US government expressed its concern about her. Herrera was horribly tortured sexually by her military captors. I also mentioned that, the day after Carter's Vice President, Walter Mondale, left Manila in June 1978, Marcos released those of us who had been detained in Camp Bicutan in connection with our demonstration against the farcical Interim Batasan elections of that year. I attributed our release, among other things, to the pressure exerted on the Marcos government by Carter's human rights policy.

Supportive Americans

It was also gratifying for me to have met separately two Americans who saw developments in the country in a different light from the way official America did. One of them was retired US Navy Admiral Gene R. La Rocque, whom I saw at the Center for Defense Information on Maryland Avenue in Washington, DC. The other was New York City Councilwoman Miriam Friedlander whom I visited at her office. The two boosted my argument against the continued presence of the US bases and of nuclear weapons in the country.

The admiral said that the US did not actually need the bases in the Philippines for its security requirements, but for the comparatively cheap repair and refueling facilities that the bases offered. I told La Rocque I was amazed but thankful that he supported the call for the removal of the bases. Now I could point to an American naval officer who disagreed with the official line of the Pentagon on the bases issue but who could not be tagged as a communist. Nonetheless, I said that the repair-and-refueling services needed by the US could still be continued but under a commercial - not a military - agreement between our two countries.

Councilwoman Miriam Friedlander, on the other hand, actively opposed the entry of nuclear powered or armed vessels into the port of New York. She expressed interest in the idea that I broached to her of establishing an anti-nuclear network covering New York, New Zealand, Japan and the Philippines. My meeting with her was a high point in my visit to New York. I found that there was international support for a ban on the proliferation of nuclear weapons — such as the one PDP-Laban called for.

Addressing Filipino Groups

Among the Filipino groups that feted me in the US capital was the University of the Philippines Alumni Association in Washington, DC. They held the affair at the National Press Club Building. They were interested to know what the post-Marcos scenario would mean for the country. I gave them the same assessment that I made before the NY and DC CFRs.

Charito Planas, Gerry Jumat and his wife Boots also organized a dinner meeting for me at the home of Dave Valderama in Virginia. Valderama, a Filipino immigrant to the US, was active in the statewide politics of Virginia and had twice been elected to its State Assembly.

In the open forums that followed my speeches, I noticed that the older persons tended to support the retention of the bases, while the younger ones argued for their removal. The pros contended that the presence of the bases was economically beneficial to the country, and that the bases lent stability and security to the State. The antis argued that the bases were no longer relevant to the times. At the Valderama forum, the age divide split the audience. The discussions between the pro-bases and the anti-bases became rather heated.

Maryland State Senator Frank Komenda pleaded that the discussants should explain their positions with candor but dispassionately so that, in his words, "the needs of the US and the Philippines might be better understood."

It was amusing that among the several audiences listening to me were many Filipino expatriates who lived in the US for at least a generation but who felt threatened by the proposals to legalize the Communist Party. They did not seem to know that Communist Parties were recognized legally in many parts of the world, including the US.

The last big Filipino anti-Marcos group that I addressed in Washington, DC, was the Movement for a Free Philippines. The MFP dinner was held at the home of its president, Raul Manglapus and his wife, Pacita LaO. Manglapus was best known as the indefatigable and uncompromising leader of the MFP in the US. He was my colleague in the 1971 Constitutional Convention and a sponsor at my and Bing's wedding. There were many Filipino and American anti-Marcos activists at the affair where I explained basically the theme that I had been repeating in all my talks before audiences in the US.

I was a little disappointed though, that Manglapus announced at the dinner, he was taking an eight-month fellowship at Harvard. To me, that meant he did not think the fall of Marcos was imminent. In any event, it was a fruitful evening during which the audience and I had a very good exchange of views on the situation back home. At the end of affair, Manglapus and I issued a joint statement calling on Marcos to respect human rights and free political detainees.

Boston & Chicago

In Boston, an anti-Marcos group gathered in the home of one of the most successful Filipino doctors in the US to hear the message that I had been delivering before other crowds in the US. At this gathering, I met a former colleague at the Constitutional Convention, Mary Rose Jacinto, who left the country shortly before martial law was imposed and never returned. Her family's steel plant in Iligan City in Mindanao had been taken over by the government and they were not paid just compensation for it, she said.

In Chicago, I spoke before two audiences — the Asian-American revelers of the Lunar Year at the McCormick Hotel and the City Council. At the Lunar Year celebration, I shared the spotlight with Sen. Alan Dixon of Illinois. At the City Council meeting, Chicago Mayor Harold Washington received me very kindly. In sum, I delivered the same message of hope for a peaceful change in the country that I spoke of earlier in New York, Washington, DC, and Boston to the Chicago crowds.

Also in Chicago, Cesar Arellano organized a dinner party for me at his home. There I met Filipino expatriates from Cagayan de Oro, like Ben Avarquez, Rafael Cecilio, Roque and Trinidad Luzon, and Oscar and Aida Feliciano.

St. Louis, San Francisco & Los Angeles

In St. Louis, in addition to my appearance before the St. Louis Committee on Foreign Relations, a crowd of MFP leaders heard me at the home of Dr. Arturo Taca. Although he had been in the US for several years and was enjoying a fairly lucrative medical practice in the city, Taca helped the MFP in a manner that bordered on the subversive. As a result, he was on the FBI's watch-list for a number of years. By sheer luck, he avoided being formally accused and tried for violating US laws on the possession and transportation of explosives.

In the West Coast, the Filipino community in San Francisco held a joint affair to hear me. It was a good example of how disparate groups of our countrymen and women in the US could join hands in expressing their desire to oust Marcos. It was made possible only because Steve Psinakis, Gasty Ortigas and Geline Avila spent time and effort to get it done. I was most happy to see my friends and relatives from Cagayan de Oro: Aurora Gayloa, who was married to Bud Bigger, Didi Daomilas and Romeo Neri at the gathering.

But when I got to Los Angeles, the story was different. I had to address three anti-Marcos groups because they could not agree to gather in one venue. Raul Daza and Dr. Rafael Fernando led one group. Serge Osmeña headed another. And a so-called "non-politician" group organized another forum for me.

Common Message

The message I articulated before the separate groups substantially embraced the following:

(1) The Opposition would back up one candidate against Marcos in the event a presidential election was called.
(2) The Convenor Group was screening the presidential probables.
(3) The Opposition has a platform that included a call for the removal of the US bases and the legalization of the Communist Party.
(4) Peaceful change was the option for us, not violence.
(5) I was going home knowing that I would be arrested because new charges of rebellion had been filed against me.

The Filipino audiences, in general, received my appraisal of the situation back home well. There were adverse views coming from those who could not understand why the Opposition advocated the removal of the US bases and the legalization of the Communist Party. Time and again, I had to repeat the justification for the controversial proposals that I had previously explained before the CFR in New York and in Washington, DC.

In Los Angeles, the Osmeña-organized forum was one of the best that I addressed in my speaking tour. He also very kindly drove me to my destinations in his latest model Toyota Lexus. I thanked him for his generosity. But there was a price to it. He lectured me for minutes on end about the need for a more mature, experienced and, inferentially, financially independent person who should take over the leadership of the nation after Marcos. It was clear that he wanted somebody else, not me, to be the Opposition's candidate for president. With as much grace as I could muster, I took all the put downs that he poured all over me as we drove in and around LA, although I was seething inside. I gave him the benefit of the doubt that he probably was saying those things with sincerity and not out of malice. We parted as friends as my tour of the US came to an end with the LA sorties. From there, my next stops were Toronto and Ottawa in Canada.

Canada

I got to Toronto on February 10. On that very evening, I was feted at the residence of a very affluent Filipino doctor, Guillermo de Villa, and his wife Nanette, also a doctor.

The following morning, despite a heavy snowfall, I addressed a symposium sponsored by the joint Center for Modern East Asia Studies of York University and the University of Toronto. I spoke basically on the topics that I had articulated before my US audiences.

The day after, I flew to Ottawa where I discussed with some members of the Canadian Cabinet and Parliament the Convenor statement of principles and the PDP Laban program of action. I returned to Toronto that same afternoon. Late in the evening, I addressed a large crowd of Filipino Canadians at an affair sponsored by the Ninoy Aquino Movement Inc. (NAMI) in a hotel. There, I discussed the Convenor approach to the problem of succession to the Marcos dictatorship and the PDP Laban vision of man and society.

In cold Toronto, I met friends and acquaintances from Cagayan de Oro: Vic Imperio, Guillermo Puyo, Rhett Abarquez and Kiddie Quiblat. Puyo, Abarquez and Quiblat so kindly rendered the popular Visayan song, *Matud Nila*, whose melodious strains brought me images of home. Before I left Canada, a popular television show, *Canada AM*, featured me in a fast question-and-answer segment.

As in the US, my audience in Toronto expressed concern about the platforms of the Convenor Group and PDP-Laban for the removal of the US bases and the legalization of the Communist Party. I explained the rationale of the proposals as I did before the CFR in New York.

Media Coverage

My trip to the US and Canada was widely covered by the media. I considered it a big bonus for me to be interviewed by *Time* and *Life* magazines, the *New York Times*, the *Wall Street Journal*, the *St. Louis Post Dispatch*, the *San Jose Mercury News, Foreign Policy*, the *San Francisco Chronicle*, the *Toronto Star* and the *Globe and Mail*. Filipino newspapers, the *Philippine News* and the *Business Day* also featured my trip.

While I was in Washington, DC, the Washington Press Club interviewed me at the Conference Center at 11 Dupont Circle. William Maynes, editor of *Foreign Policy*, presided at the conference. When I was told that Maynes would interview me, I thought that only he would do so for his publication. I was thus surprised that so many Washington-based journalists were there to grill me. As I sat down in front of the news people, I asked Maynes what the interview would cover. He said, "The Philippine situation." And so it did — the whole gamut of it.

I told the Washington Press Club that the insurgency — both communist and Muslim — had grown under Marcos. His authoritarian rule had failed to stem the growth of communist and Muslim rebels. That alone should suffice why the country should be rid of Marcos, I said.

On the issue of Opposition unity, I said that the Opposition would unite if Marcos called for a presidential election. I repeated what I had said in other forums — that the Convenor Group had started the process of winnowing the probable presidential contenders against Marcos.

Ver's Trial

As for Ver's trial for his complicity in the Aquino assassination, I emphasized that it was only for show. I foresaw a not guilty official verdict but said that, as far as the people were concerned, Ver was already held guilty. And the public's verdict of guilty also applied to Marcos. Ver's trial before the Sandiganbayan, I said was merely a strategem to make the people believe that Marcos wanted the truth to come out regarding the Aquino murder. I did not for one moment believe that Ver would be convicted.

Despite the care that attended my assessment of the Ver trial, it was twisted as an endorsement of Ver's innocence. Even the *Washington Post* of January 23, 1985 echoed that cockeyed view. The article said:

> In Washington, one Opposition leader, Aquilino Pimentel, said he did not think there was enough evidence against Ver....He said he expected Ver to be acquitted after a speedy trial and, after a previously agreed arrangement, return to his duties and then immediately retire.

I uttered those words, but the premises were not cited. *Time* magazine on February 4, 1985, recounted what I said more faithfully: "Aquilino Pimentel, leader of the Democratic Party, has called Ver's indictment a ploy 'to get acquitted and prevent any further charges against him.'"

As I had predicted, the trial resulted in the acquittal of Ver and his co-accused in October 1985.

One piece of crucial evidence of the complicity of the Armed Forces under the command of Ver as chief of staff in the murder of Aquino was not presented by the prosecution. It had to do with Philippine Air Force jets scrambling "to intercept the plane bringing Aquino to Manila from Taipei on the day he was murdered in 1983," as the *San Francisco Examiner* reported on October 28, 1985. US Air Force officers manning the Wallace Air Station were ready to testify that Philippine Air Force officers went to the station to use their facilities to track the flight path of a certain aircraft entering the country's area of responsibility on the day Aquino was assassinated. Had this testimony been introduced in the trial, it would have shown that the high echelon of the Armed Forces were preparing scenarios for the arrival of Aquino and were, therefore, involved in his tragic murder at the tarmac of the Manila International Airport.

The US media also asked about the state of health of Marcos. I said it was an open secret that Marcos was sick of *lupus erythematosus*. Marcos's illness became the subject of much speculation, I said, after Marcos uncharacteristically disappeared from public view for 12 days from November 4 to November 26, 1984. And when he reappeared he was seen by the people with his cheeks bloated that were said to be the effect of hydrocortisone treatment to check the spread of lupus.

Laudatory Items

Some laudatory items about me appeared in the US publications. The *New York Times Magazine* of January 6, 1985, for instance, reported:

> To a greater degree than his peers in the Opposition, Pimentel has won the respect of both the moderate opponents of Marcos and the more militant groups. The moderates voted in the National Assembly election and advocated working for reform within existing institutions, but the more radical of the President's opponents boycotted the election and have chosen to express their views in anti-Government demonstrations or by joining the Communist guerillas.
>
> Above all, Pimentel's rising political fortunes can probably be explained by the fact that his anti Marcos credentials are so pure. Most of Marcos's opponents at one time had links with the President or, at least, remained silent as he placed more and more of the powers of government under his personal control. Pimentel is mentioned as one of several presidential hopefuls in 1987.

Almost a month later, the *New Yorker*, in its February 4, 1985 issue, had this to say:

At the more hopeful end of the clouded spectrum, a real interest in politics and the country's future is being increasingly expressed throughout the islands by local groups of citizens as well as by the national reform bodies.

There is a demand I have not seen before for a new type of leadership, as demonstrated by Pimentel, for example, and by a number of other assemblymen of his generation, or younger, who are also beginning to make their voices heard.

Two days later, the editorial board of the *St. Louis Post Dispatch* interviewed me. The *Post Dispatch* interview came out on February 7 with a rather lengthy question-and-answer commentary, which was entitled, "On the Record: A Talk with the Philippine Opposition" and a subtitle, "Party Leader Aquilino Pimentel Discusses the Political Prospects for His Country."

In the Q&A of the *Post Dispatch*, I spoke of the danger of a coup d'etat occurring in the country to short-circuit the constitutional process of choosing the successor of Marcos. At the time I spoke about it, talk was fast and loose that the young officers of the armed forces wanted a piece of the action to replace Marcos. There was also some talk that General Ver was a probable major player in the event of a coup. I disagreed. I told the *Post Dispatch*:

A military coup can happen only with the backing of the US government because the whole military establishment in my country is structured upon total dependence on the American military. And that is the reason we in the Opposition do not believe that a coup can be staged successfully by General Fabian Ver, the chief of staff of the armed forces who, as you know, is under indictment for the assassination of Benigno Aquino.

We are more fearful of a coup being staged by General Fidel Ramos, the acting chief of staff. And the reason for this is that General Ramos is acceptable to the American military establishment and obviously to the Pentagon and the State Department. He is a West Point graduate, perceived to be a professional soldier.

There are some segments of the business community in Manila who are talking about the necessity of having Ramos head a military-led government apparently in the simplistic view that this is needed to forestall the advance of communism in my country....We are worried that the American government might just buy that line — that Ramos is needed to run the country in the meantime, maybe on an interim basis. We know for a fact from history that it is difficult to justify an interim military takeover, because the interim becomes more or less permanent and it is difficult to put the military people back in their barracks.

On February 10, the *San Francisco Examiner* had a story headlined: "Man with the right credentials to be Marcos' successor" under the byline of Phil Bronstein. It was about me. Bronstein wrote that "Pimentel has emerged as the strongest dark horse" should "Marcos die in office or call early elections." The item also mentioned that I faced "arrest upon return" to my home.

Sizing Me Up

When I accepted the CFR invitation, I knew that the American think tanks wanted to size me up if I was a viable candidate for president, one who would toe the American line. They also probably wanted to find out if I would say one thing before one group and another thing before another. With conscious effort, I kept my messages similar to the one I delivered before the New York Council on Foreign Relations, even when I was already in Canada. I also tried to picture myself as a politician who was concerned with the interests of my country first and foremost and only secondarily with Philippine-US relations.

On February 9, the *Toronto Star* had a small item on me. It said:

> [Pimentel is a] Filipino Social Democrat much given to the intellectual aspects of his philosophy and to the active Opposition to the government of President Ferdinand Marcos....Pimentel is regarded as intelligent and committed to his democratic socialist principles.

Three days later, the *Globe and Mail* had an article with the heading, "Filipino politician pulls few punches" under the byline of Paul Knox. He wrote:

> [Pimentel is] one of the parliamentary Opposition leaders least willing to compromise on questions vital to the Philippines' future. He wants to kick the US military out of the country and bar multinational corporations unless they agree to tough conditions ....He wants US military bases in the Philippines to close when their leases expire in 1991. "Our position is different from that of the radicals who want the bases removed tomorrow," he said. "We would like to negotiate...because we are concerned about the welfare of 20,000 or 30,000 Filipino workers who are directly dependent on the bases for support."
>
> Mr. Pimentel would also legalize the Communist Party of the Philippines — and offer amnesty to guerillas of the increasingly powerful New People's Army. "But over and above these two things, we have to remove the causes of injustice."

Belgium & France

From Canada, I went back to New York and flew on to Brussels on February 13, 1985. I met with Counsellor Etienne Godin of the Ministry of International Relations of Belgium; Jacques Thierry, president of the Banque

Bruselles, and Count Ferdinand D'Oultremont, a director of the Groupe Bruxelles Lambert, SA.

Banque Bruselles and Groupe Bruxelles Lambert were leading members of a consortium of banks in Belgium that extended loans to the country. Their concern was whether or not we would be honoring the debts incurred by Marcos. I told them the same thing that I had told bankers in New York. We would not renege on our loans but that a restructuring of the conditions of the loans was necessary to prevent our people from being exploited by financial agreements that benefited the crony borrowers favored by Marcos.

As in the US, the Belgian press interviewed me and the interview was aired by a television station in Brussels on February 19.

My final stop before coming home was Paris. I got there from Brussels on February 22. In the French capital, I met with Minister of Education Lionel Jospin, Minister of the Budget and Energy Philippe Busquin and Minister of Culture, Jacques Lange. They expressed deep interest in what was happening in the Philippines.

Jospin was keenly interested in the prospects for peaceful change in the country. I told him about the Convenor Group's initiative to unify the Opposition so that we would have only one candidate against Marcos. Busquin inquired about the Opposition attitude towards the external debts that Marcos had obtained. I gave him the same answers that I had expressed in the US and in Brussels.

Lange brought up an issue that I did not hear in the US, Canada or in Belgium. He asked me to relay the concern of his Ministry to the government over the arrest of movie director Lino Brocka who had been detained, along with another film director, Behn Cervantes, by the Marcos government for some utterances supposedly derogatory to the government. Brocka won critical acclaim for his entries at the Cannes Film Festival, *Insiang* and *Jaguar* while Cervantes offended the Marcos government with his "subversive" plays, *Barikada*, and the *Short, Short Life of Citizen Juan*.

Lange added that when Prime Minister Virata was in Paris months earlier, pleading the cause of the Philippine government for more loans with the Paris Club, he had asked him to work for the release of Brocka. The Manila press had downplayed the arrests of Brocka and Cervantes, but since they were notable persons in the world of cinema and the arts, their detention attracted the attention of the French Ministry of Culture. Considering my own problems with the government, all I could tell Lange was that I would see what I could do when I got back home.

The Foreign Ministry officials at Quai d'Orsay inquired about the future of the US bases in the country. I told them the position of the Opposition as expressed in the platforms of the Convenor Group and the PDP-Laban: the bases should leave probably by 1991.

Also in Paris, I had the pleasure of speaking before a large crowd of Filipinos organized by Romy Gamboa and Jun Gomez. They told me that it was the first time any politician from the Philippines had "honored" them with his presence. The migrant Filipinos brought up the main problem facing many of them in France, which was to legalize their stay. I, of course, had no definite solution to that problem, but I told them nonetheless that I would pass the matter on to our diplomats who could handle it better than I, as a legislator.

The French press gave my trip to Paris adequate coverage. The newspaper, *Le Matin*, interviewed me on February 22. It carried the story of my interview in its issue of February 24 under the headline, *"Philippines: Debut du Proces pour le Meurtre D'Aquino."* A French TV station also broadcast a news item about my visit to Paris. On the personal level, I was very happy over the fact that I met a dear friend in Paris, Joseph Enerio of Cagayan de Oro, and his wife Elizabeth, a French lady. In the heart of the city, they had a thriving shop which tourists patronized.

Due to time constraints, I could only visit Belgium and France during that trip to Europe.

From: Le Matin

André Grassart

Aquilino Pimentel, dit « Nene », président du Parti démocratique philippin : « La révolution n'est pas nécessaire pour rétablir la démocratie »

Chapter 43

My Fourth Arrest

On the first of March, I traveled home expecting to be arrested upon arrival — as the government had threatened. No such thing happened. I learned later that the military was ordered not to arrest me in the full glare of the klieg lights of local and foreign television cameras for fear of making me a martyr. Indeed, many journalists covered my arrival at the Manila International Airport.

The following day, the major dailies of Manila put their own spins to the story of my arrival. In a banner story, the *Bulletin Today* wrote, "Pimentel returns, is not arrested." *Malaya* also gave front page treatment to my arrival, "US cold to FM, says 'Nene.'" It also had a picture of me being greeted by friends with the caption in bold letters: "NO ARREST." In its news account, Malaya reported that I had been "offered asylums" in Canada and France — which were exaggerated versions of what really happened—but that I had turned them down. The newspaper was correct, though, that I had said, "This is my country and my home. I came home to continue the battle against the Marcos dictatorship."

The other major dailies, the Marcos-owned *Daily Express* and a Marcos crony-owned *Times Journal* also gave my return prominent coverage. The *Daily Express* quoted me as saying, "I was expecting to be arrested upon arrival. If they want to arrest me, I am here." The *Times Journal* wrote that I would "fight till the end the rebellion charge" against me.

If I had escaped arrest at the airport, it was only because Marcos and his minions were biding their time. They were waiting for a more opportune moment to arrest me on the basis of a warrant that was issued before I left for my CFR engagements in the US, Canada, and other European countries. The arrest came in a matter of days.

The PDP-Laban Convention

Meanwhile, since I was not arrested upon arrival, I was able to attend and preside at the National Convention of the PDP-Laban in Tagbilaran City, Bohol, on March 2 and 3.

I reported to the PDP-Laban national convention the modest gains the party had made since the last national gathering. We placed our membership at a low 70,000 and a high of 100,000. We were now present in the so-called "impossible areas" of Ilocos Sur in Luzon, Tacloban City in the Visayas, and in Tawi-Tawi, the farthest island in the south.

The magnificent performance of our members in the Batasan occupied a major portion of my report. I specifically cited Jimmy Ferrer for his masterful portrayal of the 1985 national budget as wasteful; Bobbit Sanchez for his forceful espousal of human rights; Tony Cuenco for his stand to curb the excesses of the government casinos; Dodo Cagas for his demands that victims of military operations be compensated; Monching Mitra for the cogent cuts he proposed on the budget; and Doc Martinez for his health advocacies.

I also paid tribute to Emy Lingad, Ding Tanjuatco, Inday Nita Daluz, Zaf Respicio, Rolly Marcial and Rogelio Garcia for their vigilance in denouncing all kinds of anomalies in government and for their unstinting support of Resolution No. 162. That was the Resolution that denounced the brutal dispersal on September 21 of the demonstrators at the Quezon City Welcome Rotonda and, more importantly, it upheld the right of the people to peaceably assemble for the redress of their grievances.

In the report, I condemned the continued detention in military cells for two years now of Cebu PDP-Laban stalwarts Ribomapil Holganza, his son Joey and Dr. Felimon Alberca. I had discussed the violation of the human rights of the Holganzas and Alberca with Jonathan Fine, president of the American Committee for Human Rights, in my trip to the US in early 1985. I also censured the Marcos government for the murders of our party mates Jacobo Amatong and Renato Bucag, his wife and son. Amatong was fatally shot in Dipolog City for his crusade against abusive officials. Bucag and family were massacred in Gingoog City by elements of the CHDF.

I suggested to our party mates that we should play the role of unifier of the opposition parties in the broad spectrum of national politics. The Unido, for instance, I said, was an ally even if PDP-Laban was not a member of it. We, therefore, should coalesce with Unido. By doing so, we hoped that we could fight under one flag, as it were, against Marcos.

The convention, to my mind, was a success in that about a thousand delegates attended the affair and there were a lot of new faces coming from many parts of the country, indicating in no uncertain terms that indeed our party was growing very fast.

Cagayan de Oro Arrest

After the Tagbilaran City Convention, I took a boat to Cagayan de Oro. There on March 7, 1985 at 6 p.m., I reported to some 2,000 party members in the open grounds at the back of the City Hall on my recent trip abroad and on the PDP-Laban Convention in Bohol.

When I was through speaking, police officers arrested me on charges of rebellion on the basis of an arrest warrant dated January 28, 1985, issued by Judge Leonardo Cañares, executive judge of the Regional Trial Court of Cebu.

1985: I AM ARRESTED by police officers on charges of rebellion.

I noticed that the paragraph that was usually found in arrest warrants directing "the arresting officer…not to serve the order of arrest after office hours, Saturdays-Sundays, holidays, except when the accused is notoriously dangerous" was stricken out. In its place, a note was typewritten in capital letters: "CAN BE SERVED ON ANY DAY AND ANY TIME OF THE DAY OR NIGHT." Obviously, Cañares and those who maneuvered the filing of the rebellion case against me considered me a "notoriously dangerous" rebel.

The rebellion case was a new one. It was a spin-off from the rebellion case that the Marcos government had filed against me when I was mayor of Cagayan de Oro. This time, however, the charge was directed against me personally and several John Does. The way the complaint was crafted made it look like I had a personal hand in the killing of government troopers and destruction of government properties among the acts of rebellion that I was supposed to have done in Cebu. This was the case that the government filed when I was leaving for my commitment to the Council on Foreign Relations in New York. The warrant of arrest was a reissued one. It had a more recent date than the warrant of arrest that was issued on the day when I left for my CFR engagements on January 11.

People Bail Me Out

The people of Cagayan de Oro once again came to my rescue in a lawful manner. They did not riot or act with violence against those who served the warrant of arrest on me. What they did was to generously provide bail for me. People from all walks of life — market vendors, farmers and professionals — contributed some P4,000 in coins and peso bills of small denominations to pay for the premium of the bail bond of P50,000 to secure my temporary liberty. It took one-and-a-half hours for the clerk of court to count — with manifest irritation — the coins and small bills, after which Alfredo Lagamon, the executive judge of the Regional Trial Court of Misamis Oriental, ordered my "release from the custody of the law" that very evening. I told whoever cared to listen that the new criminal case was obviously concocted out of the blue just to harass and intimidate me.

The people of the city were not the only ones who offered to bail me out. Peping Cojuangco, Jr., PDP-Laban secretary general, also offered to put up my bail. He generously sent over Dr. Fernando Carrascoso to Cagayan de Oro to provide what was needed to keep me out of jail. I decided, however, that my bond should be shouldered by the people of Cagayan de Oro, who had offered to do so. After all, my problems with the Marcos government stemmed from my desire to uphold their rights even against the wishes of the martial law regime.

The day after my arrest, *WeForum* headlined in bold letters "People Bail Out Pimentel." I told the newspaper that, by arresting me, Marcos wanted "to harass, immobilize and terrorize me...but I won't be harassed or intimidated from doing what I feel is right."

Columnists Criticize Arrest

Two days later, on March 9, *Bulletin Today* columnists Apolonio Batalla and Jesus Bigornia criticized my arrest in separate columns. Batalla wrote:

> Aquilino Pimentel will surely gain political mileage from the charges of rebellion filed against him. The basis of the charge against him is he allegedly gave a P100 contribution to a commander of the New People's Army.
>
> The administration did him a big favor by accusing him of a crime based only on that alleged act. Quite apart from the effect on the domestic scene is the effect abroad, for there are indications that Pimentel was warmly received in the cities he recently visited.

Batalla was referring to the kind reception given me by my hosts in the major cities of the US, Canada, Belgium and France in January and February of that year.

For his part, Bigornia scored the government prosecutors for building up a case against me on fatuous foundations. He said:

> At the rate real or fancied accusations are heaped on the head of Aquilino Pimentel, government prosecutors may yet succeed in

building up the former Cagayan de Oro City mayor as a national folk hero, a veritable Zorro. For while serving as mayor of a Mindanao city, he is accused of fomenting rebellion in the Central Visayan island of Cebu. Pimentel is accused by the Cebu provincial fiscal of engaging government forces in a war, destroying public property and murdering law enforcement officers in Cebu's hinterlands.

Without delving into the merits of the case, this column reflects the sentiments of many asking how a man engaged in a war against the forces of government in far-off Cebu managed to run for public office at home last year and appears to have won, according to returns so far examined by the Supreme Court.

Bigornia was obviously carried away by his feelings when he likened me to Zorro, the Mexican Robin Hood, whose life was dramatized in the popular films of our generation such as *The Mark of Zorro* and its sequels. I was most gratified that Batalla and Bigornia, who were not even personal acquaintances of mine, saw fit to place the charge of rebellion against me in its proper perspective. Their supportive columns emboldened me to tell the people that the new case of rebellion against me was patently absurd. I pointed out that if I wanted to ambush people I would have done it in Misamis Oriental were the terrain was more familiar to me than Cebu's.

The RAM

About this time, young officers of the Armed Forces were organizing the Reform the Armed Forces Movement. They said their intention was to purge the armed forces of undesirables, maintain a high standard of discipline and bolster the morale of the soldiers. The unspecified objective of the RAM was to prevent General Ver from returning to his post as chief of staff in the event of his acquittal from charges of complicity in the murder of Aquino.

To keep Marcos from being alarmed by the brewing reports of a clandestine reform movement in the Armed Forces, Ramos told Marcos in April of 1985 that the reform movement was founded on respect for law and the Constitution, and that it would conduct its activities openly.

At this time, there was much for the young idealistic officers to complain about. For one thing, Ver advanced the military careers of his sons, Irwin, Rexor, and Wyrlo, over better qualified officers. There might have been an element of jealousy in the dissatisfaction expressed by some young officers on this point but, indeed, the three sons of Ver rapidly rose to prominent ranks in the armed forces and they occupied sensitive positions. Irwin, a colonel, was chief of staff of the Presidential Security Command; Rexor, a lieutenant colonel, was some kind of a security aide of Marcos; and Wyrlo, a major, commanded the elite anti-aircraft armored carriers that were deployed around Malacanang. In fine, all the Vers — father and sons — had a direct, unlimited personal security-related access to Marcos. And that kind of access to the source of power during martial rule even perceptually was power in itself.

Also, at this time, the military was employing low-intensity conflict (LIC) tactics in many far-flung communities that reportedly had been deeply infiltrated by communist insurgents. As defined in US military manuals, low-intensity operations combine political, economic, informational and military instruments for counter-insurgency, anti-subversion and peacekeeping purposes against the so-called non-state adversaries. Set military strategies are not used. Neither are heavy weapons and aircraft. As defined, LIC operations do not sound sinister.

In the implementation of the LIC methods in my hometown, Claveria, Misamis Oriental, however, the use of heavy artillery and bombs — which were probably shells from cannons sited kilometers away — inevitably led to complaints from innocent civilian populations affected by the military operations.

One favorite LIC tactic of the armed forces was used in Claveria. They *hamleted* several barangays suspected of harboring NPA cadres. In actual terms, the *hamleting* of the barangays meant that government troops cordoned them off and prevented the residents from pursuing their normal activities. Hundreds of families were, thus, evicted from their homesteads by order of the military.

Complaints Against Brutal Campaign

While the military operations were going on, I went up to the mountain barangays of Claveria and spent a couple of days there with the peasants. In one barangay, I met with a handful of NPA regulars. The meeting was facilitated by Mayor Vicente Emano of Tagoloan, Misamis Oriental. I remember the night we went to the barangay to meet with them. As we entered the area, which was in total darkness, we were greeted by the howling of dogs. Then I heard a whistle and saw the beam of a flashlight, which apparently signaled our arrival. Soon lights from torches and other flashlights brightened up the night as we if were in the midst of a barangay fiesta dance or *baile*. I saw then that the house we were going into was surrounded by other thatched dwellings.

At the meeting, the NPA leaders complained against the brutal methods used in the campaign against the dissidents, the hamlet operations that converted targeted villages into no-man's land, the excessive use of force, and the looting that accompanied the militarization of Claveria and other parts of Misamis Oriental. I had heard those complaints before, but this time I saw for myself the ugly face of the internecine strife that was tearing apart the country right in my hometown.

I was so touched by the sight of the dissidents who were ill-clad in the cold of Claveria's weather that I took off my jacket and gave it to a young girl who apparently was a member of the NPA cadre. I took the precaution of cutting off and removing the threads that stitched my name on the jacket before I handed it over to her.

Letters to Ramos and Enrile

I documented what I saw and heard in my visit to the barangays of Claveria in a letter that I sent to Gen. Fidel Ramos, the Armed Forces chief of staff.

In my letter to Ramos, I described the desolation that greeted me in Lanise, Mat-i, Simbolan, Guimbaloran, Dal-as, Manihay, Pambugas and Don Gregorio Pelaez, all located in the hinterlands of Claveria. I saw houses razed to the ground and farmlands teeming with ripe tomatoes that were rotting away. I also met hundreds of families fleeing the areas under military siege, carrying their meager belongings in improvised carts pulled by carabaos or horses. More upsetting were the reports of torture, rapes and beatings at the hands of some soldiers or elements of the civilian home defense units that the victims themselves recounted to me.

The victims and their witnesses had a difficult time identifying the abusive soldiers and the CHDF paramilitary units involved in the mass violation of the human rights of the peasants of Claveria. The soldiers and the CHDF personnel did not have their name tags or nameplates on their uniforms when they harassed their victims. Nonetheless, some of the victims positively identified a Lt. Caballes and a Sgt. Laguitao as the leaders of the oppressive soldiers. Other victims also named CHDF men as among those who abused them: Barangay Captain Canong Oga of Tipolohan, Claveria; Toto Zarate, Dalmacio Miguela, Gelacio Miguela and Jose Ibdao of Balingasag, Misamis Oriental; and Don Cagaanan, allegedly a military informer. Cagaanan was said to be so "untouchable" in that he could snatch rebel suspects and "neutralize" (kill) them summarily.

Aside from the usual "we will look into it" reply, Ramos took no action on our complaint.

On August 8, I elevated the complaint to the office of Defense Minister Enrile and added some recent incidents where farmers and their families were victims of salvaging, sexual indignities, torture, beating and looting for his action. In the letter, I gave Enrile the names of soldiers and CHDF personnel who were identified by the victims as the perpetrators of the abuses they were complaining against. Specifically, Sgt. Gonzales, Sgt. Rodolfo Bageon, Maj. Jovencio Lalas, a PC soldier named Jack, and CHDF men Victorino Galarpe, Dickie Pacamot, Miguel Echenigue, Rogelio Akut, Cesar Tagolimot, Tomas Libunao and Ben Cagaanan were named by the victims. Like the letter that I sent to Ramos, which was ignored, my letter to Enrile suffered the same fate.

Uproar over Killing of Missionary

In April 1985, the Church was in uproar over the killing of Fr. Tulio Favali, an Italian missionary working in Tulunan, North Cotabato. The brutal manner in which Favali was killed by a band of brigands led by the Manero brothers, Norberto, Edilberto and Elpidio, further aroused the anger of the people against the Marcos regime.

The killers were reported to be members of fanatical groups that were organized by the military to counter "Catholics whom authorities brand as subversives," said the *Los Angeles Times* of June 1, 1985. Like the killers of Renato Bucag in Gingoog City who evaded arrest for a long time, it took several years before the Manero brothers were arrested, charged and convicted for the murder of Favali.

Impeaching Marcos

August 1985 was a memorable month. In the second week of the month, I went with Butz Aquino and other Opposition stalwarts to meet Raul Daza in Hong Kong. Daza was active in the anti-Marcos struggle and had been in exile in the US for 12 years. He was facing subversion charges but wanted to return home.

We thought he would be arrested upon arrival and wanted to make sure nothing untoward would happen to him at the airport. So we accompanied him to Manila. Nothing unusual happened at the airport. He was not arrested and, later, the criminal charges against him were dismissed for lack of merit.

Opposition Files Impeachment

The biggest story of the month was the Opposition's bid to impeach Marcos. Because my case against Roa had not yet been resolved, I could not discharge my duties as a member of the Batasan. I was thus terribly frustrated that I could not participate in the discussion of the resolution filed by our colleagues for the impeachment of Marcos.

With Assemblyman Antonio Cuenco as the lead complainant, Impeachment Resolution No. 644 was filed on August 13, 1985. It carried the signatures of Members of the Batasan Jose B. Laurel, Jr., Edmundo Cea, Neptali Gonzales, Marcelo Fernan, Antonio Cuenco, Homobono Adaza, Pedro Marcellana, Jr., Ciriaco Alfelor, Rolando Marcial, Rolando Andaya, Bienvenidio Marquez, Jr., Honorato Aquino, Antonio Martinez, Jose L. Atienza, Jr., Emigdio Lingad, Rogaciano Mercado, Enrique Belo, Ramon Mitra, Jr., Natalio Beltran, Jr., Cesar Bolaños, Juanita L. Nepomuceno, Douglas Cagas, Roy Padilla, Fermin Caram, Jr., Cecilia Muñoz-Palma, Hernando Perez, Nenita Cortez-Daluz, Gonzalo Puyat, II, Arthur Defensor, Isidoro Real, Jr., Emilio de la Paz, Jr., Hilario de Pedro, Zafiro Respicio, Demetrio Demetria, Virgilio Robles, Manuel Domingo, Alberto Romulo, Carlos Fernandez, Augusto Sanchez, Jaime Ferrer, Oscar F. Santos, Wilson Gamboa, Gemiliano Lopez Jr., Rogelio Garcia, Francisco Sumulong, Rolleo Ignacio, Emigdio Tanjuatco, Eva Estrada Kalaw, Luis Villafuerte, Rafael Lazatin, Victor Ziga and Hjalmar Quintana.

Women Lead Petitioners

That Opposition members of the Batasan started the impeachment proceedings against Marcos was not surprising. What was rather astonishing was that women in private life took the lead in openly in identifying themselves as "petitioners for impeachment."

Princess Tarhata Lucman of the Sultanate of Lanao and 18 other ladies signed on as private petitioners for the impeachment of Marcos on July 31, 1985. The others — all professionals — were Narzalina Lim, Margarita Cojuangco, Mary Concepcion Bautista, Victoria P. Garchitorena, Solita Monsod, Susan Sonya Severino, Maria Teresa Roxas, Narcisa Escaler, Pacita Montinola, Pilar Singian, Patricia Sison, Luisa Hilado, Cecile Araneta, Noemi Olivares, Cecilia Lazaro, Goji Velarde, Betty Nelle and Cleofe Llamas. Throwing caution to the winds, they signed the first page of the three-page list of petitioners for impeachment.

When I read the names of the women as lead petitioners in the impeachment papers, I imagined the men petitioners shouting, "There go our women, we must follow them." And follow them, they did. The next two pages of the list of impeachment petitioners included Jejomar Binay, Francisco Rodrigo, Francis Garchitorena, Gil Ramos, Johnny Baccay, Atilano Jimenez, Eduardo Galang, Ricardo Nepomuceno, Emmanuel Soriano, Teofisto Guingona, Jr., Agapito Aquino, Dick Powel, Reli German, Benjamin Gutierrez, Chito Roque, Jose Luis Alcuaz, Cesar Climaco, Jr. and Jaime Cacho.

Complaint Specifics

The major point of the resolution was that Marcos had enriched himself in office by raiding the public treasury, plundering the nation's wealth and stashing ill-gotten wealth in foreign countries. Of the specifications in the complaint, what hurt Marcos the most were the charges that he and his wife bought properties in the US and elsewhere that could not be justified on the basis of their legitimate income. Because of that allegation, the US press gave wide publicity to the impeachment move against Marcos.

Among the questionable deals included in the complaint were that Marcos and Imelda had bought personally or through dummies, the Crown Building in Manhattan, New York; the Lindenmere Estate in Long Island, New York; a 13-acre home in Princeton, New Jersey; three condominiums on 5th Avenue, Manhattan; three other condominiums in San Francisco; the Herald Shopping Center in Manhattan; and mansions in Beverly Hills, Honolulu, London and Rome.

The complaint on pages 3, 4, 5 and 6 identified Herminio Disini, Jr., Rodolfo Cuenca, Jose Yao Campos, Roberto Benedicto, Leandro Vasquez, Antonio Floirendo, Bienvenido Tantoco, Eduardo Cojuangco, Vilma H. Bautista and Jorge Ramos; two American law firms, Berstein, Carter & Deyo of New York, and Graham & James of San Francisco; and corporations such as Luna 7 Development Corp.; Ancor Holdings NV of the Netherlands Antilles; Faylin Ltd.; New York Land Company; and TRA Equities of Delaware as "fronts" or "dummies" of Marcos or Imelda.

In late July, US Ambassador Stephen Bosworth made an extraordinary offer in a speech before a civic club in Metro Manila. He said the US government would help in tracking down the properties of Philippine government officials and businessmen in the United States. It was incredible that a US Ambassador would speak so openly in Manila of a plan of the US government to undercut Marcos. But that was what he did and it was welcome news to the Opposition.

Predictably, however, Minister of Justice Estelito Mendoza ignored the offer. Mendoza was the official directed by Marcos to investigate the allegations that he, Imelda, Enrile and a few others had stashed ill-gotten wealth in the US, Europe and other countries. As the days passed by, it was getting clearer that the matter would not be seriously probed while Marcos was in power.

Committee Rejects Move

The KBL members of the Batasan Committee to which the impeachment resolution was referred showed all the world what power meant to them. As the *New York Times* reported on August 14:

> In an unusual evening session that lasted late into the night, the Committee on Justice, Human Rights and Good Government rejected the measure (for) lack of merit.

The Committee Report (No. 154) that recommended the dismissal of the impeachment complaint was endorsed by Mendoza and all the committee's KBL members: Manuel Garcia, Guardson Lood, Antonio Diaz, Juan Ponce Enrile, Leonardo Perez, Salacnib Baterina, Concordio Diel, Teodulo Natividad, Renato Cayetano, Damian Aldaba, Adelino Sitoy, Alejandro Almendras, Luis Ectubañez, Regalado Maambong, Macacuna Dimaporo and Salvador Britanico.

When the ruling of the KBL majority dismissed the impeachment complaint, I remembered what Minister Mendoza said during our 1984 debate on his committee's proposed Rules to govern impeachments. When I criticized his rules as being intended to shield Marcos, he replied arrogantly that Marcos did not need any protection from anyone from the risk of impeachment. The error of Mendoza's position was now clearly apparent. The event showed that the KBL members of his committee used his rules to protect Marcos from the impeachment try against him.

Mercury News Exposé

Had I been in the Batasan, I would have voted in favor of the impeachment resolution. In fact, as early as July 11, Eva Kalaw, Tony Cuenco, Lito Atienza, former Senator John Osmeña and I had launched the "Impeach Marcos Movement." The Comelec, at the time, had not yet secured my temporary ouster from the Batasan. What triggered our move to launch the Impeach Marcos Movement was the *Mercury News* of California exposé that reported that Marcos, Imelda and their cronies had salted away millions of dollars in the US.

Kalaw called the exposé "a great scandal." She said, "It calls for the resignation, impeachment or suicide of the Marcoses and the cronies." I seconded her observation by saying, "The impeachment of Marcos is long overdue and it is time the Opposition in the Batasan fulfilled their pledge to dismantle the oppressive Marcos regime."

With the dismissal of the impeachment complaint, I told the *Christian Science Monitor*, which reported my remarks on August 15, "More than ever, it will drive the parliamentary Opposition to the streets."

In the vote on the impeachment, we lost Rafael Recto, who voted against the complaint because he believed that it "had no legal leg to stand on." He also decried the "intercalation of his signature" on the impeachment resolution. He told *Mr&Ms* magazine in August 1985 that his signature had been inserted into the document without his consent. How that happened, Recto did not say. As expected, the KBL exploited Recto's statement and hit the Opposition for "shamelessly resorting to underhanded tactics." Marcos even peevishly suggested that the Batasan should investigate the matter. Nobody took him up on the suggestion.

In the buildup of the impeachment complaint at the committee level, the Opposition also lost — more permanently, this time — our colleague, Rafael Legaspi of Aklan. Although his name had already been typed on the impeachment complaint, he died before he could sign it. Two members of the Opposition, Fabian Sison of Pangasinan and Rufino Bañas of South Cotabato, likewise did not sign the impeachment complaint. They both had the same explanation: they faced pending cases in the Comelec and they were apprehensive that the latter, as a tool of the Marcos regime, would rule against them.

Some of our colleagues were said to have received favors from Imelda who facilitated the release of loans for housing to members of the Batasan with the intention of preventing them from signing the impeachment petition. That was probably true because, before I was temporarily ousted from the Batasan, Imelda sycophants told me that I could borrow funds from the GSIS to build a house. Fortunately, I declined. I said my house in Marikina — where I still live — was enough for my family's needs. But I know of one assemblyman who received a P3 million housing loan. His opponents in his home province said he did not support the impeachment effort against Marcos.

Because I was still ousted from the Batasan, I was also unable to vote for Orlando Mercado's motion to allow the showing to the Batasan members of the Betamax tapes that he had taken in the US of the properties of Marcos, Imelda and their cronies. By an overwhelming vote of 103-48, the KBL members drowned out the motion. Assemblyman Alejandro Almendras was so peeved by Mercado's move that, in his explanation of why he voted "No," he said that he saw no need to view Mercado's video tapes because "all of us here are corrupt."

King Macos and Lady Mida

It was a good thing that the Opposition did not allow Almendras's sweeping indictment against the integrity of the members of the Batasan to go unchallenged. On August 25, in a masterful rebuttal of Almendras's indiscriminate invective, Douglas Cagas delivered an inspired speech that so rattled the KBL majority that they moved to have the speech deleted from the records of the Batasan.

In his explanation, Cagas said he had to defend himself from Almendras's accusation because to say nothing would be to accept that the latter was right. Cagas said that, contrary to Almendras's charges, he was "now several times poorer" than when he was practicing law. He concluded, "While others are charged with unexplained wealth, I should be guilty of unexplained poverty. But I have no regrets. The opportunity to fight for the dismantling of this dictatorship is compensation enough."

The preliminaries of Cagas speech did not bother the KBL majority. What irked them was his explanation of how he came to that conclusion. He started with a story of a fictional kingdom where the king and the queen held sway by corrupting the officials of the land and holding the people hostage by the threat of arbitrary arrest and indefinite detention and keeping them in perpetual poverty.

The bubble of fiction with which he covered his story burst when he called the king, "Macos," and his famous lady, "Mida." Soon rabid Marcos supporters, Arturo Pacificador, Leonardo Perez, Alejandro Almendras and Ramon Tirol were on their feet castigating him. Perez was at his vitriolic best when he said that Cagas suffered from "gonorrhea of the mouth and a diarrhea of the brain." Like a quartet singing to the beat of a bandmaster, they all moved to delete Cagas's speech for reasons that ranged from its being "hypocritical and irresponsible" to the cover-all category of its being "unparliamentary and uncalled for."

Opposition Assemblyman Hjalmar Quintana flashed his off-and-on brilliance on the floor with a vigorous defense of Cagas. He said:

> Cagas's speech was only an allegory and yet the majority want it deleted from the record. When the President delivered his State of the Nation address, he gave us a fairy tale. But we did not move to have the entire speech expunged.

Gagging the Opposition

Quintana's and our other colleagues' opposition to the motion to delete Cagas's speech failed to save it. The KBL majority voted 86-39 to strike it out in its entirety. Seven months before, the KBL majority had previously struck out the speech of Opposition Assemblyman Rogaciano Mercado.

In January 1985, Mercado rose on a question of personal and collective privilege to answer Marcos's criticism of the Batasan Opposition as the cause for the delay of the passage of vital legislation. Mercado assailed the President as "habituated to dictatorial manners," which prevented him from seeing the Batasan as a democratic forum. Even before Mercado could finish his speech, Assemblyman Leonardo Perez moved to strike out Mercado's entire statement.

Perez's motion was clearly unparliamentary. His KBL colleague, Assemblyman Arturo Tolentino, called the Perez motion "ridiculous and dangerous." Tolentino warned:

> If the chamber has the power to delete an entire speech, what will prevent the majority…from voting to delete entire speeches in opposition of administration measures? Then, nothing will remain in the records except speeches in favor of the measure.

Three other KBL assemblymen, Camilo Cabili, Rogelio Sarmiento and Eduardo Nonato Joson supported Tolentino's position and voted with the Opposition against the motion of Perez. Nonetheless, the KBL majority mindlessly voted 83-58 to uphold it.

The deletion of Cagas's speech and the expunging of Mercado's speech were glaring manifestations that the KBL majority had no compunction about curtailing the freedom of expression of the members of the Opposition.

Censuring Benitez

Then, there was the move to censure Minister Jolly Benitez, a favorite of Imelda Marcos, for certain anomalies in housing projects under the Ministry of Human Settlements. Had I been in the Batasan, I would have voted to censure Benitez because the anomalies in the so-called "Kubeta Village" project in Carmona, Cavite, were so glaring that, as Imelda's favorite assistant incharge of the project, he was primarily responsible for them. Again, the vote went along partisan lines. 50 Opposition assemblymen voted to censure him and 98 KBL and their allies voted against it. Earlier, the Committee on Privileges, by a vote of 10 KBL members against four Opposition members, cleared Benitez on charges that he had bribed reporters to downplay adverse stories about his ministry.

In-Party Distractions

While I had my hands full with the problem of my ouster from the Batasan, I also had to cope with distractions within my party. Some individuals accused the treasurer of the party, Mordino Cua, of juggling funds supposedly coming from abroad. Since Cua was my city administrator when I was mayor of Cagayan de Oro, the implication was that I was involved in the misuse of the funds.

I denied it because it was pure poppycock. Cua, as party treasurer, also denied it and he submitted an accounting of the use of PDP-Laban funds before our National Council to whom he was accountable under party rules.

I had the consolation that writer Jesus Bigornia of *Bulletin Today*, who I had not met personally at that time, wrote in his popular column on April 16, 1985 that I was being smeared by black propaganda that appeared to have been mounted by fellow Oppositionists. He added:

> Pimentel's rise in the political firmament may be attributed to a consistent and steadfast opposition to the present regime since the declaration of martial rule. Incarceration for three times has invested Pimentel the aura of a persecuted martyr. Now he is the victim of a smear campaign both here and abroad. Filipino residents in the United States have received copies of a poison-letter that has been circulating here since January. By subjecting him to overkill efforts, Pimentel may yet rise over his detractors who should be reminded of the old Tagalog saying: Only fruit-laden mango trees are subjected to stoning.

The smear campaign notwithstanding, the National Council in our Cebu meeting voted overwhelmingly by secret ballot to retain me as the chair of the party.

Some months after the controversy hit the pages of local newspapers, Max Soliven in his column, "The Last Word," in *Mr&Ms* of October 25-26, reported that in Bonn, both foundations, the Friedrich-Ebert-Stiftung and Konrad Adenauer Stiftung earlier that month, "denied having 'donated' any funds to any Opposition politician — certainly not to former MP Aquilino 'Nene' Pimentel."

Soliven also said that Dr. Josef Thesing, the Konrad Adenauer director of the Institute for International Solidarity, told him that they were sponsoring a trip for me to observe political and parliamentary trends in France and Germany. Sponsoring my trips to the countries mentioned to enable me to learn from their political and parliamentary programs was a far cry from saying that the foundations gave me money for personal or partisan political purposes.

In any event, Soliven advised our detractors:

> So, you malicious fellows — stop whispering about that money allegedly given to poor Nene Pimentel.

Soliven's findings aside, I can truly say that I did not receive a single centavo from any foreign foundation or source for my personal benefit or to advance any partisan agenda. It must be said, however, that both the Konrad Adenauer Foundation and the Friederich-Ebert Foundation were, at the time, actively involved in promoting cooperatives and in democratizing labor groups and Cua was engaged in the promotion of both programs.

NUC Meeting

Meanwhile, the Convenor Group's efforts to unify the opposition parties got stalled. A new group called the National Unification Conference, under the leadership of Cecilia Muñoz-Palma, tried to bring the various Opposition groups together under one organization to prepare for the day when Marcos would call for presidential and vice presidential elections. A major attempt to unify the Opposition elements was made by the NUC in March 1985. Many political personalities attended the NUC meeting, but Jovy Salonga, Butz Aquino, Cory Aquino and I did not.

Salonga sent "sincere and cordial greetings" to Doy Laurel who was actually the head of the Unido which gave the NUC its power-base. Salonga said that, as no program of government had yet been agreed upon, he could not be personally present. Butz Aquino said he was supporting the Convenor's Group headed by his sister-in-law, Cory, Tañada and Ongpin. Cory, however, was represented by her mother-in-law, Aurora Aquino. Cory said she wanted to attend the NUC meet, but had been prevailed upon by the majority of the members of the Convenor Group not to attend. In my case, I said I did not go to the NUC meet because the so-called presidential candidates nominated by the Convenor Group were not invited and I was one of them.

In the end, the NUC attempts to unify the Opposition groups fizzled out. Muñoz-Palma and Doy Laurel had a falling out. At one meeting, Doy reportedly raised his voice at Muñoz-Palma and everybody thought it was so rude of him to do that to a frail lady of 72. Whatever the provocation, that was the end of the NUC's and Doy Laurel's utility in bringing together the disparate Opposition groups.

In my case, I was not too saddened by the collapse of Doy's efforts to lead the Opposition groups. That he was not too keen on clarifying his stand on the US bases was a minus factor for him, as far as I was concerned. Besides, as a *provinciano*, I felt a little unease everytime Doy would justify — and this was often — his positions on public issues on the basis of what his "Papa" had said. I thought that even if his father had been a former President and Justice of the Supreme Court, it would have been better for Doy to argue the justness of his political causes himself, rather than merely quote his father. Maybe Doy's problem was that he had a too famous father that he was typecast as the son of Jose P. Laurel, the original. His approach, I thought, was a little too familial and too conservative in a fast-changing world.

In any event, Doy's loss in the unification efforts was Cory's gain. Now she could bargain more evenly with Doy. Even then I saw that, if Doy ran for president and Cory also did, they would not only divide the Opposition vote but would also provide Marcos with the excuse for cheating massively at the polls and then toss the blame for Cory's loss to the division of the Opposition.

There was reason then for a more determined effort to unify the opposition groups. The unification, however, would not come until my birthday on December 11, 1986, over a year into the future, and not because it was my birthday but because circumstances — absolutely beyond my control — converged on that blessed day to compel the unification of the Opposition.

Graft Charges Dismissed

There was some good news for me and my family in the last quarter of the year. Ombudsman Bernardo Fernandez approved, on October 24, 1985, the dismissal of the last batch of baseless graft charges filed separately against Bing and me by my local detractors. Special Prosecutor Jane Aurora Lantion recommended the dismissals for "want of merit." Earlier, the Ombudsman also dismissed for the same reason all other charges concocted by my political opponents.

Chapter 45

Supreme Court Reinstates Me

After seven months of scrutinizing the questioned election returns in my case against Roa, Deputy Court Administrator Romeo Mendoza submitted in August 1985, the findings of Revisor Group No. 2. The report covered 12,954 ballots. Of this batch of questioned ballots, I had 6,470 votes and Roa, 5,886. The report presaged the favorable findings of the other revisor groups that were headed by Court Administrator Arturo Buena, Deputy Court Administrator Leo Medialdea, Deputy Clerks of Court Vicente Bengzon, Daniel Martinez and Damasita Aquino.

All this while, the order removing me from the Batasan caused a big problem to my family. Among other things, it inflicted a heavy toll on Bing's and my financial ability to sustain the growing demands of our brood of six children, two of whom were in college, another two in high school and the two youngest, in grade school. I had devoted practically all my waking hours to my legislative and political organizing work and Bing only had a minimal salary from her job as the Placement Director of the Ateneo de Manila in Quezon City. Thus my ouster from the Batasan strained our resources to the limit.

It was not all that bleak, however, for me and my family. One psychological consolation was that my ouster from the Batasan brought unexpected praise from the foreign press. For instance, the *Far Eastern Economic Review* of November 8, 1984, reported that:

> Congressional sources...expressed concern that the US Government has so far ignored what they consider to be a potent political development — the expulsion of a leading opposition figure, Aquilino Pimentel, from parliament on charges of voting fraud. The action is seen as being aimed at removing from the national scene a serious opposition candidate who (as Aquino could have done) might challenge Marcos in the 1986 presidential election. Pimentel's role in parliament, which has now been cut short, would have helped give him national stature.

Unprecedented Generosity

More concretely, my colleagues in the Batasan Opposition did something that was completely unprecedented and unheard of in Philippine politics. They authorized Antonio de Guzman, the Secretary General of the Batasan, to deduct P300 each from their monthly basic salary to be given to me on a monthly basis.

Their generosity enabled me to keep body and soul together, see my children through their schooling and continue my struggle for the peaceful restoration of freedom and democracy to our people and country.

My Batasan colleagues who kindly helped me during those difficult times included Antonio Cuenco and Marcelo Fernan of Cebu City; Nenita Cortez-Daluz, of Cebu; Douglas Cagas of Davao del Sur; Oscar Santos, Cesar Bolaños, Bienvenido Marquez, Jr. and Hjalmar Quintana of Quezon; Zafiro Respicio of Davao City; Homobono Adaza of Misamis Oriental; Ciriaco Alfelor, Rolando Andaya, Luis Villafuerte and Edmundo Cea of Camarines Sur; Honorato Aquino of Baguio City; Rufino Bañas, Rogelio Garcia and Hilario de Pedro of South Cotabato; Natalio Beltran, Jr. of Romblon; Fermin Caram, Jr. and Arthur Defensor of Iloilo; Demetrio Demetria and Fabian Sison of Pangasinan; Manuel Domingo of Malabon, Navotas and Valenzuela; Carlos Fernandez, Gemiliano Lopez, Jr., Gonzalo Puyat II, Eva Estrada Kalaw and Jose Atienza, Jr. of Manila; Jaime Ferrer of Las Piñas and Parañaque; Wilson Gamboa of Negros Occidental; Neptali Gonzales of San Juan and Mandaluyong, Metro Manila; Rolleo Ignacio of Mindoro Oriental; Jose B. Laurel, Jr., Hernando Perez and Rafael Recto of Batangas; Rafael Lazatin, Emigdio Lingad and Juanita Nepomuceno of Pampanga; Pedro Marcellana, Jr. and Victor Ziga of Albay; Rolando Marcial of Davao del Norte; Antonio Martinez and Virgilio Robles of Caloocan; Orlando Mercado, Cecilia Muñoz-Palma and Alberto Romulo of Quezon City; Rogaciano Mercado of Bulacan; Ramon Mitra, Jr., of Palawan; Candu Muarip of Basilan; Roy Padilla of Camarines Norte; Augusto Sanchez and Emilio de la Paz, Jr., of Pasig and Marikina, Metro Manila; Isidoro Real, Jr. of Zamboanga del Sur; and Francisco Sumulong and Emigdio Tanjuatco, Jr., of Rizal.

Supreme Court Declares Me Winner

Finally, on November 19, 1985, the Supreme Court declared me the winner over Roa. In a 31-page decision, the Court ruled that:

> The canvass by the Board of Canvassers of all the votes from all the voting centers in Cagayan de Oro City shows that petitioner Pimentel garnered 63,784 votes, while respondent Roa obtained 59,102, giving Pimentel a majority of 4,682 votes.

The decision penned by Chief Justice Felix Makasiar had the concurrence of Justices Claudio Teehankee, Vicente Abad Santos, Efren Plana, Venicio Escolin, Hugo E. Gutierrez, B.S. de la Fuente, Serafin Cuevas, Nestor Alampay and Lino Patajo. Justice Ramon Aquino, who was inclined to side with Roa, took no part in it. Justices Hermogenes Concepcion, Ameurfina Melencio-Herrera and Lorenzo Relova were on leave.

It took the Supreme Court one year and one month from the date the Comelec altered the results of the vote in Cagayan de Oro in favor of Roa to arrive at the simple conclusion that I had won over Roa by 4,682 votes. In that period, the people of Cagayan de Oro were not represented by anyone. My ouster from the Batasan machinated by Comelec officials and legitimated by some Supreme Court magistrates was clearly unjust not only to me but to the constituents of the city. Yet, two agencies of the government, one, the Comelec, that by the Constitution was mandated to ensure clean and honest elections, and two, the Supreme Court, that was ordained to see to it that justice is delivered efficiently and well, apparently ignored the need for a fast resolution of my case. While I was lucky in the sense that I finally won with almost four years still remaining in my six-year term, the time lost in terms of service that I could have rendered my constituents was no longer recoverable.

On November 19, 1985, the Supreme Court ordered that I could return to the Batasan. Four days later, I wrote my generous Batasan friends in an attempt to give back to them the amounts they had so kindly extended to me. In the note, I thanked them for their kindness and said:

> Since I am once again entitled to the emoluments of our office, without meaning any offense, kindly allow me to give back to you the little amount enclosed herein.
>
> This is not in repayment of your kindness but simply in recognition that a thousand and one demands are being made upon each and everyone of us by our constituencies. Besides, in all candor, I would not want it said by anyone that I have enriched myself at the expense of others.

In the event, some reluctantly received my offer of repayment. Others did not.

Shortly after my reinstatement to the Batasan and before we recessed for the presidential snap elections in 1986, Speaker Yñiguez sent his daughter Rosette to ask me to see him. In his office, he told me there was money left over in the coffers of the Batasan. He told me I had a share in it. When I asked what it was for, he said every assemblyman was entitled to it. I declined it. I did not see how it could be justified. After the Cory government replaced the Marcos regime, I discovered to my surprise that the Batasan records showed I had received my share of it. Obviously, someone collected the amount, pocketed it and enriched himself or herself at my and the people's expense.

Part 11

Snap Presidential Elections

1985: CORY (center), flanked by Nep Gonzales and me, explains why she is challenging Marcos for the presidency.

Chapter 46

Marcos Brazens It Out

In the closing months of 1985, like a man holding on to a lanyard for dear life, Marcos decided to brazen it out. Two actions of his weighed heavily on people's minds — the call that he made in November for snap presidential elections and his reinstatement of General Ver as chief of staff of the Armed Forces in December.

Marcos Offers Snap Elections

To a nation deprived of honest-to-goodness presidential elections since martial law was imposed, the passage of Batas Blg. 883 by the Batasang Pambansa gave our people hope that we now had a chance to peacefully replace Marcos. The law authorized the holding of presidential and vice presidential elections on February 7, 1986. Marcos told US television viewers on the *David Brinkley Show* on November 3, 1985 that he would "call snap elections in 1986 for the two positions."

While the people looked forward to it, my immediate reaction was that Marcos was trying to put one over all of us by calling for snap elections for the two offices. The proposed election for the Office of the Vice President was all right. We needed an elected vice president to succeed Marcos should he die, resign or create a vacancy in the office of the president. As things stood, Marcos had issued a decree — shrouded in mystery — that provided for his presidential successor. We did not like that. We wanted a law to take care of the contingency of a vacancy in the Office of the President.

No Vacancy

The problem, however, was that the law calling for the holding of the presidential election was like a magician's bag — full of tricks. The main deception was that there was no vacancy in the Office of the President that could be filled up by the election. Marcos was very much alive and he was occupying the office.

Under democratic precedents, snap elections cannot be held for fixed term offices that are not vacant. Which meant that for an election to be validly held for the Office of the President, Marcos would have to resign. His resignation would create the vacancy in the office that could then be filled up by an election.

Deviously, Marcos claimed that he had resigned, although he determined to hold the office until certain conditions were fulfilled. Our position was that

Marcos could not hang on to the presidential office and run for the position simultaneously.

Petitions to Supreme Court

In the event, because I believed that the law calling for the presidential and vice presidential elections was deceptively faulty, I got one of the best-known lawyers specializing in Constitutional matters, Ramon Gonzales, to challenge it before the Supreme Court. My colleagues from the Opposition, Zafiro Respicio, Antonio Cuenco, Nenita Cortez-Daluz, Emigdio Lingad, Douglas Cagas, Oscar Santos, Orlando Mercado, Ciriaco Alfelor, Isidoro Real, Jr., Rolando Marcial and Rogelio Garcia joined me in the petition.

Our principal argument was that there was no vacancy in the Office of the President. Therefore, there was no basis for the holding of the proposed elections. Marcos could have created a vacancy in the office by resigning. But he did not resign. What Marcos did was to simulate a resignation — as was evident in a letter dated November 11, 1985 in which he said:

> To pave the way for the holding of a special election for the president, I hereby irrevocably vacate the position of President effective only when the election is held and after the winner is proclaimed and qualified as President by taking his oath of office ten (10) days after his proclamation.

The proffered resignation of Marcos was merely a ploy. The resignation was not irrevocable. It was most revocable. As worded, it was dependent on (a) the election of a candidate for the presidency; (b) the winner being proclaimed; and (c) the winner qualifying by taking his oath of office within 10 days after his or her proclamation.

Clearly, the conditions had to transpire before Marcos would consider himself resigned. The Marcos-imposed conditions made the whole electoral exercise chancy. The Batasan was under his thumb with a three-to-one majority in his favor. The majority had time and again already shown its canine subservience to him. As examples, they threw out the impeachment resolution without any attempt to verify the truth of the charges and they deleted Opposition statements in the Batasan critical of Marcos without any legislative precedent as basis by relying only on the sheer force of their numbers. We had no doubt that the same KBL majority would proclaim Marcos the winning candidate after the Comelec — another agency overwhelmingly populated by rabid Marcos partisans — would have attested to the fact that a presidential election was held pursuant to law.

The other Marcos-laid condition that the winner must take his oath within 10 days from proclamation likewise raised our suspicion that Marcos sought to create a situation that could preclude his successor from taking over. This condition was absolutely unnecessary because the Constitution itself required that any person who assumes public office, including the winner in a presidential election, must take the appropriate oath of office at the proper time. We suspected that he imposed the condition, so, theoretically, he could bar the oath-taking of the winner for any number of reasons. Our apprehensions on this matter probably bordered on paranoia, but our fears were based on a 13-year national experience with Marcos's Machiavellian proclivities. The experience taught us that he was capable of doing anything to prolong his stay in power.

Ten other cases were brought to the Supreme Court to scuttle the "snap election." But when it became certain that Cory Aquino would be the standard bearer of the unified Opposition groups, the petitioners, including us, withdrew the cases. We were sure that, with a united opposition, Marcos could be beaten through the ballot, a process much more decisive for our cause than winning a legal argument or gaining a judicial verdict in our favor.

The Supreme Court did not immediately dismiss the petitions. It first sustained the constitutionality of the law by a split decision, 7-5, on December 19, 1985. Nineteen days later, on January 7, it dismissed the cases.

Marcos Reinstates Ver

Five days before the Supreme Court dismissed the petitions that challenged the constitutionality of the law calling for the elections of the President and the Vice President, the Sandiganbayan acquitted Gen. Fabian Ver of charges that he was involved in the murder of Ninoy Aquino. Upon his acquittal on December 2, Marcos rejoiced over the verdict and immediately reinstated him as the chief of staff of the Armed Forces. Unfortunately for the regime, the people in general and the American press in particular — whose approval for his policies Marcos assiduously courted — did not share his exhilaration.

I was not surprised by Ver's acquittal. The Agrava report had earlier exonerated Ver, and time and again Marcos had publicly telegraphed his wish to reinstate Ver in the event of his acquittal. Ver knew too much of the venalities of Marcos that it would have been the height of political naiveté for anyone to believe that Marcos would distance himself from Ver.

As a lawyer, I found the charge against Ver for covering up the participation of some military men in the killing of Ninoy Aquino fundamentally erroneous. Covering up for his men was a far less grievous offense than being charged as a coconspirator in the plot to kill Aquino. To me, the accusation against Ver was merely a sop to satisfy the public's clamor that he should be brought to trial. It was never meant to convict him. I conveyed that view to the Council on Foreign Relations audiences that I addressed in my trip to the US in early 1985. I continued to articulate the same view whenever the occasion arose.

Media Displeasure

In the US, on December 3, the *Los Angeles Times* editorialized its displeasure by calling Ver's acquittal "The Manila Whitewash." The newspaper said:

[The verdict] coming from a panel of Marcos appointees was not surprising. Neither was it even faintly credible....[It] can only add to the radicalization of the political opposition in the Philippines, to the benefit of the growing Communist-led insurgency.

The newspaper also said that Marcos aggravated the loss of his credibility when he reinstated "his crony and kinsman, Gen. Fabian C. Ver, as Armed Forces chief of staff immediately after Ver was acquitted of charges of trying to cover up military involvement in the Aquino assassination." In its view, that was "further good news to the insurgents." The newspaper said, "If Ver remains in his job...there will almost surely be new moves in [the US] Congress to cut military aid to the Philippines."

The *New York Times* of the same date editorialized Ver's acquittal as "The Shameless Verdict in Manila." It said:

To nobody's surprise, a court in Manila has absolved 26 Filipinos accused of murdering Benigno Aquino, including the key defendant, General Fabian Ver, now renamed to his former post as chief of staff. Worthless as law, his acquittal is a political act. It suggests, unmistakably, that those who risk their necks for President Ferdinand Marcos are legally untouchable.

To put it bluntly, Marcos reinstated Ver because he needed a man he could trust with his life in his campaign for a new mandate as president. There was no other person who could fill up the role except Ver.

Thus was the stage set for the February 7, 1986 presidential and vice presidential election.

Chapter 47

Cory Stands Up To Marcos

With the elections now fixed by law, Salvador Laurel's followers moved resolutely to ensure that he would be chosen as the standard bearer of the Opposition. His main problem was that the big names of the business community, like Jaime Ongpin, Ramon del Rosario, Ernesto Aboitiz, Jaime Zobel de Ayala and other business heavyweights, had already thrown their support behind Cory. They wanted a nontraditional politician to challenge Marcos.

The business elite reflected the people's wish as far as we could gauge it. We sensed that the people were wary of the *politicos* of the pre-and-current martial law variety who were becoming more and more visible as the presidential election approached. Unfortunately, even among the ranks of the Opposition, Doy Laurel was perceived as a Marcos-era politician who could not provide the people with much of an alternative to the politics of Marcos. Even if the perception was not necessarily true, it caused a number of Doy's potential supporters to stay away from his presidential effort.

Cory's Choice

Talk was rife that I would be Cory's vice presidential teammate. While I would have loved to be Cory's running mate, the fact was— as I told her and everybody who cared to listen — that I was dispensable. My main concern was to help unify the Opposition to strengthen our bid to oust Marcos through the ballot. That was the stand that I took ever since the possibility of holding presidential and vice presidential elections was mentioned. Even during my speaking tour in the US in early 1985, invariably, I told my inquisitors that my principal aim as an opposition leader was to seek the unification of the various opposition groups. As the preparations for the elections went into high gear, my stand hardened into a mission.

Earnest negotiations were underway to make Doy withdraw his presidential bid and agree to be Cory's running mate. The attempts, however, swirled into a whirlpool of difficulties, not the least of which was due to Doy's belief that he held the franchise to challenge Marcos. He hung on to this belief primarily because he did get many opposition groups to enroll as members of the Unido. Besides, as his wife Celia wrote in a beautiful memoir published in 2005, titled *Doy Laurel*, Doy was driven by an inflexible desire to be president for as long as she could remember. Nobody could dispute those premises in the level of theory. But, in the rough race and turbulent tumble of real life politics, those considerations were far from sufficient.

Basically, Macapagal, Tañada, Salonga, Diokno, Guingona, Kalaw and I shared that view that Doy Laurel should *not* be the candidate of the Opposition. Despite his eminent academic qualifications and his political savvy, I thought that Doy would have great difficulty besting Marcos in the presidential race. For one thing, I believed that we in the Opposition should put up as our candidate a person who was totally the opposite of Marcos, the consummate politician, so that the contrast would be perceived more easily by the people. In my view, our candidate should be a nontraditional politician, and have, aside from integrity and courage (two virtues that Doy also possessed), a platform that had a pro-people bent and espoused a nationalist orientation. Despite his rhetoric, Doy was not perceived as having a nationalist view of how the country should develop. Specifically, we could not get him to agree to two planks of the Convenor Agreement: (1) the legalization of the Communist Party and (2) the removal of the US bases.

Nonetheless, I also believed that Doy should have a major role in the electoral push against Marcos, not as the presidential standard bearer of the Opposition but perhaps as Cory's Vice President.

Only for President

As for Cory, there was no other position we wanted her to run for except the presidency. We believed that only she could truly unify the Opposition. Without Cory as the standard bearer of the Opposition, we foresaw that the Opposition would splinter into several factions. If the Opposition were disunited, fighting Marcos in the elections would be like banging our heads against a reinforced concrete wall. Marcos's machinery was formidable enough without our being split. Marcos had the KBL old-time politicians supporting him, the Comelec, the military, and the local and barangay officials. Moreover, he not only had his huge personal fortune, but also almost limitless government funds at his disposal. Thus, any attempt to dislodge him via the election process by a divided Opposition would be quixotic.

Only the widow Cory, with the magic of the Aquino name, could fully exploit the emotional content of her husband's supreme sacrifice. Only she could galvanize the people into a massive irresistible force that was needed to drive Marcos out of Malacañang. Since she had no public sins to cover up, we believed that she had the capacity to appeal to the people's latent patriotic sentiments to vote *for* her, if not at least *against* Marcos.

Thunderous Applause

At a rally in Makati, without clearing it with anyone, not even with Cory, in the midst of my speech, I endorsed her as the Opposition's candidate for President. That endorsement received a thunderous applause from the overflow crowd.

Most of the Convenor Group presidential potentials were on the stage. They were all taken aback by my announcement, but had no chance to display their disappointment over my officious announcement because the audience received it enthusiastically.

Aside from the one million signatures that Chino Roces and his band of ne'er-say-die crusaders gathered to convince Cory to run, the boost that I gave to her candidacy that afternoon prodded her brother Peping Cojuangco and the rest of her family to decide that it was time to make her bid for the presidency public. It was not that easy, however, for Cory to switch from Cory, the convenor of possible presidential candidates of the Opposition, to Cory, the candidate of the Opposition. As a private person, she also had difficulty dealing with politicians and even with the people. Moreover, there was the big problem of convincing Doy Laurel to step aside in her favor and agree to be her vice presidential candidate.

Anyway, Cory and Doy held several negotiations. All sorts of formulae were serially tried and rejected. There was the Doy offer for Cory to run for Vice President. Cory said "No." There was the Cory counter offer for Doy to run as her Vice President. Doy said "No." Then, there was the Doy offer for Cory to run as President but under the Unido. Cory said "No."

Cory Offers Me Vice Presidency

The negotiations got so rough that on the evening of December 11, 1986, the last day of the filing of certificates of candidacy for president and vice president, Cory called me up in my house in Marikina. She asked me to prepare to go with her to the Comelec so we could file our certificates of candidacy together, she for president and I for vice president. I asked her what happened to the negotiation with Doy. She told me that it had collapsed.

I then quietly asked my supporters to prepare my certificate of candidacy for Vice President. My supporters were doubly elated because they felt that, at last, the sacrifices of PDP-Laban in the struggle against Marcos would be recognized and also because December 11 happened to be my birthday. We were, in fact, commemorating the day with a few friends in our family home in Marikina.

Within the hour, however, Cory phoned me again. She said, "Can I come to your house to discuss something with you personally?" "Why not?" I replied. She then asked for directions. I described the landmarks near Fairlane Subdivision. Cory responded, "I suppose when we get there, we can just ask the guard." I had to tell her, "There is no guard. This is not a gated community. This is a poor man's subdivision." She sounded unsure if her driver could find his way to my place so I offered to see her instead at her home on Times Street, Quezon City.

Before leaving, I told my friends who stayed behind in our house, to expect the worst. I meant that Cory probably found a new vice presidential teammate — otherwise why would she have to personally tell me what she had in mind instead of just conveying it to me over the phone?

We soon found out when we got to Cory's house. Our neighbors, Celedonio Cruz, Romeo Reyes, Tony Togonon, Estelo Tumblod and Frank Ogsimer, and my daughter Inde, accompanied me to the meeting with Cory. We had a short, direct-to-the-point, 15-minute conversation. Cory told me that Cardinal Sin had finally convinced Doy Laurel to run as her Vice President.

"That's fine with me," I said. Indeed it was. I believed then and to this day that the decision to have Laurel instead of me or anyone else as her vice presidential candidate was good for the nation at that time.

Inde remembers that I nodded my head and smiled. In fact, when a sister-in-law of Cory called me later that night to "console" me, I told her not to worry about me. I said I would take care of my personal affairs and assured her that I would continue working for Cory's candidacy as best I could.

Bing, however, took it badly. She thought I had invested a lot of time and effort in building PDP-Laban into a recognized national political party that supported Cory all the way and, up to that point, there had been no reciprocal move on the part of Cory's people to even acknowledge it. Privately, Bing said, "One day, they will regret that decision." Bing's opinon proved prophetic because, years later, Cory told my daughter Maria Petrina in an interview that she found Doy Laurel difficult to work with as her Vice President.

Without losing a beat in our march to oust Marcos, the very next evening, I paid a call on Doy Laurel at his home on Shaw Boulevard in Mandaluyong. I went there to pledge my personal and our party's support for the Cory-Doy ticket. Elfren Cruz, a PDP-Laban leader of Parañaque, Assemblyman Zafiro Respicio and Lito Lorenzana accompanied me. Doy graciously received and assured us that we could now devote our efforts to defeat Marcos and work together as a team for the good of the people.

Cardinal Sin's Intervention

Soon thereafter, the nation learned that the person who had successfully brokered a Cory-Doy ticket was none other than the ebullient and politically astute Archbishop of Manila, Jaime Cardinal Sin.

My daughter Maripet, who was writing a thesis for a master's degree in Mass Communications at the California State University Northridge, recorded the Cardinal's recollection on the matter some years after the event.

The Cardinal said:

> Mr. Laurel came. He said, "Cardinal, I am running as President. I have all my posters ready." He was accompanied by Ernie Maceda and Joe Concepcion.
>
> "Let's all take lunch together. Doy," I said, "if you will run as president, and Mrs. Aquino runs for president, both of you will lose because your force and strength will be divided. Between Mrs. Aquino and yourself, I would say that Mrs. Aquino is more attractive than you are. And I think this is the will of God because I can see that God wants to humiliate this strongman. If he is defeated by a woman, that is the greatest humiliation. I feel it. Do you love your country?"
>
> "Yes," he said.

I told him, "If you love your country, do some sacrifices. Be the Vice President."

He stood up and said, and he was crying now, "If that is the case, I will do it."

"But do it right now," I said, "Go to Mrs. Aquino because this woman will not go to you. She is proud. Then, go to the Comelec."

Both of them went to the Comelec at 11:30 p.m., 30 minutes before the deadline. And there was dancing here when they signed their applications. So [the agreement for Cory and Doy Laurel to run as a ticket] was formulated here in this house. That was my role.

Incidentally, the statements attributed to Cardinal Sin in Chapters 49 and 54 were also taped recorded by Maripet in the same interview.

Chapter 48

Cory's Campaign

Shortly before the campaign began, a stream of high-level US government officials visited the country. Sen. John Kerry, State Department Assistant Secretary Richard Armitage, State Department official Paul Wolfowitz, National Security Council head Richard Childress, Congressman Stephen Solarz and CIA chief William Casey, among others, called on Marcos, Cardinal Sin and some Opposition figures. Their visits bolstered our belief that the country was in the priority radar screen of the US. We were elated by the interest shown by US government officials in the presidential election. Naively, we thought that the attention given by US officials could deter any plot to cheat on the part of the ruling party.

Just the same, I believed we had to do our share to make it difficult for Marcos to manipulate the elections. I had determined to work actively in Cory's campaign and "not to sulk," as columnist Arturo Borjal insinuated in one of his columns. I decided to strengthen our party and help smooth ruffled feelings among disparate groups of Cory supporters. It helped that Peping Cojuangco, Jr., Cory's brother, asked me to accompany her in the campaign as a frontline campaign manager. I accommodated his request and, like Cory's shadow, I went with her throughout the nation from the start of the campaign up to its end and beyond that is, even after Marcos had fled the country.

As a sort of on-the-spot political "Mr. Fix-It," I made sure that, while I stayed within her beck-and-call, I did not share the spotlight with her on the political stage. Still, a few photographs caught me on the political stage with Cory. Often, however, I was beyond camera range in the back row on a political stage or off the stage ironing out creases in our relationships with our political organizers in a particular campaign area. I made sure that important local personalities were seated or stood beside Cory, knowing that politicians needed personal recognition by the candidate they were supporting. I also had the unavoidable but pleasant task of delivering speeches endorsing Cory and Doy wherever we campaigned.

Difficult Campaign

It was a difficult campaign. We had very minimal logistics. In the beginning, we went to distant places on commercial flights. Only later in the campaign, when the contributors saw the tremendous outpouring of support for

1986: *ONE OF THE FEW* photographs that show me on the political stage with Cory during her campaign.

Cory throughout the nation, did they begin lending us their private planes. At first, they put at our disposal small planes, but, by the time the campaign was in full swing, they were lending us larger turbo prop jet planes.

The change was not lost on Cory who once mentioned it to me in Tagalog, "*O, Nene, OK na tayo ngayon, ano?* We're OK now, Nene, don't you think?" Indeed, we were more than OK. We had more speed, more mobility and more leg space than before. Aside from Eldon Cruz, husband of her daughter Ballsy, her sister Terry Lopa and me, Cory aides could already be accommodated in the bigger planes.

Apart from logistical constraints that hobbled our campaign at the start, we had another problem. The Metro Manila crowds knew Cory by sight, but the people in remote provinces didn't know her that well, although they knew her by name as Ninoy Aquino's widow.

I fared even worse in terms of public recognition especially in the provinces — not that it mattered since I wasn't the candidate. The thing, however, was that, every now and then, I had to step in as the emergency master of ceremonies or the introducer of Cory. I mention this matter because, in a sortie in a town in Samar, neither our provincial nor municipal coordinator was on hand to take charge of the rally. We were already on stage at the town plaza but there was no local politician to receive us. So I had to act as the impromptu emcee. It was funny in a sense because I had to introduce Cory to the sparse crowd that braved the hostility of the local officialdom and the military, but I myself needed to be introduced. So I did the most expedient thing. I introduced myself first. In doing so, I had to blow my own horn louder than Triton, the horn blower of Greek mythology, when he put the giants to flight.

I said I was an assemblyman who fought Marcos in the Batasan. I mentioned that I was a member of Ninoy's team that ran against Imelda in Metro Manila in the 1978 Interim Batasang Pambansa elections. I also told the incredulous crowd that Marcos had — up to that point — jailed me three times: first as a Constitutional Convention delegate, then as a protesting candidate in the 1978 IBP elections, and still later as the opposition mayor of Cagayan de Oro. All that hype about me took time, but I had to capture the attention of the crowd, and, like a barker at a circus, get the people watching from a distance to come closer to the stage so that they could see and hear Cory better. As the crowds started to trickle in, only then did I introduce Cory.

Cory Magic

Cory was not a particularly spectacular political platform speaker. But she had a certain indefinable aura that caused the people to gasp in awe of her presence and gape at her while she did her spiel. She was Ninoy's widow after all. She said she did not want to be a candidate for president, but somebody had to face up to Marcos so that democracy could be restored in the country. In a few minutes, she was done with her speech. Our local leaders

***1986:** I ENDORSE Cory and Doy all over the nation.*

were still not there, but it was time to move on to the next stop.

Happily, with the exception of some out-of-the-way towns like that municipality in Samar, Cory was always engulfed by wave upon wave of enthusiastic political fans from Day 1 of the campaign until the last. The crowds that mobbed Cory everywhere she went was unlike any that I had seen in previous campaigns. Teodoro Benigno, a hard-boiled newsman if ever there was one, then writing for Agence France Presse, told Alfonso Policarpio that he saw "an avalanche" in the making in the Cory-Doy campaign. Benigno, who had seen the legendary vote-getter, Ramon Magsaysay, draw huge political crowds as never before, told friends, "I have not seen anything like this — not even for Magsaysay." Policarpio, a Cory believer, printed Benigno's observations in his column, "Business of Truth," in the *Malaya* issue of December 21, 1985.

The frenzied multitudes that met Cory wherever she arrived by plane, car or boat were so thick and unruly that a tight cordon of Cory volunteers was always needed to keep them in check, especially at the airports where the danger of the aircraft propellers' accidentally hitting wayward greeters was greatest. Many a time as our campaign plane was about to land, I saw phalanxes of people running pell-mell onto the runway and they had to be turned back by airport security and Cory's advance team. Kept behind the security cordon, the maddened crowd would strain against the ropes or the bodies of the guards to go near Cory's plane or helicopter. When the plane or chopper landed, inevitably people would rush towards it, un-mindful of the dangers of the whirling propeller blades that could chop their heads off or slice their bodies fatally. With superhuman effort on the part of Cory's security and volunteers, no serious injuries attended our landings and takeoffs.

Ten days of nonstop campaigning in the provinces brought us to Escalante, Negros Occidental, a municipality notorious for the massacre of 21 farmers by government security forces three months before. Some 3,000 people attended our rally at the town square. I told the *New York Times* correspondent, Alice Villadolid, "What we are seeing is a real ground swell" considering that we only had "a skeletal campaign structure" in the province.

That evening, we had a mammoth rally in Bacolod City, the capital of Negros Occidental. At least 20,000 people trooped to the plaza of the provincial capitol to hear Cory's appeal to dismantle the martial law government. Cory and Doy took time to affirm their support for the sugar planters of the province to do away with the government monopoly on sugar trading by the Nasutra, the National Sugar Trading Corporation. A Marcos creation, Nasutra implemented policies that wrought difficulties in the lives of some 250,000 workers and their families in the sugar provinces of Negros Occidental, Iloilo, Bukidnon and Pampanga.

The Campaign Issues

Marcos hurled all kinds of ridiculous issues at Cory. As a woman, he sneered, she was only good for the bedroom. We capitalized on that *faux pas* and counter-charged that he demeaned women in general. We cited women leaders from the pages of our history, such as: Gabriela Silang, who led the rebels in the Ilocos against the Spanish government; Melchora Aquino or Tandang Sora, who helped Andres Bonifacio sustain his rebellion against Spain in Manila and its environs; and brilliant women leaders of the country in recent times like Yay Panlilio Marking, a guerilla who fought against the Japanese invaders; and, more recently, Senators Pacita Madrigal-Warns, Helena Benitez, Magnolia Antonino and Eva Estrada Kalaw who did their share in nation building.

Teresita Quintos-Deles, head of *Filipina*, a feminist organization, and Dr. Mita Pardo de Tavera, chair of Gabriela, a group of activist women, also took up the cudgels for Cory and condemned the male chauvinist tone of the Marcos put down.

The counter-argument was so telling that Marcos never repeated the offensive remark again. When he pounded on Cory's lack of knowledge, *walang alam*, or experience in governance, we merrily hit Marcos's vaunted exceptional knowledge or experience in corruption, human rights abuses, extrajudicial killings and selling out the interests of the country to foreign exploiters.

Ballots versus Bullets

To gain public sympathy, Marcos raised the bogeyman that the Opposition was plotting to assassinate him. His partisans heatedly threatened to kill Cory with one bullet, saying *"Isang bala ka lang! One bullet is all it takes!"* Cory had a ready repartee. "We will get rid of Marcos not by bullets but by the ballot," she orated in our sorties. *"Marcos, isang balota ka lang!* Marcos, one ballot is all it takes!"

One Marcos charge against Cory seemed to click with the rightist elements and the unthinking sectors of the country's society. It was Marcos's relentless accusation that Cory was a communist lover. Marcos led them to believe that the communists were a far greater threat to the nation's well-being than his authoritarian rule.

The controlled media fanned belief in the anti-communist line of Marcos. For instance, the *Metro Manila Times* of January 5, 1986 bannered his absolutely fantastic claim that "Cory Helped Found NPA." Marcos tossed the canard against Cory also to inveigle the Americans to support him. His line was that, if she won, she would legalize the Communist Party and remove the US military bases. That, he said, would spell more difficulties for the nation. It was, in his view, proof that Cory was either a communist or a supporter of a communist cause.

In anticipation, I tried to explain the twin issues to American audiences when I was in the US the year before and, more importantly, when I addressed domestic audiences.

We asserted that Cory's alleged communist bias had no basis whatsoever. We flatly denied that she had anything to do with the founding of the NPA. That was the easier part of our defense of Cory because it was so patently and absurdly untrue.

But the issues of the legalization of the Communist Party and the removal of the US military bases needed more rationalized explanation. The two issues were spelled out in the platform of the Convenor Group in an attempt to provide a basis for the unification of the then splintered Opposition. We explained that legalizing the Communist Party was in line with what other democratic countries like the US did. It was a way of inducing the Communist Party to shift to the parliamentary arena rather than armed struggle. As for the removal of the US military bases, Cory advocated that the bases would be phased out after the expiry date of the Bases Agreement in 1991. The removal of the bases was not asserted merely to massage the perceived national ego but also — and more importantly — to lay the basis for the fast economic development of the areas then being used primarily as advance defense perimeters of the US and as rest and recreation zones for American troops.

Marcos exploited the communism issue to exhaustion. He summed up the February 7 election as a "fight between communism and democracy" — Cory for communism and Marcos for democracy.

Assemblyman Jaime Ferrer offered the best defense against Marcos accusations that Cory was a communist lover. In a statement printed in the *WeForum* weekly of January 7-13, 1986, Ferrer said:

> Mr. Marcos should learn a lesson from Mrs. Aquino in diffusing the communist rebellion. Mr. Marcos's 20-year policy against the communists is a dismal failure. They only grew to alarming proportions under his regime of terror and injustice.
>
> Like President Magsaysay before her, Mrs. Aquino's platform of justice can attract the communists in abandoning the armed struggle and rejoin the mainstream in rebuilding the nation. As President Magsaysay said, "Communism is an idea and you cannot fight it with bullets." Make the communists feel that they are Filipinos first and communists second, and you stand a good chance in attracting them back to the fold. Mr. Marcos's credibility problem bars him from succeeding in doing this. Mrs. Aquino's credibility, sincerity and platform of justice [are] precisely the solution to the civil war Mr. Marcos keeps talking about.

Coming as it did from Ferrer, an avowed anti-communist and a close confidante of the late President Magsaysay, we believed that the rebuttal scoured Cory clean of the accusations that she was a communist or a communist lover.

Incidentally, we did not leave Marcos the luxury of defining the issues of the campaign unilaterally. We counterattacked that Marcos was the biggest recruiter to the NPA cause by his corruption, abuses and human rights violations. We also accused Marcos of malicious scheming by his introduction of Amendment No. 6 to the 1973 Constitution. Amendment No. 6 made him a super legislature and invested him with vast powers to rule by decree even after the formal structures of martial rule were seemingly removed. Thus, we made it a campaign promise to cause the repeal of Amendment No. 6.

In June 1985, Marcos made the mistake of publicly admitting that he might have to call on American troops to fight insurgency in the country. To us, the error highlighted Marcos's hidden agenda to involve American troops in the country to stamp out the NPA rebellion. It was also a clear sign that he no longer spoke for the people and was prepared to barter away the country's sovereignty in favor of the continued presence of the US troops to prop up his regime.

Failing Health

We also hit him hard on his failing health. We capitalized on the report that he had systemic *lupus erythematosus*, an incurable ailment, which was eating into his being. In early February 1986, while it sounded a little cruel, we could not help but reveal the precarious state of Marcos's health. We cited a Marcos press conference in Malacañang during which he said that he was physically strong, only to stumble as he left his chair in the presence of the media. Only the timely intervention of his aides prevented him from falling on his face. The photograph of Marcos being propped up by his aides in the *Arab News* of February 2, 1986 said it all.

Marcos was so secretive about his ailment that even the killing on November 1, 1985 of kidney specialist, Dr. Potenciano Baccay, was attributed to people close to him. Baccay was one of Marcos's doctors. He had reportedly leaked the fact that Marcos had two kidney transplants, one in August 1983, and the other in November 1984. The August 1983 operation was not successful. The new kidney was rejected. But the November 1984 transplant seemed to have worked.

Marcos did not like people talking about his ailment. In the coffee shops where the views of the rumormongers were not censored, it was the consensus that Baccay was murdered to silence him. Ver's men were suspected of having done the killing. Malacañang spokespersons denied that Marcos or Ver had anything to do with it. And while it had never been conclusively proven to be the case, three years later, Sterling Seagrave wrote in his book, *The Marcos Dynasty*, that Marcos "ordered Ver to find the leak and silence it."

When KBL propagandists peddled the slogan, *"Subok sa Krisis"*"or "Tested by Crisis," to boost Marcos's candidacy, we contended that indeed Marcos was so at home with crises that, since he was elected president in 1965 up to now, the country was constantly buffeted by one crisis after another.

Bogus War Hero

One issue pained Marcos a lot. It was the accusation that he was a fake war hero. A former military intelligence officer and a top leader of the MFP, Bonifacio Gillego, concluded, after extensive study of the documents available in US archives, that Marcos was a bogus war hero. Marcos, Gillego said, did not deserve the medals that he time and again proudly displayed. We knew that he was hurting from the issue because he appealed several times in the course of the campaign to the veterans among the audience in his rallies to help him refute the accusation.

The main reason why Marcos chafed against the fake war hero charge was that the American press had taken it up. The *New York Times* of January 23, 1986 questioned the bases of the medals awarded to Marcos. *Newsweek* in its issue of February 3, also wrote about it as a major story titled, "The Maharlika Papers." *Maharlika*, which is Tagalog for nobles, was the name of the Marcos-organized guerilla group that asked for compensation from the US for their services during the war against Japan. The magazine quoted an American guerilla leader in Pangasinan, Ray C. Hunt, Jr., as having said that war exploits of Marcos were "a cock-and-bull story."

Hunt was exaggerating. To my mind, Marcos did fight against the Japanese invaders. But not too many people were convinced that Marcos was the war hero that his propaganda machine pictured him to be. If, indeed, he fought the Japanese as a guerilla, there was nothing outstanding in his activities to merit the many medals he claimed were legitimately conferred on him for his war exploits.

Unfulfilled Promises

We also used the issues researched by our colleague from the Batasan, Oscar Santos, to show that Marcos made a lot of promises but was short on delivery. Santos documented that Marcos, instead of lowering the prices of sugar, beef and transport fare as he promised, actually triggered their increases. In a more telling analysis, Santos said a kilo of rice, which cost only P0.90 in 1965 (when Marcos first became president), was already P7.50 in this campaign. There were many other items that Santos faulted Marcos for, but the rice issue was the most effective. People readily understood it, involving as it did the politics of the stomach. Behind the scenes, Raul Contreras, Billy Esposo and their colleagues of the Cory press office also busily put out anti-Marcos propaganda.

The issues we hurled against Marcos sounded like campaign charges that one usually heard in local politics: "liar, fake war hero, killer, land-grabber and womanizer." The only national issue that, I thought, fitted him to a "T" was that he was "a discredited, decrepit and dying dictator whose continued hold on power was perilous to the nation."

In turn, Marcos called Cory names without expressly referring to her. He said that his opponent was "a communist, childish, inexperienced, a know-nothing, and one who was only good for the bedroom and whose election would be a disaster."

Cory's Superstar Appeal

Marcos's attacks against Cory did not seem to make a dent on her superstar appeal on the campaign trail. Rain or shine, people mobbed her from the time of our arrival anywhere in the country to the minute of our departure.

During the entire campaign, there were only a couple of places where we felt palpable hostility to Cory in the very air we breathed. We felt the enmity of Governor Juanito Remulla in Cavite, when we passed in a convoy of cars through several towns of the province. *"Mga komunista kayo!* You are communists! *Hindi kayo kailangan dito!* You are not wanted here!" people shouted, clenching their fists to underscore what was in store for us if we tarried any longer.

We felt the same visceral antipathy when we had a fast caravan of several cars passing through many municipalities in Ilocos Norte, the home province of Marcos. In Laoag City, we wanted to have a rally, but the person entrusted with the funds to organize it "mysteriously disappeared," as *Veritas* reported on January 12, 1986. In Vigan, Ilocos Sur, we had to be content with a lightning rally in front of a public market at 10 a.m. We used a six-by-six truck as an improvised stage. Cory spoke briefly on Aquino's supreme sacrifice and the continuing violations of human rights by the Marcos regime. A few people listened. The presence of some people in the rally was enough reason for me to tell the journalists who covered Cory's campaign with much hyperbole that "Cory has cracked the Solid North." The northernmost provinces are collectively known as the Solid North because the voters there, politicians say, invariably support Ilocano candidates.

While we did not really crack the Solid North, Narvacan in Ilocos Sur, La Union, Baguio City and even Tuguegarao in Cagayan flattered her with huge turnouts. We also received enthusiastic responses in the towns of Hilongos, Baybay, Maasin and Tacloban City in Leyte, the political bailiwick of Imelda. There, surprisingly, thousands of people cheered Cory at our rallies or when her motorcade passed by. Res Salvatierra, Bemboy Antoni, Tita Pedrosa and several unnamed volunteers did yeoman work for PDP-Laban in coordination with Unido leaders to bring in the Leyte crowds for Cory's campaign there.

In Cebu, we encountered a hostile reception in Danao City, hometown of Ramon Durano, who was widely acknowledged as Marcos's alter ego in the province. Durano controlled the municipality with an iron hand. He brooked no dissent and nobody alive dared to express disagreement in Danao with what he did in his turf. In legend, he was known as the provider of work to the residents of the town through fair means or foul. In return, he demanded feckless fealty from the townsfolk. Upon the insistence of our Cebu Opposition colleagues in the Batasan, Inday Nita Daluz, Tony Cuenco and Celing Fernan, we motored to Danao to show Marcos and Durano that we did not fear their goons.

Quiet Support

At the boundary of the city, a huge banner greeted us in Visayan, "*Ang mga komunista, dili dawaton sa Danao.* "Communists are not welcome in Danao." As we went through the main thoroughfare of Danao City, I saw a few people line up on either side of the road. There were no smiles or waving of hands or displays of the usual Cory symbols of yellow. The people were all so reserved and quiet as if an honored dead was passing by. But, to my astonishment, I saw a couple of women clandestinely express their support for Cory by pressing the back of their right hands on their breasts and flashing the "L" sign of Laban with their forefingers and thumbs. Inday Nita also whispered to us that, inside the huts we passed by, some people had clandestinely flashed the Laban sign.

The message that we were not welcome was repeated in smaller handmade placards that some individuals, presumably Danao residents, carried as they followed us into the local Church where Cory and the rest of us prayed. Ever the optimist, Inday Nita pointed out to us that some of the women who carried the placards had tears in their eyes, attesting to their sympathy for Cory. I did not see their tears, but I decided I would not lose anything if I believed Inday Nita's observation.

Despite the chilling reception in Danao, I told our campaign colleagues that, if people could not suppress their feelings for Cory even in Durano country, we were on our way to evicting Marcos after the February 7 elections. Aside from the placards that did not welcome us, no hostile acts marred our visit to Danao.

Plaza Pershing Bombing

In Zamboanga City, I had the scare of my life. Our rally on January 19, 1986 in Plaza Pershing attracted a huge crowd. Media estimates placed it at 30,000. Cory and Doy were seated on the front row on the stage with some local VIPs. After delivering my brief speech in support of our candidates, I went down to the side of the stage to talk with some of our leaders.

Suddenly, bombs exploded some distance away. The explosions sounded so near though that I thought we were being shelled by hostile fire. Thousands of people scampered in all directions. My immediate thought was to get back on stage and secure Cory.

With my heart pounding at a crazy rate, I rushed up the stage, bumping into people who were going down. On the stage, I saw a sight that would be fixed indelibly in my memory. With his back towards the crowd, Doy leaned over Cory to shield her with his body. Amid the pandemonium, Cory had not moved from her chair. To my mind, that was Doy's highest moment in the campaign. He demonstrated for all to see that Camelot had no monopoly on chivalry. He also had it in his blood.

That moment would never be repeated in the campaign. This was how Cory described years later her feelings over the incident at Plaza Pershing in a taped-interview with my daughter Maripet:

> You always think of physical danger and there were actual instances. In fact, when we were in [Zamboanga], a grenade exploded close by....Given that my husband was assassinated, well, you always think, what will prevent the perpetrators from doing something similar? But, like my husband, I am a fatalist and I believe that, so long as one believes in what one is doing, then one should go on, regardless of the consequences. I always put my trust in God, and if God wanted me to continue what I was trying to do, then He would take care of everything.

Parenthetically, the comments ascribed to Cory in Chapters 49, 50, 51, 53, and 54 were also recorded on tape by Maripet.

Evidently, even at Plaza Pershing, Cory's God protected her and wanted her to continue her campaign to oust Marcos. A few minutes after the explosions, we heard the master of ceremonies announce that everything was under control and we could continue with our rally. Cory and Doy then delivered their usual discourses and lambasted Marcos for trying to intimidate us. With our candidates' show of courage under fire, I was certain that we would get a large chunk of the votes of the city. It did not turn out that way on the day of the election, but on that scary night we had reason to be optimistic.

As the campaign progressed, my friend, Assemblyman Hjalmar Quintana, Doy Laurel's batty but occasionally brilliant sidekick, suggested that a catchy slogan should be used to introduce Cory and Doy to our audiences in lieu of the uninspired cliches that our emcees used. He was a hundred percent convinced that it would click. He said that Cory and Doy should be presented in our rallies as the "Cory-Doy Love Team." Our convent-bred candidate did not even think it funny. She just wryly smiled it away. Quintana, however, would not take a wry smile for a "No." He continued to use the phrase when Cory was not around.

In the island of Panay, the people's reception of the Cory-Doy team was nothing short of phenomenal. Everywhere they went, the people simply went gaga. In Iloilo, when we motored through the city on the way to the other parts of the island, without letup, supporters lined the Cory campaign caravan route from morning until dusk.

Yellow Everywhere

Because Cory had chosen yellow as the color of her campaign, in the urban places, people raised yellow banners, homemade placards on yellow cardboards or just anything yellow to show their support for Cory. In the rural areas, the barangay folks waved yellow papaya fruits or leaves, held aloft ripe yellow mangoes or waved yellow sunflowers. In one barangay, a young lady gaily hoisted on a stick something unique that I did not see anywhere else in the campaign trail. She waved a yellow nylon panty as if it were a banner that proudly proclaimed our victory. For its unique advertising value, I called Cory's attention to it. She smiled at the happy incongruity of it all.

In the town of San Jose, the capital of Antique, no less than 10,000 people swarmed all over the town plaza to hear Cory promise to give justice to the followers of our leader in the province, Evelio Javier. Seven of Javier's men were killed in a shoot-out with Assemblyman Arturo Pacificador and his followers in 1984. Up to the time, one year and nine months to the day of the massacre, no charges had been filed against the culprits. When my turn came to speak, I underscored Cory's promise that her administration "will seek justice for the victims of oppression under the Marcos regime."

1986: *MASSIVE CROWD FOR CORY and Doy in Cagayan de Oro*

Everywhere we went, people insisted on their right to shake the hand of Cory. As a precaution against accidental injury, I advised her not to stick her hand out of the car when we were passing by crowds of onlookers. I said that she could break her arm if she carelessly allowed her fans to hang on to her hand even as our car moved on. I suggested that she should just wave to the people from within the car but keep her hands out of reach of the fans on the roadside.

That was not, however, possible all the time. Sometimes, the surge of people towards our campaign vehicles was so insistent that we had to move at a snail's pace. The windows of the car that Cory took had to be slid down and she could not avoid offering her hand for people to shake. People would then hold her hand, shake it or pinch the back of it or any part of her arm that was within reach. Sometimes I had to remind the driver to proceed more slowly to avoid injuring Cory or those who hung on to her hand or to the sides of the car. Often, when we alighted from our lead campaign vehicle, Cory and Terry, her sister, had to hang on to my belt at my back so as not to be separated from one another and from me as her security and I barreled through the throngs to get to the campaign stage or wherever our next stop was.

When we campaigned in my home city, I was not embarrassed. We had a good crowd, some 20,000 people who filled every inch of the available space at the city amphitheater and the side streets leading to it. The rousing reception for Cory and Doy boosted our spirits no end. It was made possible only because Mayor Ambing Magtajas, Vice Mayor Henry Bacal and our band of loyal city councilors, Guilly Parrel, Roddy Villaroya, Jun Pepito and Pepe Abbu, and our party leaders, Luz Sabanal and Jun de Gracia, willingly stuck their necks out to support our presidential and vice presidential ticket.

While in the city, Cory, her sister Terry, her lady assistants and security people slept in our house on Archbishop Hayes Street in the heart of the city. The place was not exactly in good shape. The appointments were roughly the equivalent of a no-star hotel. The added problem was that Bing was not home. She had to go to the US to accompany our young nieces, Chelsea and Carmel, daughters of Paul and Tess Emata, who were immigrants there. And so, without my knowing about it, the house help did not even change the linen on the beds that were placed for the use of my very important guests. Fritzie Aragon, Cory's assistant, tactfully brought the problem to my attention. A fast order remedied it, but Cory never offered to sleep in the house again.

The only time she visited the house anew during the campaign was when we were unable to land our chopper on an airstrip near Marawi City. Clouds were so thick that the pilot, despite three tries, could not locate the landing field. Instead of returning to Butuan City, we decided to land in Cagayan de Oro as it was long past the lunch hour. There at the house, we feasted on *bulalo*, a beef-and-bone-marrow stew, that I ordered from the nearest local fastfood outlet. We were so famished that Cory thoroughly enjoyed the meal. Even when she was already installed in Malacañang as President, she would recall now and then that the lunch we had in Cagayan de Oro was the "best" she had during the entire campaign.

Marcos Partisans Switch Sides

As the campaign progressed, some known Marcos partisans like Gov. Felicisimo San Luis of Laguna, former Speaker of the House of Representatives Cornelio Villareal and his son Gov. Cornelio Villareal, Jr. of Capiz, Assemblyman Enrique Belo and Gov. Eduardo Joson of Nueva Ecija, and Gov. Carlos Fortich of Bukidnon switched their support to Cory. One big boost to Cory's candidacy was the resignation of an official of the Ministry of Foreign Affairs, Ambassador Leticia Ramos Shahani. She was also the UN assistant secretary general for Social Development and Humanitarian Affairs and the younger sister of Gen. Fidel V. Ramos. Shahani endorsed the candidacy of Cory and Doy in early January 1986. Her resignation created the impression that it carried the implicit support of General Ramos for Cory. Ramos, at the time, was chief of the Constabulary. Psychologically, the Shahani endorsement of Cory carried a lot more weight among the people than those of the switching politicians.

After the fact, I asked Shahani why she did it. She explained:

> It was my son, Ranjit, and my friend, Betty Go-Belmonte, who convinced me to support Cory Aquino, whom I did not know personally at the time. The two had urged similar reasons for me to do so.

"If you want change," they said, "you should go for Cory." Shahani
added, Then "I heard the sentimental melody and lyrics of the song "*Bayan
Ko*" being played in a neighbor's house while Ranjit was egging me to help
Cory. "Mom," Ranjit said, "listen to that song. How could you turn your
back [on] your country?"

Without considering that she could lose her jobs at the MFA and the UN,
which she did, Shahani cast her lot with Cory and abandoned the presidential
candidacy of her second cousin, President Marcos.

Zobels Weigh In

The Cory campaign, however, suffered a perceptual loss when business
tycoon Enrique Zobel, whom we thought would back Cory, didn't. On January 12, the magazine *Veritas* carried a photograph of Zobel smiling effusively
at Cory, while shaking her hand with his right and holding her elbow with his
left. The occasion was the January 6 forum of the Bishops-Businessmen Conference, the Makati Business Club and the Management Association of the
Philippines. Cory was a big hit at the forum where she explained her agenda
for the country. Soon after the publication of the picture, Marcos called Zobel
and told him the facts of life. Days later, Zobel openly declared for Marcos. It
was a good thing that Jaime Zobel, cousin of Enrique, weighed in for Cory to
tilt the electoral scale of big business for our candidate.

The Cory campaign, however, because of the perception that I had ready access to Cory, I got invited to
press forums to tangle with Marcos apologists and boldly predict what the
results of the elections would be. At the Manila Hotel on *Kapihan sa Manila's*
first anniversary, Roman Cruz, Jr., a Marcos man, who was president of the
hotel and of Philippine Airlines, invited me to join the forum. The *Times Journal* on February 4 reported that the editors of the major dailies and some foreign journalists were there. They included *Bulletin's* Pat Gonzales, *Daily Express's*
Enrique Romualdez and Neal Cruz, *Times Journal's* Manuel Salak, *Asiaweek's*
Tony Lopez and *Washington Post* bureau chief John Burgess. The *Journal* also
noted that Chief Justice Enrique Fernando, Agrarian Reform Minister Conrado
Estrella and I were among those who occupied center table. Estrella predicted
a Marcos-Tolentino victory. I contradicted him by saying that it would be a
"Cory-Doy win against the Marcos-Tolentino tandem, 55%-45%, nationwide."

The huge turnouts for Cory's rallies emboldened us to aggressively challenge Marcos to debate with Cory. To our surprise, he rejected the challenge
and left it to his subalterns to explain why. Batasan Speaker Yñiguez, among
other Marcos spokespersons, said that there was no need for the debate because Cory had no platform to speak of anyway and that the stand of the KBL
on all issues had already been spelled out. In reply, we charged that Marcos
was either too sick to appear in a public debate with Cory or was too afraid
that he would be unmasked as having done nothing through the years of his

martial law regime except to enrich himself and his cronies and cause further deterioration in the areas of law and order, poverty, human rights and good governance.

Ambassador JV Cruz, a former Marcos press secretary, frequently stood in for Marcos in televised discussions with Opposition spokespersons on the electoral issues. On one TV discussion, I exchanged views with Cruz. He lectured me on the need of the country to have a leader who had experience and knowhow, especially in the fight against communism. I countered that he probably did not know that the people saw Marcos as "experienced," but in misgovernance and in the mishandling of the resources of the nation. I also said that, "perhaps because he had been out of the country for so long, the ambassador did not know the situation that really obtained in the country especially in the provinces where human rights abuses were the rule, not the exception."

Verbal Skirmishes

We also had some verbal skirmishes with Marcos's Labor Minister Blas Ople who spoke for Marcos now and then. During one discussion at *Kapihan sa Manila*, he said the Opposition was being used "as weapons of destabilization by the hawks in the Reagan administration" to unseat Marcos and destabilize the Republic. I disputed his premises. I emphasized that Cory, as she had time and again asserted, would not allow herself to be *used* by anyone. If American public opinion favored Cory, it was because they saw that Marcos was no longer in a position to govern the country well. I also stressed that Ople got it wrong because Marcos was not the State or the Republic. He and other Marcos defenders were deliberately peddling the line that Marcos, like Louis XIV of France, and the State were one. They wanted to create the image of the Marcos's indispensability.

Despite the fact that Ople and I were on opposite sides of the political divide, I appreciated his knack for the well-turned phrase. I found one such phrase, even if it was meant to disparage our candidate's dismissive attitude towards Marcos, to be memorably acidic. Ople said that the stance of Cory was reflective of "upper-crust arrogance." To blunt his criticism, I retorted that Cory, in fact, reflected the views of the oppressed masses of our people, not the disenchantment of society's upper classes. In all, I was disappointed that Ople sided with Marcos. He was supposedly a "left of center" politician and there he was extolling to the high heavens Marcos, who was, in our view, the epitome of a rightist politician. I found Ople's behavior difficult to rationalize.

We also encountered great difficulty with the mainstream media. Marcos controlled all the TV and radio stations and the major dailies. In her words, Cory described the problem:

I had no coverage here in Manila. That was the sad part. I only had access on radio and even that was really very difficult because the opposition had very little money. But I think that also worked in my favor because the fact that people could not see me on television, they made every effort to see me at the rallies. So we were able to get really big crowds to attend our rallies because the curiosity aspect was there. And I guess they were tired of seeing Marcos on television.

Because we continued to draw the huge crowds to Cory's campaign rallies, we maintained our optimism that we could beat Marcos come Election Day. We believed that, if people braved not only the elements but also the threat of harassment by the regime to show their affection for Cory, they would translate their actions into pro-Cory votes.

The biggest turnout of people for Cory in the campign was at the Luneta on February 4, 1986, our *miting de avance*. I was with Cory and Doy at the Quirino Grandstand and I was simply amazed at the number of people who stood on every inch of the ground in front of the stage and as far as the eye could see. Some estimates placed the crowd at 2.5 million. *Asiaweek* of February 16 said it was 800,000. Having seen the magnitude of the multitude that showed up at the final rally of Cory and Doy, I think that the higher end of the pro-Cory estimates was more accurate.

Marcos had his own *miting de avance* but his crowd was much sparser than Cory's. Yet on the evening of February 7, Election Day, even as the votes were still being counted, Marcos claimed victory. Immediately, we in the Opposition asserted that Cory had won the snap elections despite the massive cheating of Marcos and his minions. The Catholic Bishops Conference of the Philippines took up our cry as the following chapter shows.

Part 12

The Purifying Days of February

PDP-Laban Files

1986*: RESPONDING TO THE CALL for People Power, PDP-Laban party members flock to Edsa to help oust the Marcos government.*

Chapter 49:

CBCP Condemns Cheating

To quell the rising clamor against his claims of victory, Marcos broached the possibility of invalidating the elections. We opposed the idea. We believed that Cory won even if Marcos had roundly cheated her in the elections. Cory spoke of the cheating in this wise:

> Up to the very last days of the counting, I was still (running) neck-to-neck with Marcos. And this in spite of the rampant cheating which was widely reported not only by Filipinos but by the American observers and also the international media. This was so blatantly done. The Marcos government did not even make any attempt to be subtle about it or to do it in a more sophisticated manner....Minister Juan Ponce Enrile admitted during the Edsa Revolution that, in his own province alone, I was cheated of something like 200,000 to 300,000 votes. So this is an admission coming from somebody within the establishment, within the Marcos administration.

As for having another election, Rene Saguisag, Cory's spokesman, in his inimitable way, told *Time* magazine of February 11, "We won the elections, there's no reason for holding new elections to prove it."

Time, in that same issue, speculated that Ramon Mitra, Jr., Neptali Gonzales and I were "prominent on that list" of Opposition assemblymen whom Cory would appoint to her cabinet. In that respect, the magazine nailed the truth. The three of us, indeed, landed positions in the Cory administration after Marcos went into exile.

Reagan's Reckless Remarks

In the US, President Ronald Reagan recklessly fueled mass hatred against Marcos and the US when he told the American media that both the KBL administration and the Opposition committed election frauds. In effect, Reagan said the Opposition had no cause to complain against fraud because it was equally guilty of it.

Cory excoriated the US President for his facile assertions that tended more to exonerate Marcos of having manipulated the results of the elections than to protect the integrity of the election process. She recalled:

> I was very upset by this and angry that he (Reagan) should say something like this. With the help of American senators and congressmen who were

here to observe the elections, he got a clearer picture of what actually happened and he no longer mentioned that earlier statement about both sides having cheated.

Unparalleled Cheating

On February 14, Cory's lament against Reagan's insidious statement that tended to shore up Marcos's claims of victory in the polls got a tremendous boost when the Catholic Bishops Conference of the Philippines condemned the results of the elections. The bishops said the electoral irregularities committed by the administration "were unparalleled" in the history of the country. The bishops focused on four major anomalies in the elections: systematic disenfranchisement of voters throughout the country; massive vote buying; tampering with election returns; and acts of intimidation, harassment, terrorism and murder perpetrated on the innocent.

The CBCP's statement put Reagan on the defensive. He then sent his personal envoy, Philip Habib, to Manila to confer with Marcos and Cory separately to get a more solid sounding of what had happened.

All this while, Marcos issued public statements offering "reconciliation with the Opposition." On the day the CBCP statement came out, I told the *Kapihan sa Maynila* forum that, "after having deprived the Opposition of its victory at the polls, the administration's invitation for reconciliation 'added insult to injury.'" I said that Marcos's sincerity in anything that he dangled before the public was always subject to proof. In fact, while he offered the hand of reconciliation to the Opposition, the Marcos police was harassing Cory supporters in Las Piñas. Fred Juntilla, PDP-Laban coordinator for the campaign of Cory and Doy in that town, complained that our party workers Elmer Jalmanza, Fortunato Caraga, Deo Mosqueda, Elmo Dermo, Rizal Mondonedo and Armando Quiman were arrested and detained without bail by police. Their crime: putting up "Marcos Concede" posters.

Batasan Proclaims Marcos

On February 15, two days before Habib's arrival, the Batasan railroaded the proclamation of Marcos and Tolentino as the winners of the elections. The KBL majority proclaimed that Marcos had won the elections over Cory with 10.8 million votes against 9.3 million for her. It was Marcos's way of telling Reagan and everybody else that nothing could now be done to stop his claims of victory over Cory at the polls.

Yet it was a sign of the uncertainty of the times that Chief Justice Ramon Aquino administered the presidential oath to Marcos at past midnight of February 16 in a private ceremony in Malacañang. There never was any instance in our history where anyone ever took his or her oath as President of the country privately and at the witching hours. Up to that point, only Marcos did it. And the reason he did it was his insecurity. He was unsure that he would survive the day without any attempt on his life or the serious challenges to his incumbency. He wanted to make sure that, if destiny took his life or forced him out of office, history would record that he was the President when it happened. Being President also gave him and his family a sense of security in that he still had security people under the command of Ver at his beck and call.

His hush-hush oath-taking was attended by his family and dyed-in-the-wool Marcos loyalists. But his Vice President, Arturo Tolentino, whom the Batasan had also proclaimed as duly elected, was not there. Neither was Marcos's Prime Minister Cesar Virata, who had resigned earlier, citing his inability to work effectively for the government.

Among the few personalities who attended the private oath-taking of Marcos, was Defense Minister Enrile, according to Arturo Aruiza in his book, *Malacañang to Makiki*. Aruiza said Enrile appeared tense and distraught. His observation had a basis because, seven days later, Enrile withdrew his support for Marcos and declared for Cory.

The Marcos oath-taking was a fantasy play that had no bearing on reality. The absence of Tolentino and Virata indicated that the two top civilian officials of his government had abandoned him. That meant that Marcos was done. The whole structure of martial law, that in his greed for power and pelf he had nurtured from 1972 up to 1986, was now tumbling down around him.

National Civil Disobedience Campaign

On February 16, Cory launched a national civil disobedience campaign in Luneta. People by the hundreds of thousands responded to her appeal for support and showed up in Luneta.

As a part of the calibrated campaign, she urged the people to delay payment of taxes to the illegitimate Marcos government and to boycott the establishments of his known cronies. Cory identified Channel 4, *Bulletin Today*, *Daily Express*, *Times Journal* and *People's Journal* for boycotting. She named San Miguel Corporation and Rustan's Department Store as among the business establishments that people should boycott. She also singled out Security Bank, Commercial Bank of Manila, United Coconut Planters Bank, Traders Royal Bank, Republic Planters Bank, Union Bank and Philippine National Bank as the banks that people should boycott for helping "the usurper [Marcos] perpetuate his hold on power."

Habib's Visit

On February 17, Habib called on Marcos in Malacañang. The meeting was well publicized by the controlled Manila media. Marcos told Habib that he had documented frauds committed by the Opposition in the elections. While Marcos dealt tactfully with Habib, KBL propagandists, using the pages of the *Metro Manila Times*, hit Habib's (read the US's) apparent officiousness and called his visit a proof of "American meddling" that was "related to the US bases."

1986: HUNDREDS OF THOUSANDS answer Cory's call at the Luneta for Civil Disobedience and boycott of the Marcos-crony establishments.

After seeing Marcos, Habib visited Cory at her office in Makati. I was in Cory's office when he came. Cory gave Habib an earful. She told him that if he wanted to suggest that she should accept a power-sharing deal with Marcos, the answer would be a flat "No." For emphasis, she added that if that was his reason for seeing her, it would have been best if he did not come at all. She wanted nothing short of Marcos's resignation and his getting out of the country. Cory said it was Marcos who cheated in the elections and it was he who was destroying the democratic foundations of the country. In so many words, Cory said Reagan should be ashamed of himself.

Years later, when Cory was already in Malacañang, she spoke of Habib's visit:

> Before Ambassador Habib came, I was told that he was going to ask me to cooperate with the Marcos government and perhaps accept a position in the Marcos cabinet. I told an American friend that if this was all that Ambassador Habib was going to tell me then it's a waste of time and he might as well not come. At any rate, when I saw Philip Habib, the first thing he told me was, "I'm sorry you had the impression that I was coming here to ask you to cooperate with Marcos. I'm not asking you to do that. I just want to find out what the situation is here."

So he asked me about the protest movement. "How long do you think you can pursue this?" And I said, "Well, probably as long as six months," although I knew that we only had enough money for maybe three or four months. It was so providential that, when Philip Habib came here, we did hold that very huge rally in the Luneta and he was staying in the Manila Hotel at that time. So he was a witness to the massive display of support coming from the Filipino people.

Backing from Cardinal Sin

Cory's stand that Reagan erred when he said both the KBL and the Opposition committed fraud received an invaluable backing from Cardinal Sin. The Cardinal said that he talked with Reagan over the phone:

> We called Reagan because his statement in the United States was confusing. He said that the anomaly in the election was done by both Aquino and Marcos. So he was trying to play politics. I said to Mr. Reagan..., "How can Mrs. Aquino commit anomalies when she is not in power?"

The Cardinal cited the walkout on February 14 of the computer technicians, then assisting the Comelec count to prove his point. The walkout was in protest against the anomalies perpetrated in the election by the Marcos political machinery.

RAM in the Shadows

While these events were unfolding, Peping Cojuangco, Jr., Ramon Mitra, Jr., and Rene Saguisag were actively in contact with the Reform the Armed Forces Movement (RAM), which spearheaded the eventual withdrawal of support of a good segment of the Armed Forces from Marcos.

Even as it operated in the shadows at the time, the names of certain RAM leaders were whispered to us in the Opposition circles. They all appeared to be the most utopian of the young officers of the nation's military, among them were: Gregorio Honasan, Rex Robles, Felix Turingan, Tirso Gador, Victor Batac, Washington Javier, Gregorio Catapang, Diosdado Valeroso and Hernani Figueroa.

RAM also had a civilian confabulator, Silvestre Afable, Jr., who was their chief propagandist. In the view of Enrile, the RAM was a group of idealistic young military officers who wanted to improve the efficiency, discipline, tactics and doctrine of the military based on their experiences in the field. Unsaid by Enrile was the fact that the members of the RAM did not like the way General Ver ran the Armed Forces and, inferentially, Marcos's support for the latter.

Because of his human rights advocacies, Rene Saguisag was not completely trusted by the RAM leaders, according to Rex Robles. RAM apparently trusted Mitra more than Rene. RAM also dealt with Peping Cojuangco, Jr., the brother of Cory, presumably because they wanted him to serve as their direct contact with her.

Chapter 50

People Power Restores Freedom

B uoyed by the success of the Manila rally, Cory decided that the next major stop of the National Civil Disobedience Campaign would be Cebu City. Little did we know that, as we brought the boycott campaign to the Visayas, the next four days of the otherwise languid month of February, circumstances would conspire with white heat intensity to unravel the fabric of Marcos's martial rule.

I was in Cagayan de Oro when I got word that Cory wanted me to join her in Cebu. With lawyer Fred Gapuz, Edwin Padla and Rene Barrientos, my ever-loyal man-Friday, we took the boat to Cebu and arrived there on the morning of February 22, the day Cory, her daughter Kris and her brother Peping arrived by plane from Manila. We had lunch in the house of Norberto Quisumbing, a big business-man in Cebu, who was into the manufacture of Japanese motorcycles.

That same afternoon of February 22, braving the early afternoon heat, we proceeded to the Fuente Osmeña Plaza where thousands of *Sugbuanons*, the people of Cebu, answered Cory's call to shift the struggle from the electoral phase to the boycott and civil disobedience arena.

Tony Cuenco and Inday Nita Daluz, along with John Osmeña, Lito Osmeña and the Bando-Osmeña political machinery ensured the vast multitude's attendance at the Fuente.

As the master-of-ceremonies, Tony Cuenco began the rally by blasting away at the dictatorial rule of Marcos. With a *basso profundo* unique to him, Tony's graphic condemnation of the KBL manipulation of the last election found sympathetic ears among the thousands at the plaza. He called on the people of Cebu to support Cory's call for the boycott of several Marcos-crony establishments and for civil disobedience.

Many speakers roused up the crowd with their anti-Marcos rhetoric. One of the most applauded, however, was not a speaker in the usual sense of the word. He was an entertainer — a singing guitarist who provided an intermission number. And he was blind. We called him in Visayan *Peryong Buta* or Peryong, the Blind Man, but his real name was Porferio Torentera. He prefaced his number by saying that, even if he was born blind, he clearly saw the misdeeds of Marcos. The audience received his teaser with much applause. He then tossed a challenge to the audience, "What about you, you have eyes to see? Do you not see what Marcos is doing to our country?" The line elicited an even more thunderous applause from the anti-Marcos crowd.

The sun was setting when I addressed the rallyists shortly before Cory's turn. Briefly, in Visayan, I exhorted them to persevere in our struggle against Marcos. After my talk, I whispered to Cory to make her speech short because dusk was setting in. I was apprehensive that, under the cover of darkness, some crazed supporter of Marcos would toss a grenade on stage and cause injuries to her and the other participants in the rally. Then I left the stage to make small talk with some friends.

Enrile, Ramos Abandon Marcos

A couple of Manila news people met me when I got down from the stage. They told me that Enrile and Ramos had withdrawn their support from Marcos. I asked if the story had been verified. They assured me that it was true. I went up the stage again as Cory wound up her speech. With Tony Cuenco, Inday Nita Cortez-Daluz, Sonny Osmeña and Monching Mitra, we told her of the developments in Manila.

Reporter Belinda Cunanan also told Cory that Eggy Apostol of the *Inquirer* had relayed the information that Enrile and Ramos had taken refuge in Camp Crame. The two officials knew that Marcos was about to arrest them, after the latter uncovered a coup plot that Enrile was linked to.

The reports were sketchy. But we were convinced that the situation in Manila was serious. Rather than linger on stage, we went to Quisumbing's house to map out our next move. There, we arrived at the conclusion that Cory should repair to a safe house for the night.

We agreed that Tony Cuenco would drive Cory to the safe house. No one of us, her political henchmen, was to know where she would lodge for the night, a precaution we took in case we were arrested before the night of uncertainties was over. If arrested, we could honestly disclaim any knowledge of her whereabouts.

US Offers Assistance

Before Cory could leave, Blaine Porter, the American consul in Cebu, arrived and offered her the use of an American frigate for as long as she needed it to ride out the emergency. Cory politely thanked him and declined the offer. She did not want to be beholden to the US.

Then somebody said that Enrile was on the line and that he wanted to speak with Cory. Suspecting that it might be a ruse to draw evidence of Cory's support for the violent overthrow of the Marcos government, I cautioned her against making precipitate statements that might provoke Marcos into rounding us up and incarcerating us in the islet of Caballo near the island of Corregidor. The threat of that happening was not an idle one. The day before, Monching Mitra phoned to warn me that Marcos had instructed Ver to prepare a Presidential Detention Arrest Order for our detention in Caballo, the rough equivalent of Alcatraz in San Francisco. The difference, of course, was that Alcatraz had the facilities to house convicts. Caballo only had grass, rocks, the remnants of World War II vintage cannons and the sea around it. Included in that PDA order, Monching said, were Cory Aquino, me, him and a few others.

I stood by Cory's side while she conversed with Enrile over the phone ready to cut off the call if I thought that she was veering towards incriminatory directions. Cory, thankfully, kept her part of the chat "short and sanitized." She made no overt statement of support, except to say that she would pray for Enrile and Ramos. Her recollection of her telephone conversation with Enrile follows:

> I was able to talk with Enrile on the telephone and...I asked him what was going on. I also told him that at that moment the only thing I could offer him were my prayers. And he said that was what he needed most.

The phone call done, we left for our respective safe houses. I was assigned to a house of a couple I did not know personally. They were so kind not only because they accepted me, a stranger, as a lodger for the night, but also because they gave me a room with a radio in it.

Developments in Manila

Since I could not sleep, I tuned in on Radio Veritas and followed the developments in Manila. Over the radio, I heard that Enrile and Ramos had indeed withdrawn their support from Marcos. Enrile told Radio Veritas that he did not recognize the results of the elections because of their fraudulent character. He said that Cory was the duly elected president and that, in his province, Cory had been cheated of some 300,000 votes.

I also heard Cardinal Sin's call for the people to mass around Camp Crame and protect Enrile, Ramos and their troops from Marcos's forces. Later, I heard Doy Laurel echo Sin's call. And Butz Aquino made a similar appeal. I thought it was critical for Cory to make a statement on the events in Manila, otherwise she would be left out of the people's consciousness as their leader at that crucial moment in the peaceful uprising against the dictator.

I was pacing in the room, fingering my rosary, at the same time trying to figure out what I could do under the circumstances when I heard knocking on the door of the house. I thought the Cebu Metropolitan District Command (Metrodiscom) agents had discovered where I was and had come to pick me up. Happily, it was only Monching Mitra and John Osmeña.

I was eager to hear the news they brought. They had nothing new. They wanted to know where Cory was hiding for the night. It was important, they said, that we get to see Cory and that she should issue a statement on the events in Manila. Their suggestion matched my own thoughts on the matter. Our problem was where to begin the search. John, a close friend of Tony Cuenco, suggested that we try the Carmelite nuns' convent a few kilometers out of the heart of the city in the Mabolo district.

Gate Closed

With John driving, Monching sitting beside him and me at the back, we took off in the night in search of our candidate. All the while, I was apprehensive that military or police stop-and-search patrol units would stop us and place us under arrest. Marcos had announced that there would be a nationwide curfew, and military and police units all over the land were instructed to enforce it. In the event, we got to the convent without anybody stopping us. We took that as a sign that Marcos had lost control at least over Cebu.

A closed gate and a high concrete fence surrounding the monastery, however, barred us from entering. We pounded on the gate as loudly as we could. Nobody opened it. So we left and proceeded to Magellan Hotel where several foreign and local journalists were billeted. The media people had flown to Cebu to cover our boycott rally.

Crafting Cory's Statement

In the car, we discussed what to say to the media who we assumed were eager to know where Cory was and what her plans were. John, Monching and I agreed that Cory had to speak out. It was not good for her not to say anything. The Cardinal had spoken. So had Doy Laurel, Butz Aquino and a clutch of other lesser-known personalities. Since she was our leader, we believed that she had to say something to express her solidarity with the people who were demanding the resignation of Marcos.

Monching asked, "What should Cory's message to the media be?" I suggested a terse statement: "How about this? 'Cory wants Marcos to step down immediately to avoid a bloodbath." Since the call for Marcos's resignation was a constant theme in Cory's speeches in the campaign, it would be fairly easy to justify the words that I fashioned. Monching and John also thought it was a credible enough statement that could be attributed to Cory without compromising her in any way.

At the hotel parking lot, we got out of the car and sprinted up to the hotel lobby where we found the media people all looking sleepy, tired and hungry for news. Like journalists anywhere in the free world, they wanted to ask questions at the same time. Above the din, I heard that they unanimously wanted to know where Cory was and what had she to say about the volatile situation in Manila.

Since John and Monching agreed that I would speak for the three of us, I told the media people that Cory was in a safe place and her message was: "Marcos should resign to avoid bloodshed." The media people were incredulous. They said, "Is that all? Why so short?" I had to respond in the only way I could, "Yes, that is all." There was really not much else we could tell them except that Cory was safe somewhere in the city and that they could probably see her on the morrow. We then went back to our safe houses.

Big Relief

The following morning, a Sunday, after I thanked my generous hosts, I went to the Carmelite Monastery. I identified myself at the gate and was allowed to enter. I went straight to the nuns' convent. There in the company of Tony Cuenco, Peping, Cory's brother, Monching and a few others, I had breakfast with Cory, courtesy of the nuns.

At breakfast, we learned that the nuns heard the loud banging at their gate the night before. But they were too scared to open the gate because they thought that the Marcos military police had come to arrest Cory. So they prayed to all the saints in heaven to make "the barbarians at the gate" go away. We all had a hearty laugh, buoyed up by the thought that we had survived the night without mishap. We also theorized that, since Marcos failed to arrest us or even implement the curfew that he had announced on the night of our boycott rally, he had lost control of the situation nationwide.

Later, Tony Cuenco told me that it was his wife Nancy's idea that Cory should take refuge in the Carmelite Monastery. Nancy said that Cory would be safest there. Quietly, Nancy phoned the Mother Superior and made arrangements for Cory and some companions to sleep there.

Lito Osmeña lent his brand new Ford Sedan to ferry Cory, her daughter Kris and her brother Peping to the monastery. Tony drove, with Nancy beside him. Behind them sat Cory, Kris and Peping.

Recalling the episode, Tony said:

> I was very nervous. I broke my eyeglasses when I hit a glass door as we left the Quisumbing house.
>
> It was the most thrilling ride I have ever taken. *Kulba-hinam!* Breathtaking! While I was driving, I sensed that there were vehicles following us. I zigzagged along the road to the monastery. I also cut corners trying to lose every vehicle that I thought was following us.
>
> We arrived at the monastery and found its gate a bit ajar. The gatekeeper waved us in. On the grounds of the monastery, we saw a sight we could hardly forget. The Mother Superior and 25 nuns holding their rosaries greeted us warmly in the still of the night. The gate was then closed and we felt safe inside its high walls.
>
> The nuns gave Cory, Kris and Nancy a big room for the three of them. They gave me and Peping a smaller room.
>
> Peping and I could not sleep. Through a transistor radio, we monitored what was happening in Manila via Radio Veritas.

The nuns apparently treated their overnight guests so well that the only complaint Tony heard came from Kris. Mosquitoes feasted on the girl. They had no mosquito nets in their room.

No Hiding for Cory

Over breakfast, we discussed what Cory should do in the light of events. Monching Mitra suggested that Cory could go to Palawan, then eventually to Malaysia. In that manner, she could stay away from the turmoil in Manila until it was safe to resurface. I disagreed with the idea that she should even go out of the country while the Manila unrest was ongoing. I suggested that she should instead go to Mindanao, perhaps to Davao where Chito Ayala and our sturdy band of PDP-Laban partisans could provide adequate protection for her, or to Cagayan de Oro.

Cory, however, would have none of our proposals. She said that she would go back to Manila because that was where the action was. I guess she knew the moment of her meeting with destiny had come. With her decision, there was not much we could do but to agree to go back to Manila with her.

After lunch, we motored to the airport. On the way to the airport, Cory, Tony Cuenco and Monching Mitra dropped by Hotel Magellan. The media people were eager to hear a statement from Cory herself regarding the developments in Manila. Cory obliged them with a prepared statement that was typewritten on a short bond paper. Dated February 23, 1986, it read:

> A week ago on February 16, I launched my nonviolent and peaceful protest in order to pressure Mr. Marcos to respect the people's mandate. Millions of our countrymen answered my call to boycott the enterprises associated with Mr. Marcos and his cronies. Yesterday, two high-ranking officials, namely, Minister of Defense Juan Ponce Enrile and Lt. General Fidel Ramos, in a surprise move, finally broke away from the Marcos government to uphold the people's choice of Cory Aquino and Doy Laurel. I appeal to our brothers and sisters throughout the nation and to those who are now in Camp Aguinaldo to continue giving their full support to this peaceful struggle. I also call on the other government officials to dissociate themselves from the Marcos regime now and to follow the lead taken by Supreme Court Justice Nestor Alampay and Postmaster General Roilo Golez, among others. For the sake of the Filipino people, I ask Mr. Marcos to step down now so that we can have a peaceful transition of government.
>
> Cebu City
> Philippines

Monching had typed the statement on an old Underwood typewriter with a battered ribbon. The typewriter imprints were hardly legible. Cory did not have any choice but to make do with what was available. Tony said that Cory made some corrections. She inserted the words "in a surprise move" to describe Enrile's and Ramos's breakaway from the Marcos government and added the phrase "to uphold the people's choice" to clarify the purpose of their seceding from the regime. He said that Cory also tucked in the words "among others" after the names of Nestor Alampay and Roilo Golez to show that they were not the only ones who had defected.

The statement had a carbon copy, which Cory left with Tony Cuenco. It bore a short handwritten note that said:

> Dear Tony,
>   This is certainly a most memorable time.
>
>   Cory
>   2/23/86

Cory Returns to Manila

Two light planes were placed at the disposal of Cory for the trip back to Manila. She took the first one, along with members of her family and Monching Mitra. I was to take the second plane with Bea Zobel and some members of Cory's entourage.

Our plane was not there when we got to the airport. Assemblyman Bono Adaza had used it to fly to Bohol where he felt that he would be safer than if he were to fly directly to Manila. Bea was rightly upset about it. She thought it was not right for anyone to take her plane without her permission. In any event, our wait at the Cebu airport really did not take too long because Bohol was only 15 minutes away by a fast jet from Cebu. Bea's plane was back sooner than we expected.

In minutes, we were in the air and on our way to Manila. We were chatting about the impending collapse of the Marcos regime when the pilot told Bea a rather disconcerting bit of news. Over the plane's radio, he heard that a PAL commercial jet full of troops from Zamboanga in Mindanao had landed at the Manila International Airport to reinforce the rebel troops of Enrile and Ramos. But soldiers loyal to Marcos had surrounded the plane and arrested the troops.

The situation at the Manila International Airport was so muddled at the time that we did not know who controlled the airport. If the Marcos soldiers were in control, we'd be in trouble if we landed there. Thus, the pilot suggested we proceed to the Calatagan airstrip of the Zobel de Ayalas in Batangas.

Although I sensed that Bea had already made up her mind, she asked me if it was all right for us to take the risk and land at the Manila International Airport. I could not give any other reply than that it was OK by me. I could not imagine giving any other answer because, if the lady was willing to risk it, why shouldn't I? Bea then ordered the pilot to land at the Manila International Airport.

In minutes, our plane taxied on the runway, veered towards the hangar of the Ayalas and parked there. Everything appeared normal. No soldiers stopped us. At the hangar, friends picked me up. They came in a convoy of several cars that were loaded with assorted firearms. They took me to the house of Josephine Cojuangco Reyes, the sister of Cory, in the plush Wack-Wack village.

Coded Call from Cebu

Meanwhile, from Cebu, Marie, the wife of Ernesto Aboitiz, thoughtfully called up Bing in Marikina. In a coded message, she said, "I am calling for you know who. He is safe. Please do not ask questions." Then she hung up. Bing extrapolated from the brief phone call that Cory and those of us who were with her at the Cebu boycott rally, had returned to Manila to join and support the demonstrations at the Epifanio de los Santos Avenue (Edsa).

With our youngest daughter Inde in tow, Bing went to Channel 4, the government TV station, to ask the new management to air the information that Cory and the rest of us were back in Manila to support the demonstrators. The station had just been taken over by pro-Cory demonstrators and some 50,000 or so rallyists were still surrounding its premises to prevent Marcos loyalists from taking it back.

Bing passed the information on to the new management. In the light of so many events taking place, we were unable to follow whether or not the information was broadcast to bolster the morale of the demonstrators.

Anyway, when I got to Josephine's house, Cory's brothers and sisters were discussing whether or not she should go to Edsa, where tens of thousands of people had massed and were repeatedly chanting "Cory! Cory! Cory!" The rallyist were publicly manifesting their support for her and were pleading that she should express her solidarity with them. A majority of the members of her family felt uneasy about her going there. They feared for her safety. They thought that she could very well express her support for the demonstrators by issuing a statement that could be disseminated by radio or by leaflets without her personally going to Edsa. Cory decided otherwise. She would go to Edsa.

Cory Speaks at Edsa

Assemblyman Alberto Romulo and I accompanied her to Edsa. We went to the Philippine Overseas Employment Administration building at the junction of Ortigas and Edsa. We got on a balcony that provided a panoramic view of the sea of humanity on the streets below. With Bert and I flanking her, Cory addressed the multitudes. Crammed only inches apart, the people filled the whole stretch of Ortigas in front of us and Edsa to the left and right of the balcony. As usual, Cory spoke briefly. Her message was that she came to show her solidarity with the people and thank them for their support. She said she wanted Marcos to resign to spare the nation from further trouble.

This is how Cory remembered the event:

> I was in the POEA building and, in fact, this was reported by the *Business Day*. Unfortunately, there were no TV people there. While it is true I announced that I would be there, we did not say exactly the time. My security felt that it was best not to let too many people know where and when I would be there. There were so many people there, many priests, seminarians and nuns...we sang *"Ama Namin,"* the "Our Father."

Years later, when they parted ways, Enrile criticized Cory as a *dakilang miron*, a great kibitzer, who was not an actual player in the people's peaceful revolt against Marcos. Enrile alleged that she had not been present at any time during the people power demonstrations against Marcos in the four days of February. Enrile was wrong. She was there at Edsa on February 23, 1986. I was there with her. So was Bert Romulo. Also, tens of thousands of the demonstrators at the Ortigas-Edsa junction saw and heard her in person.

From the POEA building we saw countless yellow banners and streamers of PDP-Laban waving in the air. Mobilized by Jojo Binay of Makati; Jimmy Ferrer, Janet Ferrer, Elfren Cruz, Wally Ferrer and Ben Allanigue of Parañaque; Dante Tinga of Taguig; Dr. Tony Martinez, Romeo Santos, Pap Masquiñas and Shirley Estrellon of Caloocan; Fred Juntilla of Las Piñas; Jun Simon, Virgilio Tordera, Tina Montiel and Mel Chavez of Quezon City; Ponciano Subido, Bert Domingo, Bernie Ang, Danny Lacuna, Toto Ty, Odi Melchor, Efren Adan and Ben Paypon, thousands of the party faithful showed their support for the peaceful ouster of Marcos at Edsa. Elfren Cruz personally handed out hundreds of the yellow banners and streamers, which held their own in the sea of red flags at the Edsa demonstrations.

The red flags called attention to the presence of the Left in the demonstrations. But whether yellow or red, the demonstrators lapped up every word of Cory's brief statement and applauded her as if they had heard the salvific word of God. When she was through, she asked me in Tagalog, *"Ano, magsalita ba kayo ni Bert?* Will you and Bert speak?"* I said "No" for both of us. I wanted her out of the place immediately. I saw how vulnerable she was to sniper fire or a grenade attack on that open balcony. Happily, we left the place without any incident and were back at Wack-Wack in no time at all.

At Josephine's house, Cory's brother, Peping, Monching Mitra, Apeng Yap, Jimmy Ongpin and other political supporters sat in one room to discuss probable nominees to her cabinet. I was told that Cory would name me her Minister of Local Government, a job that I felt I was equipped by training and experience to do relatively well. Bobbit Sanchez's name was mentioned as her Labor Minister. I thought that Sanchez was an excellent choice for it. And Mitra would be Minister of Agriculture. Mitra had wide personal experience as a farmer and a rancher in Palawan. He was thus fully qualified for the post.

Many callers flitted in and out of Josephine Reyes's house. Like bees attracted by the sweet smell of nectar, they came in droves, some apparently driven by the desire to share in the spoils of an impending victory. The politically inclined gravitated towards Cory's brother Peping and his wife Tingting. The non-political hovered around the nucleus of Cory's kitchen cabinet of Tere Lopa, Maria Montelibano, Margie Juico and Fritzie Aragon.

We were in Josephine's house when news broke that Marcos had left the country. We shouted for joy. Our happiness was, however, short-lived. A TV station that was still functioning showed him and his family in Malacañang and defiant as ever. It was a false alarm.

Contingency Plans

For a couple of nights during those exciting days in February, Bing and I stayed at a condominium "safe house," courtesy of the Jaime and Bea Zobel. I was advised not to go back to our house in Marikina as the house was being cased by military and police agents.

In Bing's absence, Gwen, our eldest daughter, took care of running the house. Koko, our eldest son, told his younger brother Jac that if anything should happen to him, Jac should continue the fight against Marcos — as if he or Jac could do anything to hasten the downfall of the martial law regime. Koko and Jac joined their classmates from the Ateneo de Manila in manning barricades at Edsa or wherever they were needed to hamper the movements of pro-Marcos elements. Jac told us after the fact that, without Bing's or my knowledge, he used the family car, a Toyota Hi-Ace, to block the main gate of Radio Veritas to help prevent the entry of "enemy" vehicles into the grounds of the radio station.

Bing and the kids had contingency plans for the safe evacuation of family members in case the situation worsened or I was picked up by the military.

Plan A sought to secure our boys from the military. Bing believed that the boys would be the first targets for harassment by the military as they were more visible than the girls in the protest movement against Marcos. The girls, aside from attending to household chores, acted mostly as assistants to Bing. Inde, the youngest, tended to cry if Bing so much as hinted that she should also leave the house and stay with some relatives where she and her sisters would be safer.

In the plan, Koko and Jac were not to go home straight from any demonstration if they sensed that they were being tailed by Marcos agents or if they felt that our house was under surveillance. The boys followed their mom's instructions to the letter. Sometimes, they would go to the house of our neighbor, Cesar Caballero, as a diversionary tactic, before proceeding to our house. At the Caballero residence, Koko and Jac would pretend to play with the Caballero boys, Jun and Nelson, who were of their age, even as they checked if any unusual movements were taking place in or near our house.

Plan B covered the contingency of the boys' having to go to the houses of Bing's sisters who lived in various places in Metro Manila should the situation worsen.

For my safety, Bing and the kids also improvised a signal to alert me of the presence of "enemy agents" in the house. A light bulb attached to the front eaves of the house — which we never lighted to conserve energy — would signal an "all clear" if it remained off. But, if it was on, that was a sign that Marcos agents were in our house or lurking in the immediate vicinity. Then I should not proceed to the house but go elsewhere.

The precaution was in addition to the alarm network that my neighbors in Fairlane had devised ever since they learned that I was opposed to the martial law regime. If our neighbors noticed strange vehicles or unknown persons in the vicinity of our house, they would call us up. One of our neighbors, Arman Belen, who was adept in electronics, even wired our house to his house and to the house of another neighbor, Ed Mojar. If our house was raided by martial law authorities, all we had to do was to press a button on the window sill next to our bed. Belen and Mojar would then alert the other residents of the subdivision about the emergency taking place in our house.

Meanwhile, at Josephine's house in Wack-Wack, we continued to monitor the developments on Edsa. More people were now crowding Josephine's house than on the day of our arrival from Cebu. Although I did not see any firearms displayed, I felt that Cory's supporters were ready for any eventuality.

Demos Stump Military

The Edsa demonstrations calling for the ouster of Marcos now attracted massive support from all sectors of society. The demonstrators occupied the whole of Edsa fronting Camp Crame and there was no moving them away. Marcos and his generals led by Ver threatened to use force to disperse the demonstrators. Fortunately, the threat remained just that: a threat. But it was not for want of trying.

General Ver, in fact, ordered his military generals to move in and scatter the crowds. Some, like Gen. Artemio Tadiar and Col. Braulio Balbas, tried to obey Ver's command. But when they saw so many innocent people and nuns and priests holding their line, offering flowers and food to the soldiers, and refusing to back off, the officers simply could not give the order to shoot. Thus it was the soldiers who backed off — tanks and all — from the confrontation with unarmed civilians, some of whom were their own children, relatives and friends.

Failing to get the military to disband the Edsa demonstrators, Marcos ordered the police do the dispersal. Police Gen. Alfredo Lim recounts in the book, *May Langit Din Ang Mahirap* or *The Poor Also Have a Heaven*, with the subtitle, *The Life Story of Alfredo Siojo Lim*, written by Nick Joaquin, that Marcos himself twice ordered him directly by phone to disperse the rallyists.

Lim said that the first telephoned order was given at 2:45 on the afternoon February 23:

> [Marcos said,] "General Lim, what's happening out there?"
>
> "Mr. President, there are many people converging on Edsa, between [Camps] Crame and Aguinaldo."
>
> "Then you tell them to go home because we are going to shell Crame. Tell them to disperse so that they won't get hurt. We are sending in tanks, mortars and artillery. So be sure to disperse them at all costs."
>
> "Yes, Sir, Mr. President."

Instead of complying with the President's order verbatim, Lim bought time by trying to get clearance from his immediate superior, Gen. Prospero Olivas. Olivas, however, could not be disturbed because, according to his deputy, Col. Mitch Templo, he was under sedation in preparation for a medical operation.

Lim did not know it then, but Olivas was also looking for a way to evade receiving a direct order from Marcos to disperse the demonstrators from Edsa. By early evening, however, Lim received another call from Marcos. Lim said:

> The President sounded furious.
>
> "General, you failed me!"
>
> "Mr. President, it is physically impossible to conduct dispersal operations."
>
> "Why? Why?"
>
> "Because there are 35,000 to 40,000 people on Edsa and I have only 126 men with me."
>
> "All right, listen. I will send you additional reinforcements: two more army battalions — but be sure you disperse at all costs! Tell the crowd to go home — that Crame is going to be shelled."
>
> "Yes, Sir, Mr. President."

Tanks Turned Away

As fate would have it, the hours flew so fast that, before Lim could implement the second order to disperse the demonstrators, Gen. Victor Natividad, the new PC chief whom Marcos appointed in lieu of Ramos, ordered him to pull out of Crame. Natividad instructed Lim to join him at the Meralco compound along Ortigas and to bring with him the military group that was placed under his command. Lim was ecstatic about this development. He could now leave Edsa. And, should Marcos call again, he no longer had to invent alibis to explain why he could not disperse the demonstrators. He would refer the matter to his superior officer.

When Lim met Natividad at the Meralco command post. Natividad asked, "But where are the tanks?" Surprised, Lim asked in turn, "What tanks?"

Some army tanks had indeed been ordered to go out of Fort Bonifacio, proceed to Edsa and blast Camp Crame, where Enrile, Ramos and their band of rebel soldiers were holding out. The tanks, however, were not placed under Lim's command.

Lim told Natividad that, on his way to the latter's command post, he had seen some tanks, but these were moving in the wrong direction. Instead of proceeding towards Camp Crame, the tanks were going towards Pasig, an adjoining town.

Lim and Natividad later learned that the tanks had been turned away from Edsa by a thick human barricade of priests, nuns and thousands of unarmed demonstrators. The demonstrators, armed only with their faith in the Almighty and trust that the soldiers would not massacre innocent civilians, caused the tanks to back off. The first People Power exercise in the country scored its first victory.

By 8 o'clock in the evening of Sunday, February 23, Lim and his men were exhausted. They had been on their toes since early morning. Very clearly, they needed rest. Lim asked permission for his men to take a break. Natividad willingly granted the request.

Lim Assures Butz Aquino

Earlier that day, unknown to Natividad, Ramos had called Lim. According to Lim, Ramos suggested that, if Lim were to obey Marcos's orders to disperse the crowds at Edsa, Enrile, General Espino, Assemblyman Renato Cayetano and many others, including Ramos, would be wiped out. Ramos told Lim their only weapons were M16s and M14s, which were no match against tanks, heavy artillery and mortars.

Ramos's tactful appeal softened Lim's heart towards the demonstrators which was one of the reasons why he could not enforce Marcos's orders to disperse them. In fact, after his phone conversation with Ramos, Lim assured Butz Aquino that he was not going to disperse the crowds at Edsa. It was then only a matter of time before Lim formally allied himself with the rebels at Camp Crame. By 6 p.m. of February 25, Lim, along with 40 other top-ranking police officers and their men, put themselves at the disposal of the rebels led by Enrile and Ramos at the camp.

Even before Lim switched to the rebels' side, Col. Antonio Sotelo, with his helicopter team, defected to the side of the rebels in Crame. So did Gen. Fidel Singson and 160 of his men. Singson's defection was most significant as he was Ver's chief of military intelligence.

Reagan Warns Against Violence

Meanwhile, the pressure on Marcos to leave Malacañang mounted relentlessly. Washington sent word to Marcos that the US government would look with extreme disfavor on any attempt on his part to use force to disperse the demonstrators at Edsa. At 6 p.m. of the 24th of February, Reagan called Marcos up to tell him that it would be futile for him to violently remove the demonstrators. The US caveat to Marcos was probably the decisive factor why

Marcos did not give General Ver permission to attack Crame and the demonstrators who ringed it.

Cory Ascends to the Presidency

On February 24, Cory Aquino and Doy Laurel decided to take their oaths of office as President and Vice President respectively. Explaining the circumstances that led her to make that decision, Cory said:

> There was talk of a civil military junta. In fact, this was discussed with… Laurel who informed me about this and asked my opinion.…I was never in favor of a junta. And I had been meeting with the opposition leaders also. On the morning of the 24th…Senators Tañada, Salonga and Diokno, and Justice Palma [told] me, "Cory, it is best that you now take your oath of office because we are reading something different in the latest pronouncements of Ponce Enrile." He was no longer mentioning my name, so I guess most people were already suspecting that he wanted to take over. So, we…all agreed that on the morning of the 25th I would take my oath of office. I would have done it on the evening of the 24th, except that it took some time for the lawyers to prepare the oath that I was going to take. We had to postpone it for the 25th.…Also, in order to safeguard and protect the people, I said it would be better to do it during daylight.

Cory chose Club Filipino, a popular clubhouse in Greenhills, in the municipality of San Juan, as the site for her and Doy Laurel's oath-taking. When Enrile was informed about it, he suggested that they take their oaths in Camp Crame. It was safer there, he said. He warned that Marcos still had the capability to militarily destroy any activity of the Opposition that diminished the legitimacy of the martial law regime.

I was among those who advised Cory against accepting Enrile's suggestion. I thought that Cory would be unnecessarily placing herself under the control of Enrile and Ramos. And, if she agreed with the Enrile proposal, in effect, she would give primacy to the military intervention in the attempt to end the Marcos regime. I believed that, at every opportunity, Cory should give emphasis to the participation of the people in overthrowing the martial law regime. Cory apparently did not need our advice. Fatalistically, she told Enrile's emissaries, "No, thanks." She would take her oath at Club Filipino regardless of the perils that Enrile spoke of.

History Unfolds at Club Filipino

Their oath-taking was thus set for 10 o'clock on the morning of February 25, 1986 at Club Filipino. I was among the very first to arrive at the club to help make the guests welcome, especially, the members of the Batasan Opposition and other political supporters. I noticed that there was not much we could do to secure the place. The club was vulnerable to attacks from all sides, top, front and back. If Marcos helicopters strafed us, hundreds would die. We simply did not have any defense against gunships. The only consolation — if it could be considered that — was that thousands of Cory partisans and our party mates were there ready to lay down our lives for the cause of freedom and democracy that she and Doy Laurel symbolized. Leaving everything to the hands of the Almighty, I banished the thought that I could die on that occasion and leave behind a widow and six children.

Most of the Manila-based Opposition leaders and Opposition members of the Batasan were there for the historic occasion. Some erstwhile Marcos men joined the happy occasion. One justice of the Supreme Court, Antonio Barredo, tried to blend in with the Cory crowd but was booed and had to leave. I also saw KBL Assemblyman Jose Zubiri who was a little bit edgy, but we, his colleagues in the Batasan, made him feel welcome.

Doy Laurel took his oath as Vice President before Supreme Court Justice Vicente Abad Santos first. Doy's oath was based on the standard wording prescribed by the Constitution.

Oath to Defend the People

Cory then took her oath before Supreme Court Justice Claudio Teehankee. The oath was not in the form prescribed by the Constitution, which past Presidents had taken. It was an oath crafted by Rene Saguisag, Neptali Gonzales and one or two other lawyers. Its main thrust was that Cory was taking the oath to defend the people.

During the event, cameras clicked to preserve it for posterity. Cory's children and mother-in-law, Aurora Aquino, were there beside her. The only prominent political figure who got into the historic photograph was Ernesto Maceda, who had been Ninoy Aquino's confidant while they were in exile in the US and who had played a significant role in the Cory campaign against Marcos.

I was seated immediately across the presidential table, mesmerized by the unfolding historic event. I could hardly believe that we had gotten this far. I knew that Cory gave Marcos the fight of his life in the presidential election, but seeing Cory take her oath as president was not on the horizon when the campaign began, nor even when it was in full swing. But, now, here we were at Club Filipino, watching the beginning of a new era for the country. It was a scene that made the hairs on my arms rise. It was unbelievable, but yet so true.

Doy and Cory then gave their inaugural speeches. Doy's speech was a statesman's dream that called for binding the nation's wounds and highlighted the need for the people to work together. I remember that his speech was longer than Cory's.

Then Cory spoke. Her speech was short, and extemporaneous. She had no prepared text. Amid the seeming unreality of events, what I remembered most of her speech was her pledge to do right by the people.

After the handshaking and back-patting with everyone within reach, I invited several PDP-Laban members, who could not witness the oath-takings inside Club Filipino, to go with me to the law office of Dante Tinga and Francisco Fuentes in Makati, where I had a room for conferences. There we discussed the post-Marcos scenario for the party. In the midst of our discussion, I got a call that Cory wanted us to go to Josephine's house. We happily went to answer the summons of our President.

Marcos Flees

Even as we were discussing in Josephine's house the details of Cory's taking over the presidency, in Malacañang, Marcos remained as defiant as ever. Delusions about his role as the only salvation of the nation kept Marcos fighting to retain power to the very end. But his resolve crumbled when an Air Force gunship piloted by Capt. Wilfredo Evangelista who had defected to Cory's side strafed Malacañang. That was when he cried enough. He sued for a way out. He called up Enrile and begged him not to shell Malacañang again. Enrile assured him that he would not. The demonstrators, however, were getting restless. Thousands were threatening to assault Malacañang and drive the Marcoses away physically.

At this point, Cardinal Sin suggested to Reagan that he should help Marcos. The Cardinal reconstructed his talk with Reagan as follows:

> That was the time when I told Reagan that Mr. Marcos should be helped. If he remained for another two hours in Malacañang, he would be assassinated because there were already young students here with red flags. They were about to go to Malacañang and I told them not to, because the moment you do that and you kill somebody there, that will be the beginning of a civil war. I told them, "Please wait, just wait." Reagan did not like Marcos to go to the US. So he phoned the President of Honduras. These are all in my diary.

Reagan apparently thought that Marcos was too hot a potato to handle. He wanted Marcos to go to Honduras, not to the US, for political asylum. He had the President of Honduras, Jose Azcona del Hoyo, call Cardinal Sin. Sin, however, thought that Marcos would die if he went toHonduras instead of to the US. He recalled:

> The Hondura[n] president said to me in Spanish, "I will accept Marcos if you insist, even though our national council has decided not to accept your president." Then I answered him in very classical Spanish, "Mr. President, don't complicate my life because this man is sick. The moment he goes to Honduras, he is going to die. He needs special attention and first-class equipment."

The Cardinal's view that Marcos needed special medical care that Honduras could not provide convinced Reagan to allow Marcos asylum in the US. In his words:

> Reagan decided to bring him to Hawaii because he [did] not like Marcos to go to the mainland. And Marcos agreed. His story that he wanted to go to Paoay is wrong. He really wanted to save himself. And because of our insistence, he was saved. As soon as he left Malacañang, in less than 45 minutes, the people were there. They started to burn his pictures and destroy his things. If he was there, he could have been killed. This is the story.

On February 26, Marcos was flown out of Malacañang to Hawaii, with a brief stopover at the Clark Air Base to enable him to rest.

This was Cory's recollection of how Marcos had a stopover in Clark:

> I was in constant touch with Ambassador Bosworth and he informed me that then President Marcos was asking if he could then go on to Paoay from Clark. I asked, "Well, is he in very poor health, is he in real danger of dying?" Ambassador Bosworth told me, "No, he's just tired." So I said, "In that case, he will have to leave as soon as possible, after he has had his night's rest in Clark."

After Marcos's stopover in Clark, he had to leave the country. He had become a pariah. Cory did not want him here. Reagan did not want him in the

Courtesy of Jake Macasaet, Malaya

1986: JOE BURGOS'S Malaya *captures the historic moment!*

US mainland either. Hawaii was the compromise place for Marcos's ignominious exile from which he was never to return.

That, then, was how the martial law story in the country ended: gloriously for the people, who dismantled the machinery of martial law with hardly a drop of blood being shed; and ingloriously for Marcos and *some* of those who had engineered the imposition of martial law with him in 1972. The phenomenon became known to the whole world as the People Power Revolution. It was, however, mainly a Metro Manila affair. People in the Visayas and Mindanao hardly had any actual participation in the events at Edsa. But they had children, relatives or friends working, studying or vacationing in Metro Manila at that time, and many of them participated in the peaceful uprising against Marcos. While parochial in its inception, the uniquely purifying four days of People Power in February 1986 ushered in the national restoration of democratic rule all over the country.

In the meantime, at Josephine's house, President Cory announced her appointment of Joker Arroyo as her Executive Secretary. It was a most welcome appointment. From the point of view of those of us who received the brunt of the oppression of martial law, Joker's appointment sort of balanced the earlier appointments she had extended to Enrile as her Defense Minister and Ramos as the Chief of Staff of the Armed Forces, both of whom were remnants of the martial law regime. I congratulated Joker for a very well-deserved appointment. During a pause in our conversation, Arroyo asked Elfren Cruz, who was with our group at the time, to report to Malacañang on Monday and assist him in his work.

Unchartered Seas

I learned in that meeting at the house of Josephine that President Cory would soon be appointing me as her Minister of Local Government. In a matter of days, she did. From the more familiar terrain of provincial politics, I was thrust inexorably into the unchartered seas of national politics. It was a new challenge. I took it up with some degree of trepidation, but with a lot of faith that the Almighty would, as He had done through the turbulent years of martial law in the country, not let me down for the sake of our people.

1986: IN MALACAÑANG, CORY administers oath of office to me as Minister of Local Government. Inde, Bing and Koko witness the simple ceremony.

2006: *BY THE GRACE OF GOD, I lived to tell my story of how we coped with the strictures of martial rule. My family, front, (left to right): Malyn, Gwen, Bing, Preet, me, AL, Terelou and Maripet. Standing: AC, Jac, Dominique, Luigi, Trina, Inde, Alain, Koko, Komart, Jewel and Sonny.*

As a family, we thanked the Almighty in heaven who worked through all sorts of people, that we all survived martial law intact in mind, body and soul. Bing continued to do her indispensable role as a full-time mother for our kids and as a part-time composer of songs; Gwen was finishing her law course at the University of the Philippines; Maripet was working her way to a master's degree in Mass Communication in California; Koko was doing freshman work in law in UP; Jac was finishing his Bachelor of Arts in Biology in Ateneo; Terelou was a sophomore in Psychology in Xavier University, and Inde was a third-year high school student at Maryknoll College.

We also especially gave thanks to the Lord that, despite four arrests, two ousters from office and several death threats, I was still up and around and did not seem the worse for the experience. And above all, for blowing the super-typhoon of martial rule away from the land and once again caressing the backs of our people with the breeze of freedom.

— *Bibliography* —

Aquino, Belinda A. *Politics of Plunder: The Philippines under Marcos.* Quezon City: University of the Philippines, 1999.

Aquino, Benigno S. Jr. *Testament from a Prison Cell.* Makati: Benigno S. Aquino, Jr. Foundation, 1984

Aquino, Ramon C. *A Chance to Die: A Biography of Jose Abad Santos, Late Chief Justice of the Philippines.* Quezon City: Alemars-Phoenix, 1967.

Aruiza, Arturo C. *Ferdinand E. Marcos: Malacañang to Makiki.* Quezon City: ACA Enterprises, 1994.

Bautista, Felix B. *Cardinal Sin and the Miracle of Asia.* Manila: Vera-Reyes, 1987.

Bernas, Joaquin G. *Dismantling Dictatorship: From MIA Tarmac 1983 to EDSA 1986: A Collection of Essays.* Manila: Ateneo de Manila University, 1994.

Bonner, Raymond. *Waltzing with a Dictator: The Marcoses and the Making of American Policy.* New York: Times Books, 1987.

Boyce, James K. *The Political Economy of Growth and Impoverishment in the Marcos Era.* Quezon City: Ateneo de Manila University Press, 1993.

Bravo, Marie Teresita, ed. *Mariani: A Woman of a Kind.* Quezon City: Task Force Detainees of the Philippines, 2001.

Burton, Sandra. *Impossible Dream: The Marcoses, the Aquinos, and the Unfinished Revolution.* New York: Warner Books, 1989.

Canoy, Reuben R. *The Counterfeit Revolution: The Philippines from Martial Law to Aquino Assassination.* Manila: Philippine Editions, 1981.

Civil Liberties Union of the Philipppines. *The State of the Nation after Three Years of Martial Law.* Makati: Civil Liberties Union, 1994.

Collins, Joseph. *The Philippines: Fire on the Rim.* San Francisco, CA: The Institute for Food and Development Policy, 1989.

Constantino, Renato. *Report of the National Press Club Seminar Committee on The State of the Philippine Press.* Quezon City: Foundation for Nationalist Studies, 1994

De Dios, Aurora Javate, Petronilo Bn. Daroy and Lorna Kalaw-Tirol, eds. *Dictatorship and Revolution: Roots of People Power,* Manila: Conspectus, 1988.

De Quiros, Conrado. *Dead Aim: How Marcos Ambushed Philippine Democracy.* Pasig City; Foundation for World Wide People's Power, 1997.

Escalante, Salvador and Augustus De la Paz. *The EDSA Uprising?: The Five Percent Revolution EDSA in Retrospect: A Deconstruction.* Quezon City: Truth and Justice, 1994.

Fajardo, Reynaldo T. *The Philippines Betrayed*. LP Young Turks, 1997.

—————————. *The Marcos Gold*. Quezon City: Jolejarsi Books, 1992.

Fortich, Chic. *Escape! Charito Planas: Her Story*. Quezon City: New Day, 1991.

Hill, Gerald N. and Kathleen Thompson Hill. *Aquino Assassination: True Story and Analysis of the Assassination of Philippine Senator Benigno S. Aquino, Jr*. California: Hilltop, 1983.

Joaquin, Nick. *May Langit Din Ang Mahirap: The Life Story of Alfredo Siojo Lim*. Atlas, 1998.

—————————. *The Quartet of the Tiger Moon: Scenes from the People-Power Apocalypse*. Manila: Book Stop, 1994.

Kessler, Richard J. *Rebellion and Repression in the Philippines*. New Haven: Yale University Press, 1994

Komisar, Lucy. *Corazon Aquino: The Story of Revolution*. New York: George Braziller, 1988

Laurel, Celia Diaz. *Doy Laurel*. Celia Diaz-Laurel, 2005.

Li, Zhisui. *The Private Life of Chairman Mao*. New York: Random House, 1994.

Mamot, Patricio R. *The Aquino Administration's Baptism of Fire*. Manila: National Book Store, 1987.

Manalang, Priscila. *The Cellophil Caper, or, How Buddies Marcos and Disini Tried to Beat the Pinoy to a Pulp*. Quezon City: Freedom from Debt Coalition, 1992.

Manapat, Ricardo. *Some Are Smarter Than Others: The History of Marcos' Crony Capitalism*. New York: Aletheia Publishing, 1991.

Maramba, Asuncion David, ed. *On the Scene : The Philippine Press Coverage of the 1986 Revolution*. Manila: Solar, 1987.

Martinez, Manuel F. *More Assassinations and Conspiracies*. Manila: Anvil, 2004.

—————————. *Footprints in the Wilderness: The Life and Times of Oscar F. Santos and His Message to the Filipino Youth*. Quezon City: Coconut Industry Reform Movement, Inc. (COIR), 1997.

Martinez, Manuel Festin. *The Grand Collision: Aquino vs. Marcos*. Quezon City: Manuel F. Martinez, 1987.

McDougald, Charles. *The Marcos File: Was He a Philippine Hero or Corrupt Tyrant?* California: San Francisco Publishers, 1987.

Mijares, Primitivo. *The Conjugal Dictatorship of Ferdinand and Imelda Marcos I*. Quezon City: CBSI, 1976.

Montiel, Cristina Jayme and Susan Evangelista. *Down from the Hill: Ateneo de Manila in the First Ten Years Under Martial Law, 1972-1982*. Quezon City: Ateneo de Manila University, 2005.

Ninoy, Ideals & Ideologies, 1932-1983 : A Rare Collection of Photographs of the Late Senator Benigno S. Aquino Jr. Highlighted by His Famous Quotations, His Thoughts, His Principles, and the Ideals He Fought, Lived, and Died For. Makati: Benigno S. Aquino Jr. Foundation, 1993.

Olaguer, Eduardo B. *Light a Fire II: Confessions of a Jesuit Terrorist-Son*. Quezon City: Ed Olaguer Family, 2005.

Ortigas, Gaston Z. and Sylvia L. Mayuga. *A Revolutionary Odyssey: The Life and Times of Gaston Z. Ortigas*. Pasig: Anvil, 1994.

Pedrosa, Carmen Navarro. *The Rise and Fall of Imelda Marcos*. Manila: Bookmark, 1994.

Permanent People's Tribunal Session on the Philippines: Repression and Resistance. Komite ng Sambayanang Pilipino, 1981.

Policarpio, Alfonso P. *Ninoy: The Willing Martyr.* Manila: Isaiah, 1986.

Political detainees in the Philippines : Documentation Report of Signs of the Times, A Publication of the Association of Major Religious Superiors in the Philippines, March 31, 1976. Manila: Anti-martial Law Coalition (Philippines), 1994.

Poole, Fred and Max Vanzi. *Revolution in the Philippines: The United States in a Hall of Cracked Mirrors.* New York: McGraw-Hill, 1984.

Psinakis, Steve. *Two "Terrorists" Meet.* California: Alchemy Books, 1981.

Rempel, William C. *Delusions of a Dictator: The Mind of Marcos as Revealed in His Secret Diaries.* Canada: Little, Brown and Company, 1984

Reyes, Rodolfo T. with Avel C. de Guzman. *Memoirs of a Newsman.* Parañaque: Rod T.Reyes Media Services, 1990.

Riordan, Patrick. *Philosophical Perspectives on People Power.* Naga City: Ateneo de Naga, 2001.

Rodrigo, Francisco Soc. *Mga Bakas ng Kahapon: Memoir.* 1987

Rodriguez, Filemon C. *The Marcos Regime: Rape of the Nation.* New York: Vintage Press, 1985.

_____. *Our Struggle for Power.* Manila: Phoenix, 1967.

Romualdez Francia, Beatriz. *Imelda and the Clans: A Story of the Philippines.* Mandaluyong: Solar Publishing, 1988.

Romulo, Beth Day. *Inside the Palace: The Rise and Fall of Ferdinand and Imelda Marcos.* New York: Putnam, 1987.

Salonga, Jovito Reyes. *The Memoir of Jovito R. Salonga: A Journey of Struggle and Hope.* Quezon City: U.P. Center for Leadership, Citizenship and Democracy ; Regina Pub., 2001.

Seagrave, Sterling. *The Marcos Dynasty.* New York: Harper & Row, 1988.

Simons, Lewis M. *Worth Dying For.* New York: William Morrow and Company, 1994

Sohmer, Karla. *Hubris: When States and Men Dare God: The Persecution of the Marcoses.* Quezon City: Katotohanan at Katarungan Fdtn., 2000.

Sta. Romana-Cruz, Neni. *Tales From EDSA.* Pasig City: Anvil, 2000.

Sycip, Cynthia Y. *Memories of a Hero.*

Tolentino, Arturo. *Voice of Dissent.* Quezon City: Phoenix, 1990.

Villadolid, Alice Colet. *Filipinos — A Century Back and Forward.* Manila: Paragon Printing, 2000.

Bello, Walden, David Kinley, and Elaine Elinson. *Development Debacle,The World Bank in the Philippines.* California: Institute for Food and Development Policy. 1982.

Wurfel, David. *Filipino Politics : Development and Decay.* Quezon City: ADMU, 1988.

Yap, Miguela Gonzalez. *The Making of Cory.* Quezon City: New Day, 1987.

— *Index* —

—*About the Book*—

In this book, ***Martial Law in the Philippines: My Story***, Aquilino "Nene" Pimentel writes primarily about the experiences that he and his family underwent during the martial law regime that President Ferdinand E. Marcos had instituted in the country in 1972 and implemented until he was forced to flee to the US in 1986.

He candidly posits the view that martial law was a gross criminal act that Marcos and his collaborators perpetrated upon the people. Also, he details how Marcos by means of cajolery, bribery and threats laid its foundations in the 1973 Constitution with the indispensable assistance of his lieutenants in the Constitutional Convention of 1971.

He recalls that soon after the declaration of martial law, he was jailed in Camp Crame and thrown into a cell for hardened criminals. That was the first of his four arrests during martial rule. He also describes how he and his fellow human rights activists like Sen. Lorenzo Tañada, Sen. Joker Arroyo, Sen. Soc Rodrigo, Fr. Archie Intengan, S.J., Tito Guingona and Ernie Rondon were incarcerated in the military camp in Bicutan for waging a demonstration against the farcical Interim Batasan elections in 1978.

Citing pertinent documents, he describes how some detainees in the martial law detention centers were tortured and who the torturers were.

In 1980, he was elected mayor of Cagayan de Oro City. But even after his election as mayor and later as a member of the regular Batasan Pambansa, the martial law harassments continued.

Through it all, he retained his faith in the Almighty, who, he says, worked through friends to see him through the martial law years.

Nene Pimentel was born in Claveria, Misamis Oriental. He is an incumbent Senator of the Republic and resides with his wife, Lourdes de la Llana, in Cagayan de Oro City in Mindanao, Philippines.